## FIGURE 3-12

The rate of growth of money is measured as the change in *M2*, and the inflation rate is measured as the change in the CPI. Periods of high money growth are accompanied by periods of high inflation, consistent with the prediction of the quantity theory of money.

### THE RATE OF GROWTH OF MONEY AND THE INFLATION RATE, 1880–2000 (DECADE AVERAGES)

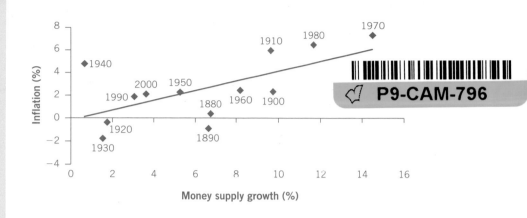

SOURCE: Historical data are taken from *New Estimates of the Canadian Money Stock, 1871–1967* by Cheri Metcalf, Angela Redish, and Ronald Shearer, University of British Columbia Discussion Paper 96-17. The data are available at www.econ.ubc.ca/dp96list.htm. From 1967 onward: *M2*: CANSIM II V37128; CPI: V375319.

## FIGURE 2-2

The upper panel of Figure 2-2 shows the nominal interest rate and the inflation rate. The difference between these two variables is the real rate of interest, which is shown in the lower panel. (Notice that the vertical scales on the two diagrams are different.) The data is graphed over the period 1961–2002. Notice that the real interest rate averaged approximately 3 to 4 percent per year until the early 1970s, when it began to decrease sharply and even became negative. Throughout the 1980s and most of the 1990s, the real interest rate averaged nearly 6 percent per year before returning to an average of 3 to 4 percent per year by the year 2000.

### NOMINAL AND REAL INTEREST RATES AND INFLATION, 1961–2002

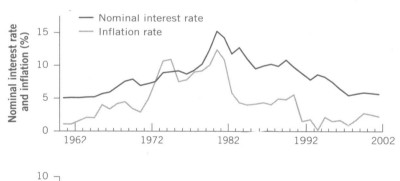

SOURCE: CANSIM II: Long-term government bond rate: V122487; Consumer Price Index: V315739.

# macroeconomics

## SEVENTH CANADIAN EDITION

Rudiger Dornbusch
Late of Massachusetts Institute of Technology

Stanley Fischer
Vice-Chairman of Citigroup

Richard Startz
University of Washington

Frank J. Atkins
University of Calgary

Gordon R. Sparks
Queen's University

McGraw-Hill
Ryerson

Toronto   Montréal   Boston   Burr Ridge, IL   Dubuque, IA   Madison, WI   New York   San Francisco
St. Louis   Bangkok   Bogotá   Caracas   Kuala Lumpur   Lisbon   London   Madrid   Mexico City   Milan
New Delhi   Santiago   Seoul   Singapore   Sydney   Taipei

**McGraw-Hill Ryerson**

**Macroeconomics**
**Seventh Canadian Edition**

ISBN 13: 978-0-07-091616-6
ISBN 10:  0-07-091616-0


 2 3 4 5 6 7 8 9 10 TCP 0 9 8 7

Printed and bound in Canada

Care has been taken to trace ownership of copyright material contained in this text; however, the publisher will welcome any information that enables them to rectify any reference or credit for subsequent editions.

Statistics Canada information is used with the permission of the Minister of Industry, as Minister responsible for Statistics Canada. Information on the availability of the wide range of data from Statistics Canada can be obtained from Statistics Canada's Regional Offices, its World Wide Web site at http://www.statcan.ca, and its toll-free access number 1-800-263-1136.

Vice President, Editorial and Media Technology: Patrick Ferrier
Executive Sponsoring Editor: Lynn Fisher
Marketing Manager:  Kelly Smyth
Developmental Editor: Daphne Scriabin
Production Coordinator: Mary Pepe
Supervising Editor: Anne Nellis
Copy Editor: June Trusty
Cover Design: Dianna Little
Cover Image Credit: © J.W. Burkey / Getty Images
Composition: Pages Design Ltd.
Printer: Transcontinental Printing Group

National Library of Canada Cataloguing in Publication

Macroeconomics / Rudiger Dornbusch ... [et al.]. -- 7th
Canadian ed.

4th Canadian ed. by Rudiger Dornbusch, Stanley Fischer, Gordon R.     Sparks.
Includes bibliographical references and index.
ISBN 0-07-091616-0

1. Macroeconomics.  I. Dornbusch, Rudiger.  Macroeconomics.
II. Dornbusch, Rudiger

HB172.5.M33525 2004             339             C2003-907371-8

*In economics, we teach that the true value of anything is what you give up to get it.
By this measure, my wife Laurie must believe that this book is very valuable.*

*FJA*

# CONTENTS IN BRIEF

# C O N T E N T S

# CONTENTS IN BRIEF

**PART 4**

## THE ECONOMY IN THE VERY SHORT RUN: SPENDING AND THE *IS-LM* MODEL OF ECONOMIC ACTIVITY 187

**PART 5**

## BEHAVIOURAL FOUNDATIONS 271

# CONTENTS

## PART 6
# MONETARY AND FISCAL POLICY AND ADVANCED TOPICS 343

# ABOUT THE AUTHORS

**RUDI DORNBUSCH** (1942–2002) was Ford Professor of Economics and International Management at MIT. He did his undergraduate work in Switzerland and held a Ph.D. from the University of Chicago. He taught at Chicago, at Rochester, and from 1975 to 2002, at MIT. His research was primarily in international economics, with a major macroeconomic component. His special research interests included the behaviour of exchange rates, high inflation and hyperinflation, and the problems and opportunities that high capital mobility pose for developing economies. He lectured extensively in Europe and Latin America, where he took an active interest in problems of stabilization policy and held visiting appointments in Brazil and Argentina. His writing includes *Open Economy Macroeconomics* and, with Stanley Fischer and Richard Schmalensee, *Economics*.

**STANLEY FISCHER** is vice-chairman of Citigroup and president of Citigroup International. From 1994 to 2002, he was first deputy managing director of the International Monetary Fund. He was an undergraduate at the London School of Economics and has a Ph.D. from MIT. He taught at the University of Chicago while Rudi Dornbusch was a student there, starting a long friendship and collaboration. He was a member of the faculty of the MIT Economics Department from 1973 to 1998. From 1988 to 1990, he was chief economist at the World Bank. His main research interests are economic growth and development; international economics and macroeconomics, particularly inflation and its stabilization; and the economics of transition. **www.iie.com/fischer**

**RICHARD STARTZ** is Castor Professor of Economics at the University of Washington. He was an undergraduate at Yale University and received his Ph.D. from MIT, where he studied under Stanley Fischer and Rudi Dornbusch. He taught at the Wharton School of the University of Pennsylvania before moving on to the University of Washington, and he has taught, while on leave, at the University of California–San Diego, the Stanford Business School, and Princeton. His principal research areas are macroeconomics, econometrics, and the economics of race. In the area of macroeconomics, much of his work has concentrated on the microeconomic underpinnings of macroeconomic theory. His work on race is part of a long-standing collaboration with Shelly Lundberg. **www.econ.washington.edu/user/startz**

**FRANK ATKINS** is an associate professor of Economics at the University of Calgary. He attended the University of Guelph and received an Honours B.A. in 1977 and an M.A. in 1979. On graduation, he spent two years at the Bank of Canada as an economic analyst, where he gained a deep appreciation for the difficulties associated with monetary policy formation. In 1981, he left the Bank of Canada to further his studies in economics at Queen's University at Kingston. He graduated in 1985 with a Ph.D. in economics, and joined the faculty at the University of Calgary. His main academic areas of interest are monetary policy and the application of time series analysis to macroeconomic data. As well as publishing many articles in leading economic journals, he is a frequent commentator on macroeconomic issues for the major national networks. He lives in Calgary, Alberta, with his wife Laurie and their children Dan and Andrea. **http://econ.ucalgary.ca/atkins.htm**

**GORDON SPARKS** has a B.A., a mathematics degree from the University of Toronto, and an M.A. and a Ph.D. in economics from the University of Michigan. He is currently a professor of Economics at Queen's University in Kingston, Ontario. He has been a consultant for the Bank of Canada, an assistant professor at MIT (1965–1967), and a visiting professor at MIT (1981–1982). His fields of interest include monetary policy and exchange rates and the use of time series methods to analyze historical data. His articles have been published in various journals, including the *Canadian Journal of Economics, Econometrica,* and *Explorations in Economic History.* In recent years, he has been teaching courses on the economics of the European Union at the International Study Centre (Queen's University) in Sussex, England.

# PREFACE

## A MODERN CANADIAN TEXT

If you ever get a chance to look at the first edition of this textbook (which was published more than 20 years ago), you will notice that it is quite a bit different from this Seventh Edition. Although there are numerous changes, the substantive differences are in two general areas. First, major developments have taken place in macroeconomics over the last 30 years. These developments have been the result of careful analysis of a great deal of macroeconomic data, as well as recent intellectual developments in macroeconomic theory and policy. This edition reflects these developments from a Canadian perspective. We believe that the learning experience is enhanced by an understanding of the relationship between the models presented and real-world data.

Second, the Canadian economy has undergone considerable structural change over the last quarter of a century, and has developed its own unique character. Canada is no longer considered to be simply a satellite economy of the United States. Indeed, John Manley, who was minister of Finance in late 2003, called the Canadian economy the "Northern Tiger." This book has been written to reflect this new stature of the Canadian economy.

## Canadian Features

In this edition, we have retained the uniquely Canadian features that were developed over the last two editions. First, each chapter contains data concerning movements of Canadian variables that are relevant to the theory developed in the chapter. Second, the popular *Working with Data* feature, which helps students to retrieve and manipulate Canadian data, has been retained. We have also added a new feature in each chapter called *Policy in Action*. The purpose of these features is to demonstrate how the theory and the data in each chapter can be used to understand major policy initiatives that have been undertaken in Canada. Finally, Chapters 18 and 19 have been rewritten to discuss monetary and fiscal policy developments in Canada.

Throughout this edition we have continued to emphasize the importance of international trade and the exchange rate. Chapter 5 deals with long run issues, such as the relationship between the balance of payments and net foreign lending, and how purchasing power parity plays a role in the long run movements of the nominal exchange rate. Chapter 9 considers how the terms of trade can be incorporated into the standard aggregate demand-aggregate supply model. Chapter 13 presents a thorough treatment of the relationship among interest rates, capital flows, exchange rate movements, and net exports in the short run. In addition, Chapter 18 has been expanded to include consideration of the Monetary Conditions Index, which is useful for analyzing how the short-term interest rate and the exchange rate play a role in the short run conduct of monetary policy decisions in Canada.

In addition to the above Canadian features, we have made a number of changes to specific chapters. Chapter 14, Consumption and Saving, now contains a section on intertemporal optimization. As well, the *IS-LM* chapters (Chapters 11, 12, and 13) have been extensively rewritten. For instance, we now consider the situation where monetary policy is conducted according to an interest rate rule.

## Organization of the Book

We have retained the general structure that was used in the last two editions, treating the analysis of the economy in the long run first, and then moving to the short run. However, this should not deter those who want to emphasize short run analysis. The book is deliberately written in a flexible manner so that short run analysis could be treated very early in any course.

Chapter 1 emphasizes the use of models in economics and introduces the aggregate demand-aggregate supply model. We stress that the assumed speed of price adjustment is reflected in the shape of the aggregate supply curve, and this determines whether our analysis pertains to the long run or the short run. Parts 2 through 5 of the book follow the theme that the long run can be differentiated from the short run by assuming that price adjustment is completely flexible, sticky, or even fixed.

Part 2 deals with long run flexible price models. Chapter 3 carefully describes the long-run Classical market clearing model and introduces the production function. This leads directly to long run growth analysis in Chapter 4. Part 2 concludes with Chapter 5, which presents an introduction to open economy analysis, with an emphasis on long run open economy issues.

The focus of Part 3 is on sticky price (Phillips curve) models. Once again, there is an open economy chapter, dealing with international adjustment in an aggregate demand and aggregate supply framework. Part 4 deals with analysis of the economy over the very short run, including a chapter on international capital mobility. Part 5 discusses behavioural foundations, with a chapter on consumption and saving, investment theory, and the demand for money. Part 6 discusses policy in general and monetary and fiscal policy in particular, and concludes with a chapter on advanced topics.

## What's New in This Edition

We have made numerous style and emphasis changes to reflect the many helpful comments we have received from our readers. In addition, we have made the following more substantive improvements:

▶ **Chapter 1:** The extensive look at Canadian data has been expanded to include graphs of the rate of growth of $M2$ and the 90-day Treasury bill rate.

▶ **Chapter 2:** The general structure of this chapter has been changed in order to put less emphasis on the details of construction of GDP measures and more emphasis on measuring data and how it fits the structure of the Canadian economy. There is a new section on unemployment and Okun's law, so the chapter now covers GDP, inflation, nominal and real interest rates, and unemployment. All material from Section 2-2 onward has been rewritten, and includes an explicit discussion of savings and investment, the current account, and wealth accumulation.

▶ **Former Chapter 10:** The Sixth Edition Chapter 10 has been moved to the new Part 6, *Monetary and Fiscal Policy and Advanced Topics*, of this edition and is now Chapter 17, *Policy*. Here it serves as a good introduction to the analysis of monetary and fiscal policy in Canada in Chapter 18, *The Money Supply and Monetary Policy*, and Chapter 19, *Deficits, Debt, and Fiscal Policy*.

▶ **Chapters 10–13:** This entire section of the book has been rewritten to reflect a more modern emphasis of this important very short run material. Chapter 10, *Income and Spending* (previously Chapter 11), has been completely rewritten and streamlined. It now serves as an introduction to early Keynesian models, including the concept of the multiplier. Students will review ideas that should have been covered in an introductory economics course and, in addition, this chapter will serve as an introduction to the *IS* curve material in Chapter 11, *Money, Interest, and Income.*

In Chapter 11 (previously Chapter 12), the material on the derivation of the *IS* curve has been rewritten in a manner that is more accessible to students. Chapter 13—*Capital Mobility and the Exchange Rate in the IS-LM Model* (previously Chapter 12)—has been completely rewritten. Among the many changes, we have provided a modern treatment of the liquidity trap and how this relates to the Canadian and U.S. economies after the events of September 11, 2001. The section on the vertical *LM* curve has been reworked and related to the Classical model. The fiscal policy section has been rewritten, and there is a new section on the conduction of monetary policy according to an interest rate rule, as compared to a money supply rule. Chapter 13 (previously Chapter 12) has been completely rewritten to centre on the results of the Mundell-Fleming model under fixed and flexible exchange rates. As well, there is an expanded treatment of the relationship between interest differentials and exchange rate expectations.

▶ **Chapter 14:** Rewritten to emphasize the short run nature of a Keynesian consumption function, this chapter also contains a completely new section covering the theoretical relationship among consumption, interest rates, and income, using the two-period intertemporal optimization model.

▶ **Chapter 18:** Revised to provide a more consistent description of how monetary policy is conducted by the Bank of Canada, this chapter also includes coverage of the Monetary Conditions Index and a discussion of the Taylor rule.

▶ **Chapter 19:** This chapter has been rewritten to reflect the importance of debt, deficits, and fiscal policy in Canada.

▶ **Epilogue: What Have We Learned?:** This is completely new material which gives an overview of the major themes of the text and discusses how these themes relate to current issues in macroeconomics.

## Customize Your Course

This edition has been deliberately organized to allow a great deal of flexibility in terms of the type of course that you may wish to present. The core introductory material is contained in Chapters 1 through 3. After these chapters, there are several ways to proceed:

### An Overview Course

After Chapters 1–3, proceed to Chapter 5, which gives an introduction to the balance of payments and exchange rates (you may want to omit Section 5-2); Chapter 6, which gives an overview of the aggregate demand-aggregate supply model; and Chapters 11 and 12, which discuss the economy in the short run and policy issues.

### A Traditional Aggregate Demand-Oriented Course

After Chapters 1–3, proceed to Part 3, with emphasis on Chapters 6, 7, and 9, and then to Part 4, Chapters 10–13. Part 4 can be done before Part 3 without loss of continuity. For advanced students, the sections on New Keynesian economics in Chapter 20 can be included.

## A Classical Market Clearing Course

A Classical market clearing course could include Parts 1 and 2; Part 3, with an emphasis on the long run results; and the microeconomic underpinnings of macroeconomics presented in Chapters 14–16. For advanced students, the sections on the random walk of GDP and real business cycles in Chapter 20 could be included.

## A Business School Course

In addition to the core chapters identified for the overview course, a business school course should add Chapter 18, which contains material on the Bank of Canada, and Chapter 19, which discusses fiscal policy. The additional open economy chapters, Chapters 9 and 13, can be added, and Chapter 4 on growth theory can be treated with less emphasis.

## Chapter Walkthrough

We believe that the learning experience is enhanced by an understanding of the relationship between the models presented and real-world data. We have worked toward updating and improving the pedagogical features in this edition to provide a more innovative approach.

### Focus on the Interaction of Theory and Data

The authors continue to refine the focus on current data and how these data can be used to understand key economic models and topics.

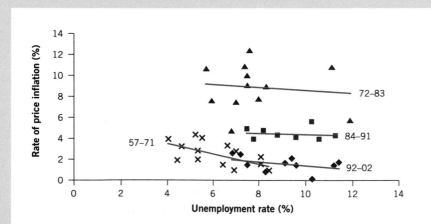

*FIGURE 7-6*

**FOUR SHORT RUN PHILLIPS CURVES**

All estimated short run Phillips curves are consistent with a very flat short run trade-off. High expected inflation in the late 1970s and early 1980s led to a higher Phillips curve. As the inflation rate gradually lowered, expectations of inflation decreased and the Phillips curve shifted downward. The Phillips curve from the 1960s is virtually identical to the Phillips curve of the late 1990s.

SOURCE: 1960–1975: Statistics Canada, *Historical Statistics of Canada*, Publication 11-516-XIE; 1976–2002: CANSIM II V2062815; inflation: CANSIM II V735319.

## New *Policy in Action* Feature

*Policy in Action* is a **new** feature that demonstrates how the theory and data in each chapter can be used to understand major policy initiatives that have been undertaken in Canada.

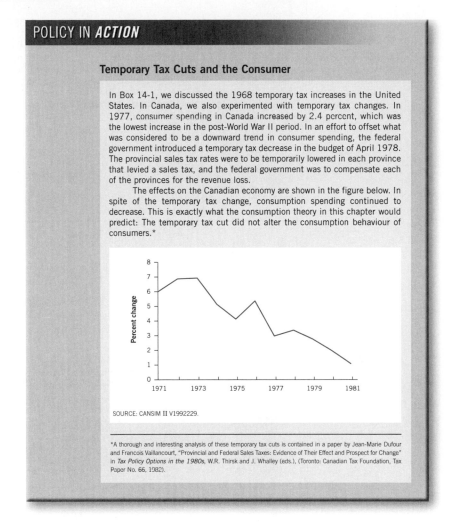

POLICY IN *ACTION*

**Temporary Tax Cuts and the Consumer**

In Box 14-1, we discussed the 1968 temporary tax increases in the United States. In Canada, we also experimented with temporary tax changes. In 1977, consumer spending in Canada increased by 2.4 percent, which was the lowest increase in the post-World War II period. In an effort to offset what was considered to be a downward trend in consumer spending, the federal government introduced a temporary tax decrease in the budget of April 1978. The provincial sales tax rates were to be temporarily lowered in each province that levied a sales tax, and the federal government was to compensate each of the provinces for the revenue loss.

The effects on the Canadian economy are shown in the figure below. In spite of the temporary tax change, consumption spending continued to decrease. This is exactly what the consumption theory in this chapter would predict: The temporary tax cut did not alter the consumption behaviour of consumers.*

SOURCE: CANSIM II V1992229.

*A thorough and interesting analysis of these temporary tax cuts is contained in a paper by Jean-Marie Dufour and Francois Vaillancourt, "Provincial and Federal Sales Taxes: Evidence of Their Effect and Prospect for Change" in *Tax Policy Options in the 1980s*, W.R. Thirsk and J. Whalley (eds.), (Toronto: Canadian Tax Foundation, Tax Paper No. 66, 1982).

## Working with Data

Each chapter ends with a section entitled *Working with Data*, which has been updated to reflect current use of CANSIM II. In this section, the student will be led through the procedure of deriving one important graph from the chapter. At the end

*Working with Data*

Okun's law is a statement about the relationship between the rate of change of real GDP and the unemployment rate, expressed by the following relationship.

$$\frac{Y - Y^*}{Y^*} = -\gamma(u_t - u^*) \tag{17}$$

In this chapter, we asserted that, in Canada $\gamma \approx 1.7$. In Chapter 8, we will discuss ways to estimate the unknown $u^*$. In this chapter, we made the convenient simplification that the term on the right-hand side of equation (17) can be approximated by the change in the unemployment rate, or $u_t - u_{t-1}$.

Go to CANSIM II and retrieve data on GDP in 1997 dollars (V1992259) and the unemployment rate (V2062815). You will need to average these data to get the annual values. In Chapter 2, we estimated Okun's law over the period 1962–2002. The data for the unemployment rate prior to 1976 are:

| Year | Unemployment Rate |
|------|-------------------|
| 1961 | 8.4 |
| 1962 | 6.9 |
| 1963 | 6.4 |

of the section, the student should be able to reproduce this graph. In addition, in the Application Questions section, students are directed to data sources and asked to manipulate data that were used in the chapter.

## Boxes

Updated "Box" features provide mini-cases focused on current economic issues.

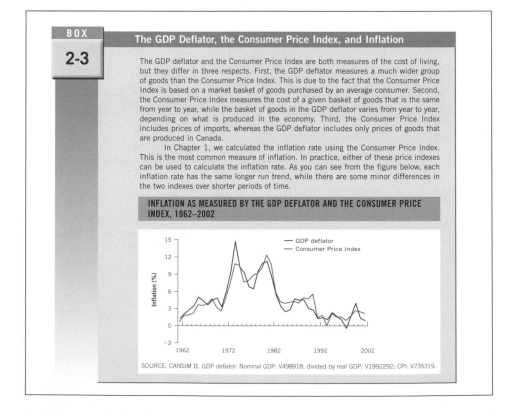

**BOX 2-3**

**The GDP Deflator, the Consumer Price Index, and Inflation**

The GDP deflator and the Consumer Price Index are both measures of the cost of living, but they differ in three respects. First, the GDP deflator measures a much wider group of goods than the Consumer Price Index. This is due to the fact that the Consumer Price Index is based on a market basket of goods purchased by an average consumer. Second, the Consumer Price Index measures the cost of a given basket of goods that is the same from year to year, while the basket of goods in the GDP deflator varies from year to year, depending on what is produced in the economy. Third, the Consumer Price Index includes prices of imports, whereas the GDP deflator includes only prices of goods that are produced in Canada.

In Chapter 1, we calculated the inflation rate using the Consumer Price Index. This is the most common measure of inflation. In practice, either of these price indexes can be used to calculate the inflation rate. As you can see from the figure below, each inflation rate has the same longer run trend, while there are some minor differences in the two indexes over shorter periods of time.

**INFLATION AS MEASURED BY THE GDP DEFLATOR AND THE CONSUMER PRICE INDEX, 1962–2002**

SOURCE: CANSIM II. GDP deflator: Nominal GDP: V498918, divided by real GDP: V1992292; CPI: V735319.

## Learning Objectives

Each chapter opens with Learning Objectives that provide students with an easy-to-follow road map of the chapter.

## Web Links

Updated Web site references provide students with a key research tool.

www.bankofcanada.ca

www.statcan.ca/english/
freepub/11-516-XIE/
free.htm

## Figures and Tables

In a book in which economic modelling plays an important role, figures and the supporting data tables are important elements for the learner. In this Seventh Edition, all graphics, captions, and supporting data have been updated from the most recent statistics available.

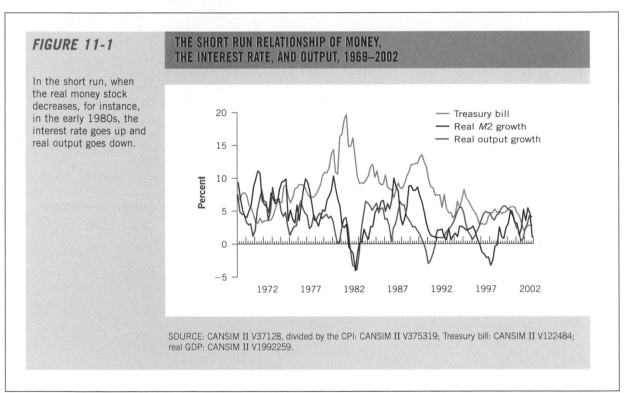

**FIGURE 11-1**

**THE SHORT RUN RELATIONSHIP OF MONEY, THE INTEREST RATE, AND OUTPUT, 1969–2002**

In the short run, when the real money stock decreases, for instance, in the early 1980s, the interest rate goes up and real output goes down.

SOURCE: CANSIM II V37128, divided by the CPI: CANSIM II V375319; Treasury bill: CANSIM II V122484; real GDP: CANSIM II V1992259.

## Chapter Summary

Each chapter concludes with a summary of the concepts and theories developed in the chapter.

## Key Terms

A list of key terms introduced in the chapter is presented, accompanied by the page number on which each term first appears.

## Discussion Questions

New questions have been added, some at a more challenging level.

## Application Questions

Application Questions have been updated to reflect the current use of the CANSIM II database.

### D I S C U S S I O N   Q U E S T I O N S

1. Most of the time, both the goods market and the money market are subject to shocks at the same time. How would you think about choosing between an interest rate rule and a money supply rule in this real-world situation?

2. Discuss the circumstances under which the monetary and fiscal policy multipliers are each, in turn, equal to zero. Explain in words why this can happen and how likely you think this is.

### A P P L I C A T I O N   Q U E S T I O N S

1. The economy is at full employment. Now the government wants to change the composition of demand toward investment and away from consumption without, however, allowing aggregate demand to go beyond full employment. What is the required policy mix? Use an *IS-LM* diagram to show your policy proposal.

2. Suppose the government cuts income taxes. Show in the *IS-LM* model the impact of the tax cut under two assumptions: (1) The government keeps interest rates constant through an accommodating monetary policy, (2) the money stock remains unchanged. Explain the difference in results.

 3. Go to CANSIM and retrieve data on the money stock, *M*1B, and the 90-day Treasury bill rate. Calculate the rate of growth of money and plot this with the Treasury bill rate. Can you relate this graph to any of the monetary policy discussions in this chapter?

# THE MACROECONOMICS ONLINE LEARNING CENTRE

More and more students are studying online. That is why we offer an Online Learning Centre (OLC) that follows *Macroeconomics* chapter by chapter. It doesn't require any building or maintenance on your part and is ready to go the moment you and your students type in the url:
**www.mcgrawhill.ca/college/dornbusch**

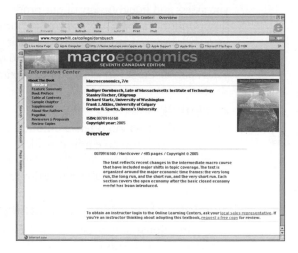

As your students study, they can refer to the OLC Web site for such benefits as:

- Self-grading quizzes
- Additional problems
- Annotated Web Links
- Access to $\Sigma$-STAT and CANSIM II database

- Chapter highlights
- Learning Objectives
- Searchable Glossary
- Graphing Exercises

Remember, the *Macroeconomics* OLC content is flexible enough to use with any course management platform currently available. If your department or school is already using a platform, we can help. For information on your course management services, contact your *i*-Learning Sales Specialist or see "Superior Service" in this preface.

## Superior Service

Service takes on a whole new meaning with McGraw-Hill Ryerson and *Macroeconomics*. More than just bringing you the textbook, we have consistently raised the bar in terms of innovation and educational research. These investments in learning and the education community have helped us to understand the needs of students and educators across the country, and allowed us to foster the growth of truly innovative, integrated learning.

## Integrated Learning

Your Integrated Learning (*i*-Learning) Sales Specialist is a McGraw-Hill Ryerson representative who has the experience, product knowledge, training, and support to help you assess and integrate any of our products, technology, and services into your course for optimum teaching and learning performance. Whether it's using our test bank software, helping your students improve their grades, or putting your entire course online, your *i*-Learning Sales Specialist is there to help you do it. Contact your local *i*-Learning Sales Specialist today to learn how to maximize all of McGraw-Hill Ryerson's resources!

## *i*-Learning Services Program

McGraw-Hill Ryerson offers a unique *i*-Services package designed for Canadian faculty. Our mission is to equip providers of higher education with superior tools and resources required for excellence in teaching. For additional information, visit **www.mcgrawhill.ca/highereducation/eservices**.

## Teaching, Technology & Learning Conference Series

The educational environment has changed tremendously in recent years, and McGraw-Hill Ryerson continues to be committed to helping you acquire the skills you need to succeed in this new milieu. Our innovative Teaching, Technology & Learning Conference Series brings faculty together from across Canada with 3M Teaching Excellence award winners to share teaching and learning best practices in a collaborative and stimulating environment. Preconference workshops on general topics, such as teaching large classes and technology integration, are also offered. We will also work with you at your own institution to customize workshops that best suit the needs of your faculty at your institution.

## Research Reports into Mobile Learning and Student Success

These landmark reports, undertaken in conjunction with academic and private sector advisory boards, are the result of research studies into the challenges professors face in helping students succeed and the opportunities that new technology presents to impact teaching and learning.

## Supplementary Material

### For the Student

The **Student Online Learning Centre, prepared by Rashid Khan, McMaster University** to accompany *Macroeconomics*, offers such study aids as Chapter Objectives, Chapter Highlights, Student Quick Quiz (with multiple-choice questions), Internet application questions, interactive graphing exercises, annotated Web links, and access to the CANSIM II database.

$\Sigma$-**STAT** is an educational resource designed by Statistics Canada and made available to Canadian educational institutions. Using 450,000 current CANSIM (Canadian Socio-economic Information Management System) Time Series and the most recent—as well as historical—census data, $\Sigma$-STAT lets you bring data to life in colourful graphs and maps. Access to $\Sigma$-STAT and the CANSIM II database is made available to purchasers of this book, via the Dornbusch Web site, by special agreement between McGraw-Hill Ryerson and Statistics Canada. The Online Learning Centre provides additional information.

The **Data Liberation Initiative (DLI)** is a cost-effective method for improving data resources for Canadian post-secondary institutions. Prior to the start of the DLI program, Canadian universities and colleges had to purchase Statistics Canada data, file by file. With the advent of the DLI, participating post-secondary institutions pay an annual subscription fee that allows their faculty and students unlimited access to numerous Statistics Canada public-use microdata files, databases, and geographic files.

**Study Guide (0-07-092214-4), prepared by Lonnie Magee, McMaster University.** A concerted effort has been made to increase the level of rigour of the Study Guide. Problems of the mathematical and model-manipulation type have been added.

## For the Instructor

The **Instructor Online Learning Centre** includes a password-protected Web site for instructors (**www.mcgrawhill.ca/college/dornbusch**). The site offers downloadable supplements, access to the CANSIM II database and PageOut, the McGraw-Hill Ryerson Web site development centre.

The **Instructor's CD-ROM** contains all of the necessary instructor supplements:

▶ **Instructor's Manual, prepared by author Frank Atkins, University of Calgary,** which outlines clearly all of the changes made to the new edition on a chapter-by-chapter basis. As well, new users will find suggestions for different approaches to use with the material in each chapter. We have also included a section on additional problems, with solutions. These can be used for extra assignment questions or mid-term exam problems.

▶ **Test Bank prepared by author Frank Atkins, University of Calgary,** which has been thoroughly updated and now includes references to the page numbers in the textbook where the answers to the questions can be found. We have included questions at three different levels of difficulty, so that you can carefully design the structure of tests.

Create a custom course Website with **PageOut**, free with every McGraw-Hill Ryerson textbook.

▶ **Microsoft® PowerPoint® Powernotes, prepared by Marc Prud'homme, University of Ottawa,** have been significantly enhanced for this edition.

Visit **www.mhhe.com/pageout** to create a Web page for your course using our resources. PageOut is the McGraw-Hill Ryerson Web site development centre. This Web page-generation software is free to adopters and is designed to help faculty create an online course, complete with assignments, quizzes, links to relevant Web sites, lecture notes, and more—all in a matter of minutes.

In addition, content cartridges are available for course management systems, such as **WebCT** and **Blackboard**. These platforms provide instructors with user-friendly, flexible teaching tools. Please contact your local McGraw-Hill Ryerson i-Learning Specialist for details.

Blackboard
www.blackboard.com

# ACKNOWLEDGEMENTS

The staff at McGraw-Hill Ryerson has been especially helpful in getting this Canadian edition into its final form. We would like to thank Lynn Fisher, Daphne Scriabin, and Anne Nellis. Special thanks to June Trusty for her careful copy editing.

Frank Atkins would like to thank Lonnie Magee (McMaster University) and David Cape (Ryerson University) for extraordinary effort on the technical check of this text.

We also appreciate the many constructive comments made by the reviewers of the Sixth Edition and of the new manuscript as it was being developed. These reviewers include:

Saud Choudhry, *Trent University*

Cristina Echevarria, *University of Saskatchewan*

Michael Fellows, *Mount Royal College*

Derek Hum, *University of Manitoba*

Gustavo Indart, *University of Toronto*

Eric Kam, *Ryerson University*

Kenneth Kasa, *Simon Fraser University*

R. Kolinski, *University of Windsor*

Lonnie Magee, *McMaster University*

Dan Otchere, *Concordia University*

Jack Parkinson, *University of Toronto*

Shmuel Sharir, *University of Alberta*

Javid Taheri, *Saint Mary's University*

Baotai Wang, *University of Northern British Columbia*

# PART 1

# INTRODUCTION AND MEASURING ECONOMIC PERFORMANCE

# CHAPTER 1

# INTRODUCTION

## *LEARNING OBJECTIVES*

After reading and studying this chapter, you should be able to:

▶ *Understand how economists use models, and how price in a market plays an important role in ensuring market equilibrium.*

▶ *Understand how price movement in some markets may be assumed to be slow or even fixed, and how macroeconomics uses these fixed and flexible price assumptions.*

▶ *Identify four different time frames for analysis—the very long run, the long run, the very short run, and the short run—and understand how these time frames are tied to the fixed and flexible price assumptions, and to assumptions concerning factors of production.*

▶ *Understand how actual macroeconomic data are consistent with the assumptions that underlie these time frames.*

For most individuals, the major source of economic news is the media. Inevitably, news reports make economics seem very interesting and important, while at the same time, these same news reports often make the economy seem very complicated. For instance, we all remember the events of late 2001, when there was widespread fear that the Canadian economy had come to a standstill. Many individuals feared that they would lose their jobs. Within months of these events, the focus shifted and, by the summer of 2002, the Canadian economy was believed to be growing too fast and that this could result in inflation.

In macroeconomics, we use the tools of economics to study major economic events such as those mentioned above. No matter how complicated the economy seems to be, you must remember that any economy is composed of individuals like ourselves, going about our daily lives. All of our individual decisions—for instance, what goods to buy, where to work—go together to make up the economy. If we study the Canadian economy from the perspective of the decisions of one individual or from the perspective of just one market, this is the study of microeconomics. Alternatively, if we view the economy from the perspective of aggregate outcomes—total production or the inflation rate for the whole economy—this is the study of macroeconomics.

It is important to remember that microeconomics and macroeconomics are both subdisciplines of economics and each applies economic theory to the problems that are studied. The only real difference between microeconomics and macroeconomics is the perspective. While microeconomics views the economy from the perspective of individual decisions and individual markets, macroeconomics views the economy in aggregate.

In macroeconomics, we study what might be called the "big picture" events in an economy. We examine economic phenomena such as business cycles, long-term growth and productivity, inflation, the exchange rate, and balance of payments. In order to understand the issues involved with macroeconomics, we have to assume that the economy can be described by a set of *aggregate* markets. For instance, in macroeconomics, we deal with the market for goods as a whole, treating all of the markets for different goods—such as the market for agricultural products, or the market for medical services—as a single market. Similarly, we deal with the labour market as a whole, abstracting from the difference between, say, unskilled labour and medical specialists.

Macroeconomics, by its nature, also deals with major policy issues. Some of the great policy questions in our past—and in our future—hinge on an understanding of the workings of the macro economy. A very old question is: *Can* the government intervene in the economy to improve economic performance and, if it can, *should* the government intervene? Of course, there are sceptics on each side of this debate. For instance, the late James Tobin of Yale University won a Nobel Prize in Economics for theories that basically showed that monetary policy has an important stabilizing role to play in the economy. On the other hand, two other Nobel Prize winners—Milton Friedman and Robert Lucas (both of whom were with the University of Chicago for most of their careers)—each developed theories purporting to show the harm that government could possibly do by intervening in the economy.

You have probably been exposed to enough economics by now—either through the media or through your principles courses—to realize that economics has its own particular language and its own manner of thinking about problems. For the remainder of this introductory chapter, we are going to introduce you to how economists think and some of the language that we use.

## 1-1 | HOW ECONOMISTS THINK: MARKETS, MODELS, AND TIME FRAMES

As we noted at the beginning of this chapter, macroeconomics can seem very confusing to some people. You will often see two macroeconomists on the news, and when they are each asked the same question, they will each give what appears to be an opposite answer. For instance, in late 2002 and early 2003, the Bank of Canada raised the bank rate several times. One group of economists claimed that this was necessary, as the economy was growing too quickly and there would be inflation if thc growth was not slowed by higher interest rates. Another group of economists disagreed, saying that a policy-induced increase in interest rates was unnecessary, and that inflation itself would have a natural tendency to slow economic growth without central bank involvement.

As we will learn in this book, both assertions could be correct, depending on the time frame involved and the different assumptions concerning how the economy works. These assumptions are part of the models that we build to understand the economy. In order to analyze economic questions, economists use these **models**, which can be thought of as simplified representations of the world. Since we will make extensive use of models throughout this book, we begin by looking at a very simple model of a labour market. The details of this model will be developed more fully in Chapter 3. For now, it is important only that you understand the general idea of how this model (and all other models) works.

**models**
Simplified representations of the world.

### How Models Work: A Simple Model of the Labour Market

A model of a typical labour market would look like the one shown in Figure 1-1.

---

**FIGURE 1-1**

### A SIMPLE MODEL OF THE LABOUR MARKET

The vertical axis measures the real wage, $w$, and the horizontal axis measures the amount of labour, $N$. The initial equilibrium is at $w_0$, $N_0$. An exogenous increase in female labour force participation shifts the labour supply curve outward to $N_1^s$. At the original real wage, $w_0$, there is an excess supply of labour. This causes the real wage to decrease and more labour to be hired, which brings the market to a new equilibrium at $w_1$, $N_1$.

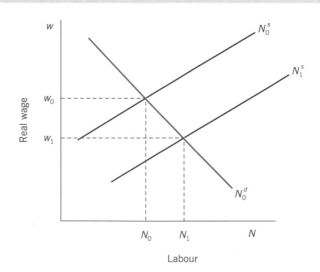

**endogenous variables**
Variables determined within the model.

**exogenous variables**
Variables determined outside of the model.

where $w$ is the real wage, which is equal to the nominal wage $W$, divided by the price level $P$, and $N$ is the number of hours of labour.[1] Models are composed of **endogenous variables** and **exogenous variables**. Endogenous variables are determined within the model and exogenous variables are determined outside of the model. In this model, the real wage and the number of labour hours are the endogenous variables, as their values are determined by the model. The exogenous variables in this model are any important labour market variables that are not determined within the model. For instance, a change in payroll taxes would be exogenous to the demand for labour, and a change in the participation rate would be exogenous to the supply of labour.

We use economic models to answer questions concerning how some change in market conditions will affect the equilibrium in the model. Any economic model works in the following way: A change in an exogenous variable, which is a shift in a curve, works through the model and leads to a change in an endogenous variable, which is a movement along a curve.

In order to illustrate how economists use models, we are going to try to answer the following question: How did the increase in female labour force participation, which started in the 1960s, affect the labour market?

In Figure 1-1, we assume a downward-sloping labour demand curve and an upward-sloping labour supply curve. Given this, the initial equilibrium real wage is $w_0$ and the equilibrium hours worked is $N_0$. These are the equilibrium values of the endogenous variables in the model. The equilibrium will be disturbed if there is a change in an exogenous variable. An increase in female labour force participation is an exogenous change, which shifts the labour supply curve outward to $N_1^s$.

At the previous equilibrium real wage, $w_0$, there is now an excess supply of labour. In economics, we assume that excess supply in any market will reduce price in that market. Here the price is the real wage, and therefore the excess supply of labour makes the real wage decrease. This real wage decrease means that more labour will be demanded (movement along the labour demand curve) and less labour will be supplied (movement along the new labour supply curve). The end result is a new equilibrium at $w_1$ and $N_1$. At the new equilibrium, the real wage is lower and employment is higher. Further, because the market is in equilibrium, all workers who want to work at the new real wage have found employment. Therefore, the unemployment rate has not changed between $N_0$ and $N_1$.

Be sure that you understand that it is the movement in the real wage, $w$, that drives the market back to equilibrium when there is an exogenous change. Therefore, the role of the real wage in this model, or any price in an economic model, is to ensure that the market remains in equilibrium. As long as the real wage is free to move after there is a shock (an exogenous change is often called a *shock*), the answer to our question would be the following: An increase in female labour force participation lowers the real wage, increases employment, and has no effect on the unemployment rate.

## Flexible Prices and Sticky Prices

It is worth emphasizing the following point: In economics, we assume that the mechanism that drives a market back to equilibrium is the movement of price in that market. For our labour market model, it was the change in the real wage that brought

---

[1] We will discuss the difference between nominal and real variables in some detail in Chapter 3.

the market back to equilibrium. Now ask yourself the following question: What if the labour market was faced with this shock, and the real wage, for some reason, moved only slowly, or did not move at all? If we assume that the real wage moves only very slowly, then the new equilibrium may not be reached for a long period of time. In this situation, there would be unemployment in the labour market after the change in the participation rate. Therefore, the answer to our question concerning the change in the participation rate depends on the assumption we are willing to make concerning the speed of market adjustment.

In macroeconomics, we accept that there are two different manners in which to view the **speed of adjustment** in a market. Another way to put this is that macroeconomics uses two paradigms. For our purposes, we can think of a paradigm as a generally accepted manner in which to analyze problems. One paradigm in macroeconomics can be called the **Classical, or market clearing, paradigm**, which uses the assumption that all **prices are flexible**, and, therefore, that all markets clear at all times.[2] The other paradigm can be called the **Keynesian, or non-market clearing, paradigm**, which uses the assumption that (at least some) prices move slowly, or, in some cases, are even fixed. These Keynesian models are sometimes called **sticky price** models.

Each of these paradigms makes sense over a different time frame. When we are analyzing the economy over long periods of time, we assume that prices move freely to ensure market equilibrium. When we are analyzing the economy over short periods of time, it is reasonable to assume that price movement is very slow, or in some cases that price does not move at all and, therefore, there will be some markets that do not clear.

## Market Clearing, Non-Market Clearing, and Time

It turns out that we need to be a bit more precise concerning the concepts of long run and short run. For instance, when we are looking at the economy over generations, we are concerned with different aspects of the economy than we would be when looking at the economy over, say, 10 to 15 years. However, each of these time frames would require models that have flexible prices and, therefore, they would fit into our definition of long run. Similarly, when we view the economy over, say, five years, we are interested in different aspects of the economy than we would be when we look at the economy over one to two years. Each of these time frames would require models with non-flexible prices and, therefore, would be considered to be short run. For these reasons, we divide the generic long run into two parts, which we will call the *very long run* and the *long run*. We also divide the generic short run into the *very short run* and the *short run*. Each of these terms is discussed below.

The first time frame is called the **very long run**, and this is where we study growth theory. We use the assumption that all prices are flexible and, therefore, all markets are in equilibrium at all times, and ask how the accumulation of inputs—investment in machinery, for example—and improvements in technology lead to an increase in standard of living. We ignore recessions and booms and related short run fluctuations in employment of people and other resources.

How can a model that ignores fluctuations in the economy possibly tell us anything sensible? Fluctuations in the economy—the ups and downs of unemployment, for example—tend to average out over the years. Over long periods of time, all that matters is how quickly the economy grows on average. Growth theory seeks to explain the growth rate averaged over many years or decades. Chapter 4 examines the

**speed of adjustment**
The amount of time it takes a price to adjust so that a market returns to equilibrium.

**Classical, or market clearing, paradigm**
A paradigm that uses the assumption that all prices are flexible, and, therefore, that all markets clear at all times.

**flexible prices**
Prices that are assumed to move very quickly after an exogenous change.

**Keynesian, or non-market clearing, paradigm**
A paradigm that uses the assumption that (at least some) prices move slowly, or, in some cases, are even fixed.

**sticky prices**
Prices that are unable to adjust quickly enough to keep markets in equilibrium.

**very long run**
The time frame in which growth theory is studied; all prices are flexible and all markets are in equilibrium at all times.

---

[2] A market is said to clear when it is in equilibrium.

causes of economic growth and the differences in growth rates among nations. In all countries, the rate of savings is a key determinant of future well-being. Countries that are willing to sacrifice today, in terms of less current consumption and more savings, have higher standards of living in the future.

Do we really care whether the economy grows at 2 percent per year rather than at 4 percent? Over a lifetime, the difference matters a great deal: At the end of one 20-year generation, our standard of living will be 50 percent higher under 4 percent growth than under 2 percent growth. Over 100 years, a 4 percent growth rate produces a standard of living seven times higher than does a 2 percent growth rate.

The second time frame is called the **long run**. In this time frame, all prices are still considered to be flexible and all markets are still assumed to be in equilibrium at all times, but the productive capacity of the economy is assumed to be fixed. In this situation, all factors of production are fully employed, but not growing, and output is at the full employment level, but not changing.

You can get an idea of how the long run and the very long run are modelled by studying Figure 1-2. The **aggregate demand–aggregate supply models** presented in this figure will be developed later in the book. The aggregate supply ($AS$) curve depicts, for each price level, the total quantity that firms are willing to supply. The position of the $AS$ curve depends on the productive capacity of the economy. The aggregate demand ($AD$) curve shows, for each given price level, the level of output at which the goods market and the money market are simultaneously in equilibrium. The position of the $AD$ curve depends on monetary and fiscal policy and the level of consumer confidence. The intersection of the $AD$ and $AS$ curves determines price and quantity.

In Figure 1-2(a), we show the long run, where we assume that factors of production are fully employed but not changing and the $AS$ curve is vertical at the level of full employment output. Therefore, in the long run, output is determined by aggregate supply alone. For a given $AS$ curve, the price level is determined by the level of aggregate demand. If $AD$ was to increase, the price level would increase, while the

**long run**
The time frame in which all prices are considered to be flexible, and all markets are assumed to be in equilibrium at all times, but the productive capacity of the economy is assumed to be fixed.

**aggregate demand–aggregate supply model**
The major macroeconomic model that will be used throughout this book. The $AD$ curve shows, for each price level, the amount of demand from the goods and money market simultaneously. The aggregate supply curve shows, for each price level, the amount that firms are willing to supply.

## FIGURE 1-2

### THE AGGREGATE DEMAND–AGGREGATE SUPPLY MODEL IN THE LONG RUN AND THE VERY LONG RUN

Figure 1-2(a) shows the $AD$–$AS$ model in the long run when we assume that all factors of production are fully employed but not changing. Output is determined by $AS$, and $AD$ determines the price. Figure 1-2(b) shows the $AS$ curve in the very long run. In the very long run, output grows by an average of approximately 2 percent per year. Therefore, in the very long run, the $AS$ curve is shifting outward by 2 percent per year.

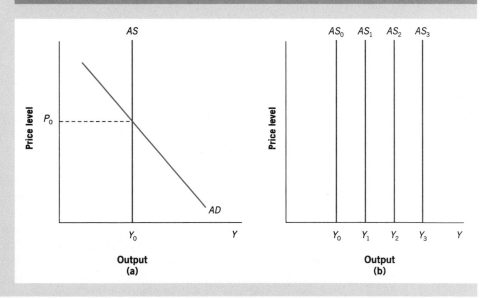

level of output would remain constant. We know that aggregate demand changes can be very large and very fast. It follows that rapid increases in the overall price level— that is, high inflation rates—are always due to changes in aggregate demand. In fact, as we will eventually learn, the only source of really high inflation rates is government-sanctioned increases in the money supply.[3]

The very long run is shown in Figure 1-2(b). Because the factors of production are increasing, the full employment level of output is increasing. Since economic growth over the very long run averages a few percentage points per year, we know that the *AS* curve typically moves to the right by a few percentage points per year

The third time frame that macroeconomists study is the **very short run**. Recall that in the short run, prices are assumed to be sticky or even fixed. In the very short run, we are considering a time frame that is short enough that we can consider prices to be fixed. Therefore, in the very short run the aggregate supply curve is horizontal. This is shown in Figure 1-3.

**very short run**

The time frame in which prices are assumed to be fixed.

---

### FIGURE 1-3

In the very short run, we assume that the price level is fixed, so the *AS* curve is assumed to be horizontal. In this situation, *AD* determines output.

## THE AGGREGATE DEMAND–AGGREGATE SUPPLY MODEL IN THE VERY SHORT RUN

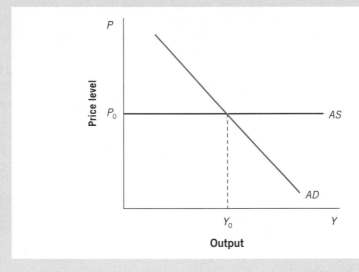

---

It can be seen from Figure 1-3 that, in the very short run, the price level is determined by the *AS* curve, and changes in aggregate demand will bring about changes in output.

**short run**

The time frame in which prices are assumed to be sticky.

The fourth time frame is called the **short run**. In the short run, prices are assumed to be sticky, as opposed to fixed. That is, prices will adjust somewhat, but not fully. In this time frame, the aggregate supply curve has a slope somewhere between horizontal and vertical. The short run aggregate demand-aggregate supply model is shown in Figure 1-4. How steep is the short run aggregate supply curve? This question represents one of the major areas of research and discussion in macroeconomics. The speed with which prices adjust is a critical parameter for our understanding of the economy. At a horizon of 20 years, not much matters except the rate of very long run growth. In the very short run, at a horizon of less than one year, not much matters except aggregate demand.

---

[3] Some temporary price increases can be due to supply shocks. For example, drought could cause crop failure.

## Models and the Real World

Models are simplified representations of the real world. A good model accurately explains the behaviours that are most important to us and omits details that are relatively unimportant. The notion that the earth revolves around the sun on an elliptical path and that the moon similarly revolves around the earth is an example of a model. The exact behaviour of sun, earth, and moon is much more complicated, but this model enables us to understand the phases of the moon. For this purpose, it is a good model. Even though the real orbits are not simple ellipses, the model "works."

In economics, the complex behaviour of millions of individuals, firms, and markets is represented by one, two, a dozen, a few hundred, or a few thousand mathematical relations in the form of graphs or equations or computer programs. The intellectual problem in model building is that humans can understand the interactions between, at most, only a handful of relations. So usable macrotheory relies on a toolbox of models, each consisting of two or three equations. A particular model is a tool based on a set of assumptions—for example, that the economy is at full employment—that is reasonable in some real-world circumstances. Understanding the macroeconomy requires a rich toolbox and the application of sound judgement regarding when to deploy a particular model. We cannot overemphasize this point: The only way to understand the very complicated world in which we live is to master a toolbox of simplifying models and to then make quite explicit decisions as to which model is best suited for analyzing a given problem.

As an illustration, consider three very specific economic questions: (1) How will your grandchildren's standard of living compare to yours? (2) What caused the great inflation of the post–World War I Weimar Republic (the inflation that contributed to Hitler's rise to power)? (3) Why did the Canadian unemployment rate, which had been just over 7 percent during 1979, reach nearly 12 percent by 1983? You can answer each of these questions by applying a model introduced in this chapter.

1.   Over a time span of a couple of generations, we want a model of very long run growth. Nothing much matters except the development of new technology and the accumulation of capital. At growth rates between 2 and 4 percent, income would more than double and less than quintuple. Your grandchildren would certainly live much better than you do. They would certainly not be as rich as Bill Gates is today.

2.   Huge inflations have one cause: great outward sweeps of the aggregate demand curve caused by the government's printing too much money. Small changes in the price level may have many contributing factors. However, huge changes in prices are the domain of the long run aggregate supply–aggregate demand model, in which a vertical aggregate supply curve remains relatively motionless, while the aggregate demand curve moves outward.

3.   Big changes over short time spans in the level of economic activity, and thus in unemployment, are explained by the short run aggregate supply–aggregate demand model—with a horizontal aggregate supply curve. At the beginning of the 1980s, the Bank of Canada clamped down on aggregate demand, driving the economy into a deep recession. The Bank's intention was to reduce inflation—eventually, this is just what happened. But as the short run model explains, over very short periods, cutting back aggregate demand reduces output, increasing unemployment.

There's a flip side to knowing which model to use to answer a question: You also need to know which models to ignore. In thinking about growth over two generations, monetary policy is pretty much irrelevant. And in thinking about the great German inflation, technological change doesn't much matter. As you study macroeconomics, you'll find that memorizing lists of equations is much less important than learning to match the model to the problem at hand.

## FIGURE 1-4

In this time frame, both price and output are determined by the inter- action of *AD* and *AS*.

### THE AGGREGATE DEMAND–AGGREGATE SUPPLY MODEL IN THE SHORT RUN

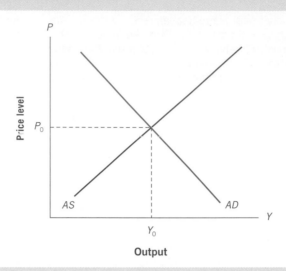

## BOX 1-2

### The Long Run and the Short Run

Whenever macroeconomic events are discussed, either by the media or in most macroeconomic textbooks, these events are generally referred to as simply long run or short run. From the perspective of the *AD-AS* model introduced in this chapter, the distinction is very easy to understand: In the long run, we assume that all prices are flexible and all markets clear; therefore, in the long run, the *AS* curve will be vertical. In the short run, we assume that (at least some) prices are not flexible and some mar- kets do not clear; therefore, in the short run, the *AS* curve is not vertical.

However, some short run events happen very, very quickly—for instance, short run interest rate changes that will be discussed in Part 4. Similarly, some long run events happen very slowly—for instance, the amount of time it takes for changes in the growth rate of the capital stock to change the average growth rate of real income, which will be discussed in Chapter 4. Because of this, we have divided the generic long run into two parts: the very long run and the long run. We have also divided the generic short run into two parts: the very short run and the short run.

#### Distinguishing between the Very Long Run and the Long Run

The difference between the very long run and the long run lies in whether or not the vertical *AS* is shifting. In the *very long run*, capital and labour are growing and there may also be technological change. Therefore, full employment output is growing and the *AS* curve is shifting. In the *long run*, the *AS* is still vertical, but it is stationary at the level of full employment output, as any growth in the factors of production has not altered the average growth rate of income.

#### Distinguishing between the Very Short Run and the Short Run

The difference between the very short run and the short run is whether the slope of the *AS* curve is horizontal or upward sloping (but not vertical). In the *very short run*, prices are assumed to be fixed and the *AS* curve is horizontal. In the *short run*, prices are beginning to adjust, so that they are not fixed, but adjusting slowly (called *sticky prices*) and the *AS* curve has slope somewhere between horizontal and vertical.

> ## BOX
> ## 1-3
>
> ### Demand and Supply Models in Microeconomics and Macroeconomics
>
> Critics of economics often state that all economists know is supply and demand. It is certainly true that supply and demand models play an important role in economics. In Figures 1-2 through 1-4, we have shown that the macroeconomic aggregate demand-aggregate supply model looks different over various time frames. There is a tendency to think of the *AD-AS* model in macroeconomics as being the same as the demand-supply model in microeconomics. This can be somewhat misleading in two important ways.
>
> First, consider the price on the vertical axis in each model. In macroeconomics, this is the *price level*, which is an index of all prices in the economy. That is, it is a measure of overall purchasing power.* Therefore, if the price level increases, there has been an increase in the price of *all goods*. In microeconomics, the price on the vertical axis is the price of one individual good, *with all other individual prices being held constant*. Therefore, if the price was to increase, there would be a relative price change for this one good.
>
> Second, consider the quantity on the horizontal axis. In macroeconomics, this is the amount of goods produced, or GDP. Of course, GDP is composed of a variety of goods, but in macroeconomics, we treat these various goods as one composite good. Therefore, an increase in this quantity is an increase in production for the *economy as a whole*. In microeconomics, the quantity on the horizontal axis is the quantity of one good in the particular market that is being studied. An increase in this quantity is simply an increase in production of that *one good*.
>
> ---
>
> *The concept of a price index will be discussed in detail in Chapter 2.

## 1-2 | THE DATA OUR MODELS ARE TRYING TO EXPLAIN

### Gross Domestic Product

The growth rate of the economy is the rate at which gross domestic product (GDP) is increasing over time. On average, most developed economies grow by approximately 2.0 percent per year over long periods of time. Figure 1-5 plots real income per person in Canada over the 133 years from 1870 to 2002. Notice that, on average, income has been growing steadily over these years. The average growth rate of real GDP in Canada from 1870 to 2002 was approximately 2.0 percent per year and, roughly speaking, we can measure this growth rate by the slope of the line in Figure 1-5. If we wanted to explain this very long run growth rate or why this growth rate might be different after the 1930s (notice that the slope of the line appears steeper after about 1930), we would use the very long run growth model, where we assume that the *AS* curve shifts outward, as in Figure 1-2(b).

Over somewhat shorter periods of time (but still the long run), we are not concerned with the trend growth of GDP. Figure 1-6 shows GDP per person over the 15-year period of 1988–2002. The average annual growth rate over this period was just over 1 percent, and you can see that the graph appears much flatter than in Figure 1-5.

## FIGURE 1-5

### REAL GDP PER CAPITA, 1870–2002 (THOUSANDS OF 1997 DOLLARS)

The vertical axis measures real GDP per person in thousands of 1997 dollars. Over the long run, output per person grows reasonably steadily. The average annual growth rate over this period is approximately 2.0 percent. For this very long run time frame, we assume that the *AS* curve is vertical and shifting outward.

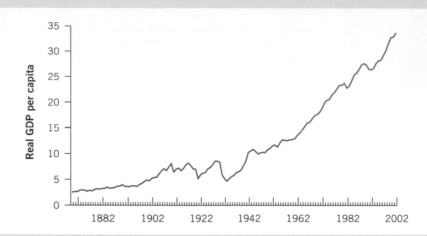

SOURCE: GDP in 1997 dollars: 1870–1926: Adapted from M.C. Urquhart, *Gross National Product, Canada, 1870–1926*; 1926–1961: Statistics Canada, *Historical Statistics of Canada*, Publication 11-516-XIE (available in electronic form at www.statcan.ca/english/freepub/11-516-XIE/free.htm); 1961–2002: CANSIM II V1992259; population: Statistics Canada, *Historical Statistics of Canada* and CANSIM II V1.

www.statcan.ca/english/
freepub/11-516-XIE/free.htm

This is the approximate period of time over which we use the long run *AD-AS* model of Figure 1-2(a), where we assume that the *AS* curve is vertical but not shifting. In this long run time frame, we make the assumption that current factors of production are fully employed, and we ignore growth in these factors.

In order to illustrate how volatile the very short run movements in GDP can be, we have graphed the rate of growth of real GDP per capita from quarter to quarter

## FIGURE 1-6

### REAL GDP PER CAPITA, 1988–2002 (THOUSANDS OF 1997 DOLLARS)

Over this 15-year period, the average annual growth rate is just over 1 percent. Within this period, you can see (if you look carefully) the downturn in the economy in the early 1990s and the long recovery through the 1990s. However, for long run analysis, we ignore these ups and downs and assume that the *AS* curve is vertical and stationary.

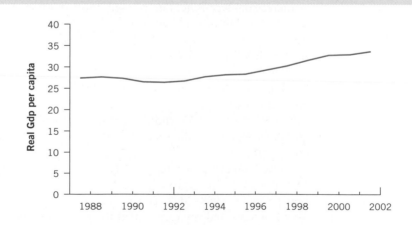

SOURCE: Real GDP: CANSIM II V1992259; population: CANSIM II V1.

over the period 1998–2002 in Figure 1-7. It can be seen from this figure that output varies quite a bit over the very short run. In this time frame, we assume that the *AS* curve is horizontal and that output changes due to demand shocks, as depicted in Figure 1-3.

**FIGURE 1-7**

Over the very short run, output varies substantially. This figure shows the rate of change in real GDP per person quarterly. In this diagram, you can see clearly the quarterly ups and downs in GDP, as well as the economic downturn in 2001, with the beginning of the recovery in 2002. In this very short run time framework, we assume that the *AS* curve is horizontal and shifts in *AD* determine changes in GDP.

**REAL GDP PER CAPITA, PERCENTAGE CHANGE, 1998 QUARTER 1 TO 2002 QUARTER 4**

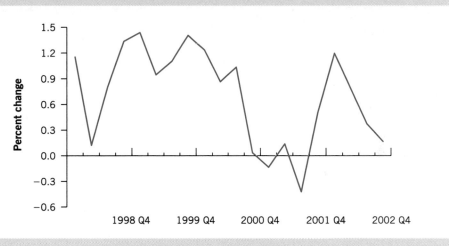

SOURCE: Real GDP: CANSIM II V1992259; population: CANSIM II V1.

**business cycle**
The more or less regular pattern of expansion (recovery) and contraction (recession) in economic activity around full employment output.

**Phillips Curve**
A measure of the speed of adjustment of prices.

The very short run fluctuations in Figure 1-7 are a rough characterization of **a business cycle**. A business cycle is the more or less regular pattern of expansion (recovery) and contraction (recession) in economic activity around full employment output. If you look carefully, you can see some business cycle patterns in Figures 1-5 and 1-6.

In the short run, when we assume that the *AS* curve has some upward slope, we are concerned with the speed of price adjustment. That is, if the *AS* curve was horizontal, then there would be no price adjustment, and if the *AS* curve was vertical, there would be full price adjustment. The speed of price adjustment can be summarized by the **Phillips Curve**, one version of which is graphed in Figure 1-8.

In Figure 1-8, the inflation rate is plotted against the unemployment rate using annual data over the period of 1992 to 2002. The slope of the line fitted to the data is −0.19. This means that, over the period of one year, if the unemployment rate increased by one percentage point, the inflation rate would decrease by only 0.19 percent. Thus, over the short run, price adjustment is quite slow and the aggregate supply curve is quite flat.

FIGURE 1-8

**PHILIPS CURVE, 1992–2002**

The vertical axis measures the rate of change of the Consumer Price Index (inflation) and the horizontal axis measures the unemployment rate. The Phillips Curve is a measure of the speed of adjustment of prices. The slope of the trend line in this graph is –0.19 This means that a fall in the unemployment rate from, say, 6 percent to 5 percent, would be accompanied by an increase in the inflation rate of just under 0.2% over one year.

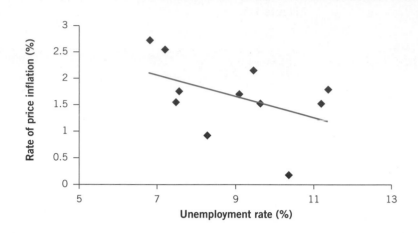

SOURCE: Consumer Price Index: CANSIM II V735319; unemployment rate: CANSIM II V2062815.

# POLICY IN *ACTION*

## Monetary Policy Immediately after September 11, 2001

By the middle of 2001, it was becoming clear that the Canadian economy was slipping into an economic slowdown. The events of September 11, 2001, served to push the economy even farther downward. We can use the tools developed in this introductory chapter to have a first look at the policy reaction to these events. We will return to this question in later chapters.

The monetary policy reaction to the events of late 2001 was swift and strong. The central bank immediately lowered interest rates to levels not seen in 40 years. From the perspective of our *AD-AS* model, the actions of the central bank served to shift the *AD* curve outward, in an attempt to soften the effects of the economic slowdown. We know that, in the very short run, the *AS* curve is horizontal. Therefore, when the *AD* curve shifts outward, output should go up. This is exactly what we observed from this policy move. If you look at Figure 1-7, you will see that GDP increased sharply in early 2002.

However, a question remains concerning what we might expect to happen over the other time frames discussed in this chapter. In the short run, we expect that there would be some price adjustment, as the *AS* curve is upward sloping (but not vertical). Interestingly, in late 2002 and into 2003, we saw increases in the inflation rate in Canada, which is consistent with some price adjustment in the short run.

It remains to be seen what the effects on the economy will be over the long run time periods.

**Consumer Price Index (CPI)**

A measure of the average cost consumers face when purchasing goods and services.

**inflation rate**

The rate of change in the CPI.

## The Price Level and the Inflation Rate

One measure of the average cost that consumers face when purchasing goods and services is the **Consumer Price Index** (CPI). The CPI is plotted from 1915 to 2002 in the upper panel of Figure 1-9. The rate of change in the CPI is called the **inflation rate**. The inflation rate is plotted over the same period as the CPI in the lower panel of Figure 1-9.

### *FIGURE 1-9*

The upper panel shows the level of consumer prices, measured as an index, with 1992 = 100. The lower panel measures the rate of change in consumer prices, or the inflation rate. There are both long run trend movements and short run cyclical movements in consumer prices. After World War II, consumer prices started a long run upward trend. However, you can see short run movements in the inflation rate due the recessionary periods in the economy in 1975, 1981, and 1991.

**PRICE LEVEL AND THE INFLATION RATE, 1915–2002**

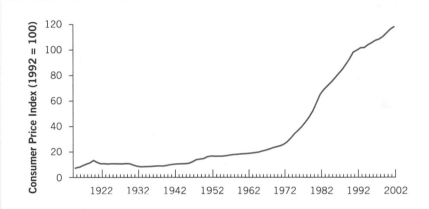

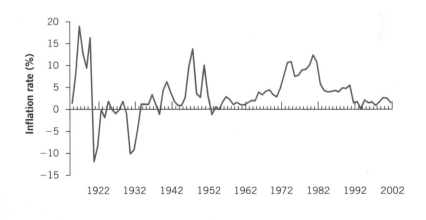

SOURCE: CANSIM II V735319.

Notice that between 1915 and the end of World War II, the CPI was roughly constant. However, within this period, there were cyclical movements in the inflation rate. There were periods of high inflation due to the two World Wars, but there were also two periods of *deflation* (when the inflation rate was negative) after World War I and during the Great Depression.

After World War II, and especially during the 1970s, the price level was continually increasing. As we will see later in the book, this period of sustained inflation was due to continual aggregate demand increases caused by excessive increases in the money supply by the government. Once again, within this period, there were also cyclical movements in the inflation rate. During the 1960s, there was a long growth period in GDP and the inflation rate was gradually increasing. However, there was a slowdown in growth in the early 1970s and in approximately 1975, when the inflation rate went down. More dramatically, you can see the reaction of the inflation rate to the recessions of the early 1980s and early 1990s.

## Money and Interest Rates

There are many ways to think about how the Bank of Canada can affect the economy in the short run and the long run. In this section, we briefly review two important monetary policy variables: the rate of growth of the money stock and the level of the short-term interest rate.

The many different definitions of money will be discussed in detail in Chapter 17, but here we focus on one commonly used measure of the money supply: $M2$. Figure 1-10 plots the annual rate of growth of $M2$ between 1915 and 2002.

## FIGURE 1-10

### MONEY STOCK, ANNUAL GROWTH RATE, 1915–2002

The rate of growth of the money supply has considerable short run fluctuation as well as longer trend movements. The rate of growth of money decreased considerably just prior to the recessions of the early 1980s and the early 1990s, indicating a tighter monetary policy stance. You can also see that the long upward trend in the growth rate of money that started in the 1950s roughly matches the upward trend in the inflation rate over the same period, which was shown in Figure 1-9.

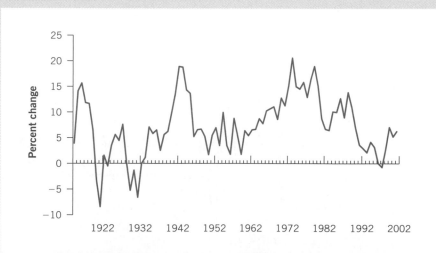

SOURCE: Historical data is taken from *New Estimates of the Canadian Money Stock, 1871–1967* by Cheri Metcalf, Angela Redish, and Ronald Shearer, University of British Columbia Discussion Paper 96-17. The data is available at www.econ.ubc.ca/dp96list.htm. From 1968–2002: CANSIM II V37128.

Figure 1-10 shows that the rate of growth of the money supply has considerable short run fluctuation as well as longer trend movements. Notice how the rate of growth of money increased during World Wars I and II and then decreased considerably at the end of each of these wars. Because the rate of growth of the money stock is controlled by the Bank of Canada, we can use Figure 1-10 as a guide to the stance

**www.bankofcanada.ca/en/
graphs/a1-table.htm**

of monetary policy.[4] The rate of growth of money decreased considerably just prior to the recessions of the early 1980s and the early 1990s, indicating a tighter monetary policy stance. You can also see that the long upward trend in the growth rate of money that started in the 1950s roughly matches the upward trend in the inflation rate over the same period, as shown in Figure 1-9. This is some indication that the Bank of Canada played a role in the inflation of the 1970s.

Another indicator of monetary policy conditions is the level of the short-term interest rate. Figure 1-11 plots the level of the 90-day Treasury bill interest rate over the period 1946–2002.

## FIGURE 1-11

The shorter business cycle movements in the interest rate roughly follow those in the rate of growth of money, especially at the onset of the recessions of the early 1980s and 1990s. The trend in the Treasury bill interest rate since the 1950s also follows the trend in the rate of growth of money and the inflation rate over the same period.

### 90-DAY TREASURY BILL INTEREST RATE, 1946–2002

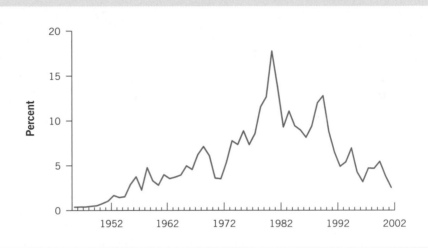

SOURCE: CANSIM II V122484.

The interest rate movements in Figure 1-11 show some interesting patterns, which will be discussed throughout the book. Notice that, in terms of shorter run monetary policy stance, the interest rate increased considerably just prior to the recessions of the early 1980s and 1990s. The relationship between these movements and the shorter run money supply movements noted above will be the focus of Chapters 12 and 13 of this book. Further, the longer run upward trend in the interest rate starting in the 1950s matches the trend in both the rate of growth of money (Figure 1-10) and the inflation rate (Figure 1-9). These longer run issues will be discussed in Chapter 3.

## The Unemployment Rate

**unemployment rate**
A measure of the number of people who are actively in the labour force seeking jobs, but who cannot find work.

The **unemployment rate** is a measure of the number of people who are actively in the labour force who are seeking jobs but cannot find work. The national unemployment rate over the period of 1921–2002 is plotted in Figure 1-12.

---

[4] You should be aware that the Bank of Canada did not exist prior to 1935, so attributing the rate of growth of money to monetary policy stance prior to this period is somewhat problematic.

## FIGURE 1-12

The unemployment rate measures the number of people in the workforce who are actively seeking jobs but cannot find employment. The unemployment rate exhibits long run trend movements as well as short run cyclical movements. From the 1960s to the early 1990s, there was a trend increase in the unemployment rate. However, during this period, the unemployment rate showed cyclical movements, such as the increase in unemployment due to the recession of the early 1980s.

### THE UNEMPLOYMENT RATE, 1921–2002

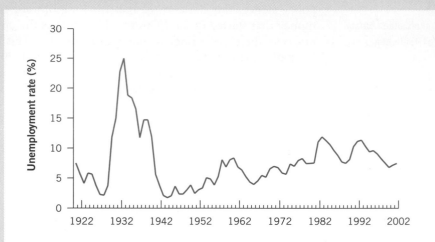

SOURCE: 1921–1945: M.C. Urquhart (ed.), *Historical Statistics of Canada* (Macmillan: 1965); 1946–1975: Statistics Canada, *Historical Statistics of Canada*, Publication 11-516-XIE; 1976–2002: CANSIM II V2062815. All historical statistics were adjusted by the authors to be consistent with the CANSIM series.

The most striking feature of Figure 1-12 is the dramatic increase in the unemployment rate during the Great Depression, when 25 percent of the labour force could not find jobs, and the equally dramatic fall during World War II, when the unemployment rate was as low as 1.8 percent. Notice that, on average, after World War II, the unemployment rate was increasing, in spite of the fact that, on average, the economy was expanding. You are asked to comment on this observation in Discussion Question 1 at the end of this chapter.

Even though the average unemployment rate was increasing after World War II, you can see the highly cyclical nature of the unemployment rate over this period. During the expansion of the early 1960s, the unemployment rate decreased, and during the recessions of the early 1980s and the early 1990s, the unemployment rate increased dramatically.

For a regional economy such as Canada's, there are important differences between the national unemployment rate and the provincial unemployment rates. These differences will be discussed in Chapter 8.

## The International Economy

One of the most prominent economic changes over the last 20 years has been the movement toward a more global economy, where countries engage in a great deal of trade with each other. This trade takes place in the form of goods and services, and also in the form of trade in financial instruments. An economy that engages in a substantial amount of international trade is known as an **open economy**. The Canadian economy has always been an open economy and international trade has taken on more prominence in our economy, given today's global economic environment.

In our economy, one of the aspects of openness with which we are concerned is the **balance of trade**, the difference in values of exports and imports. Exports and imports are plotted in Figure 1-13.

**open economy**
An economy that engages in a substantial amount of international trade.

**balance of trade**
The difference between exports and imports.

### FIGURE 1-13

**EXPORTS, IMPORTS, AND BALANCE OF TRADE, PERCENTAGE OF GDP, 1926–2002**

The vertical axis measures exports, imports, and the balance of trade (values of exports – values of imports) as a percentage of GDP. Canada has had periods of a trade deficit (when imports are greater than exports), such as the 1950s, and periods of a trade surplus (when exports are greater than imports), such as the late 1990s.

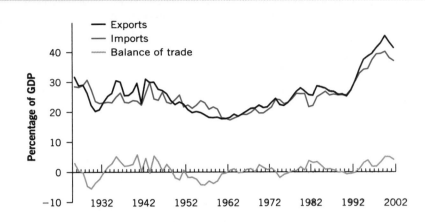

SOURCE: 1926–1960: Statistics Canada, *Historical Statistics of Canada*, Publication 11-516-XIE; 1961–2002: exports, CANSIM II V498935; imports, V498938; GDP: V498918.

You can see from Figure 1-13 that during World War II and in the late 1990s, exports exceeded imports and Canada had a trade surplus. Conversely, during the 1950s, imports exceeded exports and Canada was running a trade deficit.

In an open economy such as Canada's, another important variable is the **foreign exchange rate**. The foreign exchange rate is the price that foreign citizens must pay for one Canadian dollar or, equivalently, the price that Canadians must pay for one unit of foreign currency. There will be a foreign exchange rate for any country that Canada trades with. However, since a great deal of our trade is with the United States economy, the U.S. foreign exchange rate is important to us. The Canada-U.S. foreign exchange rate over the period 1950–2002 is shown in Figure 1-14.

**foreign exchange rate**
The price that foreign citizens must pay for one Canadian dollar, or, equivalently, the price that Canadians must pay for one unit of foreign currency.

### FIGURE 1-14

**CANADA-U.S. EXCHANGE RATE, 1950–2002**

The exchange rate was fixed in the early 1960s until 1973 at approximately $0.92 U.S. Since then, it has been a floating exchange rate.

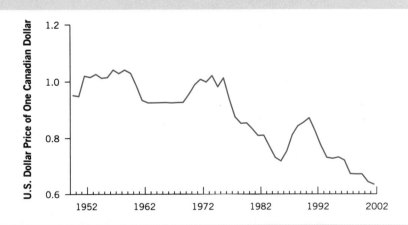

SOURCE: CANSIM II V37126.

Notice that during the 1950s, the Canadian dollar was roughly on par with the U.S. dollar. During the 1960s, the Canadian dollar was fixed in a narrow band at approximately $0.92 U.S. Since 1973, the Canadian dollar has been floating and has been subject to large changes.

## 1-3 | WHAT'S NEXT

We have organized this book around the broad themes that have been introduced in this chapter: The economy can be viewed from different time frames. Chapter 2 completes this introductory section by discussing various measures of economic activity that can be used to assess the performance of the Canadian economy.

Part 2 deals with long run issues. First we present a market clearing long run model of the economy with fixed productive capacity and then proceed to discuss the very long run growth model in Chapter 4. Chapter 5 presents an introduction to open economy issues and the exchange rate.

In Part 3, Chapters 6 and 7 present models of aggregate demand and aggregate supply that deal with the issue of price adjustment. Part 3 also contains a chapter on inflation and unemployment and a chapter on the international adjustment.

In Part 4, we examine the *IS-LM* model that underlies our aggregate demand curve. Part 5 discusses the details of the individual economic behaviour behind the broad macroeconomic models, and Part 6 deals with monetary and fiscal policy and advanced topics.

## *Working with Data*

In each chapter of the book, we are going to give you a chance to work with some of the data presented in the chapter. Almost all of this data pertaining to the Canadian economy comes from Statistics Canada's CANSIM II database, to which most universities in Canada have access.

Each data series in CANSIM II has a CANSIM II number. For instance, the GDP series that we used in this chapter has CANSIM II number V1992259. In this section, in order to get you started using CANSIM, we are going to show you how to reproduce Figure 1-7. To do this, you will need CANSIM II series V1992259 (real GDP) and V1 (population). These are shown in Columns (1) and (2) in the table on the next page. You will need to create per capita GDP by multiplying real GDP by 1,000,000 and then dividing it by population. You need to multiply, because real GDP is measured in millions of dollars, while population is raw numbers. Real GDP per capita is shown in column (3).

The last column is simply the percentage change of the numbers from column (3). So, for instance, the first number is 0.13 = [($30,201.67 − $30,162.84)/$30,162.84]. The numbers from column (4) are used to produce Figure 1-7.

| Date | Income (millions of 1997 dollars) (1) | Population (2) | Per Capita Income (3) | Growth Rate (4) |
|---|---|---|---|---|
| 1998Q1 | 908268 | 30112150 | 30162.84 | |
| 1998Q2 | 911136 | 30168395 | 30201.67 | 0.13 |
| 1998Q3 | 920924 | 30248412 | 30445.37 | 0.81 |
| 1998Q4 | 935672 | 30326130 | 30853.66 | 1.34 |
| 1999Q1 | 950072 | 30354641 | 31299.07 | 1.44 |
| 1999Q1 | 950072 | 30354641 | 31299.07 | 1.44 |
| 1999Q2 | 960912 | 30411507 | 31596.99 | 0.95 |
| 1999Q3 | 974708 | 30509323 | 31947.87 | 1.11 |
| 1999Q4 | 991276 | 30596443 | 32398.41 | 1.41 |
| 2000Q1 | 1004632 | 30629243 | 32799.77 | 1.24 |
| 2000Q2 | 1015668 | 30698567 | 33085.19 | 0.87 |
| 2000Q3 | 1029320 | 30790834 | 33429.43 | 1.04 |
| 2000Q4 | 1032852 | 30883995 | 33442.95 | 0.04 |
| 2001Q1 | 1032760 | 30921275 | 33399.66 | −0.13 |
| 2001Q2 | 1036996 | 31003581 | 33447.62 | 0.14 |
| 2001Q3 | 1036240 | 31110565 | 33308.30 | −0.42 |
| 2001Q4 | 1044860 | 31210081 | 33478.29 | 0.51 |
| 2002Q1 | 1058448 | 31240487 | 33880.65 | 1.20 |
| 2002Q2 | 1069320 | 31315287 | 34146.90 | 0.79 |
| 2002Q3 | 1076744 | 31413990 | 34275.94 | 0.38 |
| 2002Q4 | 1081044 | 31485623 | 34334.53 | 0.17 |

## C H A P T E R    S U M M A R Y

▶ Models are simplified depictions that attempt to capture the essential elements of how the macroeconomy works.

▶ Models contain endogenous variables that are determined within the model and exogenous variables that are determined outside of the model. Models work in the following way: A change in an exogenous variable, through the model, brings about a change in an endogenous variable.

▶ Our major model will be the aggregate demand-aggregate supply model.

www.mcgrawhill.ca/college/dornbusch

▶ Over the very long run, we assume that the aggregate supply curve is vertical and shifting outward as factors of production (labour and capital) grow. Analysis of the very long run is called *growth theory*.

▶ Over the long run, we assume that factors of production are fully employed but not growing. In the long run, we assume that the aggregate supply curve is vertical but not shifting.

▶ Over the long run and the very long run, prices are assumed to be flexible.

▶ In the very short run, the price level is assumed to be fixed. The aggregate supply curve is assumed to be horizontal, and aggregate demand determines output.

▶ In the short run, the aggregate supply curve has a slope intermediate between vertical and horizontal.

## K E Y   T E R M S

models, *4*

endogenous variables, *5*

exogenous variables, *5*

speed of adjustment, *6*

Classical, or market clearing, paradigm, *6*

flexible prices, *6*

Keynesian, or non-market clearing,

paradigm, *6*

sticky prices, *6*

very long run, *6*

long run, *7*

aggregate demand–aggregate supply model, *7*

very short run, *8*

short run, *8*

business cycle, *13*

Phillips Curve, *13*

Consumer Price Index (CPI), *15*

inflation rate, *15*

unemployment rate, *17*

open economy, *18*

balance of trade, *18*

foreign exchange rate, *19*

## D I S C U S S I O N   Q U E S T I O N S

1. When we discussed the simple labour market model at the beginning of the chapter, we asked the question, How has the increase in female labour force participation affected the labour market? Can you relate this discussion to the observation from Figure 1-10 that although GDP has been growing since the 1960s, the unemployment rate seems to have increased on average over this period?

2. Explain the difference between inflation and deflation and identify inflationary and deflationary periods in Figure 1-9. Can you offer any explanation for these periods?

3. Explain the essential difference between microeconomics and macroeconomics. What are the major differences between a microeconomic model of demand and supply and the macroeconomic model of aggregate supply and aggregate demand?

4. We asserted that inflation is caused by continual increases in aggregate demand. We also assumed that, over the very long run, the aggregate supply curve would be shifting out by approximately 2 percent per year. What would the inflation rate be if aggregate demand was increasing by 5 percent per year? What would it be if aggregate demand was decreasing by 1 percent per year?

## A P P L I C A T I O N   Q U E S T I O N S

1. Go to the CANSIM database and retrieve the Consumer Price Index, all items. Calculate the inflation rate for Canada over the period 1915 to 2002.

2. Go to the CANSIM database and retrieve the series on female labour force participation. Plot this series and show how it relates to Discussion Question 1.

# MEASURING THE PERFORMANCE OF THE CANADIAN ECONOMY

## *LEARNING OBJECTIVES*

After reading and studying this chapter, you should be able to:

▶ *Understand that gross domestic product (GDP) is the value of all final goods and services produced in the economy.*

▶ *Understand that we assume that goods are produced through a production function, which uses inputs of capital and labour to produce output; therefore, we can measure GDP as the value of the supply of goods and services by adding up payments to the factors of production.*

▶ *Understand that what is produced must be sold; therefore, we can also measure GDP as the value of gross domestic product by adding up spending on the components of demand: consumption, investment, government spending, and net export spending.*

▶ *Understand that in an economy, total savings is composed of private savings plus the government budget deficit, which is public savings. Total savings must equal investment spending plus the current account balance. Therefore, savings adds to the stock of wealth of a country by increasing the capital stock through investment or by increasing the stock of net foreign assets.*

▶ *Understand that the dollar value of gross domestic product can change if the level of physical production changes or if the price level changes.*

▶ *Understand that the real interest rate is equal to the nominal interest rate minus the inflation rate.*

▶ *Understand that the unemployment rate can change if the participation rate changes or if the number of people employed changes.*

A s we pointed out in Chapter 1, macroeconomics is concerned with aggregate outcomes in the economy. Most often, any assessment of the well-being of the economy will be based on the performance of a handful of macroeconomic aggregates. You will often hear that gross domestic product went up or unemployment went down, with the accompanying commentary on whether this means that the economy is doing well or doing poorly. Given this, it is very difficult to understand macroeconomics without first having an understanding of how we measure the important macroeconomic variables in our economy.

In Chapter 1, we examined graphs of several key macroeconomic variables. In this chapter, we are going to have a closer look at measurement of some of these variables. We will examine gross domestic product, the inflation rate, the unemployment rate, and the nominal and real interest rate. As we are discussing the measurement of these variables, we will also give you a first look at the overall structure of the economy. That is, we will outline how some of these variables move together over time. Of course, the details of these movements are what we will study in detail in the remaining chapters of the book.

## 2-1 | MEASURING GROSS DOMESTIC PRODUCT

**National Income and Expenditure Accounts**

A measure of current activity in the Canadian economy, published quarterly by Statistics Canada.

**gross domestic product (GDP)**

The dollar value of all final goods and services produced in an economy over some specified period of time, usually one year.

www.statcan.ca/english/freepub/13-010-XIE/free.htm

Every quarter, Statistics Canada publishes the *National Income and Expenditure Accounts*, which are a measure of current activity in the Canadian economy. One of the most widely quoted numbers from these accounts is **gross domestic product**, which is commonly referred to as GDP. Technically, GDP is defined as the dollar value of all final goods and services produced in an economy over some specified period of time, usually one year.

GDP is one of the most closely watched aggregates in economics. Millions of decisions made by millions of individuals go together to produce gross domestic product. However, we are not concerned with these individual decisions, but rather with the aggregate outcome as measured by total gross domestic product. In order to understand how GDP is constructed, though, we are going to have to disaggregate GDP somewhat and gain an understanding of its major components.

As we will discuss in this chapter, we must be very careful about distinguishing between nominal and real GDP. In any one year, the value of GDP can change, either because prices have increased from the previous year or because production has increased from the previous year, or some combination of price change and production change has occurred. Nominal GDP measures both the production change and the price change, while real GDP measures only the change in production.

In 2002, the value of output in the Canadian economy was $1,132 billion, measured in 2002 prices. Since the Canadian population was approximately 31.3 million, per capita GDP in 2002 was approximately $36,200. If you look back at Figure 1-5, you will see that per capita GDP in 2002 equalled approximately $33,700. However, in Figure 1-5, GDP is measured in constant 1997 dollars—the prices that prevailed in 1997—so the price change is taken out of the measurement. This represents real GDP per capita in 2002.

The measurement of GDP is based on a simple principle from supply and demand: Whatever is produced in an economy must be sold. If a firm produces a good that is not sold to a consumer or another business, then the firm buys the good itself and this is counted as inventory. Given this, GDP can be measured by adding up the final value of all goods produced (supply) or by adding up the final value of all goods purchased (demand).

## Measuring Supply: Output and the Payment to Factors of Production

**factors of production**
Inputs such as labour and capital.

The production side of the economy transfers inputs, such as labour and capital, into output, which is GDP. Inputs such as labour and capital are called **factors of production** and the payments to these factors, such as wages and interest payments, are called **factor payments**. As an example, suppose that an economy consisted of one economic consulting firm with you as the owner. Your output would be economic reports and your inputs would be economists (labour) and desks (capital). With some experience, you could predict the number of reports that could be produced based on the number of economists and the number of desks that you use. We could write an equation for this relationship in the form

**factor payments**
Payments made to factors, such as wages and interest payments.

$$\text{Reports} = F(\text{economists, desks}) \tag{1}$$

**production function**
Technological relation showing how much output can be produced for a given combination of inputs.

In economics, we call this type of a relationship a **production function**. We will make use of the concept of a production function throughout this book. In Chapters 3 and 4, the production function will be a focal point of our analysis, and we will think of GDP ($Y$) in an economy as being produced using capital ($K$) and labour ($N$), and we will write this in the general form $Y = F(K, N)$.[1]

In our example, once you sell the economic reports, you must make payments to the factors of production. You pay wages to the economists and you pay the owner of the desks for their use. Anything left over is profit. The factor payments could be expressed as

$$Y = (w^*N) + (i^*K) + \text{profit} \tag{2}$$

**final goods and services**
Goods and services that are sold to firms, the public, or the government for any purpose other than use as an input to production; all goods excluding intermediate ones.

This equation states that the total output ($Y$) equals the wage rate times the number of economists ($w^*N$), plus the interest rate times the number of desks ($i^*K$), plus profit.

In order to measure GDP from the supply side, we could add up the value of all **final goods and services** produced in the economy, or, equivalently, we could add up the payments to factors of production that were used to produce these goods and services.

We must be careful that we count only **final goods and services** in calculating GDP. Consider the example of the production of a car. The car manufacturer buys components of the car from other manufacturers. These components are called **intermediate goods**. GDP would count the full price of the automobile, but not the value of intermediate goods. If GDP counted the value of the car, plus the total value of the intermediate goods, there would be double counting. In practice, double counting is avoided by the concept of **value added**. At each stage of the manufacturing process, only the value added to the good at that stage of the production process is counted.

**intermediate goods**
Goods used to produce other goods or services; flour purchased by bakers is an example.

**value added**
Increase in value of output at a given stage of production. Equivalently, value of output minus cost of inputs.

---

[1] In future chapters, we will actually write the production function as $Y = AF(K,N)$. The term $A$ is meant to capture any changes in technology or productivity. In this chapter, we will ignore the term $A$, and reintroduce it in Chapter 3.

## Value Added and the Goods and Services Tax

The Goods and Services Tax (GST), introduced at the beginning of 1991, is a form of value-added tax. It is imposed on the value added at each stage of production. Each firm pays tax on its purchases of intermediate goods and receives a rebate for the tax already paid by its supplier. The following table illustrates the process for the case of a loaf of bread, assuming a GST of 7 percent.

### VALUE ADDED AT EACH STAGE AND THE GST

| Farmer | | Baker | |
|---|---|---|---|
| Value of wheat | $0.10 | Cost of flour | $0.407 |
| Miller | | Less GST rebate | −0.007 |
| Cost of wheat | 0.10 | Plus GST | 0.028 |
| Plus GST | 0.007 | Value added | 0.20 |
| Value added | 0.30 | Total | $0.628 |
| Total | $0.407 | Final consumer | |
| | | Cost of bread | $0.628 |
| | | Less GST rebate | −0.028 |
| | | Plus GST | 0.042 |
| | | Final cost | $0.642 |

The miller pays $0.107 for the wheat including the 7 percent GST. Since the flour is sold to another firm, this tax is rebated and the net cost to the baker is $0.40 plus GST of $0.028. This tax is in turn rebated so that the final cost to the consumer is $0.60 before tax. GST is again added so that the consumer's total cost is $0.642.

The reason for this system of taxes and rebates is that it ensures that the tax will be paid regardless of whether a good is sold to another firm for further processing or sold to a consumer. For example, the price of flour supplied by a miller is $0.40 plus $0.028 GST regardless of the identity of the purchaser. If it is bought by a consumer, then there will be no rebate and the total tax paid will be 7 percent of the value of the final good.

GDP also counts only the value of goods that are currently produced. Therefore, GDP excludes transactions in items such as paintings by old masters or existing housing. Notice that the construction of new houses is counted in GDP, as this is current production.

Measuring GDP as payments to factors of production for the years 1961 and 2002 is summarized in Table 2-1.

You can see from Table 2-1 that, although the current dollar amounts of each category have changed substantially over the years, the percentage of each category in total GDP has remained roughly constant.

We will outline some of the major features of the calculations.

**net domestic product at factor cost**

The total payments to factors of production.

## Net Domestic Product at Factor Cost

The first four items in Table 2-1 show total payments to factors of production. Technically, this is known as **net domestic product at factor cost**. Notice that labour

## TABLE 2-1

### THE INCOME APPROACH TO MEASURING GDP, 1961 AND 2002

| | Millions of 1961 Dollars | Percent of GDP | Millions of 2002 Dollars | Percent of GDP |
|---|---|---|---|---|
| Labour income | 21,184 | 51.5 | 590,485 | 52.2 |
| Corporate profit* | 4,467 | 10.9 | 129,105 | 11.4 |
| Unincorporated business income† | 4,381 | 10.7 | 73,723 | 6.5 |
| Interest and investment income | 1,286 | 3.1 | 50,247 | 4.4 |
| **Net domestic product at factor cost** | **31,318** | **76.2** | **843,560** | **74.5** |
| Indirect taxes less subsidies | 4,750 | 11.5 | 136,147 | 12.0 |
| **Net domestic product at market prices** | **36,068** | **87.7** | **979,706** | **86.5** |
| Depreciation | 5,104 | 12.2 | 151,145 | 13.4 |
| Statistical discrepancy | 91 | 0.1 | 1,181 | 0.1 |
| **GDP** | **41,173** | **100.0** | **1,132,033** | **100.0** |
| Net investment income from non-residents | −724 | −1.8 | −25,501 | −2.3 |
| **GNP** | **40,449** | **98.2** | **1,106,532** | **97.7** |

\* Includes pre-tax profit of government business enterprises and inventory valuation adjustment.
† Includes net income of farm operators.

SOURCE: CANSIM II table 3800016.

income is by far the largest component of factor payments, equalling nearly 70 percent of total factor payments. This same allocation of factor payments has been roughly constant since 1961 and is also roughly constant for most industrialized countries.

### Net Domestic Product at Market Prices

Business must pay indirect taxes to the federal, provincial, and municipal governments. These are items such as provincial sales taxes and the federal goods and services tax (GST). These are separate from factor payments, as they are income of the government. When indirect taxes (net of subsidies) are added to net domestic product at factor cost, the result is **net domestic product at market prices**.

### Gross Domestic Product

We know that capital wears out as it is being used to produce output. This is called **depreciation**, or capital consumption allowance. When net income is calculated by business, depreciation is subtracted, as it does not add to the productive capacity of a firm. Therefore, when depreciation is added to net domestic product, the result is *gross domestic product*.

### Gross National Product

This final category recognizes that factor payments include receipts from abroad made as factor payments to domestically owned factors of production. For instance, part of Canadian GDP corresponds to profits earned by Honda from its Canadian manufacturing operations. These profits are part of Japan's GNP, because they are income of Japanese-owned capital. Adding these payments to GDP gives **gross national product**, or GNP.

**net domestic product at market prices**
Indirect taxes (net of subsidies) are added to net domestic product at factor cost.

**depreciation**
The wearing out of capital as it is being used to produce output.

**gross national product (GNP)**
Measure of the value of all final goods and services produced by domestically owned factors of production.

## Measuring Demand: The Components of Spending

In this section, we look at the demand for output, and we discuss the components of the aggregate demand for domestically produced goods and services, the different purposes for which GDP is demanded.

Total demand for domestic output is made up of four components: (1) consumption spending by households ($C$); (2) investment spending by businesses and households ($I$); (3) government (federal, provincial, and municipal) purchases of goods and services ($G$); and (4) foreign demand for our net exports ($NX$). These four categories account, definitionally, for all spending. The fundamental **national income accounting identity** is

$$Y \equiv C + I + G + NX \tag{3}$$

Memorize this identity. You will use it repeatedly in this course and in organizing your thinking about the macroeconomy.

We now look more closely at each of the four components.

national income
accounting identity
$Y \equiv C + I + G + NX$

### Consumption

Table 2-2 presents a breakdown of the demand for goods and services in 1961 and 2002 by components of demand. The table shows that the chief component of demand is **consumption spending** by the household sector. Although the consumption category includes all current spending by consumers, there is some discussion among economists concerning the type of spending that should be included in consumption. If you look at the national accounts, you will see that consumption spending can be broken down into spending on non-durables and spending on durables. This means that when you purchase a car, for instance, the total current purchase price is included in today's consumption expenditure. However, you consume the car for several years, which prompts some economists to label this as an investment.

consumption spending
Total current spending by
consumers in the economy.

---

**TABLE 2-2**

### MEASURING GDP BY COMPONENTS OF DEMAND, 1961 AND 2002

|  | Millions of 1961 Dollars | Percent of GDP | Millions of 2002 Dollars | Percent of GDP |
|---|---|---|---|---|
| Consumption | 25,784 | 62.9 | 685,739 | 57.0 |
| Investment | 7,077 | 17.2 | 197,797 | 17.5 |
| Government | 8,519 | 20.7 | 242,103 | 21.4 |
| *Exports* | *7,310* | *17.8* | *467,080* | *41.3* |
| *Imports* | *7,517* | *18.3* | *419,417* | *37.0* |
| Net exports | −207 | −0.5 | 47,663 | 4.3 |
| Statistical discrepancy | −90 | −0.3 | −1,179 | −0.2 |
| Gross domestic product | 41,173 | 100.0 | 1,132,033 | 100.0 |

SOURCE: CANSIM II table 3800002.

## Investment

investment spending
Additions to the physical
stock of capital.

**Investment spending** requires some definitions. First, throughout this book, "investment" means additions to the physical stock of capital. As we use the term, investment does not include buying a bond or purchasing stock in General Motors. Investment includes housing construction, building of machinery, construction of factories and offices, and additions to a firm's inventories of goods.

---

**BOX**

**2-2**

www.statcan.ca/english/
IPS/Data/71F0023XIE/
1999001.htm

### Problems in Measurement of GDP

GDP data are, in practice, used not only as a measure of how much is being produced but also as a measure of the welfare of the residents of a country. Economists and politicians talk as if an increase in real GDP means that people are better off. However, GDP data are far from perfect measures of either economic output or welfare. There are at least three major problems with GDP measurement:

▶ Some outputs are poorly measured because they are not traded in the market. If you bake a home-made pie, the value of your labour isn't counted in official GDP statistics. If you buy a (no doubt inferior) pie, the baker's labour is counted. This means that the vastly increased participation of women in the labour force has increased official GDP numbers with no offsetting reduction for decreased production at home. (We officially measure the value of commercial daycare, but taking care of your own children is valued at zero.)

   Note, too, that government services aren't directly priced by the market. The official statistics assume that a dollar spent by the government is worth a dollar of value. GDP is mismeasured to the extent that a dollar spent by the government produces output valued by the public at more or less than a dollar.

▶ Some activities measured as adding to GDP in fact represent the use of resources to avoid or contain "bads" such as crime or risks to national security. Similarly, the accounts do not subtract anything for environmental pollution and degradation. This issue is particularly important in developing countries. For instance, one study of Indonesia claims that properly accounting for environmental degradation would reduce the measured growth rate of the economy by 3 percent.

▶ It is difficult to account correctly for improvements in the quality of goods. This has been the case particularly with computers, whose quality has improved dramatically while the price has fallen sharply. But it applies to almost all goods, such as cars, whose quality changes over time. The national income accountants attempt to adjust for improvements in quality, but the task is not easy, especially when new products and new models are being invented.

To shed light on just how much quality change can matter, William Nordhaus, of Yale University, has calculated how much better room lighting is now than in the past, based on estimates of energy requirements per lumen. The improvements—very few of which show up in the official statistics—are enormous. Today's electric light is about 25 times as efficient as Edison's first electric light was in 1883.

   Unmeasured quality improvements are not new. Nordhaus calculates that 5 litres of sesame oil cost a Babylonian worker about 0.5 shekel (roughly two weeks' wages). Light equivalent to two candles burning for an hour cost a Babylonian about an hour's wages.*

---

*For other serious, but fun, comparisons, see William D. Nordhaus, "Do Real Output and Real Wage Measures Capture Reality? The History of Lighting Suggests Not," in Robert J. Gordon and Timothy F. Bresnahan (eds.), *The Economics of New Goods* (Chicago: University of Chicago Press, 1997, pp. 29–66).

**human capital**
The knowledge and ability to produce that is embodied in the labour force.

If we think of investment more generally as any current activity that increases the economy's ability to produce output in the future, we would include not only physical investment but also what is known as investment in human capital. **Human capital** is the knowledge and ability to produce that is embodied in the labour force. Investment in education can be regarded as investment in human capital, but the official accounts treat personal educational expenditures as consumption and public educational expenditures as government spending.

The classification of spending as consumption or investment is to a significant extent a matter of convention. From the economic point of view, there is little difference between a household building up an inventory of peanut butter and a grocery store doing the same. Nevertheless, in the national income accounts, the individual's purchase is treated as a personal consumption expenditure, whereas the store's purchase is treated as inventory investment. Although these borderline cases clearly exist, we can apply a simple rule of thumb: Investment is associated with the business sector adding to the physical stock of capital, including inventories.[2] Officially, however, all household expenditures are counted as consumption spending. This is not quite as bad as it might seem, since the accounts do separate household purchases of durable goods such as cars and refrigerators from their other purchases.

**gross investment**
Investment including depreciation.

**net investment**
Gross investment minus depreciaton.

Finally, we note that investment can be measured as gross investment or net investment. In Table 2-2, investment is actually **gross investment** in that depreciation has not been deducted. **Net investment** is gross investment minus depreciation.

## Government

**government purchases**
Government spending on goods and services. Contrast *government expenditure*.

The next category in Table 2-2 is **government purchases** of goods and services. This component of GDP includes such items as national defence spending, costs of road paving by provincial governments, and salaries of government employees. In this category, we must be very careful how we label government spending. When any level of government spends money to purchase a good or service, we call this *government purchases*. However, governments also spend money on **transfer payments**, which are payments made to individuals where no good or service is provided in exchange. Therefore, transfer payments are not counted as part of GDP. Typical transfer payments are payments under the Employment Insurance plan or social spending such as welfare. We will refer to **government expenditure** as government purchases plus transfers.

**transfer payments**
Payments that are made to people without their providing a current service in exchange.

**government expenditure**
Purchases plus transfers.

## Net Exports

**net exports**
The difference between exports and imports.

The term "net exports" appears in Table 2-2 to account for domestic spending on foreign goods and foreign spending on domestic goods. When foreigners purchase goods we produce, their spending adds to the demand for domestically produced goods. Correspondingly, that part of our spending that purchases foreign goods has to be subtracted from the demand for domestically produced goods. Accordingly, the difference between exports and imports, called **net exports**, is a component of the total demand for our goods.

The role of net exports in accounting for GDP can be illustrated with an example. Assume that personal sector spending was higher by $20 billion. How much

---

[2] The GDP accounts record as investment business sector additions to the stock of capital. Some government spending, for instance, for roads or schools, also adds to the capital stock. This is recorded in the government category, under government gross fixed capital formation.

higher would GDP be? If we assume that government and investment spending remained unchanged, we might be tempted to say that GDP would have been $20 billion higher. That is correct if all of the additional spending had fallen on domestic goods. The other extreme, however, is that all of the additional spending had fallen on imports. In that event, consumption would have been up $20 billion *and* net exports would have been down $20 billion, with *no* net effect on GDP.

## 2-2 | ALLOCATION OF INCOME AND SAVINGS

The national income accounting identity given by equation (3) gives us a framework for thinking about the allocation of income, which we will explore in much more detail in Chapter 3. For now, we want to understand the important concept of savings and how this is related to investment in an economy.

The right-hand side of equation (3) tells us how the income generated by production is spent in the economy. Consider a very simple economy, where there is no government or foreign trade. In this economy, the national income accounting identity would be

$$Y = C + I \tag{4}$$

We know that, in aggregate, consumers do not spend all of their income. Define the excess of income over consumption as savings.

$$S = Y - C \tag{5}$$

If we substitute equation (4) into equation (5) we arrive at

$$S = I \tag{6}$$

In this very simple economy, savings identically equals investment. We will explore the behavioural relationships underlying this identity in Chapter 3.

Now suppose that we allow for government and foreign trade. The fundamental GDP identity is the familiar

$$Y \equiv C + I + G + NX \tag{3}$$

Now that we have introduced government, we must take into account that some of the income earned by consumers must be spent on taxes and that some income is earned by non-residents. We define personal **disposable income**, which is income available for consumption or saving, as

**disposable income**
Income available for consumption or saving.

$$YD = Y + YNR + TR - TA \tag{7}$$

That is, **disposable income** ($YD$) equals income ($Y$) plus net investment income from non-residents ($YNR$) plus transfers ($TR$) minus taxes ($TA$). Net income from non-residents is the difference between GNP and GDP, shown in Table 2-1. We define private savings ($S^P$) as any savings that is undertaken by the private sector (i.e., non-government savings). Private savings is equal to disposable income minus consumption

$$S^P = YD - C \tag{8}$$

Substituting the definition of disposable income from (7)

$$S^P = (Y + YNR + TR - TA) - C \tag{9}$$

Now substitute the GDP identity

$$\begin{aligned} S^P &= C + I + G + NX + YNR + TR - TA - C \\ &= (G + TR - TA) + (NX + YNR) + I \end{aligned} \tag{10}$$

The first term in brackets on the right-hand side is the excess of government spending over government revenue, which is the government budget deficit (or surplus). This is the negative of government savings, $S^G$. The second term in brackets on the right-hand side is net exports plus net income from non-residents, which is equal to the current account balance, $CA$.[3] Therefore, we can write

$$S = S^P + S^G = I + CA \tag{11}$$

Equation (11) is very important. It tells us that total savings in the economy, which is composed of private savings plus government savings, must be equal to investment plus the current account balance. It also tells us something about wealth accumulation in an economy. Total savings can be invested in the physical capital stock; that is, in the machinery and equipment that will aid in the productive process in the future. Alternatively, savings can be invested in net assets of foreigners; that is, the current account. The sum of these two terms is the net addition to the stock of national wealth in an economy.

Figure 2-1 plots the variables from equation (11) from 1961 to 2002.

**FIGURE 2-1**

**INVESTMENT, SAVINGS, AND THE CURRENT ACCOUNT, 1961–2002**

This figure illustrates that savings must equal investment plus the current account balance, as shown in equation (11). The current account balance has been negative in the past, but has been consistently positive in the last several years.

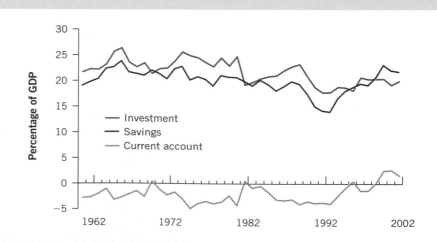

SOURCE: CANSIM II table 3800032.

[3] There are actually some other minor items in the current account, which we will discuss in detail in Chapter 5.

As you can see in Figure 2-1, the current account balance has been negative in the past, but has been consistently positive in the last several years. We will discuss these issues in Chapter 3.

## POLICY IN *ACTION*

### The Federal Government Fiscal Balance

Prior to approximately 1973, the Canadian federal government pursued a policy of producing fiscal budgets that were roughly balanced over the business cycle. However, starting in 1973, fiscal policy became very expansionary at the federal level, and the government began to run chronic budgetary deficits. The extent of these deficits can be seen in the figure below.

**FEDERAL BUDGETARY DEFICIT AS PERCENT OF GDP, 1961–2002**

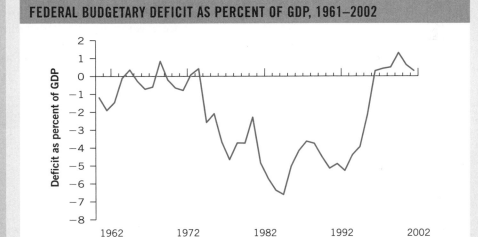

SOURCE: Federal government saving: CANSIM II V647208; divided by nominal GDP: CANSIM II V498918.

By the 1980s, the federal government came under severe criticism for this policy. One of the criticisms was that this policy could be diverting private sector savings to potentially non-productive resources. We can see how this may be true by rearranging the savings investment identity in the following manner.

$$S^P = I - S^G + CA$$

This identity shows us that when you and I save, in the form of private sector savings, it can be used by businesses for fixed investment, it can be used by the government to pay for any excess of spending over taxes (the deficit), or it can be used to acquire (or divest) net foreign assets.

The figure above shows that the federal government began to recognize the possible problems with the chronic deficit position and, by the mid-1990s, began running federal government surpluses.

2-3 # Real and Nominal GDP and Inflation

In Section 2-1, we learned that we can calculate GDP in an economy by adding up the value of all goods that are produced (supply) or by adding up the value of all goods that are sold (demand). In the example of a simple economy that produces only economic reports, calculating GDP is a straightforward task. We simply multiply the number of reports produced in any one year times the price of reports in the same year, and this would give us the value of all of the reports produced, which is equal to **current dollar, or nominal, GDP**.

**current dollar, or nominal, GDP**
Measuring GDP between two periods, while allowing the price level to change between the two periods.

Of course, in the real world, the economy is composed of many different goods and each of these goods is sold in some market; therefore, each good has a price associated with it. In order to calculate nominal GDP, we would have to multiply the price of each individual good by the number of goods produced for every type of good produced.

As an example, suppose that an economy consists of two goods: economic reports and computers. In this economy, nominal GDP could be calculated as

$$\text{Nominal GDP} = (\text{price of reports} \times \text{number of reports}) \\ + (\text{price of computers} \times \text{number of computers}) \quad (12)$$

This formula can be used to calculate the value of current dollar GDP in any year. Table 2-3 illustrates the calculation of nominal GDP for this simple economy.

## TABLE 2-3 — CALCULATING GDP IN A TWO-GOOD ECONOMY

| Year | Price | Nominal GDP Units Produced (Sold) | Value |
|---|---|---|---|
| 1995 | $1,000 per report | 10 reports | $10,000 |
| | $1,000 per computer | 5 computers | $ 5,000 |
| **Nominal GDP** | | | **$15,000** |
| 2002 | $1,100 per report | 15 reports | $16,500 |
| | $500 per computer | 10 computers | $ 5,000 |
| **Nominal GDP** | | | **$21,500** |

Table 2-3 shows that nominal GDP in 1995 would have been equal to the value of reports produced in 1995 ($1,000 × 10 reports) plus the value of computers produced in 1995 ($1,000 × 5 computers), equal to $15,000. Similarly, in 2002, nominal GDP would be equal to the value of reports produced in 2002 ($1,100 × 15 reports) plus the value of computers produced in 2002 ($500 × 10 computers), equal to $21,500.

Table 2-3 illustrates that nominal GDP can change either because physical production changes, or because the price of a good changes, or some combination of both. The concept of **constant dollar, or real, GDP** is intended to isolate the change in GDP that is due solely to a change in physical production. If there was only one good, then we could simply add up production of that good in any year. However, if there is more than one good, you cannot add up physical production. In the 1995

**constant dollar, or real, GDP**
Measuring GDP between two periods, holding the price level constant.

example in Table 2-3, you cannot add 10 reports to 5 computers to arrive at real GDP of 15. This measure has no sensible meaning, as reports and computers are not the same good. In practice, real GDP is calculated by choosing a base year for prices and holding those base year prices constant each year. This is illustrated in Table 2-4.

## TABLE 2-4

### CALCULATING REAL GDP USING DIFFERENT BASE YEARS

#### 1. REAL GDP CALCULATED USING 1995 BASE YEAR PRICES

| Year | Price | Quantity | Value in 1995 Dollars |
|---|---|---|---|
| 1995 | $1,000 per report | 10 reports | $10,000 |
| | $1,000 per computer | 5 computers | $ 5,000 |
| **1995 GDP measured in 1995 Dollars** | | | **$15,000** |
| 2002 | $1,000 per report | 15 reports | $15,000 |
| 2002 | $1,000 per computer | 10 computers | $10,000 |
| **2002 GDP measured in 1995 Dollars** | | | **$25,000** |

Growth rate of real GDP = ($25,000/$15,000) = 66.67%

#### 2. REAL GDP CALCULATED USING 2002 BASE YEAR PRICES

| Year | Price | Quantity | Value in 1995 Dollars |
|---|---|---|---|
| 1995 | $1,100 per report | 10 reports | $11,000 |
| | $500 per computer | 5 computers | $ 2,500 |
| 1995 GDP measured in 2002 Dollars | | | $13,500 |
| 2002 | $1,100 per report | 15 | $16,500 |
| | $500 per computer | 10 | $ 5,000 |
| **2002 GDP measured in 2002 Dollars** | | | **$21,500** |

Growth rate of real GDP = ($21,500/$13,500) = 59.2%

The top portion of Table 2-4 shows that, in calculating real GDP using 1995 as a base year, we multiply the quantities produced in both 1995 and 2002 by the prices from 1995. Thus, we are holding price constant in the calculation (which is why real GDP is often referred to as *constant dollar GDP*). Therefore, real GDP in 1995 is calculated as ($1,000 × 10) + ($1,000 × 5) = $15,000. Notice that if we are using 1995 as a base year, real and nominal GDP must be the same in that base year. Similarly, real GDP in 2002 is calculated as ($1,000 × 15) + ($1,000 × 10) = $25,000. Given these calculations, the growth rate of real GDP between 1995 and 2002 equals 66.6 percent (equal to $25,000/$15,000).[4]

Of course, choosing 1995 as a base year is arbitrary. We can easily recalculate real GDP using 2002 as our base year. The bottom portion of Table 2-4 shows that using

---

[4] In the Application Questions at the end of the chapter, you are asked to calculate growth rates in several different ways.

2002 as a base year, real GDP would be calculated as ($1,100 × 10) + ($500 × 5) = $13,500 in 1995, and calculated as ($1,100 × 15) + ($500 × 10) = $21,500 in 2002 (notice that this equals nominal GDP in 2002). Therefore, the growth rate of real GDP measured in 2002 dollars between 1995 and 2002 equals 59.2 percent (equal to $21,500/$13,500).

Why did real GDP appear to grow less between 1995 and 2002 when we used 2002 as a base year? The answer to this question lies in noting that, in our example, the price of computers went down in 2002. If you value production at 1995 prices, when the computer price was $1,000 per computer, the value of the change in computer production is larger than if you value computers at the 2002 price of $500. This illustrates a very important problem in constructing estimates of constant dollar GDP: The choice of base year can make a difference.

The choice of a base year would not be a problem if all individual prices changed by the same proportion each year. However, in our example, the price of computers relative to the price of reports changed. In an economy, these types of relative price changes are common. For instance, the price of computers actually did decrease substantially between 1994 and 2002.[5] What this means for the construction of constant dollar GDP is that some individual prices used in the base year can become, in a sense, out of date.

In response to this general problem, Statistics Canada has changed the GDP base year approximately every five years. However, each time that the base year is changed, historical values of real GDP must be recalculated so that there is a consistent series over time. In the year 1997, rather than continually changing the base year, Statistics Canada began calculating **chain weighted GDP**. Chain weighted GDP is calculated by averaging the base over two years, the current and the preceding year, and so the averaging moves over time as the current year moves over time. Chain weighting effectively removes the need to change the base periodically.[6]

## Price Indexes and Inflation

A price index is a measure of prices in any one year compared to the level of the same prices in some base year. The level of prices in the base year is always scaled to equal 100, and the level of prices in any other year can be compared to the index base value of 100. Notice that knowledge of the level of the price index in any one year is not of much use until it is compared to the level in some other year. Thus, price indexes are generally used to calculate rates of inflation. Inflation is defined as the rate of change in prices. If $P_t$ represents the price index in period $t$ and $P_{t-1}$ represents the price index in the previous year, then the annual rate of inflation can be written as

$$\pi_t = \frac{P_t - P_{t-1}}{P_{t-1}} \tag{13}$$

where $\pi$ stands for the inflation rate in year $t$. In order to calculate the inflation rate, we need to substitute some price index into the above formula. The price index that pertains to the goods produced in GDP is called the **GDP deflator**, and it is defined as

$$\text{GDP deflator} = \text{Nominal GDP/Real GDP} \tag{14}$$

www.statcan.ca/english/ concepts/chainfisher/ methodology.htm

**chain weighted GDP**
Chain weighted GDP is calculated by averaging the base over two years, the current and the preceding year, and so the averaging moves over time as the current year moves over time.

**GDP deflator**
The ratio of nominal GDP in a given year to real GDP of that year.

---

[5] In the Application Questions at the end of the chapter, you are asked to show that this is true.

[6] You can read about the concepts and techniques involved with chain weighting at www.statcan.ca/ english/concepts/chainfisher/methodology.htm.

Once the GDP deflator is calculated, it can be substituted into equation (13) and an inflation rate can be calculated.

There is an alternative way to look at price inflation as measured by the GDP deflator. Recall from above that any change in nominal GDP is composed of any change in physical production and any change in price, and that changes in real GDP reflect changes in production at constant prices. Therefore, it follows that the difference between the change in nominal GDP and the change in real GDP is a reflection of the change in prices. Given this, we could also calculate the inflation rate for the GDP deflator as

$$\pi_t \approx \%\Delta \text{ nominal GDP} - \%\Delta \text{ real GDP} \qquad (15)$$

The GDP deflator is not the only price index that can be used to calculate an inflation rate. The other major price index that is used in economics is the **Consumer Price Index**, which measures the cost of a fixed bundle of goods that is representative of the purchases of the average consumer. Box 2-3 discusses the differences between these two price measures.

**Consumer Price Index (CPI)**

Measures the cost of buying a fixed bundle of goods, representative of the purchases of consumers.

---

**BOX**

**2-3**

## The GDP Deflator, the Consumer Price Index, and Inflation

The GDP deflator and the Consumer Price Index are both measures of the cost of living, but they differ in three respects. First, the GDP deflator measures a much wider group of goods than the Consumer Price Index. This is due to the fact that the Consumer Price Index is based on a market basket of goods purchased by an average consumer. Second, the Consumer Price Index measures the cost of a given basket of goods that is the same from year to year, while the basket of goods in the GDP deflator varies from year to year, depending on what is produced in the economy. Third, the Consumer Price Index includes prices of imports, whereas the GDP deflator includes only prices of goods that are produced in Canada.

In Chapter 1, we calculated the inflation rate using the Consumer Price Index. This is the most common measure of inflation. In practice, either of these price indexes can be used to calculate the inflation rate. As you can see from the figure below, each inflation rate has the same longer run trend, while there are some minor differences in the two indexes over shorter periods of time.

### INFLATION AS MEASURED BY THE GDP DEFLATOR AND THE CONSUMER PRICE INDEX, 1962–2002

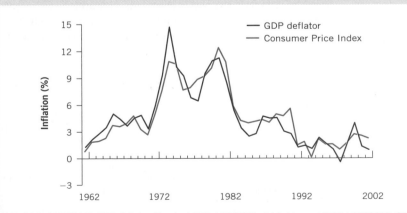

SOURCE: CANSIM II. GDP deflator: Nominal GDP: V498918, divided by real GDP: V1992292; CPI: V735319.

## 2-4 | Inflation and Nominal and Real Interest Rates

A bond is a contract between a lender and a borrower, much like a bank loan. The only difference is, if you or I buy a bond, we are the lender, but if you or I take out a loan, we are the borrower. Suppose you decide that you want to save some money, so you buy a bond for $P_t^B$ dollars. This is the same as saying that the current price of the bond is $P_t^B$. When you decide to cash the bond, you can measure your return as the amount that the price of the bond has increased. If $P_{t+1}^B$ stands for the price of the bond when you cash it in year $t + 1$, then the nominal interest rate is defined as

$$i_t = \frac{P_{t+1}^B - P_t^B}{P_t^B} \qquad (16)$$

**nominal interest rate**

Measures how much money you received (or paid) above the amount that you invested (or borrowed), expressed as a percentage.

A **nominal interest rate** measures how much money you received above the amount that you initially invested, expressed as a percentage. For instance, if you paid $1,000 for the bond today and when you cashed it the price had risen to $1,050, then the annual nominal interest rate would be 5 percent ($50/$1,000 = 0.05). Notice that, by convention, we multiply interest rates by 100, so it is common to see a 5 percent rate of return expressed as 5, rather than as a proportion, 0.05.

The famous economist Irving Fisher first pointed out that if there is inflation, even though you have more nominal dollars from holding a bond, you may not be able to purchase more goods.[7] This is because inflation erodes the purchasing power of money; that is, each dollar can purchase fewer goods and services because of inflation. To see this, consider taking $100 and putting it under your mattress for one year. If the inflation rate is 10 percent during that year, that $100 will purchase 10 percent fewer goods at the end of the year than it could at the beginning.

The difference between the increase in the value of the bond, which is measured by the nominal interest rate, and the decrease in purchasing power caused by inflation is the **real interest rate**. That is, we can define the real interest rate $r$ as the nominal interest rate with the inflation rate subtracted.[8]

**real interest rate**

The nominal interest rate with the inflation rate subtracted.

$$r = i - \pi \qquad (17)$$

The upper panel of Figure 2-2 shows the nominal interest rate and the inflation rate measured annually over the period 1961–2002. The difference between these two variables, which is the real interest rate, is graphed in the bottom panel of Figure 2-2. Notice that the real interest rate averaged approximately 3 to 4 percent per year until the early 1970s, when it began to decrease sharply and even became negative. Throughout the 1980s and most of the 1990s, the real interest rate averaged nearly 6 percent per year before returning to an average of 3 to 4 percent per year by the year 2000. This behaviour will be discussed in the next chapter.

---

[7] Irving Fisher first discussed this problem in 1896. See "Appreciation and Interest," *American Economics Association Publication*, series 3 (1896), pages 331–442.

[8] In the Application Questions at the end of this chapter, you are asked to derive this relationship mathematically.

## FIGURE 2-2

### NOMINAL AND REAL INTEREST RATES AND INFLATION, 1961–2002

The upper panel of Figure 2-2 shows the nominal interest rate and the inflation rate. The difference between these two variables is the real rate of interest, which is shown in the lower panel. (Notice that the vertical scales on the two diagrams are different.) The data is graphed over the period 1961–2002. Notice that the real interest rate averaged approximately 3 to 4 percent per year until the early 1970s, when it began to decrease sharply and even became negative. Throughout the 1980s and most of the 1990s, the real interest rate averaged nearly 6 percent per year before returning to an average of 3 to 4 percent per year by the year 2000.

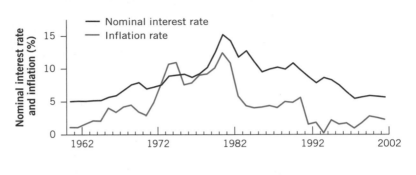

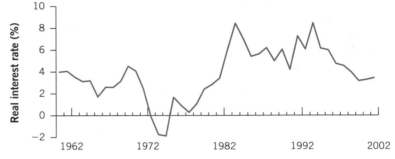

SOURCE: CANSIM II: Long-term government bond rate: V122487; Consumer Price Index: V315739.

## 2-5 | THE UNEMPLOYED AND THE UNEMPLOYMENT RATE

### Measuring the Unemployment Rate

Statistics Canada produces a wealth of information on the unemployment rate each month, through a survey of more than 50,000 households. This information is published in the *Labour Force Survey* and is also available in CANSIM II.[9] We will discuss the details of unemployment in Chapter 8. Here we present a broad overview of some measurement issues, and introduce the relationship between GDP and the unemployment rate known as Okun's law.

Earlier in this chapter, we made use of the economic concept of a production function. One of the inputs into the production function is labour. We now want to be somewhat more precise about what we mean when we use the term *labour*. The **labour force** is defined as the total number of individuals who are employed, plus the

**labour force**

The total number of individuals who are employed, plus the number of individuals who are actively seeking employment but do not have jobs.

---

[9] Details of this are available as Statistics Canada publication 71-001, *Labour Force Information*. Most of the relevant data is available in CANSIM II in Tables 282-0001 to 282-0042 and 282-0047 to 282-0095.

number of individuals who are actively seeking employment but do not have jobs. If you are in this latter category (that is, you are looking for work but are not currently employed), you are counted as being *unemployed*. One of the statistics that is most often quoted is the *unemployment rate*, which is defined as the percentage of the labour force that is unemployed. We could write an equation for the unemployment rate as

$$\text{Unemployment rate} = \frac{\text{Number of unemployed persons}}{\text{Total labour force}} \times 100 \qquad (18)$$

In Chapter 1, we saw a graph of the unemployment rate (see Figure 1-12). As with most economic data, the unemployment rate exhibits a great deal of shorter run business cycle movement as well as longer run trend movements.

In terms of the business cycle movements of the unemployment rate, notice that there are two ways in which the unemployment rate could change. First, if more individuals became unemployed out of a given labour force, the unemployment rate would increase. Second, if the total labour force increased and none of those individuals received jobs, then the unemployment rate would also increase. This highlights an important concept that is related to the unemployment rate. The **labour force participation rate** is the number of individuals in the labour force as a percentage of the total adult population.

$$\text{Labour force participation rate} = \frac{\text{Labour force}}{\text{Adult population}} \times 100 \qquad (19)$$

You can see from this equation that if the participation rate increases because more of the adult population is seeking employment and these individuals do not find jobs, then the unemployment rate will increase.[10]

In terms of longer run trends, a concept that we will use throughout this book is full employment, which is often called the **natural rate of unemployment**. This is the unemployment rate that would prevail if the labour force was fully employed. If you look at the definition of the unemployment rate in equation (18), you will immediately think that the unemployment rate should be zero at full employment. However, no matter how efficiently the economy is running, the unemployment rate will never be zero. At least two types of unemployment will always exist to ensure that the measured unemployment rate is never zero. First, there is **frictional unemployment**, which exists because the economy is very dynamic. New jobs are always being created and some jobs are always being made obsolete. Frictional unemployment exists as workers try to match their skills to the changing workforce. Second, there is **structural unemployment**, which exists because there are long-term, chronically unemployed individuals. This usually arises because the skills of some individuals no longer match the changing needs of employers in the workplace.

The survey method of determining the unemployment rate may actually underestimate the number of unemployed individuals. Some individuals who have been in the labour force and could not find employment have now given up looking for

**labour force participation rate**
Number of individuals in the labour force as a percentage of the adult population.

**natural rate of unemployment**
Rate of unemployment at which the flows into and out of the unemployment pool balance; also, the point on the augmented Phillips curve at which expected inflation equals actual inflation.

**frictional unemployment**
The unemployment that exists when the economy is at full employment.

**structural unemployment**
Long-term unemployment that arises because of a lack of matching between the skills of workers and the needs of employers.

---

[10] We asked you to think about this question in Chapter 1, Discussion Question 1.

**discouraged workers**
Individuals who have been in the labour force, could not find employment, and have now given up looking for work. Because these individuals are not in the labour force, they are not counted among the unemployed.

**Okun's law**
The hypothesized relationship between changes in the unemployment rate and changes in real GDP.

employment. These are what economists call **discouraged workers**. Statistics Canada counts these individuals as not being in the labour force and, therefore, they are not counted among the unemployed.

## The Relationship between Unemployment and GDP: Okun's Law

When the unemployment rate increases, we would expect this to result in a decrease in output. In the early 1960s, Arthur Okun studied this relationship, which came to be known as **Okun's law**.[11] We have graphed a version of Okun's law in Figure 2-3.

In Figure 2-3, the slope of the estimated line is −1.7, indicating that an increase in the unemployment rate of one percentage point will lower the growth rate of real GDP by approximately 1.7 percent. We will discuss this relationship in more detail in Chapters 7 and 8.

*FIGURE 2-3*

Okun's law postulates a negative relationship between the change in the unemployment rate and the percent change in GDP. The slope of the estimated line is −1.7, indicating that if the unemployment rate increases by 1.0 percent, output will drop by approximately 1.7 percent.

**OKUN'S LAW, 1962–2002**

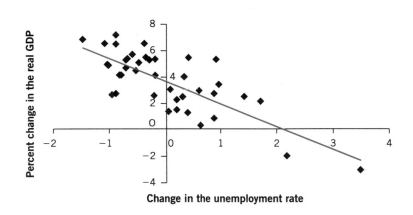

SOURCE: Unemployment rate: 1961–1975: Statistics Canada, *Historical Statistics of Canada*, Publication 11-516-XIE; 1976–2002: CANSIM II V2062815; real GDP: CANSIM II V1992259.

## *Working with Data*

Statistics Canada is responsible for producing data on gross domestic product. As well as being measured as payments to factors of production or as components of demand, GDP is also measured in current dollars and constant dollars, and as seasonally adjusted and not seasonally adjusted. In this section, we explain the difference between these different measurements.

---

[11] *Potential GDP: Its Measurement and Significance*, Proceedings of the Business and Economics Statistics Section, American Statistical Association, 1962, pages 98–103.

## Current and Constant Dollar Data

In Section 2-3, we explained the difference between current dollar GDP and constant dollar GDP. Remember that GDP in any period could change because (1) more physical goods and services were produced or (2) the price of goods and services changed. If you want to know the value of the change in GDP, this would take into account both the price change and the production change. Measured this way, this is called *current dollar GDP*. If you want to know only how production has changed, without the effects of price, this is called *constant dollar GDP*. Constant dollar GDP is always measured relative to some base year. Currently, Statistics Canada uses 1997 as a base year. This means that if you looked at current dollar GDP and constant dollar GDP, they would be the same in 1997.

To show this, go to CANSIM II and retrieve nominal GDP, quarterly, V498918, and real GDP in 1997 dollars, quarterly, V1992292. As each of these series is measured quarterly, not seasonally adjusted, you will need to sum them to get the annual GDP for each year. You should be able to show that each of these series equals $882,733 in 1997 (recall from the Chapter 1 Working with Data section that this is measured in millions of dollars). Notice also that, prior to 1997, nominal GDP is smaller than real GDP, and after 1997, nominal GDP is greater than real GDP.

## Seasonally Adjusted Data

When you use data that is seasonally adjusted at the annual rate (SAAR), this means that the data have been manipulated in two important ways. First, we know that a great many economic time series exhibit a seasonal pattern; for instance, construction slows down in the winter, retail sales increase before the December holidays, etc. If you want to know what a variable would be without the seasonal pattern, then you would seasonally adjust the data. The second important adjustment is that the data are expressed at an annual rate. That is, for each quarter, the figure for GDP measures what GDP would be annually if that quarter was repeated for all quarters of the year.

Go to CANSIM II and retrieve real GDP in 1997 dollars, seasonally adjusted, V1992259. Because these data are SAAR, to get the annual amount for GDP in any year, you would take the *average* of the quarterly values. You should be able to show that this series will also give you an annual value in 1997 of $882,733.

## CHAPTER SUMMARY

▶ GDP is the value of all final goods and services produced in an economy within a given period.

▶ GDP can be measured from the supply side as payments to factors of production or on the demand side as components of spending.

www.mcgrawhill.ca/college/dornbusch

▶ Total savings in an economy is composed of private savings plus government savings (the budget deficit). Total savings equals investment plus the current account balance.

▶ Nominal GDP is also called *current dollar GDP* and is equal to the value of output in a given period measured in the prices of that period.

▶ Real GDP is also called *constant dollar GDP* and is equal to the value of output in a given period measured in the prices of a base period.

▶ Chain weighted GDP is an alternative measure of real GDP that is calculated by averaging the base over two years: the current and the preceding year. The averaging moves over time as the current year moves over time.

▶ A price index is a measure of prices in any one year compared to the level of the same prices in some base year. The two major price indexes are the Consumer Price Index and the GDP deflator.

▶ Inflation is the rate of change in prices.

▶ Nominal interest rates give the return on bonds in current dollars and real interest rates give the return in constant dollars.

▶ The unemployment rate is defined as the percentage of the labour force that is unemployed.

▶ The labour force participation rate is defined as the percentage of the adult population that is in the labour force.

## KEY TERMS

*National Income and Expenditure Accounts, 24*
gross domestic product (GDP), *24*
factors of production, *25*
factor payments, *25*
production function, *25*
final goods and services, *25*
intermediate goods, *25*
value added, *25*
net domestic product at factor cost, *26*
net domestic product at market prices, *27*
depreciation, *27*

gross national product (GNP), *27*
national income accounting identity, *28*
consumption spending, *28*
investment spending, *29*
human capital, *30*
gross investment, *30*
net investment, *30*
government purchases, *30*
transfer payments, *30*
government expenditure, *30*
net exports, *30*
current dollar, or nominal, GDP, *34*

constant dollar, or real, GDP, *34*
chain weighted GDP, *36*
GDP deflator, *36*
Consumer Price Index (CPI), *37*
nominal interest rate, *38*
real interest rate, *38*
labour force, *39*
labour force participation rate, *40*
natural rate of unemployment, *40*
frictional unemployment, *40*
structural unemployment, *40*
discouraged workers, *41*
Okun's law, *41*

www.mcgrawhill.ca/college/dornbusch

## DISCUSSION QUESTIONS

1. We mentioned in Box 2-2 that the GDP measures do not take into account effects of production on the environment or depletion of natural resources. How do you think that taking these factors into account would affect our measures of GDP? You may want to look at the article "The Canadian National Accounts Environmental Component: A Status Report" by Philip Smith in National Income and Expenditure Accounts, Annual Estimates 1982–1993, catalogue no. 13-201.

2. Currently, Statistics Canada uses a base year of 1997 to calculate constant dollar GDP. Do you think that changing the base year will have any effect on measurement of GDP? To think about this, you may want to read "The Effect of Rebasing on GDP," which can be found online at www.statcan.ca/english/concepts/nateco/rebase.pdf.

3. Increases in real GDP are often thought of as increases in welfare. What are some problems with this interpretation? What do you think is the biggest problem with it, and why?

4. Suppose that you take out a student loan to finance your education. This loan has a fixed nominal interest rate at the time you take it out, and this interest rate does not change over the period of time you pay back the loan. Discuss how you may be better off or worse off when you pay back this loan under the following situations:

    a. Inflation unexpectedly increased.

    b. Inflation unexpectedly decreased.

5. Discuss what you think would happen to the level *and* the growth rate of GDP if Statistics Canada was to include unpaid housework in the estimates of GDP.

## APPLICATION QUESTIONS

1. Table 2-1 was calculated from the data in CANSIM II table 3800016. Using data from this table, recalculate the numbers in Table 2-1 using data from 2000.

2. In equation (16), we defined the nominal interest rate as the percentage change in the nominal price of a bond. The real price of a bond in period $t$ is given as $P_t^B / P_t$, where $P_t$ is the price level in period $t$. Show that the percentage change in the real price of a bond is approximately equal to the nominal interest rate minus inflation, as given in equation (17).

3. CANSIM II table 3800002 contains measures of chain weighted GDP as well as constant dollar GDP. Graph each of these variables over the period 1961–2002 and comment on any differences in the two series.

4. In this chapter, we stated that the price of computers has decreased. The nominal price of computers can be found in CANSIM II V735541. Calculate the percentage decrease in this variable. Using the Consumer Price Index, calculate the relative price of computers and calculate the percentage change in this variable. Plot each of these percentage changes and comment on the difference between the two.

5. Consider an economy that consists only of those who bake bread and those who produce its ingredients. Suppose that this economy's production is as follows: 1 million loaves of bread (sold at $2 each); 1.2 million pounds of flour (sold at $1 per pound); and 100,000 pounds each of yeast, sugar, and salt (all sold at $1 per pound). The flour, yeast, sugar, and salt are sold only to bakers, who use them exclusively for the purpose of making bread.

    **a.** What is the value of output in this economy (i.e., nominal GDP)?

    **b.** How much value is added to the flour, yeast, sugar, and salt when the bakers turn them into bread?

**6.** Go to CANSIM II and retrieve the 91-day Treasury bill rate. Use the inflation data from question 2 above to calculate the real interest rate over the period 1953–2000.

**7.** In the Working With Data section of this chapter, you were asked to retrieve nominal and real GDP. Use this information to calculate the GDP deflator by dividing nominal GDP by real GDP, and calculate the GDP inflation rate. Now calculate the growth rate of nominal GDP and the growth rate of real GDP and show that the difference between the two is approximately equal to the inflation rate as measured by the GDP deflator.

**8.** The Canadian federal government issues a bond that compensates the holder for inflation; that is, it is a real return bond. You can retrieve this as CANSIM II V122553. Calculate the real interest rate monthly using the federal government's long-term nominal bond rate and the inflation rate as measured by the rate of change in the Consumer Price Index. Compare these two measurements of the real interest rate.

www.mcgrawhill.ca/college/dornbusch

# P A R T

# 2

# THE ECONOMY IN THE LONG RUN AND THE VERY LONG RUN

## CHAPTER 3

# THE ECONOMY IN THE LONG RUN:

## The Classical Market Clearing Model

### *LEARNING OBJECTIVES*

After reading and studying this chapter, you should be able to:

▶ *Understand that the difference between the long run (this chapter) and the very long run (Chapter 4) involves the assumption that, in the long run, the capital stock and technology are assumed to be fixed.*

▶ *Understand that over the long run, we assume that all factors of production are fully employed and all prices in all markets are completely flexible.*

▶ *Understand that a very simple Classical model assumes that the supply of goods and services is based on the production function, with technology and capital assumed to be fixed. Therefore, equilibrium output depends on equilibrium labour use.*

▶ *Understand that the demand for goods and services is based on the allocation of income among spending by consumers, the business sector, the government, and the foreign sector.*

▶ *Understand that in a long run Classical world, the price level is determined by the level of the money supply and the inflation rate is determined by the rate of growth of the money supply.*

I n this chapter we are going to examine the economy over the long run. In Chapter 4, we will examine the economy over the very long run and discuss growth theory. Remember that the difference between the long run and the very long run centres on our assumptions concerning the productive capacity of the economy. In this chapter, we assume that the productive capacity of the economy is fixed. Be careful that you understand the nature of this assumption. In this chapter and in Chapter 4, we assume that all prices are flexible and all markets are clear at all times. Therefore, the economy operates at full employment. However, the time frame for analysis of the long run, say, 10 to 15 years, is short enough that the capital stock is not growing quickly enough to increase full employment output. Recall from Chapter 1 that this is the period of time over which we assume that the aggregate supply curve is vertical (refer back to Figure 1-2). This vertical aggregate supply curve is often called the *Classical aggregate supply curve*, and the model that we develop in this chapter is called the *Classical model*.

## 3-1 | THE SUPPLY OF GOODS AND SERVICES: THE PRODUCTION FUNCTION AND THE LABOUR MARKET

### The General Form of the Production Function

**production function**
Technological relationship showing how much output can be produced for a given combination of inputs.

As we saw in Chapter 2, output ($Y$) is assumed to be produced through a **production function**, which combines factors of production, capital ($K$), and labour ($N$). The production function that we will use throughout this book is of the form

$$Y = AF(K, N) \tag{1}$$

The term $A$ accounts for the level of technology or, more generally, the level of productivity.

We can demonstrate how a production function is a useful tool for thinking about combining factors of production and technology to produce output. Equation (1) is a generic form of a production function. Economists have found that a specific form of the production function, called the *Cobb-Douglas production function*, appears to provide a relatively accurate description of the economy. The **Cobb-Douglas production function** can be written

**Cobb-Douglas production function**
$Y = AK^\theta N^{1-\theta}$

$$Y = AK^\theta N^{1-\theta} \tag{2}$$

In equation (2), $\theta$ and $(1-\theta)$ are weights equal to capital's share of income and labour's share of income. By *labour's share of income*, we mean the fraction of total output that goes to compensate labour. For Canada, it is approximately true that capital's share ($\theta$) equals 0.3 and labour's share ($1-\theta$) equals 0.7.[1] Given this, we could write a production function for Canada as

$$Y = AK^{0.3} N^{0.7} \tag{3}$$

In Table 3-1, we have used equation (3) to illustrate how the Cobb-Douglas production function can be used to describe the production of output in Canada over the period 1975 to 2002.

[1] If you look back at Table 2-1, you can see that labour's share of factor payments fluctuates somewhat, but on average equals approximately 0.7.

| TABLE 3-1 | AN EMPIRICAL PRODUCTION FUNCTION FOR CANADA, 1975–2002 ($Y = AK^{0.3} N^{0.7}$) | | | | |
|---|---|---|---|---|---|
| Year | GDP, (billions of 1997 dollars) ($Y$) | Capital, (billions of 1997 dollars) ($K$) | Labour, (millions of persons) ($N$) | Total Factor Productivity ($A$) | %$\Delta A$ |
| 1975 | 480.3 | 390.8 | 10.0 | 16.0 | — |
| 1976 | 506.7 | 407.2 | 10.5 | 16.1 | 0.7 |
| 1977 | 524.2 | 422.1 | 10.8 | 16.2 | 0.6 |
| 1978 | 545.6 | 436.3 | 11.1 | 16.3 | 0.7 |
| 1979 | 568.5 | 455.1 | 11.5 | 16.4 | 0.5 |
| 1980 | 576.4 | 477.7 | 11.9 | 16.0 | −2.1 |
| 1981 | 594.1 | 507.4 | 12.2 | 15.9 | −0.9 |
| 1982 | 576.7 | 525.1 | 12.3 | 15.2 | −4.3 |
| 1983 | 592.7 | 537.5 | 12.5 | 15.3 | 0.7 |
| 1984 | 626.4 | 550.8 | 12.7 | 15.9 | 3.7 |
| 1985 | 660.3 | 566.9 | 13.0 | 16.4 | 3.0 |
| 1986 | 677.8 | 585.6 | 13.3 | 16.4 | 0.3 |
| 1987 | 705.7 | 607.9 | 13.5 | 16.7 | 1.6 |
| 1988 | 740.6 | 636.8 | 13.8 | 17.0 | 2.1 |
| 1989 | 759.8 | 667.3 | 14.0 | 17.0 | −0.2 |
| 1990 | 762.4 | 692.3 | 14.2 | 16.7 | −1.7 |
| 1991 | 747.9 | 709.9 | 14.3 | 16.2 | −3.1 |
| 1992 | 754.8 | 724.1 | 14.4 | 16.2 | 0.2 |
| 1993 | 772.5 | 735.5 | 14.5 | 16.4 | 1.2 |
| 1994 | 810.0 | 750.4 | 14.6 | 17.0 | 3.6 |
| 1995 | 832.1 | 766.4 | 14.8 | 17.2 | 1.5 |
| 1996 | 845.2 | 785.7 | 14.9 | 17.3 | 0.1 |
| 1997 | 882.7 | 817.4 | 15.2 | 17.6 | 2.0 |
| 1998 | 919.0 | 849.8 | 15.4 | 17.9 | 1.7 |
| 1999 | 967.6 | 887.8 | 15.7 | 18.4 | 2.5 |
| 2000 | 1013.1 | 928.8 | 16.0 | 18.7 | 2.0 |
| 2001 | 1026.9 | 963.7 | 16.2 | 18.6 | −0.8 |
| 2002 | 1053.1 | 994.9 | 16.4 | 18.7 | 0.8 |

SOURCE: GDP: CANSIM II V1992259; capital stock: CANSIM II V1078499 and V1078501; labour force: CANSIM II V2091051.

The second column of Table 3-1 contains data on GDP in billions of 1997 dollars, which is simply real (or constant dollar) GDP that we examined in Chapter 2. The third column is the value of the capital stock in Canada measured in billions of constant 1997 dollars. The fourth column is the labour force in Canada, measured in millions of persons. Ideally, we would also like to have a measure of $A$, total factor productivity. Unfortunately, it is very difficult to construct a direct measure of total factor productivity. Instead, we measure $A$ indirectly, by assuming that the production function is correct and that anything that is not explained by capital and labour must be explained by factor productivity. That is, $A$ is calculated as

$$A = \frac{Y}{K^{0.3} N^{0.7}} \tag{4}$$

## Changes in Factor Productivity

In Table 3-1, we used the Cobb-Douglas production function to estimate values for *A*, total factor productivity. The final column of this table calculates the percentage change in *A*. This measure does not depend on the units in which each of the variables is measured. The percentage change in total factor productivity contains some interesting information about the evolution of the economy. To see this, we have graphed this variable in the figure below.

### PERCENT CHANGE IN TOTAL FACTOR PRODUCTIVITY, 1976–2002

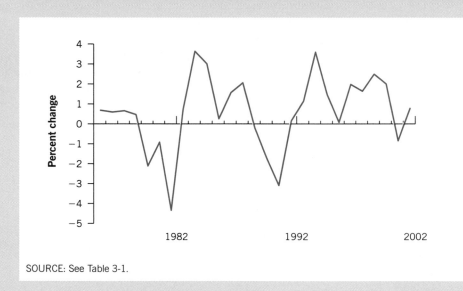

SOURCE: See Table 3-1.

You can see from the figure that factor productivity varies quite substantially from year to year. We would expect that factor productivity would decrease during economic slowdowns and increase during recoveries. The figure shows clear decreases in factor productivity during the slowdowns in 1981, 1991, and 2001, and increases in the recoveries.

Measured in this way, *A* is sometimes called the *Solow residual*.[2] Unfortunately, this method of estimating total factor productivity has a major drawback, in that the units in which *A* is measured can change if we change the units in which any of the other variables are measured. However, we can overcome this problem by measuring how total factor productivity has changed over the years. This is shown in the final column of Table 3-1. The change in total factor productivity will be an important variable when we discuss growth accounting in Chapter 4.

[2] Named after Robert Solow, one of the earliest contributors to growth theory and the 1987 Nobel Prize winner in Economic Sciences.

## The Production Function in the Long Run: Fixed Capital and Technology

For our long run Classical model, we make two important assumptions concerning the production function. Remember that the term $A$ accounts for the level of technology or, more generally, the level of productivity. Productivity changes will play a large role in the growth theory model in Chapter 4. In this chapter, we abstract from productivity changes and assume that $A$ can be ignored. The second important assumption is that changes in the capital stock are small enough that their effect on full employment output can be ignored. Both of these assumptions will be relaxed in the next chapter.

Given these assumptions, our production function becomes

$$Y = F(\overline{K}, N) \tag{5}$$

The production function tells us that, for a given technology and capital stock, the amount of output produced depends on the amount of labour input. We can use the Cobb-Douglas production function given in equation (3) to graph the production function given in equation (5). We assume that capital and technology are both fixed at their 2002 levels (949.9 and 18.7, respectively; see Table 3-1). Given these assumptions, the production function becomes

$$Y = 18.7 * (949.9^{0.3}) N^{0.7} \tag{6}$$

Notice that the only variable factor of production is labour. Equation (6) is graphed in Figure 3-1.

### FIGURE 3-1

THE PRODUCTION FUNCTION WITH FIXED CAPITAL AND TECHNOLOGY

The production function relates the amount of output that can be produced using various amounts of the labour input, holding capital and technology constant. If you solve equation (6) for $N = 5$, you will find that $Y = \$458.0$ billion (point A); if you solve for $N = 10$, $Y = \$744.1$ billion (point B). The slope of the production function gives the marginal product of labour, $MPN$. Notice that the $MPN$ is smaller at point B than at point A, illustrating the concept of diminishing marginal product of labour.

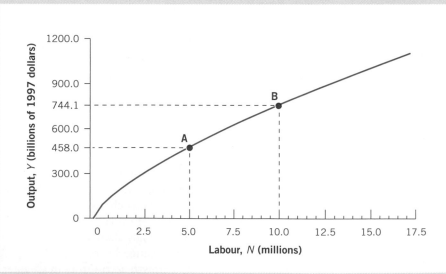

SOURCE: Derived using equation (6).

Equation (6) and Figure 3-1 show how output will change if the amount of labour used in the production process changes, holding capital and technology constant. Firms are assumed to use this production function to choose the amount of labour they wish to employ. That is, this production function will be used to derive the demand for labour curve.

The production function in Figure 3-1 has a positive slope, which means that when a unit of labour is added to the production process, even though capital and technology are fixed, output goes up. The information a firm needs is: How much does output change when a unit of labour is added? (For our production function, a unit of labour is 1 million workers.) We can use equation (6) to show that, for instance, when labour use increases from 4 to 5, output goes up by $66.2 billion, and when labour use increases from 9 to 10, output goes up by $52.9 billion.

**marginal product of labour (*MPN*)**

The amount that output increases for each additional unit increase in labour input.

This concept, the amount that output increases for each additional unit increase in labour input, is called the **marginal product of labour** (*MPN*). In Figure 3-1, the *MPN* is given by the slope of the production function.[3] Notice that when one unit of labour is added at 9 million, output increases less ($52.9 billion) than when one unit of labour is added at 4 million ($66.2 billion). This means that as labour use increases, the amount of extra output that is gained from an increase in labour input becomes smaller. This is known as the **diminishing marginal product of labour**.

**diminishing marginal product of labour**

As labour use increases, the amount of extra output that is gained from an increase in labour input becomes smaller.

Given the diminishing marginal product of labour, if we graph the marginal product of labour against labour use, we would have a downward-sloping curve. This is illustrated in Figure 3-2.

## Marginal Product of Labour and Labour Demand

We assume that the goal of any firm is to maximize profit, which equals total revenue minus total cost. When a firm hires an additional unit of labour, it incurs a marginal cost and receives a marginal benefit. The marginal cost is measured by *W*, the nominal wage that must be paid to the extra unit of labour that is hired. The marginal benefit to the firm is the value of the additional unit of output that is produced by that additional unit of labour. This marginal benefit is called the *value of the*

**FIGURE 3-2**

The *MPN* curve is downward sloping, as each additional unit of labour contributes less to output than the previous unit did. This is called the *diminishing marginal product of labour*.

### THE MARGINAL PRODUCT OF LABOUR

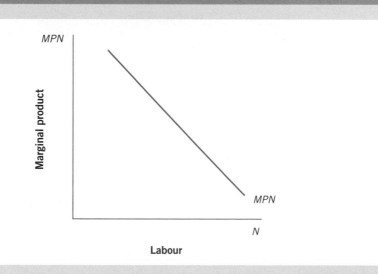

[3] Technically, the *MPN* is given by the slope of a tangent to the production function at any one point.

*marginal product* and is measured as the marginal product of labour, *MPN*, multiplied by the price, *P*. A profit-maximizing firm will hire labour until marginal benefit equals marginal cost.

$$W = MPN \times P \tag{7}$$

The profit maximizing condition in equation (7) can be rearranged in terms of the **real wage,** $w = \frac{W}{P}$,

$$w = MPN \tag{8}$$

Equation (8) states that a profit-maximizing firm will hire labour until the real wage equals the marginal product of labour. We can put equation (8) together with Figure 3-2 to derive the demand for labour curve. The demand for labour curve is simply the *MPN* curve drawn with the real wage on the vertical axis. We can do this because the real wage and the *MPN* are both measured in units of goods. The demand for labour curve is shown in Figure 3-3.

## The Supply of Labour

We assume that workers, in deciding how much labour to supply, compare the benefits and costs of working more hours. Obviously, individuals choose to work in order to earn an income, which enables them to purchase goods and services. Therefore, the marginal benefit of working an extra hour is measured by how much this extra hour of work will increase consumption. When a person works an extra hour, he or she receives a nominal wage, *W*. Given this nominal wage, the amount of extra goods and services that can be consumed depends on the price of goods and services, as measured by the price level, *P*. We know that the ratio of *W* to *P*, *W/P*, is the real wage, and this is measured in terms of goods and services. For instance, if you work 20 extra hours at $5.00 per hour, and jeans cost $100.00, then 20 hours of your work equals one pair of jeans. In this manner, the marginal benefit of working an extra hour is measured by the real wage, *w*.

**FIGURE 3-3**    DEMAND FOR LABOUR CURVE

The demand for labour curve is derived from the condition that the marginal product of labour equals the real wage. It is downward sloping due to the diminishing-returns property of the production function.

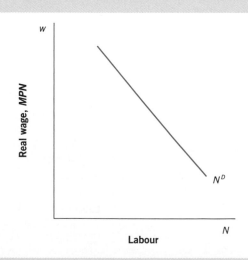

**leisure**
Non-work activities.

The marginal cost of working an extra hour is that the worker must give up other non-work activities, which economists call **leisure**. Therefore, workers will supply labour up to the point where the marginal benefit from an extra hour of work, measured by the real wage, equals the marginal cost of giving up an extra hour of leisure. We assume that increases in the real wage will make it more attractive to give up an extra hour of leisure.[4] Therefore, the labour supply curve slopes upward. This is shown in Figure 3-4.

## FIGURE 3-4

The labour supply curve is upward sloping, reflecting the assumption that a higher real wage will induce workers to give up more leisure and work more hours.

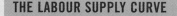

### THE LABOUR SUPPLY CURVE

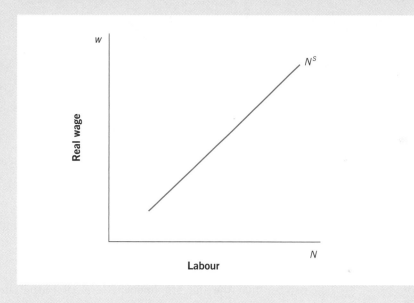

## Equilibrium in the Labour Market

Figure 3-5 depicts equilibrium in the labour market. Given the supply and demand curves, $w^*$ is the equilibrium real wage and $N^*$ is the equilibrium amount of employment. Remember that in this long run Classical model, all prices are assumed to be flexible, which ensures that markets are in equilibrium at all times. Therefore, in the labour market, the real wage is assumed to move very quickly, which means that the equilibrium amount of labour in Figure 3-5, equal to $N^*$, represents **full employment** of the labour force.[5] Be sure that you understand this important implication of Classical analysis of the labour market. At the equilibrium real wage, $w^*$, all workers who are in the labour force are employed. Any individuals who do not have a job are not in the labour force, because the real wage is too low for them to seek employment. These workers are *choosing* not to enter the labour force, and therefore cannot be counted as being unemployed.

**full employment**
Occurs when all members of the labour force are employed; individuals not working are not in the labour force and therefore are not counted as being unemployed.

Once the full employment amount of labour is determined, we can return to the production function given in equation (5). Substituting the full employment level of

[4] Be careful that you understand that this is based on an assumption.

[5] We discussed full employment in Chapter 2.

## FIGURE 3-5

**EQUILIBRIUM IN THE LABOUR MARKET**

Due to the assumption that the real wage moves very quickly to ensure constant market equilibrium, the equilibrium amount of employment, $N^*$, represents full employment in the labour market.

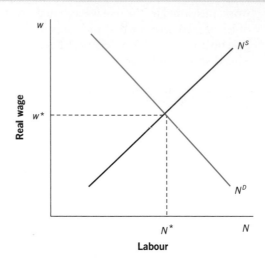

employment, $N^*$, into equation (5) determines the full employment level of output.

$$Y^* = F(\overline{K}, N^*) \tag{9}$$

Remember that the full employment level of output depends only on the full employment level of labour, as technology and capital are assumed to be fixed. We can think of $Y^*$ as the level of output the economy would reach if all prices were flexible and all factors of production were fully employed but not growing.

## The Classical Aggregate Supply Curve

In Chapter 1, we introduced the aggregate demand-aggregate supply model and demonstrated how the aggregate supply curve would take different shapes depending on the time frame under analysis. Recall that in the long run, we assumed that the aggregate supply is vertical. Now that we have derived the long run full employment level of output, we know that the aggregate supply curve will be vertical at the level of full employment output, $Y^*$. The Classical aggregate supply curve is shown in Figure 3-6.

In the long run, the supply of goods and services depends only on the production function, as given in equation (9). This equation tells us that $Y^*$ depends only on $N^*$ (given capital and technology), and we know from the labour market that $N^*$ depends on the real wage (and perhaps some exogenous variables, which we will ignore for now). Therefore, production, or supply, in the long run is independent of the price level.[6] This is the reason why the Classical aggregate supply curve is vertical.

---

[6] The determinants of the price level are discussed in Section 3-3.

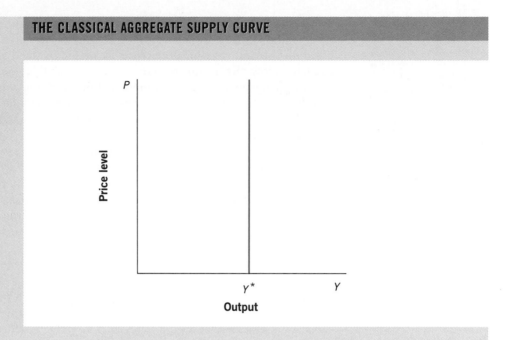

**FIGURE 3-6**

In the long run, full employment output depends only on the production function and is independent of the price level. Therefore, the Classical *AS* curve is vertical at the level of full employment output.

**THE CLASSICAL AGGREGATE SUPPLY CURVE**

## 3-2 | THE DEMAND FOR GOODS AND SERVICES

We saw in Chapter 2 that the demand for goods and services is made up of four components: consumption spending by households *(C)*, investment spending by business *(I)*, government purchase of goods and services *(G)*, and demand for net exports *(NX)*. In this chapter, we make the simplifying assumption that government spending is exogenous and concentrate on the consumption/savings decisions of households and the investment decisions of businesses. In addition, we defer any discussion of net export spending until Chapter 5.

This section primarily discusses aggregate demand, which explains how income is allocated among the different spending units listed in the previous paragraph. However, there is another allocation that is important for this chapter and especially important in Chapter 4, where we discuss growth theory—the question of how a consumer allocates current income between consumption today and consumption in the future. A decision by consumers to spend less today, which is savings, is really a decision to consume more tomorrow. The channel through which this happens in an economy is that savings by consumers feeds into investment by firms, and investment is an increase in the capital stock. In this chapter, we discuss the consumption savings decisions made by consumers and the investment decisions of firms. In Chapter 4, we discuss the ramifications of these decisions for the very long run growth of the capital stock and output.

### Consumption and Savings

When we developed the labour market sector of the Classical model, we assumed that workers and firms made decisions by equating marginal benefit to marginal cost. We can apply the same basic framework to the consumption/savings decision that consumers face. Picture yourself, as a consumer, as being in the following position. You receive income today, and you must decide how much of this income you

**rate of time preference**

The rate at which you are willing to give up consumption today if you are compensated by increased consumption in the future.

**real rate of interest**

Return on an investment measured in dollars of constant value; roughly equal to the difference between the nominal interest rate and the rate of inflation.

**private savings**

Saving by individuals, by families, and by firms; saving by everyone other than government.

will consume today and how much you will put aside as savings. The cost to you of saving more is that you must consume less today. We assume that you evaluate this based on your **rate of time preference**. If you are inclined to be a saver, we say that you have a low rate of time preference. This means that you do not perceive a large cost to giving up current consumption. Conversely, if you have a preference for spending your income on current consumption, we say that you have a high rate of time preference. This means you perceive a large cost to giving up current consumption in the form of savings.

Giving up current consumption in the form of savings is translated into increased future consumption possibilities through the return you earn on those savings. Thus, the marginal benefit of savings is given by the **real rate of interest**. We assume that as the real rate of interest increases, consumers' desire to save will also increase. Therefore, the savings curve slopes upward.[7] This is shown in Figure 3-7. Notice that we have called this $S^P$, for **private savings**, in order to distinguish it from government savings, which will be discussed below.

## Investment

Recall that firms purchase machinery and equipment to increase their productive capacity in terms of capital stock.[8] We will study investment demand in detail in Chapter 16. For now, we need to know that investment demand depends on the real rate of interest. Consider a simple example: Suppose that a firm is planning a $1-million expansion. This firm expects to make $100,000 per year from its expanded capacity. The firm wishes to borrow the money at a rate of interest of 10 percent. How will the firm know whether borrowing the money is profitable? The firm will compare the cost of borrowing the money to the expected return from borrowing the money. The

---

**FIGURE 3-7**

The savings curve shows the amount consumers are willing to save for each real rate of interest. The curve slopes upward, as we assume that an increased return on savings (the real rate of interest) makes current consumption less attractive.

**THE SAVINGS CURVE**

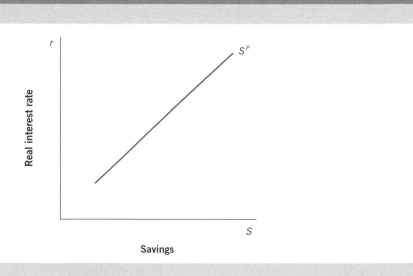

---

[7] As with the upward-sloping labour supply curve, please keep in mind that this is based on an assumption.

[8] Households also purchase capital in the form of housing. We will ignore this complication for the time being.

## Rate of Time Preference

We have all been faced with the decision of whether to purchase some goods now or save money now and delay our purchase until some point in the future. We make this decision based on several variables, such as our current income, our expected income in the future, and the amount of real return we earn on our savings. In this chapter, we stress the relationship between the return on savings—measured by the real rate of interest—and the rate of time preference.

The rate of time preference is nothing more than a concept concerning how much you worry about the future. Some individuals simply do not care a lot about the future. These people are inherently spenders—they prefer to consume as much of their current income as possible—and we say that they have high rates of time preference. Other individuals are constantly worried about their economic well-being in the future. They are inherently savers, and they have low rates of time preference.

expected return from borrowing the money is 10 percent per year ($1 million/$100,000), so the firm would borrow the money if the interest rate was less than 10 percent and not borrow the money if the interest rate was higher than 10 percent. From this example, we can see that investment spending is negatively related to the real rate of interest. This is shown in Figure 3-8.

## Government and Net Export Spending

In this chapter, we assume that government spending is exogenous. We also defer the discussion of net export spending until Chapter 5.

*FIGURE 3-8*

**THE INVESTMENT DEMAND CURVE**

The desire of a firm to build more machinery and equipment, which is investment spending, depends negatively on the real rate of interest.

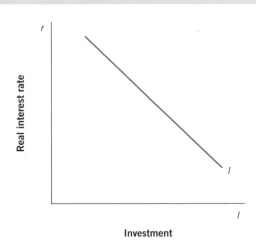

## Equilibrium: Savings Equals Investment

Remember that in this Classical model, aggregate demand is concerned with the allocation of income. Think of this in the following manner: Consumers face a decision concerning how much to consume and how much to save. When consumers save, they can be thought of as lenders, or suppliers of funds. Businesses make a decision on whether to borrow in order to expand, which is investment. Firms can be thought of as demanders of funds. There would be aggregate demand equilibrium when lenders supplied just the amount that borrowers demanded. That is, equilibrium would exist where savings equals investment.

Consider the national accounts identity for a closed economy:[9]

$$Y = C + I + G \tag{10}$$

We can rearrange this in the following manner:

$$Y - C - G = I \tag{11}$$

In Chapter 2, equation (9), we defined disposable income ($YD$) as income ($Y$) plus transfers ($TR$) minus taxes ($TA$).

$$YD = Y + TR - TA \tag{12}$$

Therefore, we can write

$$(YD - C) + (TA - TR - G) = I \tag{13}$$

$$S = S^P + S^G = I$$

government savings
The budgetary surplus or deficit; the difference between total revenue and total expenditure.

Notice that the second term on the left-hand side, $TA - TR - G$, is equal to government revenue minus government spending, which is the government budgetary surplus (if it is positive) or budgetary deficit (if it is negative). When the government is running a budgetary surplus, **government savings** is positive. Thus, equation (13) states that for aggregate demand equilibrium, savings equals investment. Savings is composed of private savings $S^P = YD - C$ and government savings $S^G = TA - TR - G$. The savings investment equilibrium is shown in Figure 3-9.

## Fiscal Policy and Savings

Consider the effect on the above equilibrium of an increase in government purchases. Notice from equation (13) that an increase in $G$ reduces government savings. As long as private sector savings does not change, total savings decreases, and the $S$ curve shifts to the left. This is shown in Figure 3-10. This shift causes the real interest rate to rise, and in the new equilibrium, savings and investment are lower. The prediction of this model is that a government budget deficit will lower savings and raise the real rate of interest.

---

[9] It may be helpful for you to review Section 2-2 in Chapter 2. In this chapter, we are considering a closed economy.

## FIGURE 3-9

For aggregate demand equilibrium, total savings equals investment. Total savings is composed of private sector savings and government savings in terms of the budgetary surplus or deficit.

### SAVINGS AND INVESTMENT

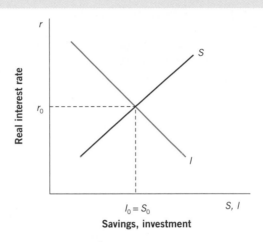

## FIGURE 3-10

When the government runs a budget deficit, government savings is negative. Therefore, the S curve, which is composed of private savings and government savings, shifts to the left. The result is that a government budget deficit causes a higher real interest rate and lower total savings.

### THE EFFECTS OF A GOVERNMENT BUDGET DEFICIT

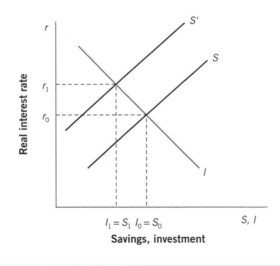

## The Effects of Fiscal Policy Since the Mid-1970s

From the mid-1970s onward, most Western countries, including Canada, began a dramatic shift in the manner of conducting fiscal policy. Prior to this period, most countries ran a budget that was roughly balanced. Starting in approximately 1975, Canada and other countries began to run consistent budgetary deficits. Our model predicts that this will shift the savings curve to the left and raise real interest rates. Figure 3-11 shows that the data for Canada are consistent with this prediction.

*FIGURE 3-11*

**THE EFFECTS OF THE CANADIAN BUDGET DEFICITS, 1972–2002**

In this figure, *r* is the real rate of interest and $S^G$ is the federal government budget deficit. The real rate of interest is measured as the long-term government bond rate less inflation, and the deficit is multiplied by minus one for illustration purposes. A chronic government budget deficit is consistent with high real interest rates.

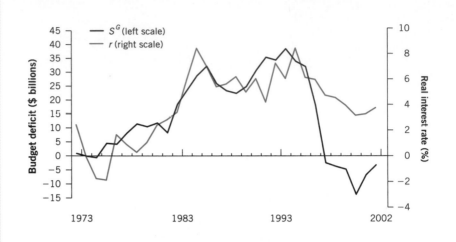

SOURCE: The long-term government bond rate is from CANSIM II V122487; the inflation rate is adapted from the CPI: CANSIM II 735319; and the federal deficit is from CANSIM II V646208.

## 3-3 | THE MONEY STOCK, THE PRICE LEVEL, AND THE INFLATION RATE

So far in our long run Classical model, we have discussed what is commonly called the *real* side of the economy. All of the variables we have discussed so far are real variables: The production function describes real output, the labour market equilibrium depends on the real wage, and savings and investment depend on the real rate of interest. In this section, we discuss how nominal variables, such as the nominal money stock and the price level, are determined in a Classical model.

We begin with a brief discussion of money and describe the relationship between money and the price level. We then show that in the long run, the rate of inflation in an economy is determined by the rate of growth of nominal money.

### Money

www.bankofcanada.ca/en/res/wp99-5.htm

**quantity equation**
$MV = PT$

The details of money supply and money demand will be discussed later in the book (Chapters 16 and 18). For now, we need to understand that the major function of money is as a medium of exchange. The fact that money is a medium of exchange can be summarized through the **quantity equation**

$$MV = PT \tag{14}$$

The quantity equation has a very natural interpretation. Think about adding up all of the real transactions in an economy over some period of time, and call this *T. P* represents the average price of all of these transactions. Because money is the

**money stock (or money supply)**
The total amount of money available in an economy; consists of any asset that can be used for immediate payment.

**velocity of money**
A measure of the speed with which money circulates in an economy.

medium of exchange, all transactions are assumed to take place through money. Therefore, $PT$ is a measure of the number of dollars exchanged in a period of time. $M$ is the size of the **money stock** (or **money supply**) in an economy. Given this, the quantity equation defines $V$ as the velocity of circulation.

$$V = \frac{PT}{M} \qquad (15)$$

The **velocity of money** is a measure of the speed with which money circulates in an economy.

This quantity equation should be thought of as an identity. If we could actually add up the nominal value of all transactions in an economy, then it must be true that this nominal value must equal money times the velocity of circulation.

In reality, it is very difficult to measure $T$, the number of transactions in an economy. Typically, we use a proxy for $T$, in the form of $Y$, which is our measure of real GDP. You will most often see the quantity equation written as

$$MV = PY \qquad (16)$$

Notice that $PY$ is a measure of the dollar value of the transactions in an economy, which is just nominal GDP, which we discussed in Chapter 2.

We are going to treat money as a commodity just like other commodities that we have studied in this chapter. We assume that there exists a money market with money supply and money demand. We have in mind a very simple money demand equation. When individuals demand money, they do so in order to purchase goods. Remember that money is a nominal variable. We can express nominal money in terms of the number of goods it can purchase as $\frac{M}{P}$, which is the real money stock. Our demand for money equation will be expressed in terms of real money demand as

$$\frac{M^D}{P} = kY \qquad (17)$$

Equation (17) says that real money demand will depend positively on real income. Here $k$ is a parameter, which determines how much real money demand will change for any given change in income.[10]

We assume that the nominal money supply is exogenously controlled by the central bank, and denote this as $\overline{M}$. Therefore, the real money supply is $\frac{\overline{M}}{P}$. In equilibrium, the real supply of money must equal the real demand for money

$$\frac{\overline{M}}{P} = kY \qquad (18)$$

We can rewrite this equilibrium condition as

$$\overline{M}\left[\frac{1}{k}\right] = PY \qquad (19)$$

Under the assumption that $V = \frac{1}{k}$, the equilibrium condition that money supply equals money demand is simply the quantity equation. We now make the assumption that velocity is constant, so that we can write

$$\overline{MV} = PY \qquad (20)$$

---

[10] You may recognize $k$ as being (almost) an elasticity. As we will see in the chapter on money demand later in the book (Chapter 16), $k$ is essentially the income elasticity of money demand.

**quantity theory of money**
Predicts that if the nominal money stock increases, the nominal price level will increase and real income will remain constant.

Of course, velocity is not really constant. Technological innovations in the banking industry, such as automated teller machines, have changed velocity in the past. However, as with many assumptions that we make in economics in general, and macroeconomics in particular, we will consider this assumption to be a convenient approximation to reality.

We can now use these relationships to discuss a very important long run proposition called the *quantity theory of money*. The **quantity theory of money** predicts that if the nominal money stock increases, the nominal price level will increase, and real income will remain constant.

$$\Delta M = \Delta P \tag{21}$$

Remember that real income is determined by the production function and the labour market, as we discussed in Section 3-1. The quantity theory of money predicts that a change in the nominal money stock will not have any effects on this production process. This is an alternative explanation for why the Classical aggregate supply curve is vertical.

We can think of the quantity theory of money as a statement that money is neutral. Money is said to be neutral when a change in the nominal money stock changes only nominal variables (the price level) and all real variables (real income) remain constant.

You should think of the quantity theory of money as a proposition that should hold in the long run. If money is not neutral in the long run, then the central bank could increase the nominal money stock forever, and everyone would be better off in real terms. This clearly does not happen. However, there are very important channels in the short run that make money non-neutral, and these will be discussed in detail in Part 4 of this textbook.

## Money Growth and Inflation

The quantity theory of money relationship can be thought of in dynamic terms as a relationship between the rate of growth of the nominal money stock and the inflation rate.

To see this, rewrite equation (20) as

$$\% \Delta \overline{M} + \% \Delta \overline{V} = \%\Delta P + \Delta\% Y \tag{22}$$

We have made the assumption that velocity is constant, so the second term on the left-hand side of equation (22) is constant. Our model also tells us that real income changes come about due to change in the production process, and that this is not related to money supply changes. Therefore, we can write equation (22) as

$$\%\Delta \overline{M} = \% \Delta P \tag{23}$$

Equation (23) states that in the long run, the rate of inflation is determined by the rate of growth of nominal money. Note that $\% \Delta P$ is the rate of change in prices (which is just the inflation rate) that we have denoted as $\pi$ throughout most of the text.

## The Quantity Theory of Money in Canada

Figure 3-12 plots the rate of growth of nominal money, as measured by *M2*, and the rate of inflation for Canada for each decade between 1870 and 2000.[11] You can see from Figure 3-12 that periods of high money growth are consistent with high inflation, and periods of low money growth are consistent with low inflation. This is evidence that the predictions of the quantity theory of money hold over the long run.

**FIGURE 3-12**

The rate of growth of money is measured as the change in *M2*, and the inflation rate is measured as the change in the CPI. Periods of high money growth are accompanied by periods of high inflation, consistent with the prediction of the quantity theory of money.

### THE RATE OF GROWTH OF MONEY AND THE INFLATION RATE, 1880–2000 (DECADE AVERAGES)

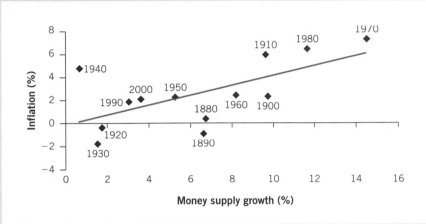

SOURCE: Historical data are taken from *New Estimates of the Canadian Money Stock, 1871–1967* by Cheri Metcalf, Angela Redish, and Ronald Shearer, University of British Columbia Discussion Paper 96-17. The data are available at www.econ.ubc.ca/dp96list.htm. From 1967 onward: *M2*: CANSIM II V37128; CPI: V375319.

**BOX**

**3-3**

## Does the Quantity Theory of Money Really Hold?

The answer to this question is yes, with two qualifications. The quantity theory of money holds only approximately, and only in the long run. This is the essential message of Figure 3-12. It takes a long time (decades) for inflation to arise due to excessive money growth. Also, the points in Figure 3-12 are only approximately consistent with the prediction that high money growth will lead to high inflation.

There is an intuitive way to look at the quantity theory of money. If the quantity theory of money does not hold in some form, then it must be true that monetary policy can change real income. This is an extremely important question: Can monetary policy change real income? As we will see in Parts 3 and 4 of this book, the answer is yes, *but only in the short run*. If monetary policy could change long run, real income, then why are we not all rich? The answer is that over the long run, output is determined by our ability to produce goods. That is, in the long run, the production function, technology, labour, capital, and whatever other resources your economy possesses, all determine your real output and real income. Changing the money stock does not use up resources to produce goods that can be consumed. Think about one definition of economics: Economics is the study of the allocation of scarce resources to satisfy unlimited human wants. If money is not neutral in the long run, this would violate the scarcity constraint.

---

[11] *M2* is one of the many measures of the money stock in Canada. These money stock measures will be discussed in detail in Chapter 16.

## The Real Interest Rate in the Long Run

In its most general form, the quantity theory of money states that monetary policy cannot affect real variables in the long run. The quantity theory prediction from equation (23) is that high money growth will lead to inflation. However, an increase in inflation could have an effect on the real rate of interest. In Chapter 2, we defined the real interest rate as

$$r = i - \pi \tag{24}$$

If inflation increases and the nominal interest rate remains constant, then the real interest rate would decrease and this would violate the quantity theory of money. Given this, one extension of the quantity theory of money, called the **Fisher effect**, is that a long run increase in the inflation rate will increase the nominal interest rate, so that the real interest rate will not change due to inflation.

To see how the Fisher effect works, rewrite equation (24).

$$i = r + \pi \tag{25}$$

Equation (25) says that, in the long run, the nominal interest rate can be thought of as having two components. First, there is the real return, $r$, which measures your ability to purchase goods and services. Second, there is a compensation for the change in purchasing power, given by the inflation rate, $\pi$. The Fisher effect states that as inflation goes up, the consumer will be compensated for this potential loss in purchasing power by an increase in the nominal interest rate and, therefore, inflation will not affect the real return.

Figure 3-13 graphs the nominal interest rate, as measured by the return on long-term government bonds, and the rate of inflation, as measured by the change in the Consumer Price Index. Each series is measured as a 10-year moving average in an attempt to isolate the long run movements. With the exception of the years immediately

**Fisher effect**

A long run increase in the inflation rate will increase the nominal interest rate, so that the real interest rate will not change due to inflation.

www.bankofcanada.ca/en/res/r963a-ea.htm

---

**FIGURE 3-13**

The nominal interest rate is the long-term government bond rate. Inflation is measured as the rate of change in the Consumer Price Index. Each series is measured as a 10-year average. Notice that when inflation is high, as in the 1970s and 1980s, the nominal interest rate tends to be high also.

**THE NOMINAL INTEREST RATE AND THE INFLATION RATE, 1945–2002 (10-YEAR AVERAGES)**

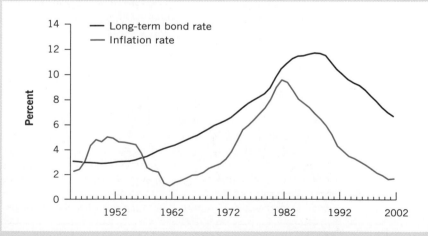

SOURCE: Long-term government bond rate: CANSIM II V122487; Consumer Price Index: V735319.

following World War II, the long run real interest rate has been positive. Figure 3-13 shows that over the long run, there is a tendency for the nominal interest rate and the inflation rate to move together.

## POLICY IN *ACTION*

### The Canadian Monetarists Experiment

By the early 1970s, Canada (and many other countries) found that the inflation rate was getting higher and showing signs of increasing further. In response to this, the Bank of Canada announced in 1975 that it would begin running monetary policy by announcing annual target rates for the rate of growth of the money supply. It would also annually lower these targets, in order to bring down the long run rate of inflation. This policy was termed *monetary gradualism* (or *monetarist*), and it was based on a belief that, in the long run, the rate of growth of money is a primary determinant of the inflation rate. In the words of the governor of the Bank of Canada:

*There is one proposition that must never be forgotten, and that is that in a free market society no strategy for dealing with inflation will succeed unless it is well supported by firm and continuing control of the rate of monetary expansion in the society. That proposition is, I assure you, as reliable as any general proposition in the whole field of economics. Every central banker in the world knows it to be true, and I doubt that any serious experienced student of financial affairs would question it. It is a very firm proposition indeed, and anyone who wants to participate responsibly in the debate on how to deal with inflation would be well advised to keep it uppermost in his mind.\**

The governor also recognized the role of the Fisher effect in the Canadian economy:

*The basic reason why interest rates are so high is because current and expected rate of inflation are so high. If you make allowance for the current rate of inflation, interest rates are not in fact unusually high.\**

You can see from Figure 3-13 that the inflation rate eventually decreased, bringing the nominal interest rate with it.

---

\*From a statement by the governor of the Bank of Canada before the House of Commons Standing Committee on Finance, Trade and Economic Affairs, reprinted in the *Bank of Canada Review*, November 1980. The earliest statement of these principles was given in an address by the governor to the Chamber of Commerce in Saskatoon in September 1975. This speech has been dubbed the "Saskatoon monetary manifesto" by Thomas Courchene. See Thomas J. Courchene, *Monetarism and Controls: The Inflation Fighters* (Toronto: C.D. Howe Research Institute, 1976).

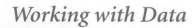

## Working with Data

In this chapter, we have used a Cobb-Douglas production function in the following form

$$Y = AK^{0.3} N^{0.7} \qquad (3)$$

Remember that in CANSIM, we can retrieve data on output ($Y$), capital ($K$), and labour ($N$), but no data are available on factor productivity ($A$). In order to calculate factor productivity, we used the formula

$$A = \frac{Y}{K^{0.3} N^{0.7}} \qquad (4)$$

Go to CANSIM II and retrieve the data that are referenced in the source for Table 3-1. You will find that the GDP data are quarterly and the labour force data are monthly. You should convert each of these to annual data using the average value. The unemployment data are available only from 1976 onward. The historical data was gathered from www.statcan.ca/english/freepub/11-516-XIE/free.htm. Here are the historical data you need.

| | |
|---|---|
| 1961 | 6521 |
| 1962 | 6615 |
| 1963 | 6748 |
| 1964 | 6933 |
| 1965 | 7141 |
| 1966 | 7420 |
| 1967 | 7694 |
| 1968 | 7919 |
| 1969 | 8162 |
| 1970 | 8374 |
| 1971 | 8631 |
| 1972 | 8891 |
| 1973 | 9279 |
| 1974 | 9662 |
| 1975 | 10015 |

You should now be able to reproduce Table 3-1.

## C H A P T E R   S U M M A R Y

▶  In this chapter, we have studied a long run Classical model of the economy. In the long run, we assume that all factors of production are fully employed and all prices are flexible in all markets.

▶ This model has three key ingredients: the supply of goods and services, the demand for goods and services, and the quantity theory of money.

▶ Aggregate supply is determined by the production function, which relates factors of production, capital, labour, and technology to output. We assume that capital is fixed at its full employment level and is not growing, and that there is no technological change. Therefore, aggregate supply depends on the labour market.

▶ Labour demand depends on the marginal product of labour, and supply depends on workers choosing between work and leisure.

▶ Aggregate demand determines the allocation of income among consumption, investment, government spending, and net export spending.

▶ Consumers choose between current consumption and savings.

▶ Government savings is measured by the budgetary deficit (negative savings) or budgetary surplus (positive savings).

▶ In equilibrium, total savings (private plus government) equals investment.

▶ In the long run, the quantity theory of money predicts that the price level is determined by the level of the money stock, and the inflation rate is determined by the rate of growth of money.

▶ In the long run, changes in the nominal money stock have no real effect on variables.

▶ The Fisher effect states that a change in the inflation rate will bring about a change in the nominal interest rate in the long run.

## K E Y   T E R M S

production function, *49*
Cobb-Douglas production
   function, *49*
marginal product of labour
   (*MPN*), *53*
diminishing marginal product of
   labour, *53*

real wage, *54*
leisure, *55*
full employment, *55*
rate of time preference, *58*
real rate of interest, *58*
private savings, *58*
government savings, *60*

quantity equation, *62*
money stock (or money
   supply), *63*
velocity of money, *63*
quantity theory of money, *64*
Fisher effect, *66*

## D I S C U S S I O N   Q U E S T I O N S

1. Discuss why the labour market model developed in this chapter could not be used to analyze unemployment.

2. Figure 3-1 exhibits the diminishing marginal product of labour. Discuss why the production function that was used to generate Figure 3-1 may have this property.

3. In deriving Figure 3-7, we assumed that savings was positively related to the real rate of interest. Can you think of reasons why this may be a good assumption or, alternatively, why this may be a bad assumption?

www.mcgrawhill.ca/college/dornbusch

4.  In Figure 3-10, we illustrated that a government budget deficit will lead to a higher real interest rate and reduced total savings. Discuss how this result could be altered if private savings reacted to the change in public savings.

5.  We used equation (22) to illustrate that the long run rate of inflation is caused by the rate of money growth. However, we know that if real income is increasing, then real money demand is also increasing. How would you alter equation (22) to allow for real income increases, and how would this change your view of the relationship between money growth and inflation in the long run?

6.  In Figure 3-13, we plotted the annual inflation rate and the annual nominal interest rate. These variables appear to be related in terms of trend, but there are periods when there is a large divergence in their movement. Discuss reasons why the Fisher effect may not hold in the short run.

## A P P L I C A T I O N     Q U E S T I O N S

1.  In constructing Figure 3-12, we used decade averages of the inflation rate and the rate of growth of money. Go to CANSIM and retrieve monthly data on these same two variables. Plot the rate of growth of money and the inflation rate over the period January 1965 to December 1970. Do you think that these data are consistent with the quantity theory of money?

2.  In Table 3-1, we assumed that capital's share of output was 0.3 and labour's share was 0.7. Recalculate total factor productivity and its percentage change under the assumption that capital's share is 0.25 and labour's share is 0.75. Do you think that this makes a big difference to Table 3-1?

3.  Use the new Table 3-1 from question 2 above to derive a new Figure 3-1.

4.  Suppose that Knarf's Pub has the following production function:

| $N$ | $K$ | $Y$ |
|-----|-----|-----|
| Servers | Taps | Glasses Served |
| 0 | 2 | 0 |
| 1 | 2 | 10 |
| 2 | 2 | 19 |
| 3 | 2 | 26 |
| 4 | 2 | 30 |

a.  Calculate $MPN$ for each level of employment.

b.  Suppose that beer costs $2.00. If the nominal wage is $18.00, how many workers will Knarf hire? If the nominal wage drops to $8.00, how many workers will be hired?

c.  Graph Knarf's demand for labour curve.

# CHAPTER 4

# THE ECONOMY IN THE VERY LONG RUN:

## The Economics of Growth

### *LEARNING OBJECTIVES*

After reading and studying this chapter, you should be able to:

▶ *Understand that economic growth is due to growth in inputs, such as capital and labour, and to improvements in technology.*

▶ *Understand that capital accumulates through savings and investment.*

▶ *Understand that the long run level of output per person depends positively on the savings rate and negatively on the rate of population growth.*

▶ *Understand that the basic economic growth model predicts that standards of living in different countries will eventually converge.*

I f you look back at Figure 1-5 in Chapter 1, you can see a very important fact: Prior to World War II, real GDP per capita (measured in 1997 dollars) was less than $10,000 in Canada. In 2002, this same real GDP per capita is more than $33,000. Clearly, we have enormously higher incomes than did our great-grandparents several generations back. In this chapter, we are going to look at this very long run span of income growth and try to explain it using growth accounting and growth theory. Growth accounting attempts to determine what portion of total growth in output is due to growth in different factors of production, such as capital and labour. Growth theory helps us to understand how economic decisions control the accumulation of factors of production, or how savings today affects the capital stock in the future.

Figure 4-1 shows GDP for four countries over more than 180 years. The graph has three striking characteristics. First, the long-term growth record of Canada is remarkable, with average income increasing more than twentyfold over the nineteenth and twentieth centuries. Second, Japan has gone from being a moderately poor country before World War II to being a wealthy country with a standard of living slightly higher than that of Canada. Third, Bangladesh was miserably poor 180 years ago and—growthless—remains that way today.

Our goal in this chapter is to explain Figure 4-1. Why is income in Canada so much higher today than it was a century ago? Why has Japan surpassed Canada, and why has Bangladesh not? We will learn that economic growth results from the accumulation of factors of production, particularly capital, and from increased productivity.

## 4-1 | GROWTH ACCOUNTING

In Chapters 2 and 3, we used a general production function that had the following form.

$$Y = AF(K, N) \tag{1}$$

---

**FIGURE 4-1**

Canada, the United States, and Japan have all experienced strong growth in GDP per capita, while Bangladesh has experienced virtually no growth.

www.imf.org/external/pubs/ ft/weo/2003/01/data/ index.htm

**GDP PER CAPITA FOR FOUR COUNTRIES, 1820–2002**

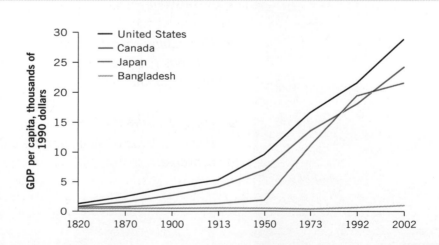

SOURCE: Angus Madison, *Monitoring the World Economy* 1820–1992 (Paris: Organisation for Economic Co-operation and Development, 1995), Table 1-3. Updated to 2002 using International Monetary Fund, World Economic Outlook Database, available online at www.imf.org/external/pubs/ft/weo/2003/01/data/index.htm.

**growth accounting
equation**
A summary of the
contributions of input
growth and changes in
productivity to the growth
of output.

In this chapter, we relax the assumption that capital ($K$) and productivity ($A$) are constant, and use the production function to study sources of growth over the very long run. This is summarized by the **growth accounting equation** (derived in the appendix to this chapter).

$$\Delta Y/Y = [(1 - \theta)(\Delta N/N)] + [\theta(\Delta K/K)] + \Delta A/A \qquad (2)$$

Equation (2) summarizes the contributions of input growth and changes in productivity to the growth of output. Recall from Chapter 3 that $\theta$ and $(1 - \theta)$ are the share of income attributable to capital and labour, respectively. Notice that labour and capital each contributes an amount equal to its individual growth rate multiplied by the share of that input in income. The last term, the growth rate of **total factor productivity**, is the amount by which output would increase as a result of improvements in methods of production, with all inputs unchanged. In other words, there is a growth in total factor productivity when we get more output from the same factors of production.[1]

**total factor productivity**
Rate at which productivity
of inputs increases;
measure of technological
progress.

## BOX 4-1   Human Capital

In industrialized countries, raw labour is less important than the skills and talents of workers. Society's stock of such skills is increased by investment in *human capital* through schooling, on-the-job training, and other means in the same way that physical investment leads to increased physical capital. (In poor countries, investments in health are a major contributor to human capital. In times of extreme poverty, the critical investment can be providing workers with enough calories to enable them to bring in the harvest.) Adding human capital, $H$, we can write the production function as

$$Y = AF(K, H, N)$$

The factor share of human capital is large in industrialized countries. An influential article by Mankiw, Romer, and Weil suggests that the production function is consistent with factor shares of one-third each for physical capital, raw labour, and human capital. Differential growth in these three factors can explain about 80 percent of the variation in GDP per capita across a wide sample of countries, emphasizing the critical role of factor accumulation in the growth process.

A large physical capital stock, the result of a high investment ratio, should lead to high GDP. Panel (a) of the figure on the next page plots (the logarithm of) per capita GDP against investment (as a fraction of GDP) for a cross-section of countries. It's apparent that high investment does lead to high income. But is there a similar relationship between human capital and output? Human capital is difficult to measure precisely, but average years of schooling can serve as a proxy for human capital. In panel (b), we see that the evidence strongly supports the positive relationship between human capital and output. In the next chapter, we will see that human capital, like physical capital, can continue to accumulate and therefore can be a contributor to permanent growth.

*cont'd...*

---

[1] There is a distinction between total factor productivity and labour productivity. Labour productivity is simply the ratio of labour input to total output, $Y/N$. Labour productivity certainly grows as a result of technical progress, but it also grows because of accumulation of capital per worker.

## Human Capital cont'd

*Relationship of (a) Investment Ratio and (b) Average Years of Schooling to GDP*

The higher the rate of investment—in capital or human capital—the higher the GDP.

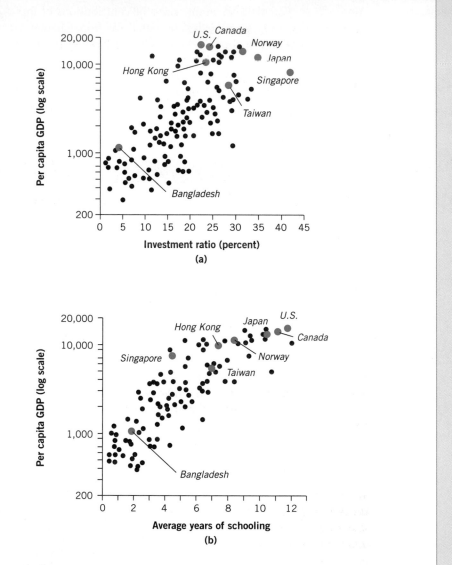

SOURCE: Data taken from R. Barro and J. Lee, "International Comparisons of Educational Attainment," National Bureau of Economic Research working paper, 1993.

As an example of one way to use equation (2), suppose that capital was growing at 3.3 percent, the labour force was growing at 2.0 percent, and total factor productivity grew at 0.3 percent. Substituting into equation (2)

$$2.7 = (0.7 \times 2.0) + (3.3 \times 0.3) + 0.3 \qquad (3)$$

In this situation, output would be growing at 2.7 percent. If we did the same calculation, but assumed that capital was growing at 6.6 percent, double its previous growth rate, then the growth in output would be 3.7 percent, rising by just over one percentage point, even though the growth rate of capital doubled.

In order to get an idea of the contributions of the factors of production to Canadian growth, Table 4-1 uses data from the Canadian economy to estimate the growth accounting equation for Canada over the period 1962 to 2002.

---

**TABLE 4-1**

### ACCOUNTING FOR GROWTH IN CANADA, 1962–2002 (AVERAGES)

| Year | $(1 - \theta)(\Delta N/N)$ | $\theta(\Delta K/K)$ | $\Delta A/A$ | $\Delta Y/Y$ |
|------|------|------|------|------|
| 1962–1973 | 2.1 | 1.4 | 1.9 | 5.4 |
| 1974–1992 | 1.6 | 1.1 | 0.0 | 2.8 |
| 1993–2002 | 0.9 | 1.0 | 1.5 | 3.4 |

SOURCE: GDP: CANSIM II V1992259; capital stock: CANSIM II V1078499 and V1078501; labour force: CANSIM II V2091051, adapted from equation (2).

---

www.oecd.org/home

There are two important points to notice about the data in Table 4-1. First, the annual growth rates of GDP in the period 1974–1992 are much smaller than those in the earlier period. This dramatic slowdown in GDP growth was accompanied by an equally dramatic slowdown in productivity growth over the same period. Annual productivity growth over 1962–1973 averaged just under 2 percent per year, while over the period 1974–1992, it averaged 0 percent per year. This productivity slowdown over the period between 1973 and the early 1990s was not confined to Canada, as most countries in the Organisation for Economic Co-operation and Development also experienced slower productivity growth over this same period. This productivity slowdown is discussed in Box 4-2.

The second interesting feature of the data in Table 4-1 is that there may be evidence that this productivity slowdown has reversed. Average factor productivity growth was 1.5 percent per year over 1993–2002, and average GDP growth was 3.4 percent per year over the same period. Many analysts believe that this recovery is due to the boom in computers and related equipment.

BOX

4-2

## The Post-1973 Productivity Slowdown

One of the most interesting and largely unsolved developments in recent economic history is the worldwide slowdown in productivity and economic growth after 1973. The following table gives an example of this from four countries.

|  | Average Annual Growth in Total Factor Productivity | |
| Country | 1959–1973* | 1973–1992 |
| --- | --- | --- |
| Canada | 1.99 | 0.45 |
| Japan | 5.08 | 1.04 |
| United Kingdom | 1.48 | 0.69 |
| United States | 1.72 | 0.18 |

* Canadian\ calculations start in 1962.

SOURCE: Angus Maddison, *Monitoring the World Economy 1820–1992*  (Paris: Organisation for Economic Co-operation and Development, 1995), Table K-2. Canada was calculated by the authors based on Table 4-1.

Although there is no single accepted explanation for this phenomenon, several theories have been put forth. We will briefly discuss a few of these theories.

### THIS IS SIMPLY A MEASUREMENT PROBLEM

This explanation centres on our ability to measure quality changes. It is argued that there may be no actual slowdown in productivity because the production function measures only numbers and not quality. For instance, if we produced fewer computers, but they were all faster, the production function would not measure this increased productivity.

### THE SLOWDOWN WAS A RESULT OF THE OIL PRICE SHOCKS

One important economic event of the 1970s was the series of oil price shocks that began with the Organization of the Petroleum Exporting Countries (OPEC) embargo in 1973. This explanation presumes that the productivity of some portion of the capital stock was dependent on cheap energy and could not easily be modified. Therefore, dramatically increased input prices in terms of oil may have rendered this portion of the capital stock obsolete.

### THE PACE OF INNOVATION SLOWED

This argument is really that the pace of innovation after World War II was abnormally high, because the war (and the depression before it) suppressed the ability to use innovation. Once the backlog of innovations was cleared, the economy reverted to a lower growth path.

There are other explanations for this slowdown, and this topic is still under active research.

## Growth Accounting and the Asian Tigers

Until the recent economic problems experienced in Southeast Asia, growth in Hong Kong, Singapore, South Korea, and Taiwan had been so remarkable that the four nations were sometimes called the "Asian Tigers." They had been held up to the rest of the world as examples of effective development. What can we learn by examining the experience of the Asian Tigers?

The table below is taken from a very careful study of East Asian growth by Alwyn Young. Between 1966 and 1990, all four countries had remarkable growth, but their growth was mostly explained by increased input, not by higher productivity. Growth in total factor productivity (TFP: a measure of output per unit of input) was high, but not remarkable, in Hong Kong, South Korea, and Taiwan. Singapore's TFP growth was notably small. All four countries had a drastic increase in the fraction of the population that works, largely due to increased labour force participation by women. Each country also greatly increased its human capital, moving educational attainment to levels close to those of the leading industrialized nations.

The Asian Tigers had several other characteristics in common. All four had relatively stable governments. The four shared an outward-looking economic policy, encouraging their industries to export, compete, and learn to survive in the world market.

The near-zero productivity growth in Singapore is nonetheless noteworthy. In an influential article comparing Singapore and Hong Kong, Alwyn Young draws attention to the fact that Hong Kong has had an essentially laissez-faire, free market government while Singapore's government maintains tight control over the economy, with most of the economy's investments being indirectly directed by the government. He argues that the government of Singapore has tried to force the pace of development, relying on foreign investment to bring in new technologies, but has moved on too rapidly to ever-more sophisticated goods before local entrepreneurs and workers have mastered the current technology.

### GROWTH IN THE ASIAN TIGERS (PERCENT)

| | Hong Kong (1966–91) | Singapore (1966–90) | South Korea (1966–90) | Taiwan (1966–90) |
|---|---|---|---|---|
| GDP per capita growth | 5.7 | 6.8 | 6.8 | 6.7 |
| TFP growth | 2.3 | 0.2 | 1.7 | 2.6 |
| Δ % labour force participation | 38 → 49 | 27 → 51 | 27 → 36 | 28 → 37 |
| Δ % secondary education or higher | 27.2 → 71.4 | 15.8 → 66.3 | 26.5 → 75.0 | 25.8 → 67.6 |

SOURCE: Alwyn Young, "The Tyranny of Numbers: Confronting the Statistical Realities of the East Asian Growth Experience," *Quarterly Journal of Economics*, August 1995.

## 4-2 | GROWTH THEORY: THE NEOCLASSICAL MODEL

**neoclassical growth theory**

Focuses on capital accumulation and its link to savings decisions and the like.

There have been two periods of intense work on growth theory, the first in the late 1950s and the 1960s and the second 30 years later, in the late 1980s and early 1990s. Research in the first period created **neoclassical growth theory**. Neoclassical growth theory focuses on capital accumulation and its link to savings decisions and the like. The best-known contributor is Robert Solow.[2]

We begin our study of the neoclassical growth model by making the simplifying assumption that there is no technological progress. We will relax this assumption once the model is developed more fully. In Section 4-1, when we discussed growth accounting based on equation (2), we were interested in the growth of total output in an economy. In growth theory, we are interested in the concept of per capita GDP. Therefore, we begin with the standard production function as given by equation (1), with two changes. First, as we are ignoring technological change, we drop the term $A$. Second, for certain types of functions (the Cobb-Douglas, for example), we can modify the expression into per capita form as follows.

$$\frac{Y}{N} = f\left(\frac{K}{N}, 1\right) \tag{4}$$

**capital-labour ratio**

The number of machines per worker.

Define $y = \frac{Y}{N}$ as per capita output and $k = \frac{K}{N}$ as the **capital-labour ratio**. Therefore, we can write the production function as

$$y = f(k) \tag{5}$$

This production function says that output per worker is a function of the capital-labour ratio. Equation (5) is graphed in Figure 4-2.

### FIGURE 4-2

The production function $y = f(k)$ is the relationship between per capita output and the capital-labour ratio.

**PER CAPITA PRODUCTION FUNCTION**

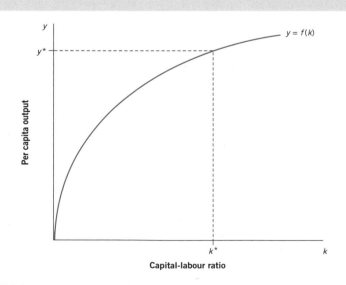

Capital-labour ratio

[2] R. Solow, "A Contribution to the Theory of Economic Growth," *Quarterly Journal of Economics*, February 1956. The collection of papers in Joseph Stiglitz and Hirofumi Uzawa (eds.), *Readings in the Theory of Economic Growth* (Cambridge, MA: MIT Press, 1969), contains many of the most important papers of that period.

The production function graphed in Figure 4-2 exhibits two important characteristics:

**marginal product of capital (MPK)**
Increment to output obtained by adding one unit of capital, with other factor inputs held constant.

1.  As $k$ increases, $y$ increases, so that the **marginal product of capital** is positive; that is, the production function has a positive slope.

2.  Output rises less at high levels of $k$ than at low levels. This is called the *diminishing marginal product of capital*. This is shown by the fact that the slope of the production function is continually decreasing. (These are the same properties possessed by the marginal product of labour discussed in Chapter 3.)

In order to keep the analysis as simple as possible, we assume a model with no government and no foreign trade. We now use the GDP identity from Chapters 2 and 3, written in per capita terms.

$$y = c + i \qquad (6)$$

where $c = C/N$ is per capita consumption and $i = I/N$ is per capita investment. We assume that per capita consumption is a function of income.

$$c = (1 - s)y \qquad (7)$$

Here, $s$ is the marginal propensity to save, so that $(1 - s)$ is the marginal propensity to consume.

Recall that in long run equilibrium, investment equals savings.[3] We can write this as

$$i = sy \qquad (8)$$

Recall that $y = f(k)$; therefore,

$$i = sf(k) \qquad (9)$$

Therefore, total output is divided between consumption and investment. This is shown in Figure 4-3.

## Steady-State Equilibrium

**steady-state equilibrium**
The combination of per capita GDP and the capital-labour ratio where the economy will remain at rest.

The **steady-state equilibrium** for the economy is the combination of per capita GDP and the capital-labour ratio where the economy will remain at rest; that is, where per capita economic variables are no longer changing: $\Delta y = 0$ and $\Delta k = 0$. In equilibrium, we define the steady-state values of output per capita and the capital-labour ratio as $y^*$ and $k^*$. This steady state will occur when the investment required to provide capital for new workers and to replace machinery that is worn out equals savings generated by the economy.

Assume that there is some exogenous rate of growth of population.

$$n = \frac{\Delta N}{N} \qquad (10)$$

---

[3] Recall that this happens because of the role of the real rate of interest. We assume that, in the background, the real rate of interest is doing its job to ensure that savings always equals investment, as discussed in Chapter 3.

FIGURE 4-3

**CONSUMPTION AND INVESTMENT IN THE NEOCLASSICAL GROWTH MODEL**

Savings is a constant proportion of income, given by $sf(k)$, where $s$ is the marginal propensity to save. In long run equilibrium, savings equals investment. The remainder of income is consumption, given that we assume no government or foreign trade.

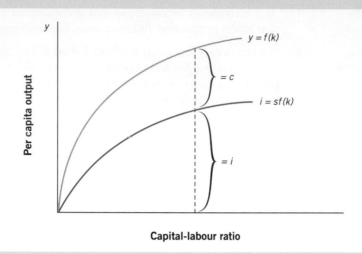

and that depreciation each year equals $d$. Therefore, in steady state,

$$i = (n + d)k \qquad (11)$$

This defines for us the amount of required investment in steady state. This must equal savings. Therefore, in the steady state

$$sy = (n + d)k \qquad (12)$$

Equilibrium is defined as a state where there is some $k^*$ and $y^*$, such that $\Delta k = 0$.

$$sf(k^*) = (n + d)k^* \qquad (13)$$

Figure 4-4 presents a graphical solution for the steady state. With individuals saving a constant fraction of their incomes, the curve $sy$, which is a constant proportion of output, shows the level of saving at each capital-labour ratio. The straight line $(n + d)k$ shows the amount of investment that is needed at each capital-labour ratio to keep the capital-labour ratio constant by supplying machines both as replacements for those that have worn out and as additions for workers newly entering the labour force. Where the two lines intersect at point C, saving and required investment balance with steady-state capital $k^*$. Steady-state income is read off the production function at point D.

## The Growth Process

In Figure 4-4, we study the adjustment process that leads the economy from some initial capital-labour ratio over time to the steady state. The critical element in this transition process is the rate of saving and investment compared with the rate of depreciation and population growth.

## FIGURE 4-4

### STEADY-STATE OUTPUT AND INVESTMENT

The economy reaches steady-state equilibrium at point C. At C, there is a matching between actual investment and required investment, so the capital-labour ratio and output per capita do not change.

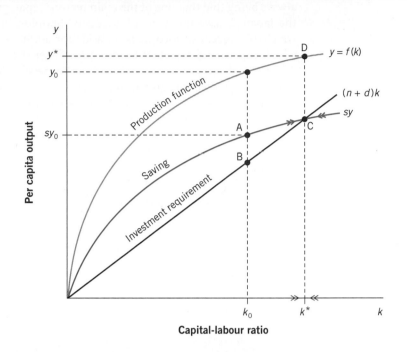

The key to understanding the neoclassical growth model is that when saving, $sy$, exceeds the investment requirement line, then $k$ is increasing, as specified by equation (12). Accordingly, when $sy$ exceeds $(n + d)k$, $k$ must be increasing, and over time the economy is moving to the right in Figure 4-4. For instance, if the economy starts at capital-output ratio $k_0$, then with saving at A exceeding the investment needed to hold $k$ constant at B, the horizontal arrow shows $k$ increasing.

The adjustment process comes to a halt at point C. Here we have reached a capital-labour ratio, $k^*$, for which saving and investment associated with that capital-labour ratio exactly match the investment requirement. Given the exact matching of actual and required investment, the capital-labour ratio neither rises nor falls. We have reached the steady state.

Note that this adjustment process leads to point C from any initial level of income. An important implication of neoclassical growth theory is that countries with equal savings rates, rates of population growth, and technology (that is, the same production function) should eventually converge to equal incomes, although the convergence process may be quite slow.

At that steady state, both $k$ and $y$ are constant. With per capita income constant, aggregate income is growing at the same rate as population, that is, at rate $n$. *It follows that the steady-state growth rate is not affected by the savings rate.* This is one of the key results of neoclassical growth theory.

## An Increase in the Savings Rate

Why should the long run growth rate be independent of the savings rate? Aren't we always being told that one of the main reasons Japan grows faster than Canada is that the Japanese save more than Canadians? Shouldn't it be true that an economy in which 10 percent of income is set aside for additions to the capital stock is one in which capital and therefore output grow faster than in an economy in which only 5 percent of income is saved? According to neoclassical growth theory, the savings rate does not affect the growth rate *in the very long run*.

In Figure 4-5, we show how an increase in the savings rate affects growth. In the short run, an increase in the savings rate raises the growth rate of output. It does not affect the *long run growth rate* of output, but *it raises the long run level of capital and output per head*.

In Figure 4-5, the economy is initially in steady-state equilibrium at point C, at which saving precisely matches the investment requirement. Now people want to save a larger fraction of income. This causes an upward shift of the savings schedule, to the dashed schedule.

At point C, at which we initially had a steady-state equilibrium, saving has now risen relative to the investment requirement; as a consequence, more is saved than is required to maintain capital per head constant. Enough is saved to allow the capital stock per head to increase. The capital stock per head, $k$, will keep rising until it reaches point C'. At C', the higher amount of saving is just enough to maintain the higher stock of capital. At point C', both capital per head and output per head have risen.

---

### FIGURE 4-5

If the savings rate increases from $s$ to $s'$, the steady-state capital-labour ratio increases from $k^*$ to $k^{**}$.

**INCREASE IN SAVINGS RATE MOVES THE STEADY STATE**

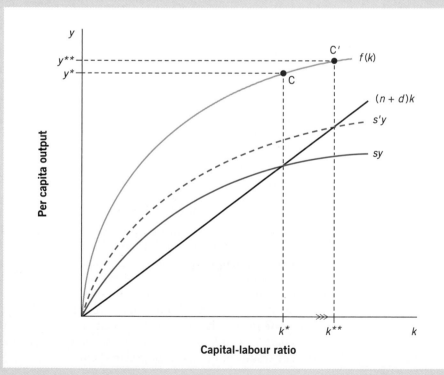

However, at point C′, the economy has returned to its steady-state growth rate of $n$. Thus, with this constant-returns-to-scale production function, an increase in the savings rate will in the long run raise only the level of output and capital per head, and not the growth rate of output per head.

In the transition process, however, the higher savings rate increases the growth rate of output and the growth rate of output per head. This follows simply from the fact that the capital-labour ratio rises from $k^*$ at the initial steady state to $k^{**}$ in the new steady state. The only way to achieve an increase in the capital-labour ratio is for the capital stock to grow faster than the labour force (and depreciation).

Figure 4-6 summarizes the effects of an increase in the savings rate, paralleling the shift shown in Figure 4-5. Figure 4-6(a) shows the level of per capita output. Starting from an initial long run equilibrium at time $t_0$, the increase in the savings rate causes saving and investment to increase, the stock of capital per head grows, and so does output per head. The process will continue at a diminishing rate. Figure 4-6(b) shows the growth rate of output, plotting the rate of change of the level of output in panel (a). The increase in the savings rate immediately raises the growth rate of output because it implies faster growth in capital and therefore in output. As capital accumulates, the growth rate decreases, falling back toward the level of population growth.

**FIGURE 4-6**

**ADJUSTMENT TO NEW STEADY STATE**

Panels (a) and (b) show the adjustment of output and of the output growth rate following the increase in the savings rate depicted in Figure 4-5.

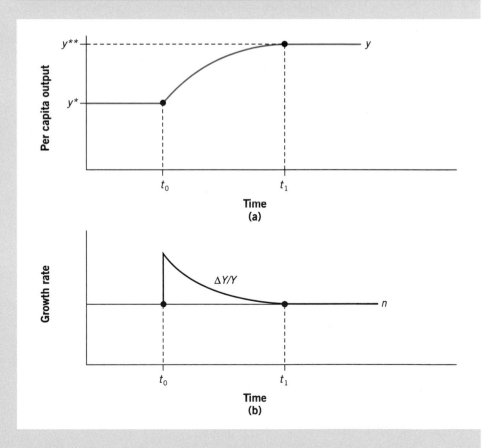

## Population Growth

The preceding discussion of saving and the influence of the savings rate on steady-state capital and output makes it easy to discuss the effects of increased population growth. An increase in the population growth rate affects the $(n + d)k$ line in the diagram, rotating it up and to the left. In the end-of-chapter Application Questions, we ask you to show the following results:

▶  An increase in the rate of population growth *reduces* the steady-state *level* of capital per head, $k$, and output per head, $y$.

▶  An increase in the rate of population growth *increases* the steady-state rate of growth of *aggregate* output.

## The Golden Rule Steady State

Is higher income always better? Not necessarily. There is a trade-off inherent in the neoclassical growth model. We know that the higher the savings rate chosen by a society, the higher will be the steady-state capital and income. However, the higher that $k$ is, the greater the investment required just to maintain the capital-labour ratio, as opposed to being used for current consumption.

We want to answer the question: Is there a steady state that is, somehow, optimal? One way to view this is that, since individuals get utility out of consumption and we want to maximize utility, we assume that the optimal steady state is one that maximizes steady-state consumption per capita. Notice that steady-state consumption per capita is the vertical distance between the $y = f(k)$ line and the $i = (n + \delta)k$ line. Consumption per capita is maximized at the value of $k$ where the slopes of these two lines are equal. This is illustrated in Figure 4-7.

---

### FIGURE 4-7

**THE GOLDEN RULE MAY NOT BE THE STEADY STATE**

The Golden Rule level of the capital stock is $k^{**}$. If the steady-state capital stock is at $k^*$, as in this figure, then the savings rate is too high and consumption per capita is not maximized. The Golden Rule may not be the steady state.

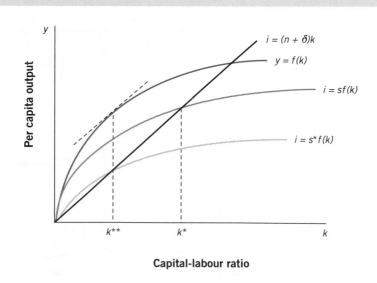

In Figure 4-7, the steady-state equilibrium is at a capital stock of $k^*$. However, the level of capital that maximizes consumption per capita is $k^{**}$. This is the Golden Rule level of the capital stock. In order to attain the Golden Rule level of the capital stock, the savings rate would have to change from $s$ to $s^*$. Notice, however, that there is nothing inherent in the economy to guarantee that the economy will ever reach this Golden Rule steady state.

## Growth with Exogenous Technological Change

Figure 4-2 and the analysis that followed set $\Delta A/A = 0$ as a simplification. This simplification helped us understand steady-state behaviour, but it eliminated the long-term-growth part of growth theory. We reinstate growth in GDP per capita by allowing technology to improve over time, that is, $\Delta A/A > 0$.

The production function in Figure 4-2 can be thought of as a snapshot of $y = Af(k)$ taken in a year in which $A$ is normalized to 1. If technology improves at 1 percent per year, then a snapshot taken a year later will be $y = 1.01 f(k)$; two years later, $y = (1.01)^2 f(k)$; and so forth. In general, if the rate of growth is defined as $g = \Delta A/A$, then the production function rises at $g$ percent per year, as shown in Figure 4-8. The savings function grows in a parallel fashion. As a result, in growth equilibrium, $y$ and $k$ both grow over time.

**FIGURE 4-8**

An exogenous increase in technology causes the production function and savings curve to rise. The result is a new steady-state point at a higher per capita output and higher capital-labour ratio. Thus, increases in technology over time result in growth of output over time.

**EXOGENOUS TECHNOLOGICAL CHANGE**

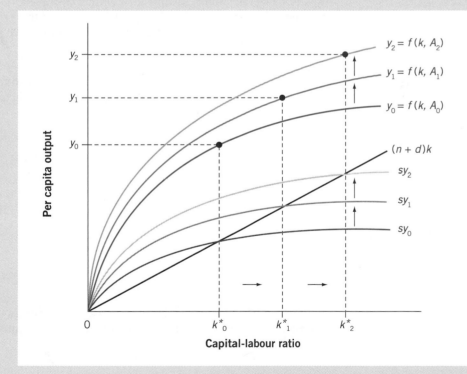

## Endogenous Growth

The neoclassical growth theory model that we developed above attributes long run growth to technological progress but leaves unexplained the economic determinants of that technological progress. In addition to this, an empirical prediction of the model is that economic growth and savings rates should be uncorrelated in a steady state. The data appear to contradict this prediction.

The solution to both the theoretical and empirical problems with the neoclassical model lies in modifying the assumed shape of the production function in a way that allows for self-sustaining growth, that is, **endogenous growth**. We can illustrate the essence of endogenous growth through Figure 4-9.

Figure 4-9(a) reproduces the basic neoclassical model diagram from Figure 4-4. Recall that the steady state occurs at point C, where the savings and investment requirement lines cross. Anywhere the savings line is above the investment requirement line, the economy is growing because capital is being added. Starting at point A, for example, the economy moves, over time, to the right. How do we know that this process eventually comes to a halt (i.e., reaches a steady state)? Because of the *diminishing marginal product of capital,* the production function and parallel savings curve eventually flatten out. Since the investment requirement line has a constant positive slope, the investment requirement line and savings curve are guaranteed to cross.

Contrast Figure 4-9(b), where we have changed the assumed shape of the production function to show a *constant marginal product of capital.* The production function, like the parallel savings curve, is now a *straight line.* Since the savings curve no longer flattens out, saving is everywhere greater than required investment. The higher the savings rate, the bigger the gap of saving above required investment and the faster the growth.

The economy described in Figure 4-9(b) can be illustrated with a simple algebraic model leading to endogenous growth. Assume a production function with a constant marginal product of capital and with capital as the only factor. Specifically, let

$$Y = aK \tag{14}$$

That is, output is proportional to the capital stock. The marginal product of capital is simply the constant $a$.

Assume that the savings rate is constant at $s$ and that there is neither population growth nor depreciation of capital. Then all saving goes to increase the capital stock. Accordingly,

$$\Delta K = sY = saK \tag{15}$$

or

$$\Delta K/K = sa$$

The growth rate of capital is proportional to the savings rate. Further, since output is proportional to capital, the growth rate of output is

$$\Delta Y/Y = sa \tag{16}$$

In this example, the higher the savings rate, the higher the growth rate of output.

You can see from the above that endogenous growth relies on constant returns to scale to generate ongoing growth. Current empirical evidence suggests that endogenous growth theory is not very important for explaining international differences in growth rates.

**endogenous growth**
Self-sustaining growth.

## FIGURE 4-9

The neoclassical growth model [panel (a)] assumes diminishing marginal product of capital, so the production function and the savings curve become flatter as *k* increases. For the endogenous growth model [panel (b)], we assume constant marginal product of capital, so the production function and the savings curve are now straight lines. Therefore, the higher the savings rate, the greater is the gap between savings and required investment, and the faster the growth.

### (a) SOLOW GROWTH MODEL VS. (b) ENDOGENOUS GROWTH

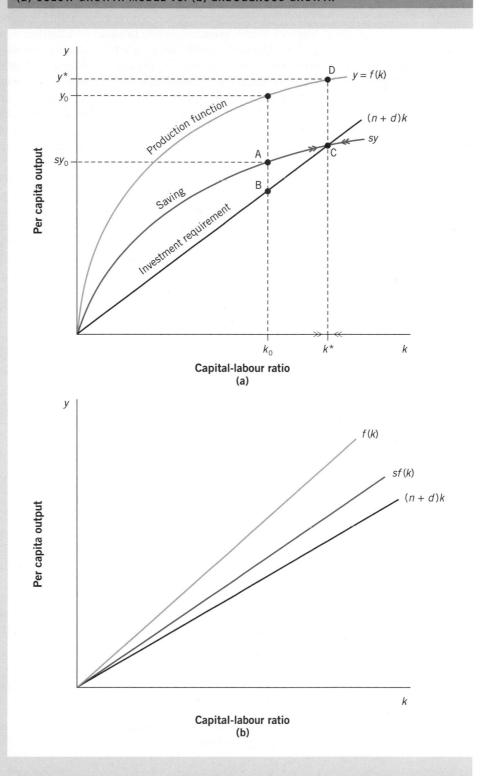

## Convergence

The question of *convergence* centres on whether economies with different initial levels of output eventually grow to equal standards of living.

Neoclassical growth theory predicts **absolute convergence** for economies with equal rates of savings and population growth and with access to the same technology. In other words, they should all reach the same steady-state income. (If Figure 4-9(a) is the same for two economies, they eventually reach the same steady state even if one economy begins farther to the left.) **Conditional convergence** is predicted for economies with different rates of savings or population growth; that is, steady-state incomes will differ as predicted by the Solow growth diagram, but *growth rates* will eventually equalize.

Contrast conditional convergence with the prediction of endogenous growth theory that a high savings rate leads to a high growth rate. In a series of papers, Robert Barro has shown that while countries that invest more tend to grow faster, the impact of higher investment on growth seems to be transitory:[4] Countries with higher investment will end in a steady state with higher per capita income but not with a higher growth rate. This suggests that countries do converge *conditionally,* and thus endogenous growth theory is not very important for explaining international differences in growth rates, although it may be quite important for explaining growth in countries on the leading edge of technology.

Barro's evidence suggests that conditional convergence is taking place at a rate of 2 percent per year. For instance, if India's income level is now 5 percent of that of the United States, in 35 years it would be approximately 10 percent of the U.S. level[5]— provided that the other variables that affect the level of income, such as the savings rate, are the same between the two countries. This convergence is very slow; it means that people in India today cannot look forward to catching up any time soon with the United States merely by relying on the "natural" neoclassical force of convergence.

## Reform and Growth in Eastern Europe

In the 1990s, the formerly communist countries of Eastern Europe and of the former Soviet Union faced an economic growth and reform challenge of unprecedented nature and scale. Each of these economies had been run through a highly centralized planning system. In most of them, nearly all property and all industry were owned by the state, and unemployment was virtually unknown. Several of them, including the former Soviet Union and Poland, ended the communist period with massive budget deficits and large external debts.

As the countries themselves, agencies such as the International Monetary Fund and the World Bank, and academic economic advisers to the new governments wrestled with the question of how to reform, a basic reform strategy was developed:[6]

---

**absolute convergence**
Tendency of both the levels and growth rates of output in different countries to approach each other over time, and for their steady-state values to be the same.

**conditional convergence**
Tendency of growth rates of output in different countries to approach each other over time, and for their steady-state values to be the same.

www.worldbank.org

---

[4] See, for example, Robert Barro's "Economic Growth in a Cross Section of Countries," *Quarterly Journal of Economics*, May 1991, and his *Determinants of Economic Growth: A Cross-Country Empirical Study* (Cambridge, MA: MIT Press, 1997).

[5] It takes 35 years for an economy growing at 2 percent to double its size. In this case, the doubling is relative to another economy.

[6] See "Symposium on Economic Transition in the Soviet Union and Eastern Europe," *Journal of Economic Perspectives*, Fall 1991.

**BOX**

**4-4**

## A Nobel Laureate's Words

*I do not see how one can look at figures like these without seeing them as possibilities. Is there some action a government of India could take that would lead the Indian economy to grow like Indonesia's or Egypt's? If so, what, exactly? If not, what is it about the "nature of India" that makes it so? The consequences for human welfare involved in questions like these are simply staggering: Once one starts to think about them, it is hard to think about anything else.\**

### GDP PER CAPITA (ANNUAL PERCENT)

| | 1990 DOLLARS\* | | |
|---|---|---|---|
| | 1950 | 1992 | Cumulative growth, % |
| United States | 9,573 | 21,558 | 125.20 |
| Bangladesh | 551 | 720 | 30.67 |
| China | 614 | 3,098 | 404.56 |
| Egypt | 517 | 1,927 | 272.73 |
| India | 597 | 1,348 | 125.80 |
| Indonesia | 874 | 2,749 | 214.53 |
| Mexico | 2,085 | 5,112 | 145.18 |
| South Korea | 876 | 10,010 | 1,042.69 |
| Taiwan | 922 | 11,590 | 1,157.05 |
| Tanzania | 427 | 604 | 41.45 |
| Thailand | 848 | 4,694 | 453.54 |
| U.S.S.R. | 2,834 | 4,671 | 64.82 |
| Zaire | 636 | 407 | −36.01 |

\*Including errors and ommissions.

SOURCE: Angus Maddison, *Monitoring the World Economy 1820–1992* (Paris: Organisation for Economic Co-operation and Development, 1995).

\*Robert E. Lucas, Jr., "On the Mechanics of Economic Development," *Journal of Monetary Economics,* July 1988.

1. Restore macroeconomic stability by bringing the budget close to balance and pursuing tight monetary and credit policies.

2. Liberalize prices by removing price controls and allowing markets to begin operating.

3. Privatize government-owned firms by selling them, or even by giving them away to the citizens.

4. Liberalize foreign trade, allowing domestic firms and consumers to have access to world markets.

5. Establish a social safety network so that people who become unemployed do not become destitute.

6.  Develop, as rapidly as possible, the legal framework that a market economy needs in order to operate (e.g., contract and bankruptcy laws).

This agenda is overwhelming; accomplishing its directives will take decades. It includes such things as the necessity to develop banks and train business managers and accountants. Since the changes are interdependent, ideally they should all take place at once. However, no government can operate that quickly—least of all a new government made up of people who have spent their working lives in a very different type of economy. That is why the reform process is bound to look chaotic at the outset and will take time.

The initial stages of reform are very difficult. Table 4-2 shows estimates of the decline in output during the period 1989–1994. These data are rough, but they show a massive decline in each country. For comparison, note that real output in Canada declined by 30 percent in the Great Depression, between 1929 and early 1933. The drop in per capita GDP in the former U.S.S.R. pushed living standards to the levels of 1960. In some parts of what had been the Soviet Union, the economy essentially stopped working.

East Germany is a special case. Since its unification with West Germany, it has been receiving massive subsidies from the western part of the country. The unification made the adjustment more difficult in some respects, for wages in the east have risen very quickly and eastern Germans are therefore less employable than they otherwise would be. The German government is spending massively on retraining, on subsidizing investment in the eastern part of Germany, and on making welfare payments to eastern Germans. The estimate is that half of the income of eastern Germans comes from the German government. Still, there is no doubt that the living standards of eastern Germans have risen and will continue to rise far more rapidly than the standards of citizens of other countries that had been behind the Iron Curtain.

| TABLE 4-2 | GDP DECLINES IN FORMERLY SOCIALIST ECONOMIES, 1989–1994 | | |
|---|---|---|---|
| | Country | Year of Lowest Output | Decline, % |
| | Albania | 1992 | 39.9 |
| | Bulgaria | 1993 | 27.4 |
| | Czech Republic | 1993 | 21.4 |
| | Poland | 1991 | 17.8 |
| | Russia | 1994 | 48.3 |

SOURCE: S. Fischer, R. Sahay, and C. Végh, "Stabilization and Growth in Transition Economics," *Journal of Economic Perspectives*, Spring 1996.

## The Truly Poor Countries

The growth line for Bangladesh (see Figure 4-1) and the nation's GDP data (see the table in Box 4-4) illustrate a striking problem: Compared to the rest of the world, Bangladesh hasn't had any economic growth! (Bangladesh is used as an example. The same holds true for a number of other countries.) Income is so low that much of the population lives at the borderline of subsistence.

Have we explained Bangladesh? In part, yes. Saving in Bangladesh is very low. Barro and Sala-i-Martin report that between 1960 and 1985, investment in Bangladesh averaged 4.6 percent of GDP, as compared to 36.6 percent and 24 percent in Japan and the United States, respectively.[7] Population growth in Bangladesh and in other extremely poor countries, was also much higher than in Japan or the United States. So the effect of both saving and population growth is as theory would predict. The poorest countries are hard-pressed to invest in human capital. Many of the poorest countries also have hostile climates for foreign investment, either because of deliberate policies that attempt to encourage domestic production instead or simply because the economic and legal environment is uncertain and the nations are unwilling or unable to guarantee investors the ability to repatriate profits.

## Natural Resources: Limits to Growth?

Production uses up natural resources, in particular, energy. Is it true, as is sometimes alleged, that exponential growth in the economy will eventually use up the fixed stock of resources? Well, yes, it is true in the limited sense that current theories suggest the universe will one day run down. However, this seems more of a concern for a course in astrophysics, or perhaps theology, than for a course in economics. Over any interesting horizon, the economy is protected from resource-depletion disasters by two factors. First, technical progress permits us to produce more using fewer resources. For example, the energy efficiency of room lighting has increased by a factor of 4500 since Neolithic times.[8] Second, as specific resources come into short supply, their prices rise, leading producers to shift toward substitutes.

Environmental protection is important, however. Even here, technology can be directed to assist us. For example, the conversion of urban transportation systems from horses to internal combustion engines has eliminated most of the pollution associated with transportation. As incomes rise and populations move away from the edge of survival, people and governments choose to spend more on protecting the environment. Unlike other consumption choices, environmental protection is often "bought" through political choices rather than in the marketplace. Because the benefits of environmental protection flow across property boundaries, there is greater reason for the government to intervene on environmental issues than there is with respect to purely private goods.

## 4-3 | GROWTH POLICY

According to our neoclassical growth model, one of the most important determinants of growth is the savings rate in an economy. It would be tempting to simply assert that we would all be better off if somehow everyone just saved more. However, we saw in Chapter 3 that consumers make decisions concerning savings and consumption based on their rates of time preference. Therefore, it is possible to argue that, whatever the savings rate is, it is a market outcome that consumers have chosen.

In spite of this, there are those who argue that if it was left up to the market, consumers would not save enough. Certainly, compared to Japan, Canadians save very

---

[7] Robert Barro and Xavier Sala-i-Martin, *Economic Growth* (Cambridge, MA: MIT Press), Table 10.1.

[8] Actually, people in Neolithic times probably didn't have "rooms" per se. For a more recent benchmark, the energy efficiency of room lighting has improved by a factor of 20 since 1900. See William D. Nordhaus, "Do Real Output and Real Wage Measures Capture Reality? The History of Lighting Suggests Not," in Robert J. Gordon and Timothy F. Bresnahan (eds.), *The Economics of New Goods* (Chicago: University of Chicago Press, 1997), pp. 29–66.

little. However, compared to the United States, we save a lot. It is helpful to look at the reasons for these differences in savings rates.

One of the reasons we save more than the United States may be that our tax laws favour savings. For instance, in Canada, we give tax breaks to individuals who save through Registered Retirement Savings Plans (RRSPs). The United States has a similar plan, called Individual Retirement Account, but this plan was introduced later than the RRSP in Canada, and it has been limited since 1986. There is also some belief that the U.S. tax system favours borrowing and current consumption. Finally, the argument has been made that one reason Canadians save more than U.S. citizens is that our public pension plans (CPP and QPP) are weaker than the U.S. public pension plan and, therefore, consumers need to save more. In the Discussion Questions at the end of this chapter, you will be asked to comment on some of the studies that have made these arguments.

There appears to be no consensus on why the savings rate in Japan is so high. Some of the arguments are that Japanese culturally save more, perhaps in a desire to produce larger bequests. Another reason may be that land prices in Japan are very high, and down payment requirements to buy a house are stricter than in Canada. Therefore, in order to buy a house, Japanese people would have to save more.

Given the above, is there anything the government can do to encourage savings? The most obvious channel centres on the realization that if the government spends more than it raises in tax revenue, that is, if the government runs a budgetary deficit, this is negative public savings. We saw in Chapter 3 that budget deficits are associated with higher real interest rates, which crowds out private investment spending and decreases the rate of growth of capital. Figure 4-10 shows that there is some tendency for a government budget deficit to be associated with lower private savings.[9] By the late 1990s, the Government of Canada had eliminated this deficit problem.

## FIGURE 4-10

Personal and government savings are each measured as a percentage of nominal GDP. Fiscal deficits, which became chronic in the early 1970s, eventually lead to lower personal savings rates.

### PERSONAL AND GOVERNMENT SAVINGS, 1961–2002

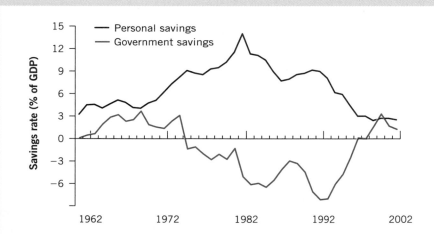

SOURCE: Personal savings: CANSIM II V499302; government savings: CANSIM II V499304; nominal GDP: CANSIM II V498918.

---

[9] You may wish to use this information to have another look at Discussion Question 4 in Chapter 3.

## Different Forms of Capital

The neoclassical growth model assumes that there is only one capital stock. However, in reality, the capital stock can take different forms. For instance, we saw in Box 4-1 that human capital can make a difference to the growth rate of an economy. Increasing human capital would require an investment in education, which is largely publicly funded in Canada. It has also been argued that there is a link between the infrastructure of an economy—roads, bridges, etc.—and the productivity of an economy. Exploiting this link would appear to have been the intent of the Liberal government's infrastructure program that was instituted in 1993.

## Technological Innovation

One of the lessons of the neoclassical growth model is that technological innovation will increase the long run growth rate in an economy. Therefore, the government could aid technological innovation through incentives in the tax system for investment in technology. Compared to other countries in the world, Canada has one of the most favourable tax systems toward investment expenditures in research and development. The interesting problem is that, in spite of this tax treatment, Canada has one of the lowest ratios of research and development expenditure to GDP in the world. One possible explanation for this is that the overall corporate tax structure needs to be changed in order for firms to be able to respond properly to the research and development incentives.

## POLICY IN *ACTION*

### Politics and Infrastructure

We have mentioned several times in this chapter that the concept of one single type of physical capital is somewhat restrictive. One type of capital stock that has not been mentioned is infrastructure; that is, the roads, bridges, etc., in an economy. In a very influential and controversial article, D.A. Aschauer* concluded that the slowdown in productivity in the U.S. economy in the 1970s (see Box 4-2) was attributable to the decline in the rate of public infrastructure investment. Some of the discussion that followed was not so much a question of whether infrastructure capital is good for the economy, but rather, whether the government or the private sector should be undertaking this type of investment.

When it was first elected in 1993, the Liberal government of Jean Chrétien implemented an infrastructure investment program. One of the goals of this program was to upgrade the highways and bridges in Canada, which would allow future higher growth in output. At the end of 2002, there appeared to be renewed interest in government infrastructure investment.

*D.A. Aschauer, "Is Public Expenditure Productive?" *Journal of Monetary Economics*, March 23, 1989, pp. 177–200.

## *Working with Data*

Equation (2) is the fundamental growth accounting equation. Table 4-1 used the data from Table 3-1 to apply this growth accounting equation to the Canadian experience. In any year, $\Delta N/N$ is the percentage change in labour, $\Delta K/K$ is the percentage change in the capital stock, and each can be calculated from Table 3-1. Go to CANSIM and get the data that are referenced in Table 4-1. Remembering that $\theta = 0.3$, try to reproduce the data in Table 4-1.

## C H A P T E R   S U M M A R Y

▶ Neoclassical growth theory accounts for growth in output as a function of growth in inputs, particularly capital and labour.

▶ Each input contributes to growth by an amount equal to its factor share times its growth rate.

▶ Long run growth can result from improvements in technology.

▶ Steady-state output per person depends positively on the savings rate and negatively on the rate of population growth.

## K E Y   T E R M S

growth accounting equation, *73*
total factor productivity, *73*
neoclassical growth theory, *78*
capital-labour ratio, *78*

marginal product of capital
  (*MPK*), *79*
steady-state equilibrium, *79*
endogenous growth, *86*

absolute convergence, *88*
conditional convergence, *88*

## D I S C U S S I O N   Q U E S T I O N S

1. We discussed the divergent savings rates in Canada and the United States. Discuss reasons why these savings rates may have diverged. You may want to consult two interesting papers on this topic: C. Carroll and Lawrence Summers, "Why Have Private Savings Rates in the United States and Canada Diverged?" *Journal of Monetary Economics*, September 1987, and John Sebalhaus, "Public Policy and Saving in the United States and Canada," *Canadian Journal of Economics*, May 1997.

2. The standard production function used in Chapters 3 and 4 included labour and capital as inputs. We used this to derive the "Solow residual." What sort of mistakes could we be making by attributing this residual to technological progress? How could you expand the model to accommodate this?

3. Figure 4-4 is a basic illustration of the neoclassical growth model. Interpret this figure, being careful to explain the meaning of the savings and investment requirement lines. Why does steady state occur where these lines cross?

4.  What factors determine the growth rate of steady-state per capita output? Are there any other factors that could affect the growth rate of output in the short run?

5.  Discuss the difference between absolute and conditional convergence as predicted by the neoclassical growth model.

## A P P L I C A T I O N    Q U E S T I O N S

1.  In a simple scenario with only two factors of production, suppose that capital's share of income is 0.4 and labour's share is 0.6 and that annual growth rates of capital and labour are 6 and 2 percent, respectively. Assume there is no technical change.

    **a.** At what rate does output grow?

    **b.** How long will it take for output to double?

    **c.** Now suppose technology grows at a rate of 2 percent. Recalculate your answers to (a) and (b).

2.  Suppose that output is growing at 3 percent per year and capital's and labour's shares of income are 0.3 and 0.7, respectively.

    **a.** If both labour and capital grow at 1 percent per year, what would the growth rate of total factor productivity have to be?

    **b.** What if both the labour and the capital stocks are fixed?

3.  Suppose again that capital's and labour's shares of income are 0.3 and 0.7, respectively.

    **a.** What would be the effect (on output) of increasing the capital stock by 10 percent?

    **b.** What would be the effect of increasing the pool of labour by 10 percent?

    **c.** If the increase in labour is due entirely to population growth, will the resulting increase in output have an effect on people's welfare?

    **d.** What if the increase in labour is due, instead, to an influx of women into the workplace?

4.  Consider a production function of the form $Y = AF(K, N, Z)$, where $Z$ is a measure of natural resources used in production. Assume this production function has constant returns to scale and diminishing returns in each factor.

    **a.** What will happen to output per head if capital and labour both grow but $Z$ is fixed?

    **b.** Reconsider (a), but add technical progress (growth in $A$).

    **c.** In the 1970s, there were fears that we were running out of natural resources and that this would limit growth. Discuss this view using your answers to (a) and (b).

5.  Consider the following production function: $Y = K^{0.5}(AN)^{0.5}$, where both the population and the pool of labour are growing at a rate $n = 0.07$, the capital stock is depreciating at a rate $d = 0.03$, and $A$ is normalized to 1.

    **a.** What are capital's and labour's shares of income?

    **b.** What is the form of this production function?

    **c.** Find the steady-state values of $k$ and $y$ when $s = 0.20$.

    **d.** At what rate is per capita output growing at the steady state? At what rate is total output growing? What if total factor productivity is increasing at a rate of 2 percent per year ($g = 0.02$)?

www.mcgrawhill.ca/college/dornbusch

6. Suppose the level of technology is constant. Then it jumps to a new, higher constant level.

   a. How does this technological jump affect output per head, holding the capital-labour ratio constant?

   b. Show the new steady-state equilibrium. What has happened to per capita saving and the capital–labour ratio? What happens to output per capita?

   c. Chart the time path of the adjustment to the new steady state. Does the investment ratio rise during transition? If so, is this effect temporary?

7.* For a Cobb-Douglas production function $Y = AK^{\theta}N^{(1-\theta)}$, verify that $1 - \theta$ is labour's share of income. (*Hint:* Labour's share of income is the piece of income that results from that labour ($MPL^*N$) divided by total income.)

8. Go to CANSIM and retrieve real GDP and population, and calculate real GDP per capita. Calculate the growth rate of this series over the periods 1962–1973, 1973–1992, and 1992–2000. Relate these growth rates to the discussion in Box 4-2.

## Appendix

In this appendix we briefly show how the fundamental growth equation (equation (2) in this chapter) is obtained. We start with the production function $Y = AF(K, N)$ and ask how much output changes if labour changes by $\Delta N$, capital changes by $\Delta K$, and technology changes by $\Delta A$. The change in output will be

$$\Delta Y = MPN \times \Delta N + MPK \times \Delta K + F(K, N) \times \Delta A \qquad (A1)$$

where $MPN$ and $MPK$ are the marginal products of labour and capital, respectively. Dividing both sides of the equation by $Y = AF(K, N)$ and simplifying yields

$$\frac{\Delta Y}{Y} = \frac{MPN}{Y} \Delta N + \frac{MPK}{Y} \Delta K + \frac{\Delta A}{A} \qquad (A2)$$

Now we multiply and divide the first term by $N$ and the second term by $K$:

$$\frac{\Delta Y}{Y} = \left(\frac{MPN \times N}{Y}\right) \Delta N/N + \left(\frac{MPK \times K}{Y}\right)\frac{\Delta K}{K} + \frac{\Delta A}{A} \qquad (A3)$$

These transformations follow from rules of mathematics. To get the rest of the way to equation (2), we need to make a strong, but very reasonable, assumption: The economy is *competitive*.

In a competitive economy, factors are paid their marginal products. Thus $MPN = w$, where $w$ is the real wage. Total payment to labour is the wage rate times the amount of labour, $w \times N$; the total payment to labour as a fraction of all payments—which is to say, "labour's share"—is $MPN \times N/Y$. (The argument for capital is analogous.) Now substitute $1 - \theta \equiv$ labour's share for $MPN \times N/Y$ and $\theta \equiv$ capital's share for $MPK \times K/Y$ into equation (A3) to reach equation (2):

$$\Delta Y/Y = [(1 - \theta) \quad (\Delta N/N)] + [\quad \theta \quad (\Delta K/K)] + \Delta A/A$$

$$\text{Output growth} = \left(\begin{array}{c}\text{Labour}\\\text{share}\end{array} \times \begin{array}{c}\text{Labour}\\\text{growth}\end{array}\right) + \left(\begin{array}{c}\text{Capital}\\\text{share}\end{array} \times \begin{array}{c}\text{Capital}\\\text{growth}\end{array}\right) + \begin{array}{c}\text{Technical}\\\text{progress}\end{array} \qquad (2)$$

---

*An asterisk denotes a more difficult problem.

**BOX**

**A4-1**

## Following Along with the Cobb-Douglas

The phrase *constant returns to scale* (CRTS) means that if all inputs increase in equal proportion, output increases in that same proportion. Mathematically, if we multiply both inputs by a constant, $c$, output will also be multiplied by $c$: $AF(cK, cN) = cAF(K, N) 5 cY$. CRTS is a believable assumption because of the replication argument: If one factory using X workers produces output Y, then two factories using X workers each should produce output 2Y, three factories using X workers each should produce output 3Y, and so forth. In addition to this attractive logical argument, empirical evidence also suggests that returns to scale are roughly constant.

To show that the Cobb-Douglas has constant returns to scale, multiply both $K$ and $N$ by $c$:

$$A(cK)^{\theta}(cN)^{1-\theta} = A(c^{\theta}K^{\theta})(c^{1-\theta}N^{1-\theta}) = c^{\theta}c^{1-\theta}AK^{\theta}N^{1-\theta} = c^{\theta + (1-\theta)}Y = cY$$

To show that capital's share is $\theta$, multiply the marginal product of capital (which is what a unit of capital gets paid in a competitive market) by the number of units of capital and divide by total output:

$$MPK \cdot K/Y = (\theta Y/K) \cdot K/Y = \theta$$

And yes, the exponent $\theta$ in the Cobb-Douglas is the same $\theta$ that appears in the growth accounting equation (equation (2)).

# CHAPTER 5

# INTERNATIONAL TRADE AND EXCHANGE RATES

## LEARNING OBJECTIVES

After reading and studying this chapter, you should be able to:

▶ Understand that the balance of payments is composed of the current account and the capital account.

▶ Understand that the current account balance and the capital account balance must sum to zero.

▶ Understand that a small open economy takes the foreign (world) real interest rate as exogenous.

▶ Understand that given the foreign real rate of interest, domestic savings does not have to equal domestic investment in equilibrium.

▶ Understand that if domestic savings is greater than domestic investment, then there is a balance of trade surplus and net foreign lending is positive. If domestic savings is less than domestic investment, then there is a balance of trade deficit and net foreign lending is negative.

▶ Understand that Canada has operated under both a floating and a flexible exchange rate system.

▶ Understand that purchasing power parity predicts that the exchange rate will move to equate purchasing power internationally.

www.dfait-maeci.gc.ca/
menu-en.asp

E arly in the twenty-first century, national economies are becoming more closely interrelated, and the notion of globalization—that we are moving toward a single global economy—is increasingly accepted. Economic influences of other countries have a powerful effect on the Canadian economy. Canada is linked to the rest of the world through two broad channels: trade in goods and services, and finance.

The trade linkages arise from the fact that some of Canada's output is exported to foreign countries (exports), while some of the goods that are purchased in Canada are produced elsewhere in the world (imports). In 2002, exports accounted for 41 percent of GDP, while imports were 37 percent (refer back to Table 2-2). Given the amount that Canada engages in international trade, Canada is called an **open economy**. Compared to Canada, the United States engages in relatively little international trade—in 2002, U.S. exports were 11 percent of GDP, while U.S. imports were 16 percent of GDP. Given this, the U.S. economy is a relatively **closed economy**.

**open economy**
An economy that trades goods, services, and assets with other countries.

**closed economy**
An economy that does not engage in any international trade.

The international linkages in the area of finance arise from the fact that Canadian residents, whether households, banks, or corporations, can hold assets in foreign countries, and foreigners can choose to hold Canadian assets. Although households are likely to hold mainly domestic assets, portfolio managers for banks and corporations consider the relative attractiveness of lending and borrowing in other countries.

## 5-1 | THE BALANCE OF PAYMENTS ACCOUNTS

**balance of payments**
A record of the transactions of a country with the rest of the world.

The **balance of payments** is a record of the transactions of a country with the rest of the world. Table 5-1 summarizes the balance of payments for Canada in 2002.

There is a simple rule for balance of payments accounting: Any transaction that gives rise to a payment by Canadian residents to a foreign country is an outflow and is recorded as a debit item; these are listed in Table 5-1 with minus signs. Conversely, any transaction that gives rise to a payment by foreigners to a Canadian resident is an inflow and is a credit item.

In Table 5-1, you will see that the balance of payments is made up of two major accounts: the current account and the capital and financial account.[1]

### Current Account

**current account**
Net exports, net income from assets, and net transfers.

The **current account** has three major components: net exports; net income from assets; and net transfers. We have already seen **net exports** in Chapter 2 as a component of the national accounts. In 2002, exports, which give rise to a receipt, were greater than imports, which give rise to a payment. Therefore, net exports is a receipt item and enters as a credit of $49.5 billion.

**net exports**
The difference between exports and imports.

You will often hear the term **merchandise trade balance** used by the media. This is due to the fact that both exports and imports can be broken down into trade in goods (merchandise) and trade in services. Thus, the merchandise trade balance is the difference between exports of goods and import of goods only. Trade in services refers to items such as tourism and education.

**merchandise trade balance**
The difference between exports of goods and import of goods.

Net income from assets refers to returns on financial instruments. For instance, if you held a bond that was issued by the U.S. government, any interest you earn on

---

[1] Since 1997, Statistics Canada has divided the capital account into capital account and financial account. Generally speaking, we will refer to this as the *capital account*.

| TABLE 5-1 | CANADA'S INTERNATIONAL BALANCE OF PAYMENTS, 2002 (BILLIONS OF DOLLARS) |
|---|---|

| | | | |
|---|---:|---:|---:|
| **Current Account** | | | |
| Net Exports | | **49.5** | |
|     Exports | 472.6 | | |
|     Imports | 423.1 | | |
| Net Income from Assets | | **−27.5** | |
|     Receipts on Investments | 31.6 | | |
|     Payments on Investments | −59.1 | | |
| Net Transfers | | **1.4** | |
|     Transfer Receipts | 7.0 | | |
|     Transfer Payments | −5.6 | | |
| **Current Account Balance** | | | **23.4** |
| **Capital and Financial Account** | | | |
| Capital Account Net Flow | | **4.8** | |
| Inflow | **5.6** | | |
| Outflow | −0.8 | | |
| Financial Account Net Flow | | **−18.0** | |
| Canadian Liabilities Net Inflow | 62.9 | | |
| Canadian Assets Net Outflow | −80.8 | | |
|     Official Reserves | 0.3 | | |
|     Other Assets | −81.1 | | |
| **Capital and Financial Account balance** | | | **−13.2** |
| **Statistical Discrepancy** | | | **−10.2** |

SOURCE: CANSIM II tables 3760001 and 3760002.

that bond is a credit in the income from assets account. Conversely, payments to foreigners who own Canadian financial instruments would be a debit item in income from assets. Net income from assets refers to the difference between these two items. In 2002, this account was in a net debit position of $27.5 billion.

The final item, transfers, refers to items such as foreign aid or a gift from family members in one country to family members in another country. This small item was in a net credit position of $1.4 billion in 2002.

The current account balance is the sum of the above three items. In 2002, Canada had a current account surplus of $23.4 billion.

**capital and financial account**

Financial account records direct investment and portfolio investment, while capital account includes items such as inheritances and trade in intellectual property.

## Capital and Financial Account

The current account transactions discussed above refer to trade in currently produced goods and services. Trade between countries in existing assets is recorded in the **capital and financial account**. As its title suggests, the capital and financial account is broken down into two items: capital account and financial account. The financial account records direct investment and portfolio investment, while the capital account includes items such as inheritances and trade in intellectual property. As we noted earlier, we will most often refer to these accounts together as *capital account*.

**official reserves**

Assets held by central banks that can be used to make international payments.

One final item in the balance of payments accounts that is of particular importance is **official reserves**, which are listed under Canadian assets, net outflow. If this item is positive (as it is in 2002: $0.3 billion), this means that the Bank of Canada has sold foreign reserves (i.e., a flow of funds into Canada in receipt of these reserves). Notice that the sum of the current account ($23.4 billion) and capital account not including official reserves ($–12.9 billion) plus the statistical discrepancy (–$10.2 billion) equals $0.3 billion, representing a balance of payments deficit. This is exactly matched by the sale of foreign reserves of $0.3 billion. In general, a country that has a balance of payments surplus will have an increase in foreign reserves, and a country that has a balance of payments deficit will have a reduction in foreign reserves.

It should be clear that the overall balance of payments must be zero. Individuals and firms must pay for what they buy abroad. If you were to spend more than your income, your deficit would need to be financed by selling assets or borrowing. Similarly, if a country runs a deficit in current account, spending more abroad than it receives from sales to the rest of the world, the deficit needs to be financed by selling assets thereby borrowing abroad. Therefore, any current account deficit must be financed by an offsetting capital account inflow.

$$\text{Current account} + \text{Capital account} = 0 \tag{1}$$

Remember two points about equation (1). First, *capital account* refers to capital and financial account and, second, capital account includes official reserves.

## 5-2 | SAVINGS AND INVESTMENT IN A SMALL OPEN ECONOMY

In Chapter 3, we discussed the long run goods market equilibrium condition that savings equals investment, and we did not discuss the role of net exports. Therefore, in Chapter 3, we were assuming that Canada was a closed economy. In this section, we extend the analysis of Chapter 3 and explicitly take account of the fact that Canada is an open economy. Recall the GDP identity

$$Y = C + I + G + NX \tag{2}$$

We know from Chapter 2 that the following equation must hold.

$$S = I + (NS + YNR) \tag{3}$$

where $NX$ stands for *net exports*, equal to exports minus imports, and $YNR$ is net investment income from non-residents. Remember that the sum of net exports plus net investment income from non-residents equals the current account (assuming no current transfers). Therefore, we can write

$$S = I + CA \tag{4}$$

We can write equation (4) slightly differently as

$$S - I = CA \tag{5}$$

Equation (5) tells us that, in an open economy, the excess of domestic savings over domestic investment must equal the current account. Notice how this equilibrium condition is related to the balance of payments equilibrium condition given in equation (1). Recall from Table 5-1 that the major components of the current account are net exports and net income from assets. Net income from assets is essentially the same as net investment income from non-residents, which is part of GNP but not GDP.[2] For the most part for the remainder of this chapter, we will assume that current account and net exports are the same, and the terms will be used interchangeably. We know from equation (1) that the current account and capital account must offset each other for balance of payments equilibrium. Therefore, equation (5) can be interpreted in terms of trade in goods and services equalling capital flows in terms of net lending or borrowing.

$$S - I = NX \qquad (6)$$
$$\text{Net foreign lending} = \text{Trade balance}$$

Suppose that domestic savings is greater than domestic investment. In this situation, the excess domestic savings is loaned to foreigners. Therefore, the left-hand side of equation (6) is equal to **net foreign investment**, which is the amount that domestic residents are lending to foreigners. Therefore, another way to look at the equilibrium condition is that net foreign investment must equal the trade balance in equilibrium.

**net foreign investment**
The amount that domestic residents are lending to foreigners.

## The Role of the World Real Rate of Interest

In the closed economy model that we developed in Chapter 3, the domestic real rate of interest played an important role in keeping the market in equilibrium. Recall that if savings were greater than investment, then the domestic real interest rate would decline to ensure market equilibrium. However, in an open economy, equation (6) says that domestic savings can be greater than domestic investment in equilibrium. The reason for this is that in open economy analysis, all market participants are assumed to have access to the **foreign (or world) real rate of interest**.[3] We assume that Canada is a small open economy, so that any action by market participants in Canada will not affect the foreign real rate of interest. This means that in Canada we take the foreign real interest rate as given, or exogenous.

**foreign (or world) real rate of interest**
The real interest rate that prevails in international capital markets; individuals, businesses, and governments are assumed to be able to borrow and lend at this rate.

Now consider a situation where the foreign real interest rate, $r_f$, is greater than the domestic real interest rate, $r$. This is illustrated in Figure 5-1.

In Figure 5-1, if the foreign real rate of interest, $r_f$, equalled the domestic real interest rate, then the equilibrium would be identical to the closed economy equilibrium where domestic savings equals domestic investment. However, given that $r_f > r$, there is an excess of domestic savings over domestic investment. Therefore, there is a trade surplus and positive net foreign lending.

Figure 5-2 shows the opposite case, where $r_f < r$ and there is a trade deficit and net foreign borrowing.

---

[2] You may want to refer back to Table 2-1 in Chapter 2 to remind yourself of this.

[3] Technically, the assumption that we are making here is called *perfect capital mobility*. This assumption will be discussed later in the book.

## FIGURE 5-1

If the foreign real rate of interest, $r_f$, is greater than the domestic real rate of interest, $r$, then net exports are greater than zero. In this situation, net foreign investment (lending) must also be positive.

**SAVINGS AND INVESTMENT IN A SMALL OPEN ECONOMY**

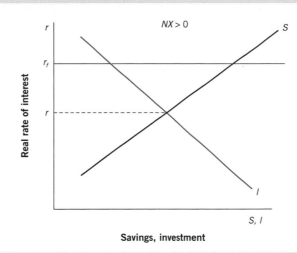

## Fiscal Policy and the Twin Deficits

Now we wish to consider how fiscal policy affects the equilibrium in our model. Suppose that the economy is at a position of equilibrium where the domestic real interest rate equals the foreign rate, as shown in Figure 5-3. We know from our analysis in Chapter 3 that if the government runs a budget deficit, the savings curve shifts to the left. Given the new savings curve, $S'$, domestic savings is now less than domestic investment at the foreign real rate of interest. The result is that there is a balance of trade deficit and net foreign borrowing, given by the distance $S' - I$.

## FIGURE 5-2

If the foreign real rate of interest, $r_f$, is less than the domestic real rate of interest, $r$, then net exports are negative (there is a trade deficit). In this situation, net foreign investment (lending) must also be negative.

**SAVINGS AND INVESTMENT IN A SMALL OPEN ECONOMY**

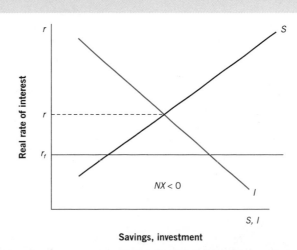

### FIGURE 5-3

A government budget defect shifts the savings curve left to $S'$. At the foreign real rate of interest, savings is less than investment, and there is a balance of trade deficit equal to $S' - I$.

**A GOVERNMENT BUDGET DEFICIT CAN CAUSE A BALANCE OF TRADE DEFICIT**

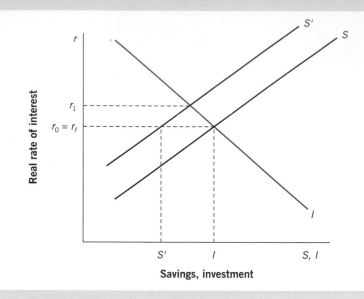

The preceding result implies that, in a small open economy such as Canada's, a government budget deficit leads to a balance of trade deficit. This is what many refer to as the **twin deficit** problem. It is important to understand that a government budget deficit will lead to a trade deficit only if total savings decreases. We have assumed that private savings does not increase to compensate for the decrease in government savings.[4] Figure 5-4 graphs the federal government budget deficit and trade balance between the years 1961 and 2002. Notice that the period of large fiscal deficits in the 1970s and 1980s was accompanied by a trade deficit.

**twin deficit**

In a small open economy, a government budget deficit leads to a balance of trade deficit.

### FIGURE 5-4

The government budget deficit and the current account balance are both measured as a percent of GDP. In this figure, when the government budget balance is positive, there is a budgetary deficit. There is a tendency for the fiscal deficits of the 1970s and 1980s to be coincident with a current account deficit.

**THE TWIN DEFICITS, 1961–2002**

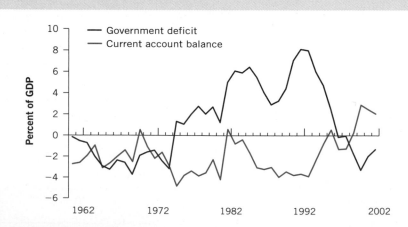

SOURCE: Government fiscal: CANSIM II V647356; current account balance: CANSIM II V113713; nominal GDP: CANSIM II V498933.

---

[4] You may want to refer back to Figure 4-10.

## 5-3 | EXCHANGE RATES

### Exchange Rate Determination

**nominal exchange rate**
The number of Canadian dollars that must be given up in order to purchase a unit of foreign currency.

**flexible (or floating) exchange rate**
The central bank allows the exchange rate to be determined by the foreign exchange market.

**currency appreciation or depreciation**
A change in the price of foreign exchange under flexible exchange rates.

www.economist.com/
markets

**fixed rate system**
Central banks buy and sell currency at a fixed rate in terms of foreign exchange.

**intervention**
Occurs when the central bank has to buy or sell foreign currency to make up for any excess supply or demand arising from private transactions.

In this section, we discuss the determination of the nominal exchange rate. We define the **nominal exchange rate** as the number of Canadian dollars that must be given up in order to purchase a unit of foreign currency. For instance, it currently costs approximately $1.17 Canadian to purchase 100 Japanese yen, or it currently costs approximately $1.40 Canadian to purchase one U.S. dollar. We call this the *nominal exchange rate* to distinguish it from the real exchange rate, which will be discussed in the next section.

The nominal exchange rate is a price that is determined by supply and demand in the foreign exchange market. Under a **flexible (or floating) exchange rate system**, the central bank allows the exchange rate to be determined by activity in the foreign exchange market, without intervention. A change in the foreign exchange rate under a flexible rate system is referred to as a *currency appreciation* or *depreciation*. We say that we experience a **currency appreciation** when it becomes less expensive to buy foreign currency. Therefore, if the Canadian dollar price of one U.S. dollar changes from $1.40 to $1.35, this is a currency appreciation. Conversely, we say that we experience a **currency depreciation** when it becomes more expensive to buy foreign currency. In this case, if the Canadian dollar price of one U.S. dollar changes from $1.40 to $1.45, this is a currency depreciation.[5]

In Figure 5-5, we illustrate the determination of the nominal exchange rate. The supply of foreign currency offered in exchange for Canadian dollars arises from exports and capital inflows. It is upward sloping, since an increase in the Canadian dollar price of foreign exchange (i.e., a depreciation) reduces the cost of exports in foreign markets. The demand curve in Figure 5-5 arises from imports and capital outflows. It is downward sloping, since an increase in the Canadian dollar price of foreign exchange raises the cost of imports. In a flexible rate system, the equilibrium exchange rate is determined by the usual intersection of the supply and demand curves, shown at $e_1$ in Figure 5-5.

In a **fixed rate system**, central banks stand ready to buy and sell their currency at a fixed price in terms of foreign exchange. Figure 5-5 illustrates that a fixed exchange rate is like any other price support scheme, such as one in an agricultural market. If the price is fixed below the equilibrium level, say at $e_2$ in Figure 5-5, the central bank can keep the exchange rate fixed only by meeting the excess demand for foreign exchange by buying Canadian dollars with foreign exchange

A change in the price of foreign exchange under a fixed exchange rate is referred to as *devaluation* or *revaluation*. A devaluation (revaluation) takes place when the value of the currency in terms of foreign exchange is reduced (increased) by official action.

### Exchange Market Intervention

In a fixed rate system, the central bank has to buy or sell foreign currency to make up for any excess supply or demand arising from private transactions. Such purchases and sales are referred to as exchange market **intervention**. In order to be able to ensure that the rate stays fixed, it is obviously necessary to hold an inventory of foreign

---

[5] Discussion Question 3 at the end of this chapter asks you to rewrite this paragraph, expressing the exchange rate in U.S. dollars.

**FIGURE 5-5**

To fix the exchange rate at $e_2$ below the equilibrium rate $e_1$, the central bank has to meet the excess demand by selling international reserves.

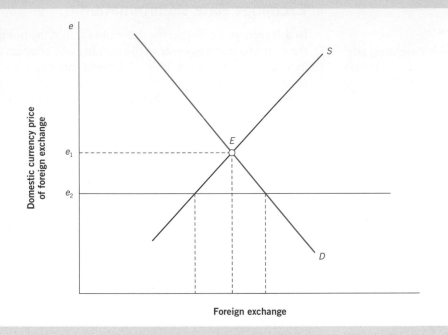

**THE FOREIGN EXCHANGE MARKET**

exchange that can be sold in exchange for domestic currency. Thus, the Bank of Canada holds reserves of U.S. dollars, and gold that can be sold for U.S. dollars, for the purpose of exchange market intervention.

The ability of a country to maintain the value of its currency depends on its stock of foreign exchange reserves. If it persistently runs deficits in the balance of payments, the central bank eventually will run out of reserves and will be unable to continue intervention. Before that point is reached, the central bank is likely to resort to a devaluation. In 1967, for instance, Britain devalued sterling from $2.80 per pound to $2.40 per pound.

Under flexible exchange rates, intervention is not required. In a system of clean floating, central banks do not intervene in foreign exchange markets and thus allow exchange rates to be freely determined. In practice, the flexible rate system has not been one of clean floating, but rather one of **managed,** or **dirty, floating.** Under managed floating, central banks intervene by buying or selling foreign currency and attempt to influence exchange rates.

**managed, or dirty, floating**

Central banks intervene by buying or selling foreign currency and attempt to influence exchange rates.

## The Evolution of the Canadian Exchange Rate

The value of the Canadian dollar has been determined at various times under both fixed and flexible exchange rate regimes. Figure 5-6 shows the fluctuations in the value of the Canadian dollar since 1913. Until 1929, Canada and most other countries fixed their rates by maintaining convertibility into gold at a fixed price. A floating rate was in effect during the 1930s until the outbreak of World War II, when a fixed rate of $1.10 Canadian was established.

In 1946, the *Bretton Woods system* was established in an attempt to avoid the unstable exchange rates and restrictive trade policies of the 1930s. Under this system, countries fixed their exchange rates in terms of the U.S. dollar by specifying the rate at which the central bank would buy or sell U.S. dollars. Canada participated initially in

www.polsci.ucsb.edu/
faculty/cohen/inpress/
bretton.html

## FIGURE 5-6

The Canadian dollar has been subject to both fixed and floating exchange rate regimes in the past. The exchange rate was approximately fixed until 1930 and again between 1939 and 1973. Since 1973, the Canadian dollar has been floating, and went through a long period of depreciation until the end of 2002. In early 2003, the Canadian dollar appreciated sharply.

### THE CANADIAN DOLLAR, 1913–2003

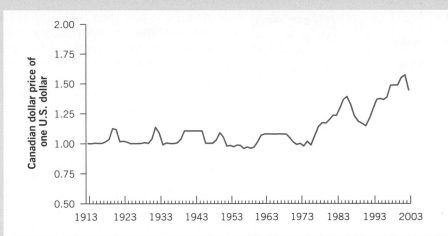

SOURCE: 1913–1950: Statistics Canada, *Historical Statistics of Canada*, Publication 11-516-XIE (available in electronic format at www.statcan.ca/english/freepub/11-516-XIE/free.htm), table J563; 1951–2003: CANSIM II V37426.

the Bretton Woods system with its currency revalued to $1.00 Canadian per U.S. dollar, but this rate was abandoned in 1950 in favour of a floating rate. Under the influence of market forces, our dollar soon appreciated to the range of $0.95– $0.98 Canadian per U.S. dollar, where it remained until 1961.

After a rapid depreciation in 1961 and early 1962, it was decided to return to a fixed rate, and a value of $1.08 Canadian was established in May 1962. The framers of the Bretton Woods system saw the fixed exchange rate system as a means of facilitating world trade. With fixed rates, firms can invest in facilities to supply export markets and make contracts for the delivery of goods without uncertainty concerning the future level of exchange rates.

In 1970, however, the Canadian dollar came under strong appreciation pressure. In addition, there was instability in the world economy, arising particularly from sharp increases in the price of oil. These events forced the abandonment of the fixed exchange rate system in 1973. After initially appreciating to under $1.00 Canadian in the early 1970s, the Canadian dollar began a slow depreciation that continued, on average, until early 2003, when the Canadian dollar experienced a sharp, sudden appreciation.

## Alternative Measures of the Exchange Rate

Table 5-2 shows several measures of the exchange rate. All of the exchange rates listed in Table 5-2 are measured in Canadian dollars.[6] The first three columns are bilateral exchange rates. The term *bilateral* simply means that the exchange rates measure the value of one currency against one other currency.

---

[6] The C-6 exchange rate is an index of the weighted-average foreign exchange value of the Canadian dollar against major foreign currencies. Weights for each country are derived from Canadian merchandise trade flows with other countries over the three years from 1994 through 1996. The index has been based to 1992 (i.e., C-6 = 100 in 1992). The C-6 index broadens the coverage of the old G-10 index to include all of the countries in the European Monetary Union.

BOX

5-1

http://europa.eu.int/
euro/entry.html

### The Euro

Western Europe has gone through five decades of increasing economic integration, from inconvertible currencies, trade quotas, and prohibitive tariffs at the end of World War II to unrestricted free trade within borders, total mobility of labour across borders, and indeed the abolition of internal borders, along with common passports, a European parliament, and a central economic authority in Brussels. Many decisions remain at the national level, but it is formidable just how much Europe has moved from segmented national economies to an integrated political and economic area.

This process of economic and political integration has led to the European Union (EU). A controversial crowning piece of that economic agenda has been the creation of a monetary union, the European Monetary Union (EMU), and its common money, the euro. This currency started in January 1999 with exchange rates immutably fixed and was to be completed in January 2002 with the introduction of the actual currency—coins and notes. No more lira, Deutschmarks, francs, or pesetas—just euros, with the symbol € denoting the new money.

The new money was highly controversial for one simple reason: For much of the post-war period, Germany had a good economy—low inflation—and most other European economies, France or Italy in particular, did not. No surprise then that Germans worried about their money. The key issue was the creation of a convergence process in which countries would have to reach specific targets (the "Maastricht criteria," named after the Dutch town where the agreements were reached). These qualifying hurdles were, specifically, 2 percent inflation or less, no restrictions on capital flows and no devaluation in the preceding two years, a budget deficit of less than 2 percent of GDP, and a debt ratio below 60 percent of GDP or at least committed to falling to that level over time. Convergence has happened—as evidenced by the fact that Italian interest rates, debts and deficits notwithstanding, have fallen to German levels.

### THE EVOLUTION OF THE EURO SINCE 1999

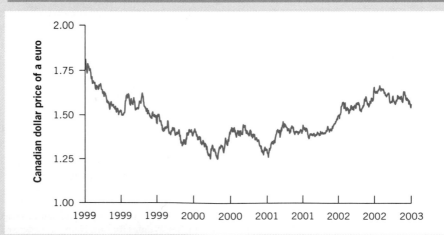

SOURCE: CANSIM II V121742.

| TABLE 5-2 | ALTERNATIVE MEASURES OF THE EXCHANGE RATE, 1990–2003 (CANDIAN DOLLARS) | | | |
|---|---|---|---|---|
| Year | U.S. Dollar | U.K. Pound | Japanese Yen | C-6 |
| 1990 | 1.17 | 2.08 | 0.0081 | 104.44 |
| 1991 | 1.15 | 2.03 | 0.0085 | 106.12 |
| 1992 | 1.21 | 2.13 | 0.0096 | 99.97 |
| 1993 | 1.29 | 1.94 | 0.0116 | 94.03 |
| 1994 | 1.37 | 2.09 | 0.0134 | 88.29 |
| 1995 | 1.37 | 2.17 | 0.0147 | 86.84 |
| 1996 | 1.36 | 2.13 | 0.0125 | 88.21 |
| 1997 | 1.38 | 2.27 | 0.0115 | 88.06 |
| 1998 | 1.48 | 2.46 | 0.0114 | 82.67 |
| 1999 | 1.49 | 2.40 | 0.0131 | 82.14 |
| 2000 | 1.49 | 2.25 | 0.0138 | 82.85 |
| 2001 | 1.55 | 2.23 | 0.0128 | 80.21 |
| 2002 | 1.57 | 2.36 | 0.0126 | 78.87 |
| 2003 | 1.54 | 2.34 | 0.0122 | 79.37 |

SOURCE: CANSIM II table 1760064

**multilateral exchange rate**

Measures the value of one currency against a basket of other currencies.

Often we want to measure the movement of the Canadian dollar relative to some basket of other currencies in a single index, just as we use a price index to show how the prices of goods in general have changed. The final column in Table 5-2 shows an index of the value of the Canadian dollar against the countries in the C-6 group. This is called a **multilateral exchange rate**.

## 5-4 | THE EXCHANGE RATE IN THE LONG RUN: PURCHASING POWER PARITY

**purchasing power parity (PPP)**

In the long run, the nominal exchange rate moves primarily as a result of difference in price level behaviour between two countries.

The **purchasing power parity (PPP)** theory of the exchange rate states that, in the long run, the nominal exchange rate moves primarily as a result of difference in price level behaviour between two countries. Under this theory, the nominal exchange rate will appreciate or depreciate to the point where the average price of goods, as measured by some overall price index, will be the same when measured in a common currency.

We can gain an understanding of PPP by looking at this theory from the perspective of a single good that is produced in two different countries.[7] If PPP holds for a single good, the nominal exchange rate should adjust to the point where the good costs the same amount when purchased in either country, as long as the price is measured in a common currency. One good that is almost identical no matter what country it is produced in is a Big Mac. Consider the case of a Big Mac bought in Canada and a Big Mac bought in the United States. In April 2000, a Big Mac cost $2.51 U.S. in the United States and in Canada it cost $2.85 Cdn.[8]

---

[7] Technically speaking, when we apply the PPP theory to a single good, rather than to overall price levels, the theory is called the *Law of One Price*.

[8] See the Web page of *The Economist* at www.economist.com/markets/bigmac.

The first problem is that the two Big Macs are measured in different currencies. We can compare these two prices by converting the U.S. price into Canadian dollars.

$$P_{U.S.}^C = P_{U.S.}^{U.S.} \times e \qquad (7)$$
$$= \$2.51 \text{ U.S.} \times 1.47$$
$$= \$3.69 \text{ Cdn.}$$

where $e$ is the nominal exchange rate, measured as the Canadian dollar price of one U.S. dollar. Here the subscript denotes the country of origin and the superscript denotes the currency in which the price is measured. Therefore, the Canadian dollar price of a U.S. Big Mac in April 2000 equalled $3.69 Cdn. Now, because we have two prices that are both measured in Canadian dollars, we can calculate the relative price of a Big Mac in the two countries.

$$\text{Relative Big Mac price} = \frac{P_{U.S.}^{U.S.} \times e}{P_C^C} \qquad (8)$$

$$= \frac{\$3.69 \text{ Cdn.}}{\$2.85 \text{ U.S.}}$$

$$= 1.29$$

This equation tells us that, measured in a common currency, the U.S. Big Mac costs 29 percent more than the Canadian Big Mac.

In this example, the PPP level of the nominal exchange rate is the level that would make this relative price equal 1. This can be calculated as

$$e_{PPP} = \frac{P_C^C}{P_{U.S.}^{U.S.}}$$

$$= \frac{\$2.85 \text{ Cdn.}}{\$2.51 \text{ U.S.}} \qquad (9)$$

$$= 1.14$$

Notice that if you were to calculate the relative Big Mac price from equation (8) using 1.14 as the exchange rate, this relative price would equal 1. This Big Mac standard implies that the Canadian dollar is undervalued by 29 percent and, therefore, PPP would predict that the nominal exchange rate would appreciate 29 percent to reach 1.14.

We think of PPP as a theory about the general level of prices in two economies, as opposed to the relationship between a single good, as in the Big Mac example. Therefore, the PPP level of the exchange rate is the one that would equate price levels in two countries. The **real exchange rate** is the measure of foreign prices to domestic prices, measured in a common currency. The real exchange rate, $R$, is defined as

**real exchange rate**
The ratio of foreign prices to domestic prices, measured in a common currency.

$$R = \frac{eP_f}{P} \qquad (10)$$

where $P$ is the domestic price level, $P_f$ is the foreign price level, and $e$ is the nominal exchange rate, measured as the domestic price of a unit of foreign currency.

If the real exchange rate equals 1, currencies are at purchasing power parity. A real exchange rate above 1 means that goods abroad are more expensive than goods at home. Other things being equal, this implies that people—both at home and abroad—are likely to switch some of their spending to goods produced at home. This is often described as an increase in the competitiveness of our products. As long as $R$

| BOX | Burgernomics |
|:---:|:---|
| **5-2** | The information concerning the Big Mac example in the text was taken from an annual feature in *The Economist*. Each year *The Economist* gathers information on the price of a Big Mac in local currencies around the world and puts this information together with exchange rates in an attempt to test PPP. *The Economist* labels this "Burgernomics." You can examine the Burgernomics data at www.economist.com/markets/bigmac. |

If PPP held around the world, all Big Mac prices would be the same, measured in U.S. dollars. In the Big Mac Index that can be accessed at this Web site, column 2 shows that Big Mac prices vary widely around the world. Column 3 shows the exchange rate that would prevail if PPP held, and column 4 shows the actual exchange rate at the time of the price survey.

is greater than 1, we expect the relative demand for domestically produced goods to rise. Eventually, this should either drive up domestic prices or drive down the exchange rate, moving us closer to purchasing power parity.

Market forces prevent the exchange rate from moving *too* far from PPP or from remaining away from PPP indefinitely. However, pressures to move to PPP work only slowly. There are several reasons for slow movement toward PPP. The first reason is that market baskets differ across countries. The second reason for slow movement toward PPP is that there are many barriers to the movement of goods between countries. Some are natural barriers—transportation costs are one obvious extra cost—while others, tariffs for example, are imposed by governments. Sometimes movement of final goods isn't enough: Workers and capital would have to move. Third, and probably of greatest importance, many goods—land is the classic example—are "non-traded" and cannot move.

Figure 5-7 plots the real exchange rate between Canada and the United States for the period 1914 to 2002. Notice that although there are large deviations, the long run

*FIGURE 5-7*

**THE REAL EXCHANGE RATE, 1914–2002**

The real exchange rate is measured using the Canadian and U.S. Consumer Price Indexes, and scaled to 1973 = 1.00. There is some tendency for the real exchange rate to return to its long run level, but substantial deviations are evident in the short run.

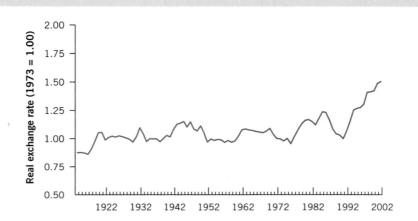

SOURCE: Canada-U.S. exchange rate: see Figure 5-6; Canadian price level: CANSIM II V735319; U.S. price level: CANSIM V11123.

real exchange rate has a tendency to return to a mean value of approximately 1.0. This may indicate that the large deviation from equilibrium that began in the early 1990s may be a short run phenomenon, and the nominal exchange rate may appreciate to bring the real exchange rate back to equilibrium. This, of course, is the same prediction of the Big Mac PPP index.

Since both $P_f$ and $P$ in the formula for the real exchange rate represent baskets of goods specific to each country, PPP does not necessarily imply that the real exchange rate should be equal to 1. Rather, in practice, PPP is taken to mean that in the long run, the real exchange rate will return to its average level. (This is sometimes called *relative PPP*.) Thus, if the real exchange rate is above its long run average level, PPP implies that the exchange rate will fall.

## POLICY IN *ACTION*

### Monetary Policy, Inflation, and the Exchange Rate

In Chapter 3, we learned that, in the long run, monetary policy controls the rate of inflation through the quantity theory of money. In this chapter, we discussed how, in the long run, purchasing power parity (PPP) will determine the long run value of the nominal exchange rate. If we look at PPP in a more dynamic framework, we can see that it predicts that changes in the nominal exchange rate will come about because of inflation differentials between two countries. For instance, if the inflation rate in Canada is greater than the inflation rate in the United States, over the long run, PPP would predict that the nominal exchange rate should depreciate. Since the long run inflation rate is determined by monetary policy, this is the sense in which monetary policy also controls long run appreciation or depreciation in the nominal exchange rate.

You can see from Figure 5-6 that there was a long, slow depreciation of the Canadian dollar, starting shortly after Canada went to a flexible exchange rate system in the early 1970s. Some of this depreciation was caused by the fact that through much of the three decades starting in the 1960s, Canada's inflation performance was worse than that of the United States. Thus, monetary policy played some role in this depreciation.

However, through the 1990s, Canadian inflation was somewhat lower than that in the United States, even though the exchange rate appeared to be almost continually under depreciation pressure. This prompted a great number of economists to predict that the Canadian dollar was undervalued and would have to appreciate at some point. In early 2003, the Canadian dollar underwent a sharp appreciation. Some of this appreciation has to be attributed to the Bank of Canada's continuing successful fight against inflation in Canada.

# Working with Data

In this section, we are going to help you reproduce the real exchange rate, graphed in Figure 5-7. First, you will need the Canadian and U.S. Consumer Price Indexes. You will find the CANSIM numbers for these series in the source note for Figure 5-7. These series are available monthly, so you should convert them to annual figures by taking the average. The Canada-U.S. exchange rate is available on CANSIM from 1951. Again, you should convert from monthly to annual by taking the average. The exchange rate from the historical statistics for 1914 to 1950 are given below.

| | | | | | | | |
|---|---|---|---|---|---|---|---|
| 1914 | 0.9992 | 1924 | 1.0127 | 1934 | 0.99 | 1944 | 1.105 |
| 1915 | 1.0039 | 1925 | 1.0002 | 1935 | 1.0051 | 1945 | 1.1045 |
| 1916 | 1.0018 | 1926 | 0.9998 | 1936 | 1.0006 | 1946 | 1.0025 |
| 1917 | 1.0018 | 1927 | 1 | 1937 | 0.9999 | 1947 | 1.0025 |
| 1918 | 1.0159 | 1928 | 1.0009 | 1938 | 1.0056 | 1948 | 1.0025 |
| 1919 | 1.0357 | 1929 | 1.0076 | 1939 | 1.037 | 1949 | 1.0308 |
| 1920 | 1.1247 | 1930 | 1.0016 | 1940 | 1.105 | 1950 | 1.0892 |
| 1921 | 1.1164 | 1931 | 1.0381 | 1941 | 1.105 | | |
| 1922 | 1.0154 | 1932 | 1.1352 | 1942 | 1.105 | | |
| 1923 | 1.0196 | 1933 | 1.0874 | 1943 | 1.105 | | |

The real exchange rate is given by the equation

$$R = \frac{eP_f}{P} \tag{10}$$

In Figure 5-7, we chose 1973 = 100 as a base year for $R$. If you have calculated equation (10) correctly, you will find that in 1973, $R = 1.580071$. Therefore, you should divide $R$ in every year by 1.580071. If you plot this, you will find that you have reproduced Figure 5-7.

## C H A P T E R   S U M M A R Y

▶ The balance of payments is a record of transactions of Canadians with foreigners. It is composed of the current account and the capital account. Current account balance and capital account balance must sum to zero.

▶ Canada is a small open economy, which takes the foreign (world) real interest rate as exogenous. In equilibrium, the foreign real interest rate does not have to equal the domestic real interest rate, and domestic savings does not have to equal domestic investment.

▶ If domestic savings is greater than domestic investment, then there is a balance of trade surplus and net foreign lending is positive. If domestic savings is less than domestic investment, then there is a balance of trade deficit and net foreign lending is negative.

www.mcgrawhill.ca/college/dornbusch

▶ The foreign exchange rate can be measured as a nominal exchange rate or as a real exchange rate. The nominal exchange rate is the dollar price of a unit of foreign exchange. The real exchange rate is a measure of foreign prices to domestic prices, measured in a common currency.

▶ Purchasing power parity predicts that the exchange rate will move to equate purchasing power internationally.

## K E Y   T E R M S

open economy, *99*
closed economy, *99*
balance of payments, *99*
current account, *99*
net exports, *99*
merchandise trade balance, *99*
capital and financial account, *100*
official reserves, *101*

net foreign investment, *102*
foreign (or world) real rate of
   interest, *102*
twin deficit, *104*
nominal exchange rate, *105*
flexible (or floating) exchange
   rate, *105*
currency appreciation or
   depreciation, *105*

fixed rate system, *105*
intervention, *105*
managed, or dirty, floating, *106*
multilateral exchange rate, *109*
purchasing power parity
   (PPP), *109*
real exchange rate, *110*

## D I S C U S S I O N   Q U E S T I O N S

1. Carefully explain the relationship between current account balance and net exports.

2. It is sometimes said that a central bank is a necessary element for a balance of payments deficit. What is the explanation for this argument?

3. In the text, we measured the nominal exchange rate as the Canadian dollar price of one U.S. dollar. You will often hear the exchange rate expressed as the U.S. dollar price of one Canadian dollar. In order to be sure that you understand the difference, rewrite the paragraph on depreciation and appreciation, measuring the exchange rate in U.S. dollars.

4. What is the difference between depreciation and devaluation?

5. Explain the purchasing power parity (PPP) theory of the exchange rate. Indicate whether there is any circumstance in which you would not expect this theory to hold.

6. Why do economists care whether PPP holds or not?

7. Explain why, in a small open economy, national savings does not have to equal investment.

## A P P L I C A T I O N   Q U E S T I O N S

1. In Canada, we worry a great deal about our exchange rate with the United States. Exchange rates for other countries are available in CANSIM II table 1760064. Plot some of these and comment on whether Canada is depreciating against currencies other than that of the United States.

2. Go to *The Economist* Web page (see Box 5-2) and look at the data on implied Big Mac PPP level of the exchange rates for all of the countries in the sample. List which exchange rates are undervalued and which are overvalued according to the Big Mac PPP index.

3. In Box 5-1, we discussed the euro. You can find data on the Canada-euro exchange rate in CANSIM II V121742. Plot these data and discuss the evolution of the Canada-euro exchange rate.

www.mcgrawhill.ca/college/dornbusch

4. Assume a small open economy where GDP equals $100 billion and government spending is $25 billion. Consumption, investment, and the foreign (world) real interest rate are given by:

| $r_f$ | $C$ | $I$ |
|---|---|---|
| 6% | $50 billion | $15 billion |
| 5% | $55 billion | $17 billion |
| 4% | $60 billion | $20 billion |
| 3% | $65 billion | $23 billion |

For each value of $r^f$, calculate national savings and foreign lending.

5. Figure 5-8 shows the cost of barley in England relative to its cost in Holland, measured in a common currency, over a long span of time. What can be concluded about PPP from this figure?

**FIGURE 5-8**

Price is silver price.

**LOG RELATIVE ENGLISH TO DUTCH BARLEY PRICES, 1367–1985**

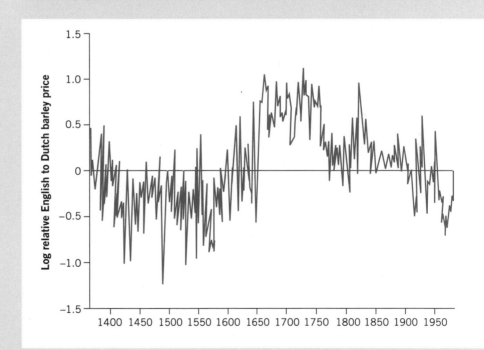

SOURCE: Kenneth A. Froot, Michael Kim, and Kenneth Rogoff, "The Law of One Price over 700 Years," NBER Working Paper 5132, 1996.

www.mcgrawhill.ca/college/dornbusch

# 3

# THE ECONOMY IN THE SHORT RUN: BUSINESS CYCLES AND ADJUSTMENT

# BUSINESS CYCLES AND THE AGGREGATE DEMAND-AGGREGATE SUPPLY MODEL

## *LEARNING OBJECTIVES*

After reading and studying this chapter, you should be able to:

▶ *Identify business cycle movements in output, the unemployment rate, and the inflation rate.*

▶ *Understand that output and prices are determined by the interaction of aggregate supply and aggregate demand.*

▶ *Understand that the slope of the aggregate supply curve reflects assumptions concerning the economy's price adjustment mechanism.*

▶ *Understand that in the very short run, we assume that there is no price adjustment and the aggregate supply curve is horizontal.*

▶ *Understand that in the long run, we assume that prices are completely flexible and the aggregate supply curve is vertical.*

▶ *Understand that the aggregate demand curve slopes downward and shifts due to change in monetary or fiscal policy.*

▶ *Understand that changes in aggregate demand change output in the short run and change prices in the long run.*

A s we noted at the beginning of Chapter 1, macroeconomics is concerned with the behaviour of the economy as a whole—with booms and recessions, the economy's total output of goods and services, and the rates of inflation and unemployment. Having explored long run economic growth in the preceding chapters, we turn to the short run fluctuations that constitute the business cycle.

Business cycle swings can be large. For instance, in the Great Depression, output fell by nearly 30 percent; between 1931 and 1940, the unemployment rate averaged 18.8 percent. The Great Depression was the defining event for a generation. Post–World War II recessions have been much milder, but they still dominated the political scene when they occurred.

Inflation rates vary widely. A dollar stored under your mattress in 1975 would have bought less than 31 cents' worth of goods in 2000. In contrast, during the Great Depression, prices *dropped* by one-fourth.

The aggregate supply-aggregate demand model is the basic macroeconomic tool for studying output fluctuations and the determination of the price level and the inflation rate. We use this tool to understand why the economy deviates from a path of smooth growth over time and to explore the consequences of government policies intended to reduce unemployment, smooth output fluctuations, and maintain stable prices.

## 6-1 | BUSINESS CYCLES

**business cycle**

The more or less regular pattern of expansion (recovery) and contraction (recession) in economic activity around full employment output.

**expansion (recovery)**

A sustained period of rising real income.

**contraction (recession)**

That period of time in a business cycle when output is falling below full employment.

**potential GDP**

Output that is produced when all factors of production are fully employed.

**output gap**

Measures the difference between actual output and the output that could be produced at full employment, or potential output.

Changes in GDP, inflation, and unemployment are related through the **business cycle**. In Chapter 1, we defined a business cycle as the more or less regular pattern of **expansion (recovery)** and **contraction (recession)** in economic activity around full employment output. A stylized view of a business cycle is presented in Figure 6-1.

In Figure 6-1, the relatively straight line represents a hypothetical trend path of real GDP. This would be analogous to the very long run economic growth path of an economy, such as the one shown in Figure 1-5 in Chapter 1. This trend path of GDP represents full employment, or **potential GDP**. The other line in Figure 6-1 depicts hypothetical business cycle movements around trend GDP. During an expansion (or recovery), employment of factors of production increases, and production increases. Output can rise above potential because people work overtime and machinery is used for several shifts. Conversely, during a recession, unemployment increases and less output is produced than could be with the existing factors of production and technology.

Deviations of actual output from potential output are referred to as the **output gap**, as shown in equation (1).

$$\text{Output gap} = \text{Potential output} - \text{Actual output} \qquad (1)$$

Potential output is the amount of goods and services that could be produced if the economy was operating at full employment. We never actually know what potential output is, and estimates of potential output vary depending on the methodology used. In Figure 6-2, we show one measure of potential output, along with actual output, over the period 1961–2002.[1]

---

[1] The details of the calculation of potential output are shown in the Working with Data section of this chapter.

## FIGURE 6-1

The business cycle is the movement of current GDP around its trend path. At a cyclical peak, economic activity is high; at a trough, output is below trend.

### A STYLIZED GDP BUSINESS CYCLE

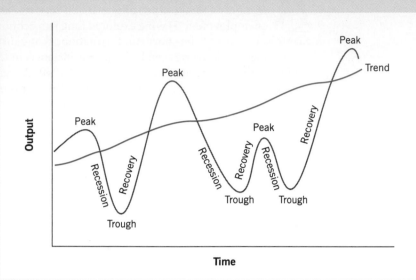

www.bankofcanada.ca/en/
backgrounders/bg-p5.htm

Figure 6-2 shows how actual output declines relative to potential output during recessionary periods. For instance, in the large recessions of the early 1980s and early 1990s, the output gap became quite large.

In addition to business cycle movements in output, the unemployment rate and the inflation rate also exhibit clear cyclical patterns. Figure 6-3 shows the cyclical movements in the unemployment rate over the period 1968 to 2002.

You can see in Figure 6-3 that unemployment increases very quickly during recessions, especially during the recession of the early 1980s. Notice that the response of unemployment during a cycle is not symmetric. In recovery, the unemployment rate decreases only slowly. Between the middle of 1981 and the end of 1982 (a period

## FIGURE 6-2

In this figure, recessions are shown as the shaded areas. During the recessions of the early 1980s and early 1990s, current output fell well below estimated potential output.

### ACTUAL AND POTENTIAL GDP, 1961–2002

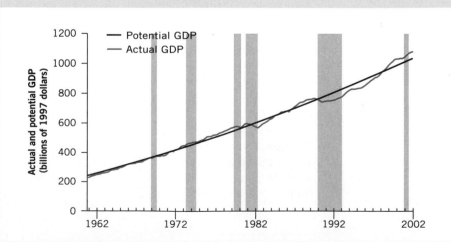

SOURCE: CANSIM II V1992259; potential GDP estimated by the authors.

## FIGURE 6-3

The unemployment rate increases during recessions, and decreases during expansions.

### THE CYCLICAL BEHAVIOUR OF THE UNEMPLOYMENT RATE, 1968–2002

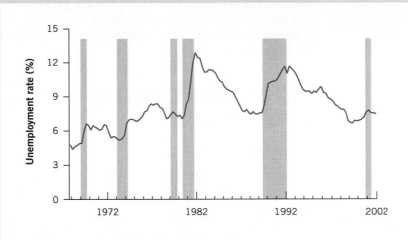

SOURCE: 1968–1975: *Bank of Canada Review*, various issues; 1976–2002: CANSIM II V2062815.

www.bankofcanada.ca/en/
inflation/index.htm

of recession), the unemployment rate rose from 7.1 percent to 12.9 percent. However, in the recovery of the mid-1980s, it took until 1989 for the unemployment rate to return to the 7 percent range.

The cyclical behaviour of the inflation rate is shown in Figure 6-4.

You can see in Figure 6-4 that there was a substantial build-up of inflation through the 1960s and 1970s. As we will see, this was caused primarily by expansionary aggregate demand policies on the part of the government. Notice how the inflation rate responds to the cycle in the economy. The recession of the early 1980s caused the inflation rate to drop from over 10 percent to approximately 5 percent, and the recession of the early 1990s brought the inflation rate down to less than 2 percent.

## FIGURE 6-4

During periods of recession, the inflation rate decreases.

### THE CYCLICAL BEHAVIOUR OF THE INFLATION RATE, 1961–2002

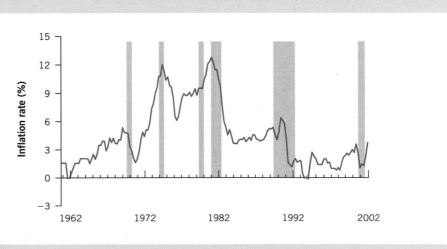

SOURCE: CANSIM II V735319.

www.canadianeconomy.gc.
ca/english/economy

The three preceding figures show how GDP, the unemployment rate, and the inflation rate are all related through the business cycle. Our model of aggregate demand and aggregate supply is designed to explain these cyclical movements. In the remainder of this chapter, we provide an introduction and overview of the aggregate demand-aggregate supply model. In Chapter 7, we develop the short run aggregate supply model more fully.

## 6-2 | INTRODUCTION TO AGGREGATE DEMAND AND AGGREGATE SUPPLY

### Aggregate Demand

**aggregate demand (AD) curve**
Shows combinations of the price level and the level of output for which the demanders of goods and services are in equilibrium.

The **aggregate demand (AD) curve** shows combinations of the price level and the level of output for which the demanders of goods and services—households, business, and government—are in equilibrium.[2] A typical AD curve is shown in Figure 6-5.

You can see in Figure 6-5 that the AD curve is downward sloping. The exact technical reasons for this downward slope will be detailed in Part 4 of this book. For now, we offer the following simplified explanation: Aggregate demand depends on the level of the *real* money stock. Along an AD curve, the level of the *nominal* money stock is constant. For a given nominal money stock, the real money stock depends on the level of prices. A higher price level with a given nominal money stock translates to a lower real money stock and lower aggregate demand. Therefore, the AD curve slopes downward.

**FIGURE 6-5**

The AD curve slopes downward, because, as the price level increases, with the nominal money stock held constant, the real money stock decreases. An increase in the nominal money stock shifts the AD curve outward. The vertical shift in the AD curve is proportional to the change in the nominal money stock. For a given level of income, $Y_0$, the level of the real money stock is unchanged after the shift in AD.

**THE AGGREGATE DEMAND (AD) CURVE**

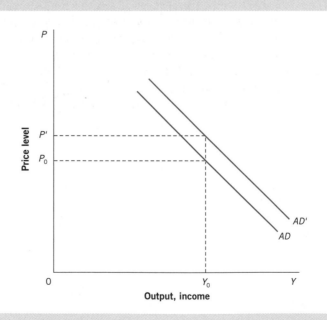

---

[2] This definition actually simplifies the theory of aggregate demand somewhat. As we will see in Chapter 12, aggregate demand involves an interaction of agents in the goods and money markets. We also defer discussion of the role of the foreign sector in the aggregate demand curve until Chapter 9.

Recall that any curve will shift due to an exogenous change. Therefore, a change in fiscal or monetary policy will shift the *AD* curve. For instance, an increase in the nominal money stock will shift the *AD* curve up and to the right. This shift is shown in Figure 6-5.

It is important for what follows to understand that an increase in the nominal money stock shifts the *AD* schedule up exactly in proportion to the increase in the nominal money stock. In Figure 6-5, this means that, for instance, a 10 percent increase in the nominal money stock will leave real spending unchanged if prices rise by 10 percent. Therefore, at point *P′* in Figure 6-5, the level of the real money stock is unchanged and the level of real spending is unchanged.

## Aggregate Supply

**aggregate supply (*AS*) curve**

Relationship between the amount of final goods and services produced in an economy and the price level.

**Keynesian aggregate supply curve**

Very short run horizontal aggregate supply curve.

**Classical aggregate supply curve**

Long run vertical *AS* curve.

In Chapter 1, we introduced the basic shapes that the **aggregate supply (*AS*) curve** could take. You will recall that these depended on the time frame being analyzed. The Keynesian and Classical *AS* curves are shown in Figure 6-6.

In the very short run, the **Keynesian aggregate supply curve** is horizontal, indicating that firms will supply whatever amount of goods are demanded at the existing price level. You can think of the Keynesian *AS* curve as being relevant for the very short run when firms can hire more labour without increasing the current wage.

As we saw in Chapter 3, the **Classical aggregate supply curve** is vertical, indicating that the same amount of goods will be supplied no matter what the price level. Remember that the Classical *AS* curve is based on the assumption of full market clearing, so that the labour market is in equilibrium with full employment of the labour force. In Chapter 7, we will expand our view of aggregate supply in the short run and develop an *AS* curve that is upward sloping. The time frame will be in between the very short run, when prices are assumed to be fixed (Keynesian *AS*), and the long run, when prices are assumed to be completely flexible (Classical *AS*).

---

**BOX 6-1**

### "Aggregate Supply" and "Aggregate Demand"—What's in a Name?

In Box 1-3 in Chapter 1, we discussed the important differences between the aggregate demand and supply models used in this book, and microeconomic demand and supply models. It is worth reiterating some of these important points here.

The aggregate demand and aggregate supply curves used in this chapter have the friendly, familiar appearance that you probably remember from your study of microeconomics. What's more, the mechanical workings of the model (demand shifts up...prices and quantities both rise..., etc.) are the same as the workings of a microeconomic supply and demand diagram. However, the economics underlying the aggregate supply–aggregate demand diagram is unrelated to the microeconomic version. (It's too bad that our macroeconomic version wasn't given a different name.) In particular, "price" in microeconomics means the ratio at which two goods trade: I'll give you two bags of candy in exchange for one economics lecture, for example. In contrast, in macroeconomics, "price" means the nominal price level, the cost of a basket of all of the goods we buy measured in money terms.

One particular item from macroeconomics provides a special opportunity for confusion. In microeconomics, supply curves are relatively flatter in the long run than in the short run, at least as a rough rule of thumb. The behaviour of aggregate supply is just the opposite. The aggregate supply curve is vertical in the long run and horizontal in the short run. (We will, of course, discuss why this is so.)

## FIGURE 6-6

### THE KEYNESIAN AND CLASSICAL AGGREGATE SUPPLY (AS) CURVES

The Keynesian *AS* curve is horizontal, indicating that any amount of output will be supplied at a given price. This is a very short run model. The Classical *AS* curve is vertical at the level of full employment income, $Y^*$. This is based on the assumptions of the Classical market clearing model discussed in Chapter 3.

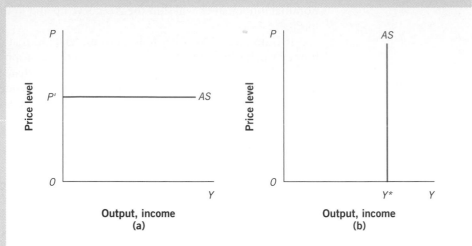

## 6-3 | AGGREGATE DEMAND POLICY UNDER ALTERNATIVE SUPPLY ASSUMPTIONS

Now we use the aggregate demand and supply model to study the effects of aggregate demand policy in the two extreme supply cases—Keynesian and Classical.

### The Keynesian Case

In Figure 6-7, we combine the aggregate demand schedule with the Keynesian aggregate supply schedule. The initial equilibrium is at point E, where *AS* and *AD* intersect.

Consider an increase in aggregate demand—such as increased government spending, a cut in taxes, or an increase in the money supply—that shifts the *AD* curve

## FIGURE 6-7

### AGGREGATE DEMAND EXPANSION: THE KEYNESIAN CASE

In the very short run, the *AS* curve is horizontal. When the *AD* shifts to the right, output increases, while the price level remains constant.

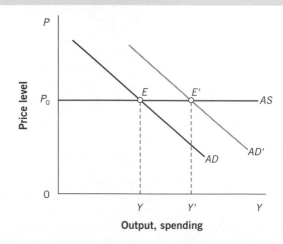

BOX
6-2

## Vertical or Horizontal: Is It All a Matter of Timing?

The text describes the aggregate supply curve as vertical in the long run, horizontal in the very short run, and implicitly having an intermediate slope in the short run. This picture oversimplifies in a way that can be very important for policy. The truth is that the aggregate supply curve, even in the short run, is really a curve and not a straight line.

The figure below shows that at low levels of output, below potential output $Y^*$, the aggregate supply curve is quite flat. When output is below potential, there is very little tendency for prices of goods and factors (wages) to fall. Conversely, where output is above potential, the aggregate supply curve is steep and prices tend to rise continuously. The effects of changes in aggregate demand on output and prices therefore depend on the level of actual relative to potential output.

In a recession, we are on the flat part of the aggregate supply curve, so demand management policies can be effective at boosting the economy without having much effect on the price level. However, as the economy approaches full employment, policy makers must be wary of too much stimulus to avoid running the aggregate demand curve up the vertical portion of the aggregate supply curve shown in the figure.

### AGGREGATE DEMAND AND NON-LINEAR AGGREGATE SUPPLY

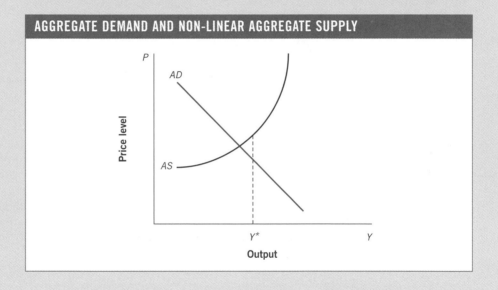

out and to the right, from $AD$ to $AD'$. The new equilibrium is at point $E'$, where output has increased. Because firms are willing to supply any amount of output at the level of prices $P_0$, there is no effect on prices. The only effect in Figure 6-7 is an increase in output and employment.

## The Classical Case

In the Classical case, the aggregate supply curve is vertical at the full employment level of output. Firms will supply the level of output $Y^*$ whatever the price level. Under this supply assumption, we obtain results very different from those reached using the Keynesian model. Now the price level is not given but, rather, depends on the interaction of supply and demand.

**FIGURE 6-8**    **AGGREGATE DEMAND EXPANSION: THE CLASSICAL CASE**

Due to the assumption of full market clearing, a shift in the *AD* curve leads to only a price level increase in the long run.

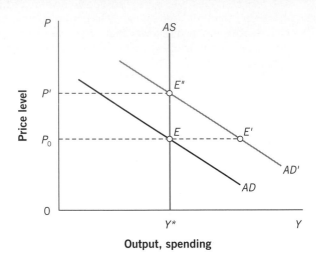

In Figure 6-8, we study the effect of an aggregate demand expansion under Classical supply assumptions. The aggregate supply curve is *AS*, with equilibrium initially at point *E*. Note that at point *E* there is full employment because, by assumption, there is full market clearing.

The expansion shifts the *AD* curve from *AD* to *AD'*. In the very short run, if the price level was to remain at $P_0$, the economy would move to point *E'*, as shown in Figure 6-7. However, this would cause excess demand in the goods and labour markets, which would force up wages and prices. As the Classical model assumes instant adjustment, the economy would go directly to point *E''*, with no change in output, and a higher price level. Chapter 7 is devoted to discussing the adjustment of the economy to points like *E''*.

**BOX 6-3**

## Keynesian and Classical—Short Run and Long Run

We have repeatedly used the terms "Keynesian" and "Classical" to describe assumptions of a horizontal or vertical aggregate supply curve. Note that these are not alternative models providing alternative descriptions of the world. Both models are true: The Keynesian model holds in the short run, and the Classical model holds in the long run. Economists do have contentious disagreements over the time horizons in which each model applies. Almost all economists agree that the Keynesian model holds over a period of a few months or less and the Classical model holds when the time frame is a decade or more. Unfortunately, the interesting time frame for policy relevance is several quarters to a few years. The speed with which prices adjust—that is, how long it takes the aggregate supply curve to rotate from horizontal to vertical—is an area of active research.

# POLICY IN *ACTION*

## Supply-Side Economics: Was This a Demand or Supply-Side Policy?

In the 1980s, supply-side economics began to be considered seriously by politicians in Canada and the United States. In the United States, the Reagan administration actually pursued a supply-side economics policy for a period of time. Supply-side economics is basically the idea that cutting tax rates will increase the long run aggregate supply enough that total tax collection will rise.

However, not realized at the time was that cutting tax rates will affect both the supply and demand sides of the economy, as illustrated in the figure below.

As a result of a tax cut, the aggregate demand curve shifts from $AD$ to $AD'$, and the aggregate supply curve shifts from $AS$ to $AS'$. However, it is now well known that the shift in the aggregate supply curve will be less than the shift in the aggregate demand curve. In the short run, the economy moves from $E$ to $E'$. As a result, total tax revenues fall proportionately less than does the tax rate. This is purely an aggregate demand effect. In the long run, the economy moves to $E''$. GDP is higher, but only by a very small amount. As a result, total tax collections fall and the deficit rises. In addition, prices are permanently higher. This appears to be exactly what happened as a result of the Reagan experiment.

### EFFECTS OF CUTTING TAX RATES ON AGGREGATE DEMAND AND SUPPLY

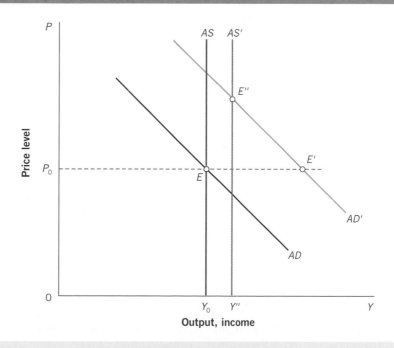

## *Working with Data*

In this section, we are going to help you reproduce the fluctuations of output around potential GDP that we graphed in Figure 6-2. The data that were used for actual GDP were quarterly observations on GDP measured in constant 1997 dollars, seasonally adjusted: CANSIM II V1992259. We created potential output by running an ordinary least squares regression of GDP on a constant, time and time squared. The estimated equation is

$$GDP = 239.42 + 3.52(time) + 0.00719(time^2)$$

This equation can be used to create a synthetic series for potential GDP. Time is a variable that equals 1,2,…,168. Therefore, the first observation on potential GDP equals

$$Potential\ GDP = 239.42 + 3.52(1) + 0.00719(1^2)$$

The second observation is

$$Potential\ GDP = 239.42 + 3.52(2) + 0.00719(2^2)$$

You should be able to calculate the entire potential GDP series in this manner. The dates of the recessions are: 70:02 – 70:03; 74:02 – 75:01; 80:01 – 80:03; 81:03 – 82:04; 90:02 – 92:04; and 01:04 – 02:01. You should now be able to reproduce Figure 6-2.

## CHAPTER SUMMARY

▶ The business cycle is the more or less regular pattern of expansion (recovery) and contraction (recession) in economic activity around full employment output.

▶ Movements in output, the unemployment rate, and the inflation rate are related through the business cycle.

▶ The output gap measures deviations of current output from potential output.

▶ The aggregate supply-aggregate demand model is used to show the determination of the equilibrium levels of both output and prices.

▶ The aggregate demand curve shows for each price level the quantity of goods demanded.

▶ For any given *AD* curve, the level of the nominal money stock is constant. As the price level increases for a given nominal money stock, the real money stock decreases. Therefore, the aggregate demand curve slopes downward.

▶ A change in the level of the nominal money stock or a change in fiscal policy will shift the aggregate demand curve.

www.mcgrawhill.ca/college/dornbusch

▶ An increase in the nominal money stock will shift the aggregate demand curve upward by an amount proportional to the change in the money stock.

▶ The Keynesian aggregate supply curve is horizontal, and the Classical aggregate supply curve is vertical.

▶ Supply-side economics makes the claim that reducing tax rates generates very large increases in aggregate supply.

## K E Y   T E R M S

business cycle, *119*
expansion (recovery), *119*
contraction (recession), *119*

potential GDP, *119*
output gap, *119*
aggregate demand (*AD*) curve, *122*
aggregate supply (*AS*) curve, *123*

Keynesian aggregate supply
   curve, *123*
Classical aggregate supply curve, *123*

## D I S C U S S I O N   Q U E S T I O N S

1. What do the aggregate supply and aggregate demand curves describe?

2. Explain why the Classical supply curve is vertical. What are the mechanisms that ensure continued full employment of labour in the Classical case?

3. What relationship is captured by the aggregate supply curve? Can you provide an intuitive justification for it?

4. How does the Keynesian aggregate supply curve differ from the Classical one? Is one of these specifications more appropriate than the other? Explain, being careful to state the time horizon to which your answer applies.

5. The aggregate supply and demand model looks, and sounds, very similar to the standard supply and demand model of microeconomics. How, if at all, are these models related?

## A P P L I C A T I O N   Q U E S T I O N S

1. **a.** If the government was to reduce income taxes, how would the reduction affect output and the price level in the short run? In the long run? Show how the aggregate supply and demand curves would be affected in both cases.

   **b.** What is supply-side economics? Is it likely to be effective, given your answer to (a)?

2. Suppose that the government increases spending from $G$ to $G'$ while simultaneously raising taxes in such a way that, at the initial level of output, the budget remains balanced.

   **a.** Show the effect of this change on the aggregate demand schedule.

   **b.** How does this affect output and the price level in the Keynesian case?

   **c.** How does this affect output and the price level in the Classical case?

 3. In CANSIM, there is a series called Industrial Capacity Utilization (CANSIM II V142812), which is one measure of the state of the economy relative to the business cycle. Retrieve this series and plot it together with the recession dates used for Figures 6-2 through 6-4. These dates are 1970:01–1070:02; 1974:02–1975:01; 1980:01–1980:03; 1981:01–1982:04; 1990:02–1992:04; 01:04–02:01. Comment on the cyclical behaviour of capacity utilization.

# CHAPTER 7

# WAGE AND PRICE ADJUSTMENT:

## The Phillips Curve and Aggregate Supply

### *LEARNING OBJECTIVES*

After reading and studying this chapter, you should be able to:

▶ *Understand that the Phillips curve relates the change in wages to the unemployment rate. The Phillips curve gradually came to mean the relationship between the change in prices (inflation) and the unemployment rate.*

▶ *Understand that the short run aggregate supply curve and the Phillips curve both describe the price adjustment mechanism of the economy.*

▶ *Understand that the short run aggregate supply curve shifts due to changes in expectations of the price level.*

▶ *Understand that expectations can be modelled as being formed in an adaptive manner or in a rational manner.*

## 7-1 | THE PHILLIPS CURVE

I n Chapter 3, we derived the Classical aggregate supply (*AS*) curve from the production function

$$Y = F(\overline{K}, N) \tag{1}$$

Remember that we assumed that the capital stock was fixed ($\overline{K}$) and that there was no technological change. In this situation, output depended only on supply and demand in the labour market. In this chapter, we maintain these assumptions.

In long run Classical labour market analysis, we assume fully flexible wages and prices, so that the nominal wage is assumed to move quickly and the labour market will always be in equilibrium. Given the Classical market clearing assumptions, the equilibrium amount of employment, $N^*$, is considered to be full employment in the labour market. The unemployment rate is related to the level of employment through the equation

$$u_t - u^* = \frac{N^* - N_t}{N_t} \tag{2}$$

where $u^*$ is the full employment level of the unemployment rate, which we have referred to as the *natural rate of unemployment*. Therefore, when the current level of employment equals the full employment level ($N_t = N^*$), the current level of unemployment equals the full-employment level of the unemployment rate ($u_t = u^*$). Also, given the production function [equation (1)], the equilibrium amount of output produced, $Y^*$, is full employment output.

In this chapter, we are considering the transition period between the very short run (horizontal aggregate supply) and the long run (vertical aggregate supply). In this period, the Classical long run assumption of fully flexible wages and prices is no longer appropriate. We assume that wage and price adjustment is sluggish or, in the terminology used in Chapter 1, that wages and prices are sticky. If the nominal wage rate does not move infinitely quickly, then there can be some level of employment, $N$, that is not equal to the full employment level of employment, $N^*$. Put another way, slowly adjusting wages will lead to some unemployment rate, $u$, that is not the full employment level of the unemployment rate $u^*$. We can describe this adjustment by the equation

$$g_w = -\epsilon(u_t - u^*) \tag{3}$$

where $g_w$ is the growth rate of the nominal wage, or wage inflation, given by

$$g_w = \frac{W_t - W_{t-1}}{W_{t-1}} \tag{4}$$

Notice that equation (3) describes the same type of adjustment as was assumed in deriving the Classical *AS*: Excess demand or supply, as measured by deviations of the current unemployment rate from the full employment level of the unemployment rate, will lead to nominal wage change. However, we now assume that this wage change is sticky, or slower than the speed of adjustment that was assumed in the Classical model. The amount of stickiness in wage adjustment is measured by the parameter $\epsilon$. Notice that under the Classical fully flexible assumption, $\epsilon = \infty$ (vertical *AS*) and in the very short run, $\epsilon = 0$ (horizontal *AS*). In this chapter, we assume that $\epsilon$ is somewhere in between these two extremes.

## The Phillips Curve

**Phillips curve**

An inverse relationship between the rate of unemployment and the rate of change in the nominal wage.

It turns out that equation (3) is nothing more than a simple **Phillips curve**. In 1958, A.W. Phillips, then a professor at the London School of Economics, published a comprehensive study of wage behaviour in the United Kingdom for the years 1861 to 1957.[1] The main finding of Phillips' article is that there is an inverse relationship between the rate of unemployment and the rate of change in the nominal wage. This became known as the *Phillips curve*. A typical Phillips curve is shown in Figure 7-1.

Notice that the Phillips curve describes sticky adjustment in the labour market, given by equation (3). The slope of the Phillips curve is given by $\epsilon$, the speed of adjustment in the labour market. The higher $\epsilon$ is, the faster wages are assumed to adjust and the steeper the Phillips curve is.

The Phillips curve implies that wages and prices adjust slowly to changes in aggregate demand. Why? Suppose the economy is in equilibrium, with prices stable and unemployment at the natural rate. Now, assume that there is an increase in the money stock of, say, 10 percent. Prices and wages both have to rise by 10 percent for the economy to get back to equilibrium. However, the Phillips curve shows that for wages to rise by an extra 10 percent, the unemployment rate will have to fall. That will cause the rate of wage increase to go up. Wages will start rising, prices will also rise, and eventually the economy will return to the full employment level of output and unemployment. This point can be readily seen by rewriting equation (3), using the definition of the rate of wage inflation, in order to look at the level of wages today relative to the past level.

$$W_t = W_{t-1}[1 - \epsilon(u_t - u^*)] \tag{5}$$

For wages to rise above their previous level, unemployment must fall below the natural rate. The original Phillips curve estimate by A.W. Phillips is reproduced as Figure 7-2.

---

**FIGURE 7-1**

**THE PHILLIPS CURVE**

The Phillips curve is an inverse relationship between the rate of unemployment and the rate of change in nominal wages. The higher the rate of unemployment, the lower the rate of wage inflation.

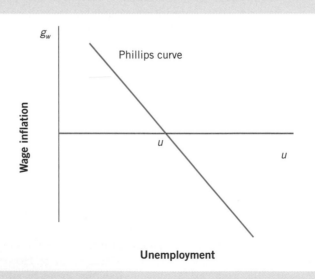

---

[1] A.W. Phillips, "The Relation Between Unemployment and the Rate of Change of Money Wages in the United Kingdom, 1861–1957," *Economica*, November 1958.

## *FIGURE 7-2*

When A.W. Phillips first estimated the original Phillips curve, he was interested in the relationship between the rate of change of the nominal wage (vertical axis) and the unemployment rate (horizontal axis). The fitted curve is non-linear, as opposed to the linear curves that we estimate in this chapter.

### THE ORIGINAL PHILLIPS CURVE FOR THE UNITED KINGDOM

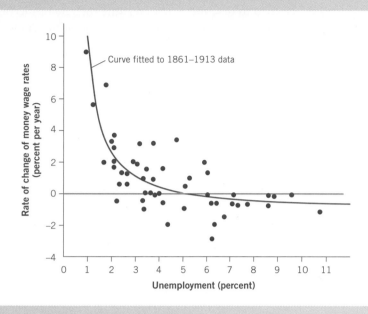

Curve fitted to 1861–1913 data

SOURCE: A.W. Phillips, "The Relation Between Unemployment and the Rate of Change of Money Wages in the United Kingdom, 1861–1957," *Economica*, November 1958.

### BOX 7-1

## The Canadian Wage Phillips Curve, 1940–2002

When A.W. Phillips first estimated the curve that bears his name, he was investigating the relationship between the rate of change in nominal wages and the unemployment rate. In the text, we have estimated Phillips curves using the rate of change of consumer prices (price inflation). Below, we show an estimated Phillips curve for Canada, using the rate of change of nominal wages and the unemployment rate, over the period 1940 to 2002.

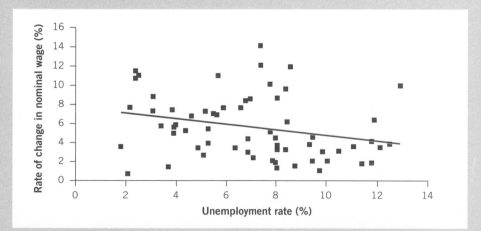

SOURCE: 1921–1945: *Historical Statistics of Canada*, M.C. Urquhart (ed.), (Macmillan: 1965); 1946–1975: Statistics Canada, *Historical Statistics of Canada*, Publication 11-516-XIE; 1976–2002: CANSIM II V2062815; wage rate: Statistics Canada, *Historical Statistics of Canada*, Publication 11-516-XIE and CANSIM II V174072. All historical statistics were adjusted by the authors to be consistent with the CANSIM II series.

Although Phillips' own curve relates the rate of increase of wages, or wage inflation, to unemployment, as in equation (3), the term *Phillips curve* gradually came to be used to describe a curve relating the rate of increase in prices, or price inflation, to the unemployment rate. This version of the Phillips curve is described by

$$\pi_t = - \epsilon(u_t - u^*) \tag{6}$$

where $\pi_t$ is price inflation, given by

$$\pi_t = \frac{P_t - P_{t-1}}{P_{t-1}} \tag{7}$$

Figure 7-3 shows the version of a Phillips curve given by equation (6) for the Canadian economy over the period 1960 to 1969.

This figure shows that the Phillips curve appears consistent with the data over the period of the 1960s. As inflation increased almost steadily over the 1960s, the unemployment rate fell continually.

The Phillips curve rapidly became a cornerstone of macroeconomic policy analysis. It suggested that policy makers could *choose* different combinations of unemployment and inflation rates. This choice is often referred to as a **policy trade-off**. For instance, if low unemployment was a policy goal, this could be attained at the cost of high inflation. This would be consistent with the situation in the late 1960s, as shown in Figure 7-3. Conversely, if low inflation was a policy goal, this could be attained at the price of higher unemployment, as in the early 1960s.

However, we must be careful in interpreting this early Phillips curve. The suggestion that there is some policy trade-off must be only a short run possibility. We have already seen that, in the long run, the aggregate supply curve is vertical. Therefore, even if a short run trade-off does exist, there can be no long run policy trade-off between inflation and unemployment. We can reconcile these two views by altering the simple Phillips curve to include expectations.

**policy trade-off**

The choice made by policy makers of different combinations of unemployment and inflation rates.

**FIGURE 7-3**

The Phillips curve for the 1960s gives a fairly accurate representation of the short run trade-off between inflation and unemployment over that period.

**THE CANADIAN PHILLIPS CURVE, 1960–1969**

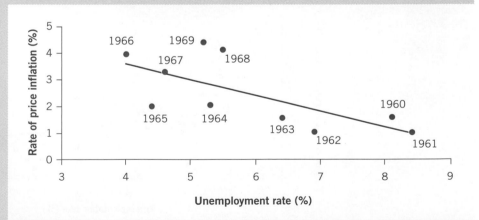

SOURCE: Unemployment rate: Statistics Canada, *Historical Statistics of Canada*, Publication 11-516-XIE; price inflation: CANSIM II V735319.

## The Role of Expectations

One major problem with the simple Philips curve described above is that it did not seem to give an accurate representation of the data after the 1960s. Figure 7-4 plots pairs of unemployment and inflation for the period 1960 to 2002.

It appears from Figure 7-4 that the Phillips curve does not fit the data after the 1960s.

**expected or anticipated inflation**

Inflation that people expect.

What is missing from the simple Phillips curve described above is **expected** or **anticipated inflation**. We know from our analysis of the labour market in Chapter 3 that workers and firms are concerned with the real wage. Consider the following situation: Suppose that you are offered a wage increase of 2 percent for next year. Whether you will be able to buy 2 percent more goods depends on what you expect the inflation rate to be over the next year. Suppose you believe (expect) that inflation will be 4 percent for the next year. In this situation, a 2 percent raise would make you 2 percent $(2 - 4)$ worse off. Therefore, you compare any wage increase to the expected inflation rate.

www.bankofcanada.ca/en/res/wp01-4.htm

We can rewrite equation (3), the original wage-inflation Phillips curve, to show that it is the excess of wage inflation over expected inflation that matters.

$$(g_w - \pi^e) = -\epsilon(u_t - u^\star) \tag{8}$$

where $\pi^e$ is the level of expected price inflation.

Maintaining the assumption of a constant real wage, actual inflation, $\pi$, will equal wage inflation. Thus, the equation for the modern version of the Phillips curve, the (inflation-) **expectations-augmented Phillips curve**, is

**expectations-augmented Phillips curve**

Phillips curve that includes inflationary expectations as a determinant of the inflation rate.

$$\pi_t = \pi^e - \epsilon(u_t - u^\star) \tag{9}$$

Note two critical properties of the modern Phillips curve:

▶  Expected inflation is passed one for one into actual inflation.

▶  Unemployment is at the natural rate when actual inflation equals expected inflation.

---

*FIGURE 7-4*

No single Phillips curve appears to accurately represent the data over the period 1960–2002.

### INFLATION AND UNEMPLOYMENT, 1960–2002

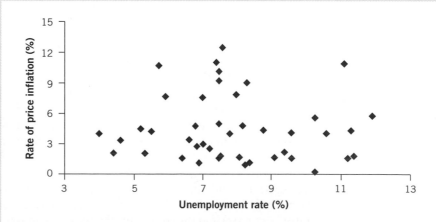

SOURCE: 1960–1975: Statistics Canada, *Historical Statistics of Canada*, Publication 11-516-XIE; 1976–2002: CANSIM II V2062815; inflation: CANSIM II V735319.

**adaptive expectations**

Individuals are assumed to take an average of past actual price levels to form their expectation of the current price level.

**static expectations**

Individuals form their expectations by assuming that the expected price level equals last period's actual price level.

**rational expectations**

Individuals do not make systematic errors in forming their expectations; expectational errors are corrected immediately, so that on average, expectations of the price level are correct.

We know that the Phillips curve will shift if expectations of the price inflation rate change. The crucial question is: How do expectations change? It is possible that individuals form their expectations by looking at the recent past. The assumption underlying this possibility is called **adaptive expectations**. Under the adaptive expectations assumption, individuals are assumed to take an average of past actual price levels to form their expectation of the current price level. A very simple form of adaptive expectations is called **static expectations**, which says that individuals form their expectations by assuming that the expected price level equals last period's actual price level.

$$\pi_t^e = \pi_{t-1} \tag{10}$$

One of the problems with assuming static expectations is that, if the inflation rate is moving, expectations of the inflation rate are always one period behind and, therefore, always wrong. In spite of this, given that expectations may be very difficult to form in the real world, static expectations may represent a convenient rule of thumb. However, it has been suggested that a better manner in which to model expectations would be to assume that expectations are formed in a rational manner. The assumption that underlies **rational expectations** is that individuals do not make systematic errors in forming their expectations. An equation that describes rational expectations is

$$\pi_t^e = \pi_t + \eta_t \tag{11}$$

Under rational expectations, the expected inflation rate equals the actual inflation rate with a random error, $\eta_t$, which has a mean of zero. Under rational expectations, if there is an expectational error, it is corrected immediately so that, on average, expectations of the price level are correct.

We now have an additional factor determining the height of the short run Phillips curve. Instead of intersecting the natural rate of unemployment at zero, the modern Phillips curve intersects the natural rate at the level of expected inflation. Figure 7-5 shows stylized Phillips curves for the early 1980s (when inflation had been running 8 to 10 percent) and the late 1990s (when inflation had been running at about 2 percent).

Firms and workers may adjust their expectations of inflation in light of the recent history of inflation.[2] The short run Phillips curves in Figure 7-5 reflect the low level of inflation that was expected in the late 1990s and the much higher level that was expected in the early 1980s. The curves have two properties you should note. First, the curves have the same short run trade-off between unemployment and inflation; that is to say, the *slopes are equal*. Second, in the late 1990s, full employment was compatible with roughly 2 percent annual inflation; in the early 1980s, full employment was compatible with roughly 9 percent inflation.

The height of the short run Phillips curve, the level of expected inflation, $\pi^e$, moves up and down over time in response to the changing expectations of firms and workers. *The role of expected inflation in moving the Phillips curve adds another automatic adjustment mechanism to the aggregate supply side of the economy.* When high aggregate demand moves the economy up and to the left along the short run Phillips curve, inflation results. If the inflation persists, people come to expect inflation in the future ($\pi^e$ rises) and the short run Phillips curve moves up.

---

[2] How quickly firms and workers adjust and the extent to which they look to the future rather than to recent history are matters of some dispute.

**FIGURE 7-5**

**INFLATION EXPECTATIONS AND THE SHORT RUN PHILLIPS CURVE**

In the short run, a Phillips curve is indexed by the level of expected inflation. Thus, the short run Phillips curve from the early 1980s, when expected inflation was approximately 9 percent, is much higher than the short run Phillips curve from the late 1990s, when expected inflation was approximately 2 percent.

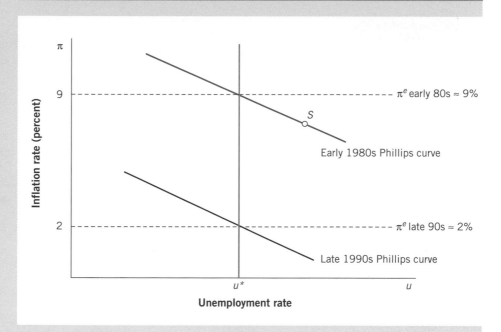

## Does the Augmented Phillips Curve Fit the Data?

We saw in Figure 7-4 that the simple Phillips curve does not fit the data particularly well. The above discussion suggests that adding expectations of inflation to the Phillips curve should give us different Phillips curves for different expected inflation regimes, as summarized in Figure 7-5. The problem with trying to graph equation (8) is that there is no generally accepted manner in which to measure expectations of inflation. For now, we adopt the assumption used in Figure 7-5 that expectations of inflation are adjusted according to the recent history of the actual inflation rate. If we make this assumption, then the data are consistent with equation (8), with three different expected inflation regimes. This is plotted in Figure 7-6

There are two important features to notice about Figure 7-6. First, the data appear generally consistent with the theoretical augmented Phillips curves shown in Figure 7-5. When inflation was in the neighbourhood of 8 to 10 percent in the 1970s and early 1980s, the Phillips curve was very high. As inflation came down in the 1980s, expectations began to shift downward, as did the Phillips curve. By the 1990s, inflation was approximately equal to that in the 1960s, and the Phillips curves from the two periods are virtually identical.

The second important point to notice is that, as asserted above, each of the estimated Phillips curves in Figure 7-6 appears to have approximately the same slope. That is, the short run trade-off appears relatively flat. For instance, the slope of the Phillips curve from the 1960s equals approximately −0.5, indicating that an increase of one percentage point in unemployment reduces inflation by only about one-half of one percentage point.

### FIGURE 7-6

### FOUR SHORT RUN PHILLIPS CURVES

All estimated short run Phillips curves are consistent with a very flat short run trade-off. High expected inflation in the late 1970s and early 1980s led to a higher Phillips curve. As the inflation rate gradually lowered, expectations of inflation decreased and the Phillips curve shifted downward. The Phillips curve from the 1960s is virtually identical to the Phillips curve of the late 1990s.

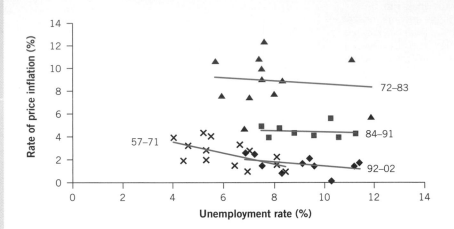

SOURCE: 1960–1975: Statistics Canada, *Historical Statistics of Canada*, Publication 11-516-XIE; 1976–2002: CANSIM II V2062815; inflation: CANSIM II V735319.

### BOX 7-2

## Why Are Wages Sticky?

In the Classical theory of supply, wages adjust instantly to ensure that output is always at the full-employment level. But output is not always at the full employment level, and the Phillips curve suggests that wages adjust slowly in response to changes in unemployment. The key question in the theory of aggregate supply is: Why does the nominal wage adjust slowly to shifts in demand? In other words: Why are wages sticky? *Wages are sticky, or wage adjustment is sluggish, when wages move slowly over time, rather than being fully and immediately flexible, so as to ensure full employment at every point in time.*

Although there are different approaches to macroeconomics, each school of thought has had to try to explain why there is a Phillips curve or, equivalently, the reasons for wage stickiness. The explanations are not mutually exclusive, and we shall therefore briefly mention several of the leading approaches.

### IMPERFECT INFORMATION—MARKET CLEARING

Some economists have sought to explain the Phillips curve in a context in which markets clear: Wages are fully flexible but adjust slowly because expectations are temporarily wrong. In the 1960s, Milton Friedman and Edmund Phelps developed models in which, when nominal wages go up because prices have risen, workers mistakenly believe their real wage has risen and so are willing to work more.[*] Thus, in the short run, until workers realize that the higher nominal wage is merely a result of a higher price level, an increase in the nominal

---

[*] Milton Friedman, "The Role of Monetary Policy," *American Economic Review*, March 1968; Edmund S. Phelps, "Phillips Curves, Expectations of Inflation, and Optimal Unemployment over Time," *Economica*, August 1967. See also Edmund Phelps, "A Review of Unemployment," *Journal of Economic Literature*, September 1992.

**BOX**

**7-2**

## Why Are Wages Sticky? cont'd

wage is associated with a higher level of output and less unemployment. In these models, the slow adjustment of wages arises from workers' slow reactions to, or *imperfect information* about, changes in prices.

### COORDINATION PROBLEMS

The *coordination approach* to the Phillips curve focuses more on the process by which firms adjust their prices when demand changes than it does on wages.[*] Suppose there is an increase in the money stock. Ultimately, as we know from Chapter 6, prices will go up in the same proportion as the money supply, and output will be unchanged. However, if any one firm raises its price in proportion to the increase in the money stock, and no other firm does, then the single firm that has raised its price will lose business to the others. Of course, if all firms raised their prices in the same proportion, they would move immediately to the new equilibrium. But because the firms in an economy cannot get together to coordinate their price increases, each will raise prices slowly as the effects of the change in the money stock are felt through an increased demand for goods at the existing prices.

Coordination problems can also help explain why wages are sticky downward, that is, why they do not fall immediately when aggregate demand declines. Any firm cutting its wages while other firms do not will find its workers both annoyed and leaving the firm. If firms coordinated, they could all reduce wages together; however, since they generally cannot coordinate, wages go down slowly as individual firms cut the nominal wages of their employees, probably with those firms whose profits have been hardest hit moving first.[†]

### EFFICIENCY WAGES AND COSTS OF PRICE CHANGE

Efficiency wage theory focuses on the wage as a means of motivating labour. The amount of effort workers make on the job is related to how well the job pays relative to alternatives. Firms may want to pay wages above the market clearing wage to ensure that employees work hard to avoid losing their good jobs.

Efficiency wage theory offers an explanation for slow changes in real wages but by itself does not explain why the average *nominal* wage is slow to change, although it does help explain the existence of unemployment. However, taken in combination with the fact that there are costs of changing prices, efficiency wage theory can generate some stickiness in nominal wages even if the costs of resetting prices are quite small.[††] Combining that stickiness with problems of coordinating, this theory can help account for nominal wage stickiness.

---

[*]See the papers under the heading "Coordination Failures" in N. Gregory Mankiw and David Romer (eds.), *New Keynesian Economics*, vol. 2 (Cambridge, MA: MIT Press, 1991).

[†]A very similar explanation for downward wage rigidity was presented by Keynes in his *General Theory* (New York: Macmillan, 1936).

[††]See George A. Akerlof and Janet L. Yellen, "A Near-Rational Model of the Business Cycle, with Wage and Price Inertia," *Quarterly Journal of Economics*, Supplement, 1985, and, edited by the same authors, *Efficiency Wage Models of the Labor Market* (New York: Cambridge University Press, 1986). See, too, "Costly Price Adjustment" in N. Gregory Mankiw and David Romer (eds.), *New Keynesian Economics*, vol. 1 (Cambridge, MA: MIT Press, 1991), and the discussion in Richard Layard, Stephen Nickell, and Richard Jackman, *Unemployment: Macroeconomic Performance and the Labor Market* (New York: Oxford University Press, 1991).

## 7-2 | FROM PHILLIPS CURVE TO AGGREGATE SUPPLY

An aggregate supply curve is a macroeconomic relationship between the price level and the level of real output. In Chapter 1, we introduced several shapes that an aggregate supply curve could take: horizontal in the *very* short run; upward sloping in the short run; and vertical in the long run. In this section, we are going to discuss the short run aggregate supply curve and examine why it may be upward sloping.

After many years of research, macroeconomists have come to believe that any short run aggregate supply curve can be represented by the equation

$$Y_t^s = Y^* + \alpha(P_t - P_t^e) \tag{12}$$

This equation tells us that any deviations of actual output from full employment output are a result of deviations of actual price from expected price. Even though

## POLICY IN *ACTION*

### Using the Phillips Curve in Both Directions

In this chapter, we have emphasized that there may be a *short run* trade-off available to policy makers. Indeed, the empirical evidence suggests that policy makers have exploited this short run trade-off in the recent past. In the late 1970s, inflation was above 10 percent in Canada and the United States. In both countries, the monetary authorities pursued a tight money policy that shifted the aggregate demand curve inward. The result was a severe economic downturn and decreased inflation. Essentially, the economy moved along a short run Phillips curve, with unemployment increasing, while inflation decreased. We had a similar episode, although smaller in magnitude, at the end of the 1980s.

However, the most interesting period of policy exploiting a short run trade-off came toward the end of the 1990s. There was a strong belief that stock markets in North America were overheated and that this was making the Canadian and U.S. economies grow too quickly, which would ultimately lead to inflation. In response to this threat, both the Bank of Canada and the Federal Reserve Board began tightening aggregate demand. This had the desired effect because, by mid-2001, both economies were slowing down substantially and inflationary pressures were cooling. However, after the events of September 11, 2001, the Canadian and U.S. economies came to a virtual standstill. There were now fears of deflation, rather than inflation. In response to this, both the Bank of Canada and the Federal Reserve Board eased monetary policy considerably, hoping to exploit the Phillips curve in the opposite direction—allow inflation to go up with short run economic growth. This policy had the desired effect in Canada, as output growth increased quite strongly in 2002.

most macroeconomists believe this description of short run aggregate supply, they disagree on how this supply curve can be derived and how it can be interpreted. We will present two main derivations and interpretations of this curve: one based simply on the sticky adjustment Phillips curve from the previous section, using an assumption of static expectations, and one based on the Classical model from Chapter 3, using rational expectations.

## Short Run Aggregate Supply Derived from the Phillips Curve

We begin with the naïve Phillips curve given by equation (6).

$$\pi_t = -\epsilon(u_t - u^*) \tag{13}$$

Notice that inflation can be written as

$$\pi_t = \frac{P_t}{P_{t-1}} - 1 \tag{14}$$

Given this, we can write equation (13) as

$$P_t = P_{t-1}[1 - \epsilon(u_t - u^*)] \tag{15}$$

Written in this manner, the naïve Phillips curve can be viewed as a theory of price adjustment, rather than inflation adjustment. Equation (15) says that the current price level will adjust according to two factors: excess demand or supply $(u - u^*)$ and last period's price level $(P_{t-1})$. If we assume static expectations, then today's expected price equals yesterday's actual price. Therefore, we can write (15) as

$$P_t = P_t^e[1 - \epsilon(u_t - u^*)] \tag{16}$$

**Okun's law**

States that there is a relationship between changes in unemployment and change in real GDP.

The final step is to link the unemployment rate, $u$, to changes in output, $Y$. We can do this through Okun's law, which we introduced in Chapter 2. **Okun's law** states that there is a relationship between changes in unemployment and change in GDP. We can express this relationship as

$$\frac{Y_t - Y^*}{Y^*} = -\gamma(u_t - u^*) \tag{17}$$

where $\gamma$ is a parameter that relates the size of changes in the unemployment rate to change in output. In Canada, $\gamma \approx 1.7$.[3] That is, if the current unemployment rate rises above full employment by 1.0 percent, output will drop by approximately 1.7 percent. We can substitute Okun's law into equation (16).

$$P_t = P_t^e\left[1 + \frac{\epsilon}{\gamma}\left(\frac{Y_t - Y^*}{Y^*}\right)\right] \tag{18}$$

---

[3] If you look back at Chapter 2, Figure 2-6, you will see a graph of Okun's law.

**short run aggregate supply (SRAS) curve**
A relationship derived from the Phillips curve that shows how output can deviate from its full employment level in the short run.

Defining $\lambda = \epsilon/\gamma Y^*$, we have an equation for the **short run aggregate supply (SRAS) curve**.

$$P_t = P_t^e \left[ 1 + \lambda (Y_t - Y^*) \right] \tag{19}$$

Notice that this equation can be rearranged as

$$P_t \approx P_t^e + \lambda (Y_t - Y^*) \tag{20}$$

This equation can be rewritten as

$$Y_t = Y^* + \alpha (P_t - P_t^e) \tag{21}$$

where $\alpha = 1/\lambda$ . Thus, this is a form of the generally accepted SRAS curve. The difference between equation (19) and equation (21) is interpretation. Many economists who believe in Phillips curves write the short run aggregate supply curve as in (19), as a theory of price adjustment. As we will see below, there is a different interpretation of short run aggregate supply curve.

## Short Run Aggregate Supply Derived from the Classical Model

In this derivation of the short run aggregate supply curve, we begin with all of the assumptions of the Classical labour market. We assume that supply is based on the production function, with fixed capital stock.

$$Y = F(\bar{K}, N) \tag{22}$$

Therefore, if the amount of labour, $N$, was to change, the amount of output would change. We assume that labour supply and output will go up if labour expects an increase in the real wage (of course, labour and output will go down if labour expects a decrease in the real wage). We can write the expected real wage (in natural logarithms) as[4]

$$\omega_t = W_t - P_t^e \tag{23}$$

If we assume that changes in the actual price level are the same as changes in the actual wage rate (this is the same assumption used in the Phillips curve), then we can write the SRAS curve as

$$Y_t^s = Y^* + \alpha (P_t - P_t^e) \tag{24}$$

---

[4] If we take the natural logarithm of the expected real wage, $W_t/P_t^e$, we get $Ln(W_t/P_t^e) = LnW_t - LnP_t^e$
We assume that each of the variables in equation (23) is written in natural logarithms.

In this formulation, deviations of current output from full employment output are a function of mistakes in expectations of the price level. That is, if nominal wage and price increase, and workers did not expect the increase, then the expected real wage will increase, workers will offer more labour services, and current output will go up. This formulation of aggregate supply is usually combined with the assumption of rational expectations, and is sometimes called the *New Classical macroeconomic model.*

## Comparing the Two Aggregate Supply Curves

In the text accompanying Figure 6-8, we discussed the reaction of the economy to an increase in the nominal money stock. We can now see how the economy adjusts to the Classical long run equilibrium.

## Adjustment under the Static Expectations Assumption

Adjustment under the static expectations assumption is shown in Figure 7-7.

Assume that the initial equilibrium is at point $E$, with a price level of $P_0$ and output of $Y^*$. In period 1, assume that the Bank of Canada increases the nominal money stock. This causes the $AD$ curve to shift outward and the economy moves to point $E'$, with a price level of $P'$ and output of $Y'$.[5]

| **FIGURE 7-7** | **ADJUSTMENT TO AN INCREASE IN THE NOMINAL MONEY STOCK** |
|---|---|

The initial equilibrium is at point $E$. When the nominal money stock increases, the $AD$ curve shifts outward, and there is a short run equilibrium at point $E'$. As the price level increases, and expectations adjust, the economy reaches a new equilibrium at point $E''$. Real output has returned to full employment and the price level has risen in proportion to the change in the nominal money stock.

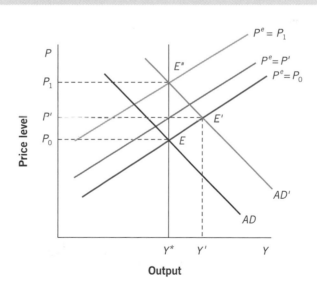

---

[5] You can see that, in Chapter 6, $E'$ was farther to the right, as a result of the assumption that the SRAS curve is horizontal. In this chapter, we are assuming some wage and price adjustment in the short run, and the SRAS curve has some slope.

We know that the SRAS curve will shift if expectations of the price level change. Under the static expectations assumption, today's expected price is equal to last period's actual price. Therefore, in period 1, agents still expect the price level to be $P_0$, and the SRAS curve does not shift. In period 2, the increase in the price level causes expectations to increase, and the SRAS curve shifts to $P^e = P'$. The new SRAS intersects the Classical AS at precisely the same price level that occurred in period 1 ($P'$). In each successive period, the AS curve will continue to shift as the actual price changes and the expected price changes in response. The economy will eventually reach a new equilibrium at $E''$.

This new equilibrium is the same as the Classical long run equilibrium. At this point, the price level has risen in proportion to the change in the nominal money stock and real output has not changed. However, in Classical macroeconomics, it is assumed that the economy would reach this point instantly, as wages and prices are assumed to adjust quickly. The only difference between the Classical result and the result in Figure 7-7 is the speed of adjustment. In Figure 7-7, the economy takes a finite period of time to reach the new equilibrium.

## Adjustment under Rational Expectations

In relation to Figure 7-7, under rational expectations, if there was an increase in the money supply, individuals would expect the price level to be the new equilibrium price level, $P_t^e = P_1$. In this situation, only if there were expectational mistakes would there be a short run aggregate supply curve.[6] If expectations are on average correct, then the economy will be on average at $Y^*$. In this sense, equation (24) is an equation for the Classical AS curve. When individuals make an expectational error, the economy could be at a point such as $E'$ in Figure 7-7. However, under rational expectations, as soon as the mistake is made, it is corrected and the economy would then go instantly to the Classical equilibrium.

In terms of the long run equilibrium, there is no difference among the Classical model, the adaptive expectations model, or the rational expectations model. The difference lies in the timing. Under adaptive expectations, the economy takes some period of time to reach the Classical equilibrium. In this view of the economy, there is a short run trade-off that is available to policy makers. Under rational expectations, the economy is, on average, at the Classical equilibrium. In this view of the economy, there is no trade-off available to policy makers.

## *Working with Data*

Okun's law is a statement about the relationship between the rate of change of real GDP and the unemployment rate, expressed by the following relationship.

$$\frac{Y - Y^*}{Y^*} = -\gamma(u_t - u^*) \tag{17}$$

---

[6] These ideas are elaborated on in Chapter 20.

In this chapter, we asserted that, in Canada $\gamma \approx 1.7$. In Chapter 8, we will discuss ways to estimate the unknown $u^*$. In this chapter, we made the convenient simplification that the term on the right-hand side of equation (17) can be approximated by the change in the unemployment rate, or $u_t - u_{t-1}$.

Go to CANSIM II and retrieve data on GDP in 1997 dollars (V1992259) and the unemployment rate (V2062815). You will need to average these data to get the annual values. In Chapter 2, we estimated Okun's law over the period 1962–2002. The data for the unemployment rate prior to 1976 are:

| Year | Unemployment Rate |
|------|-------------------|
| 1961 | 8.4 |
| 1962 | 6.9 |
| 1963 | 6.4 |
| 1964 | 5.3 |
| 1965 | 4.4 |
| 1966 | 4.0 |
| 1967 | 4.6 |
| 1968 | 5.5 |
| 1969 | 5.2 |
| 1970 | 6.6 |
| 1971 | 7.0 |
| 1972 | 6.8 |
| 1973 | 5.9 |
| 1974 | 5.7 |
| 1975 | 7.4 |

In order to calculate Okun's law, you must first calculate the rate of change of GDP and $u - u_{t-1}$. This is why you need the data for 1961. If you graph these in Excel with the growth of real GDP on the vertical axis and the change in the unemployment rate on the horizontal axis (see Figure 2-6, Chapter 2) and fit a trend line, you should find that the slope of the trend line equals approximately –1.7.

## CHAPTER SUMMARY

▶ The Phillips curve describes the adjustment of nominal wages to change in the unemployment rate. Nominal wages adjust slowly in the short run. The term *Phillips curve* gradually came to be used to describe the adjustment of prices to the unemployment rate.

▶ A Phillips curve that includes expectations of inflation is called an *expectations-augmented Phillips curve.*

▶ Expectations of inflation determine the height of the Phillips curve.

▶ The short run Phillips curve is quite flat. An increase of one percentage point in unemployment reduces inflation by only about one-half of one percentage point.

▶ The short run aggregate supply (SRAS) curve is derived from the Phillips curve.

▶ The slope of the SRAS curve depends on the amount of wage and price adjustment, and the SRAS curve shifts due to changes in expected price.

▶ A shift in the aggregate demand curve increases the price level and output in the short run, but increases the price level only in the long run.

## KEY TERMS

Phillips curve, *132*
policy trade-off, *134*
expected or anticipated
   inflation, *135*

expectations-augmented Phillips
   curve, *135*
adaptive expectations, *136*
static expectations, *136*

rational expectations, *136*
Okun's law, *141*
short run aggregate supply (SRAS)
   curve, *142*

## DISCUSSION QUESTIONS

1. Explain how the aggregate supply and Phillips curves are related to each other. Can any information be derived from one that cannot be derived from the other?

2. How do short and long run Phillips curves differ? (*Hint*: In the long run, we return to a Classical world.)

3. This chapter has discussed a number of different models that can be used to justify the existence of sticky wages, and hence the ability of aggregate demand to affect output. What are they? What are their similarities and differences? Which of these models do you find the most plausible?

4. Explain how the ability of inflation expectations to shift the Phillips curve helps the economy to adjust, automatically, to aggregate supply and demand shocks.

5. Discuss the differences in adjustment under the assumption of static expectations and under the assumption of rational expectations.

## APPLICATION QUESTIONS

1. Analyze the effects of a reduction in the nominal money stock on the price level, on output, and on the real money stock when the aggregate supply curve is positively sloped and wages adjust slowly over time.

2. Suppose the Bank of Canada adopts a policy of complete transparency; that is, suppose it announces beforehand how it will change the money supply. According to rational expectations theory, how will this policy affect the Bank of Canada's ability to move the real economy (e.g., the unemployment rate)?

3.  **a.** Show, in an aggregate supply and demand framework, the long and short run effects of a decline in the real price of materials (a favourable supply shock).

    **b.** Describe the adjustment process, assuming that output began at its natural (full-employment) level.

4.  Go to CANSIM and retrieve the unemployment rate for individuals 15 and older, and the Consumer Price Index. Calculate the inflation rate and plot a Phillips curve for the period 1992–2002. Compare this to the Phillips curve in Figure 7-3.

www.mcgrawhill.ca/college/dornbusch

## CHAPTER 8

# THE ANATOMY OF INFLATION AND UNEMPLOYMENT

## LEARNING OBJECTIVES

After reading and studying this chapter, you should be able to:

▶ *Understand that the costs of unemployment, which are mainly forgone output, are very large.*

▶ *Understand that the costs of anticipated inflation are very small, at least at the moderate levels experienced in industrialized countries.*

▶ *Understand that the costs of unanticipated inflation, which can be quite large, are mainly distributional. There are big winners and losers.*

▶ *Understand that unemployment rates vary widely across demographic groups and provinces.*

W
e have concentrated so far on how various economic factors determine output and prices, unemployment, and inflation. Now we turn to the actual details of unemployment and inflation. Both inflation and unemployment should be avoided as much as possible. Since, as we saw in Chapter 7, short run trade-offs between inflation and unemployment exist, it is important to get a better understanding of the relative costs of inflation and unemployment. This information provides the input for policy-makers' evaluation of the trade-offs.

This chapter focuses on the details of the costs of unemployment and inflation. Before discussing the details, you should be aware of the "big picture" costs:

▶ There are two main costs of unemployment: lost production and possible undesirable effects on the distribution of income.

▶ The costs of anticipated inflation are small. The costs of unanticipated inflation are probably small on net, but unanticipated inflation may cause significant redistributions of wealth within the economy.

## 8-1 | THE ANATOMY OF UNEMPLOYMENT

The Canadian unemployment rate exhibits the following general characteristics:

▶ There are large variations in unemployment rates across age groups and across provinces.

▶ There are substantial flows of individuals in and out of unemployment each month, and most people who become unemployed in any given month remain unemployed for only a short period of time.

▶ People who will be unemployed for a long period of time account for much of the unemployment rate.

**unemployed person**
Someone who is out of work and (1) has actively looked for work in the previous four weeks, or (2) is waiting to be recalled to a job after having been laid off, or (3) is waiting to report to a new job within four weeks.

Table 8-1 shows aspects of the Canadian labour market as of December 2002. The working-age population in Canada then was approximately 21.6 million people. Of these people, nearly 16 million, or almost 76 percent, were in the labour force. The labour force is composed of those who are employed and those who are unemployed. An **unemployed person** is defined as someone who is out of work and (1) has actively looked for work in the previous four weeks, or (2) is waiting to be recalled to

| **TABLE 8-1** | **CANADIAN LABOUR FORCE AND UNEMPLOYMENT, DECEMBER 2002** (thousands of persons, 15–64 years old) |
|---|---|

| | |
|---|---|
| Population 15–64 Years | 21,616 |
| Not in Labour Force | 4,872 |
| Labour Force | 16,744 |
| Employed | 15,548 |
| Unemployed | 1,195 |

SOURCE: Population: CANSIM II V466971; labour force: CANSIM II V3404669; employed: CANSIM II V3404703; unemployed: CANSIM II V3404805.

a job after having been laid off, or (3) is waiting to report to a new job within four weeks. The condition of having looked for work in the past four weeks tests that the person is actively interested in working.[1]

## The Unemployment Pool

**unemployment pool**
The number of unemployed people at any point in time.

At any point in time there is a given number, or pool, of unemployed people, and there are flows in and out of the **unemployment pool**. A person may become unemployed for one of four reasons:

1.  He or she may be a new entrant into the labour force—someone looking for work for the first time—or may be a re-entrant—someone returning to the labour force after not having looked for work for more than four weeks.

2.  A person may quit a job in order to look for alternative employment, and may register as unemployed while searching.

3.  A person may be laid off. A layoff means that the worker was not fired and will return to the old job if demand for the firm's product recovers. A firm will typically adjust to a decline in product demand by laying off some labour. A firm may also rotate layoffs among its labour force so that individual laid-off workers may expect a recall even before product demand has fully recovered.

4.  A worker may lose a job, either by being fired or because the firm closes down.

There are essentially three ways of moving out of the unemployment pool:

1.  A person may be hired into a new job.

2.  Someone laid off may be recalled by his or her employer.

3.  An unemployed person may stop looking for a job and thus, by definition, leave the labour force.

The concept of the unemployment pool provides a good way of thinking about changes in unemployment. Unemployment is rising when more people are entering the pool than leaving. Thus, other things equal, increases in quits and layoffs increase unemployment, as does an increase in the flow of new entrants into the labour market. Job loss accounts for about half of new unemployment. Voluntary separations, new entrants, and re-entrants into the labour force together account for the other half.

The contemporaneous link between unemployment and output embodied in Okun's law is an accurate first approximation, but the dynamics of the output-unemployment link are somewhat more complicated. Consider the typical adjustment pattern of labour use during a recession. Employers first adjust hours per worker—for example, by cutting overtime—and only then trim their workforce. Next, layoffs and firings increase, increasing the flow into unemployment. But, at the same time, quits decrease, as workers sensibly decide to hold on to their current jobs. During a prolonged recession, many of the unemployed become discouraged and leave the labour force, making the *reported* unemployment rate lower than it would otherwise be. As a result of all of these effects, unemployment changes usually lag behind output changes.

---

[1] Those who are of working age but not in the labour force are not counted as unemployed. "Out of the labour force" includes retired persons, homemakers, and full-time students. It also includes discouraged workers—people who would like to work but have given up looking—as discussed in Chapter 2.

## Variation in Unemployment Across Groups

At any point in time, there is a given aggregate level of unemployment or, expressed as a fraction of the labour force, an unemployment rate. For example, in December 2002, the unemployment rate was 7.1 percent. But this aggregate number conceals wide variations across various segments of the population. For instance, Figure 8-1 shows that the unemployment rate for individuals in the 15–24 age group is consistently higher than for other age groups. In addition, the unemployment rate for young people rises more sharply in recessions. Notice also that female unemployment was higher than male unemployment until the early 1990s, but in 2002, the female unemployment rate was slightly lower than that for males.

Figure 8-2 shows unemployment rates for the regions of Canada. The Atlantic provinces have consistently had a higher unemployment rate than the other regions, while the Prairies and Ontario have had lower unemployment rates.

The variation in unemployment rates across different groups in the labour force can be examined using the relationship between the overall unemployment rate, $u$, and the unemployment rates, $u_i$, of groups within the labour force. The overall rate is a weighted average of the unemployment rates of the groups:

$$u = w_1 u_1 + w_2 u_2 + \ldots + w_n u_n \qquad (1)$$

The $w_i$ weights are the fraction of the labour force that falls within a specific group, such as teenagers.

Equation (1) makes it clear that the overall unemployment rate may conceal dramatic differences in unemployment rates among regions or groups. For instance, in December 2002, the aggregate unemployment rate was 7.1 percent. For the age group 15–24, the rate was 11.8 percent, while for the age group 25 and over, it was 6.3 percent. In terms of equation (1), we have

$$7.1\% = (0.842)6.3\% + (0.158)11.8\%$$

where the shares of the two groups in the labour force were 84.2 percent and 15.8 percent, respectively.

www.statcan.ca/english/
freepub/89F0133XIE/
free.htm

---

### FIGURE 8-1

The unemployment rate for individuals in the 15–24 age group is consistently higher than that for any other age group. Also, in the 1990s, the female unemployment rate was slightly lower than the male unemployment rate.

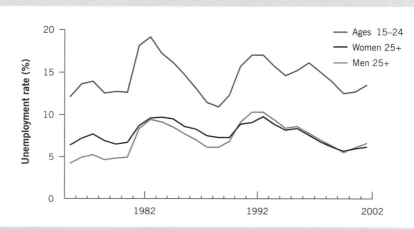

**UNEMPLOYMENT ACROSS VARIOUS DEMOGRAPHIC GROUPS, 1976–2002**

SOURCE: Individuals 15–24: CANSIM II V2461225; males 25+: CANSIM II V2461436; females 25+: CANSIM II V2461646.

*FIGURE 8-2*

**THE UNEMPLOYMENT RATE ACROSS REGIONS, 1976–2002**

The Atlantic provinces have consistently had higher unemployment rates than the other regions of Canada.

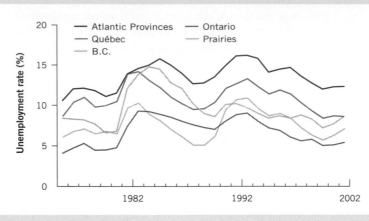

SOURCE: CANSIM II table 2820009.

## Cyclical and Frictional Unemployment

**frictional unemployment**

The unemployment that exists when the economy is at full employment.

There is an important distinction between cyclical and frictional unemployment. **Frictional unemployment** is the unemployment that exists when the economy is at full employment. Frictional unemployment results from the structure of the labour market—from the nature of jobs in the economy and from the social habits and labour market institutions (e.g., unemployment benefits) that affect the behaviour of workers and firms. The frictional unemployment rate is the same as the natural unemployment rate, which we discuss in more detail below. **Cyclical unemployment** is unemployment in excess of frictional unemployment: It occurs when output is below its full employment level.

**cyclical unemployment**

Unemployment in excess of frictional unemployment; occurs when output is below its full employment level.

With this preliminary discussion in mind, we now turn to a closer examination of unemployment.

## 8-2 | FULL EMPLOYMENT

The notion of full employment—or the natural, or frictional, rate of unemployment—plays a central role in macroeconomics and also in macroeconomic policy. We start by discussing the theory of the natural rate and then examine estimates of the rate.

## Determinants of the Natural Rate

**natural rate of unemployment**

Rate of unemployment at which the flows into and out of the unemployment pool balance; also the point on the augmented Phillips curve at which expected inflation equals actual inflation.

The determinants of the **natural rate of unemployment**, $u^*$, can be thought of in terms of the *duration* and *frequency* of unemployment. The duration of unemployment depends on cyclical factors and, in addition, on the following structural characteristics of the labour market:

▶ The organization of the labour market, including the presence or absence of employment agencies, youth employment services, and the like.

▶ The demographic make-up of the labour force.

▶ The ability and desire of the unemployed to keep looking for a better job, which depends in part on the availability of unemployment benefits.

The last point deserves special notice. A person may quit a job to have more time to look for a new and better one. We refer to this kind of unemployment as *search unemployment*. If all jobs are the same, an unemployed person will take the first one offered. If some jobs are better than others, it is worthwhile searching and waiting for a good one. The higher the Employment Insurance benefits, the more likely people are to keep searching for a better job, and the more likely they are to quit a current job to try to find a better one. Thus, an increase in Employment Insurance benefits will increase the natural rate of unemployment.

The behaviour of workers who have been laid off is also important when considering the duration of unemployment. Typically, a worker who has been laid off returns to her or his original job and does not search much for another job. The reason is quite simple: A worker who has been with a firm for a long time has special expertise in the way that firm works and may have built up seniority rights, including a pension. Hence, such an individual is unlikely to find a better-paying job by searching. The best course of action may be to wait to be recalled, particularly if the individual is eligible for unemployment benefits while waiting.

The *frequency of unemployment* is the average number of times, per period, that workers become unemployed. There are two basic determinants of the frequency of unemployment. The first is the variability of the demand for labour across different firms in the economy. Even when aggregate demand is constant, some firms are growing and some are contracting. The contracting firms lose labour, and the growing firms hire more labour. The greater the variability of the demand for labour across different firms, the higher the unemployment rate. The second determinant is the rate at which new workers enter the labour force: The more rapidly new workers enter the labour force—that is, the faster the growth rate of the labour force—the higher the natural rate of unemployment.

The three factors affecting duration and the two factors affecting frequency of unemployment are the basic determinants of the natural rate of unemployment. These factors obviously change over time. The structure of the labour market and the labour force can change. The variability of the demand for labour by differing firms can shift. As Edmund Phelps has noted, the natural rate is *not* "an intertemporal constant, something like the speed of light, independent of everything under the sun."[2]

## Estimates of the Natural Rate of Unemployment

Estimates of the natural rate of unemployment typically try to adjust for changes in the composition of the labour force, and for changes in the natural rate of unemployment in the various groups in the labour force. We can write an equation very similar to equation (1) for the natural rate, $u^*$.

$$u^* = w_1 u_1^* + w_2 u_2^* + \ldots + w_n u_n^* \tag{2}$$

Equation (2) states that the natural rate is a weighted average of the natural rates of unemployment for the subgroups of the labour force.

Equation (2) is somewhat difficult to estimate. In Figure 8-3, we present an estimate of the natural rate of unemployment, using a simpler method, over the period 1950 to 2002.

---

[2] See E.S. Phelps, "Economic Policy and Unemployment in the Sixties," *Public Interest*, Winter 1974.

## FIGURE 8-3

The natural rate of unemployment is not constant. The actual rate of unemployment moves cyclically around the natural rate of unemployment.

### THE ACTUAL RATE OF UNEMPLOYMENT AND THE ESTIMATED NATURAL RATE OF UNEMPLOYMENT, 1950–2002

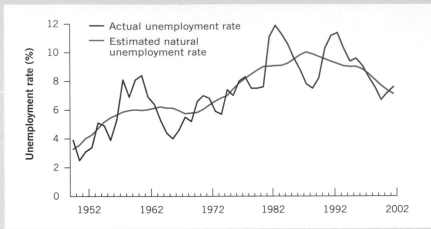

SOURCE: Actual unemployment rate: 1950–1975: Statistics Canada, *Historical Statistics of Canada*, Publication 11-516-XIE; 1976–2002: CANSIM II V3404839. The natural rate was estimated by averaging the previous six years with the future six years of the unemployment rate. After 2002, the actual unemployment rate was set at 6.0.

You can see in Figure 8-3 that the natural rate of unemployment is not constant. The natural rate appears to have increased gradually from the 1950s until the 1990s, when it seems to be decreasing toward its previous level. In the 1970s, the actual unemployment rate was fairly close to the natural rate. The recessions of the early 1980s and the early 1990s pushed the actual unemployment rate well above the natural rate.

## Hysteresis and the Rising Natural Rate of Unemployment

**unemployment hysteresis**
The phenomenon that when unemployment is high, it tends to remain high and come down only slowly.

Figure 8-3 shows that the actual and natural rates of unemployment both tended to increase from the 1950s onward. Although the Canadian economy was doing very well in the mid-1990s, the actual unemployment rate was still greater than the unemployment rate in the 1970s. This phenomenon—when unemployment is high, it tends to remain high and comes down slowly—is known as **unemployment hysteresis**. There are various ways in which this could happen. The unemployed might become accustomed to not working. They might find out about unemployment benefits, how to obtain them, and how to spend the day doing odd jobs. Or the unemployed may become discouraged and apply less than full effort to locating a job.

The problem may be reinforced by the actions of potential employers. For instance, they may believe that the longer a person has been unemployed, the more likely it is that the person lacks either the energy or the qualifications to work. Long unemployment spells thus signal to firms the possibility (not the certainty!) that the worker is undesirable and, accordingly, firms shy away from hiring such workers. Hence, the higher the unemployment rate (and therefore the longer the unemployment spells), the more unbreakable the vicious circle of lengthening unemployment spells.

## Reducing the Natural Rate of Unemployment

Discussion of methods for reducing the natural rate of unemployment tends to focus on the high unemployment rates of teenagers and on the very high proportion of total unemployment accounted for by the long-term unemployed.

We start with teenage unemployment. Teenagers enter and leave the labour force in part because the jobs they hold are not particularly attractive. To improve jobs, the emphasis in some European countries, especially Germany, is to provide technical training for teenagers and thus make holding on to a job more rewarding. The European apprenticeship system, in which young people receive on-the-job training, is also widely credited not only with providing serious jobs for the young but also with making youths productive workers for the long term.

Teenagers' wages (on average) are closer to the minimum wage than are those of more experienced workers. Many teenagers earn the minimum wage and some earn less, as in Ontario, where that is currently permissible. Accordingly, reducing the minimum wage might be one way of reducing the teenage unemployment rate. However, programs allowing "subminimum" wages for teenagers appear to have had little impact.[3]

## Employment Insurance

www.hrdc-drhc.gc.ca/
insur/histui/hrdc.html

It is possible that the existence of the Employment Insurance Program[4] may have an effect on the unemployment rate. The effect of such programs on the *measured* rate of unemployment depends on the replacement ratio—that is, the ratio of after-tax income while unemployed to after-tax income while employed. There are three channels of influence.

First, the presence of unemployment benefits allows *longer job search*. The higher the replacement ratio, the less urgent the need to take a job. Second, the measured unemployment rate may reflect *reporting effects*. To collect unemployment benefits, people have to be "in the labour force," looking for work even if they do not really want a job. They therefore are counted as unemployed. In the absence of unemployment benefits, some people might not be in the labour force, and hence participation and unemployment rates would be lower.

The third channel is *employment stability*. With unemployment insurance, the consequences of being in and out of jobs are less severe, so workers and firms do not find it as much in their interest to create highly stable employment. Further, there is an incentive favouring seasonal jobs for which layoffs in the off-season are not a risk but a virtual certainty, so that the unemployment insurance system becomes a subsidy to seasonal industries.

The substantial liberalization of the benefits payable to the unemployed under Canada's Unemployment Insurance Act in the early 1970s provides an interesting case study of these effects. In general there is substantial evidence that the participation rate and the average duration of unemployment were increased.[5] Thus, there

---

[3] For example, Charles Brown, in "Minimum Wages Laws: Are They Overrated?" *Journal of Economic Perspectives*, Summer 1988, finds little evidence that these measures have affected teenage unemployment.

[4] In Canada, the program was originally called the Unemployment Insurance Program, and was amended substantially in the 1970s under the Unemployment Insurance Act. In 1996, the name was changed to the Employment Insurance Program.

[5] See Jean-Michel Cousineau, "Unemployment Insurance and Labour Market Adjustments," in F. Vaillancourt, *Income Distribution and Economic Security in Canada*, Research Study No. 1, Royal Commission on the Economic Union and Develoment Prospects for Canada (Toronto: University of Toronto Press, 1985).

seems to be little doubt that unemployment compensation does add to the natural rate of unemployment. This does not imply, though, that unemployment compensation should be abolished. Individuals need time to do some searching if the economy is to allocate people efficiently among jobs. It would not make sense to put a skilled worker in an unskilled job the moment a previous job is lost, just because the worker cannot afford to search. Thus, even from the viewpoint of economic efficiency, zero is not the ideal level of unemployment benefits. Beyond that, society may be willing to give up some efficiency so that the unemployed can maintain a minimal standard of living. What is appropriate is a scheme that will create less incentive for firms to lay off labour, while at the same time ensuring that the unemployed are not exposed to economic distress. This is obviously difficult to implement.

## 8-3 | THE COSTS OF UNEMPLOYMENT

As individuals, the unemployed suffer both from their income loss while unemployed and from the related social problems that long periods of unemployment cause. Society on the whole loses from unemployment because output is below its potential level.

This section provides some estimates of the costs of forgone output resulting from unemployment, and it clarifies some of the issues connected with the costs of unemployment and the potential benefits of reducing unemployment. We emphasize the costs of cyclical unemployment, which is associated with short run deviations of the unemployment rate from the natural rate.

---

**BOX 8-1**

### Percent Change, Percentage Points, and Basis Points

In this section, we have tried to be very careful in our use of some basic mathematical terms. If a variable changes, it is often convenient to express this change in percentage terms. The most obvious use of this in macroeconomics is the inflation rate, which is the percentage change in the price level. However, potential confusion arises when we want to talk about a change in the inflation rate. As an example, suppose the inflation rate changes from 5 percent to 10 percent. Mathematically, the inflation rate has changed by 100 percent. However, this would also be true if the inflation rate went from 1 percent to 2 percent, but the macroeconomic consequences of these two changes are quite different. To avoid this type of confusion, we say the inflation rate went up by 5 percentage points in the first case, and the inflation rate went up by 1 percentage point in the second case.

Another important variable that is expressed as a percentage is the unemployment rate. Remember that the unemployment rate is the percentage of the labour force that is unemployed.* As with the inflation rate, if the unemployment rate increases from 5 percent to 10 percent, we say that the unemployment rate has increased by 5 percentage points.

You will sometimes hear the term *basis point* used. A basis point is 1/100th of a percentage point. For instance, if the inflation rate changes from 3.25 to 3.30, we say that the inflation rate has changed by 5 basis points.

---

*Notice that, even though both the inflation rate and the unemployment rate are expressed as percentages, the inflation rate is a percentage change, while the unemployment rate is a percentage of the labour force.

## Costs of Cyclical Unemployment

The largest single cost of unemployment is lost production; the cost of lost output can be very high. In Chapter 2, we introduced Okun's law, which postulates a relationship between changes in the unemployment rate and changes in real GDP. If you look back at Figure 2-6 in Chapter 2, you will see that the estimated relationship between unemployment and GDP for Canada over the period 1962–2002 is that the economy appears to lose about 1.7 percent of output for every 1 percent that the actual unemployment rate exceeds the natural unemployment rate.

**sacrifice ratio**

The percentage of output lost for each 1 percentage-point reduction in the inflation rate

In the short-run, when the Bank of Canada wants to reduce the inflation rate, the cost of this policy is increased unemployment and reduced output. The **sacrifice ratio** is the percentage of output lost for each 1 percentage-point increase in the inflation rate. There are many ways to calculate the sacrifice ratio, and estimates will vary depending on the time period and the methodology used.

We can combine the information on the slope of the short run Phillips curve and the slope of the Okun's law curve to obtain an approximation of the sacrifice ratio in Canada. We know from Okun's law that a 1 percentage-point increase in unemployment is consistent with a lowering of the growth rate of real GDP by 1.7 percent. From the short run Phillips curve estimates in Chapter 7, we know that the slope of the short run Phillips curve equals approximately –0.5. This means that a 1 percentage-point increase in the unemployment rate is consistent with a 0.5 percentage-point decrease in the inflation rate. Therefore, the Phillips curve is telling us that if inflation is reduced by 1 percentage point, unemployment increases by 2 percentage points. Using this methodology and putting these two estimates together, our estimate of the sacrifice ratio is that it equals approximately 3.4. This is in the range of reasonable published estimates of the sacrifice ratio in Canada of between 1 and 5.[6] We discuss the interaction of the sacrifice ratio and monetary policy in the Policy in Action feature in this chapter. You can see some international evidence of the size of the sacrifice ratio in Box 8-2.

We can also use Okun's law to calculate the cost of unemployment during a recession. For instance, at the height of the recession in the early 1990s, the unemployment rate reached 11.4 percent. According to the estimate of the natural rate of unemployment shown in Figure 8-3, the natural rate was approximately 9.2 percent at this time. Therefore, the loss of unemployment was 2.2 percentage points. According to our Okun's law estimate, this translates into a loss in output of 3.7 percent, or approximately $26 billion.

## Distributional Impact of Unemployment

While the Okun's law estimate provides the basic measure of the overall costs of cyclical unemployment, the distributional impact of unemployment also has to be taken into account. In general, unemployment hits poorer people harder than it hits the rich, and this aspect should increase concern about the problem.

The Okun's law estimate encompasses *all* of the lost income, including that of all individuals who lose their jobs. That total loss could, in principle, be distributed among different people in the economy in many different ways. For instance, one

---

[6]See, for instance, estimates in *Some Evidence on Hysteresis and the Costs of Disinflation in Canada*, Barry Cozier and Gordon Wilkinson, Bank of Canada Technical Report 55 (1991), available online at www.bankofcanada.ca/en/trlist.htm#1991; and William Scarth, "Fighting Inflation: Are the Costs Getting Too High?" in Robert York (ed.), *Taking Aim: The Debate on Zero Inflation*, Study No. 10, C.D. Howe Institute, 1990, pages 81–103.

POLICY IN *ACTION*

## The Disinflation of the Early 1980s

If you look back at various figures showing the inflation rate in Canada (for instance, see Figure 1-9 in Chapter 1), you will see that the inflation rate in Canada increased steadily through the 1960s and 1970s. By 1981, the inflation rate was above 12 percent, and the Bank of Canada raised interest rates abruptly in order to bring down the rate of inflation.

The cost of bringing down the inflation rate was a short run increase in the unemployment rate. In Chapter 7, we learned that the short run Phillips curve is very flat, so that any reduction in inflation will be accompanied by a large increase in the unemployment rate. However, the trade-off is a short run phenomenon, so that eventually the economy will return to a reasonable unemployment rate. You can see the nature of how this happened in the following graph that shows two estimated Phillips curves, one for the period 1979–1982 and another for the period 1983–1988.

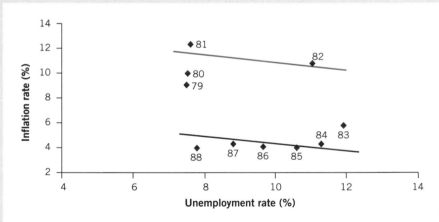

SOURCE: Unemployment: CANSIM II V2062815; inflation: CANSIM II V735319.

In 1979, the unemployment rate was approximately 7.5 percent, while the inflation rate was 9 percent. By 1982, the inflation rate was above 10 percent, while the unemployment rate had risen to nearly 12 percent. In this period, inflationary expectations were in the neighbourhood of 10 percent, and the short run Phillips curve was quite high to reflect this. Once inflationary expectations decreased and the Phillips curve shifted downward, the actual inflation rate became lower but the unemployment rate remained high. The economy then had to move along another flat short run Phillips curve until the unemployment rate reached under 8 percent, approximately the same level that it was in 1979.

What did the disinflation cost in terms of forgone output? We have calculated one estimate of the sacrifice ratio as approximately 3.4. Remember that the sacrifice ratio tells us that a 1 percentage-point decrease in inflation costs approximately 3.4 percent of GDP. Since inflation went down by 6 percentage points, the disinflation may have cost more than 15 percent of output.

## The "Sacrifice Ratio"—An International Perspective

We know that in the short run, when monetary policy reduces inflation, the cost is increased unemployment and reduced output. We can measure this cost through the sacrifice ratio, which is the percentage of output lost for each 1 percentage-point reduction in the inflation rate. Estimates of the sacrifice ratio vary, depending on the time frame and the methodology used. The table below provides estimates of the sacrifice ratio for a number of countries, including Canada.

### ESTIMATED AVERAGE SACRIFICE RATIOS

| Country | Ratio, % |
| --- | --- |
| Australia | 1.00 |
| Canada | 1.50 |
| France | 0.75 |
| Germany | 2.92 |
| Italy | 1.74 |
| Japan | 0.93 |
| Switzerland | 1.57 |
| United Kingdom | 0.79 |
| United States | 2.39 |

SOURCE: Laurence Ball, "How Costly Is Disinflation? The Historical Evidence," *Business Review*, Federal Reserve Bank of Philadelphia, November–December 1993.

Notice that the above estimate of the sacrifice ratio for Canada is 1.5, which is quite a bit lower than our estimate of 3.4. This reflects the different methodology used and, to some extent, different time periods. The difference in methodology is interesting and of some importance. Our estimate of 3.4 is only for movements along any one short run Phillips curve and, therefore, holds inflationary expectations constant. As we have seen, during a disinflation, expected inflation falls, causing a downward shift in the Phillips curve as well as a movement along a Phillips curve. We can include this drop in inflationary expectations in our calculation of the sacrifice ratio in the following manner. In Policy in Action, we stated that during the disinflation of the early 1980s, inflation went down by 6 percentage points, and this may have caused a loss of 15 percent of output. We can use this information to calculate a sacrifice ratio of $15/6 = 2.5$, which is somewhat closer to the estimate of 1.5 shown in the table in this box.

could imagine that the unemployed would continue to receive benefit payments totalling close to what their income had been while employed, with the benefit payments financed through taxes on working individuals. In that case, the unemployed would not suffer an income loss from being unemployed, but society would still lose from the reduction in total output. The unemployment compensation system partially, but by no means fully, spreads the burden of unemployment.

## Other Costs and Benefits

Are there any other costs of unemployment or, for that matter, any offsetting benefits? A possible offsetting benefit occurs because the unemployed, by not working, have more leisure. However, the value that can be placed on that leisure is small. In the first place, much of it is unwanted leisure.

Second, because people pay taxes on their wages, society in general receives a benefit in the form of tax revenue when workers are employed. When a worker loses a job, society bears the additional cost of lost tax revenue on top of the worker's lost wages. This is an additional reason that the benefit of increased leisure provides only a partial offset to the Okun's law estimate of the cost of cyclical unemployment.

## 8-4 | THE COSTS OF INFLATION

**perfectly/imperfectly anticipated inflation**

Inflation is perfectly anticipated when all agents correctly anticipate the future inflation rate. Inflation is imperfectly anticipated when inflation is unexpected.

There is no direct loss of output from inflation, as there is from unemployment. In considering the costs of inflation, it is important to distinguish between inflation that is **perfectly anticipated**, and taken into account in economic transactions, and **imperfectly anticipated**, or unexpected, inflation. We start with perfectly anticipated inflation.

## Perfectly Anticipated Inflation

Suppose that an economy has been experiencing a given rate of inflation, say, 5 percent, for a long time and that everyone correctly anticipates that the rate of inflation will continue to be 5 percent. In such an economy, all contracts would build in the expected 5 percent inflation.

Borrowers and lenders would know and agree that the dollars in which a loan is repaid will be worth less than the dollars given up by the lender when making the loan. Nominal interest rates would be raised by 5 percentage points to compensate for the inflation. Long-term labour contracts would increase wages at 5 percent per year to compensate for the inflation and would then build in whatever changes in real wages are agreed to. Long-term leases would take account of the inflation. In brief, any contracts in which the passage of time is involved would take the 5 percent inflation into account. In that category we include the tax laws, which we are assuming would be indexed. The tax brackets themselves would be increased at the rate of 5 percent per year.[7]

In such an economy, inflation has no real costs—with two qualifications. The first qualification arises because no interest is paid on currency—notes and coins—not least because it is very difficult to do so. This means that the costs of holding currency rise along with the inflation rate.

The cost to the individual of holding currency is the interest forgone by not holding an interest-bearing asset.[8] When the inflation rate rises, the nominal interest rate rises, the interest lost by holding currency increases, and the cost of holding currency therefore increases. Accordingly, the demand for currency falls. Individuals have to make do with less currency, making more trips to the bank to cash smaller

---

[7] The taxation of interest would have to be on the real (after-inflation) return on assets for the tax system to be properly indexed.

[8] Note that cash holders are effectively making an interest-free loan to the government. The direct effect of higher interest rates is a transfer of revenue from the private to the public sector. This is sometimes called an *inflation tax*, and will be discussed in Chapter 19.

BOX

8-3

## Unemployment in International Perspective

In the early post-World War II period—indeed, through the 1960s—European unemployment was typically far less than unemployment in Canada. But this is no longer the case, as can be seen in the table below. European unemployment in the 1980s averaged more than twice its 1970s level, which in turn was almost twice the 1960s level and was still very high in 2001.

### UNEMPLOYMENT RATES AND LONG-TERM UNEMPLOYED, SELECTED COUNTRIES, 1983 AND 2001

| | Unemployment Rate, Percent | | Unemployed More Than One Year, Percent of Total Unemployment* | |
|---|---|---|---|---|
| | 1983 | 2001 | 1983 | 2001 |
| North America | | | | |
| Canada | 11.2 | 7.2 | 7.8 | 9.5 |
| United States | 7.4 | 4.8 | 13.3 | 6.1 |
| Japan | 2.7 | 5.0 | 12.9 | 26.6 |
| Central and Western Europe | | | | |
| Belgium | 12.1 | 6.6 | 64.8 | 51.7 |
| France | 9.7 | 8.6 | 42.2 | 37.6 |
| Germany (western) | 7.1 | 7.9 | 41.6 | 51.5 |
| Ireland | 15.5 | 3.8 | 36.7 | 57.0 |
| Netherlands | 11.8 | 2.4 | 48.8 | 47.9 |
| United Kingdom | 11.7 | 5.0 | 45.6 | 27.7 |
| Southern Europe | | | | |
| Italy | 9.4 | 9.5 | 69.8 | 63.4 |
| Spain | 19.7 | 13.0 | 52.4 | 44.0 |
| Nordic countries | | | | |
| Finland | 5.2 | 9.1 | 19.2 | 26.2 |
| Norway | 3.1 | 3.6 | 6.3 | 4.9 |
| Sweden | 3.1 | 5.1 | 10.3 | 27.3 |
| Australia | 8.9 | 6.7 | 25.4 | 21.5 |

*The unemployment measure attempts to standardize across countries and so may differ from official statistics. For further discussion and an earlier version of this table, see R. Ehrenberg and J. Smith, *Modern Labor Economics*, 6th ed. (Reading, MA: Addison-Wesley, 1997).

SOURCE: Organisation for Economic Co-operation and Development (OECD), *Employment Outlook*: www.OECD.org/dataoecd/29/42/1939233.pdf.

With the European unemployment rate averaging more than 9 percent for a decade, it became a prime public issue and topic of academic research.* Many reasons have been advanced for the continuation of high unemployment, among them high unemployment benefits and the hysteresis theory discussed in the text.

* An extensive study of the European labour market appears in *The OECD Jobs Study: Evidence and Explanations* (Paris: OECD, 1995). See also Olivier J. Blanchard and Justin Wolfers, "The Role of Shocks and Institutions in the Rise of European Umemployment: The Aggregate Evidence," MIT working paper, March 1999.

*continued*

## Unemployment in International Perspective cont'd

Other prominent explanations include the inflexibility of European labour markets, specifically the downward inflexibility of real wages and the high firing costs imposed by law. The argument is that firms were reluctant to hire workers because it would be so expensive to fire them if necessary later.[†]

The strength of European unions receives part of the blame. The insider-outsider theory of the labour market says that firms bargain with the insiders (the already employed) and have no reason to take account of the outsiders, the unemployed. Of course, if unions were not so strong, the firms might be willing to hire the outsiders at lower wages, or new firms would be set up to take advantage of the cheap labour.[‡] High European unemployment benefits also contribute to high unemployment, with some potential workers being better off unemployed than in a job.

European unemployment is a problem especially because of its incidence. The share of youth among the unemployed is very high, as is the share of the unemployed who experience long-term unemployment. Unemployment has for many gone on so long that most have greatly reduced their lifetime earnings potential. For example, in 1993, the long-term unemployment rate was about one-tenth the overall unemployment rate in the United States but was more than half the overall unemployment rate in much of Europe.

Notice that unemployment rates in Europe vary widely and are especially low in Sweden and Norway. In part, this reflects the relatively robust state of the Scandinavian economies in 1983 and 1998. But Sweden, in particular, has a very activist policy for finding jobs for the unemployed—including public sector employment when necessary.

---

[†] See Edmond Malinvaud, *Mass Unemployment* (Oxford: Basil Blackwell, 1988), and Charles Bean, Richard Layard, and Stephen Nickell (eds.), *Unemployment* (Oxford: Basil Blackwell, 1987).

[‡] See Assar Lindbeck and Dennis Snower, *The Insider-Outsider Theory* (Cambridge, MA: MIT Press, 1989). For a discussion of the linkages between the economics and the politics of European unemployment, see Gilles Saint-Paul, "Exploring the Political Economy of Labour Market Institutions," *Economic Policy*, October 1996.

---

cheques than they did before. The costs of these trips to the bank are often described as the "shoe-leather" costs of inflation. They are related to the amount by which the demand for currency is reduced by an increase in the anticipated inflation rate, and they are estimated to be small.

**menu costs**

Small costs incurred when the nominal price of a good is exchanged; for example, the cost for a restaurant of reprinting its menus when it raises/ lowers its prices.

The second qualification is the **menu costs** of inflation. These arise from the fact that with inflation—as opposed to price stability—people have to devote real resources to marking up prices and changing pay telephones and vending machines as well as cash registers. Those costs are there, but one cannot get too excited about them.

We should add that we are assuming here reasonable inflation rates—say, in the single or low double digits—that are low enough not to disrupt the payments system. At such low-to-moderate inflation rates, the costs of fully anticipated inflation are small.[9]

---

[9] There is clear cross-country evidence that high rates of inflation are associated with low rates of sustained growth. The negative link is not due to costs of inflation per se. Rather, "The inflation rate serves as an indicator of the overall ability of the government to manage the economy. Since there are no good arguments for very high rates of inflation, a government that is producing high inflation is a government that has lost control" (Stanley Fischer, "Macroeconomic Factors in Growth," *Journal of Monetary Economics*, December 1993). See also Steve Ambler and Emanuela Cardia, "Testing the Link Between Inflation and Growth," available online at www.bankofcanada.ca/publications/conf/con97/cn97-5.pdf.

The notion that the costs of fully anticipated inflation are small does not square well with the strong aversion to inflation reflected in policy making and politics. The most important reason for that aversion is that the inflationary experience of Canada is one of varying, imperfectly anticipated inflation, the costs of which are substantially different from those discussed in this section.

## Imperfectly Anticipated Inflation

The idyllic scenario of full adjustment to inflation does not describe economies in the real world. Modern economies include a variety of institutional features representing different degrees of adjustment to inflation. Economies with long inflationary histories, such as those of Brazil and Israel, have made substantial adjustments to inflation through the use of indexing. Those in which inflation has been episodic, such as the Canadian economy, have not.

## Wealth Redistribution Through Inflation

One important effect of inflation is a change in the real value of assets fixed in nominal terms. Between 1966 and 2002, the price level in Canada rose more than fivefold, cutting the purchasing power of all claims or assets fixed in money terms to more than one-fifth of their initial value. Thus, someone who bought a 30-year government bond in 1966 and expected to receive principal of, say, $100 in constant purchasing power at the 2002 maturity date actually wound up with a $100 principal that had a purchasing power of less than $20 in 1966 dollars. Similarly, a worker who retired on a fixed-dollar pension in 1966 finds that his or her income will buy less than one-fifth of what it did at retirement. The near quintupling of the price level has—if it was unanticipated—transferred wealth from the creditors or holders of bonds to the borrowers and from pensioners to firms.

**wealth redistribution**
When inflation is not anticipated, those who hold financial assets have some of their purchasing power transferred to those who issue financial assets.

This **wealth redistribution** effect operates with respect to all assets fixed in nominal terms, in particular, money, bonds, savings accounts, insurance, contracts, and some pensions. It implies that realized real interest rates might have been negative. Obviously, it is an extremely important effect, since it can wipe out the purchasing power of a lifetime's saving that is supposed to finance retirement consumption. Table 8-2 shows real returns on various assets. We note that currency earns negative real returns whenever inflation is positive.

Who gains and who loses from unanticipated inflation? There is a popular belief that the old are more vulnerable to inflation than the young in that the old own more nominal assets. Offsetting this, however, is the fact that social security benefits are indexed, so a substantial part of the income of retirees is protected from unanticipated inflation. Common political rhetoric also alleges that the poor are especially vulnerable to unanticipated inflation. There appears to be little evidence supporting this view.[10]

Inflation redistributes *wealth* between debtors and creditors. It could also redistribute income. A popular line of argument has always been that inflation benefits capitalists or recipients of profit income at the expense of wage earners. Unanticipated inflation, it is argued, means that prices rise faster than wages and therefore allow profits to expand. For Canada and the United States in the post–World

---

[10] See Rebecca Blank and Alan Blinder, "Macroeconomics, Income Distribution and Poverty," in Sheldon Danziger and Daniel Weinberg (eds.), *Fighting Poverty* (Cambridge, MA: Harvard University Press, 1986).

| *TABLE 8-2* | **REAL ASSET RETURNS** (percent per year) | | | |
|---|---|---|---|---|
| | | 1960–69 | 1970–79 | 1980–89 | 1990–2002 |
| | Currency | −2.55 | −7.39 | −6.50 | −2.27 |
| | Treasury Bills | 1.89 | −0.37 | 4.77 | 3.15 |
| | Bonds | 2.55 | 1.10 | 5.21 | 5.15 |

SOURCE: CANSIM II: currency: V735319; Treasury bills: V122484; bonds: V122487.

War II period, there is no persuasive evidence to this effect. There is evidence that the real return on common stocks—that is, the real value of dividends and capital gains on equity—is reduced by unanticipated inflation. Thus, equity holders are hurt by unanticipated inflation.[11]

The last important distributional effect of inflation concerns the real value of tax liabilities. A failure to index the tax structure implies that inflation moves the public into higher tax brackets and thus raises the real value of its tax payments or reduces real disposable income. Without indexed tax brackets, inflation is effectively the same as an increase in tax schedules. In Canada, tax brackets were fully indexed until 1985, at which point they were partially de-indexed. The federal government recently reinstituted full tax bracket indexation.[12]

The fact that unanticipated inflation serves mainly to redistribute wealth has led to some questioning of the reasons for public concern over inflation. The gainers, it seems, do not shout as loudly as the losers. Since some of the gainers (future taxpayers) have yet to be born, this is hardly surprising. There is also a notion that the average wage earner misperceives the connection between the nominal wage and price level increases (see Box 8-4).

**BOX 8-4**

## Surely, Anticipated Inflation Isn't Really Costless?

*It mainly is,* but the view of the average citizen seems to be closer to "5 percent inflation costs me 5 percent." Probably the misperception arises from a point of view something like the following: We understand that in a 5 percent anticipated inflation, nominal prices and nominal wages both rise 5 percent and so real wages are unchanged. Workers, however, see the 5 percent wage increase and attribute it to their own hard work, to the bargaining power of their unions, or to the success of their companies. The increase in prices is seen as eroding these "earned" gains.

While students of economics understand that the increases in nominal wages and prices are linked consequences of the inflation rate, it is hard to convince the general public of this view.

[11] See Charles R. Nelson, "Inflation and Rates of Return on Common Stocks," *Journal of Finance*, May 1976, for one of the earliest articles with this result—which has stood up to repeated testing. See also Franco Modigliani and Richard Cohn, "Inflation, Rational Valuation and the Market," *Financial Analysts Journal*, March–April 1979, for a controversial view of the reasons inflation affects the stock market.

[12] Inflation also affects the real rate of taxation of interest and other asset returns when taxes are not adjusted for inflation.

8-5

# INFLATION AND INDEXATION: INFLATION-PROOFING THE ECONOMY

In this section, we look briefly at two kinds of contracts that are especially affected by inflation: long-term loan contracts and wage contracts. We then discuss the possibility of reducing people's vulnerability to inflation by **indexation**, which ties the terms of contracts to the behaviour of the price level.

**indexation**
Ties the terms of contracts to the behaviour of the price level.

## Inflation and Interest Rates

There are many long-term nominal loan contracts, including 30-year government bonds and 25- or 30-year mortgages. For example, a firm may sell 20-year bonds in the capital markets at an interest rate of 8 percent per year. Whether the real (after-inflation) interest rate on the bonds turns out to be high or low depends on what the inflation rate will be over the next 20 years. The rate of inflation is thus of great importance to long-term lenders and borrowers, and this is especially true in housing.

## Inflation and Housing

The typical Canadian or U.S. household buys a home by borrowing from a bank or trust company. In Canada, interest payments on home mortgages are not tax-deductible. However, inflation still affects the real cost of financing a home. Consider someone buying a home in 1963 and financing it with a 25-year mortgage at a rate of 6 percent. Now, if the average rate of inflation over the 25 years is 5.5 percent, then the real cost of borrowing will be only 0.5 percent. In an interesting difference in tax laws, in the United States, interest payments on home mortgages are tax-deductible. Now consider the same home buyer, living in the United States. If the mortgage rate and inflation rate are the same, then the pre-tax cost of borrowing will be 0.5 percent. However, the home buyer in the United States can deduct the interest paid on the mortgage from his or her taxable income. At an interest rate of 6.0 percent and a tax rate of 30 percent, the tax reduction is worth 1.8 percent per year (30 percent of 6.0 percent), so the after-tax real cost of borrowing is minus 1.3 percent. Of course, the inflation rate may turn out to be lower than expected, and then the borrower will have done worse than he or she expected, and the lender will have made, rather than lost, money.

Uncertainty concerning the outlook for inflation was one of the reasons why *adjustable rate mortgages* became popular. These mortgages, which are essentially the same as floating rate loans, are simply long-term loans with an interest rate that is periodically (every year, for example) adjusted in line with prevailing short-term interest rates. To the extent that nominal interest rates roughly reflect inflation trends, adjustable rate mortgages reduce the effects of inflation on the long-term real costs of financing home purchases. There have been adjustable rate mortgages in Canada for many years.

www.statcan.ca/english/
IPS/Data/62F0014MIE200
3016.htm

## Indexed Debt

In countries where inflation rates are high and uncertain, long-term borrowing using nominal debt becomes impossible: Lenders are simply too uncertain about the real value of the repayments they will receive. In such countries, governments typically issue *indexed debt. A bond is indexed (to the price level) when either the interest or the principal or both are adjusted for inflation.*[13]

---

[13] It is also common to index debt to the value of a foreign currency, frequently the U.S. dollar.

The holder of an indexed bond will typically receive interest equal to the stated real interest rate (e.g., 3 percent) plus whatever the inflation rate turns out to be. Thus, if inflation is 18 percent, the bondholder receives 21 percent; if inflation is 50 percent, the *ex post* nominal interest payment is 53 percent. That way, the bondholder is compensated for inflation.

Many economists have argued that governments should issue indexed debt so that citizens can hold at least one asset with a safe real return. However, it is generally only governments in high-inflation countries, such as Brazil, Argentina, and Israel, that issue such debt, and they do it because they could not otherwise borrow.

Among low-inflation countries, the Canadian and British governments have been issuing indexed bonds for some time. The U.S. Treasury began issuing indexed debt in 1997, hoping that the value of "inflation insurance" would lower the real interest rate the government pays. Of course, since social security payments in many countries are effectively indexed, the citizens of those countries do hold an asset that protects them against inflation. However, the stream of social security payments is not an asset they can buy and sell.

We will now consider the arguments for and against indexation.

## Indexation of Wages

**cost-of-living adjustment (COLA)**

Links increases in money wages to increases in the price level.

Formal labour contracts sometimes include automatic **cost-of-living adjustment (COLA)** provisions. COLA provisions link increases in money wages to increases in the price level. COLA clauses are designed to allow workers to recover, wholly or in part, purchasing power lost through price increases since the signing of the labour contract.

This form of indexation is a quite common feature of labour markets in many countries. Indexation strikes a balance between the advantages of long-term wage contracts and the interests of workers and firms in not having real wages get too far out of line.

Because wage bargaining is time-consuming and difficult, wages are not negotiated once a week or once a month but, rather, in the form of one- or three-year contracts. However, since prices will change over the term of these contracts, some adjustment has to be made for inflation. Broadly, there are two possibilities. One is to index wages to the CPI or the GDP deflator and, through periodic—say, quarterly—reviews, to increase wages by the increase in prices over the period. The other is to schedule periodic, preannounced wage increases based on the expected rate of price increase. If inflation was known with certainty, the two methods would produce the same result. But since inflation can differ from expectations, there will be discrepancies.

We should expect to find indexation, rather than preannounced wage increases, when uncertainty about inflation is high. Inflation is more uncertain when the inflation rate is high than when it is low, and therefore wage indexation is more prevalent in high-inflation countries than in low-inflation countries.

## Why Not Index?

Economists have often argued that governments should adopt indexation on a broad scale, indexing bonds, the tax system, and everything else they control. That way, inflation would be much easier to live with, and most of the costs of unanticipated inflation would disappear. Governments, by contrast, have been very reluctant to index.

**BOX**

**8-5**

## Is a Little Inflation Good for the Economy?

More than 25 years ago, James Tobin argued that a small amount of inflation is good for the economy—and reduces the natural rate of unemployment—because it provides a necessary mechanism for lowering real wages without cutting nominal wages.* This idea has been revived in an influential article by George Akerlof, William Dickens, and George Perry.**

The argument is as follows: In a changing world, some real wages need to go up and some need to go down in order to achieve economic efficiency and low unemployment. It is easy to raise real wages by simply raising nominal wages faster than inflation. To decrease real wages, firms must hold nominal wage increases below the rate of inflation. For example, if the inflation rate is 10 percent, a 3 percent real wage cut can be accomplished by holding nominal wage increases to 7 percent. But at zero inflation, nominal wages have to be cut by 3 percent to accomplish a 3 percent real wage cut.

Workers are extraordinarily resistant to accepting cuts in nominal wages (the exception may be when firms are facing bankruptcy). Therefore, at zero inflation, firms would have a difficult time getting workers to accept a nominal wage cut. However, if inflation is low—say, 3 percent—then real wage cuts can be accomplished without nominal wage decreases.

The counterargument to this is that eventually workers would realize that a 7 percent wage increase with 10 percent inflation is actually a 3 percent real wage cut. In this case, it would not matter if inflation was zero, as workers would react in the same manner as when inflation was 10 percent.

The idea that positive inflation has a significant benefit is very controversial. The very existence of this controversy is a departure from the traditional view that zero is the best inflation target.

---

* See James Tobin, "Inflation and Unemployment," *American Economic Review*, March 1972.

** See G.A. Akerlof, W.T. Dickens, and G.L. Perry, "The Macroeconomics of Low Inflation," *Brookings Papers on Economic Activity*, 1 (1996).

There are three good reasons. First, as we see in the case of wage indexation, indexing makes it harder for the economy to adjust to shocks whenever changes in relative prices are needed. Second, indexing is in practice complicated, adding another layer of calculation to most contracts. Third, governments fear that by making inflation easier to live with, indexation will weaken the political will to fight inflation, lead to higher inflation, and possibly make the economy worse off, since indexation can never deal perfectly with the consequences of inflation.[14]

## *Working with Data*

The public dislikes both unemployment and inflation. One attempt to measure the effects of inflation and unemployment is called the *misery index*, which is simply the sum of unemployment and inflation.

$$\text{Misery index} = u + \pi$$

---

[14] Indexation cannot be perfect because there are lags in measuring the price level and making payments.

There are those who believe that the political party that holds power will do well if the misery index is low or falling. You can easily calculate the misery index from the sources provided so far. You should plot this index and see if you can correlate movements in this index to the outcomes of elections in Canada.

## C H A P T E R  S U M M A R Y

▶ In Canada, in any given month, most people who become unemployed remain unemployed for only a short period of time. Nonetheless, much of Canadian unemployment is accounted for by people who will be unemployed for a long period of time.

▶ There are significant differences in unemployment rates across age groups and regions in Canada. The unemployment rate for individuals in the 15–24 age group is significantly higher than for other age groups. Unemployment is highest in the Atlantic provinces and lowest in Ontario and the Prairies.

▶ The concept of the natural rate of unemployment is used to describe how much unemployment would exist even if the economy was at full employment.

▶ The major costs of unemployment are in terms of lost output. In addition, unemployment tends to be concentrated among the poor, and thus there is a distributional aspect to unemployment.

▶ The economy can adjust to perfectly anticipated inflation by moving to a system of indexed taxes and to nominal interest rates that reflect the expected rate of inflation. If inflation was perfectly anticipated and adjusted to, the only costs of inflation would be shoe-leather and menu costs.

▶ In Canada, the government issues real return bonds, which are indexed to the rate of change in the Consumer Price Index.

▶ Imperfectly anticipated inflation has important redistributive effects among sectors. Unanticipated inflation benefits monetary debtors and hurts monetary creditors. The government gains real tax revenue, and the real value of government debt declines.

▶ While very high inflation rates are considered to be bad, there is some evidence that a small, positive inflation rate lubricates the economy by reducing real wage rigidity.

## K E Y  T E R M S

unemployed person, *149*
unemployment pool, *150*
frictional unemployment, *152*
cyclical unemployment, *152*
natural rate of unemployment, *152*

unemployment hysteresis, *154*
sacrifice ratio, *157*
perfectly/imperfectly anticipated
  inflation, *160*
menu costs, *162*

wealth redistribution, *163*
indexation, *165*
cost-of-living adjustment
  (COLA), *166*

www.mcgrawhill.ca/college/dornbusch

## DISCUSSION QUESTIONS

1. Discuss reasons why the unemployment rate may be so much higher for the 15–24 age group.

2. Discuss why the Atlantic provinces may have higher unemployment rates than Ontario and the Prairies.

3. We say that the natural rate of unemployment is the rate of unemployment that would exist when the economy is at full employment. Is this a contradiction?

4. Some people say that since inflation can be reduced in the long run without an increase in unemployment, we should reduce inflation to zero. Others believe that a steady rate of inflation of, say, 3 percent should be our goal. What are the pros and cons of these two arguments?

5. Define the sacrifice ratio. At what horizons is it not zero? Explain.

6. State Okun's law. How does it help us evaluate the cost (to society) of unemployment?

7. What costs are associated with perfectly anticipated inflation? Do these costs change as the rate of inflation changes?

8. What costs are associated with imperfectly anticipated inflation? Discuss them carefully. Who loses and who gains when inflation is higher than we expect?

9. Should Canada index its wages and prices? Detail the pros and cons of such a plan. How would your answer differ if you expected the country would face a period of extremely high inflation (say, 300 percent)?

## APPLICATION QUESTIONS

1. The following information is to be used for calculation of the unemployment rate: Suppose there are two major groups, adults and teenagers, with adults divided into men and women. Teenagers account for 10 percent of the labour force; adults account for 90 percent. Women make up 35 percent of the labour force. Suppose also that the unemployment rates for these groups are as follows: teenagers, 19 percent; men, 7 percent; and women, 6 percent.

   a. Calculate the aggregate unemployment rate.

   b. What if the share in the labour force of teenagers increases from 10 to 15 percent? How will this affect the aggregate unemployment rate?

2. Use CANSIM to find unemployment and participation rates for both men and women over the age of 25 for the years 1981 to 2000.

3. Use CANSIM to find unemployment rates for the five regions of Canada for the years 1981 to 2000.

www.mcgrawhill.ca/college/dornbusch

# INTERNATIONAL ADJUSTMENT:

## Aggregate Demand and Supply in an Open Economy

### *LEARNING OBJECTIVES*

After reading and studying this chapter, you should be able to:

▶ *Understand that national economies are linked through trade flows and exchange rates.*

▶ *Understand that the real exchange rate is a measure of the price of Canadian goods relative to the price of foreign goods measured in one currency.*

▶ *Understand that an increase in the real exchange rate, which is called an* improvement in the terms of trade, *will lead to an increase in net exports, through a decrease in imports and an increase in exports.*

▶ *Understand that, in the long run, a monetary expansion will depreciate the nominal exchange rate and raise the domestic price level, leaving the real exchange rate unaltered.*

▶ *Understand that the monetary approach to the balance of payments emphasizes the connection between the changing domestic money supply and the level of the balance of payments.*

A s the world moves toward increasing globalization and freer trade among nations, countries are becoming more and more interdependent. Booms and recessions in one country spill over into other countries through trade flows and exchange rate movements. For example, in early 2003, the U.S. dollar began a long-awaited depreciation. Of course, from the Canadian perspective, this translated into a rather large, fast appreciation in the Canadian dollar relative to the U.S. dollar. There were fears that this would push the Canadian economy into a slow-growth, or even recessionary, period. These types of issues will be examined in this chapter.

## 9-1 | Aggregate Demand, Aggregate Supply, and Net Exports

In this section, we discuss how the *AD-AS* model that was developed in Chapters 6 and 7 can be used to discuss open economy issues. Central to our discussion will be an understanding of the role of the real exchange rate as a relative price that is important for net exports. In Chapter 5, we defined the real exchange rate as

$$R = \frac{eP_f}{P} \tag{1}$$

where $e$ is the nominal exchange rate, measured as the Canadian dollar price of foreign currency; $P_f$ is the nominal price of foreign goods, measured in foreign currency; and $P$ is the Canadian dollar price of Canadian goods. The numerator of equation (1) is the nominal price of foreign goods, expressed in Canadian dollars. Therefore, the **real exchange rate**, which is often called the **terms of trade**, is a measure of the relative price of Canadian and foreign goods.

> **real exchange rate (or terms of trade)**
>
> The ratio of foreign prices to Canadian prices, measured in a common currency.

To understand the role of the real exchange rate in macroeconomics, consider the following thought exercise. Suppose that the price of domestic goods, $P$, was to decrease, while the nominal exchange rate, $e$, and the foreign price level, $P_f$, were to remain constant. In this situation, we would say that there has been a relative price decrease in domestic goods. You can see from equation (1) that this would result in an increase in the real exchange rate. An increase in the real exchange rate will be referred to as an *improvement in the terms of trade.*

An increase in the real exchange rate will have an effect on both exports and imports. First, in the foreign economy, Canadian goods are now relatively cheaper than foreign goods, measured in foreign currency.[1] This should increase the demand for Canadian exports in the foreign country. Second, in the Canadian economy, the relative price of foreign goods, *measured in Canadian dollars*, has increased. This means that the price of imported goods in Canada relative to the price of Canadian goods would be higher. To the extent that consumers can (and are willing) to substitute between domestic and foreign goods, the Canadian demand for imports should decrease. Therefore, this increase in the real exchange rate should increase net exports. This is why the real exchange rate is often referred to as the terms of trade. In the situation described in this paragraph, we would say that the Canadian economy has experienced an improvement in the terms of trade. In general, the real exchange rate will rise (that is, there will be an improvement in the terms of trade) whenever there is an *increase* in foreign prices, a *decrease* in domestic prices, or a *depreciation* of the Canadian dollar.

---

[1] Remember that, in our example, the Canadian dollar price of goods decreased, while the nominal exchange rate remained constant. Therefore, the foreign currency price of Canadian goods has decreased.

In Chapter 6, we briefly discussed the Keynesian aggregate demand curve. Remember that this curve is downward sloping in $(P, Y)$ space because, as the price level increases, with the nominal money stock held constant, the real money stock decreases, which decreases aggregate demand. We can incorporate the real exchange rate into this aggregate demand curve by noting that when the real exchange rate increases, Canadian goods become relatively cheaper; therefore, exports increase and imports decrease, causing net exports to increase. Of course, if the real exchange rate decreases, then net exports will fall. Remember that, along an $AD$ curve, the Canadian price level, $P$, is an endogenous variable. The other components of the real exchange rate, $P_f$ and $e$, are exogenous variables for the $AD$ curve. Therefore, for a given nominal exchange rate and foreign price level, in an open economy, a decrease in the domestic price level will increase net exports and aggregate demand. This is an additional reason why the Keynesian aggregate demand curve slopes downward.

In Chapter 6, we also showed that an increase in the nominal money stock or an increase in government spending will shift the $AD$ curve outward. In our **open economy aggregate demand curve**, an increase in the foreign price level or a depreciation in the nominal exchange rate will also shift the $AD$ curve outward. This is shown in Figure 9-1.

**open economy aggregate demand curve**

The aggregate demand curve that takes into account changes in the real exchange rate.

## External Equilibrium

In Chapter 5, we discussed the balance of payments, concluding with an important identity.

$$S - I = NX$$

$$\text{Net foreign lending} = \text{Trade balance} \qquad (2)$$

We know that, for balance of payments equilibrium, the current account and

---

### FIGURE 9-1

**THE OPEN ECONOMY *AD* CURVE**

In an open economy, an additional reason for the *AD* curve to slope downward is that, for a given foreign price level and nominal exchange rate, a decrease in the Canadian price level improves the terms of trade and increases net exports. Additionally, for a given Canadian price level, a depreciation in the nominal exchange rate or an increase in the foreign price level will increase the terms of trade and shift the *AD* curve outward.

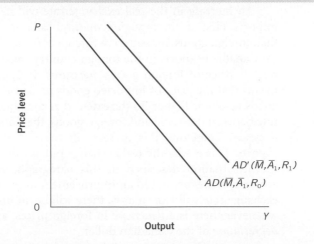

## Appreciation and Depreciation: Is That Up or Down?

When dealing with foreign exchange rates, we introduce a degree of complexity that requires us to be very careful about how we label variables and describe changes in variables. Remember that a nominal exchange rate is the relative price of two currencies. Consider the case of the Canada-U.S. nominal exchange rate. Because this is the relative price of Canadian and U.S. money, it can be expressed in Canadian dollars or in U.S. dollars. The convention that we have adopted in this book is to express the nominal exchange rate in Canadian dollars. Therefore, if the Canadian dollar price of a U.S. dollar increases (that is, $e$ goes up), this is referred to as a *depreciation* of the Canadian dollar. Notice that if we measured the nominal exchange rate in U.S. dollars, *then a depreciation would be a decrease in the U.S. dollar price*.

Now apply this logic to the construction of the real exchange rate.

$$R = \frac{eP_f}{P}$$

The numerator of the real exchange rate contains the nominal exchange rate, measured in Canadian dollars. Therefore, a depreciation in the nominal exchange rate, which is an increase in $e$, results in an increase in the real exchange rate (for a given $P$ and $P_f$), which we call an *improvement in the terms of trade*. This should lead to an increase in net exports.

Notice that the real exchange rate has a numerator and a denominator that are both measured in Canadian dollars. We could construct the same real exchange rate with the numerator and denominator both measured in U.S. dollars. Define the Canada-U.S. exchange rate, measured in U.S. dollars, as $E$ and construct the real exchange rate as given below.

$$\tilde{R} = \frac{EP}{P_f}$$

Be sure that you understand that this is the same *relative* price of Canadian and U.S. goods, but each *nominal* price is now measured in U.S. dollars. Therefore, the interpretation of $\tilde{R}$ is different from the interpretation of $R$. A depreciation in the nominal exchange rate, which is a decrease in $E$, results in $\tilde{R}$ decreasing, which is an improvement in the terms of trade.

You are strongly urged to attempt Application Question 7 at the end of the chapter to make certain that you understand these concepts.

capital account must offset each other.[2] Therefore, equation (2) states that any surplus in current account must equal capital account flows in terms of net lending or borrowing.

In this chapter, we will interpret equation (2) as a model of supply and demand for Canadian dollars in the foreign exchange market, where the price in this market is the real exchange rate, *R*. As an example, suppose that both net exports and net foreign investment are greater than zero. We assume that net foreign investment represents the quantity of Canadian dollars *supplied* to the exchange market that is used

---

[2] You should recognize equation (2) as being the same as equation (6) in Chapter 5. We repeat the assumption concerning some components of the balance of payments that we used in Chapter 5: In Table 5-1, net income from assets is essentially the same as net investment income from non-residents, which is part of GNP but not GDP. Since we are concerned with GDP, current account and net exports are assumed to be the same, and the terms will be used interchangeably.

to buy foreign assets, such as foreign bonds. We also assume that net exports represents the *demand* for Canadian dollars in the foreign exchange market, which is used to pay for the Canadian goods.

Given these assumptions concerning supply and demand for Canadian dollars in the foreign exchange market, we have depicted this market for Canadian dollars in the foreign exchange market in Figure 9-2.

In Figure 9-2, we have assumed that the supply of Canadian dollars is not dependent on the real exchange rate, so it is a vertical line. The demand for Canadian dollars is an upward sloping line, where an increase in the real exchange rate (an improvement in the terms of trade) increases the demand for net exports, as discussed above. In Figure 9-2, the point where demand and supply are equal determines the equilibrium real exchange rate, $R_0$.

---

**FIGURE 9-2**

**SUPPLY AND DEMAND FOR CANADIAN DOLLARS**

The supply of Canadian dollars comes from net foreign investment that is supplied to the exchange market to buy foreign assets, such as foreign bonds. The demand for dollars comes from the need to pay for our net exports. Supply and demand determine the equilibrium real exchange rate, $R$.

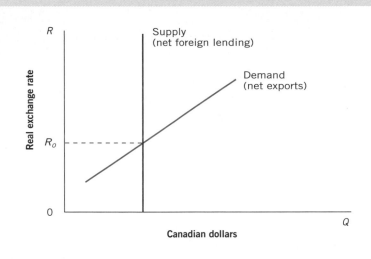

---

## The Effects of Expansionary Monetary Policy

In Chapter 7, we discussed how expansionary monetary policy could result in sticky price adjustment in the short run, and how the economy will eventually adjust to a new long run equilibrium position. In this section, we repeat this exercise, allowing for adjustment of net exports, capital flows, and the exchange rate. Figure 9-3(a) shows the *AD-AS* model initially in long run equilibrium at point *E*, where the economy is at full employment. Figure 9-3(b) shows equilibrium in the foreign exchange market. In this initial long run equilibrium, the domestic and foreign price levels are such that the nominal exchange rate is consistent with purchasing power parity (PPP).[3]

Now consider the effects of expansionary monetary policy. An increase in the nominal money supply, *M*, shifts the *AD* curve outward to *AD'*. Assuming that agents

---

[3] You may want to briefly review the section on PPP in Chapter 5.

have static expectations, the Canadian price level increases to $P'$. In the short run, for a given nominal exchange rate and a given foreign price level, this increase in the Canadian price level causes the terms of trade to worsen.[4] This is shown as a new short run real exchange rate of $R'$ in Figure 9-3(b). Because of the higher price level, Canada's competitive position in world markets has been eroded.

In the foreign exchange market, there is excess supply at the level of the real exchange rate, $R'$. This excess supply causes the nominal exchange rate to depreciate. Notice that this depreciation is needed to restore Canada's international competitive position. However, at the same time as the nominal exchange rate is depreciating, the Canadian price level continues to increase, as price expectations shift the SRAS curve to the left. Therefore, in order to reach long run equilibrium and restore our competitive position internationally, in the long run, there must be a real exchange rate depreciation from the lower level of $R'$. That is, on the adjustment path, the nominal exchange rate must depreciate more than the price level increases. This will ensure that the real exchange rate reverts to $R_0$.

At the new long run equilibrium, the price level in the Canadian economy is $P_1$, [at point $E_1$ in Figure 9-3(a)], which is consistent with the quantity theory of money result derived in Chapter 7. This price level is also consistent with PPP, as the real

---

**FIGURE 9-3**

An increase in the nominal money supply shifts the *AD* curve outward to *AD'*, and the Canadian price level to increases to *P'*. In the short run, for a given nominal exchange rate and a given foreign price level, the terms of trade worsen. This is shown as a new short run real exchange rate of *R'* in Figure 9-3(b). At the new long run equilibrium, the price level in the Canadian economy is $P_1$, which is consistent with the quantity theory of money. This price level is also consistent with PPP, as the real exchange rate and the level of net exports are the same as they were prior to the monetary expansion.

**OPEN ECONOMY ADJUSTMENT TO A MONEY SHOCK**

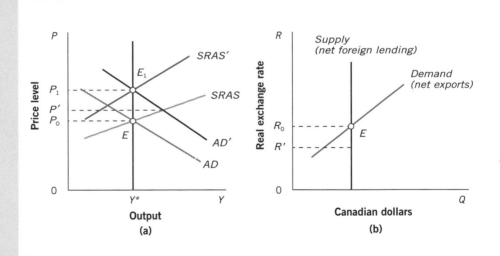

(a)

(b)

---

[4]An interesting facet of the adjustment path, which is not shown here, is that the initial increase in the money stock causes the nominal interest rate to decrease. In the very short run, this causes capital outflow and a temporary depreciation in the nominal exchange rate. Therefore, in the very short run, net exports actually show a temporary initial increase.

exchange rate and the level of net exports are the same as they were prior to the monetary expansion. The nominal exchange rate has depreciated enough to offset the increase in the price level caused by the monetary expansion, so in the new long run equilibrium, the real exchange rate is unchanged.

## Do Net Exports Respond to Changes in the Real Exchange Rate?

The adjustment described above is predicated on the assumption that net exports are positively related to changes in the real exchange rate. In Figure 9-4, we have graphed these two variables over the period 1972–2002.

Although it is difficult to tell from Figure 9-4 that there is an overall positive relationship between net exports and the real exchange rate, there are some periods where the co-movement is clear. Throughout the last half of the 1980s, the terms of trade slowly worsened. Between the first quarter of 1985 and the fourth quarter of 1991, the real exchange rate fell by 24 percent. You can see the resultant large decline in net exports over this period. Also, the long gradual increase in the real exchange rate over the latter half of the 1990s is matched by an increase in net exports.

*FIGURE 9-4*

**THE REAL EXCHANGE RATE AND NET EXPORTS, 1972–2002**

There is some tendency for the real exchange rate and net exports to move together. Throughout the last half of the 1980s, the terms of trade slowly worsened. Between the first quarter of 1985 and the fourth quarter of 1991, the real exchange rate fell by 24 percent. You can see the resultant large decline in net exports over this period. Also, the long gradual increase in the real exchange rate over the latter half of the 1990s is matched by an increase in net exports.

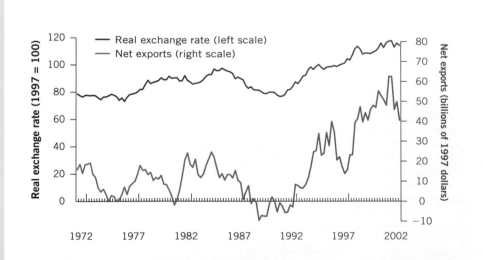

SOURCE: The real exchange rate is constructed as in equation (1), with 1997 = 100. Canadian price level: CANSIM II V735319; U.S. price level: CANSIM II V11123; nominal exchange rate: CANSIM II V37426; exports and imports: CANSIM II V1992249 and V1992253, respectively.

Then BOX
9-2

## Relative Prices and the Trade Balance: The J-Curve

It is possible that an improvement in the terms of trade could worsen the trade balance. To make this point clear, we write out the trade balance, measured in terms of domestic goods, as

$$NX = X - \frac{eP_f}{P} Q$$

where $X$ denotes the foreign demand for our goods or exports and $Q$ denotes our own import quantity. The term $(eP_f/P)Q$ thus measures the *value* of our imports in terms of domestic goods.

Suppose that we now have an exchange depreciation and that, in the first instance, domestic and foreign prices, $P$ and $P_f$, are unchanged. Then the relative price of imports, $eP_f/P$, rises. This leads to two effects. First, if the physical *volume* of imports does not change, their *value* measured in domestic currency unambiguously increases because of the higher price. This means higher import spending (measured in terms of the domestic currency) and thus a worsening of the trade balance. This is the source for the potentially perverse response of the trade balance to exchange depreciation.

However, there are two *volume* responses that run in the opposite direction: Exports should rise because our goods are now cheaper for foreigners to buy, and the volume of imports should decline because imports are more expensive.

The question, then, is whether the volume effects on imports and exports are sufficiently strong to outweigh the price effect, that is, whether depreciation raises or lowers net exports. Some of the empirical evidence on this question shows the following result:* *The short-term volume effects, say, within a year, are quite small and thus do not outweigh the price effect. The long-term volume effects, by contrast, are quite substantial, and certainly enough to make the trade balance respond in the normal fashion to a relative price change.*

Why does this pattern of responses take place? First, the low short-term and high longer-term volume effects result from the length of time consumers and producers take to adjust to changes in relative prices. Some of these adjustments may be instantaneous, but it is clear that tourism patterns, for example, may take six months to a year to adjust and that relocation of production internationally in response to changes in relative costs and prices may take years.

The lag in the adjustment of trade flows to changes in relative prices is thus quite plausible. What do these lags imply about the impact of relative price changes on the trade balance? Suppose that at a particular time, starting with a deficit, we have a depreciation that raises the relative price of imports. The short-term effects result primarily from increased import prices with very little offsetting volume effects. Therefore, the trade balance initially worsens. Over time, as trade volume adjusts to the changed relative prices, exports rise and import volume progressively declines. The volume effects come to dominate, and in the long run, the trade balance shows an improvement. This pattern of adjustment is referred to as the *J-curve effect*, because diagrammatically the response of the trade balance looks like a "J."

The medium-term problem of sticky real wages and the J-curve effect provides important clues for the interpretation of macroeconomic experiences across countries, particularly in showing why depreciations typically do not lead to improvements in the current account in the short term.

*See Ellen Meade, "Exchange Rate Adjustment and the J Curve," *Federal Reserve Bulletin*, October 1988, and Paul Krugman, "The J-Curve, the Fire Sale and the Hard Landing," *American Economic Review*, May 1989.

**BOX**

**9-3**

**www.bankofcanada.ca/
en/res/r984b-ea.htm**

## Fixed Exchange Rates and Devaluation

Prior to the early 1970s, most countries, including Canada, were on a fixed exchange rate system. Fixed exchange rate systems raise interesting questions concerning the financing of any external imbalance. Suppose that Canada was in a balance of payments deficit position. In this situation, there would be an excess supply of Canadian dollars (or an excess demand for foreign currency, which is the same thing), which would put depreciation pressure on the Canadian dollar. This could be remedied in the short run by the Bank of Canada supplying this excess demand for foreign currency at the level of the fixed exchange rate (that is, buying Canadian dollars and paying for them with foreign currency). Essentially, the Bank of Canada would be financing the current account deficit. However, maintaining and financing current account deficits over long periods of time is impossible.

In this situation, ultimately a country must restore its competitive position. This could happen through automatic adjustment in the domestic economy. For instance, the economy could adjust to a lower price level through aggregate demand and short run aggregate supply adjustment. This implies a recession to bring down the price level. The unemployment that typically accompanies this adjustment suggests that a less painful adjustment could be achieved through a devaluation in the nominal exchange rate. For given foreign and domestic prices, a devaluation in the nominal exchange rate will improve the terms of trade and, through an increase in exports and a decrease in imports, will ultimately correct the trade imbalance.

## 9-2 | THE MONETARY APPROACH TO THE BALANCE OF PAYMENTS

It is frequently suggested that external balance problems are monetary in nature and that, in particular, balance of payments deficits are a reflection of an excessive money supply.

There is a simple first answer to that suggestion. It is obviously true that, for any given balance of payments deficit, a sufficient contraction of the money stock will restore external balance. The reason is that a monetary contraction, by raising interest rates and reducing spending, reduces income and therefore imports. It is equally true that this result could be achieved by tight fiscal policy, and so there is nothing especially monetary about this interpretation of remedies for external imbalance.

A more sophisticated interpretation of the problem recognizes the links among the balance of payments deficit, foreign exchange market intervention, and the money supply in a fixed exchange rate system. The automatic mechanism is for a sale of foreign exchange—as arises in the case of a balance of payments deficit—to reduce the stock of high-powered money and hence the money stock. In a surplus country, the central bank increases the outstanding stock of high-powered money when it buys foreign exchange, thereby expanding the money stock. Given this link between the money supply and the external balance, it is obvious that this adjustment process must ultimately lead to the right money stock so that external payments will be in balance. This is the adjustment process discussed in Section 9-1.

## Sterilization

The only way the automatic adjustment process can be suspended is through *sterilization operations*. Central banks frequently offset, or sterilize, the impact of foreign exchange market intervention on the money supply through open market operations. Thus, a deficit country that is selling foreign exchange and correspondingly reducing its money supply may offset this reduction by open market purchases of bonds that restore the money supply.[5]

With sterilization, persistent external deficits are possible because the link between the external imbalance and the equilibrating changes in the money stock is broken. It is in this sense that persistent external deficits are a monetary phenomenon: By sterilizing, the central bank actively maintains the stock of money too high for external balance.

## The Monetary Approach and the IMF

**monetary approach**
The emphasis on monetary considerations in the interpretation of external balance problems.

The emphasis on monetary considerations in the interpretation of external balance problems is called the **monetary approach** to the balance of payments.[6] The monetary approach has been used extensively by the International Monetary Fund (IMF) in its analysis and design of economic policies for countries in balance of payments trouble. We give the flavour of the approach by describing typical IMF procedure in analyzing a balance of payments problem.

We start with the balance sheet of the monetary authority, usually the central bank, as in Table 9-1. The monetary authority's liabilities are high-powered money.[7] But on the asset side, it can hold both foreign assets—including foreign exchange reserves, gold, and claims on other central banks or governments—and domestic assets, or *domestic credit*. Domestic credit consists of the monetary authority's holdings of claims on the public sector—government debt—and on the private sector—usually loans to banks.

From the balance sheet identity, we have

www.imf.org/external/
pubs/cat/longres.cfm?sk=
16691.0

$$\Delta NFA = \Delta H - \Delta DC \qquad (3)$$

where $\Delta NFA$ denotes the change in net foreign assets, $\Delta H$ the change in high-powered money, and $\Delta DC$ the change in the central bank's extension of domestic credit. In words, the change in the central bank's holdings of foreign assets is equal to the change in the stock of high-powered money minus the change in domestic credit.

---

[5] *Currency boards*, such as those set up in Lithuania and Estonia, fix their country's exchange rate and permit high-powered money to be created only if it is fully backed by holdings of foreign currency. Currency boards amount to a fixed exchange rate system strictly without sterilization. Because sterilization is ruled out, adjustment is automatic, although of course not painless. Excellent references on currency boards include Steve Hanke and K. Schuler, *Currency Boards for Developing Countries* (San Francisco: International Center for Economic Growth, 1994), and Anna Schwartz, "Currency Boards: Their Past, Present, and Possible Future Role," *Carnegie-Rochester Conference on Public Policy*, December 1993.

[6] For a collection of essays on this topic, see Jacob Frenkel and Harry G. Johnson (eds.), *The Monetary Approach to the Balance of Payments* (London: Allen & Unwin, 1976). See also IMF, *The Monetary Approach to the Balance of Payments* (Washington, DC: International Monetary Fund, 1977), and Nadeem Haque, Kajal Lahiri, and Peter Montiel, "A Macroeconometric Model for Developing Countries," *IMF Staff Papers*, September 1990.

[7] The details of the Bank of Canada balance sheet will be discussed in Chapter 18.

The important point about equation (3) is that $\Delta NFA$ is the balance of payments: Official reserve transactions, which are all that $\Delta NFA$ is, are equal to the balance of payments.

The first step in developing a monetary approach-type of stabilization policy package is to decide on a balance of payments target, $\Delta NFA^*$. The IMF asks how much of a deficit the country can afford and then suggests policies to make the projected deficit no larger. The target is based largely on the availability of loans and credit from abroad and the possibility of drawing down existing reserves or the need to add revenues.

The next step is to ask how much the demand for money in the country will increase. The planned changes in the stock of high-powered money, $\Delta H^*$, will have to be just sufficient to produce, via the money multiplier process, the right increases in the stock of money to meet the expected increase in demand. Then, given $\Delta NFA^*$ and $\Delta H^*$, equation (3) tells the monetary authority how much domestic credit it can extend consistent with its balance of payments target and expected growth in money demand. Typically, a stabilization plan drawn up by the IMF will include a suggested limit on the expansion of domestic credit.

The limit provides a *ceiling on domestic credit expansion*. The adoption of such a ceiling helps the central bank avoid the temptation of expanding its loans to the government or private sector in the face of rising interest rates or government budget deficits.

**TABLE 9-1**

## BALANCE SHEET OF THE MONETARY AUTHORITIES

| Assets | Liabilities |
|---|---|
| Net foreign assets *(NFA)* | High-powered money *(H)* |
| Domestic credit *(DC)* | |

## How Does It Work?

The simplicity of equation (3) raises an obvious question. Since all it takes to improve the balance of payments is a reduction in the rate of domestic credit expansion, why not balance payments immediately and always? To answer this question, we need to understand the channels through which the curtailment of domestic credit improves the balance of payments.

Controlling domestic credit means operating tight monetary policy. Consider an economy that is growing and has some inflation, so demand for nominal balances is rising. If domestic credit expansion is slowed, an excess demand for money develops. This, in turn, causes interest rates to rise and spending to decline. The increase in interest rates leads to a balance of payments improvement. That is, the monetary approach as used by the IMF relies on restrictive monetary policy to control the balance of payments. There is, though, a subtle difference between domestic credit ceilings and ordinary tight money. In an open economy with fixed exchange rates, the money stock is endogenous. The central bank cannot control the money stock, since it has to meet whatever demand arises for foreign currency. But it can make "money" tight by reducing the growth of domestic credit. That will imply that the only source of money growth becomes an increase in foreign exchange reserves or foreign borrowing. The economy has to go through enough of a recession or rise in interest rates to generate a balance of payments surplus.

The use of domestic credit ceilings is a crude but easy-to-understand policy to improve the balance of payments. But the simplicity of the conceptual framework, and the apparent definiteness of the policy recommendations to which it leads, frequently makes it the best policy tool available, particularly if dramatic action is needed and the credibility of the government's policies needs to be restored.

## The Monetary Approach and Depreciation

Proponents of the monetary approach have argued that depreciation of the exchange rate cannot improve the balance of payments except in the short run. The argument is that in the short run, the depreciation does improve a country's competitive position and that this very fact gives rise to a trade surplus and therefore to an increase in the money stock. Over the course of time, the rising money supply raises aggregate demand and therefore prices until the economy returns to full employment and external balance. Devaluation thus exerts only a transitory effect on the economy, which lasts as long as prices and the money supply have not yet increased to match fully the higher import prices.

The analysis of the monetary approach is entirely correct in its insistence on a longer-run perspective in which, under fixed exchange rates, prices and the money stock adjust and the economy achieves internal and external balance. It is also correct in arguing that monetary or domestic credit restraint will improve the balance of payments. Typically, the tight money policy produced by slow domestic credit growth produces a recession.

The monetary approach is misdirected when it suggests that exchange rate policy cannot, even in the short run, affect a country's competitive position. More importantly, exchange rate changes frequently arise from a position of deficit and unemployment. In that case, a devaluation can be used to speed up the adjustment process.

## 9-3 | EXCHANGE RATE FLUCTUATIONS AND INTERDEPENDENCE

In the late 1960s, there was growing dissatisfaction with fixed exchange rates. The Bretton Woods system was called a crisis system because, from time to time, exchange rates would get out of line and expectations of exchange rate changes would precipitate massive capital flows that often forced the exchange rate changes that speculators expected. Is the flexible rate system put into effect in the 1970s better? Is it less crisis-prone, and does it provide a better framework for macroeconomic stability?

At one time it was argued that flexible exchange rates have the advantage of permitting countries to pursue their own national monetary and fiscal policies without having to worry about the balance of payments. This is certainly correct, but it is also misleading. There are important linkages between countries, whatever the exchange rate regime.

### Interdependence

**spillover (interdependence) effects** Occur when policy changes or supply/demand shocks in one country affect output in another.

**Spillover, or interdependence, effects** are at the centre of the discussion about flexible exchange rates. The effects of the tight U.S. monetary policy in 1981 created problems for all industrialized countries. The reason is clear from our models: As the United States tightens monetary policy, U.S. interest rates rise, and this attracts capital flows. The U.S. dollar appreciates and other currencies depreciate. The U.S.

appreciation implies a loss in U.S. competitiveness. World demand shifts from U.S. goods to those produced by other countries. Therefore, U.S. income and employment decline, while income and employment expand in other countries.

There are also spillover effects through prices. When the U.S. dollar appreciates, there is downward pressure on U.S. prices directly through import prices and indirectly through the decline in demand for U.S. goods. However, the opposite occurs in other countries. Their currencies depreciate and their prices increase. Thus there is inflation in other countries, which may welcome an increase in employment as a side effect of U.S. monetary policy but will not welcome the inflation.

In the same way, U.S. fiscal policies exert effects elsewhere. A U.S. fiscal expansion such as occurred during the early 1980s will lead to appreciation of the U.S. dollar and a loss in competitiveness. The direct increase in U.S. spending and the deterioration in U.S. competitiveness are the channels through which U.S. expansion is shared with other countries, which experience increased exports.

Policy makers in other countries therefore must decide whether to accept the higher employment-higher inflation effects of U.S. policies or to change their own

# POLICY IN *ACTION*

## One Mad Cow, Policy, and Interdependence

In mid-2003, the Canadian economy was hit with a series of shocks. The two most important of these were the spread of severe acute respiratory syndrome (SARS) in Ontario and bovine spongiform encephalopathy (BSE, or mad cow disease) in Alberta, both of which reminded of us of interdependence and the need for policy coordination internationally. Both of these shocks had almost immediate effects on the provincial and Canadian economies, but mad cow disease seemed to have particularly intricate international policy ramifications.

As soon as the one case of mad cow disease became public, the United States immediately closed the border to Canadian beef. High-level policy negotiations began with the United States in what appeared to be a vain attempt to reopen the U.S. border to Canadian beef. Suddenly, Japan announced that if the United States opened its border to Canadian beef, then Japan would no longer allow imports of U.S. beef. So, because of a policy decision in Japan, the United States would not immediately consider reopening its border to Canadian beef. There seemed to be no way for Canadian policy makers to overcome this problem. Meanwhile, a large number of other countries closed their borders to Canadian beef, and the Alberta beef industry was losing approximately $5 million per day.

The economic policy response in Canada was to offer some aid to the cattle industry but, of course, this could be considered as only a temporary measure, until policy negotiations opened the borders again. The lesson here is that policy decisions in all countries have international ramifications.

policies. If the rest of the world does not want *imported inflation,* then their response must be to tighten money. This response by Canada and other countries led to a spreading of the 1981–1982 recession throughout the world.

## Policy Coordination

www.imf.org/external/
pubs/ft/fandd/2003/06/pdf
/brooks.pdf

The large changes in exchange rates that arise when policies are not fully synchronized between countries pose a major threat to a world of free trade. A substantial appreciation and loss of competitiveness can cause large shifts in demand. Domestic workers become unemployed, and they recognize that foreign workers have gained the jobs they have lost. Thus, there will be pressure for protective tariffs or quotas to keep out imports that are "artificially cheap" because of the appreciation.

On the question of independence under flexible exchange rates, the experience of the last 20 years offers a clear answer. Under flexible rates, there is as much interdependence as there is under fixed rates, or more. Moreover, because exchange rates react so quickly to policies (good or bad), macroeconomic management does not become easier. To make the system work better than it has in the past clearly requires more coordination of policies.

## *Working with Data*

### The Nominal and Real Exchange Rates

In Working with Data in Chapter 5, we asked you to graph the real exchange rate. One way to look at PPP is to graph the real exchange rate together with the nominal exchange rate. You should be able to do this with the data that were used in Chapter 5. According to PPP, when the nominal exchange rate changes, the real exchange rate should not change. You should be able to see the close movement between the nominal and real exchange rates, and thus see that PPP does not seem to hold in the short run.

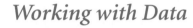

## C H A P T E R   S U M M A R Y

▶ The real exchange rate, which is often called the *terms of trade,* measures the relative price of domestic goods to foreign goods.

▶ An increase in the real exchange rate, which is referred to as an *improvement in the terms of trade,* will lead to an increase in net exports, through a decrease in imports and an increase in exports.

▶ In the long run, a monetary expansion increases the price level and depreciates the nominal exchange rate. All real variables, including the real exchange rate, are unchanged, so that the quantity theory of money and purchasing power parity hold in long run equilibrium.

▶ The monetary approach to the balance of payments draws attention to the fact that a payments deficit is always a reflection of a monetary disequilibrium and is always self-correcting. But the correction mechanism, because it involves unemployment, may be excessively painful compared with policy actions such as devaluation.

▶ Even under flexible exchange rates, economies are closely tied to one another. A monetary expansion at home will lead to unemployment and disinflation abroad. A fiscal expansion will cause an expansion abroad, along with inflation. These interdependent effects make a case for coordinating policies.

## K E Y   T E R M S

real exchange rate (or terms of trade), *171*
terms of trade, *171*

open economy aggregate demand curve, *172*
monetary approach, *179*

spillover (interdependence) effects, *181*

## D I S C U S S I O N   Q U E S T I O N S

1. Consider a country that is in a position of full employment and balanced trade. Which of the following types of disturbance can be remedied with standard aggregate demand tools of stabilization? Indicate in each case the impact on external and internal balance as well as the appropriate policy response.

   **a.** A loss of export markets

   **b.** A reduction in saving and a corresponding increase in the demand for domestic goods

   **c.** An increase in government spending

   **d.** A shift in demand from imports to domestic goods

   **e.** A reduction in imports with a corresponding increase in saving

2. In relation to external imbalance, a distinction is frequently made between imbalances that should be "adjusted" and those that should be "financed." Give examples of disturbances that give rise, respectively, to imbalances that require adjustment and those that should more appropriately be financed.

3. Should countries intervene to stabilize the exchange rate?

4. In Box 9-3, we stated that maintaining and financing current account deficits over long periods of time is impossible. Discuss why this is so.

5. In the early 1970s, Canada moved from a system of fixed exchange rates to a system of floating ones. Is the current flexible system less crisis-prone, or does it provide a better framework for macroeconomic stability? Discuss.

6. Discuss the lures and dangers in exchange market intervention when exchange rates are flexible. Do you think such intervention is a good idea?

7. Is the importance of spillover effects larger or smaller under flexible exchange rates, as opposed to fixed ones? Is macroeconomic management easier under one regime than the other?

## A P P L I C A T I O N     Q U E S T I O N S

1. Assume that there is perfect mobility of capital. How does the imposition of a tariff affect the exchange rate, output, and the current account? (Hint: Given the exchange rate, the tariff reduces our demand for imports.)

2. Use the central bank balance sheet to show how a balance of payments deficit affects the stock of high-powered money under fixed exchange rates. Show, too, how sterilization operations are reflected in the central bank's balance sheet.

3. Suppose your country's exports were to permanently increase. Explain how income, price adjustments, and adjustments to the real money supply would interact to lead it back to full employment and external balance.

4. What are the short-term and long-term volume effects of an exchange depreciation? Does empirical evidence suggest that they are of sufficient size to outweigh price effects and therefore improve the trade balance?

5. Show, graphically, the short and long run effects of a monetary expansion when both exchange rates and prices are flexible and capital is perfectly mobile. What happens during the period of adjustment from the short run to the long run?

 6. Go to CANSIM and retrieve the data needed to construct the real exchange rate, as given in Figure 9-4. Construct the real exchange rate as a relative price in Canadian dollars and as a relative price in U.S. dollars. Graph both of these variables and describe when there has been a terms of trade improvement and a worsening of the terms of trade for each variable.

# THE ECONOMY IN THE VERY SHORT RUN: SPENDING AND THE *IS-LM* MODEL OF ECONOMIC ACTIVITY

# INCOME AND SPENDING

### *LEARNING OBJECTIVES*

After reading and studying this chapter, you should be able to:

▶ *Understand that in the most basic model of aggregate demand, spending determines output and income, but output and income also determine spending. In particular, consumption depends on income, but increased consumption increases aggregate demand and, therefore, output.*

▶ *Understand that increases in autonomous spending increase output more than one for one. In other words, there is a multiplier effect.*

▶ *Understand that the size of the multiplier depends on the marginal propensity to consume and on tax rates.*

▶ *Understand that increases in government spending increase aggregate demand and, therefore, tax collections. However, tax collections rise by less than the increase in government spending, so increased government spending increases the budget deficit.*

P art 3 of this book discussed business cycle behaviour in a situation where prices are assumed to be sticky. In Chapter 7, we described the Phillips curve, which explains the short run co-movement of output and inflation over the business cycle. In this chapter and in Chapters 11 through 13 (all of Part 4), we are going to discuss business cycles in the very short run, under the assumption that the price level is fixed. Recall from Chapter 1 that in the very short run, we assume that the aggregate supply curve is horizontal. In this situation, any changes in aggregate demand will change equilibrium output only, with no change in price. Therefore, in this part of the book, we will concentrate on theories of aggregate demand. You can look at the models in this section as filling in the background behind the aggregate demand curve that was introduced in Chapters 6 and 7.

In Chapter 10, we present a very simple model of aggregate demand, one that discusses spending only. In later Part 4 chapters, we will enhance our definition of aggregate demand to include spending and the money market—that is the whole *IS-LM* model—which is the actual model that underlies the aggregate demand curve in Chapters 6 and 7.

This chapter gives a brief introduction to these very short run models of business cycle activity but concentrates primarily on consumption spending and its relationship to aggregate demand. In the next chapter, we also consider investment spending and the money market to complete our model of aggregate demand.

## 10-1 | AGGREGATE DEMAND AND EQUILIBRIUM INCOME

### The Consumption Function

In this section, we focus on the determinants of consumption demand. We do this primarily because consumption spending is very large, and because it is easy to see the link between consumption spending and income. In Chapters 2 and 3, we introduced the concept of *disposable income* ($YD$), which is equal to income ($Y$) minus taxes ($\overline{TA}$) plus transfers ($\overline{TR}$), as in equation (1).[1]

$$YD = Y - \overline{TA} + \overline{TR} \tag{1}$$

**consumption function**
Describes the relationship between consumption spending and disposable income.

We define the **consumption function** as a relationship between consumption spending ($C$) and disposable income ($YD$).

$$C = \overline{C} + cYD \tag{2}$$

This consumption function is shown in Figure 10-1.

**marginal propensity to consume**
The increase in consumption per unit increase in income.

The coefficient $\overline{C}$ is the intercept and represents the level of consumption spending when disposable income is zero.[2] The coefficient $c$ is the **marginal propensity to consume**, which tells us how much consumption increases for a unit increase in disposable income. For example, if $c = 0.9$, then every $1.00 increase in disposable

---

[1] Remember that a variable with a "bar" over it is assumed to be exogenous.

[2] In our formulation, you can think of the role of the intercept as representing factors that affect consumption other than income. One of these factors would be the ownership of assets such as stocks, bonds, and houses.

income will increase consumption spending by $0.90. Notice that the marginal propensity to consume is the slope of the consumption function in Figure 10-1.

---

**FIGURE 10-1**

The consumption function shows the level of consumption spending at each level of disposable income. The slope of the consumption function is given by the marginal propensity to consume, *c*.

**THE CONSUMPTION FUNCTION**

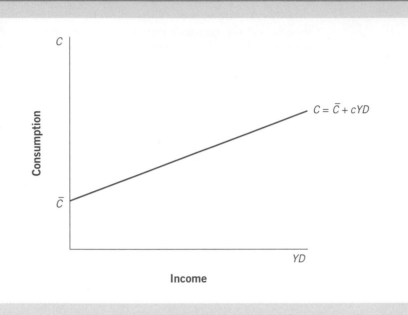

## The Consumption Function and Aggregate Demand

We know that consumption spending is only one component of aggregate demand.[3] For now, we will make the assumption that the other components of aggregate demand (investment spending, *I*; government spending, *G*; and net export spending, *NX*) are all exogenous. Gathering all of our aggregate demand terms together

$$AD = C + I + G + NX$$
$$= \bar{C} + cYD + \bar{I} + \bar{G} + \overline{NX}$$
$$= [\bar{C} + c(\overline{TR} - \overline{TA}) + \bar{I} + \bar{G} + \overline{NX}] + cY$$
$$= \bar{A}_0 + cY \tag{3}$$

Notice that we have grouped all of the exogenous terms into one variable called $\bar{A}_0$, and we define $\bar{A}_0 = \bar{C} + c(\overline{TR} - \overline{TA}) + \bar{I} + \bar{G} + \overline{NX}$—that is, all of the terms in the square brackets in equation (3). The aggregate demand function from equation (3) is shown in Figure 10-2.

---

[3] Remember that the concept of aggregate demand used in this chapter includes spending only. In the next chapter, we will broaden our view of aggregate demand to include spending on goods and services and the holding of money and bonds.

BOX

10-1

## The Consumption-Income Relationship

The consumption function of equation (2), $C = \overline{C} + cYD$, provides a good initial description of the consumption-income relationship. Annual per capita consumption and disposable personal income data for Canada for the years since 1961 are plotted in the figure below. Recall from Chapter 2 that disposable personal income is the amount of income households have available for either spending or saving after paying taxes and receiving transfers.

The figure reveals a very close relationship between consumption and disposable income. The actual relationship is

$$C = 0.28 + 0.89YD$$

where $C$ and $YD$ are each measured in thousands of 1997 dollars per person. Although the relationship between consumption and disposable income is close, there are some substantial deviations from the straight line, especially in the latter years. This means that something other than disposable income is affecting consumption in any given year. We turn our attention to the other factors determining consumption in Chapter 14. Meanwhile, it is reassuring that equation (2) is a quite accurate description of Canada's consumption-income relationship.

### RELATIONSHIP OF TOTAL CONSUMPTION TO DISPOSABLE INCOME

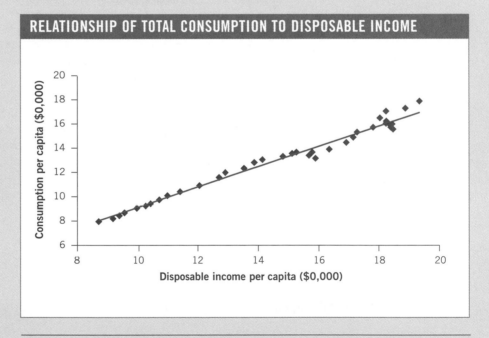

SOURCE: Consumption: CANSIM II V1992229; disposable income adapted from CANSIM II V501126 and V691803, deflated by the GDP deflator: CANSIM II V1997776; all series are divided by population: CANSIM II V1.

## Equilibrium Income

We know that in economics, equilibrium is almost always defined by the condition that supply equals demand. Equation (3) defines demand for us. However, we know that the supply curve for this model is a horizontal line in $P$, $Y$ space (as in Figure 6-7 in Chapter 6). It is impossible to draw this supply curve with the demand curve in

## FIGURE 10-2

### THE CONSUMPTION FUNCTION, AGGREGATE DEMAND AND EQUILIBRIUM OUTPUT

The vertical distance between the consumption function and the *AD* curve is given by $\bar{I} + \bar{G} + \overline{NX}$. Equilibrium income is given by the intersection of the *AD* curve with the 45° line, at point *E*, for income $Y_0$. At that point, $AD = Y$, which is the condition that supply equals demand.

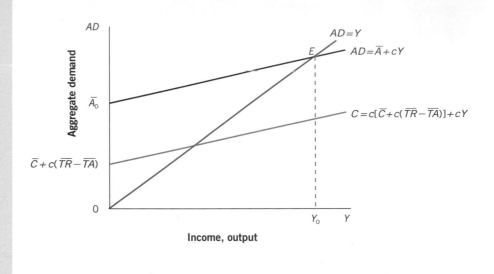

Figure 10-2 (the axes are different). In this model, we can think of income ($Y$) as being supply at any point in time. Therefore, equilibrium, which is defined as supply equals demand, will be anywhere that $Y = AD$. Therefore, instead of drawing the supply curve with the demand curve, we draw the equilibrium condition $Y = AD$ with the demand curve. The equilibrium condition is given by the $Y = AD$ line in Figure 10-2. Any point on a 45° line has the property that $Y = AD$. Therefore, equilibrium is defined where the *AD* curve intersects a 45° line, shown at point *E*, for income $Y_0$ in Figure 10-2.

It is fairly easy to write an equation for the equilibrium level of income. We know that *AD* is given by equation (3), which is repeated here

$$AD = \bar{A}_0 + cY$$

and the equilibrium condition is that supply equals demand.

$$Y = AD \tag{4}$$

Therefore, substituting equation (3) into equation (4)

$$Y = \bar{A}_0 + cY \tag{5}$$

Since $Y$ is on both sides of the equation, we can collect terms and solve for the equilibrium level of income.

$$Y_0 = \frac{1}{1-c}\bar{A}_0 \tag{6}$$

Equation (6) shows how the level of output is related to the marginal propensity to consume and the exogenous components of spending given in A–0. Frequently, we are interested in how a change in some component of A–0 (for instance, a change in government spending, $\bar{G}$) will change output. Starting from equation (6), we can relate changes in output to changes in exogenous spending through the equation

$$\Delta Y_0 = \frac{1}{1-c} \Delta \bar{A}_0 \qquad (7)$$

For example, if the marginal propensity to consume is 0.9, then $\frac{1}{1-c} = 10$, and a $1-billion increase in government spending ($\bar{G}$) will lead to a $10-billion increase in output. Notice that the change in output is a multiple of the change in spending, and this is why the term $\frac{1}{1-c}$ is called the *multiplier*. We will discuss this in detail in the next section.

## BOX 10-2

## Consumption, Savings, Investment, and Equilibrium: Why Is Chapter 3 Different from Chapter 10?

In Chapter 3 and in this chapter, we have based theories of aggregate demand on the GDP identity

$$Y = C + I + G + NX$$

In equilibrium, supply ($Y$) must equal the sum of all of the demand components ($C + I + G + NX$). No matter what the underlying model is, the first equation can always be manipulated in the following manner. Income can be either spent or saved or paid in taxes.

$$Y = C + S + \overline{TA} + \overline{TR}$$

Combining the two equations,

$$I + NX = S + (\overline{TA} - \bar{G} - \overline{TR})$$

The final equation is a form of the familiar condition that savings must equal investment (both private and government) in equilibrium. One lesson here is that you can always write the equilibrium condition that supply of goods and services equals demand for goods and services ($Y = AD$) as the condition that savings equals investment ($S = I$).

So, is the analysis in Chapter 3 different from the analysis in this chapter? The answer is that the model is different, so the results are different. In Chapter 3, we made the assumption that, in the long run, the *AS* curve is vertical and the level of output is determined by the amount of capital and labour through the production function. In this model, consumption, savings, and investment are dependent on the real rate of interest. A change in any exogenous component of aggregate demand will change the real rate of interest and also change the allocation of the level of income. This makes good sense in the long run.

In this chapter, we make the very short run assumption that the aggregate supply curve is horizontal and the level of output is determined by aggregate demand. Savings and consumption are related to the level of income, so a change in any exogenous component of *AD* will change actual output, which makes sense over the very short run.

## 10-2 | THE MULTIPLIER

In this section, we develop an answer to the following question: By how much does a $1 increase in autonomous spending raise the equilibrium level of income? There appears to be a simple answer: Since, in equilibrium, income equals aggregate demand, it would seem that a $1 increase in (autonomous) demand or spending should raise equilibrium income by $1. That answer is wrong. Let us now see why.

Suppose first that output increased by $1 to match the increased level of autonomous spending. This increase in output and income would in turn give rise to further *induced* spending as consumption rises, because the level of income has risen. How much of the initial $1 increase in income would be spent on consumption? Out of an additional dollar of income, a fraction ($c$) is consumed. Assume, then, that production increases further to meet this induced expenditure, that is, that output and thus income increase by $1 + c$. That will still leave us with an excess demand, because the expansion in production and income by $1 + c$ will give rise to further induced spending. This story could clearly take a long time to tell. Does the process have an end?

In Table 10-1, we lay out the steps in the chain more carefully. The first round begins with an increase in autonomous spending, $\Delta\overline{A}$. Next, we allow an expansion in production to meet exactly that increase in demand. Production accordingly expands by $\Delta\overline{A}$. This increase in production gives rise to an equal increase in income and, therefore, via the marginal propensity to consume, $c$, gives rise in the second round to induced expenditures of size $c\Delta\overline{A}$. Assume again that production expands to meet this increase in spending. The production adjustment this time is $c\Delta\overline{A}$, and so is the increase in income. This gives rise to a third round of induced spending equal to the marginal propensity to consume times the increase in income, $c(c\Delta\overline{A}) = c^2\Delta\overline{A}$. Since the marginal propensity to consume, $c$, is less than 1, the term $c^2$ is less than $c$, and therefore induced expenditures in the third round are smaller than those in the second round.

If we write out the successive rounds of increased spending, starting with the initial increase in autonomous demand, we obtain

$$\Delta AD = \Delta\overline{A} + c\Delta\overline{A} + c^2\Delta\overline{A} + c^3\Delta\overline{A} + \ldots$$
$$= \Delta\overline{A}(1 + c + c^2 + c^3 + \ldots) \tag{8}$$

For a value of $c<1$, the successive terms in the series become progressively smaller. In fact, we are dealing with a geometric series, so the equation simplifies to

$$\Delta AD = 1/(1 - c)\Delta\overline{A} = \Delta Y_0 \tag{9}$$

| TABLE 10-1 | THE MULTIPLIER | | |
|---|---|---|---|
| Round | Increase in Demand This Round | Increase in Production This Round | Total Increase in Income (All Rounds) |
| 1 | $\Delta\overline{A}$ | $\Delta\overline{A}$ | $\Delta\overline{A}$ |
| 2 | $c\Delta\overline{A}$ | $c\Delta\overline{A}$ | $(1 + c)\Delta\overline{A}$ |
| 3 | $c^2\Delta\overline{A}$ | $c^2\Delta\overline{A}$ | $(1 + c + c^2)\Delta\overline{A}$ |
| 4 | $c^3\Delta\overline{A}$ | $c^3\Delta\overline{A}$ | $(1 + c + c^2 + c^3)\Delta\overline{A}$ |
| . . . | . . . | . . . | . . . |
| . . . | . . . | . . . | |
| . . . | . . . | . . . | $\dfrac{1}{1-c}\Delta\overline{A}$ |

From equation (9), therefore, we find that the cumulative change in aggregate spending is equal to a multiple of the increase in autonomous spending—just as we deduced from equation (7). The multiple $1/(1-c)$ is called the *multiplier*.[4] The **multiplier** is the amount by which equilibrium output changes when autonomous aggregate demand increases by one unit.

The concept of the multiplier is sufficiently important to create new notation. The general definition of the multiplier is $\Delta Y/\Delta \overline{A}$, the change in equilibrium output when autonomous demand increases by one unit. In this specific case, omitting the government sector and foreign trade, we define the multiplier as $\alpha$, where

$$\alpha \equiv \frac{1}{1-c} \qquad (10)$$

Inspection of the multiplier in equation (10) shows that the larger the marginal propensity to consume, the larger the multiplier. For a marginal propensity to consume of 0.6, the multiplier is 2.5; for a marginal propensity to consume of 0.8, the multiplier is 5. This is because a high marginal propensity to consume implies that a larger fraction of an additional dollar of income will be consumed, and thus added to aggregate demand, thereby causing a larger induced increase in demand.

Why focus on the multiplier? The reason is that we are developing a very short run explanation of fluctuations in output. The multiplier suggests that output changes when autonomous spending (including investment) changes *and* that the change in output can be larger than the change in autonomous spending. The multiplier is the formal way of describing a common-sense idea: If the economy for some reason—for example, a loss in confidence that reduces investment spending—experiences a shock that reduces income, people whose incomes have gone down will spend less, thereby driving equilibrium income down even further. The multiplier is therefore potentially part of the explanation of why output fluctuates.

## 10-3 | FISCAL POLICY IN THE VERY SHORT RUN

We define fiscal policy as the policy of the government toward the level of government spending ($\overline{G}$), the level of transfers ($\overline{TR}$), or the level of taxes ($\overline{TA}$).[5] We now make the assumption that, rather than being exogenous, the government imposes a proportional income tax, collecting a fraction, $t$, of income in the form of taxes.

$$TA = tY \qquad (11)$$

With this specification of fiscal policy, we can rewrite the consumption function as

$$C = \overline{C} + cYD$$
$$= \overline{C} + c(Y + \overline{TR} - tY)$$
$$= \overline{C} + c\overline{TR} + c(1-t)Y \qquad (12)$$

**multiplier**

The amount by which equilibrium output changes when autonomous aggregate demand increases by one unit.

---

[4] Table 10-1 and equation (9) derive the multiplier using the mathematics of geometric series. If you are familiar with calculus, you will realize that the multiplier is nothing other than the derivative of the equilibrium level of income, $Y_0$, in equation (6) with respect to autonomous spending. Use calculus on equation (6) to check the statements in the text.

[5] In Chapter 2, we defined G as government purchases, and purchases plus transfers as government expenditure. In this chapter, we follow the convention that is often used in the very short run—that government purchases are labelled *government spending*.

Now we can add the other components of aggregate demand.

$$AD = C + I + G + NX$$
$$= \bar{C} + cYD + \bar{I} + \bar{G} + \overline{NX}$$
$$= \bar{C} + c(Y + \overline{TR} - tY) + \bar{I} + \bar{G} + \overline{NX}$$
$$= [\bar{C} + c\overline{TR} + \bar{I} + \bar{G} + \overline{NX}] + c(1-t)Y$$
$$= \bar{A}_1 + c(1-t)Y \tag{13}$$

where $\bar{A}_1 = \bar{C} + c\overline{TR} + \bar{I} + \bar{G} + \overline{NX}$, which is larger than the previous intercept term, $\bar{A}_0$. In addition to this, while the marginal propensity to consume out of disposable income remains $c$, the marginal propensity to consume out of total income is now $c(1-t)$, where $c(1-t)$ is the fraction of income left after taxes. Therefore, the marginal propensity to consume out of total income is smaller than the marginal propensity to consume out of disposable income. For example, if the marginal propensity to consume, $c$, is 0.8 and the tax rate, $t$, is 0.15, the marginal propensity to consume out of total income, $c(1-t)$ is $0.6[= 0.8 \times (1 - 0.25)]$.

The effects of introducing fiscal policy in terms of a marginal tax rate are shown in Figure 10-3. The new aggregate demand curve, denoted $AD'$, has a higher intercept but a flatter slope. The intercept is larger because the term $cTA$ is no longer in the intercept, and the slope is smaller because the marginal propensity to consume out of total income is now $c(1-t)$, which is smaller than $c$. Notice that, with the slope of the $AD$ curve flatter, the multiplier is now smaller. If the marginal propensity to consume, $c$, is 0.8 and the tax rate, $t$, is zero, the multiplier is $5[= (1/1 - 0.8)]$ with the same marginal propensity to consume, and a tax rate of 0.25, the multiplier is $2.5[= 1/1 - 0.8(1 - 0.25)]$. Income taxes reduce the multiplier because they reduce the induced increase in consumption out of changes in income.

## FIGURE 10-3    ENDOGENOUS TAXES AND AGGREGATE DEMAND

The new aggregate demand curve, denoted $AD'$, has a higher intercept but a flatter slope. The intercept is larger because the term $-c\overline{T}A$ is no longer in the intercept, and the slope is smaller because the marginal propensity to consume out of total income is now $c(1 - t)$, which is smaller than $c$.

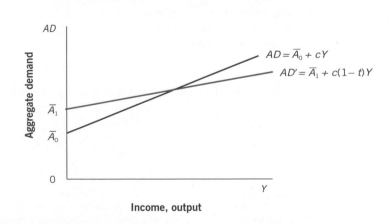

We can now determine the equilibrium in this model by combining the new aggregate demand equation given by equation (13) with the equilibrium condition $Y = AD$.

$$Y = \bar{A}_1 + c(1-t)Y \tag{14}$$

and solving for the equilibrium value of $Y$.

$$Y = \frac{1}{1 - c(1-t)}\,\bar{A}_1 \tag{15}$$

## Automatic and Discretionary Fiscal Policy

We can think of the government enacting fiscal policy in two ways. First, fiscal policy could be thought of as being a set of rules that are in place that will automatically have effects on the economy. We define an **automatic stabilizer** as any mechanism in the economy that automatically—that is, with case-by-case government intervention—reduces the amount that output changes in response to a change in some exogenous component of demand. The second type of fiscal policy is called **discretionary fiscal policy**. The government is said to undertake discretionary fiscal policy when it changes a variable under its control—say, government spending or the tax rate—in response to an observed change in the economy.

The proportional income tax is one example of an automatic stabilizer. One explanation of the business cycle is that it is caused by exogenous shifts in demand, especially investment demand. These shifts in investment demand have a smaller effect on output when automatic stabilizers are in place, as the existence of a proportional income tax lowers the multiplier. The proportional income tax is not the only automatic stabilizer. Employment Insurance benefits enable the unemployed to continue consuming even though they do not have jobs, so $TR$ rises when output falls. This means that demand falls less when someone becomes unemployed and receives benefits than it would if there were not benefits. This, too, makes the multiplier smaller and output more stable.

One example of a discretionary fiscal policy change is an increase in government purchases, $\bar{G}$. This is illustrated in Figure 10-4.

In Figure 10-4, the initial equilibrium level of income is $Y_0$ at point $E$. An increase in government purchases shifts the $AD$ curve upward by the change in $\bar{G}$, which we have shown as $\Delta\bar{G}$. This increase causes income and output to rise until the new equilibrium is reached at $Y_1$.

We can use the multiplier to determine how much equilibrium income changes. In this case, because we have introduced a proportional tax, $t$, the multiplier is $\frac{1}{1-c(1-t)}$ rather than $\frac{1}{1-c}$, so that the change in income is given by[6]

$$\Delta Y = \frac{1}{1 - c(1-t)}\,\Delta\bar{G} = \alpha_G \Delta\bar{G} \tag{16}$$

---

[6] Notice that $\bar{G}$ is one component of $\bar{A}$. The other components ($\bar{C}$, $\overline{TR}$, $\bar{I}$, and $\overline{NX}$) are all held constant. Therefore, in equation (16), $\Delta\bar{G}$ is identical to $\Delta\bar{A}$.

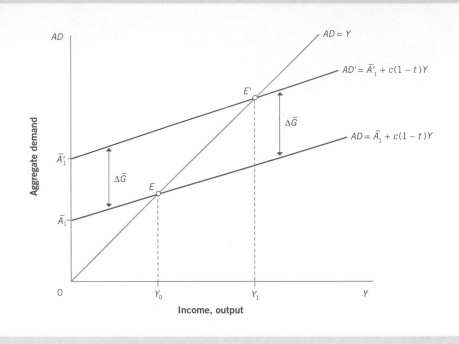

**FIGURE 10-4**

An increase in government spending shifts the aggregate demand curve up from *AD* to *AD'*. Income rises from $Y_0$ to $Y_1$.

**THE EFFECTS OF AN INCREASE IN GOVERNMENT PURCHASES**

where

$$\alpha_G = \frac{1}{1 - c(1-t)} \qquad (17)$$

Therefore, a $1.00 increase in government purchases leads to an increase in income in excess of $1.00.

## 10-4 | THE GOVERNMENT BUDGET IN THE VERY SHORT RUN

In Chapter 3, we introduced the concept of the government budget deficit. In Figure 3-11, we showed that the federal government ran budgetary deficits in each year from approximately 1974 to 1997. We showed that one of the long run consequences of this chronic government budgetary deficit was an increase in the real rate of interest. In this section, we are going to look at the very short run mechanics of the government budget deficit and see how very short run fiscal policy affects the government budget position.

The basic framework for discussing the government fiscal position is the concept of a budgetary deficit or surplus, which is identical to government savings. When government savings is positive, the government is said to be running a **budget surplus**, and when government savings is negative, the government is said to be running a **budget deficit**. In order to be consistent with how most analysts discuss the government fiscal position in the very short run, we will refer to government savings as a deficit or surplus for the remainder of this chapter.

**budget surplus**
The excess of the government's revenues, taxes, over its total expenditures, consisting of purchases of goods and services and transfer payments.

**budget deficit**
An excess of expenditures over revenues.

## POLICY IN *ACTION*

### Short Run and Long Run Effects of Fiscal Policy

Broadly speaking, fiscal policy can be viewed as a change in either government spending or tax rates. The federal government infrastructure initiative that was announced in late 2002 is one example of fiscal policy. However, we must be very careful if we wish to place this fiscal policy in the framework of Figure 10-4. The idea behind this initiative was that government money could be spent on items that would increase the amount of infrastructure capital.

Clearly, as the money is spent, this would increase the *AD* curve as in Figure 10-5. However, the fiscal multiplier presented in this chapter is only a very short run phenomenon. The *AD* curve will stay in its new high position only as long as the government money continues to be spent. As soon as the spending ends, the curve will shift back down and income will also decrease to its previous position. The longer run effects of this initiative may be through increases in the capital stock, as in Chapter 4.

Define a budget surplus (*BS*) as the excess of tax revenue over government spending.

$$BS \equiv TA - \overline{G} - \overline{TR} \qquad (18)$$

www.fin.gc.ca/wp/2002-10e.html

Of course, a negative budget surplus, which would be an excess of government spending over government revenue, would be called a budget deficit. Continuing the assumption of a proportional income tax that yields tax revenues $TA = tY$, we can write the government budget surplus as

$$BS = tY - \overline{G} - \overline{TR}$$

Notice that equation (19) says that there is a positive relationship between the level of GDP and the level of the budget surplus for given levels of government purchases and transfers. We have graphed this relationship in Figure 10-5.

Figure 10-5 plots the budget surplus as a function of the level of income for a given level of government purchases, transfers, and the tax rate. Notice that, for income less than the point where the *BS* line crosses the *Y* axis, the government is in a deficit position, while for income higher than this point, the government is in a surplus position.

Be sure to understand that in Figure 10-5, we are not determining the level of income, but rather we can calculate the budget deficit or surplus only for some given level of income. Consider the situation where there is an increase in the level of income caused by, say, an increase in exogenous investment demand. This would be a rightward movement along the *BS* curve and the deficit would fall (or the surplus

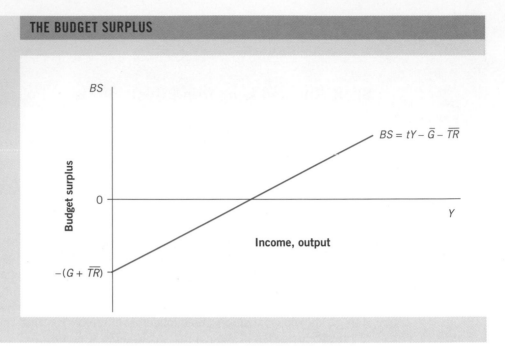

*FIGURE 10-5*

**THE BUDGET SURPLUS**

The budget surplus of deficit depends in part on the level of income. Given the tax rate, *t*, and $\overline{G}$ and $\overline{TR}$, the budget surplus will be high if income is high—because the government takes in a lot of taxes. If the level of income is low, there will be a budget deficit because government tax receipts are small.

would increase, depending on where income was prior to the change) without any change in government fiscal policy.

Fiscal policy can be viewed in two ways using Figure 10-5. First, an increase in government spending ($\overline{G}$ or $\overline{TR}$) would shift the *BS* line outward (remember that the intercept ($\overline{G} + \overline{TR}$) has a negative sign in front of it). Therefore, for every level of income, the deficit would be larger or the surplus would be smaller. Second, an increase in the marginal tax rate (*t*) would increase the slope of the *BS* line, making the deficit smaller (or the surplus larger) for every level of income.

In either of these cases, however, we do not know the size of the deficit or surplus after the change until we know the level of income before and after the change. Consider expansionary fiscal policy through an increase in $\overline{G}$. This would shift the *BS* curve to the right. If the level of income did not change, then clearly this increase in $\overline{G}$ would increase the deficit. However, this increase in $\overline{G}$ will cause a multiple increase in income. Whether or not the increase in $\overline{G}$ leads to an increase or a decrease in the budget position depends on the relative size of these two increases. It turns out that an increase in $\overline{G}$ unambiguously increases the deficit (reduces the surplus). This is discussed in the next section.

## Effects of Government Purchases and Tax Changes on the Budget Surplus

Next we show how changes in fiscal policy affect the budget. In particular, we want to find out whether an increase in government purchases must reduce the budget surplus. At first sight, this appears obvious, because increased government purchases, from equation (18), are reflected in a reduced surplus or an increased deficit. On further thought, however, the increase in government purchases will cause a multiple increase in income and, therefore, increased income tax collection. This raises the interesting possibility that tax collection might increase by more than government purchases.

A brief calculation shows that the first guess is right: Increased government purchases reduce the budget surplus. From equation (16) we see that the change in income due to increased government purchases is equal to $\Delta Y_0 \equiv \alpha_G \Delta \overline{G}$. A fraction of that increase in income is collected in the form of taxes, so tax revenue increases by $t\alpha_G \Delta \overline{G}$. The change in the budget surplus, using equation (17) to substitute for $\alpha_G$, is therefore

$$\Delta BS = \Delta TA - \Delta \overline{G}$$

$$= \alpha_G \Delta \overline{G} - \Delta \overline{G}$$

$$= \left[ \frac{t}{1-c(1-t)} - 1 \right] \Delta \overline{G}$$

$$= -\frac{(1-c)(1-t)}{1-c(1-t)} \Delta \overline{G} \tag{20}$$

which is unambiguously negative.

We have, therefore, shown that an increase in government purchases will reduce the budget surplus, although in this model by considerably less than the increase in purchases. For instance, for $c = 0.8$ and $t = 0.25$, a \$1.00 increase in government purchases will create a \$0.375 reduction in the surplus.

In the same way, we can consider the effects of an increase in the tax rate on the budget surplus. We know that the increase in the tax rate will reduce the level of income. It might thus appear that an increase in the tax rate, keeping the level of government spending constant, could reduce the budget surplus. In fact, an increase in the tax rate increases the budget surplus, despite the reduction in income that it causes, as you are asked to show in Application Question 3 at the end of this chapter.[7]

**balanced budget multiplier**

Increase in output that results from equal increases in taxes and government purchases.

This leads to another interesting result known as the **balanced budget multiplier**. Suppose government spending and taxes are raised in equal amounts and thus in the new equilibrium, the budget surplus is unchanged. By how much will output rise? The answer is that for this special experiment, the multiplier is equal to 1—output rises by the increase in government spending and no more.

## The Full Employment Budget Surplus

The final topic to be treated here is the concept of the full employment budget surplus.[8] Recall that increases in taxes add to the surplus and that increases in government expenditures reduce the surplus. Increases in taxes have been shown to reduce the level of income; increases in government purchases and transfers have been shown to increase the level of income. It thus seems that the budget surplus is a convenient, simple measure of the overall effects of fiscal policy on the economy. For instance, when the budget is in deficit, we would say that fiscal policy is expansionary, tending to increase GDP.

---

[7] The theory that tax rate cuts would increase government revenue (or tax rate increases reduce government revenue) is associated with Arthur Laffer, formerly at the University of Chicago and University of Southern California. Laffer's argument, however, did not depend on the aggregate demand effects of tax cuts but, rather, on the possibility that a tax cut would lead people to work more.

[8] The concept has a long history; it was first used by E. Cary Brown, "Fiscal Policy in the Thirties: A Reappraisal," *American Economic Review*, December 1956.

However, the budget surplus by itself suffers from a serious defect as a measure of the direction of fiscal policy. The defect is that the surplus can change because of changes in autonomous private spending—as can be seen in Figure 10-5. Thus, an increase in the budget deficit does not necessarily mean that the government has changed its policy in an attempt to increase the level of income.

Since we frequently want to measure the way in which fiscal policy is being used to affect the level of income, we require some measure of policy that is independent of the particular position of the business cycle—boom or recession—in which we may find ourselves. Such a measure is provided by the full employment budget surplus, which we denote by $BS^*$. The **full employment budget surplus** measures the budget surplus at the full employment level of income or at potential output. Using $Y^*$ to denote the full employment level of income, we can write

**full employment budget surplus**

The budget surplus at the full employment level of income or at potential output.

$$BS^* = tY^* - \overline{G} - \overline{TR} \qquad (21)$$

There are other names for the full employment surplus. Among them are the *cyclically adjusted surplus* (or deficit), the *high-employment surplus*, the *standardized employment surplus*, and the *structural surplus*. These new names all refer to the same concept as the full employment surplus, but they avoid implying that there is a unique level of full employment output that the economy has not yet reached. They suggest, reasonably, that the concept is merely a convenient reference point that fixes a given level of employment as the reference point.

To see the difference between the actual and the full employment budgets, we subtract the actual budget surplus in equation (19) from the full employment budget surplus in equation (21) to obtain

$$BS^* - BS = t(Y^* - Y) \qquad (22)$$

The only difference arises from income tax collection.[9] Specifically, if output is below full employment, the full employment surplus exceeds the actual surplus. Conversely, if actual output exceeds full employment (or potential) output, the full employment surplus is less than the actual surplus. The difference between the actual and the full employment budget is the *cyclical* component of the budget. In a recession, the cyclical component tends to show a deficit, and in a boom, there may even be a surplus.

We next look at the full employment budget deficit shown in Figure 10-6. Public concern about the deficit mounted in the 1980s. For many economists, the behaviour of the deficit during the high-unemployment years 1982 and 1983 was not especially worrisome. The actual budget is usually in deficit during recessions. But the shift toward deficit of the full employment budget was regarded as an entirely different matter.

Two final words of warning: First, there is no certainty as to the true full employment level of output. Various assumptions about the level of unemployment that corresponds to full employment are possible. Estimates of the full employment deficit or surplus will differ depending on the assumptions made about the economy at full employment.

---

[9] In practice, transfer payments, such as welfare and unemployment benefits, are also affected by the state of the economy, so *TR* also depends on the level of income. But the major cause of differences between the actual surplus and the full employment surplus is taxes.

## FIGURE 10-6

### ACTUAL AND CYCLICALLY ADJUSTED BUDGET DEFICIT, 1970–2002

After 1974, the federal government began running large budgetary deficits. In the recession of the early 1980s, the cyclically adjusted deficit was lower than the actual deficit, reflecting the fact that the economy was below full employment.

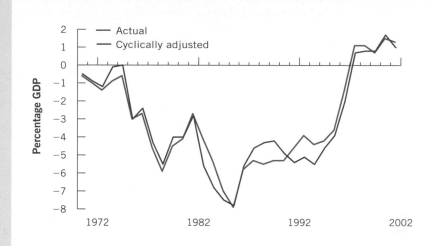

SOURCE: Department of Finance, Fiscal Reference Tables, Table 46. Available online at www.fin.gc.ca/toce/2002/frt00e.html.

www.fin.gc.ca/wp/2003-06e.html

Second, the high-employment surplus is not a perfect measure of the thrust of fiscal policy. There are several reasons for this: A change in spending with a matching increase in taxes, leaving the deficit unchanged, will raise income; expectations about future fiscal policy changes can affect current income; and in general, because fiscal policy involves the setting of a number of variables—the tax rate, transfers, and government purchases—it is difficult to describe the thrust of fiscal policy perfectly with a single number. But the high-employment surplus is nevertheless a useful guide to the direction of fiscal policy.[10]

## 10-5 | THE FOREIGN SECTOR

For a country like Canada, which exports about 40 percent of its total output and spends a similar fraction of its income on imports, foreign trade plays an important role in the determination of equilibrium income. When foreign trade is taken into account, we return to equation (1)

$$AD = C + I + G + NX$$

Denoting exports by $X$ and imports by $Q$, we have

$$NX = X - Q$$

---

[10] For a more detailed discussion of these issues see D. Purvis and C. Smith, "Fiscal Policy in Canada, 1963–84," in J. Sargent, ed., *Fiscal and Monetary Policy*, Research Studies of the Royal Commission on the Economic Union and Development Prospects for Canada, vol. 21 (Toronto: University of Toronto Press, 1986).

As in the case of planned investment and government spending, we assume that exports are fixed at a given level (denoted by $\overline{X}$). On the other hand, since imports represent part of domestic demand, they are assumed to depend on income.[11] Using a linear relationship we have

$$Q = \overline{Q} + mY \qquad (23)$$

**marginal propensity to import**

The increase in the demand for imports that results from a one-unit increase in domestic income.

where the slope $m$ is called the **marginal propensity to import**.

To determine the equilibrium level of income, we use the equilibrium condition, $Y = AD$, together with the consumption function (2) and the import function (23)

$$
\begin{aligned}
Y &= (\overline{C} + c\overline{TR}) + c(1 - t)Y + \overline{I} + \overline{G} + \overline{X} - \overline{Q} - mY \\
&= (\overline{C} + c\overline{TR} + \overline{I} + \overline{G} + \overline{X} - \overline{Q}) + [c(1 - t) - m]Y \\
&= \overline{A}_2 + [c(1 - t) - m]Y
\end{aligned}
$$

Solving for the equilibrium level of income $Y_0$, we obtain

$$Y_0 = \frac{1}{1 - c(1 - t) + m} \overline{A}_2 \qquad (24)$$

Comparing equation (24) with equation (15), we see that exports add to autonomous spending. Imports subtract from autonomous spending and reduce the increases in demand for domestic output induced by increases in income, and thereby lower the multiplier. The higher the marginal propensity to import, the lower the multiplier.

## *Working with Data*

The data that were used to produce Figure 10-6 are available online at www.fin.gc.ca/toce/2002/frt00e.html. This is a very rich source of fiscal data, not only for the federal government, but also for provincial and local governments. If you go to Table 46, you will find the data for Figure 10-6. You should use these data to try to reproduce Figure 10-6. In addition, the data are available in raw form, that is, not measured as a percentage of GDP, in Table 45. You may want to reproduce Figure 10-6 in actual numbers.

## C H A P T E R   S U M M A R Y

▶  Output is at its equilibrium level when the aggregate demand for goods is equal to the level of output.

---

[11] We are assuming here that the exchange rate is fixed. The effect of changes in the exchange rate on exports and imports is discussed in Chapter 14.

www.mcgrawhill.ca/college/dornbusch

▶ Aggregate demand consists of planned spending by households on consumption, by firms on investment goods, and by government on its purchases of goods and services, and also includes net exports.

▶ When output is at its equilibrium level, there are no unintended changes in inventories and all economic units are making precisely the purchases they had planned to make. An adjustment process for the level of output based on the accumulation or rundown of inventories leads the economy to the equilibrium output level.

▶ The level of aggregate demand is itself affected by the level of output (equal to the level of income) because consumption demand depends on the level of income.

▶ The consumption function relates consumption spending to income. Consumption rises with income. Income that is not consumed is saved, so the savings function can be derived from the consumption function.

▶ The multiplier is the amount by which a $1.00 change in autonomous spending changes the equilibrium level of output. The greater the propensity to consume, the higher the multiplier.

▶ Government purchases and government transfer payments act like increases in autonomous spending in their effects on the equilibrium level of income. A proportional income tax has the same effect on the equilibrium level of income as a reduction in the propensity to consume. A proportional income tax thus reduces the multiplier.

▶ The budget surplus is the excess of government receipts over expenditures. When the government is spending more than it receives, the budget is in deficit. The size of the budget surplus (or deficit) is affected by the government's fiscal policy variables—government purchases, transfer payments, and tax rates.

▶ The actual budget surplus is also affected by changes in tax collection and transfers resulting from movements in the level of income that occur because of changes in private autonomous spending. The full employment (high employment) budget surplus is used as a measure of the active use of fiscal policy. The full employment surplus measures the budget surplus that would exist if output was at its potential (full employment) level.

▶ When foreign trade is taken into account, exports add to and imports subtract from autonomous spending. The dependence of imports on income affects the size of the multiplier: The higher the marginal propensity to import, the lower the multiplier.

## KEY TERMS

consumption function, *189*
marginal propensity to
    consume, *189*
multiplier, *195*

automatic stabilizer, *197*
discretionary fiscal policy, *197*
budget surplus, *198*
budget deficit, *198*

balanced budget multiplier, *201*
full employment budget
    surplus, *202*
marginal propensity to import, *204*

## D I S C U S S I O N    Q U E S T I O N S

1.  We call the model of income determination developed in this chapter a *Keynesian* one. What makes it Keynesian, as opposed to Classical?

2.  What is an autonomous variable? What components of aggregate demand have we specified, in this chapter, as being autonomous?

3.  Using your knowledge of the amount of time required for the many components of the federal government to agree on and implement changes in policy (i.e., tax codes, the welfare system), can you think of any problems with using fiscal policy to stabilize the economy?

4.  Why do we call mechanisms such as proportional income taxes and the welfare system *automatic stabilizers*? Choose one of these mechanisms and explain carefully how and why it affects fluctuations in output.

5.  What is the full employment budget surplus, and why might it be a more useful measure than the actual, or unadjusted, budget surplus? The text provides other names for this measure, such as *cyclically adjusted surplus* and *structural surplus*. Why might we prefer to use these other terms?

## A P P L I C A T I O N    Q U E S T I O N S

1.  Here we investigate a particular simple example of the model studied in this chapter with no government or foreign sector. Suppose the consumption function is given by $C = 100 + 0.8Y$, while investment is given by $I = 50$.

    a.  What is the equilibrium level of income in this case?

    b.  What is the level of saving in equilibrium?

    c.  If, for some reason, output is at the level of 800, what will be the level of involuntary inventory accumulation?

    d.  If $I$ rises to 100 (we discuss what determines $I$ in later chapters), what will be the effect on the equilibrium income?

    e.  What is the value of the multiplier, $\alpha$, here?

    f.  Draw a diagram indicating the equilibria in both (a) and (d).

2.  Suppose the consumption behaviour in Application Question 1 changes so that $C = 100 + 0.9Y$, while $I$ remains at 50.

    a.  Is the equilibrium level of income higher or lower than it was in Application Question 1(a)? Calculate the new equilibrium level, $Y^1$, to verify this.

    b.  Now suppose investment increases to $I = 100$, just as in Application Question 1(d). What is the new equilibrium income?

    c.  Does this change in investment spending have more or less of an effect on $Y$ than it did in Application Question 1? Why?

    d.  Draw a diagram indicating the change in equilibrium income in this case.

3.  Now we look at the role taxes play in determining equilibrium income. Suppose we have an economy of the type studied in this chapter, described by the following functions:

$$C = 50 + 0.8YD$$

$$\bar{I} = 70$$

$$\bar{G} = 200$$

$$\overline{TR} = 100$$

$$t = 0.20$$

    **a.** Calculate the equilibrium level of income and the multiplier in this model.

    **b.** Calculate the budget surplus, *BS*.

    **c.** Suppose that *t* increases to 0.25. What is the new equilibrium income? The new multiplier?

    **d.** Calculate the change in the budget surplus. Would you expect the change in the surplus to be more or less if $c = 0.9$ rather than 0.8?

    **e.** Can you explain why the multiplier is 1 when $t = 1$?

**4.** Suppose the economy is operating at equilibrium, with $Y_0 = 1000$. If the government undertakes a fiscal change whereby the tax rate, *t*, increases by 0.05 and government spending increases by 50, will the budget surplus go up or down? Why?

**5.** Suppose the federal government decides to reduce transfer payments (such as welfare) but to increase government purchases of goods and services by an equal amount. That is, it undertakes a change in fiscal policy such that $\Delta G = -\Delta TR$.

    **a.** Would you expect equilibrium income to rise or fall as a result of this change? Why? Check your answer with the following example: Suppose that, initially, $c = 0.8$, $t = 0.25$, and $Y_0 = 600$. Now let $\Delta G = 10$ and $\Delta TR = -10$.

    **b.** Find the change in equilibrium income, $\Delta Y_0$.

    **c.** What is the change in the budget surplus, $\Delta BS$? Why has *BS* changed?

**6.** Go to CANSIM and retrieve Total Expenditures, Federal Government. Plot this with the recession dates given in Chapter 6, Application Question 3. Can you see any relationship between federal government spending and the business cycle?

## CHAPTER 11

# MONEY, INTEREST, AND INCOME

## LEARNING OBJECTIVES

After reading and studying this chapter, you should be able to:

▶ *Understand that the IS-LM model is the core of short run macroeconomics.*

▶ *Understand that the IS curve describes the combinations of income and interest rates at which the goods market is in equilibrium.*

▶ *Understand that the LM curve describes the combinations of income and interest rates at which the money market is in equilibrium.*

▶ *Understand that, together, the IS and LM curves constitute a model of aggregate demand.*

▶ *Understand that, in the short run, increases in government spending raise output and interest rates, while increases in the real money supply raise output and lower interest rates.*

**www.rich.frb.org/pubs/eq/
pdfs/summer2000/king.pdf**

**IS-LM model**

Interaction of *IS* and *LM*
curves determines the real
interest rate and the level
of income for a given
price level, for which both
goods and money markets
are in equilibrium.

**C**hapter 10 introduced a model of aggregate demand in the very short run. However, the model in Chapter 10 is very limited in the sense that there was no role for the Bank of Canada or interest rates. In this chapter, we extend the model developed in the previous chapter.

This chapter introduces money and monetary policy and builds an explicit framework of analysis within which to study the interaction of goods markets and assets markets. This new framework leads to an understanding of the determination of interest rates and of their role in the business cycle and introduces an avenue by which monetary policy affects output. Figure 11-1 shows the Treasury bill interest rate, the growth rate of real money, and the growth rate of real output. Notice that in the two most recent recessions, the early 1980s and the early 1990s, the real money stock decreased, the interest rate increased, and real output decreased. This chapter explores the link from money to interest rates to output.

The model we introduce in this chapter, the ***IS-LM*** **model**, is the core of short run macroeconomics. It maintains the spirit and, indeed, many details of the model in the previous chapter. The model is broadened, though, by introducing the interest rate as an additional determinant of aggregate demand. In Chapter 10, autonomous spending and fiscal policy were the chief determinants of aggregate demand. Now we add the interest rate as a determinant of investment and therefore aggregate demand. We then have to ask what determines the interest rate. That question extends our model to include the money markets and forces us to study the interaction of goods and money markets. The Bank of Canada enters the picture through its role in setting the supply of money. Interest rates and income are jointly determined by equilibrium in the goods and money markets. As in the previous chapter, we maintain the assumption that the price level does not respond when aggregate demand shifts.

---

## FIGURE 11-1

In the short run, when
the real money stock
decreases, for instance,
in the early 1980s, the
interest rate goes up and
real output goes down.

### THE SHORT RUN RELATIONSHIP OF MONEY, THE INTEREST RATE, AND OUTPUT, 1969–2002

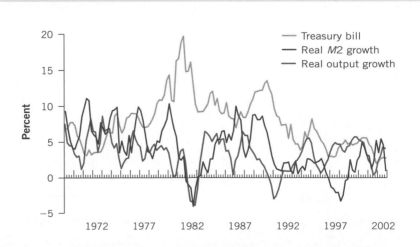

SOURCE: CANSIM II V37128, divided by the CPI: CANSIM II V375319; Treasury bill: CANSIM II V122484; real GDP: CANSIM II V1992259.

# THE GOODS MARKET AND THE *IS* CURVE

**IS curve (goods market equilibrium curve)**

Shows combinations of the interest rate and income for which the goods market is in equilibrium.

In this section, we derive a goods market equilibrium relationship called the *IS curve*. The **IS curve** shows combinations of the interest rate and income for which the goods market is in equilibrium. The concept of equilibrium in the goods market is identical to the one that we used in Chapter 10—aggregate demand equals aggregate supply. We build on the concept of aggregate demand that was introduced in Chapter 10 by adding an interest-sensitive component to the investment relation.

## Investment and the Interest Rate

In Chapter 3, we introduced the concept of a negative relationship between investment demand and the rate of interest.[1] We can specify a simple equation for this relationship.

$$I = \bar{I} - bi \qquad (1)$$

This equation is graphed in Figure 11-2, which shows, for each level of the interest rate, the amount that firms are willing to spend on investment. The coefficient $b$ measures the responsiveness of investment spending to the interest rate. If investment spending is highly responsive to the interest rate, a small decline in interest rates will lead to a large increase in investment spending, so the curve in Figure 11-2 would be quite flat. Conversely, if investment responds very little to interest rate changes ($b$ is very small), the investment curve will be much steeper. An increase in the exogenous component of investment spending, $\bar{I}$, means that, at every level of the interest rate, firms wish to spend more on investment, and this is represented by an outward shift in the investment curve.

**FIGURE 11-2**    **THE INVESTMENT DEMAND CURVE**

The investment demand curve shows how investment spending is negatively related to the rate of interest.

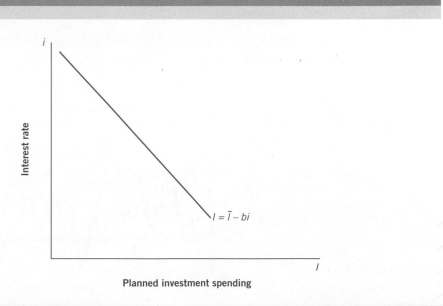

$$I = \bar{I} - bi$$

Interest rate

Planned investment spending

---

[1] In Chapter 3, investment demand depends on the real interest rate. Recall that in this chapter, we are assuming that the aggregate supply curve is horizontal, so the price level is fixed and there is no inflation. Therefore, the real and the nominal interest rates are identical.

In order to derive the *IS* curve, we begin with the *AD* equation from Chapter 10.

$$AD = C + I + G + NX$$
$$= [\overline{C} + c\overline{TR} + \overline{I} + \overline{G} + \overline{NX}] + c(1 - t)Y$$
$$= \overline{A}_1 + c(1 - t)Y \tag{2}$$
$$\overline{A}_1 = \overline{C} + c\overline{TR} + \overline{I} + \overline{G} + \overline{NX}$$

Recall that, in Chapter 10, we made the assumption that all of investment spending was exogenous, $I = \overline{I}$. We now assume that investment spending is given as in equation (1), and our aggregate demand curve becomes

$$AD = C + I + G + NX$$
$$= [\overline{C} + c\overline{TR} + \overline{I} + \overline{G} + \overline{NX}] + c(1 - t)Y - bi \tag{3}$$
$$= \overline{A}_1 + c(1 - t)Y - bi$$

Equation (3) is graphed in Figure 11-3, which can be used to derive an *IS* curve.

For a given level of the interest rate, say, $i_1$, the last term of equation (3) is a constant ($bi_1$), and we can, in Figure 11-3(a), draw the aggregate demand function of Chapter 10, this time with an intercept, $\overline{A}_1 - bi_1$. The equilibrium level of income obtained in the usual manner is $Y_1$ at point $E_1$. Since that equilibrium level of income was derived for a given level of the interest rate ($i_1$), we plot that pair ($i_1$, $Y_1$) in the bottom panel as point $E_1$. This gives us one point, $E_1$, on the *IS* curve—that is, one combination of interest rate and income that clears the goods market.

Consider next a lower interest rate, $i_2$. Investment spending is higher when the interest rate falls. In terms of Figure 11-3(a), that implies an upward shift of the aggregate demand schedule. The curve shifts upward because the previous intercept, $\overline{A}_1 - bi$, has increased. Given the increase in aggregate demand, the equilibrium shifts to point $E_2$, with an associated income level $Y_2$. At point $E_2$, in panel (b), we record the fact that interest rate $i_2$ implies the equilibrium level of income $Y_2$—equilibrium in the sense that the goods market is in equilibrium (or that the goods market *clears*). Point $E_2$ is another point on the *IS* curve.

We can apply the same procedure to all conceivable levels of the interest rate and thereby generate all of the points that make up the *IS* curve. They have in common the property that they represent combinations of interest rates and income (output) at which the goods market clears. That is why the *IS* curve is called the *goods market equilibrium relationship*.

Figure 11-3 shows that the *IS* curve is negatively sloped, reflecting the increase in aggregate demand associated with a reduction in the interest rate. We can also derive the *IS* curve by using the goods market equilibrium condition, that income equals planned spending, or

$$Y = AD = \overline{A}_1 + c(1 - t)Y - bi \tag{4}$$

which can be simplified to

$$Y = \alpha_G(\overline{A}_1 - bi) \qquad \alpha_G = \frac{1}{1 - c(1 - t)} \tag{5}$$

where $\alpha_G$ is the multiplier from Chapter 10. Note from equation (5) that a higher interest rate implies a lower level of equilibrium income for a given $\overline{A}_1$, as Figure 11-3 shows.

## FIGURE 11-3

### DERIVATION OF THE *IS* CURVE

At a particular interest rate, equilibrium in panel (a) determines the income level. A decrease in the interest rate raises aggregate demand. The *IS* curve shows the resulting negative relationship between interest rates and income.

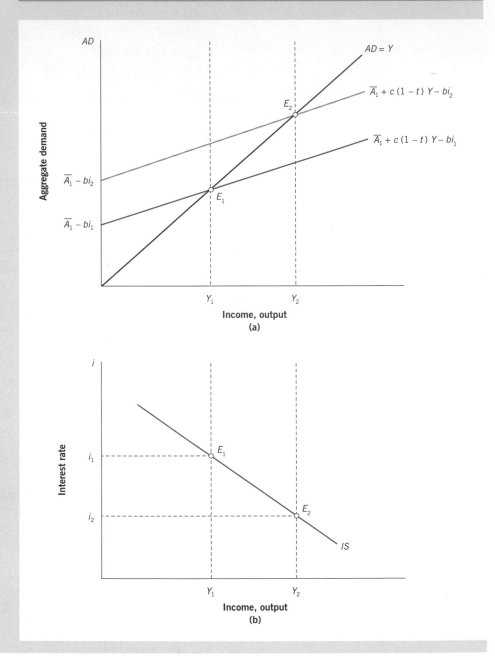

The construction of the *IS* curve is quite straightforward and may even be deceptively simple. We can gain further understanding of the economics of the *IS* curve by asking and answering the following questions:

▶ What determines the slope of the *IS* curve?

▶ What determines the position of the *IS* curve, given its slope, and what causes the curve to shift?

**BOX**

**11-1**

### Savings, Investment, and Equilibrium: Why Is Chapter 3 Different from Chapter 11?

In Box 10-2 in Chapter 10, we discussed the different short run and long run interpretations of the equilibrium condition that investment equals savings, and discussed the relationship of the long run models in Chapter 3 to the very short run models in this section. The *IS* curve is a short run relationship that can be related to the long run model in Chapter 3.

The figure below reproduces the investment-savings model from Chapter 3, with one important change. We now assume that savings is not a function of the interest rate, but rather depends only on income. You will recall that this is the assumption used in Chapter 10. Notice how this model can now be used to derive an *IS* curve using a slightly different approach from the one used previously. At interest rate $i_0$, savings equals investment. If income was to increase to $Y_1$, the savings curve would shift outward and there would be a new equilibrium. This traces out a downward sloping *IS* curve. Of course, in the background of this derivation of the *IS* curve is the assumption of a horizontal aggregate supply curve.

**DERIVING THE *IS* CURVE FROM THE SAVINGS EQUALS INVESTMENT RELATIONSHIP**

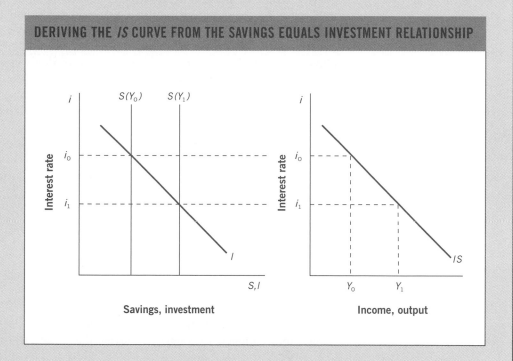

Savings, investment                Income, output

## The Slope of the *IS* Curve

We have already noted that the *IS* curve is negatively sloped because a higher level of the interest rate reduces investment spending, thereby reducing aggregate demand and thus the equilibrium level of income. The steepness of the curve depends on how sensitive investment spending is to changes in the interest rate and also depends on the multiplier, $\alpha_G$, in equation (5).

Suppose that investment spending is very sensitive to the interest rate, and so $b$ in equation (5) is large. Then, in terms of Figure 11-3, a given change in the interest rate produces a large change in aggregate demand, and thus shifts the aggregate demand curve in Figure 11-3(a) up by a large amount. A large shift in the aggregate demand schedule produces a correspondingly large change in the equilibrium level of income. If a given change in the interest rate produces a large change in income, the *IS* curve is very flat. This is the case if investment is very sensitive to the interest rate, that is, if $b$ is large. Correspondingly, if $b$ is small and investment spending is not very sensitive to the interest rate, the *IS* curve is relatively steep.

## The Role of the Multiplier

Consider next the effects of the multiplier, $\alpha_G$, on the steepness of the *IS* curve. Figure 11-4 shows aggregate demand curves corresponding to different multipliers. The coefficient $c$ on the solid flatter aggregate demand curves is smaller than the corresponding coefficient $c'$ on the steeper dashed aggregate demand curves. The multiplier is accordingly larger on the steeper aggregate demand curves. The initial levels of income, $Y_1$ and $Y'_1$, correspond to the interest rate $i_1$ in panel (b).

A given reduction in the interest rate, to $i_2$, raises the intercept of the aggregate demand curves by the same vertical distance, as shown in panel (a). However, the implied change in income is very different. On the steeper curve, income rises to $Y'_2$, while it rises only to $Y_2$ on the flatter line. The change in equilibrium income corresponding to a given change in the interest rate is accordingly larger as the aggregate demand curve is steeper; that is, the larger the multiplier, the greater the rise in income. As we see in panel (b), the larger the multiplier, the flatter the *IS* curve. Equivalently, the larger the multiplier, the larger the change in income produced by a given change in the interest rate.

We have thus seen that the smaller the sensitivity of investment spending to the interest rate and the smaller the multiplier, the steeper the *IS* curve. This conclusion is confirmed using equation (5). We can turn equation (5) around to express the interest rate as a function of the level of income.

$$i = \frac{1}{b}\overline{A}_1 - \frac{1}{\alpha_G b}Y \qquad (5a)$$

Thus, for a given change in $Y$, the associated change in $i$ will be larger in size as $b$ is smaller and as $\alpha_G$ is smaller.

Given that the slope of the *IS* curve depends in part on the multiplier, fiscal policy can affect that slope. The multiplier, $\alpha_G$, is affected by the tax rate: An increase in the tax rate reduces the multiplier. Accordingly, the higher the tax rate, the steeper the *IS* curve.[2]

## The Position of the *IS* Curve

Figure 11-5 shows two different *IS* curves, one of which lies to the right and above the other. What might cause the *IS* curve to be at *IS'* rather than at *IS*? The answer is an increase in the level of autonomous spending.

In Figure 11-5(a) we show an initial aggregate demand curve drawn for a level of autonomous spending $\overline{A}_1$ and for an interest rate $i_1$. Corresponding to the initial

---

[2] In the Application Questions we ask you to relate this fact to the discussion of automatic stabilizers in Chapter 10.

**FIGURE 11-4**

A higher marginal propensity to spend results in a steeper aggregate demand curve and, consequently, a flatter *IS* curve.

## EFFECT OF THE MULTIPLIER ON THE SLOPE OF THE *IS* CURVE

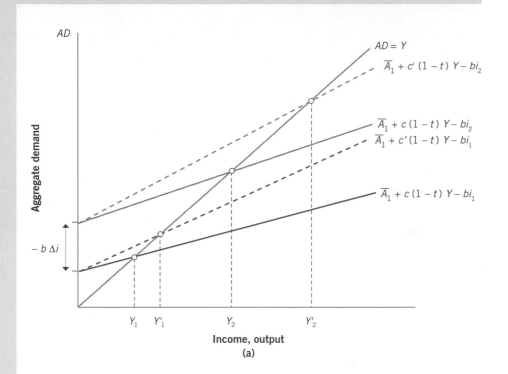

(a)

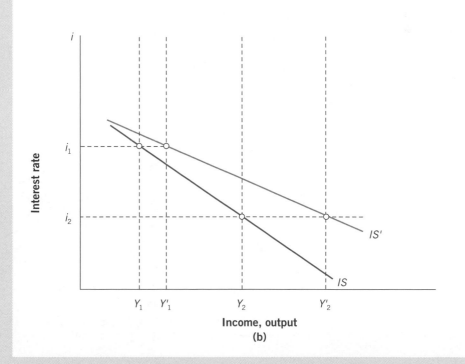

(b)

**FIGURE 11-5**

**A SHIFT IN THE *IS* CURVE CAUSED BY A CHANGE IN AUTONOMOUS SPENDING**

An increase in autonomous spending increases aggregate demand and increases the income level at a given interest rate. This is represented by a rightward shift of the *IS* curve.

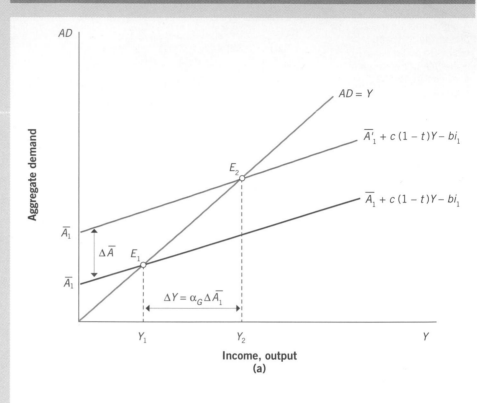

(a)

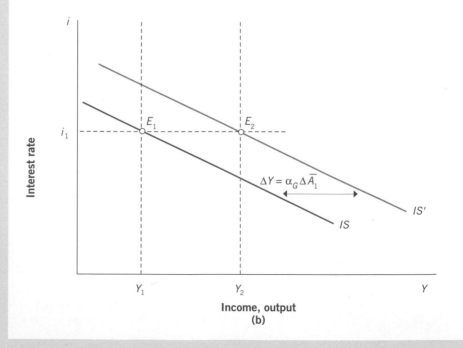

(b)

aggregate demand curve is the point $E_1$ on the *IS* curve in Figure 11-5(b). Now, at the same interest rate, let the level of autonomous spending increase to $\overline{A}'_1$. The increase in autonomous spending increases the equilibrium level of income at the interest rate $i_1$. The point $E_2$ in panel (b) is thus a point on the new goods market equilibrium curve, *IS'*. Since $E_1$ was an arbitrary point on the initial *IS* curve, we can perform the exercise for all levels of the interest rate and thereby generate the new curve, *IS'*. Thus, an increase in autonomous spending shifts the *IS* curve out to the right.

By how much does the curve shift? The change in income as a result of the change in autonomous spending can be seen from panel (a) to be just the multiplier times the change in autonomous spending. This means that the *IS* curve is shifted horizontally by a distance equal to the multiplier times the change in autonomous spending, as in panel (b).

The level of autonomous spending, from equation (2), is

$$\overline{A}_1 = \overline{C} + c\overline{TR} + \overline{I} + \overline{G} + \overline{NX}$$

Accordingly, an increase in government purchases or transfer payments shifts the *IS* curve out to the right, with the extent of the shift depending on the size of the multiplier. A reduction in transfer payments or in government purchases shifts the *IS* curve to the left.

## A Summary of the *IS* Curve

In Section 11-1, we have covered a great deal of material concerning the *IS* curve. To make certain that you understand this material, here is a summary of the major points with which you should be familiar:

▶ The *IS* curve is the schedule of combinations of the interest rate and level of income such that the goods market is in equilibrium.

▶ The *IS* curve is negatively sloped because an increase in the interest rate reduces planned investment spending and therefore reduces aggregate demand, thus reducing the equilibrium level of income.

▶ The smaller the multiplier and the less sensitive investment spending is to changes in the interest rate, the steeper the *IS* curve.

▶ The *IS* curve is shifted by changes in autonomous spending. An increase in autonomous spending, including an increase in government purchases, shifts the *IS* curve out to the right.

Now we turn to the money market.

## 11-2 | THE MONEY MARKET AND THE *LM* CURVE

**LM curve (money market equilibrium curve)**

Shows combinations of interest rates and levels of output such that money demand equals money supply.

In this section, we derive a money market equilibrium relationship, the *LM* curve. *The **LM** curve shows combinations of interest rates and levels of output such that money demand equals money supply.* The *LM* curve is derived in two steps. First, we explain why money demand depends on interest rates and income, emphasizing that because people care about the purchasing power of money, the demand for money is a theory of *real* rather than *nominal* demand. Second, we equate money demand with money supply—set by the central bank—and find the combinations of income and interest rates that keep the money market in equilibrium.

## Real and Nominal Variables in the Very Short Run

Throughout all of Part 4 of this book, we have made the assumption that the aggregate supply curve is horizontal. Thus, we are assuming that the price level is fixed. In this situation, inflation does not play a role in our models. While this is a realistic assumption for the very short run, it obscures the difference between nominal and real variables.

First, consider the real rate of interest, which we showed in Chapter 1 to be approximately equal to the nominal interest rate minus the inflation rate. Because we are ignoring the inflation rate, the nominal and real interest rates are the same variable throughout Part 4 of this book.

Second, consider money demand. We discussed the distinction between real money and nominal demand in Chapter 3: The real demand for money is the demand for money expressed in terms of the number of units of goods that money will buy. We measure this as nominal demand for money divided by the price level. However, as the price level is assumed to be fixed, any change in nominal money demand is equivalent to a change in real money demand.

## The Demand for Money

**demand for real balances**

Quantity of real money balances people wish to hold.

We turn now to the money market and initially concentrate on the **demand for real balances**.[3] The demand for money is a demand for *real* balances because people hold money for what it will buy. The higher the price level, the more nominal balances a person has to hold to be able to purchase a given quantity of goods. If the price level doubles, an individual has to hold twice as many nominal balances in order to be able to buy the same amount of goods.

The demand for real balances depends on the level of real income and the interest rate. It depends on the level of real income because individuals hold money to pay for their purchases, which, in turn, depend on income. The demand for money depends also on the cost of holding money. The cost of holding money is the interest that is forgone by holding money rather than other assets. The higher the interest rate, the more costly it is to hold money and, accordingly, the less cash will be held at each level of income.[4] Individuals can economize on their holdings of cash when the interest rate rises by being more careful in managing their money and by making transfers from money to bonds whenever their money holdings become large. If the interest rate is 1 percent, there is very little benefit from holding bonds rather than money. However, when the interest rate is 10 percent, it is worth some effort not to hold more money than is needed to finance day-to-day transactions.

On these simple grounds, then, the demand for real balances increases with the level of real income and decreases with the interest rate. The demand for real balances, which we denote as *L*, is accordingly expressed as

$$L = kY - hi \qquad k,h > 0 \qquad (6)$$

---

[3] The demand for money was introduced in Chapter 3 and is examined in depth in Chapter 16; here we present only briefly the arguments underlying the demand for money.

[4] Some types of money, including most bank deposits, earn interest, but at a lower rate than bonds. Several sizeable parts of money holding—including currency—earn no interest; so, overall, money earns less interest than other assets. Thus, there is an interest cost to holding money.

The parameters $k$ and $h$ reflect the sensitivity of the demand for real balances to the level of income and the interest rate, respectively. A $5.00 increase in real income raises money demand by $k \times 5$ real dollars. An increase in the interest rate of 1 percentage point reduces real money demand by $h$ real dollars.

The demand function for real balances, equation (6), implies that for a given level of income, the quantity demanded is a decreasing function of the rate of interest. Such a demand curve is shown in Figure 11-6 for a level of income $Y_1$. The higher the level of income, the larger the demand for real balances and, therefore, the further to the right the demand curve. The demand curve for a higher level of real income, $Y_2$, is also shown in Figure 11-6.

## The Supply of Money, Money Market Equilibrium, and the *LM* Curve

In order to complete our model of the money market, we need a money supply curve. The supply of money depends on the monetary policy stance of the central bank, which is the Bank of Canada. In this chapter, we make the assumption that the Bank of Canada controls the supply of money.[5] This assumption serves to make the supply of money exogenous, which we denote as $\bar{M}$. Since the price level is also exogenous in the very short run, the level of the real money supply is $\bar{M}/\bar{P}$. Therefore, the real money supply curve is a vertical line, as shown in Figure 11-7.

---

**FIGURE 11-6**

**DEMAND FOR REAL BALANCES AS A FUNCTION OF THE INTEREST RATE AND REAL INCOME**

The higher the rate of interest, the lower the quantity of real balances demanded, given the level of income. An increase in income raises the demand for money, as shown by the rightward shift in the money demand curve.

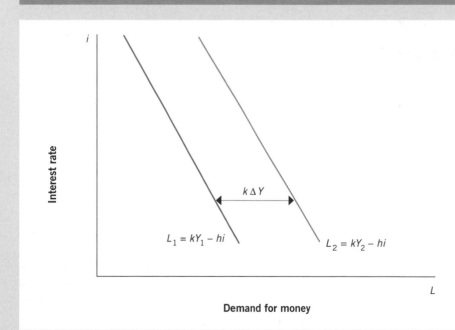

---

[5]In Chapter 12, we make an alternative, and perhaps more realistic, assumption that the Bank of Canada controls the short-term interest rate.

In Figure 11-7, we show combinations of interest rates and income levels such that the demand for real balances exactly matches the available supply. Starting with the level of income, $Y_1$, the corresponding demand curve for real balances, $L_1$, is shown in Figure 11-7(a). It is drawn, as in Figure 11-6, as a decreasing function of the interest rate. The existing supply of real balances, $\overline{M/P}$, is shown by the vertical line, since it is given and therefore is independent of the interest rate. At interest rate $i_1$, the demand for real balances equals the supply. Therefore, point $E_1$ is an equilibrium point in the money market. That point is shown in Figure 11-7(b) as a point on the *LM* curve.

## FIGURE 11-7

### DERIVATION OF THE *LM* CURVE

At the initial equilibrium, $E_1$, the level of the real money supply equals real money demand for a given level of income equal to $Y_1$. If income increases to $Y_2$, with the real money supply remaining constant, the interest rate must increase to $i_2$ to maintain money market equilibrium at point $E_2$. Therefore, for a given real money supply, a higher level of income is consistent with a higher interest rate for money market equilibrium, and the *LM* curve slopes upward.

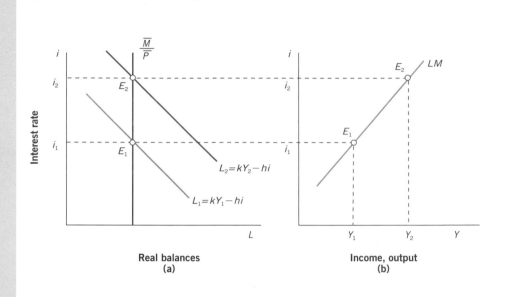

**Real balances**
**(a)**

**Income, output**
**(b)**

Consider next the effect of an increase in income to $Y_2$. In Figure 11-7(a), the higher level of income causes the demand for real balances to be higher at each level of the interest rate, so the demand curve for real balances shifts up and to the right, to $L_2$. The interest rate increases to $i_2$ to maintain equilibrium in the money market at that higher level of income. Accordingly, the new equilibrium point is $E_2$. In Figure 11-7 (b), we record point $E_2$ as a point of equilibrium in the money market. Performing the same exercise for all income levels, we generate a series of points that can be linked to give us the *LM* curve.

*The LM curve, or money market equilibrium curve, shows all combinations of interest rates and levels of income such that the demand for real balances is equal to the supply. Along the LM curve, the money market is in equilibrium.*

The *LM* curve is positively sloped. An increase in the interest rate reduces the demand for real balances. To maintain the demand for real balances equal to the fixed supply, the level of income has to rise. Accordingly, money market equilibrium implies that an increase in the interest rate is accompanied by an increase in the level of income.

The *LM* curve can be obtained directly by combining the demand curve for real balances, equation (6), and the fixed supply of real balances. For the money market to be in equilibrium, demand has to equal supply, or

$$\frac{\overline{M}}{P} = kY - hi \tag{7}$$

Solving for the interest rate,

$$i = \frac{1}{h}\left(kY - \frac{\overline{M}}{P}\right) \tag{7a}$$

The relationship (7a) is the *LM* curve.

Next we ask the same questions about the properties of the *LM* curve that we asked about the *IS* curve.

## The Slope of the *LM* Curve

In order to understand the slope of the *LM* curve, examine Figure 11-7. The slope of the *LM* curve that we derived in Figure 11-7 depends on how much the money demand curve shifts upward (from $L_1$ to $L_2$) when income changes from $Y_1$ to $Y_2$. You can see graphically that the more the money demand curve shifts, the larger the interest rate change and the steeper the resultant *LM* curve. It turns out that this depends on the ratio $\frac{k}{h}$. This can be seen easily as the slope of the *LM* curve from equation (7a).[6] Therefore, for *larger k*, the income elasticity of money demand, and for *smaller h*, the interest elasticity of money demand, the *LM* curve is steeper. This may seem like a needless technical point, but it will be used to discuss the effects of monetary policy in Chapter 12.

## Shifts in the *LM* Curve

The real money supply is held constant along an *LM* curve. It follows that a change in the real money supply will shift the *LM* curve.[7] In Figure 11-8, we show how an increase in the real money supply shifts the *LM* curve outward. Figure 11-8(a) shows the money market equilibrium, which is initially at point $E_1$, where the initial real money supply is $\overline{M}/\overline{P}$ and real money demand is given by $L_1$. Point $E_1$ is also one point on the *LM* curve in Figure 11-8(b). Now assume that the real money supply increases to $\overline{M}'/\overline{P}$, which is represented by a rightward shift in the money supply line. Since money demand does not change, with a higher money supply, the interest rate must decrease in order to maintain supply equals demand in the money market. This occurs at point $E_2$ in Figure 11-8(a). Notice that the new equilibrium is given for a lower interest rate but the same level of income. Therefore, in Figure 11-8(b) point $E_2$ is on a new *LM* curve.

---

[6] For those students who do not have the benefit of calculus, slope is simply "rise over run," which is the change in the interest rate over the change in income, or $\Delta i/\Delta Y$ in equation (7a).

[7] Remember that the price level is being held constant, so a change in the nominal money supply will change the real money supply.

## FIGURE 11-8

**SHIFTING THE *LM* CURVE**

An increase in the real money supply shifts the *LM* curve outward.

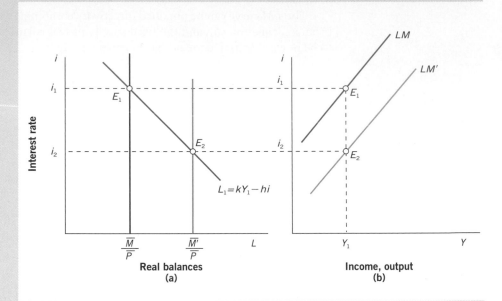

**Real balances**
**(a)**

**Income, output**
**(b)**

Notice the following technical point. For the exercise of increasing the real money supply in Figure 11-8, the amount of the shift in the *LM* curve is given by the amount of the change in the interest rate. This in turn is determined by the slope of the money demand curve. The slope of the money demand curve is given by $-1/h$. Therefore, the higher that $h$ is, the flatter the money demand curve will be, and the smaller the shift in the *LM* curve for a given change in the real money stock. Notice that $h$ also plays a role in the slope of the *LM* curve. You should convince yourself that the following is true: The higher that $h$ (the interest elasticity of money demand) is, the flatter the money demand curve and the flatter the *LM* curve (for a given $k$, the income elasticity of money demand) and the smaller the shift in the *LM* curve for a given change in the real money stock.

## A Summary of the *LM* Curve

In Section 11-2, we have covered a great deal of material concerning the *LM* curve. To make certain that you understand this material, the following is a summary of the major points with which you should be familiar:

▶ The *LM* curve shows the combinations of interest rates and levels of income such that the money market is in equilibrium.

▶ The *LM* curve is positively sloped. Given the fixed money supply, an increase in the level of income, which increases the quantity of money demanded, has to be accompanied by an increase in the interest rate. This reduces the quantity of money demanded and thereby maintains money market equilibrium.

▶ The *LM* curve is shifted by changes in the money supply. An increase in the money supply shifts the *LM* curve to the right.

BOX

**11-3**

## Money Demand and the Quantity Theory of Money

In Chapter 3, we derived a long run money demand function from the quantity theory of money

$$MV = PY$$

which can be rearranged as a money demand equation

$$\frac{M^D}{P} = kY$$

where $k = \frac{1}{V}$. We made the assumption that velocity is constant in the long run. Notice that there is no interest rate in the long run money demand equation. When there is disequilibrium in the money market (for instance, money supply is greater than money demand), then the price level will increase according to the quantity theory of money.

We write the short run money demand equation as

$$\frac{M^D}{\overline{P}} = kY$$

We use the letter $L$ for money demand in this chapter, as opposed to $M^D$ as we did in Chapter 3 because, in this chapter, short run money demand is a different sort of equation from the long run money demand equation above: It is a demand for liquidity over holding bonds. Notice that the price level is assumed to be fixed (that is, the aggregate supply curve is horizontal in the very short run), so the price level cannot adjust to an increase in the money supply. Therefore, in the short run, when money supply is greater than money demand, the interest rate decreases to bring the money market back into equilibrium.

We are now ready to discuss the joint equilibrium of the goods and assets markets. That is to say, we can now discuss how output and interest rates are determined.

## 11-3   EQUILIBRIUM IN THE GOODS AND MONEY MARKETS

The *IS* and *LM* curves summarize the conditions that have to be satisfied in order for the goods and money markets, respectively, to be in equilibrium. The task now is to determine how these markets are brought into *simultaneous* equilibrium. For simultaneous equilibrium, interest rates and income levels have to be such that both the goods market *and* the money market are in equilibrium. This condition is satisfied at point $E$ in Figure 11-9. The equilibrium interest rate is therefore $i_0$ and the equilibrium level of income is $Y_0$, given the exogenous variables, in particular the real money supply and fiscal policy.[8] At point $E$, both the goods market and the money market are in equilibrium.

---

[8] Remember that exogenous variables are those whose values are not determined within the system being studied.

*FIGURE 11-9*

**GOODS AND MONEY MARKET EQUILIBRIUM**

At point *E*, interest rates and income levels are such that the public holds the existing money stock and planned spending equals output.

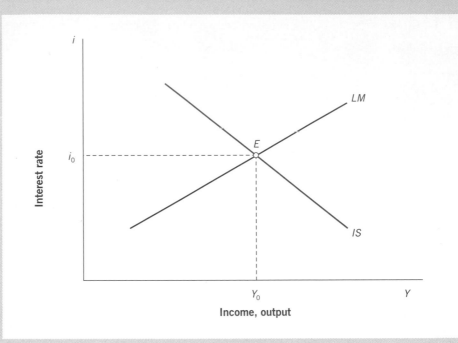

As with every model that we have discussed in this book, our conclusions are subject to the assumptions that underlie the development of the model. The *IS-LM* model, summarized in Figure 11-9, is a very short run model of economic activity. Therefore, underlying this model is the assumption that the aggregate supply curve is horizontal. Given this, the *IS-LM* model is often referred to as a *demand-driven model*: When demand changes, because the aggregate supply curve is horizontal, supply will also change. It is important to remember this when discussing the *IS-LM* model.

## Changes in the Equilibrium Income and Interest Rate: A First Look at Policy

The equilibrium levels of income and the interest rate will change when either the *IS* or the *LM* curve shifts. We know that, in order for a curve to shift, there must be a change in an exogenous variable. For the *IS* curve, the exogenous variables are contained in $\bar{A}_1 = \bar{C} + c\overline{TR} + \bar{I} + \bar{G} + \overline{NX}$. So a change in any of the individual variables in $\bar{A}_1$ will shift the *IS* curve. For now, we can think of fiscal policy as a change in $\bar{G}$. For the *LM* curve, the exogenous variable is the level of the real money stock, $\bar{M}/\bar{P}$, which will change if the Bank of Canada changes the nominal money stock, $\bar{M}$. Figure 11-10 compares the effects of expansionary fiscal policy (an increase in $\bar{G}$) with the effects of expansionary monetary policy (an increase in $\bar{M}$).

In Figure 11-10(a), expansionary fiscal policy shifts the *IS* curve outward and raises income and the interest rate. Notice how this is an extension of the result from the simple model introduced in Chapter 10, where we saw that expansionary fiscal

**FIGURE 11-10**

Expansionary fiscal policy increases output while raising interest rates, while expansionary monetary policy raises output while lowering interest rates.

**COMPARING THE EFFECTS OF MONETARY AND FISCAL POLICY**

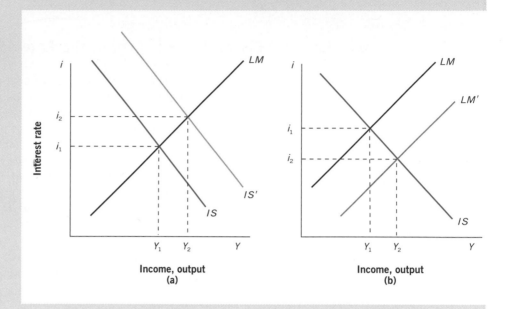

Income, output
(a)

Income, output
(b)

www.bankofcanada.ca/en/
speeches/sp02-9.pdf

policy raised income by the amount of the multiplier times the change in $\overline{G}$. Indeed, this is the amount that the *IS* curve actually shifts, as shown in Figure 11-5. Now, because we have a money market represented by the *LM* curve, when income goes up due to the multiplier, interest rates also go up and this prevents income from increasing by the full multiplier effect. This is called *crowding out*, and we will discuss the details of this sort of adjustment in Chapter 12.

In Figure 11-10(b), we can see that expansionary monetary policy also increases income but *lowers* interest rates, because, as with fiscal policy, there is now an interaction between the goods market and the money market. In the case of monetary policy, increasing the money supply initially lowers interest rates, as shown in Figure 11-8. However, this lowering of interest rates causes output to go up in the goods market. So, once again, any changes in the *IS-LM* model involve interaction of the goods and the money markets. These interactions will be studied in detail in Chapter 12.

## 11-4 | DERIVING THE AGGREGATE DEMAND CURVE

**aggregate demand curve**
Maps out the *IS-LM* equilibrium holding autonomous spending and the nominal money supply constant and allowing prices to vary.

In Chapter 10, we introduced a very simple aggregate demand curve that depended only on spending on goods and services. This simple aggregate demand curve was then used as the basis for the *IS* curve in this chapter. The term *aggregate demand*, as it is generally used in macroeconomics, refers not only to the goods market equilibrium, but also to the combination of goods and money markets equilibrium—that is, the *IS-LM* model studied in this chapter. The **aggregate demand curve** maps out the *IS-LM* equilibrium holding autonomous spending and the nominal money supply constant and allowing prices to vary. In other words, in learning to use the *IS-LM*

# POLICY IN *ACTION*

## Monetary and Fiscal Policy Stance in the Late 1970s

**policy mix**

A combination of monetary and fiscal policies.

We have seen in this chapter that both monetary and fiscal policy can have effects on the levels of interest rates and income. The policy choice concerning how monetary and fiscal policy are combined is often referred to as the **policy mix**. Remember that tight monetary policy (shifting the *LM* curve leftward) raises interest rates, while loose fiscal policy (shifting the *IS* curve rightward) also raises interest rates. In the late 1970s, we had exactly this combination of fiscal and monetary policies. The Bank of Canada was following a policy of slowly reducing the rate of growth of the nominal money supply, thus shifting the *LM* curve to the left. At the same time, on the fiscal side, the government was running budgetary deficits, thus shifting the *IS* curve outward. This is illustrated in the figure below

You can see the net result of this particular policy mix is that interest rates rise. We have drawn this figure to show output unchanged in response to these policies; however, what actually happens to output depends on the relative strength of the two policies.

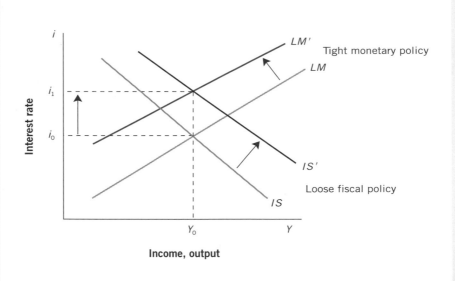

model, you've already learned everything about deriving the aggregate demand curve. Put simply, a higher price level means a lower *real* money supply, an *LM* curve shifted to the left, and lower aggregate demand.

Suppose the price level in the economy is $P_1$. Panel (a) of Figure 11-11 shows the *IS-LM* equilibrium. Note that the real money supply, which determines the position of the $LM_1$ curve, is $\overline{M}/P_1$. The intersection of the *IS* and $LM_1$ curves gives the level of aggregate demand corresponding to price $P_1$ and is so marked in the lower panel. Suppose, instead, that the price is higher, say $P_2$. The curve $LM_1$ shows the *LM* curve based on the real money supply $\overline{M}/P_2$. $LM_2$ is to the left of $LM_1$ since $\overline{M}/P_2 < \overline{M}/P_1$. Point $E_2$ shows the corresponding point on the aggregate demand curve. Repeat this operation for a variety of price levels, and connect the points to derive the aggregate demand schedule.

---

**O P T I O N A L**

## 11-5 | A FORMAL TREATMENT OF THE *IS-LM* MODEL

Our exposition so far has been verbal and graphical. We now round off the analysis with a more formal algebraic treatment of the *IS-LM* model.

### EQUILIBRIUM INCOME AND THE INTEREST RATE

The intersection of the *IS* and *LM* curves determines equilibrium income and the equilibrium interest rate. We now derive expressions for these equilibrium values by using the equations of the *IS* and *LM* curves. Recall from earlier in the chapter that the goods market equilibrium equation is

$$IS \text{ curve:} \qquad Y = \alpha_G(\overline{A}_1 - bi) \qquad (5)$$

and that the equation for the money market equilibrium is

$$LM \text{ curve:} \qquad i = \frac{1}{h}\left(kY - \frac{\overline{M}}{P}\right) \qquad (7a)$$

The intersection of the *IS* and *LM* curves in Figure 11-10 corresponds to a situation in which both the *IS* and the *LM* equations hold: The *same* interest rate and income levels ensure equilibrium in both the goods *and* the money markets. In terms of the equations, that means we can substitute the interest rate from the *LM* equation, (7a), into the *IS* equation, (5).

$$Y = \alpha_G\left[\overline{A} - \frac{b}{h}\left(kY - \frac{\overline{M}}{P}\right)\right]$$

Collecting terms and solving for the equilibrium level of income, we obtain

$$Y = \gamma\overline{A} + \gamma\frac{b}{h}\frac{\overline{M}}{P} \qquad (8)$$

where $\gamma = \alpha_G/(1 + k\alpha_G b/h)$. Equation (8) shows that the equilibrium level of income depends on two exogenous variables: autonomous spending ($\overline{A}$), including autonomous consumption and investment ($\overline{C}$ and $\overline{I}$) and fiscal policy parameters ($G$,

**FIGURE 11-11**          **DERIVATION OF THE AGGREGATE DEMAND SCHEDULE**

For a given *nominal* money stock, a price level decrease increases the *real* money stock. This shifts the *LM* curve outward, and the interest rate goes down and income increases. Therefore, along the *AD* curve, a price level decrease (holding the nominal money stock constant) is consistent with an income increase, and the *AD* curve slopes downward.

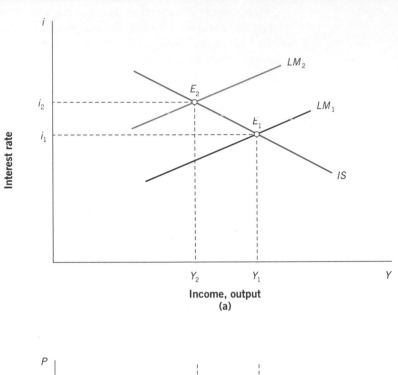

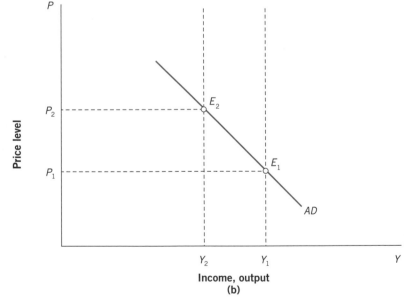

$\overline{TR}$), and the real money stock ($\overline{M}/\overline{P}$). Equilibrium income is higher the higher the level of autonomous spending, $\overline{A}$, and the higher the stock of real balances.

*Equation (8) is the aggregate demand curve. It summarizes the IS-LM relationship, relating Y and P for given levels of $\overline{A}$ and $\overline{M}$.* Since $P$ is in the denominator, the aggregate demand curve slopes downward.

The equilibrium rate of interest, $i$, is obtained by substituting the level of income from the *IS* equation, equation (5), into the *LM* equation, equation (7a).

$$i = \frac{k}{h}\,\gamma\overline{A} - \frac{1}{h + kb\alpha_G}\frac{\overline{M}}{\overline{P}} \qquad (9)$$

Equation (9) shows that the equilibrium interest rate depends on the parameters of fiscal policy captured in the multiplier and the term $\overline{A}$ and on the real money stock. A higher real money stock implies a lower equilibrium interest rate.

For policy questions we are interested in the precise relationship between changes in fiscal policy or changes in the real money stock and the resulting changes in equilibrium income. Monetary and fiscal policy *multipliers* provide the relevant information.

## THE FISCAL POLICY MULTIPLIER

**fiscal policy multiplier**

Shows how much an increase in government spending changes the equilibrium level of income, holding the real money supply constant.

The **fiscal policy multiplier** shows how much an increase in government spending changes the equilibrium level of income, holding the real money supply constant. Examine equation (8) and consider the effect of an increase in government spending on income. The increase in government spending, $\Delta\overline{G}$, is a change in autonomous spending, so $\Delta\overline{A} = \Delta\overline{G}$. The effect of the change in $\overline{G}$ is given by

$$\frac{\Delta Y}{\Delta\overline{G}} = \gamma \qquad \gamma = \frac{\alpha_G}{1 + k\alpha_G\dfrac{b}{h}} \qquad (10)$$

The expression $\gamma$ is the fiscal or government spending multiplier once interest rate adjustment is taken into account. Consider how this multiplier, $\gamma$, differs from the simpler expression $\alpha_G$ that applied under constant interest rates. Inspection shows that $\gamma$ is less than $\alpha_G$ since $1/(1 + k\alpha_G b/h)$ is a fraction. This represents the dampening effect of increased interest rates associated with a fiscal expansion in the *IS-LM* model.

We note that the expression in equation (10) is almost zero if $h$ is very small and that it is equal to $\alpha_G$ if $h$ approaches infinity. This corresponds, respectively, to vertical and horizontal *LM* curves. Similarly, a large value of either $b$ or $k$ serves to reduce the effect of government spending on income. Why? A high value of $k$ implies a large increase in money demand as income rises and hence a large increase in interest rates required to maintain money market equilibrium. In combination with a high $b$, this implies a large reduction in private aggregate demand.

## THE MONETARY POLICY MULTIPLIER

**monetary policy multiplier**

Shows how much an increase in the real money supply increases the equilibrium level of income, keeping fiscal policy unchanged.

The **monetary policy multiplier** shows how much an increase in the real money supply increases the equilibrium level of income, keeping fiscal policy unchanged. Using equation (8) to examine the effects of an increase in the real money supply on income, we have

$$\frac{\Delta Y}{\Delta (\overline{M/P})} = \frac{b\gamma}{h} \qquad (11)$$

In trying to understand the result given in equation (11), it would help to think in terms of the slopes of the *IS* and *LM* curves. First, any given change in the real money stock will have more effect on the interest rate if the *LM* curve is steeper. Therefore, monetary policy will be more powerful with a higher *k* and a lower *h*, each of which gives rise to a steeper *LM* curve.

Second, for any given change in the interest rate, there will be more change in output if the *IS* curve is flatter. Therefore, monetary policy is more effective if *b* and $\alpha_G$ are large, each of which gives rise to a flatter *IS* curve.

# *Working with Data*

Figure 11-4 shows the relationship between real money growth, the interest rate, and real output growth. Sometimes it is much easier to see a relationship between variables when you graph only two at a time. You may be able to gain more insight into how these variables move together by graphing the following pairs: the interest rate and output growth; the interest rate and money growth; and the rate of money growth and output growth.

# C H A P T E R   S U M M A R Y

▶ The *IS-LM* model presented in this chapter is the basic model of aggregate demand that incorporates the money market as well as the goods market. It places particular stress on the channels through which monetary and fiscal policy affect the economy.

▶ The *IS* curve shows combinations of interest rates and levels of income such that the goods market is in equilibrium. Increases in the interest rate reduce aggregate demand by reducing investment spending. Thus, at higher interest rates, the level of income at which the goods market is in equilibrium is lower: The *IS* curve slopes downward.

▶ The demand for money is a demand for *real* balances. The demand for real balances increases with income and decreases with the interest rate, the cost of holding money rather than other assets. With an exogenously fixed supply of real balances, the *LM* curve, representing money market equilibrium, is upward-sloping.

▶ The interest rate and level of output are jointly determined by simultaneous equilibrium of the goods and money markets. This occurs at the point of intersection of the *IS* and *LM* curves.

www.mcgrawhill.ca/college/dornbusch

▶ Monetary policy affects the economy first by affecting the interest rate and then by affecting aggregate demand. An increase in the money supply reduces the interest rate, increases investment spending and aggregate demand, and thus increases equilibrium output.

▶ The *IS* and *LM* curves together determine the aggregate demand curve.

▶ Changes in monetary and fiscal policy affect the economy through the monetary and fiscal policy multipliers.

## K E Y   T E R M S

*IS-LM* model, *209*
*IS* curve (goods market equilibrium curve), *210*

*LM* curve (money market equilibrium curve), *217*
demand for real balances, *218*
aggregate demand curve, *225*

policy mix, *226*
fiscal policy multiplier, *229*
monetary policy multiplier, *229*

## D I S C U S S I O N   Q U E S T I O N S

1. How does the *IS-LM* model developed in this chapter relate to the model of aggregate demand developed in Chapter 10?

2. **a.** Explain in words how and why the multiplier $\alpha_G$ and the interest sensitivity of aggregate demand affect the slope of the *IS* curve.

   **b.** Explain why the slope of the *IS* curve is a factor in determining the working of monetary policy.

3. Explain in words how and why the income and interest sensitivities of the demand for real balances affect the slope of the *LM* curve.

4. **a.** Why does a horizontal *LM* curve imply that fiscal policy has the same effects on the economy as those derived in Chapter 10?

   **b.** Under what circumstances might the *LM* curve be horizontal?

5. It is possible that the interest rate might affect consumption spending. An increase in the interest rate could, in principle, lead to increases in saving and therefore a reduction in consumption, given the level of income. Suppose that consumption is, in fact, reduced by an increase in the interest rate. How will the *IS* curve be affected?

\*6. Between January and December 1991, while the Canadian economy was falling deeper into its recession, the interest rate on Treasury bills fell from 10.8 to 7.3 percent. Use the *IS-LM* model to explain this pattern of declining output and interest rates. Which curve must have shifted? Can you think of a reason—historically valid or simply imagined—that this shift might have occurred?

## A P P L I C A T I O N   Q U E S T I O N S

1. The following equations describe an economy. (Think of *C, I, G*, etc., as being measured in billions and *i* as a percentage; a 5 percent interest rate implies *i* = 5.)

---

\* An asterisk denotes a more difficult problem.

$$C = 0.8(1 - t)Y$$
$$t = 0.25$$
$$I = 900 - 50i$$
$$\overline{G} = 800$$
$$L = 0.25Y - 62.5i$$
$$\overline{M}/\overline{P} = 500$$

   **a.** What is the equation that describes the *IS* curve?

   **b.** What is the general definition of the *IS* curve?

   **c.** What is the equation that describes the *LM* curve?

   **d.** What is the general definition of the *LM* curve?

   **e.** What are the equilibrium levels of income and the interest rate?

   **f.** Describe in words the conditions that are satisfied at the intersection of the *IS* and *LM* curves, and explain why this is an equilibrium.

2. Continue with the same equations.

   **a.** What is the value of $\alpha_G$ that corresponds to the simple multiplier (with taxes) of Chapter 10?

   **b.** By how much does an increase in government spending of $\Delta G$ increase the level of income in this model, which includes the money market?

   **c.** By how much does a change in government spending of $\Delta G$ affect the equilibrium interest rate?

   **d.** Explain the difference between your answers to parts (a) and (b).

3. Suppose that the money supply, instead of being constant, increases (slightly) with the interest rate.

   **a.** How will this change affect the construction of the *LM* curve?

   **b.** Can you see any reason why the Bank of Canada might follow a policy of increasing the money supply along with the interest rate?

4.  **a.** How does an increase in the tax rate affect the *IS* curve?

   **b.** How does the increase affect the equilibrium level of income?

   **c.** How does the increase affect the equilibrium interest rate?

\*5.  **a.** Show that a given change in the money stock has a larger effect on output the less interest-sensitive is the demand for money. Use the formal analysis of Section 11-5.

   **b.** How does the response of the interest rate to a change in the money stock depend on the interest sensitivity of money demand?

6. Discuss, using the *IS-LM* model, what happens to interest rates as prices change along a given *AD* curve.

7. Show, using *IS* and *LM* curves, why money is neutral in the Classical supply case.

8. Suppose there is a decline in the demand for money. At each output level and interest rate the public now wants to hold lower real balances.

   **a.** In the Keynesian case, what happens to equilibrium output and to prices?

   **b.** In the Classical case, what is the effect on output and on prices?

9. Go to CANSIM and retrieve the money supply as measured by *M*1B and the Consumer Price Index. Calculate the real money stock, and plot this variable. Can you relate this graph to any economic events?

## CHAPTER 12

# MONETARY AND FISCAL POLICY IN THE VERY SHORT RUN

## LEARNING OBJECTIVES

After reading and studying this chapter, you should be able to:

▶ *Understand that both fiscal and monetary policy can be used to stabilize the economy in the short run.*

▶ *Understand that the output effect of expansionary fiscal policy is reduced by crowding out: Increased government spending increases interest rates, reducing investment and partially offsetting the initial expansion in aggregate demand.*

▶ *Understand that the slope of the LM curve has an important bearing on the effectiveness of fiscal and monetary policy.*

T here are many interesting examples of the effects of monetary and fiscal policy on the economy. For example, the long period of deficit-financed expansionary fiscal policy that started in the early 1970s contributed to strong GDP growth. We have previously discussed the severe recessions of the early 1980s and 1990s, when monetary policy makers chose to raise interest rates and the economy went into a downturn.

Figure 12-1 illustrates one of the most recent responses of the economy to monetary policy intervention. In 1997 and 1998, real GDP was growing at an average annual rate of approximately 4 percent. The governor of the Bank of Canada considered this growth to be to be excessively strong and, therefore, began to slowly raise interest rates. Notice in Figure 12-1 how, by the beginning of 2001, output growth began to slow in response to these interest rate increases. However, after the events of September 11, 2001, output fell dramatically. In response to this, interest rates were lowered in an equally dramatic fashion. The result was a strong rebound in output growth in early 2002.

In this chapter we use the *IS-LM* model developed in Chapter 11 to show how monetary policy and fiscal policy work. These are the two main macroeconomic policy tools the government can call on to try to keep the economy growing at a reasonable rate, with low inflation. They are also the policy tools the government uses to try to shorten recessions, as in 1991, and to prevent booms from getting out of hand. Generally speaking, fiscal policy has its initial impact in the goods market, and monetary policy has its initial impact mainly in the assets markets. However, because the goods and assets markets are closely interconnected, both monetary and fiscal policies have effects on both the level of output and interest rates.

Figure 12-2 will refresh your memory about our basic framework. The *IS* curve represents equilibrium in the goods market. The *LM* curve represents equilibrium in the money market. The intersection of the two curves determines output and interest rates in the very short run, that is, for a given price level. Expansionary monetary policy moves the *LM* curve to the right, raising income and lowering interest rates.

---

*FIGURE 12-1*

**90-DAY TREASURY BILL RATE AND REAL GDP GROWTH, QUARTERLY, 1997–2002**

Between 1997 and 2001, monetary policy raised interest rates in order to slow output growth. However, after the events of September 11, 2001, monetary policy was forced to lower interest rates to prevent output from falling further.

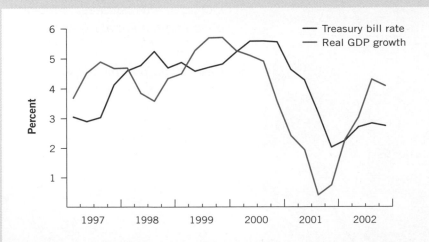

SOURCE: Treasury bill: CANSIM II V122484; real GDP: CANSIM II V1992259..

Contractionary monetary policy moves the *LM* curve to the left, lowering income and raising interest rates. Expansionary fiscal policy moves the *IS* curve to the right, raising both income and interest rates. Contractionary fiscal policy moves the *IS* curve to the left, lowering both income and interest rates.

## 12-1 | MONETARY POLICY

**monetary policy**

Any choice made by the Bank of Canada concerning the level of the nominal money stock.

**www.bankofcanada.ca/en/ monetary/index.htm**

For the purposes of this chapter, **monetary policy** will be defined as any choice made by the Bank of Canada concerning the level of the nominal money stock. Figure 12-2 describes the case of expansionary monetary policy, which is defined as an increase in the nominal money stock.

The initial equilibrium is at point *E*, which corresponds to a real money supply of $\overline{M}/\overline{P}$. Expansionary monetary policy, which increases the nominal money stock, also increases the real money stock, as we assume that the price level is fixed, and shifts the *LM* curve outward to *LM'*. The new equilibrium is at point *E'*, with a lower interest rate and a higher level of income. This is exactly the result shown in Figure 11-10(b) in Chapter 11.

Simply comparing the new equilibrium to the old (which is technically called *comparative statics*) hides the more interesting story concerning the adjustment path of the economy while it is in transition to the new equilibrium. In order to understand the dynamic adjustment, we make an important assumption: The money market adjusts very rapidly, while the goods market adjusts less quickly. This assumption actually is consistent with observed behaviour of the economy over the very short run. We often observe a change of interest rates engineered by the Bank of

**FIGURE 12-2**

An increase in the real money stock shifts the *LM* curve to the right.

**MONETARY POLICY**

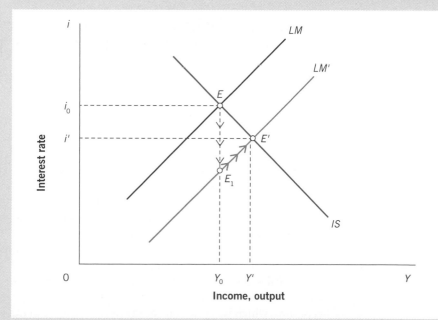

Canada, which is followed, after some time lag, by a change in real economic activity.

Now consider the adjustment path to the new equilibrium in Figure 12-2. Because the money market is assumed to adjust rapidly, the initial response of the economy is to move to point $E_1$, where the interest rate is lower but output has not yet changed. At point $E_1$, the money market is in equilibrium (the economy is on the new *LM* curve) but the goods market is not in equilibrium. In the goods market, the new interest rate, given the existing level of income, $Y_0$, is too low for equilibrium, so the economy is not on the IS curve. Given the decrease in the interest rate, there is now excess demand for goods, so output starts to increase.

In this very short run model, whenever there is adjustment, there will be feedback between the goods and money markets. Notice that as income and output increase, the demand for money increases, which causes interest rates to increase, so the economy moves along the *LM* curve toward the new equilibrium at $E'$.

Therefore, the adjustment path of the economy in response to an increase in the money stock is for interest rates to first decrease, while income and output remain constant. After the interest rate decreases, output begins to increase in response to the interest rate change. While on the path from $E_1$ to $E'$, output is increasing and interest rates must also increase.

It is important to understand that the adjustment of the economy as a result of this monetary policy change is dependent on two general responses. First, monetary policy must have the ability to lower interest rates. The fact that the interest rate decreases to $i'$ initially is one measure of the effectiveness of monetary policy in the very short run. Remember from Chapter 11 that (*ceteris peribus*) the flatter the *LM* curve, the smaller the interest rate change will be. Second, the ability of monetary policy to change real output in the very short run depends on the interest rate response in the *IS* curve. It is fairly easy to see from Figure 12-2 that for any given *LM* shift, output will change more if the *IS* curve is flatter and less if the *IS* curve is steeper.

## Is There a Situation When Monetary Policy Cannot Lower Interest Rates? The Case of the Liquidity Trap

Consider the situation where the interest elasticity of money demand, $h$, is infinite. Given that we know that the slope of the *LM* curve is given by the ratio $k/h$, when $h$ is infinite, the *LM* curve is horizontal. Remember that the slope of the money demand curve is given by $-1/h$, so in this situation, the money demand curve is also horizontal. Therefore, when $h$ is infinite, monetary policy cannot shift the *LM* curve. Put another way, monetary policy has no ability to lower interest rates.

The situation described above is the famous **liquidity trap**. The idea of a liquidity trap arose from the theories of John Maynard Keynes. Keynes himself stated that he was not aware of any practical situation in which the economy would be in a liquidity trap. Technically, a liquidity trap would exist at zero nominal interest rate, and this is something that we do not observe.

Given the above discussion, the liquidity trap remained a "theoretical curiosity" for many years, and was included in textbooks only as a technical exercise, without much real-world appeal. However, a series of events over the past several years has led economists to revive a form of the liquidity trap. In the 1990s, the Japanese economy, which was once one of the most powerful in the world, began to show signs of serious trouble. There were many policy responses to this slowdown, but one of

**liquidity trap**
A situation that arises when the *LM* curve is horizontal because the interest elasticity of money demand is infinite.

the most interesting was the intervention on the part of the Japanese central bank, which aggressively lowered Japanese interest rates in an attempt to stimulate the economy, much along the lines depicted in Figure 12-2.

However, the intervention did not produce the desired result because, even though the Japanese central bank was successful in lowering interest rates, output did not respond. In Figure 12-2, we would explain this as a very steep, or vertical, *IS* curve. In spite of this lack of success, the Japanese central bank continued to put downward pressure on interest rates. The failure of this policy promoted *The Economist* to publish an article entitled "Is Japan in a Liquidity Trap?"

After this series of events, the concept of a liquidity trap took on a new real-world meaning: An economy is sometimes said to be in a liquidity trap when interest rates are so low that a central bank has no scope to lower them further. Notice that this is somewhat different than the technical condition for a liquidity trap outlined above. One important difference is that in the modern version of a liquidity trap, the central bank can raise interest rates, something that cannot be done in the earlier technical version of a liquidity trap. For another important event that gave rise to the question of a liquidity trap, see the following Policy in Action feature.

## POLICY IN *ACTION*

### The Liquidity Trap in Canada and the United States

In this chapter, we discussed how the liquidity trap has taken on new meaning in modern macroeconomics, describing a situation in which monetary policy would like to lower interest rates but may have no scope to do so. After the events of September 11, 2001, there was a general fear that the economies of Canada and the United States would slip into a severe recession. In response to this, the Bank of Canada and the Federal Reserve Board very quickly began lowering interest rates. In a short period of time, interest rates in each country were at a 40-year low. The hope was that this sudden large drop in interest rates would stimulate output. This immediately gave rise to the question of whether interest rates were low enough to generate some growth on the output side, and if not, could monetary policy lower interest rates any further. That is, were the two economies each in a liquidity trap?

In Canada, the lowering of interest rates had the desired effect, as output growth rebounded strongly in the first quarter of 2002. However, in the United States, output growth remained sluggish and there was talk of the U.S. economy entering a period of deflation, when prices would be falling. Of course, this led to more calls for a lowering of interest rates in the United States and more talk of the U.S. economy experiencing a liquidity trap.

## Can the *LM* Curve Be Vertical? Classical Economics Again

Can the *LM* curve be vertical? The answer to this question is that, technically, the *LM* curve could be vertical if either the interest elasticity of money demand is zero or the income elasticity of money demand is infinite. We can dismiss the latter of these two possibilities immediately.[1] The interest elasticity of money demand could possibly be zero but, in this case, the money demand curve would be vertical and the money supply curve would also be vertical, as depicted in Figure 12-3. Therefore, there would either be no equilibrium, as shown in Figure 12-3, or an infinite number of equilibria in the special case where the money demand and money supply curves coincide. Neither of these cases is very appealing from an economic modelling point of view. That is, if the interest elasticity of money demand is zero, then there is no manner in which to determine the equilibrium interest rate in the money market, which leaves the model with no sensible role for the interest rate in the very short run.

### FIGURE 12-3

**THE MONEY MARKET WHEN *h* = 0**

When the interest elasticity of money demand (*h*) is zero, the money demand curve is vertical. Since the money supply curve is also vertical, there is either no equilibrium (as shown here) or an infinite number of equilibria if the money demand and money supply are superimposed.

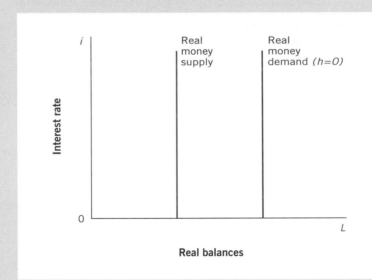

It is helpful to think of this problem in terms of markets and prices. The money market, like any other market, has a price that coordinates supply and demand. In the long run Classical model studied in Chapter 3, the quantity theory of money was assumed to hold. In that model, if there was, for instance, an increase in the nominal money stock, then the price level would increase. Therefore, the price of money was assumed to be (the inverse of) the general price level.[2] When we moved to the Keynesian *IS-LM* model in this chapter, we assumed that the price level was fixed and, therefore, the quantity theory of money could not hold. In the Keynesian *IS-LM*

---

[1] The income elasticity of money demand is relevant only over a range of $0 < k \leq 1$. See Chapter 16 for a discussion of this point.

[2] It may be helpful to have another look at Box 11-3 in Chapter 11.

model, the price of money is assumed to be the nominal interest rate. Now, if we assume that the interest elasticity of money demand is zero, then the interest rate is no longer the price of money.

In any event, the above theoretical discussion notwithstanding, it is fairly clear that, empirically, the nominal interest rate plays a prominent role in money market adjustment in the very short run, and removing it by assuming that the interest elasticity of money demand is zero would remove our ability to explain very short run movements in the economy.

---

**BOX 12-1**

## A Classical *IS-LM* Model

In this chapter, we have discussed the situation in which the interest elasticity of money demand is zero. In this situation, monetary policy can no longer work through the interest rate channel to affect output in the usual manner described in this chapter. Instead, the money market is actually a Classical money market, which behaves according to the quantity theory of money. This situation gives rise to the Classical *IS-LM* model shown in the figure below.

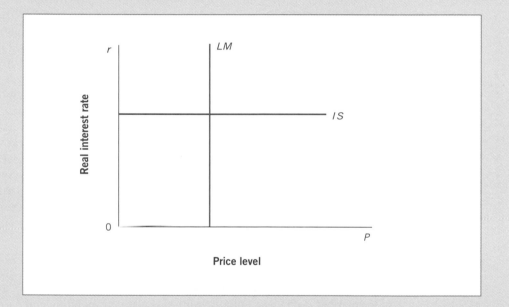

Notice that in the Classical *IS-LM* model, the price level is on the horizontal axis, not real income. This is because in a Classical world, the money market determines the price level. On the vertical axis is the real interest rate, which is the important interest rate in a Classical model. In the Classical model, the real interest rate is determined by the interaction of savings and investment, and this is exogenous to the money market. Therefore, the Classical *IS-LM* model, although logically correct, does not really tell us much. We are asking about the relationship between the real rate of interest and the nominal price level, and in a Classical model, these two variables are not related to each other.

## 12-2 | FISCAL POLICY AND CROWDING OUT

www.fin.gc.ca/access/
ecfisce.html

This section shows how changes in fiscal policy shift the *IS* curve, the curve that describes equilibrium in the goods market. Recall that the *IS* curve slopes downward because a decrease in the interest rate increases investment spending, thereby increasing aggregate demand and the level of output at which the goods market is in equilibrium. Recall also that changes in fiscal policy shift the *IS* curve. Specifically, a fiscal expansion shifts the *IS* curve to the right.

The equation of the *IS* curve, derived in Chapter 11, is repeated here for convenience:

$$Y = \alpha_G(\overline{A}_1 - bi) \qquad \alpha_G = \frac{1}{1 - c(1 - t)} \tag{1}$$

Note that $\overline{G}$, the level of government spending, is a component of autonomous spending, $\overline{A}_1$, in equation (1). The income tax rate, $t$, is part of the multiplier. Thus, both government spending and the tax rate affect the *IS* schedule.

### An Increase in Government Spending

We now show, in Figure 12-4, how a fiscal expansion raises equilibrium income and the interest rate. At unchanged interest rates, higher levels of government spending increase the level of aggregate demand. To meet the increased demand for goods, output must rise. In Figure 12-4, we show the effect of a shift in the *IS* schedule. At each level of the interest rate, equilibrium income must rise by $\alpha_G$ times the increase in government spending. For example, if government spending rises by 100 and the multiplier is 2, equilibrium income must increase by 200 at each level of the interest rate. Thus, the *IS* schedule shifts to the right by 200.

If the economy is initially in equilibrium at point *E* and government spending rises by 100, we would move to point *E″ if the interest rate stayed constant.* At *E″*, the goods market is in equilibrium in that planned spending equals output. However, the money market is no longer in equilibrium. Income has increased, and therefore the quantity of money demanded is higher. Because there is an excess demand for real balances, the interest rate rises. Firms' planned investment spending declines at higher interest rates, and thus aggregate demand falls off.

What is the complete adjustment, taking into account the expansionary effect of higher government spending and the dampening effects of the higher interest rate on private spending? Figure 12-4 shows that only at point *E′* do the goods *and* money markets both clear. Only at point *E′* is planned spending equal to income and, at the same time, the quantity of real balances demanded equal to the given real money stock. Point *E′* is therefore the new equilibrium point.

### Crowding Out

Comparing *E′* to the initial equilibrium at *E*, we see that increased government spending raises both income and the interest rate. But another important comparison is between points *E′* and *E″*, the equilibrium in the goods market at unchanged interest rates. Point *E″* corresponds to the equilibrium we studied in Chapter 11, when we neglected the impact of interest rates on the economy. In comparing *E″* and *E′*, it becomes clear that the adjustment of interest rates and their impact on aggregate demand dampen the expansionary effect of increased government spending. Income, instead of increasing to level *Y″*, rises only to *Y′*.

**FIGURE 12-4**

Increased government spending increases aggregate demand, shifting the *IS* curve to the right.

## EFFECTS OF AN INCREASE IN GOVERNMENT SPENDING

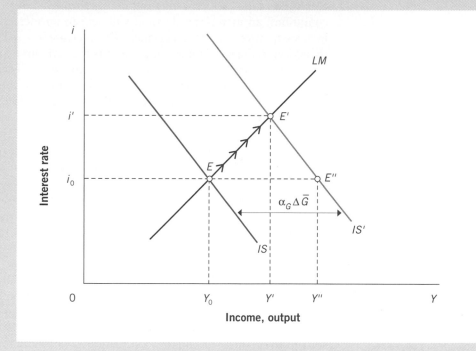

**crowding out**

Occurs when expansionary fiscal policy causes interest rates to rise, thereby reducing private spending, particularly investment.

The reason that income rises only to $Y'$ rather than to $Y''$ is that the rise in the interest rate from $i_0$ to $i'$ reduces the level of investment spending. We say that the increase in government spending *crowds out* investment spending. **Crowding out** occurs when expansionary fiscal policy causes interest rates to rise, thereby reducing private spending, particularly investment.

What factors determine how much crowding out takes place? In other words, what determines the extent to which interest rate adjustments dampen the output expansion induced by increased government spending? By drawing for yourself different *IS* and *LM* schedules, you will be able to show the following:

▶ Income increases more and interest rates increase less, the flatter the *LM* schedule.

▶ Income increases less and interest rates increase less, the flatter the *IS* schedule.

▶ Income and interest rates increase more the larger the multiplier, $\alpha_G$, and thus the larger the horizontal shift of the *IS* schedule.

In each case, the extent of crowding out is greater the more the interest rate increases when government spending rises.

## Is Crowding Out Important?

How seriously must we take the possibility of crowding out? Here, three points must be made. The first point is also an important warning. In this chapter, as in the two preceding chapters, we are assuming an economy with prices given, in which output is below the full employment level. In these conditions, when fiscal expansion increases demand, firms can increase the level of output by hiring more workers. But in fully employed economies, crowding out occurs through a different mechanism. In such conditions, an increase in demand will lead to an increase in the price level. The increase in price reduces *real* balances. (An increase in $\overline{P}$ reduces the ratio $\overline{M}/\overline{P}$.) This reduction in the real money supply moves the *LM* curve to the left, raising interest rates until the initial increase in aggregate demand is fully crowded out.

The second point, however, is that in an economy with unemployed resources, there will *not* be full crowding out because the *LM* schedule is not, in fact, vertical. A fiscal expansion will raise interest rates, but income will also rise. Crowding out is therefore a matter of degree. The increase in aggregate demand raises income, and with the rise in income, the level of saving rises. This expansion in saving, in turn, makes it possible to finance a larger budget deficit without *completely* displacing private spending.

The third point is that with unemployment and, thus, a possibility for output to expand, interest rates need not rise at all when government spending rises, and there need not be any crowding out. This is true because the monetary authorities can *accommodate* the fiscal expansion by an increase in the money supply. *Monetary policy is accommodating when, in the course of a fiscal expansion, the money supply is increased in order to prevent interest rates from increasing.* **Monetary accommodation** is also referred to as *monetizing budget deficits*, meaning that the Bank of Canada prints money to buy the bonds with which the government pays for its deficit. When the Bank of Canada accommodates a fiscal expansion, both the *IS* and the *LM* schedules shift to the right, as in Figure 12-5. Output will clearly increase, but interest rates need not rise. Accordingly, there need not be any adverse effects on investment.

**monetary accommodation**

The central bank prints money to buy the bonds with which the government pays for its deficit.

## FIGURE 12-5

If the Bank of Canada increases the money supply when there is a fiscal expansion, both the *IS* and the *LM* curves shift to the right. Because interest rates do not rise, there is no crowding out.

### MONETARY ACCOMMODATION OF A FISCAL EXPANSION

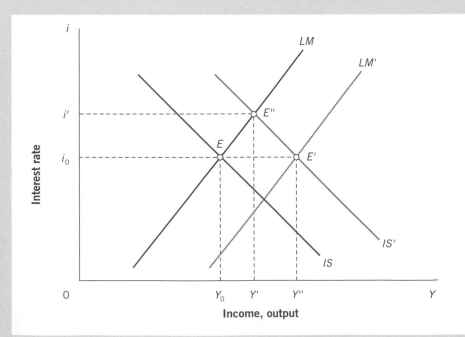

BOX

**12-2**

## The Policy Mix

In the Policy in Action feature in Chapter 11, we discussed how tight monetary policy and loose fiscal policy could lead to high interest rates. This is generally called the *policy mix*.

The policy mix of the early 1980s featured highly expansionary fiscal policy and tight money. The tight money succeeded in reducing the inflation rate at the expense of a serious recession. The continued expansionary fiscal policy then drove a recovery during which real interest rates increased.

This recovery continued until mid-1988, when both the Bank of Canada and the U.S. Federal Reserve Board, fearing that inflation was rising again, began to tighten monetary policy again, and interest rates began rising. The table below shows that the real interest rate reached 7 percent in 1989 and 8.1 percent in 1990, which forced the economy into a recession in 1990 and 1991. In 1992, inflation fell dramatically from 5.6 percent to 1.5 percent. Also, in 1992, the Bank of Canada allowed interest rates to drop and a modest recovery began. This recovery was aided by the continuation of full employment deficits throughout the 1990s.

An interesting feature of this recession and recovery is the behaviour of the unemployment rate. You can see from the table below that the unemployment rate increased from 1988 to 1992. After 1992, the unemployment rate remained above 10 percent until the late 1990s.

### THE RECESSION OF THE EARLY 1990s

| | | | (PERCENT) | | |
|---|---|---|---|---|---|
| | **1988** | **1989** | **1990** | **1991** | **1992** |
| Nominal interest rate | 9.4 | 12.0 | 12.8 | 8.8 | 6.5 |
| Real interest rate | 5.4 | 7.0 | 8.1 | 3.2 | 5.0 |
| Full-employment deficit | 4.0 | 3.9 | 3.9 | 3.6 | 3.0 |
| Unemployment rate | 7.7 | 7.5 | 8.1 | 10.4 | 11.3 |
| GDP growth | 4.9 | 2.4 | −0.2 | −1.9 | 0.76 |
| Inflation | 4.0 | 5.0 | 4.7 | 5.6 | 1.5 |

## 12-3 | MONETARY POLICY AND THE INTEREST RATE RULE

Until now, we have made the assumption that monetary policy is conducted by making discrete changes in the money supply, so that the nominal money supply was an exogenous variable. In this case, we specified the behaviour of monetary policy as

$$M^s = \overline{M} \tag{2}$$

**money supply rule**

A policy stance where the central bank holds the level (or growth rate) of the money supply constant.

This type of policy stance is technically known as a **money supply rule**.

Now imagine a situation where the money demand curve is subject to random shocks. As an example, suppose there was a major world event that caused people to hold a great deal of money—perhaps because they felt that they would not be able to liquidate other forms of wealth fast enough. This type of event would suddenly increase the demand for money, as illustrated in Figure 12-6.

---

**FIGURE 12-6**      **CHANGING THE MONEY SUPPLY WHEN THE DEMAND FOR MONEY SHIFTS**

If the money supply is increased when the demand for money shifts outward, then the interest rate would not rise as it would if the money supply was not changed.

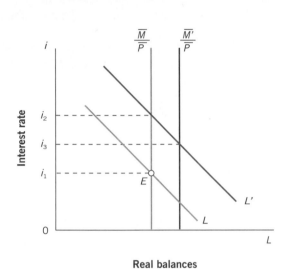

---

The initial equilibrium is at point *E*, with an interest rate of $i_1$. The shock to money demand shifts the money demand curve to *L'*. If the Bank of Canada continues to run policy according to a money supply rule, the interest rate will rise to $i_2$.

Suppose that the Bank of Canada, for whatever reason, felt that the economy should not be subject to as large of an interest rate change as given by the movement from $i_1$ to $i_2$. In response to this shock, the Bank of Canada could increase the money supply when the interest rate goes up, which would make the interest rate increase smaller than in the absence of the money supply increase. For instance, in Figure 12-6, the Bank of Canada could change the money supply to $\overline{M}'$, and the interest rate would increase to only $i_3$.

If the Bank of Canada did this every time there was a shock to money demand (of course, the shocks could be both positive and negative), the money supply would no longer be completely exogenous but would now have an endogenous component. We could write the money supply equation that describes this stance on monetary policy as

$$M^s = \overline{M} + \gamma i \; ; \gamma > 0 \tag{3}$$

The parameter $\gamma$ measures the amount that the central bank increases the money supply in response to an interest rate change. We call $\gamma$ the **interest elasticity of the money supply**. The more that the Bank of Canada reacts to changes in the interest rate, the larger $\gamma$ will be.

If we want to graph the money supply curve, we can rearrange equation (3).

$$i = \frac{1}{\gamma} (M^s - \overline{M}) \tag{4}$$

where the slope of the money supply curve is given by $1/\gamma$. Therefore, the more the Bank of Canada reacts, the larger $\gamma$ is and the flatter the money supply curve is. (Of course, the reverse is also true.) The effects of running policy in this manner are shown in Figure 12-7, where you can see that the interest rate change under a money supply rule $(i_0 - i_2)$ is greater than the interest rate change if the central bank conducts policy according to equation (4) $(i_0 - i_1)$.

## FIGURE 12-7    MONETARY POLICY REACTS TO INTEREST RATE CHANGES

If monetary policy changes the money supply every time that interest rates change, as given by equation (4), then the money supply curve is upward sloping, rather than vertical. In this situation, there is less interest rate change for any given money demand shift.

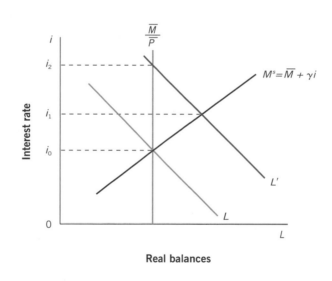

Now consider the extreme case where $\gamma = \infty$. In this case, the Bank of Canada changes the money supply by any amount that is needed, as soon as there is any small change in the interest rate. In this case, the money supply curve is horizontal and the shifts in money demand do not cause any change in the interest rate. This is known as conducting monetary policy according to an **interest rate rule**. Notice that, under an interest rate rule, the money supply is endogenous and the interest rate is exogenous.

Now consider deriving an *LM* curve under the monetary policy of an interest rate rule. For an *LM* curve, money supply equals money demand. Our money demand equation is assumed to be the same as before, and we put this together with our new money supply curve in Figure 12-8.

## FIGURE 12-8

### DERIVING THE *LM* CURVE UNDER AN INTEREST RATE RULE

If monetary policy is conducted according to an interest rate rule, then the money supply is changed any time there is a small change in the interest rate, and the *LM* curve is horizontal.

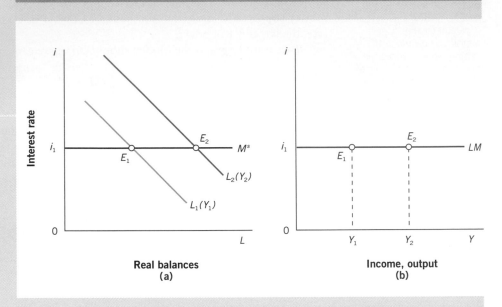

Real balances
(a)

Income, output
(b)

www.bankofcanada.ca/en/
res/r03-1-ec.htm

Figure 12-8 shows that, when monetary policy is conducted according to an interest rate rule, the *LM* curve is horizontal. It is important to understand that, in this case, the *LM* curve is horizontal by policy design. To make sure that you understand this, contrast the *LM* curve shown in Figure 12-8 with the liquidity trap discussed earlier. Remember that, theoretically, the liquidity trap would occur when the interest elasticity of money *demand* is infinite. There is nothing that policy can do about this situation. However, in the case of an interest rate rule, the *LM* curve is horizontal because monetary policy makers have chosen to make the interest elasticity of money *supply* infinite; that is, they are continually intervening in the money market. Therefore, in the case of an interest rate rule, monetary policy is capable of doing something: It acts to hold the interest rate constant. Theoretically, the Bank of Canada could choose any interest rate it wanted, so the *LM* curve under an interest rate rule, even though it is horizontal, can be shifted by policy.

You can think of conducting monetary policy according to a money supply rule as a special case where $\gamma = 0$, and the *LM* curve will be the familiar upward-sloping curve. When policy is conducted according to an interest rate rule, $\gamma = \infty$ and the *LM* curve is horizontal. These two *LM* curves are shown in Figure 12-9.

## Money Supply Rule and Interest Rate Rule: When Would Policy Makers Choose One Over the Other?

The difference between a money supply rule and an interest rate rule is more than just a textbook exercise. Under a money supply rule, the central bank sets the money supply and then does nothing else.[3] This is a policy of minimal intervention in the

---

[3] For this section, we rule out discrete, one-time changes in the money supply under a money supply rule.

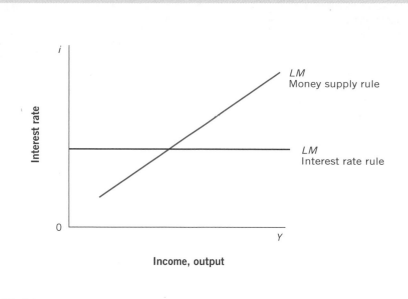

**FIGURE 12-9**

*LM* CURVE FOR A MONEY SUPPLY RULE AND FOR AN INTEREST RATE RULE

If monetary policy is conducted according to a money supply rule, then the *LM* curve has the familiar upward slope. If monetary policy is conducted according to an interest rate rule, then the *LM* curve is horizontal.

money market. Under an interest rate rule, the central bank must be intervening in the money market at all times. This is an activist monetary policy. (We will discuss activist policy in detail in Chapter 17.) Therefore, the choice of conducting monetary policy using a money supply rule or an interest rate rule is a choice of activist stabilization policy (interest rate rule) versus conducting policy by a fixed rule with a minimum of interference (money supply rule).

In order to compare the two policy stances, we assume that the goal of the central bank is to minimize the fluctuations in income, and we ask the question: Within the framework of the *IS-LM* model, will fluctuations in income be smaller under a money supply rule or under an interest rate rule? In the *IS-LM* model, fluctuations in income can arise from shocks in the goods market (the *IS* curve fluctuates) or from shocks in the money market (the *LM* curve fluctuates). We know that, at any point in time, the economy is subject to both goods market and money market shocks. However, this makes analysis very difficult. In order to make this exercise simple and understandable, we will look first at a situation where there are only goods market shocks, and then we will look at a situation where there are only money market shocks.

## Goods Market Shocks Only

In this section, we consider the situation where the goods market is subject to shocks, while the money market is not. Therefore, in this situation, the IS curve is subject to fluctuations, while the LM curve is not. This is depicted in Figure 12-10.

**FIGURE 12-10**

**MONETARY POLICY WITH SHOCKS TO THE GOODS MARKET**

If monetary policy is conducted according to a money supply rule, income varies between $Y_2$ and $Y_1$, and if it is conducted according to an interest rate rule, income varies between $Y_3$ and $Y_4$. In this case, the variance of income is minimized by a money supply rule.

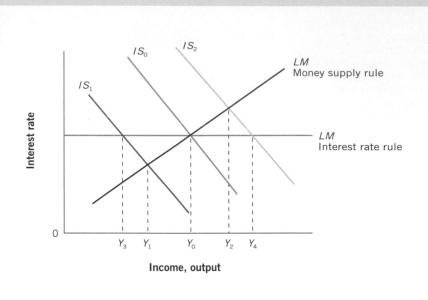

In Figure 12-10, when the *IS* curve is not subject to a shock, income is at $Y_0$, where either of the *LM* curves intersects the *IS* curve marked $IS_0$. The *IS* curve marked $IS_1$ pertains to a negative goods market shock, and the curve marked $IS_2$ pertains to a positive goods market shock.

Consider first conducting monetary policy using a money supply rule. In this case, the *IS-LM* equilibrium varies between $Y_1$ and $Y_2$. These are the equilibrium points where the *LM* (money supply rule) curve intersects the $IS_1$ and the $IS_2$ curves. Now consider conducting monetary policy using an interest rate rule. In this case, the *IS-LM* equilibrium varies between $Y_3$ and $Y_4$. These are the equilibrium points where the *LM* (interest rate rule) curve intersects the $IS_1$ and the $IS_2$ curves. Clearly, in this case, the variance in output is minimized under a money supply rule.

## Money Market Shocks Only

The situation of money market shocks only is depicted in Figure 12-11. Notice immediately from this figure that if the money market is subject to shocks, these do not affect the *LM* (interest rate rule), as the interest rate rule was designed to remove shocks from the money market. Therefore, in a situation of money market shocks only, and conducting monetary policy according to an interest rate rule, there is no variance in output. Alternatively, if the money market is fluctuating and the monetary authorities use a money supply rule, income will vary between $Y_1$ and $Y_2$. Clearly, in this situation, an interest rate rule has the minimum variance in output.

## FIGURE 12-11

If monetary policy is conducted according to a money supply rule, income varies between $Y_2$ and $Y_1$, and if it is conducted according to an interest rate rule, income does not change. In this case, the variance of income is minimized by an interest rate rule.

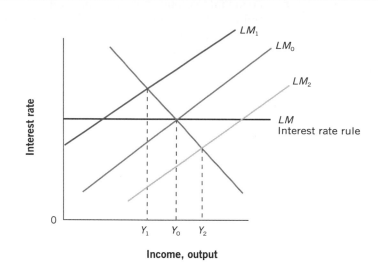

**MONETARY POLICY WITH SHOCKS TO THE MONEY MARKET**

*Working with Data*

In the introduction to this chapter, we discussed the relationship between the interest rate and growth in real GDP over the cycle. In Figure 12-1, we graphed the nominal Treasury bill rate with the growth rate of GDP. Go to CANSIM II and retrieve the Consumer Price Index (V735319), as well as the other data referred to in Figure 12-1. Construct the annual inflation rate, quarterly, and then the real rate of interest, quarterly. Plot the real rate of interest with the growth rate of GDP over the period 1975–2002. You should be able to identify the negative relationship between these two variables, especially during recessions.

## C H A P T E R   S U M M A R Y

▶ Monetary policy affects the economy, first by affecting the interest rate and then by affecting aggregate demand. An increase in the money supply reduces the interest rate, increases investment spending and aggregate demand, and thus increases equilibrium output.

▶ There are two extreme cases in the operation of monetary policy. In the Classical case, the demand for real balances is independent of the rate of interest. In that case, monetary policy is highly effective. The other extreme is the liquidity trap, the case in which the public is willing to hold *any* amount of real balances at the going interest rate. In that case, changes in the supply of real balances have no impact on interest rates and therefore do not affect aggregate demand and output.

▶ Taking into account the effects of fiscal policy on the interest rate modifies the multiplier results of Chapter 8. Fiscal expansion, except in extreme circumstances, still leads to an income expansion. However, the rise in interest rates that comes about through the increase in money demand caused by higher income dampens the expansion.

▶ Fiscal policy is more effective the smaller the induced changes in interest rates and the smaller the response of investment to these interest rate changes.

▶ The two extreme cases, the liquidity trap and the Classical case, are useful to show what determines the magnitude of monetary and fiscal policy multipliers. In the liquidity trap, monetary policy has no effect on the economy, whereas fiscal policy has its full multiplier effect on output and no effect on interest rates. In the Classical case, changes in the money stock change income, but fiscal policy has no effect on income—it affects only the interest rate. In this case, there is complete crowding out of private spending by government spending.

▶ A fiscal expansion, because it leads to higher interest rates, displaces, or crowds out, some private investment. The extent of crowding out is a sensitive issue in assessing the usefulness and desirability of fiscal policy as a tool of stabilization policy.

▶ If the central bank wants to minimize fluctuations in the interest rate, it can conduct policy according to an interest rate rule, manipulating the money supply every time interest rates change.

▶ If all of the variation in income arises from fluctuations in the goods market, then a money supply rule reduces the variance of income. If all of the variation in income arises from fluctuations in the money market, then an interest rate rule reduces the variance of income.

## KEY TERMS

monetary policy, *235*                monetary accommodation, *242*        interest elasticity of the money
liquidity trap, *236*                 money supply rule, *244*                supply, *245*
crowding out, *241*                                                          interest rate rule, *245*

## DISCUSSION QUESTIONS

1. Most of the time, both the goods market and the money market are subject to shocks at the same time. How would you think about choosing between an interest rate rule and a money supply rule in this real-world situation?

2. Discuss the circumstances under which the monetary and fiscal policy multipliers are each, in turn, equal to zero. Explain in words why this can happen and how likely you think this is.

www.mcgrawhill.ca/college/dornbusch

3. What is a liquidity trap? If the economy was stuck in one, would you advise the use of monetary or fiscal policy?

4. What is crowding out, and when would you expect it to occur? In the face of substantial crowding out, which will be more successful—fiscal or monetary policy?

5. What would the *LM* curve look like in a Classical world? If this really was the *LM* curve that we thought best characterized the economy, would we lean toward the use of fiscal policy or monetary policy? (You may assume that your goal is to affect output.)

6. What happens when the Bank of Canada monetizes a budget deficit? Is this something it should *always* try to do? (*Hint:* Outline the benefits and costs of such a policy, over time.)

7. "We can have the GDP path we want equally well with a tight fiscal policy and an easier monetary policy, or the reverse, within fairly broad limits. The real basis for choice lies in many subsidiary targets, besides real GDP and inflation, that are differentially affected by fiscal and monetary policies." What are some of the subsidiary targets referred to in this quote? How would they be affected by alternative policy combinations?

## A P P L I C A T I O N     Q U E S T I O N S

1. The economy is at full employment. Now the government wants to change the composition of demand toward investment and away from consumption without, however, allowing aggregate demand to go beyond full employment. What is the required policy mix? Use an *IS-LM* diagram to show your policy proposal.

2. Suppose the government cuts income taxes. Show in the *IS-LM* model the impact of the tax cut under two assumptions: (1) The government keeps interest rates constant through an accommodating monetary policy, (2) the money stock remains unchanged. Explain the difference in results.

3. Go to CANSIM and retrieve data on the money stock, *M*1B, and the 90-day Treasury bill rate. Calculate the rate of growth of money and plot this with the Treasury bill rate. Can you relate this graph to any of the monetary policy discussions in this chapter?

# CAPITAL MOBILITY AND THE EXCHANGE RATE IN THE *IS-LM* MODEL

## *LEARNING OBJECTIVES*

After reading and studying this chapter, you should be able to:

▶ *Understand that when capital mobility is perfect, the domestic interest rate cannot diverge very far from the foreign interest rate.*

▶ *Understand that under a flexible exchange rate, fiscal policy cannot affect the level of output, but under a fixed exchange rate, fiscal policy changes output.*

▶ *Understand that under a flexible exchange rate, monetary policy can change output, but under a fixed exchange rate, the monetary authority cannot engage in domestic stabilization.*

▶ *Understand that exchange rate expectations can drive the domestic interest rate away from the foreign interest rate.*

n Chapter 5, we introduced the basic concepts of international trade and finance. In Chapter 9, we applied these open economy concepts to our aggregate demand-aggregate supply model. In this chapter, we discuss capital mobility and the exchange rate in the very short run. Therefore, this chapter is an open economy extension of the *IS-LM* model that was developed in previous chapters.

## 13-1 | CAPITAL MOBILITY AND INTEREST PARITY

One of the striking facts about the international economy is the high degree of integration, or linkage, among financial, or capital, markets—the markets in which bonds and stocks are traded. In most industrial countries today, there are no restrictions on holding assets abroad. Canadian residents, or residents in Germany or the United Kingdom, can hold their wealth either at home or abroad. They therefore search around the world for the highest return (adjusted for risk), thereby linking together yields in capital markets in different countries. For example, if rates in New York rose relative to those in Canada, investors would turn to lending in New York, while borrowers would turn to Toronto. With lending up in New York and borrowing up in Toronto, yields would quickly fall into line.

As a consequence of these capital flows, interest rate differentials among major industrialized countries, adjusted to eliminate the risk of exchange rate changes, are quite small in practice. Consider the case of the United States and Canada. Once interest rates are measured on a "covered" basis, so that the exchange risk is eliminated, they should be exactly the same.[1] In fact, the differential is very small, averaging less than 0.5 percent, a result primarily of tax differences. We take this evidence to support the view that capital is very highly mobile across borders, as we assume henceforth.

In this chapter, we will make the assumption that, at least in the very short run, the world is characterized by **perfect capital mobility**. Capital is perfectly mobile internationally when investors can purchase assets in any country they choose, quickly, with low transaction costs, and in unlimited amounts. When capital is perfectly mobile, asset holders are willing and able to move large amounts of funds across borders in search of the highest return or lowest borrowing cost.

In Chapter 12, we introduced the assumption that financial markets clear quickly and goods markets clear slowly. In this chapter, we extend this assumption to open economy considerations. We assume that, given perfect capital mobility and the speed with which financial markets adjust relative to goods markets, the balance of payments position of the domestic economy will be determined by capital flows in the very short run. Given the above assumptions, the balance of payments will be said to be in equilibrium when there are no capital flows. Given this, we must have an understanding of short run capital flows.

**perfect capital mobility**
Occurs when investors can purchase assets in any country they choose, quickly, with low transaction costs, and in unlimited amounts.

### Capital Flows and Interest Parity

Capital flows respond to interest rates in Canada relative to the interest rates of our trading partners. Assume that what is important for capital flows is a representative interest rate in Canada, relative to a representative interest rate in the United States.

---

[1] Cover, or protection, against the risk of exchange rate changes can be obtained by buying a futures contract, which promises (of course, at a cost) to pay a given amount of one currency in exchange for a specified amount of another currency at a given future date. There are, in practice, simpler ways of obtaining foreign exchange risk cover, but the essential mechanism is the same.

Assume that you have $1.00 Canadian to invest. The rate of return in Canada is

$$1 + i_t \tag{1}$$

We wish to compare this to the rate of return from investing this same $1.00 Canadian in the U.S. economy. The U.S. dollar equivalent of $1.00 Canadian is

$$\frac{1}{e_t} \tag{2}$$

where, you will recall, $e_t$ is the current exchange rate, measured as the Canadian dollar price of one U.S. dollar. This is the amount of U.S. dollars that you have available to invest, given your initial $1.00 Canadian. We assume that you take this money and buy U.S. bonds. The rate of return from this is given by

$$\frac{1}{e_t}(1 + i^f_t) \tag{3}$$

where $i^f_t$ is the nominal interest rate in the United States. Be sure that you understand what this is: It is the rate of return from investing one Canadian dollar in the U.S. economy (by buying U.S. bonds), *measured in U.S. dollars*. Since we wish to compare this to the rate of return from buying a Canadian bond, we assume that at the end of the period, you take your U.S. return and buy Canadian dollars at a rate of $e_{t+1}$. This leaves you with

$$(\frac{1}{e_t}(1 + i^f_t)e_{t+1} \tag{4}$$

Again, be careful that you understand what this is: It is the rate of return from investing $1.00 Canadian in the U.S. economy, *measured in Canadian dollars*. Of course, you do not know, in period $t$, what $e_{t+1}$ will be, so we assume that you make an expectation of the unknown future exchange rate. We call this expectation $e^e_{t+1}$. Given all of this, we can construct the following equation.

$$(1 + i_t) = (1 + i^f_t)(\frac{e^e_{t+1}}{e^t}) \tag{5}$$

This is known as the *interest parity equation*.[2] If this equation holds, we say that interest parity holds. In this situation, there will be no capital flows. If this equation does not hold, then interest parity does not hold, and there will be capital flows chasing the highest rate of return. For instance, if the right-hand side of equation (5) was greater than the left-hand side, then there would be a higher (expected) rate of return in the U.S. economy, and there would be capital flows out of Canada and into the United States.

We can simplify this interest parity condition by making the (very naïve) assumption that agents do not expect exchange rate changes.

$$e^e_{t+1} = e_t \tag{6}$$

---

[2] Technically, this is the nominal interest parity equation.

We will relax this assumption in the last section of this chapter. This simplifies interest parity to

$$i_t = i_t^f \tag{7}$$

Equation (7) is now our interest parity condition. When the domestic interest rate equals the foreign interest rate, the interest parity condition holds. In a situation when interest parity holds, there will be no capital flows. Conversely, when the domestic interest rate does not equal the foreign interest rate, there will be capital flows and these capital flows will have exchange rate ramifications.

Consider the situation where the domestic interest rate is above the foreign rate. In this case, there is incentive to purchase Canadian bonds. Under perfect capital mobility, there will be large capital inflows. Therefore, in the foreign exchange market, there will be an excess demand for Canadian dollars. This will give rise to appreciation pressure in the foreign exchange market. The opposite will be true for a situation where the domestic interest rate is below the foreign interest rate. This is summarized in Figure 13-1.

| *FIGURE 13-1* | INTEREST PARITY, CAPITAL FLOWS, AND EXCHANGE RATE CHANGES |

If the domestic interest rate is greater than the foreign interest rate, there will be capital inflows, which will cause the Canadian dollar to appreciate. If the domestic interest rate is less than the foreign interest rate, there will be capital outflows, which will cause the Canadian dollar to depreciate.

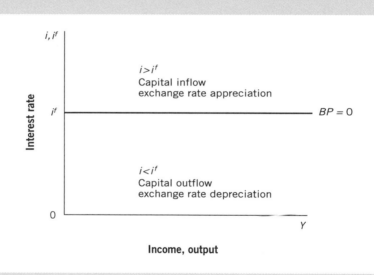

In this very short run model, the interest parity line represents balance of payments equilibrium. Remember from Chapters 5 and 9 that any balance of payments surplus is composed of a trade surplus (net exports) plus a capital account surplus (net foreign borrowing). When the domestic interest rate equals the foreign rate, there are no capital flows and, therefore, there is no trade surplus. Therefore, the balance of payments is in equilibrium. Whether or not the domestic interest rate is equal to the foreign interest rate will be determined by the intersection of the *IS* and *LM* curves. Therefore, we can now put the interest parity condition together with the *IS-LM* model. This is shown in Figure 13-2.

## FIGURE 13-2

### THE *IS-LM-BP* MODEL

Internal equilibrium is given by the usual intersection of the *IS* and *LM* curves. External equilibrium is given by the interest parity line, which is horizontal at the level of the foreign interest rate. Because of the assumption of perfect capital mobility, the interest parity line is often called the *balance of payments (BP) line.*

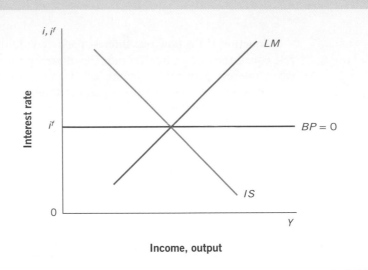

Income, output

---

**Mundell-Fleming model**

The analysis extending the standard *IS-LM* model to the open economy under perfect capital mobility.

http://jdi.econ.queensu.ca/
Publications/Mundell.html

The model depicted in Figure 13-2 is often called the **Mundell-Fleming model** or the *IS-LM-BP* model.[3] In this figure, the interest parity line is labelled *BP*, for balance of payments equilibrium line.

A helpful way to think about this model is that it has two concepts of equilibrium. First, the intersection of *IS* and *LM* gives internal equilibrium, and second, the interest parity line defines external equilibrium, or balance of payments equilibrium. As we will see in the analysis below, the economy ultimately must be in internal and external equilibrium simultaneously. What this means is that, in an open economy with perfect capital mobility, the domestic interest rate cannot differ from the foreign interest rate.[4]

We will now consider the effects of monetary and fiscal policy under both flexible and fixed exchange rate regimes.

## 13-2 | THE MUNDELL-FLEMING MODEL WITH FLEXIBLE EXCHANGE RATES

In this section, we examine the interaction of capital flows and the exchange rate in the situation where monetary policy does not intervene in the foreign exchange market to try to keep the exchange rate fixed. In Chapter 9, we saw that the level of net exports (that is, exports minus imports) depends on the level of the real exchange rate. The real exchange rate is defined as

$$R = \frac{eP^f}{P} \tag{8}$$

---

[3] Nobel Laureate Robert Mundell, now at Columbia University, and the late Marcus Fleming, who was a researcher for the International Monetary Fund, developed this model in the 1960s.

[4] This statement needs to be qualified somewhat. It is true only under the assumption made in equation (7). We will alter this assumption in the last section.

where $P^f$ is the foreign price level (measured in foreign dollars) and $e$ is the nominal exchange rate, measured in the Canadian dollar price of foreign currency. Therefore, the numerator of the real exchange rate is the level of foreign prices, measured in Canadian dollars. Throughout all of Part 4 of this book, we have been maintaining the assumption that the aggregate supply curve is horizontal, so that the domestic price level is fixed. We assume that the foreign price level is exogenous, so that we can write the real exchange rate in the very short run as

$$R = \frac{e\bar{P}^f}{\bar{P}} \tag{9}$$

Therefore, in the very short run, changes in the nominal exchange rate, $e$, will be the same as changes in the real exchange rate, $R$. Any change in the real or nominal exchange rate will shift the *IS* curve. For instance, consider the situation where the Canadian currency undergoes a nominal depreciation. Given the domestic price level, $P$, and the foreign price level, $P^f$, a nominal exchange rate depreciation makes the Canadian economy more competitive, or improves the terms of trade. That is, $R$ increases. The resultant increase in net exports causes the *IS* curve to shift to the right. Conversely, a nominal exchange rate appreciation is synonymous with a worsening of the terms of trade ($R$ goes down) and the resultant decrease in net exports shifts the *IS* curve to the left. These movements are summarized in Figure 13-3.

We can combine the information in Figure 13-3 concerning shifts in the *IS* curve caused by exchange rate movements with the information in Figure 13-1 concerning how interest rates and capital flows are related to exchange rate movements. Figure 13-1 tells us that, for instance, if the Canadian nominal interest rate is above the foreign nominal interest rate, there will be capital inflows and the nominal exchange rate will appreciate. This will worsen the terms of trade. Figure 13-3 tells us that this

---

**FIGURE 13-3**      **EXCHANGE RATE CHANGES AND THE *IS* CURVE**

In the short run, we assume that the domestic and foreign price levels are fixed, so that a depreciation causes an improvement in the terms of trade, which shifts the *IS* curve to the right.

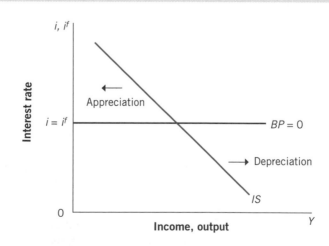

worsening in the terms of trade will cause the *IS* curve to shift to the left. Therefore, if $i > i^f$, the *IS* curve will shift leftward, and if $i < i^f$, the *IS* curve will shift to the right.

Next, we examine how various disturbances affect the variables in the model.

## A Change in the Foreign Price Level

In this section, we examine how a change in the foreign price level affects the levels of output, the interest rate, and the exchange rate in our model. In Figure 13-4, the initial equilibrium is at point *E*, where the domestic interest rate equals the foreign interest rate, and output is at $Y_0$. Now assume that the foreign price level increases. Notice that, for a given nominal exchange rate *e* and domestic price level *P*, an increase in the foreign price level improves the terms of trade. Given the above discussion, the *IS* curve shifts to the right. This is shown as a movement to *IS'* at an equilibrium of *E'* in Figure 13-4. However, at *E'*, the domestic interest rate is greater than the foreign, which causes capital inflows. These capital inflows cause the nominal exchange rate to appreciate and the terms of trade to worsen. This leads to a decline in net exports, and the *IS* curve shifts from *IS'* to the left, back toward the initial *IS* curve.

---

**FIGURE 13-4**     **EFFECTS OF AN INCREASE IN THE FOREIGN PRICE LEVEL**

Aan increase in foreign demand shifts the *IS* curve outward. However, at *E'*, because the Canadian interest rate is above the foreign interest rate, the exchange rate will appreciate and the economy will be driven back to *E*.

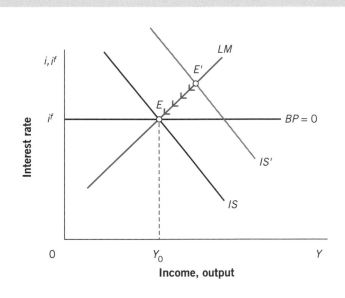

---

The nominal exchange rate will continue to appreciate as long as the Canadian interest rate is above the foreign interest rate. Further, as long as the nominal exchange rate is appreciating, the *IS* curve will continue shifting leftward. This process will end when the *IS* curve has shifted back to its original position. In Figure 13-4, this adjustment is shown by the arrows along the *LM* curve. Once the economy has returned to point *E*, it is in a position of internal and external balance.

## Fiscal Policy

We demonstrated above that an increase in the foreign price level leaves the level of output and the interest rate unchanged. With perfect capital mobility, whenever a shock leads to a change in the interest rate, the nominal and real exchange rates will respond, causing net exports to change, and the *IS* curve will shift until internal and external equilibria are reached. This general analysis can be used to examine how the economy responds to a change in fiscal policy in the very short run. Expansionary fiscal policy will shift out the *IS* curve in a manner similar to that shown in Figure 13-4. Once again, the result would be that the domestic interest rate would be higher than the foreign rate, and the adjustment back to the original equilibrium would be identical to that shown in Figure 13-4. Therefore, expansionary fiscal policy with a flexible exchange rate and perfect capital mobility cannot change the level of income in the very short run. Notice that this is a form of crowding out. This crowding out is somewhat different from the crowding out that we discussed in Chapter 12, where higher interest rates reduced investment spending (see Figure 12-4). In this chapter, the higher interest rates caused by the expansionary fiscal policy lead to an exchange rate appreciation and a decrease in net exports.

An important lesson from this fiscal policy result is that, although the level of income remains unchanged after the adjustment, the composition of income is different. To see this, assume that the expansionary fiscal policy was the result of an increase in $\bar{G}$. In the final equilibrium, the level of income is unchanged. However, the level of $\bar{G}$ is higher and this is exactly offset by a decrease in net exports.

## Monetary Policy

We describe the response of the economy to an increase in the money stock in Figure 13-5. The initial equilibrium is at point *E*, where the domestic interest rate

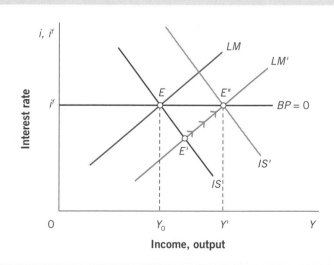

**FIGURE 13-5**

**EFFECTS OF AN INCREASE IN THE MONEY STOCK**

An increase in the money stock decreases the domestic interest rate. Because the domestic interest rate is below the foreign, the exchange rate will depreciate and net exports will increase, shifting the *IS* curve outward.

equals the foreign rate, and income is at $Y_0$. We know from Chapters 11 and 12 that expansionary monetary policy in the form of an increase in the nominal money stock (which, given a fixed price level, is an increase in the real money stock) shifts the *LM* curve to the right.

In Figure 13-5, this is shown as a movement to the new *LM* curve, *LM'*, and an equilibrium at point *E'*. At *E'* we have internal equilibrium (the *IS* and *LM* curves intersect), but the Canadian interest rate is below the foreign rate, so the economy is not in external equilibrium. In this situation, there are capital outflows and the nominal exchange rate depreciates. This leads to an improvement in the terms of trade, which increases net exports, and the *IS* curve shifts outward. The nominal exchange rate will continue to depreciate as long as the Canadian interest rate is below the foreign interest rate. Further, as long as the nominal exchange rate is depreciating, the *IS* curve will continue shifting outward. This process will end when the *IS* curve has shifted to *IS'*, at point *E''*. At point *E''*, the Canadian interest rate equals the foreign interest rate, and the economy is in internal and external equilibria. This is an interesting result, as it appears to show that a monetary expansion improves the current account and domestic income through a policy-induced depreciation. This result is discussed in the next section.

## Beggar-Thy-Neighbour Policy and Competitive Depreciation

We have shown that a monetary expansion in Canada leads to exchange depreciation, an increase in net exports, and therefore an increase in output and employment. But our increased net exports correspond to a deterioration in the trade balance abroad. The domestic depreciation shifts demand from foreign goods toward domestic goods. Abroad, output and employment decline. It is for this reason that a depreciation-induced change in the trade balance has been called a **beggar-thy-neighbour policy**—it is a way of exporting unemployment or of creating domestic employment at the expense of the rest of the world.

It is important to understand that this beggar-thy-neighbor policy is essentially a manner in which to shift demand from one country to another, rather than to change the level of world demand. It implies that exchange rate adjustment can be a useful policy when countries find themselves in different stages of the business cycle—for example, one in a boom (with overemployment) and the other in a recession. In that event, a depreciation by the country experiencing a recession would shift world demand in its direction and thus work to reduce divergence from full employment in each country.

By contrast, when countries' business cycles are highly synchronized, such as in the 1930s or in the aftermath of the oil shock of 1973, exchange rate movements will not contribute much toward worldwide full employment. If total world demand is at the wrong level, exchange rate movements do not correct the level of aggregate demand but essentially affect only the allocation of a *given* world demand among countries.

Similarly, exchange rate changes within a group of countries experiencing similar shocks can only move demand among them and have a beggar-thy-neighbour quality.

Nevertheless, from the point of view of an individual country, exchange depreciation works to attract world demand and raise domestic output. If every country tried to depreciate to attract world demand, we would have **competitive depreciation** and a shifting around of world demand rather than an increase in the worldwide level of spending. And if everyone depreciated to roughly the same extent, we would end up

**beggar-thy-neighbour policy**
A depreciation-induced change in the trade balance that exports unemployment or creates domestic employment at the expense of the rest of the world.

www.bankofcanada.ca/en/ res/wp99-12.htm

**competitive depreciation**
Occurs when every country tries to depreciate to attract world demand.

with exchange rates about where they started. Coordinated monetary and/or fiscal policies rather than depreciations are needed to increase demand and output in each country when worldwide aggregate demand is at the wrong level.

## 13-3 | PERFECT CAPITAL MOBILITY AND FIXED EXCHANGE RATES

In this short run model, if there are capital flows, the exchange rate will change. Capital flows will occur when interest parity does not hold; that is, when the domestic nominal interest rate does not equal the foreign nominal interest rate. Accordingly, capital flows and exchange rate change could be prevented if the monetary authorities ensured that the domestic nominal interest rate always equalled the foreign nominal interest rate. Given this reasoning, in this model, in order to run a fixed exchange rate regime, the monetary authorities must run an interest rate rule. Further, there is no independent choice of the domestic interest rate: It must be held constant at the level of the foreign nominal interest rate. Notice further that if the monetary authorities choose to run a fixed exchange rate by running an interest rate rule, then they can no longer aim domestic policy at changing domestic income, as they did with a flexible exchange rate. The monetary authorities must make a choice: Either choose to aim policy at domestic stabilization (e.g., changing domestic income) and allow the exchange rate to be flexible, or use monetary policy to hold the exchange rate fixed and give up domestic stabilization.

Given the above, if the monetary authorities are running a fixed exchange rate policy, the *LM* curve is horizontal and it is the same curve as the *BP* curve, as shown in Figure 13-6.

Notice that under this policy, the *LM* curve cannot be shifted. If the central bank attempted to change the interest rate in order to try to affect domestic output (domestic stabilization policy), then there would be capital flows and the exchange

**FIGURE 13-6**    THE *BP* CURVE AND THE *LM* CURVE UNDER FIXED EXCHANGE RATES

Under fixed exchange rates, the *BP* curve and the *LM* curve are identical. In order to hold the exchange rate fixed in the very short run, the Bank of Canada must run monetary policy as an interest rate rule, at the level of the foreign interest rate.

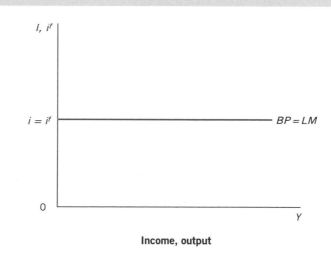

Income, output

rate would change. Since the policy is one of fixing the exchange rate, this would be the wrong thing to do. Therefore, monetary policy can do one of two things: Either pursue domestic stabilization policy and allow the exchange rate to be flexible, or fix the exchange rate and give up domestic stabilization policy.

## Fiscal Policy with a Fixed Exchange Rate

While monetary policy is essentially infeasible, fiscal expansion under fixed exchange rates with perfect capital mobility is, by contrast, extremely effective. We describe the effects in terms of the *IS-LM* model, but we do not draw the diagram, leaving that for Application Question 4 at the end of the chapter.

With the money supply initially unchanged, a fiscal expansion moves the *IS* curve up and to the right, tending to increase both the interest rate and the level of output. The higher interest rate sets off a capital inflow that would lead the exchange rate to appreciate. To maintain the exchange rate, the central bank *has* to expand the money supply, thus increasing income further. Equilibrium is restored when the money supply has increased enough to drive the interest rate back to its original level, $i = i^f$. In this case, with an endogenous money supply, the interest rate is effectively fixed, and the simple Keynesian multiplier of Chapter 10 applies for a fiscal expansion.

## The Endogenous Money Stock

Although the assumption of perfect capital mobility is extreme, it is a useful benchmark case that in the end is not too far from reality for many countries. The essential point is that *the commitment to maintain a fixed exchange rate makes the money stock endogenous* because the central bank has to provide the foreign exchange or domestic money that is demanded at the fixed exchange rate. Thus, even when capital mobility is less than perfect, the central bank has only limited ability to change the money supply without having to worry about maintaining the exchange rate.

Box 13-1 describes the effects of the fiscal expansion set off by German unification, and the consequences for Germany's neighbours, whose exchange rates were fixed against the Deutschmark.

---

**BOX**

**13-1**

### German Unification and External Problems

In fall 1989, the Berlin Wall came down and soon the unification of West and East Germany was under way. The West German government began transferring large amounts of resources to East Germany. The fiscal program included massive investment in East Germany's infrastructure, investment in industry, and an extensive income support program for the unemployed and for those working in loss-making firms.

The large fiscal expansion helped moderate the economic collapse in East Germany, but it came at the expense of a massive budget deficit. The expansionary fiscal policy brought with it a deterioration of the current account, higher interest rates, and an appreciation of the Deutschmark, as the Mundell-Fleming model predicts.

While Germany had been a net lender in world markets, starting in 1991, there was a deficit in the current account. German resources were being redirected from supplying the world market to reconstructing East Germany.

*continued*

### German Unification and External Problems continued

The German fiscal expansion had undesirable side effects on Germany's European trading partners, with whom Germany has a fixed exchange rate. In West Germany the economy overheated since demand from the East fell mostly on West German goods. In response to the overheating, the Bundesbank tightened monetary policy, raising interest rates sharply.

Countries like France and Italy in principle faced the choice of devaluing within the European monetary system or allowing their interest rates to increase along with German interest rates. Because they valued stable exchange rates, they defended their currencies by raising interest rates to match those in Germany. Without the benefit of a fiscal expansion, as had occurred in Germany, their economies slowed down sharply. Germany's trading partners kept urging the Bundesbank to cut interest rates, but the Bundesbank argued that it had to keep on fighting inflation. This episode makes the point that fixed exchange rates are hard to maintain when countries' policies go in opposite directions or when they face disturbances that are not the same for everyone.

**GERMAN UNIFICATION** (percent of GNP)

|                  | 1989 | 1990 | 1991 | 1992 |
|------------------|------|------|------|------|
| Current account  | 4.8  | 3.3  | −1.1 | −1.1 |
| Budget deficit   | −0.1 | 2.1  | 3.3  | 2.8  |
| Interest rate    | 7.1  | 8.5  | 9.2  | 9.5  |

SOURCE: OECD, *Economic Outlook*, December 1995.

## 13-4 | INTEREST DIFFERENTIALS AND EXCHANGE RATE EXPECTATIONS

In Section 13-1, we introduced the concept of interest parity through the equation

**interest differential**
The level of domestic interest rate minus the level of the foreign interest rate.

**exchange rate expectations**
When individuals feel that the current exchange is about to appreciate or depreciate.

$$(1 + i_t) = (1 + i_t^f)(\frac{e_{t+1}^e}{e_t}) \tag{10}$$

We made the convenient assumption that $e_{t+1}^e = e$, so that, with perfect capital mobility, interest parity would hold where the domestic interest rate equals the foreign interest rate; that is, interest parity would hold when the interest differential is zero. The **interest differential** is defined as the level of domestic interest rate minus the level of the foreign interest rate. Figure 13-7 graphs the 90-day Treasury bill rates for Canada and the United States. The two rates follow a similar pattern over time, but are by no means equal. We can reconcile this by adding **exchange rate expectations** to our discussion.

## POLICY IN *ACTION*

### The Policy Option of the Late 1970s

In the 1970s, both the Bank of Canada and the U.S. Federal Reserve Board were following a policy of controlling the money supply to reduce the long run rate of inflation. This policy was implemented by manipulating interest rates to control the money stock. Until approximately 1979, the interest differential between Canada and the United States ($i - i^f$), as a result of this policy in each country, was such that there was no substantive fear of exchange rate depreciation.

In 1979, the Federal Reserve Board decided to tighten monetary policy drastically, raising U.S. nominal interest rates to approximately 20 percent. This was an exogenous shock to the Canadian economy and, as a result of this shock, the *BP* curve shifted upward. At this point, the Bank of Canada faced a policy choice: react to the shock with a fixed exchange rate policy or with a flexible exchange rate policy.

From the perspective of the model in this chapter, if the Bank of Canada chose to follow a flexible exchange rate policy, then, with the Canadian interest rate lower than the U.S. interest rate, there would be capital outflows and an exchange rate depreciation. This would lead to an increase in net exports and domestic output. Alternatively, if the Bank of Canada chose to follow a fixed exchange rate policy, the domestic interest rate would have to be increased along with the U.S. interest rate, in order to prevent the exchange rate from depreciating. The model in this chapter predicts that this would lead to a decrease in output.

In Application Question 7 you are asked to show these effects using the model and to comment on the actual Bank of Canada response.

### Exchange Rate Expectations

We can think of the last term in equation (10) as being a measure of how much agents expect the exchange rate to depreciate in the future. Given this, it is possible to rewrite equation (10) as

$$i = i^f + x \tag{11}$$

where $x$ is defined as the expected percentage change in the exchange rate. If $x > 0$, agents expect a depreciation, and if $x < 0$, agents expect an appreciation. To see how $x$ plays a role in the interest parity equation, consider the example in Table 13-1.

The first line of Table 13-1 shows a typical situation that we had assumed in the earlier sections. The domestic interest rate equals the foreign interest rate and $x = 0$, so there are not capital flows. On the second line, we have shown the situation where the domestic interest rate is greater than the foreign interest rate. However, because

## FIGURE 13-7

The two interest rates move together, but they are not equal. The difference may be explained by exchange rate expectations.

**CANADIAN AND U.S. 90-DAY TREASURY BILL RATES, 1970–2002**

— Canadian Treasury bill rate
— U.S. Treasury bill rate

SOURCE: Canadian Treasury bill rate: CANSIM II V122484; U.S. Treasury bill rate: CANSIM II V122151.

$x = 0$, there would be capital inflow. This is, again, a situation that we considered above. On line 3, we demonstrate the situation where the domestic interest rate is greater than the foreign interest rate, but there will be no capital flows. The reason for this is that $x = 5$, so equation (11) is satisfied. Investors are willing to hold foreign bonds even though they bear less return than Canadian bonds, because if you hold Canadian bonds, you expect to lose 5 percent on depreciation of the Canadian dollar.

Expected depreciation helps account for differences in interest rates among low- and high-inflation countries. When the inflation rate in a country is high, its exchange rate is expected to depreciate. In addition, the Fisher relationship suggests that the nominal interest rate in that country will be high when inflation is high.[5] Thus, high-inflation countries tend to have high interest rates and depreciating currencies. This is an international extension of the Fisher equation, which relies on PPP to argue that inflation differentials internationally are matched by depreciation. Our long-term relationship, then, is

$$\text{Inflation differential} \cong \text{Interest differential} \cong \text{Depreciation rate} \qquad (12)$$

## TABLE 13-1

**INTEREST PARITY AND EXCHANGE RATE EXPECTATIONS**

| $i$ | $i^f$ | $e^e_{t+1}$ | $e$ | $x$ |
| --- | --- | --- | --- | --- |
| 10 | 10 | 100 | 100 | 0 |
| 10 | 5 | 100 | 100 | 0 |
| 10 | 5 | 105 | 100 | 5 |

---

[5] Recall from Chapter 3 that the Fisher relationship states that the nominal interest rate equals the expected real interest rate plus expected inflation, $i = r + \pi^e$.

The ≅ means "approximately equal to." The relation is only approximate because exchange rates can move independently of prices and also because obstacles to capital flows may create long-term interest differentials.

## Speculative Capital Flows

Changes in exchange rate expectations can affect the actual exchange rate as well as the domestic interest rate and output. The point is made with the help of Figure 13-8, which assumes perfect capital mobility, as specified in equation (11). Here the *BP* schedule is drawn for a given foreign interest rate and a given expected rate of change of the exchange rate, say, zero.

Suppose that we start in full equilibrium at point *E* and that the market develops the expectation that the home currency will appreciate. This implies that even with a lower home interest rate, domestic assets are attractive, and so the *BP* schedule shifts downward by the amount of expected appreciation.

Point *E* is no longer an equilibrium, given the shift of the *BP* schedule to *BP′*, but rather a position of surplus with large-scale capital inflows motivated by the anticipation of appreciation. The surplus at *E* causes the exchange rate to start appreciating, and we move in a southwesterly direction, as indicated by the arrows. The speculative attack causes appreciation, a loss in competitiveness, and, consequently, falling output and employment. Thus, the expectation of an exchange rate appreciation leads to a *self-fulfilling expectation*.

This analysis confirms that exchange rate expectations, through their impact on capital flows and thus on actual exchange rates, are a potential source of disturbance to macroeconomic equilibrium—something that policy makers who try to fix exchange rates when capital is fully mobile keep having to learn.

## FIGURE 13-8

### RESPONSE TO AN EXPECTED APPRECIATION OF THE CANADIAN DOLLAR

Expectations of a currency appreciation shift the *BP* curve downward. In anticipation of the appreciation, there is a speculative attack on the currency, which reduces competitiveness and causes output to fall.

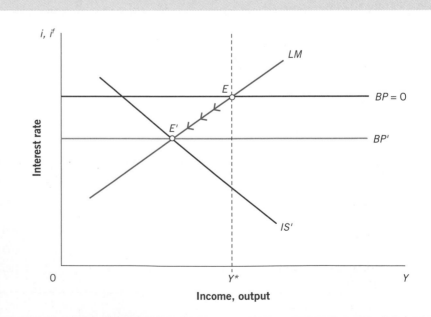

## *Working with Data*

In the final section of this chapter, we suggested that one reason why the interest differential between two countries is not zero might be exchange rate expectations. We can test this by looking at the relationship between the rate of change in the exchange rate and the interest differential between Canada and the United States. In order to do this, you will need the two CANSIM sources used for Figure 13-7, plus the Canada–U.S. exchange rate, which is CANSIM II V37426. You should try to make a scatter diagram (similar to the Phillips curve diagrams in Chapter 7) between the interest differential and the rate of change of the exchange rate.

## C H A P T E R    S U M M A R Y

▶ In the very short run, capital flows respond to the interest parity condition given by

$$(1 + i_t) = (1 + i^f_t)(\frac{e^e_{t+1}}{e_t}) \qquad (10)$$

The left-hand side of this equation is the rate of return from investing $1.00 Canadian in the Canadian economy, and the left-hand side is the (expected) rate of return from investing $1.00 Canadian in the U.S. economy. Both returns are measured in Canadian dollars. If we make the simplifying assumption that

$$e^e_{t+1} = e_t$$

then the interest parity condition becomes

$$i_t = i^f_t$$

In this situation, if $i > i^f$, there will be capital inflows and an exchange rate appreciation; if $i < i^f$, there will be capital outflows and an exchange rate depreciation.

▶ In the very short run, a nominal appreciation worsens the terms of trade and net exports decrease; conversely a nominal depreciation improves the terms of trade and net exports increase.

▶ With perfect capital mobility and a flexible exchange rate, fiscal policy cannot change the level of income. This is because a change in fiscal policy will change the level of the interest rate, which will cause capital flows. Capital flows will change the terms of trade and counteract the effects of fiscal policy. Fiscal policy in this framework will change the composition of income.

▶ With perfect capital mobility and a flexible exchange rate, monetary policy can change the level of income. This change works through the usual channel of a change in the interest rate, causing a change in the level of income, as well as the

www.mcgrawhill.ca/college/dornbusch

open economy channel of a change in the interest rate leading to a change in the terms of trade and a resultant change in net exports.

▶ With perfect capital mobility and a fixed exchange rate, the balance of payments curve (*BP*) and *LM* curve are identical. In this situation, monetary policy must be conducted in a manner that keeps the Canadian interest rate equal to the foreign interest rate. Therefore, with perfect capital mobility and a fixed exchange rate, monetary policy cannot be aimed at domestic stabilization.

▶ With perfect capital mobility and a fixed exchange rate, fiscal policy can change the level of income. This is due to the fact that, as fiscal policy tends to change the interest rate, monetary policy must react to keep the interest rate constant. Therefore, fiscal policy will have the full multiplier effect on the economy.

▶ Expectations of exchange rate change allow the domestic nominal interest rate to be different from the foreign nominal interest rate.

## K E Y   T E R M S

perfect capital mobility, *253*         beggar-thy-neighbour policy, *260*        interest differential, *263*
Mundell-Fleming model, *256*          competitive depreciation, *260*          exchange rate expectations, *263*

## D I S C U S S I O N   Q U E S T I O N S

1. Discuss why you might want to hold a U.S. Treasury bill if the return was 5 percent, when you could make 10 percent by holding a Canadian Treasury bill.

2. Use the Mundell-Fleming model to discuss the adjustment of the economy if there was an exogenous increase in the level of the foreign interest rate if:

   **a.** Monetary policy was operating under a flexible exchange rate.

   **b.** Monetary policy was operating under a fixed exchange rate.

3. Explain how and why monetary policy retains its effectiveness when there is perfect mobility of capital.

4. For each of the following questions, assume that $e_{t+1}^e = e_t$.

   **a.** When exchange rates are fixed, will fiscal or monetary policy be more successful? Explain.

   **b.** When exchange rates are flexible, will fiscal or monetary policy be more successful? Explain.

5. Your country is in recession. You feel that a policy of exchange rate depreciation will stimulate aggregate demand and bring the country out of the recession.

   **a.** What can be done to trigger this depreciation?

   **b.** How might other countries react?

   **c.** When would this be a beggar-thy-neighbour policy?

www.mcgrawhill.ca/college/dornbusch

# APPLICATION QUESTIONS

1. Assume that capital is perfectly mobile, the price level is fixed, and the exchange rate is flexible. Now let the government increase purchases. Explain first why the equilibrium levels of output and the interest rate are unaffected. Then show whether the current account improves or worsens as a result of the increased government purchases of goods and services.

2. In 1990–1992 Finland experienced serious difficulties. The collapse of exports to the Soviet Union and a dramatic fall in the prices of pulp and paper—important export items—led to both a recession and a current account deficit. What adjustment policies would you recommend for such a case?

3. Suppose you expect the pound to depreciate by 6 percent over the next year. Assume that the Canadian interest rate is 4 percent. What interest rate would be needed on pound securities, such as government bonds, for you to be willing to buy those securities with your dollars today and then sell them in a year in exchange for dollars?

4. What is the effect of a fiscal expansion on output and interest rates when exchange rates are fixed and capital is perfectly mobile? Show this rigorously, using the model developed in Section 13-3.

5. The beggar-thy-neighbour result derived in this chapter is often called a *competitive depreciation*. In early 2003, the Canadian dollar appreciated sharply against the U.S. dollar. Use the Mundell-Fleming model to discuss the possible ramifications of this change.

6.  Go to CANSIM and retrieve the Canada and United States 90-day Treasury bill rates, and the Canada–U.S. exchange rate. Calculate the interest differential between the two countries and then plot this against the rate of change in the exchange rate. Comment on this relative to Section 13-4 and the graph you produced in Working with Data.

7. In the Policy in Action feature in this chapter, we discussed the policy options that the Bank of Canada faced in the late 1970s in response to a large sudden increase in the U.S. nominal interest rate.

   a. Use the Mundell-Fleming model developed in this chapter to show the predicted response of the Canadian economy under both a fixed and a flexible exchange rate regime.

   b.  Go to CANSIM II and retrieve the Canadian and U.S. nominal interest rates as well as Canadian GDP. Use these data to discuss the actual response of the Canadian economy to this shock. Do you think that the data are consistent with any of the predictions of the model?

www.mcgrawhill.ca/college/dornbusch

# PART

# 5

# BEHAVIOURAL FOUNDATIONS

## CHAPTER 14

# CONSUMPTION AND SAVING

## *LEARNING OBJECTIVES*

After reading and studying this chapter, you should be able to:

▶ *Understand that consumption is a large but relatively stable fraction of GDP.*

▶ *Understand the relationship between changes in the real interest rate and changes in consumption and savings.*

▶ *Understand that modern theories of consumption behaviour link lifetime consumption to lifetime income. These theories suggest that the marginal propensity to consume out of transitory income should be small.*

▶ *Understand that empirical evidence suggests that both modern theories and simple Keynesian "psychological rule-of-thumb" models contribute to explaining consumption.*

onsumption accounts for just under 60 percent of aggregate demand, more than all other sectors combined. Fluctuations in consumption are proportionately smaller than fluctuations in GDP. These two facts—that consumption makes up a large fraction of GDP and that it is relatively stable—give the focus for this chapter.

We seek to understand what drives consumption, and we particularly wish to understand the dynamic link between consumption and income. In Chapter 11, we modelled consumption as a simple function of current income. Here we study several more advanced theories of consumption. The central finding is that lifetime consumption is linked to lifetime income, but the link between *this* year's consumption and *this* year's income is fairly weak.

The debate about different consumption theories can be viewed as a debate over whether the marginal propensity to consume (*MPC*) is large or small. Early Keynesian "psychological rule-of-thumb" models suggested a high *MPC*, while modern theories based on rational consumer decisions sometimes indicate a very low *MPC*. In introductory macromodels, the marginal propensity to consume, *c*, directly determines "the multiplier," $1/(1 - c)$. Even in more sophisticated models, a high *MPC* causes a large multiplier. The modern theories discussed below assign different values to the marginal propensity to consume out of income changes expected to persist for different lengths of time. The *MPC* out of income expected to be permanent is high, just as in earlier models, but the *MPC* out of transitory income is close to zero.

## 14-1 | THE KEYNESIAN CONSUMPTION FUNCTION

In Chapter 10, we introduced the Keynesian consumption function. The equation for this consumption function is

$$C = \overline{C} + cYD, \ 0 < c \leq 1 \tag{1}$$

The idea behind the Keynesian consumption function is that consumers will increase their consumption spending as disposable income increases. This consumption function arose out of the early work of John Maynard Keynes. In his *General Theory*, Keynes postulated that consumption spending is based on the "fundamental psychological law" that as income increases, this will increase consumption.[1]

In Figure 14-1, we have used data on consumption and disposable income to see what a Keynesian consumption function actually looks like.[2] In this figure, total consumption per capita, in thousands of 1997 dollars, is measured on the vertical axis and disposable income per capita, again in thousands of 1997 dollars, is measured on the horizontal axis. Total consumption is composed of consumption of durables, nondurables, and services. As we will see in later sections, modern consumption theories often argue that consumption of durables should be omitted, as you consume a durable over more than one period of time, and thus durables are more like investment than consumption. The data is measured annually from 1961–2002. The estimated values for the parameters in equation (1), given the data in Figure 14-1, are $\overline{C} = 0.29$ and $c = 0.87$.

[1] Keynes actually wrote in *General Theory* "… the fundamental psychological law, upon which we are entitled to depend with great confidence, … is that men are disposed, as a rule, and on the average, to increase their consumption as their income increases, but not by as much as their income increases."

[2] This is the same data and consumption function that was first introduced in Box 10-1.

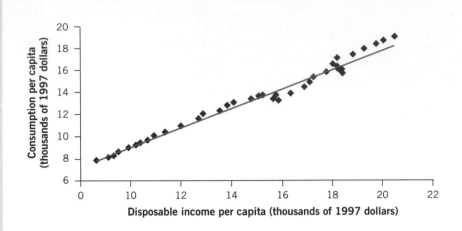

**FIGURE 14-1**

*FIGURE 14-1*    **AN ESTIMATED EARLY KEYNESIAN CONSUMPTION FUNCTION, 1961–2002**

The early Keynesian consumption function attempted to explain the relationship between total consumption and disposable income. This figure uses annual data in per capita terms over the period 1961–2002. The estimated equation is $C = 0.29 + 0.87\,YD$, which indicates that consumption rises on average by 87 cents for each additional dollar of disposable income.

SOURCE: Consumption in 1997 dollars: CANSIM II V1992229; disposable income in current dollars: CANSIM II V501125, 1961–1990, and V691803, 1991–2002; deflated by the GDP deflator: CANSIM II V3839799; population: CANSIM II V1.

The fact that the marginal propensity to consume (*MPC*) is quite large is confirmation of the appropriateness of the Keynesian consumption function over the very short run. Remember the manner in which we used the Keynesian consumption function in Chapter 10. A large *MPC* will lead to a large multiplier and, in the very short run, policy may be concerned with the size of the multiplier.

However, there are at least two features of the Keynesian consumption function that make it unsuitable for any time frame other than the short run. First, notice that there is no interest rate in the equation and, therefore, there is no channel for interest rate changes to influence consumption spending. You will recall from Chapter 3 that the real rate of interest was a prime determinant of consumption and savings in our Classical model. The Keynesian consumption function stresses the role of income and the feedback between income and consumption spending through the multiplier, as we discussed in Chapter 10, but ignores the effects of changes in the interest rate on consumption and savings.

Second, notice that current consumption depends only on current income in the Keynesian consumption function. That is, the idea behind this consumption function is somewhat static, in that consumers do not look at their lifetime earnings. More recent theories of the consumption function are based on rational consumer decisions, rather than a psychological rule of thumb and sometimes indicate a much lower *MPC* than that of the Keynesian consumption function. These modern theories, which are discussed in Sections 14-3 and 14-4, assign different values for the *MPC* out of income changes expected to persist for different lengths of time. The *MPC* out of income expected to be permanent is high and the *MPC* out of transitory income is expected to be low.

## Temporary Tax Changes and Consumption

Modern consumption theories stress that the *MPC* out of permanent changes in income should be high and the *MPC* out of temporary changes in income should be low. Therefore, if a tax change was announced to be temporary, it should have little effect on consumption. There have been several episodes of temporary tax changes in both the Canadian and U.S. economies. We discuss a major temporary initiative undertaken in Canada in this chapter's Policy in Action feature. In this box, we describe an early attempt to cool off the U.S. economy using a temporary tax increase.

In 1968, Lyndon Johnson was president of the United States, and spending associated with the Vietnam War was believed to be temporarily overheating the U.S. economy. In response to this, Johnson and the U.S. Congress passed a temporary tax increase. The U.S. economy reacted as modern consumption theory predicted—the temporary tax increase had almost no effect in the economy.

## 14-2 | CONSUMPTION, SAVINGS, AND THE REAL INTEREST RATE: INTERTEMPORAL CHOICE

**intertemporal choice**
Choice that involves decisions over more than one period of time.

In this section, we will move beyond the Keynesian consumption function and begin to think of consumption in the framework of rational utility maximizing individuals. This section provides the microeconomic foundations for the theories of the consumption function presented later in the chapter. **Intertemporal choice** in the title of this section simply means that we are going to consider the consumer's choice of consumption and savings in more than one period. The model developed in this section can be viewed as a more complete description of the Classical view of the consumption-savings choice that we first introduced in Chapter 3.

For now, we make the convenient assumption that life consists of two periods of time. We will relax this assumption in Section 14-4. Consumers are assumed to get utility from current consumption, which we denote as $u(C_t)$, and from the next period's consumption, which we denote as $u(C_{t+1})$.[3] We assume that consumers try to maximize utility, subject to some budget constraint.

### Maximizing Utility: Indifference Curves

**indifference curve**
A graphical representation of consumer preferences, showing combinations of current and future consumption for which total utility is constant.

We represent the utility maximization process through indifference curves. We define an **indifference curve** as a downward sloping line along which you trade current consumption for future consumption in such a manner that your total utility over both periods does not change. In Figure 14-2, we have drawn two indifference curves, labelled $IC_1$ and $IC_2$. Total utility (satisfaction) is considered to be constant (i.e., the consumer is indifferent) along each indifference curve, and total utility is higher along the higher indifference curve, $IC_2$.

---

[3] Utility is simply economists' mathematical way to describe consumer satisfaction. Students who have taken a good microeconomics course will recognize most of the concepts in this section.

*FIGURE 14-2*

**INDIFFERENCE CURVES**

An indifference curve is a downward-sloping line that shows how a consumer is willing to trade current consumption for future consumption. Total utility (satisfaction) is considered to be constant along each indifference curve, and total utility is higher along the higher indifference curve, $IC_2$.

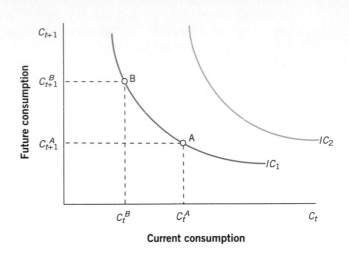

Consider two points on the indifference curve $IC_1$. At point A, the consumer is consuming $C_t^A$ in period $t$ and $C_{t+1}^A$ in period $t + 1$, while at point B, the consumer is consuming $C_t^B$ in period $t$ and $C_{t+1}^B$ in period $t + 1$. Because they are both on the same indifference curve, the consumer is indifferent between the bundle of consumption at point A and the bundle of consumption at point B.[4] This means that the consumer is *willing* to trade from A to B, without any decrease in utility.

Now consider the hypothetical situation where the consumer moves from point A to point B. Because total utility is constant in moving from A to B, a consumer is *willing* to give up the amount of current consumption equal to $C_t^A - C_t^B$, as long as the consumer is given an extra amount of tomorrow's consumption equal to $C_{t+1}^B - C_{t+1}^A$. If you draw a line between these two points (called a *chord*), then the slope of this line measures the rate at which a consumer is willing to give up current consumption for future consumption.[5]

This trade-off implied in giving up some amount today in order to receive some extra amount in the future is called the *rate of substitution*. Now suppose that point A and B are infinitely close together, so that the slope of the chord becomes the slope of the tangent at one point. In this situation, the slope of the tangent to any point on an indifference curve is equal to the **marginal rate of substitution**. The marginal rate of substitution tells us the rate at which the consumer is willing to give up an amount

**marginal rate of substitution**

The rate at which a consumer is willing to give up an amount of consumption today in order to receive increased consumption in the next period, holding total utility constant.

---

[4] Consumption in each period consists of a variety of different goods, which we call *consumption bundles*.

[5] Remember that slope is defined as rise over run. Therefore, the slope of the chord is $(C_{t+1}^B - C_{t+1}^A)/(C_t^B - C_t^A)$, which is exactly the rate at which the consumer is willing to trade. Notice that the numerator of this expression is positive, while the denominator is negative. Therefore, the indifference curve slopes downward, so that the slope of the chord and the marginal rate of substitution are both negative numbers.

of consumption today in order to receive increased consumption in the next period, holding total utility constant.

The marginal rate of substitution takes on an important meaning in this model. Consumption today differs from consumption next period because of the time difference. That is, the marginal rate of substitution tells us how the consumer is willing to trade consumption through time. Remember from Chapter 3 that when that substitution involves time, we call the marginal rate of substitution the *rate of time preference*.

## The Budget Constraint

The indifference curve analysis discussed above tells us various combinations of consumption today and next period that the consumer is willing to choose, holding total utility constant along any particular indifference curve. However, we must also take into account the consumption bundles that the consumer can afford to choose, given that person's income. Therefore, we must now consider the consumer's budget constraint.

**budget constraint**

The rate at which a consumer is willing to give up an amount of consumption today in order to receive increased consumption in the next period, holding total utility constant.

The **budget constraint** is a line that shows the combinations of consumption today and consumption next period that the consumer can choose, given real income and the real interest rate. A typical budget constraint is illustrated in Figure 14-3.

The budget constraint shown in Figure 14-3 can be derived in the following manner. Assume that the consumer has a known income of $Y_t$ and $Y_{t+1}$ in each period. In period $t$, the consumer could choose one of three possibilities: consume less than total period $t$ income, in which case, savings is positive; choose to consume an amount equal to period $t$ income, in which case, savings is 0; or choose to borrow from period $t+1$ income, in which case, consumption is greater than period $t$ income, making savings is negative, which is an alternative expression for borrowing.

---

### *FIGURE 14-3*

**THE BUDGET CONSTRAINT**

The budget constraint is a line that shows the combinations of consumption today and consumption next period that the consumer can choose, given real income and the real interest rate.

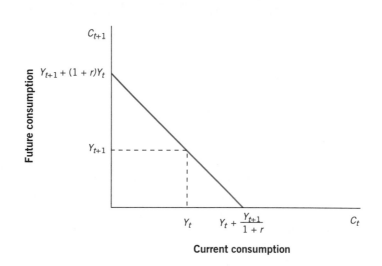

Suppose that the consumer wanted to consume everything possible in period $t$. This would entail borrowing all of period $t + 1$ income, so that the total possible consumption in period $t$ would be equal to period $t$ income, $Y_t$ plus period $t + 1$ income discounted by the cost of borrowing, given by the real rate of interest, $r$. Therefore, total possible consumption in period $t$ is equal to $Y_t + Y_{t+1}(1 + r)$. This is the point at which the budget constraint intersects the horizontal axis in Figure 14-3.

Now consider what the total consumption possibilities are in period $t + 1$. Suppose that the consumer saved all income from period $t$, so that in period $t + 1$, the consumer could consume period $t + 1$ income as well period $t$ income augmented by the interest rate. This amount is equal to $Y_t + Y_{t+1}(1 + r)$, which is the point where the budget constraint intersects the vertical axis.

The straight line joining these two intercepts is the budget constraint. Remember that the budget constraint shows the combinations of consumption today and consumption next period that the consumer can choose, given income and the interest rate. Figure 14-4 illustrates the effects on the budget constraint of changing income or the interest rate. In Figure 14-4(a), we have illustrated the effects on the budget constraint of an increase in income, holding the interest rate constant. Notice that an increase in income in either period $t$ or period $t + 1$ (or both) will shift the budget constraint outward.

In Figure 14-4(b), we have illustrated the effects of an increase in the real rate of interest on the budget constraint, holding income constant in each period. This change in the real interest rate increases borrowing costs in period $t$, thus reducing the horizontal intercept, and also increases the return to savings, which increases the vertical intercept. Therefore, the increase in the real rate of interest rotates the budget constraint. This example illustrates that the slope of the budget constraint depends on the real rate of interest. Higher real rates of interest are consistent with a steeper budget constraint and lower real rates of interest are consistent with a flatter budget constraint.

## Equilibrium: Utility Maximization Subject to the Budget Constraint

We began this section by stating that the consumer maximizes utility subject to a budget constraint. This maximization process is illustrated in Figure 14-5.

In this problem, the optimum is defined as the point where the consumer reaches the highest indifference curve possible, given the budget constraint. In Figure 14-5, the optimum is at point $E$, and the consumer chooses consumption bundles of $C_t^*$ and $C_{t+1}^*$. Given these consumption choices, and given period $t$ income of $Y_t$, the consumer has also chosen savings equal to $Y_t - C_t^*$.

At the optimum point, the budget constraint is tangent to the highest indifference curve. This illustrates a very important point about the equilibrium. The slope of the indifference curve at the optimum point is given by the marginal rate of substitution, which, in this problem, equals the rate of time preference.[6] The slope of the budget constraint at the optimum point is given by the (negative of) real rate of interest. Therefore, in equilibrium, *the rate of time preference equals the real rate of interest*.

---

[6] Remember that indifference curves slope downward, so that the marginal rate of substitution at the optimum point is a negative number.

## FIGURE 14-4

### CHANGES IN THE BUDGET CONSTRAINT

**(a)** An increase in income in either period will shift out the budget constraint, increasing the consumption possibilities in both periods.

**(b)** An increase in the real rate of interest will rotate the budget constraint, making the slope steeper.

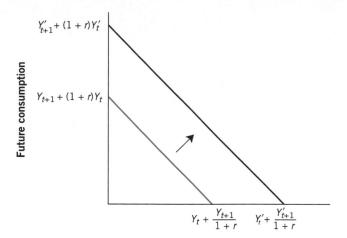

**(a) An increase in income shifts the budget constraint outward.**

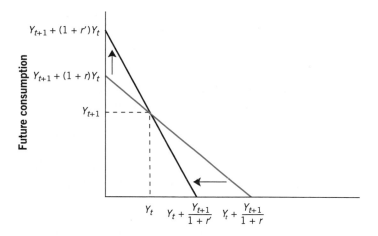

**(b) An increase in the interest rate rotates the budget constraint.**

There is an intuitive interpretation of this equilibrium condition. Along any indifference curve, the rate of time preference tells us the manner in which a consumer is willing to give up current consumption to receive more future consumption, holding total satisfaction constant. The slope of the budget constraint is given by the real rate of interest, which tells us how the market will reward the consumer for saving. Therefore, in equilibrium, the consumer is willing to trade current consumption for future consumption at a rate that is equal to the rate at which the market will reward the consumer for trading.

*FIGURE 14-5*

**CHOOSING OPTIMUM CONSUMPTION AND SAVINGS**

Optimum consumption in each period is given by point $E$, where the consumer reaches the highest indifference curve, given the budget constraint. At point $E$, the slope of the budget constraint equals the slope of the indifference curve, which means that the marginal rate of substitution equals the real rate of interest at the optimum.

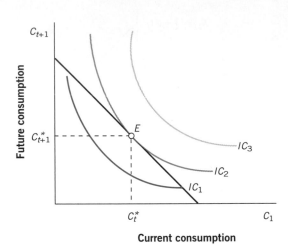

## Consumption and Changes in Income

As we saw in Figure 14-4(a), an increase in either period $t$ or period $t + 1$ income shifts the budget constraint outward, which means that the consumer can now reach a higher indifference curve. The change in consumption in periods $t$ and $t + 1$ will depend on where the new budget constraint is tangent to the higher indifference curve. In Figure 14-6, we have shown the situation where the consumer chooses more consumption in each of period $t$ and period $t + 1$. This is the situation that would arise if consumption in each period is a **normal good**. Any good is said to be a normal good if an increase in income causes the demand for this good to increase.[7]

The assumption that consumption in each period is a normal good is probably the most empirically relevant situation. However, if consumption in either period is not a normal good, then an increase in income will lead to a decrease in consumption in at least one of the periods. You are asked to investigate this is in Application Question 2 at the end of the chapter.

**normal good**
Any good is said to be a normal good if an increase in income causes the demand for this good to increase.

## Consumption, Savings, and the Real Interest Rate

We can use the model developed in this section to understand the relationship between changes in the real rate of interest and changes in consumption and savings. This is illustrated in Figure 14-7, where we consider the situation in which the consumer is a saver. You can see this from the fact that period $t$ consumption is less than period $t$ income.

---

[7] If consumption in either period is not a normal good, then an increase in income will not increase consumption in each period.

## FIGURE 14-6

An increase in income in either period $t$ or period $t + 1$ shifts the budget constraint outward. If consumption in each period $t$ and period $t + 1$ is a normal good, then the consumer will choose more consumption in each period.

### EFFECTS OF AN INCREASE IN INCOME

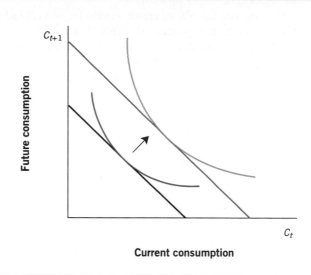

In Figure 14-7, the initial equilibrium is at point $E$. An increase in the real rate of interest is shown by the budget line rotating around the point $Y_{t+1}$, $Y_t$, to become steeper. The new equilibrium is at point $E'$. We have illustrated the situation where an increase in the real rate of interest has resulted in a decrease in current consumption and an increase in future consumption. Notice that, given current income, this

## FIGURE 14-7

An increase in the real rate of interest makes the budget constraint steeper. If the income effect is smaller than, or in the same direction as, the substitution effect, the net result is that an increase in the real rate of interest lowers period $t$ consumption and raises savings.

### EFFECTS OF AN INCREASE IN THE REAL INTEREST RATE

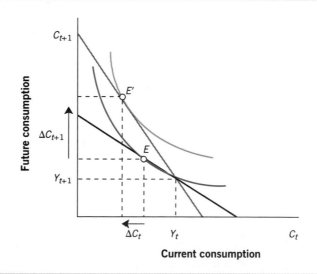

also implies an increase in savings. This is the result that we asserted in Chapter 3: There is a positive relationship between the real rate of interest and savings, or, the savings curve slopes upward.

However, the above result should be considered to be a theoretical result only that rests on an important theoretical assumption. In order to see this, ask yourself the following question: How do we know that the new equilibrium in Figure 14-7 will result in lower current consumption? To answer this question, consider thinking about the movement between the old equilibrium and the new equilibrium as being composed of two different movements.

First, if the real rate of interest goes up, the opportunity cost of current consumption is higher, as you are being offered a higher return to give up current consumption in the form of savings. In economics, we call this the *substitution effect*. The **substitution effect** states that, all else being equal, an increase in the real rate of interest will cause current consumption to go down and savings to go up.

Second, if the real rate of interest goes up, because the consumer is assumed to be a saver, then any amount of savings from period $t$ will result in higher consumption possibilities in period $t + 1$. This is called the *income effect*. The **income effect** is the change in consumption due to the fact that the consumer can now reach a higher indifference curve. If consumption in each period is a normal good, then the income effect will tend to increase consumption in both periods.

In the example illustrated in Figure 14-7, we have assumed that the income effect, which increases period $t$ consumption, is outweighed by the substitution effect, which decreases period $t$ consumption, so that an increase in the real rate of interest leads to a decrease in current consumption and an increase in savings. Ultimately, this is an empirical matter. Unfortunately, on an aggregate macroeconomic level, there is no strong evidence supporting this assumption. This is illustrated in Figure 14-8.

In Figure 14-8, we have graphed the savings rate on the vertical axis and the real rate of interest on the horizontal axis. The slope of an estimated line between these two variables is slightly positive but statistically insignificant. Therefore, empirical confirmation of the upward-sloping savings curve remains elusive.

**substitution effect**
All else being equal, an increase in the real rate of interest will cause current consumption to go down and savings to go up.

**income effect**
The change in consumption due to the fact that the consumer can now reach a higher indifference curve.

## 14-3 | THE LIFE-CYCLE–PERMANENT-INCOME THEORY OF CONSUMPTION AND SAVING

Modern consumption theory emphasizes lifetime decision making. Originally, the **life-cycle hypothesis** emphasized choices about how to maintain a stable standard of living in the face of changes in income over the course of life, while **permanent-income theory** focused on forecasting the level of income available to a consumer over a lifetime. Today, these two theories have largely merged.

### Life-Cycle Theory

The Keynesian consumption function [equation (1)] assumes that individuals' consumption behaviour in a given period is related to their income in that period. The *life-cycle hypothesis* views individuals, instead, as planning their consumption and savings behaviour over long periods, with the intention of allocating their consumption in the best possible way over their entire lifetimes. Instead of relying on a single value (based on a psychological rule of thumb) for the marginal propensity to con-

**life-cycle hypothesis**
Emphasizes choices about how to maintain a stable standard of living in the face of changes in income over the course of life.

**permanent-income theory**
Says that people form expectations of their future income and choose how much to consume based on those as well as their current income.

## FIGURE 14-8

### THE SAVINGS RATE AND THE REAL INTEREST RATE, 1961–2002

There is only a weak link between the savings rate (vertical axis) and the real rate of interest (horizontal axis). The slope of the line in this figure is slightly positive but statistically indistinguishable from 0.

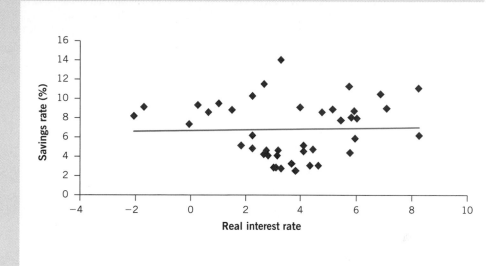

SOURCE: Savings: Persons and unincorporated businesses: CANSIM II V647354, divided by nominal GDP: CANSIM II V418918; the real interest rate is the long-term bond rate: CANSIM II V122487, minus the CPI inflation rate: CANSIM II V735319.

sume, life-cycle theory (based on maximizing behaviour) implies different marginal propensities to consume out of permanent income, transitory income, and wealth. The key assumption is that most people choose stable lifestyles—not, in general, saving furiously in one period to have a huge spending spree in the next but, rather, consuming at about the same level in every period. In its simplest form, the assumption is that individuals try to consume the same amount each year.

---

### BOX 14-2

### Linking Demography and Consumption

Life-cycle theory helps link consumption and savings behaviour to demographic considerations, especially to the age distribution of the population. Note that the marginal propensity to consume out of permanent income, *WL/NL*, changes with age. In the text example, the *MPC* out of permanent income at age 20 is 45/60. As a person ages, both the number of working years and the number of years of life decline. By age 50, for example, the *MPC* would have declined to 15/30. (The exact argument holds only for labour income, since *WL* isn't relevant to income from investments.) The *MPC* out of transitory income would rise from 1/60 at age 20 to 1/30 at age 50.

The economy is a mix of people of many different ages and life expectancies, so the *MPC* for the economy is a mix of corresponding *MPC*s. As a result, economies with different age mixtures have different overall marginal propensities to save and consume.

A numerical example illustrates the theory: Suppose that a person starts working at age 20, plans to work until 65, and will die at 80, and that annual labour income, *YL*, is $30,000. Lifetime resources are annual income times years of working life (*WL* = 65 − 20 = 45)—in this example, $30,000 × 45 = $1,350,000.[8] Spreading lifetime resources over the number of years of working life (*NL* = 80 − 20 = 60) allows for annual consumption of *C* = $1,350,000/60 = $22,500. The general formula is

$$C = \frac{WL}{NL} \times YL \qquad (2)$$

So the marginal propensity to consume is *WL/NL*. Figure 14-9 illustrates the pattern of consumption and saving.

Continuing with the numerical example, we can compute marginal propensities to consume by considering variations in the income stream. Suppose income was to

---

## FIGURE 14-9    LIFETIME INCOME, CONSUMPTION, SAVING, AND WEALTH IN THE LIFE-CYCLE MODEL

Consumption is constant throughout a lifetime. During the working life, lasting *WL* years, the individual saves, accumulating assets. At the end of the working life, the individual begins to live off these assets, dissaving for the remaining years (*NL − WL*) of life so that assets equal exactly zero at the end of life.

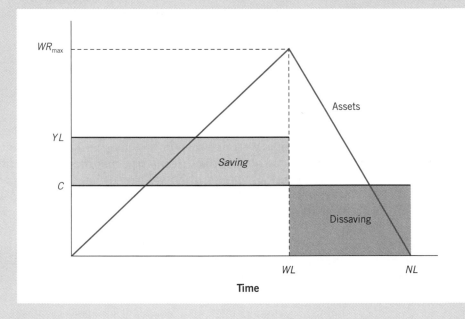

---

rise permanently by $3000 per year. The extra $3000 times 45 working years spread over 60 years of life would increase annual consumption by $3000 × (45/60) = $2250. In other words, the *marginal propensity to consume out of permanent income* would be *WL/NL* = 45/60 = 0.75. In contrast, suppose income was to rise by $3000 but only in one year. The extra $3000 spread over 60 years would increase annual consumption by $3000 × (1/60) = $50. In other words, the *marginal propensity to consume out of transitory income* would be 1/*NL* = 1/60 ≈ 0.017. While the exact examples are slightly contrived, the clear message is that the *MPC* out of *permanent income* is large and the *MPC* out of *transitory income* is small, fairly close to zero.

---

[8] Note that as a simplification we ignore the effect of interest earned on saving.

### Life-Cycle Consumption and Permanent-Income Theory: Why Can't Economists Ever Agree?

Modern consumption theory is due largely to Franco Modigliani of MIT (life-cycle theory) and Milton Friedman of the University of Chicago (permanent-income theory), both of whom have won Nobel Prizes. Modigliani is a leading Keynesian, and Friedman is the "father of modern monetarism." Their theories are quite similar. (So much so that economists frequently call the combination the life-cycle–permanent-income hypothesis, abbreviated LC-PIH.) Like much of good macroeconomics, both theories pay careful attention to microeconomic foundations. While the theories differed in their developmental stage, the two have largely merged and today are largely accepted by all economists.

The history of these theories offers an important methodological lesson. Economists seem to derive enjoyment from disagreeing with one another. This is a good thing, because progress comes from examining disputes, not from singing as a chorus. As disputes are resolved, the frontier moves on. What people often don't see is that this process leads economists to agree on 90 percent of how the economy works, even while still fiercely contesting the frontiers of the science.

The life-cycle theory implies that the marginal propensity to consume out of wealth should equal the *MPC* out of transitory income and, therefore, be very small. The reasoning is that spending out of wealth, like spending out of transitory income, is spread out over the remaining years of life. The *MPC* out of wealth is used to link changes in the value of assets to current consumption. For example, an increase in the value of the stock market will increase current consumption. Changes in the value of the stock market can be very large in comparison to income changes, so even though the *MPC* out of wealth is small, the effect of a large dollar change in the stock market multiplied by a small *MPC* can generate a significant change in consumption.

## Permanent-Income Theory

**permanent income**
The steady rate of consumption a person could maintain for the rest of his or her life, given the present level of wealth and the income earned now and in the future.

Like the life-cycle hypothesis, the permanent-income theory of consumption argues that consumption is related not to current income but to a longer-term estimate of income, which Milton Friedman, who introduced the theory, calls *permanent income*. Friedman provides a simple example: Consider a person who is paid or receives income only once a week, on Fridays. We do not expect that person to consume only on Friday, with zero consumption on the other days of the week. People prefer a smooth consumption flow rather than plenty today and scarcity tomorrow or yesterday.

The idea that consumption spending is geared to long-term, or average or permanent, income is appealing and essentially the same as the life-cycle theory. **Permanent income** is the steady rate of consumption a person could maintain for the rest of his or her life, given the present level of wealth and the income earned now and in the future.

BOX

14-4

### Durable Goods Consumption

The LC-PIH makes sense for consumption of non-durables and services, things from which we derive pleasure around the time of purchase. Durable goods, such as cars, refrigerators, and stereos, provide a stream of utility long after the purchase. The LC-PIH model explains the stream of utility, not the expenditure pattern. The theory of durable goods purchases is really the theory of investment applied to households instead of firms. This has two implications for durable goods expenditures. First, they are not smoothed out the way purchases of non-durables and services are. Second, durable goods purchases are quite sensitive to interest rates, at least in countries like Canada and the United States, where consumer finance is readily available. Automobiles and household appliances are examples of goods that respond positively to swings in GDP and negatively to interest rates.

In its simplest form the theory argues that consumption is proportional to permanent income:

$$C = cYP \tag{3}$$

where $YP$ is permanent (disposable) income.

To think about the measurement of permanent income, imagine someone trying to figure out what her permanent income is. The person has a current level of income and has formed some idea of the level of consumption she can maintain for the rest of her life. Now income goes up. The person has to decide whether the increase is permanent or merely transitory or temporary. In any particular case, an individual may know whether an increase is permanent or transitory. An associate professor who is promoted to professor and given a raise will think that the increase in income is permanent; a worker who has exceptionally high overtime in a given year will likely regard that year's increased income as transitory. But in general, a person is not likely to be so sure whether a change is permanent or transitory. A good Christmas bonus might be due to a change in your employer's compensation scheme (permanent) or it might signal that your firm had an unusually good year (transitory). The difference matters because transitory income is assumed not to have any substantial effect on consumption. (Note that the weak link between consumption and transitory income parallels the worked-out example, above, for the *MPC* out of transitory income.) According to the LC-PIH, consumption should be *smoother* than income because spending out of transitory income is spread over many years.

## 14-4 | CONSUMPTION UNDER UNCERTAINTY: THE MODERN APPROACH

If permanent income was known exactly, then according to the LC-PIH, consumption would never change.[9] The modern version of the LC-PIH emphasizes the link

---

[9] If a consumer knew total lifetime resources in advance, she could figure out once and for all how to spread consumption evenly. However, saying that "consumption would never change" is not quite right, because the statement ignores the effects of impatience and the financial return to saving. See footnote 10.

between income uncertainty and changes in consumption and takes a more formal approach to consumer maximization. According to this newer version, changes in consumption arise from *surprise* changes in income. Absent income surprises, consumption this period should be the same as consumption last period.

The modern approach to the LC-PIH begins by formally stating the lifetime utility maximization problem of a representative consumer. In a particular period, a consumer enjoys utility from consumption in that period, $u(C_t)$. **Lifetime utility** is the sum of period-by-period utilities, and the **lifetime budget constraint** is the sum of period-by-period consumption:[10]

$$\text{Lifetime utility} = u(C_t) + u(C_{t+1}) + \ldots + u(C_{T-1}) + u(C_T)$$
$$\text{subject to } C_t + C_{t+1} + \ldots + C_{T-1} + C_T$$
$$= \text{Wealth} + YL_t + YL_{t+1} + \ldots + YL_{T-1} + YL_T \qquad (4)$$

**lifetime utility**

The sum of period-by-period utilities.

**lifetime budget constraint**

The sum of period-by-period consumption.

**marginal lifetime utility of consumption**

The increase in utility from a small increase in consumption.

Consumers choose consumption each period to maximize lifetime utility subject to total lifetime consumption equalling lifetime resources. The optimal choice is the consumption path that equates the **marginal lifetime utility of consumption** across periods, $MU(C_{t+1}) = MU(C_t)$, and so on. Why? Consider the alternative: If marginal utility was a little higher in period $t$ than in period $t + 1$, lifetime utility could be increased by shifting consumption into $t$ from $t + 1$ because the gain from the former would outweigh the gain from the latter. (By definition, marginal utility is the increase in utility from a small increase in consumption.)

Now add considerations of uncertainty. The consumer cannot actually implement an equate-marginal-utilities rule because future marginal utility, $MU(C_{t+1})$, is uncertain at time $t$. The consumer *can* equate marginal utility today with a best guess of marginal utility at time $t + 1$, so the modified rule is to equate today's marginal utility with the expected value of tomorrow's marginal utility, $E[MU(C_{t+1})] = MU(C_t)$.[11]

Marginal utility functions aren't observable, but in this simple case, the functions will be equal only if their arguments are equal, so the rule can be rewritten as $E(C_{t+1}) = C_t$. Expected values aren't observable either, but in the late 1970s, Robert Hall realized that rational expectations theory could be applied to the problem—and in so doing, he revolutionized macroeconometrics.[12] Observed consumption can be written as expected consumption plus a surprise: $C_{t+1} = E(C_{t+1}) + \text{Surprise}$.

---

[10] Equation (4) leaves out two factors that were discussed in Section 14-2 People prefer to consume now rather than later, so a high rate of time preference, represented by the parameter $\delta$, moves consumption earlier. Counteracting this effect, deferred spending accrues interest at rate $r$, allowing greater consumption if one is patient. Measuring both $\delta$ and $r$ in percent per period, a more fully specified version of equation (4) is

$$\text{Lifetime utility} = u(C_t) + (1 + \delta)^{-1}u(C_{t+1}) + \ldots + (1 + \delta)^{-T}u(C_T)$$
$$\text{subject to } C_t + (1 + r)^{-1}C_{t+1} + \ldots + (1 + r)^{-T}C_T$$
$$= \text{Wealth} + YL_t + (1 + r)^{-1}YL_{t+1} + \ldots + (1 + r)^{-T}YL_T$$

[11] To fully account for the rate of time preference and the interest rate, the equate-expected-marginal-utilities rule needs to be modified to read

$$E[MU(C_{t+1})] = \left(\frac{1+\delta}{1+r}\right)MU(C_t)$$

This is actually a more sophisticated version of the equilibrium condition that the rate of time preference equals the real rate of interest, which we discussed in Chapter 3.

[12] Robert E. Hall, "Stochastic Implications of the Life Cycle–Permanent Income Hypothesis: Theory and Evidence," *Journal of Political Economy*, December 1978.

# POLICY IN *ACTION*

## Temporary Tax Cuts and the Consumer

In Box 14-1, we discussed the 1968 temporary tax increases in the United States. In Canada, we also experimented with temporary tax changes. In 1977, consumer spending in Canada increased by 2.4 percent, which was the lowest increase in the post-World War II period. In an effort to offset what was considered to be a downward trend in consumer spending, the federal government introduced a temporary tax decrease in the budget of April 1978. The provincial sales tax rates were to be temporarily lowered in each province that levied a sales tax, and the federal government was to compensate each of the provinces for the revenue loss.

The effects on the Canadian economy are shown in the figure below. In spite of the temporary tax change, consumption spending continued to decrease. This is exactly what the consumption theory in this chapter would predict: The temporary tax cut did not alter the consumption behaviour of consumers.*

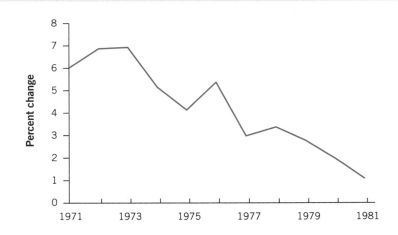

SOURCE: CANSIM II V1992229.

*A thorough and interesting analysis of these temporary tax cuts is contained in a paper by Jean-Marie Dufour and Francois Vaillancourt, "Provincial and Federal Sales Taxes: Evidence of Their Effect and Prospect for Change" in *Tax Policy Options in the 1980s*, W.R. Thirsk and J. Whalley (eds.), (Toronto: Canadian Tax Foundation, Tax Paper No. 66, 1982).

According to rational expectations theory, the surprise is truly random and unpredictable. Combining this rational expectations formula with the equate-expected-consumption rule, $E(C_{t+1}) = C_t$, leads to Hall's famous **random-walk model**.[13]

$$C_{t+1} = C_t + \epsilon \qquad (5)$$

which states that consumption tomorrow should equal consumption today plus a truly random error, $\epsilon = C_{t+1} - C_t$. Can such a strong implication of the LC-PIH possibly hold in the real world?

In Figure 14-10, we have plotted current consumption per capita on the vertical axis, and consumption per capita lagged one period on the horizontal axis. Each series is measured in thousands of 1997 dollars over the period 1961–2002. Notice that consumption in Figure 14-10 is composed of consumption spending on non-durable goods plus consumption spending on services. Modern theories of consumption behaviour usually omit consumption durables. Milton Friedman defines consumption as anything that is purchased and consumed during the period of a year. If a good is purchased and not consumed in that period, such as consumer durables, then it is not part of consumption. Notice that this distinction is not made for the Keynesian consumption theory, which uses total consumption, as shown in Figure 14-1.

The model appears to work nearly perfectly.[14] The random-walk model predicts that the line relating $C_{t+1}$ to $C_t$ should have an intercept of zero and a slope of 1. The

**random-walk model of consumption**

Consumption tomorrow should equal consumption today plus a truly random error.

www.investopedia.com/terms/r/randomwalktheory.asp

---

*FIGURE 14-10*

Consumption this period is almost perfectly predicted by consumption last period plus an allowance for growth.

**CURRENT AND LAGGED CONSUMPTION PER CAPITA, 1961–2002 (THOUSANDS OF 1997 DOLLARS)**

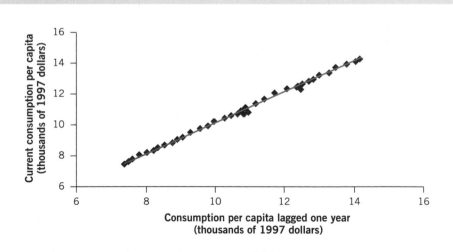

SOURCE: Consumption: non-durables: CANSIM II V1992232, plus services: CANSIM II V1992233; population: CANSIM II V1.

---

[13] At the time of Hall's discovery, everyone "knew" that consumption adjusted with long lags. Hall himself initially expected to *disprove* the LC-PIH. The random-walk model was so outlandish that Hall was the subject of much ribbing and good-natured abuse from his colleagues and his students—until everyone realized that he had found exactly the right approach to the problem.

[14] For those curious about formal statistical measures, 99.67 percent of the variance of $C_{t+1}$ in Figure 14-10 is explained by $C_t$. (In the language of statistics, $R^2 = 0.9967$.)

actual equation has an intercept of $170 (compared to a mean consumption of $10,900) and a slope of 0.999, so these predictions of the random-walk model fail only in the third decimal place.

## The LC-PIH: The Traditional Model Strikes Back

Based on rational consumer behaviour, the LC-PIH is very attractive to economists. However, empirical evidence suggests that both the traditional rule-of-thumb consumption function and the LC-PIH contribute to explaining consumption behaviour.[15] The actual behaviour of consumption exhibits both **excess sensitivity** and **excess smoothness**. The former means that consumption responds too strongly to predictable changes in income; the latter, that it responds too little to surprise changes in income.[16]John Campbell and Greg Mankiw have developed a clever way of combining the LC-PIH and the traditional consumption function in order to test for excess sensitivity.[17]According to the LC-PIH, the change in consumption equals the surprise element, $\epsilon$, so $\Delta C_{\text{LC-PIH}} = \epsilon$. According to the traditional theory, $C = \overline{C} + cYD$, so $\Delta C_{\text{trad}} = c\Delta YD$. If $\lambda$ percent of the population behaves in accordance with the traditional model and the remaining $1 - \lambda$ follow the LC-PIH, the total change in consumption is

$$\Delta C = \lambda \Delta C_{\text{trad}} + (1 - \lambda)\Delta C_{\text{LC-PIH}} = \lambda c\Delta YD + (1 - \lambda)\epsilon \tag{6}$$

Empirically estimating this equation yields

$$\Delta C = 0.486\Delta YD \tag{7}$$

suggesting that half of consumption behaviour is explained by current income rather than permanent income.[18]

## Liquidity Constraints and Myopia

Why might a theory as elegant as the LC-PIH miss explaining so much of consumption behaviour? Two explanations are **liquidity constraints** and **myopia**. The first argues that when permanent income is higher than current income, consumers are unable to borrow to consume at the higher level predicted by the LC-PIH. The second suggests that consumers simply aren't as forward-looking as the LC-PIH suggests.

A liquidity constraint exists when a consumer cannot borrow to sustain current consumption in the expectation of higher future income. Students in particular

**excess sensitivity**
Consumption responds too strongly to predictable changes in income.

**excess smoothness**
Consumption responds too little to surprise changes in income.

**liquidity constraints**
Exist when a consumer cannot borrow to sustain current consumption in the expectation of higher future income.

**myopia**
The idea that consumers are not as forward-thinking as the LC-PIH suggests.

---

[15] The first crack in the LC-PIH wall was discovered by one of Hall's students, now a professor at the University of California–San Diego, Marjorie Flavin. See her article, "The Adjustment of Consumption to Changing Expectations about Future Income," *Journal of Political Economy,* October 1981.

[16] To see how this works in a formal model, see David Romer, *Advanced Macroeconomics* (New York: McGraw-Hill, 1996), Chapter 7.

[17] John Y. Campbell and N. Gregory Mankiw, "Consumption, Income, and Interest Rates: Reinterpreting the Time Series Evidence," *NBER Macroeconomics Annual,* 1989. For earlier evidence on the same topic, see Robert E. Hall and Frederic S. Mishkin, "The Sensitivity of Consumption to Transitory Income: Estimates from Panel Data on Households," *Econometrica,* March 1982. A contrary view is presented in Joseph DeJuan and John Seater, "The Permanent Income Hypothesis: Evidence from the Consumer Expenditure Survey," *Journal of Monetary Economics,* April 1999.

[18] This equation was estimated by an advanced version of regression called *instrumental variables.* Consumption with lags 2 through 5 were used as instruments. The *t* statistic was 3.73. (Promise: This footnote will *not* be on the exam.)

should appreciate the possibility that liquidity constraints exist. Most students can look forward to a much higher income in the future than they receive as students. The life-cycle theory holds that they should be consuming on the basis of their lifetime incomes, which means they should be spending much more than they currently earn. To do that, they would have to borrow. They can borrow to some extent, through student loan plans. However, it is entirely possible that they cannot borrow enough to support consumption at its permanent level.

Such students are liquidity-constrained. When they leave college and take jobs, their incomes will rise and their consumption will rise, too. According to the life-cycle theory, consumption should not rise much when income rises, as long as the increase in income was expected. In fact, because the liquidity constraint is relieved, consumption will rise a lot when income rises. Thus consumption will be more closely related to *current* income than is implied by the LC-PIH. Similarly, individuals who cannot borrow when their incomes decline temporarily would be liquidity-constrained.[19]

The alternative explanation for the sensitivity of consumption to current income—that consumers are myopic—is hard to distinguish in practice from the liquidity constraints hypothesis. For instance, in a U.S. study, David Wilcox of the Federal Reserve Board of Governors has shown that the announcement that social security benefits will be increased (which always happens at least six weeks before the change) does not lead to a change in consumption *until the benefit increases are actually paid.*[20] Once the increased benefits are paid, recipients certainly do adjust spending—primarily on durables. The delay could be either because recipients do not have the assets to enable them to adjust spending before they receive higher payments (liquidity constraints), or because they fail to pay attention to the announcements (myopia), or perhaps because they do not believe the announcements.

## Uncertainty and Buffer-Stock Saving

The life-cycle hypothesis is that people save largely to finance retirement. However, additional savings goals also matter. The evidence on bequests suggests that some saving is done to provide inheritances for children. There is also a growing amount of evidence to support the view that some saving is *precautionary,* undertaken to guard against rainy days. In other words, savings are used as a **buffer stock**, added to when times are good in order to maintain consumption when times are bad.

One piece of evidence for these other motives is that old people rarely actually dissave. They tend to live off the income (e.g., interest and dividends) from their wealth—not to draw down wealth, as predicted by the LC-PIH. One explanation is that the older they are, the more they fear having to pay large bills for medical care

**buffer stock**

Excess consumer savings used to maintain consumption when income is lower than usual (saving for a rainy day).

---

[19] Estimates of the importance of liquidity constraints in the United States are presented in Marjorie Flavin, "Excess Sensitivity of Consumption to Current Income: Liquidity Constraints or Myopia?" *Canadian Journal of Economics,* February 1985; Stephen P. Zeldes, "Consumption and Liquidity Constraints: An Empirical Investigation," *Journal of Political Economy,* April 1989; and Tullio Jappelli, "Who Is Credit Constrained in the U.S. Economy?" *Quarterly Journal of Economics,* February 1989.

Even in developing countries, where the paucity of financial institutions makes borrowing difficult for the typical consumer, people try to smooth out their consumption in the face of income fluctuations. See the articles by Anne Case, Robert M. Townsend, Jonathan Morduch, and Timothy Besley in "Symposium on Consumption Smoothing in Developing Countries," *Journal of Economic Perspectives,* Summer 1995.

[20] David W. Wilcox, "Social Security Benefits, Consumption Expenditure, and the Life Cycle Hypothesis," *Journal of Political Economy,* April 1989.

and, therefore, the more reluctant they are to spend. Evidence from surveys of consumers, who were asked why they are saving, also indicates that saving is undertaken to meet emergency needs.

This evidence is consistent with a version of the life-cycle model in which uncertainty about future income and future needs is explicitly included.[21] Recent work by Christopher Carroll uses these ideas to explain why the LC-PIH may be off the mark for the typical consumer.[22] Income fluctuations create considerable downside risk for the consumer, because the pain caused by a large drop in spending is greater than the pleasure caused by an equal-size increase in spending. One way consumers can avoid having to cut their consumption sharply in bad times is to save up a buffer stock of assets, which they can draw on in emergencies. On the other hand, most consumers are impatient; they would prefer to spend now rather than save for the future. Under these conditions, consumers will have a "target" wealth level. The target will be the point where impatience exactly balances the precautionary (or buffer-stock) saving motive. If the wealth is below the target, the precautionary saving motive will be stronger than impatience and the consumer will try to build up wealth toward the target; if wealth is above the target, impatience will be stronger than caution and the consumer will dissave. These effects lead to a much higher *MPC* than would be predicted by the standard LC-PIH model.

## *Working with Data*

In Figure 14-1, we plotted the data that is usually presented in support of a Keynesian consumption function. In that figure, we used total consumption. If you try to reproduce Figure 14-1 using only data on consumption of non-durables and consumption of services per capita (as in Figure 14-10) plotted against disposable income per capita, you will get a smaller *MPC*. To see why this is the case, plot the two series together as across time (as opposed to a scatter plot). You should be able to see that changes in per capita disposable income are much more volatile than changes in per-capita consumption. You should be able to use this information to convince yourself that the long run MPC is high but the short run *MPC* is low.

### C H A P T E R    S U M M A R Y

▶   Theoretically, if the income effect, which increases current consumption, is outweighed by the substitution effect, which decreases current consumption, an increase in the real rate of interest leads to a decrease in current consumption and an increase in savings. Thus, the savings curve should slope upward. However, there is not strong empirical evidence in support of this proposition.

---

[21] For example, Stephen Zeldes, "Optimal Consumption with Stochastic Income: Departures from Certainty Equivalence," *Quarterly Journal of Economics*, May 1989.

[22] See C. Carroll, "Buffer-Stock Saving and the Life Cycle/Permanent Income Hypothesis," *Quarterly Journal of Economics*, February 1997. Carroll writes, "It seems plausible that many consumers ensure that retirement is taken care of by joining a pension plan, buy a house, and then subject the post-pension-plan, post-mortgage-payment income and consumption streams to buffer-stock saving rules."

▶ The life-cycle–permanent-income hypothesis (LC-PIH) predicts that the marginal propensity to consume out of permanent income is large and that the marginal propensity to consume out of transitory income is very small. Modern theories of consumption assume that individuals want to maintain relatively smooth consumption profiles over their lifetimes. Their consumption behaviour is geared to their long-term consumption opportunities—permanent income or lifetime income plus wealth. With such a view, current income is only one of the determinants of consumption spending. Wealth and expected income play a role, too.

▶ Observed consumption is much smoother than the simple Keynesian consumption function predicts. Current consumption can be very accurately predicted from last period's consumption. Both these observations accord well with the LC-PIH.

▶ The LC-PIH is a very attractive theory, but it does not give a complete explanation of consumption behaviour. Empirical evidence shows that the traditional consumption function appears to also play a role.

▶ The life-cycle hypothesis suggests that the propensities of an individual to consume out of disposable income and out of wealth depend on the person's age. It implies that saving is high (low) when income is high (low) relative to lifetime average income. It also suggests that aggregate saving depends on the growth rate of the economy and on such variables as the age distribution of the population.

## KEY TERMS

intertemporal choice, *275*
indifference curve, *275*
marginal rate of substitution, *276*
budget constraint, *277*
normal good, *280*
substitution effect, *282*
income effect, *282*

life-cycle hypothesis, *282*
permanent-income theory, *282*
permanent income, *285*
lifetime utility, *287*
lifetime budget constraint, *287*
marginal lifetime utility of
 consumption, *287*

random-walk model of
 consumption, *289*
excess sensitivity, *290*
excess smoothness, *290*
liquidity constraints, *290*
myopia, *290*
buffer stock, *291*

## DISCUSSION QUESTIONS

1. In June 2003, in both the United States and the European Union countries, strong policy discussions took place concerning returning to fiscal deficit positions. In Section 14-1, we discussed the Keynesian consumption function. Discuss how the marginal propensity to consume may play a role in this policy discussion

2. The text implies that the ratio of consumption to accumulated saving declines over time until retirement.
   a. Why? What assumption about consumption behaviour leads to this result?
   b. What happens to this ratio after retirement?

3. a. Suppose you earn just as much as your neighbour but are in much better health and expect to live longer than she does. Would you consume more or less than she does?

www.mcgrawhill.ca/college/dornbusch

Why? Derive your answer using the equation from the text, $C = (WL/NL) \times YL$.

    **b.** According to the life-cycle hypothesis, what would be the effect of the social security system on your average propensity to consume out of (disposable) income? Is the credibility of the social security system an issue here?

**4.** In terms of the permanent-income hypothesis, would you consume more of your year-end bonus if (a) you knew there would be a bonus every year, or (b) this was the only year the bonus would be given?

**5.** Explain why successful gamblers (and thieves) might be expected to live very well even in years when they don't do well at all.

**6.** What are the similarities between the life-cycle and the permanent-income hypotheses? Do they differ in their approaches to explaining why the long run *MPC* is greater than the short run *MPC*?

**7.** Canada, during the 1980s, found its rate of personal saving declining. It also, during that time, had a demographic "blip"—the baby-boomer generation, then in its late twenties to early thirties.

    **a.** Does the life-cycle hypothesis suggest a reason why these two facts might be connected?

    **b.** What does this hypothesis suggest we should see as this generation ages?

**8.** Rank the following marginal propensities to consume:

    **a.** Marginal propensity to consume out of permanent income

    **b.** Marginal propensity to consume out of transitory income

    **c.** Marginal propensity to consume out of permanent income when consumers are liquidity-constrained

    **d.** Marginal propensity to consume out of transitory income when consumers are liquidity-constrained

**9.** What is a random walk? How is Hall's random-walk model of consumption related to the life-cycle and permanent-income hypotheses?

**10.** What are the problems of excess sensitivity and excess smoothness? Does their existence disprove or invalidate the LC-PIH? Explain.

**11.** What assumption(s) regarding consumers' knowledge and behaviour in the life-cycle–permanent-income hypothesis do we need to change in order for it to explain the presence of precautionary, or buffer-stock, saving? Do these assumptions, in your opinion, bring the model closer to or further from the world as you know it?

**12. a.** Explain why the interest rate might affect saving.

    **b.** Has this relationship been confirmed empirically?

## APPLICATION QUESTIONS

**1.** In Figure 14-7, we presented the relationship between the savings rate and the real rate of interest. The definition that we used for savings was for persons and unincorporated businesses. Redo Figure 14-7 using the different definitions of savings that are available on CANSIM. Comment on how the results differ.

**2.** Show how consumption in period $t$ and period $t + 1$ will change when income increases, if income in either of the periods is not a normal good.

www.mcgrawhill.ca/college/dornbusch

3. Suppose that permanent income is calculated as the average of income over the past five years; that is,

$$YP = 1/5(Y + Y_{-1} + Y_{-2} + Y_{-3} + Y_{-4}) \qquad (P1)$$

Suppose further that consumption is given by $C = 0.9YP$.

a. If you have earned $20,000 per year for the past 10 years, what is your permanent income?

b. Suppose that next year (period $t + 1$) you earn $30,000. What is your new $YP$?

c. What is your consumption this year and next year?

d. What is your short run marginal propensity to consume? Long run $MPC$?

e. Assuming you continue to earn $30,000 starting in period $t + 1$, graph the value of your permanent income in each period, using equation (P1).

4. The graph below shows the lifetime earnings profile of a person who lives for four periods and earns incomes of $30, $60, and $90 in the first three periods of the life cycle. There are no earnings during retirement. Assume that the interest rate is 0.

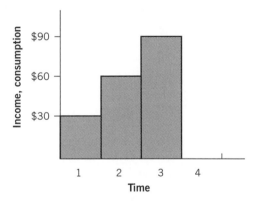

a. Determine the level of consumption, compatible with the budget constraint, for someone who wants an even consumption profile throughout the life cycle. Indicate in which periods the person saves and dissaves and in what amounts.

b. Assume now that, contrary to part (a), there is no possibility of borrowing. The credit markets are closed to the individual. Under this assumption, what is the flow of consumption the individual will pick over the life cycle? In providing an answer, continue to assume that, if possible, an even flow of consumption is preferred. (Note: You are assuming here that there are liquidity constraints.)

c. Assume next that the person described in part (b) receives an increase in wealth, or non-labour income. The increase in wealth is equal to $13. How will that wealth be allocated over the life cycle with and without access to the credit market? How would your answer differ if the increase in wealth was $23?

5. Suppose that 70 percent of a country's population, as a consequence of liquidity constraints, behaves in accordance with the traditional model of consumption and thus consumes, every period, a given fraction of its disposable income. The other 30 percent of the population behaves in accordance with the LC-PIH.

a. If the $MPC$ in the traditional model is 0.8 and disposable income changes by $10 million (you may assume that this change is due entirely to a change in transitory income), by how much will consumption change?

    **b.** What if 70 percent of the population behaves in accordance with the LC-PIH, and 30 percent behaves in accordance with the traditional model?

    **c.** What if 100 percent of the population behaves in accordance with the LC-PIH?

**6.** Suppose the real interest rate has increased from 2 to 4 percent.

    **a.** What will happen to the opportunity cost of consuming a set of goods today, as opposed to tomorrow? Explain how this will affect the fraction of income you choose to save.

    **b.** Now suppose that you save only to finance your retirement and that your goal is to have $1 million tucked away by the time you're 70. Explain how your rate of saving will respond to the rise in the interest rate in *this* context.

    **c.** Can you make a prediction regarding the net effect of this increase in *r* on the rate of saving? Why, or why not?

**7.** Go to CANSIM and retrieve real GDP. Calculate permanent income using equation (P1) from Application Question 3. Plot permanent income and actual income (GDP). Comment on the relationship between these two variables.

## CHAPTER 15

# INVESTMENT SPENDING

## *LEARNING OBJECTIVES*

After reading and studying this chapter, you should be able to:

▶ *Understand that investment is the most volatile sector of aggregate demand.*

▶ *Understand that the demand for capital depends on interest rates, output, and taxes.*

▶ *Understand that investment reflects the adjustment of the existing capital stock to the current demand for capital.*

▶ *Understand that investment spending is the primary link from monetary policy to aggregate demand.*

nvestment analysis is an important topic in macroeconomics, since its influence on the economy can be seen from both the demand side and the supply side. On the demand side, we have seen in earlier chapters that investment spending is a component of aggregate demand and therefore plays a role in the very short run models that were developed in Part 4 of the text. On the supply side, we examined the role of investment and the capital stock in Chapter 4, when discussing the very long run growth model. Investment links the present to the future.

Investment links the money markets to goods markets. And investment fluctuations drive much of the business cycle. Following are some interesting features of the investment sector:

▶  Investment spending is very volatile and thus responsible for much of the fluctuation of GDP across the business cycle.

▶  Investment spending is a primary link through which interest rates, and therefore monetary policy, affect the economy. Tax policies affecting investment, under the control of Parliament, are important tools of fiscal policy.

▶  On the supply side, investment over long periods determines the size of the stock of capital and thus helps determine long run growth.

In this chapter we study how investment relationships depend on interest rates and income. Recall from Chapter 11 that these relationships are principal determinants of the slope of the *IS* curve. We also see how government policy can increase or decrease investment, thus shifting the *IS* curve and increasing or decreasing aggregate demand.

Figure 15-1 illustrates the volatility of investment spending by comparing the growth rate of GDP with the growth rate of investment. You can see how the growth rate of investment spending decreased dramatically in the recession of the early 1980s

*FIGURE 15-1*

**INVESTMENT SPENDING AND GDP, ANNUAL GROWTH RATES, 1962–2002**

Investment spending is very volatile compared to GDP. Investment spending dropped much more rapidly than GDP in the recession of the early 1980s and grew much more erratically than GDP in the 1990s.

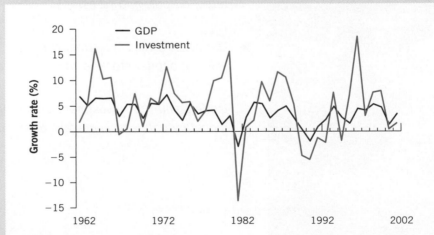

SOURCE: GDP: CANSIM II V1992259; investment: CANSIM II V1992238.

and grew much more erratically than GDP in the 1990s. Investment spending as a proportion of GDP climbed from approximately 10 percent in 1961 to approximately 17 percent in 2002.

The theory of investment is the theory of the demand for capital. We develop this theory carefully in Section 15-1, and then in Section 15-2, we apply the theory to **business fixed investment, residential investment**, and **inventory investment**. First, though, you should understand that the dynamics of investment and capital are driven by a "stylized fact": The **flow of investment** is quite small compared to the **stock of capital**.

Stocks and flows are inevitably explained with a bathtub metaphor, with the level of the bathwater playing the role of the stock of capital and the flow from the tap being analogous to the flow of investment. Businesses and individuals decide on the desired capital stock (how high they want the bathwater) and then invest (turn up the faucet) to top up the capital stock from where it is today (the height of the bathwater right now) to the desired level. A key fact, at least for the Canadian economy, is that the size of the tub is very large relative to the flow from the tap. At typical rates of investment, it would take about 15 years' flow to fill the stock of capital to its usual level. As a result, even a pretty small increase in the desired level of capital turns the investment faucet to full open, and a pretty small decrease in the desired level of capital shuts investment down to a dribble. This large-stock-to-small-flow fact explains why investment is such a volatile sector of aggregate demand. It also explains why investment has little effect on aggregate supply in the short run: Full open or shut down, the investment flow is just a ripple on the capital stock. Of course, over the long run, investment flow entirely determines the height of the capital stock and is therefore one of the most important determinants of aggregate supply.

Before getting down to business, we have to clarify terminology. In common usage, *investment* often refers to buying *existing* financial or physical assets. For example, we say someone *invests* in stocks, bonds, or a house when he or she buys the asset. In macroeconomics, *investment* has a more narrow, technical meaning: *Investment* is the flow of spending that adds to the physical stock of capital, and is often referred to as *gross fixed capital formation*.

In Section 15-1 we emphasize two elements: the demand for capital, and investment as a flow that adjusts the level of the *capital stock*. Capital is a *stock,* the given dollar value of all of the buildings, machines, and inventories at a point in time. Both GDP and investment refer to spending *flows*. Investment is the amount spent by businesses to *add* to the stock of capital over a given period.

---

**business fixed investment**
Annual increase in machinery, equipment, and structures used in production.

**residential investment**
Investment in housing.

**inventory investment**
Increase in the stock of goods on hand.

**flow of investment**
The addition to the capital stock over some period of time.

**stock of capital**
The value of all building machinery and inventories at a point in time.

www.statcan.ca/english/
freepub/31-532-GIE/
Invest.htm

---

**BOX 15-1**

## Why Investment Is Volatile—The Back-of-an-Envelope Explanation

Following along with the bathtub metaphor, we can easily rough out expected magnitudes for changes in investment. In Canada, private capital is roughly equal to 2.5 years' GDP. Investment is equal to about one-sixth of GDP. So the stock of capital is approximately 15 years' worth of investment. If the demand for capital was to drop 1 percent, the investment-GDP ratio would have to drop from around 16 percent of GDP to around 13.5 percent to satisfy the change within one year. Put differently, a 1 percent drop in the capital stock is produced by a 15 percent change in annual investment flow.

## 15-1 | THE STOCK DEMAND FOR CAPITAL AND THE FLOW OF INVESTMENT

Businesses and consumers demand a stock of capital in the form of machines and homes, but the supply of capital can be thought of as a fixed stock at a point in time. When the demand exceeds the existing stock, a flow of investment in the form of new machines and new home construction starts to fill the gap. We work through a formal analysis of the demand for capital in this section. But we start with a familiar example, the market for private homes, in order to build intuition.

The stock of existing owner-occupied homes is very large compared to the number of new homes built in any given year. The number of new homes varies greatly with economic conditions but is never more than a few percent of the existing housing stock—if only because of the limited number of rough carpenters, finish carpenters, plumbers, electricians, and so on. The demand for private homes depends primarily on three factors: income, mortgage interest rates, and taxes. When income rises, more families buy first homes or trade up to larger ones. Since a home is a long-term investment, families look ahead, increasing their demand for housing when they expect high incomes to persist. Housing demand is extraordinarily sensitive to mortgage interest rates. Since mortgage payments are almost entirely composed of interest, a small rise in interest rates can cause a big drop in housing demand. Finally, owner-occupied housing may benefit from some preferential tax treatments, such as allowing first-time buyers to use the proceeds from cashing in an RRSP toward the purchase of a home, without a tax penalty.

Suppose mortgage rates drop. The monthly cost of homeownership drops and the demand for housing rises. There isn't any way to make new homes appear overnight, so the initial reaction is an increase in the price of existing homes. The higher prices give builders the incentive to start new projects—which comprise the flow of new housing investment. Over time, enough homes are built to satisfy the new higher level of demand, and housing prices and new housing investment drop back toward their original levels. (Since the stock of housing would now be larger, there will now be more homes around to wear out. The home repair and remodelling business will be permanently greater. In other words, housing depreciation increases, so gross housing investment will have increased permanently even if net housing investment returns to its original level.)

Two results from this informal analysis apply to investment more generally. First, investment is a principal conduit of monetary policy into the goods markets. Interest rates are a prime determinant of the cost of owning capital. Loose monetary policy lowers interest rates, lessens the cost of owning capital, and increases the demand for capital. Second, fiscal policy in the form of lower taxes on capital can directly increase investment.

As we move into the formal analysis you may find it helpful to refer back to two familiar concepts. In what follows, the *price of capital* is a generalization of the price of a house and the *rental cost of capital* generalizes the example of a *monthly mortgage payment*.

### The Desired Capital Stock: Overview

In Part 2 of this textbook, we made extensive use of the production function, which tells us that a typical firm uses capital and labour to produce goods and services. In deciding

## Investment: Gross, Net, and More Inclusive Concepts

The distinction between *gross* and *net* investment is essential even though the difference, depreciation, is hard to measure. Again using the bathtub metaphor, the flow from the faucet is gross investment and the water down the drain is depreciation. The difference between inflow and outflow (gross investment less depreciation) is net investment. Aggregate supply depends on net investment, since in the long run net investment determines the capital stock. Aggregate demand, in contrast, depends on gross investment—a job building an additional machine or building a replacement machine is still a job.

Depreciation is more than just the physical wear and tear that results from use and age. A piece of capital may become economically obsolete, for instance, because input prices change—as gas-guzzlers became obsolete when oil prices increased. Economic depreciation may be much more rapid than physical depreciation. Technological obsolescence may also cause rapid economic depreciation. This is particularly true of computers, for which quality improvements have been dramatic.

The rate of depreciation depends on the type of capital. For example, structures have a useful life of decades, while office equipment has a life of only a few years. This has an important implication: If investment shifts toward capital goods with a short life (e.g., computers), then those goods make up a larger share of the capital stock and, as a result, the overall rate of depreciation will rise. This is what happened in Canada starting in the 1980s.

Although it is traditional, the focus on private sector additions to the capital stock in this chapter takes a too-restricted view of investment in two respects. First, it ignores *government investment*. As anyone who attends a public school or travels on the public highways can tell, government investment also contributes to economic productivity. There has been much recent work on the productivity of government capital, and there is no question that government investment should be included in aggregate investment. Estimates are that the government capital stock is about 15 to 20 percent of the private capital stock; therefore, Canadian capital stock and investment are 15 to 20 percent larger than the magnitudes discussed in this chapter.

Second, individuals invest not only in physical capital but also in *human capital,* in increasing the productive capacity of people through schooling and training. Recall that we discussed human capital when studying growth theory in Chapter 4. There is much evidence that this investment, like that in physical capital, yields a positive real return; indeed, the return on human capital typically exceeds that on physical capital.

In thinking about investment as spending that increases future productivity, we should look beyond just private sector gross investment.

**rental (user) cost of capital**
The cost of using one more unit of capital in production.

how much capital to use in production, firms have to balance the contribution that more capital makes to revenues against the cost incurred by using more capital. Remember that the marginal product of capital is the increase in output that results from increasing capital use by one unit. We define the **rental (user) cost of capital** as the cost incurred from using one more unit of capital in the production process.

Whether a firm actually buys its own capital or leases it, the rental cost is the right measure of the opportunity cost.[1] As long as the value of the marginal product of capital is above the rental cost, it pays the firm to add to its capital stock. Thus the firm will keep investing until the value of the output produced by adding one more unit of capital is equal to the cost of using that capital—the rental cost of capital.

To derive the rental cost of capital, we think of the firm as financing the purchase of the capital by borrowing, at an interest rate, $i$. In the presence of inflation, the nominal dollar value of capital rises over time, so the real cost of using capital over a year is the nominal interest payment less the change in the nominal value of capital. At the time that a firm makes an investment, the nominal interest rate is known, but the inflation rate over the *coming* year is not. So the firm must base its decision on the expected inflation rate, $\pi^e$. In other words, the real cost of borrowing is the expected real interest rate $r = i - \pi^e$. Of course, capital also wears out over time, so the cost of depreciation must be added. A conventional assumption is that depreciation is $d$ percent per year. Thus, the complete formula for rental cost is $rc = r + d = i - \pi^e + d$. (Taxes matter, too. They're discussed below.)

Firms desire to add capital until the marginal return to the last unit added drops to the rental cost of capital. Recall that the diminishing marginal product of capital means that the *marginal* product of capital drops as capital is increased. Figure 15-2 shows a *marginal-product-of-capital curve*. A high rental cost can be justified only by a high marginal product. So an increase of the rental cost from $rc_0$ to $rc_1$ decreases the desired capital stock from $K_0^*$ to $K_1^*$.

---

### FIGURE 15-2

Given the marginal-product-of-capital curve, a higher rental cost of capital corresponds to a lower desired capital stock.

**MARGINAL PRODUCT OF CAPITAL IN RELATION TO THE CAPITAL STOCK**

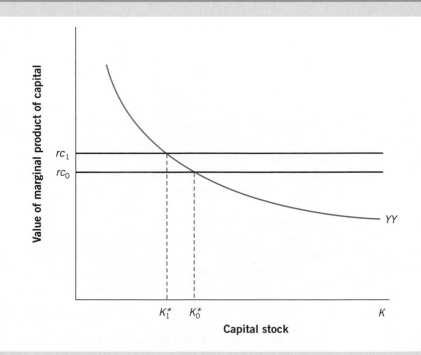

---

[1] Even if the firm finances the investment out of profits it has made in the past—retained earnings—it should still think of the interest rate as the basic cost of using the new capital, since it could have loaned those funds and earned interest on them or paid them out as dividends to shareholders.

An increase in the size of the economy moves the entire marginal-product-of-capital curve to the right, as in Figure 15-3. The rightward shift increases the demand for capital at any given rental cost.

The general relationship among the desired capital stock, $K^*$, the rental cost of capital, $rc$, and the level of output is given by

$$K^* = g(rc, Y) \qquad (1)$$

where an increase in the rental cost decreases $K^*$ and an increase in GDP increases $K^*$.

---

**FIGURE 15-3**

An increase in the size of the economy shifts the marginal-product curve to the right, increasing the desired capital stock at any given rental cost.

SHIFT OF THE MARGINAL-PRODUCT SCHEDULE

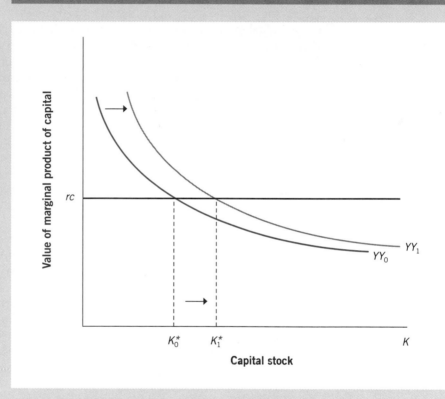

## Expected Output

Equation (1) shows that the desired capital stock depends on the level of output. However, that must be the level of output for some future period, during which the capital will be in production. For some investments, the future time at which the output will be produced is a matter of months or only weeks. For other investments, such as power stations, the future time at which the output will be produced is years away.

This suggests that the notion of permanent income (in this case, permanent output) introduced in Chapter 14 is relevant to investment as well as consumption. The demand for capital, which depends on the normal or permanent level of output, thus depends on expectations of future output levels, rather than the current level of output. However, current output is likely to affect expectations of permanent output.

www.fin.gc.ca/toce/2003/
taxratered_e.html

## Taxes and the Rental Cost of Capital

In addition to interest and depreciation, the rental cost of capital is affected by taxes. The two main tax variables are the corporate income tax and the investment tax credit. The corporate income tax is essentially a proportional tax on profits; that is, the firm pays a proportion, say, $t$, of its profits in taxes. In Canada, the general federal corporate tax rate was 28 percent in 2000, and was gradually reduced to 21 percent, effective January 2004. There are also provincial corporate tax rates that vary by province.

Surprisingly, a good argument can be made that the corporate income tax has no effect on the desired stock of capital. In the presence of the corporate income tax, the firm will want to equate the *after-tax* value of the marginal product of capital with the *after-tax* rental cost of capital in order to ensure that the marginal contribution of the capital to profits is equal to the marginal cost of using it. The key to understanding the impact of the corporate income tax is the fact that interest payments are deducted from the firm's income before its taxes are calculated.

Now consider the following example: Suppose there is no corporate income tax, no inflation, no depreciation, and an interest rate of 10 percent. The desired capital stock will be that level of the capital stock, say, $K_0^*$, such that the marginal product of capital is 10 percent. Next suppose that the corporate income tax rises to 34 percent and the interest rate remains constant. At the capital stock $K_0^*$, the after-tax marginal product of capital is now 6.6 percent (since 34 percent of the profits are paid in taxes). However, if the interest rate stays at 10 percent and the firm gets to deduct 34 percent of its interest payments from taxes, the after-tax cost of capital will be 6.6 percent too. In this example, the desired capital stock is unaffected by the rate of corporate taxation.

However, this sharp message is no longer true when investment is financed in part by equity, as it often is. When dividends are paid out to equity holders, they are not deducted from the firm's income for tax purposes. *This means that the cost of capital tends to rise with the corporate tax rate.*

The second tool of investment tax policy, the investment tax credit, was largely in place in Canada until the tax reform of the 1980s. There are still some investment tax credits in Canada, the most prominent of which is the research and development (R&D) tax credit. It allows firms to deduct from their taxes a fraction, say, 10 percent, of their investment expenditures in each year. Thus, a firm spending $1 million for investment purposes in a given year could deduct 10 percent of the $1 million, or $100,000, from the taxes it would otherwise have to pay the federal government. The investment tax credit reduces the price of a capital good to the firm, since the federal government returns to the firm a proportion of the cost of each capital good. The investment tax credit therefore reduces the rental cost of capital.

## The Effects of Fiscal and Monetary Policy on the Desired Capital Stock

Equation (1) states that the desired capital stock increases when the expected level of output rises and when the rental cost of capital falls. The rental cost of capital, in turn, falls when the real interest rate and the rate of depreciation fall and when the investment tax credit rises. An increase in the corporate tax rate is likely, through the equity route, to reduce the desired capital stock.

The major significance of these results is that they imply that monetary and fiscal policy affect the desired capital stock. Fiscal policy exerts an effect through both the corporate tax rate and the investment tax credit.

## POLICY IN *ACTION*

### Investment and the Tax System

Beginning in approximately 2000, the federal government, along with some of the provincial governments, began cutting corporate and personal tax rates. The aim is to encourage business expansion, through increased investment in the capital stock. These tax cuts were well received by business leaders in Canada. However, in an interesting article, Duanjie Chen and Jack Mintz of the C.D. Howe Institute argue that the effective tax rate on capital in Canada is still very high, thus discouraging further investment in the capital stock. Effective tax rates are calculated by following a sophisticated economic model, and the rates can differ substantially from the statutory tax rates that have been lowered recently in Canada.

According to information in this C.D. Howe article, the aggregate effective tax rate on capital in Canada was 24.3 percent in 2002 and will drop to 22.6 percent in 2006. However, the same aggregate tax rate in the United States is estimated to have been only 16.8 percent in 2002. The authors conclude that, even though Canada has lowered its statutory tax rates, the effective tax rate on capital in Canada is still too high to encourage further substantial investment increases.*

---

*Duanjie Chen and Jack M. Mintz, "How Canada's Tax System Discourages Investment," C.D. Howe Institute, *Backgrounder*, no. 68, January 2003. This article can be obtained from www.cdhowe.org/pdf/backgrounder_68.pdf.

Fiscal policy also affects capital demand by its overall effects on the position of the *IS* curve and thus on the interest rate. A high-tax–low-government-spending policy keeps the real interest rate low and encourages the demand for capital. A low-tax–high-government-spending policy that produces large deficits raises the real interest rate and discourages the demand for capital.

Monetary policy affects capital demand by affecting the market interest rate. A lowering of the nominal interest rate by the Bank of Canada (given the expected inflation rate) induces firms to desire more capital. This expansion in capital demand, in turn, will affect investment spending.

### The Stock Market and the Cost of Capital

Rather than borrowing, a firm can also raise the financing it needs to pay for its investment by selling shares, or equity. The people buying the shares expect to earn a return from dividends and/or, if the firm is successful, from the increase in the market value of their shares, that is, **capital gains**.

**capital gains**
The amount an asset appreciates in value over time.

When its share price is high, a company can raise a lot of money by selling relatively few shares. When stock prices are low, the firm has to sell more shares to raise a given amount of money. The owners of the firm, the existing shareholders, will be more willing to have the firm sell shares to raise new money if it has to sell few shares to do so, that is, if the price is high. Thus, we expect corporations to be more willing to sell equity to finance investment when the stock market is high than when it is low. That is why a booming stock market is good for investment.

## The *q* Theory of Investment

**q theory of investment**
Investment theory emphasizing that investment will be high when assets are valuable relative to their reproduction cost. The ratio of asset value to cost is called *q*.

The **q theory of investment** emphasizes this connection between investment and the stock market. The price of a share in a company is the price of a claim on the capital in the company. The managers of the company can, then, be thought of as responding to the price of the stock by producing more new capital—that is, investing—when the price of shares is high and as producing less new capital or not investing at all when the price of shares is low.

What is $q$?[2] It is an estimate of the value the stock market places on a firm's assets relative to the cost of producing those assets. In its simplest form, $q$ is the ratio of the market value of a firm to the replacement cost of capital. When the ratio is high, firms will want to produce more assets, so investment will be rapid. In fact, the most simple version of this theory has a stronger prediction than "high $q$ means high investment." Whenever $q$ is greater than 1, a firm should add physical capital because for each dollar's worth of new machinery, the firm can sell stock for $q$ dollars and pocket a profit $q - 1$. This implies a flood of investment whenever $q > 1$. In reality, adjustment costs make such a flood inefficient, so investment rises moderately with $q$.

## From Desired Capital Stock to Investment

http://active.boeing.com/
commercial/orders/
index.cfm

Figure 15-4 illustrates an increase in the demand for the stock of capital by a right-ward shift of the demand for capital schedule. At the initial capital stock, $K_0$, the price of capital is just high enough to generate enough investment, $I_0$ in panel (b), to replace depreciating capital. In the long run, the supply of new capital is very elastic so eventually the increase in demand will be met without much change in price. In the short run, the price rises to $P_1$, increasing the investment flow to $I_1$. Implicitly the unit of measurement in panel (a) is units of capital, so the shift from $K_0$ to $K_1$ might mean from 100 Boeing 737s to 150. The unit of measure meant in panel (b) is units

---

**BOX**

**15-3**

### The Demand for Capital: A Cobb-Douglas Example

The generic formula for the production function is $Y = AF(K, N)$. If you prefer to follow the discussion with a specific formula, you can use the *Cobb-Douglas production function*, $Y = AK^\theta N^{1-\theta}$, which, with $\theta \approx 0.30$, gives a very good approximation to the production function in Canada. Using the Cobb-Douglas, the marginal product of capital is $MPK = \theta AK^{\theta-1}N^{1-\theta} = \theta A(K/N)^{-(1-\theta)} = \theta Y/K$. We find the demand-for-capital function by setting marginal product equal to rental cost, $\theta Y/K = rc$, and solving for $K$. So for the Cobb-Douglas production function, the demand for capital can be written $K^* = g(rc, Y) = \theta Y/rc$.

---

[2] You will often see $q$ referred to as "Tobin's $q$." Nobel Prize winner James Tobin first put forth this way of connecting the stock market and investment.

BOX

**15-4**

## Temporary Investment Tax Credit Carries a Big Punch

It's natural to think that permanent changes to fiscal policy have bigger impacts than do temporary changes. However, the temporary investment tax credit provides an interesting counterexample. Imagine that, faced with a recession, the government decided to provide an investment tax credit. What is the effect of a temporary, as contrasted with a permanent, investment tax credit?

Suppose, as a firm manager, you were told you could get a 10 percent tax credit, *but only this year.* You would rush all your near-future capital spending plans into the current year. So a temporary credit gives a big boost to current investment. (Of course, the next few years might see substantially decreased investment, as the capital spending pipeline had been emptied.) In this way a temporary investment tax credit can be a particularly effective policy tool for boosting current investment spending. Unfortunately, governments are rarely able to so finely time tax changes.

of capital per period of time. The move from $I_0$ to $I_1$ would correspond to one new plane per year versus 10 new planes per year. Note that investment at rate $I_1$ needn't close the capital gap in a single period. The horizontal scales in panels (a) and (b) are not commensurable.

Why doesn't investment rise to instantaneously close the gap between the desired and existing capital stock? For one thing, the factors of production used to produce new capital are often themselves in limited short run supply. (When the Calgary area experienced a major construction boom in 2000, skilled tradespersons were working 10-hour days, seven days a week.) And many kinds of production just can't be sped up at any price, at least not in the short run.

*FIGURE 15-4*

### DEMAND FOR CAPITAL STOCK AND FLOW OF INVESTMENT

Panel (a) shows an increase in demand for the capital stock raising prices from $P_0$ to $P_1$ in the short run and raising the capital stock from $K_0$ to $K_1$ in the long run. Panel (b) shows the corresponding increase in investment flow.

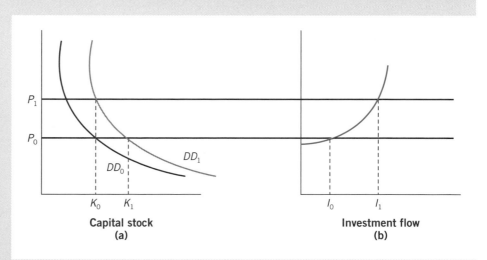

Capital stock
(a)

Investment flow
(b)

## Capital Stock Adjustment

**flexible accelerator model**

Asserts that firms plan their investment to close a fraction of the gap between their actual capital stock and their desired capital stock; a result is that more firms with a larger gap between their actual and desired capital stocks accumulate capital more quickly than other firms.

There are a number of hypotheses about the speed at which firms plan to adjust their capital stock over time; we single out the **flexible accelerator model**.[3] The basic notion behind this model is that the larger the gap between the existing capital stock and the desired capital stock, the more rapid a firm's rate of investment.

According to the flexible accelerator model, firms plan to close a fraction, $\lambda$, of the gap between the desired and actual capital stocks each period. Denote the capital stock at the end of the last period by $K_{-1}$. The gap between the desired and actual capital stocks is $(K^* - K_{-1})$. The firm plans to add to last period's capital stock $K_{-1}$ a fraction $\lambda$ of the gap $(K^* - K_{-1})$ so that the actual capital stock at the end of the current period $K$ will be

$$K = K_{-1} + \lambda(K^* - K_{-1}) \tag{2}$$

To increase the capital stock from $K_{-1}$ to the level of $K$ indicated by equation (2), the firm has to achieve the amount of net investment, $I \equiv K - K_{-1}$, indicated by equation (2). We can therefore write net investment as

$$I = K - K_{-1} = \lambda(K^* - K_{-1}) \tag{3}$$

which is the gradual adjustment formulation of net investment.

In Figure 15-5 we show how the capital stock adjusts from an initial level of $K_1$ to the desired level $K^*$. The upper panel shows the stock of capital and the lower shows the corresponding flow of investment. The assumed speed of adjustment is $\lambda = 0.5$. Starting from $K_1$, one-half the gap between target capital and current actual capital is made up in every period. First-period net investment is therefore $0.5(K^* - K_{-1})$. In the second period, investment will be one-half the previous period's rate, since the gap has been reduced by half. Investment continues until the actual capital stock reaches the level of target capital. The larger $\lambda$ is, the faster the gap is reduced.

In equation (3), we have reached our goal of deriving an investment function that shows current investment spending determined by the desired stock of capital, $K^*$, and the actual stock of capital, $K_{-1}$. Any factor that increases the desired capital stock increases the rate of investment. Therefore, an increase in expected output, a reduction in the real interest rate, or an increase in the investment tax credit will each increase the rate of investment. The flexible accelerator demonstrates that investment contains aspects of **dynamic behaviour**—that is, behaviour that depends on values of economic variables in periods other than the current period. Empirical evidence shows that the dynamics of the flexible accelerator are somewhat too rigid—for example, investment takes about two years to peak after a change in capital demand—but the basic principle of gradual adjustment is clear.

**dynamic behaviour**

Behaviour that depends on values of economic variables in periods other than the current period.

## 15-2 | INVESTMENT SUBSECTORS—BUSINESS FIXED, RESIDENTIAL, AND INVENTORY

Figure 15-6 demonstrates the volatility of each of the three investment subsectors: *business fixed investment*, *residential investment*, and *inventory investment*. Fluctuations are on the order of several percent of GDP. Business fixed investment is

---

[3] The flexible accelerator model can be given a rigorous justification as a response to adjustment costs, but we don't pursue this avenue.

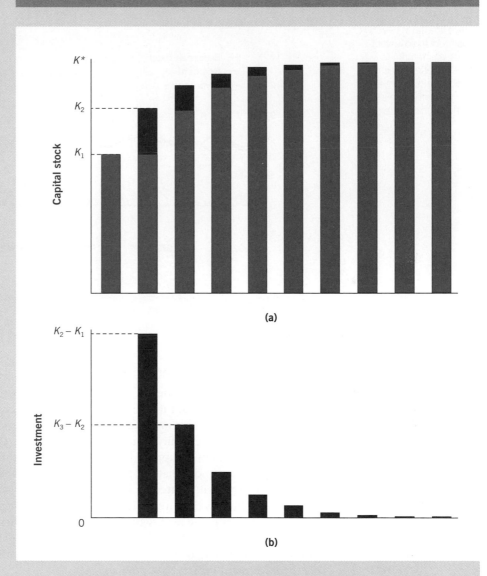

**FIGURE 15-5**

If the desired capital stock changes, the capital stock adjusts to the new desired level over time, with investment in each period determined by the speed-of-adjustment parameter, λ.

**ADJUSTMENT OF THE CAPITAL STOCK**

(a)

(b)

the largest of the three, but all three subsectors undergo swings that are substantial fractions of swings in GDP. Inventory investment is considerably smaller than the other two portions, but as you can see, it is particularly volatile.

## Business Fixed Investment

Figure 15-6 shows fixed investment as a share of GDP. In a recession, the share of investment in GDP falls sharply; then investment begins to rise as the recovery gets under way. The cyclical relationships extend much further back in history. For instance, gross investment fell to just over 4 percent of GDP in the Great Depression year 1933.

## FIGURE 15-6

### COMPONENTS OF INVESTMENT AS A PERCENTAGE OF GDP, 1961–2002

Since the late 1970s, business fixed investment has been the largest percentage of GDP. Inventory investment is rather small, and sometimes negative.

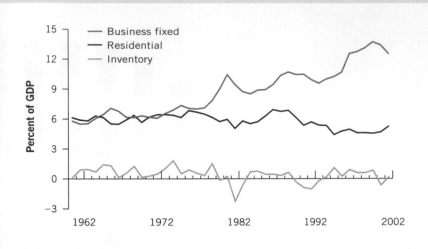

SOURCE: CANSIM II: Business fixed: V1992240; residential: V1992239; inventory: V1992245; measured as a percentage of GDP: V1992259.

## The Timing of Investment

The flexible accelerator model of investment provides a useful summary of the dynamics of investment, but it does not sufficiently emphasize the timing of investment. Because investment is undertaken for the long run and often takes several years to complete, there is flexibility as to the dates on which the investment is actually undertaken. For example, suppose that there was an investment tax credit in place, and that it was announced that this tax credit would be substantially increased a year from now. A firm that wanted to have machinery in place three years from now would be wise to delay the investment for a year, and make or acquire the machinery at a faster rate during the next two years, receiving a higher investment tax credit as a reward for waiting one year. Similarly, if a firm anticipated that the cost of borrowing next year would be much lower than this year, it might wait a year to undertake the investment project.

The flexibility in the timing of investment leads to an interesting contrast between the effects of an investment tax credit and the income tax on investment and consumption, respectively. We saw in Chapter 14 that a permanent change in income tax has a much larger impact on consumption than a transitory change. However, the rate of investment during the period that a temporary investment tax credit is in effect would be higher than the rate of investment that would occur over the same period during which a permanent credit of the same magnitude was in effect. The reason is that if firms knew that the investment tax credit was temporary, they would advance the timing of their planned investments in order to take advantage of the higher tax credit during the current period. If there was a permanent change in the investment tax credit, then the desired capital stock would rise and there would be more investment, but there would not be a bunching of investment.

BOX

## 15-5

## Credit Rationing

In the *IS-LM* model, interest rates are the only channel of transmission between financial markets and aggregate demand. Credit rationing is an important additional channel of transmission of monetary policy.* Credit rationing takes place when lenders limit the amount individuals can borrow, even though the borrowers are willing to pay the going interest rate on their loans.

Credit rationing can occur for two different reasons. First, a lender often cannot tell whether a particular customer (or the project the customer is financing) is good or bad. A bad customer will default on the loan and not repay it. Given the risk of default, the obvious answer seems to be to raise the interest rate.

However, raising interest rates works the wrong way: Honest or conservative customers are deterred from borrowing because they realize their investments are not profitable at higher interest rates. But customers who are reckless or dishonest will borrow because they do not in any case expect to pay if the project turns out badly. However carefully they try to evaluate their customers, the lenders cannot altogether escape this problem. The answer is to limit the amount loaned to any one customer. Most customers get broadly the same interest rate (with some adjustments), but the amount of credit they are allowed is rationed, according to both the kind of security the customer can offer and the propects for the economy.

When times are good, banks lend cheerfully because they believe that the average customer will not default. When the economy turns down, credit rationing intensifies—and this may happen even though interest rates decline.

Credit rationing provides another channel for monetary policy. If lenders perceive that the Bank of Canada is shifting to restraint and higher interest rates to cool down the economy, lenders fearing a slowdown will tighten credit. Conversely, if they believe that policy is expansionary and that times will be good, they ease credit, via both lower interest rates and expanded credit rationing.[†]

A second type of credit rationing can occur when the central bank imposes credit limits on commercial banks and other lenders. Banks are then not allowed to expand their loans during a given period by more than, say, 5 percent or even less. Such a credit limit can bring a boom to an abrupt end.

Credit controls thus are an emergency brake for the central bank. They work, but they do so in a very blunt way. For that reason, their use is very infrequent and remains reserved for occasions when dramatic, fast effects are desired.

---

*For a comprehensive survey on credit rationing, see Dwight Jaffee and Joseph Stiglitz, "Credit Rationing," in Ben Friedman and Frank Hahn (eds.), *Handbook of Monetary Economics* (Amsterdam: North-Holland, 1990).

†For a discussion of these and other points regarding credit and monetary policy see *Credit, Interest Rate Spreads and the Monetary Policy Transmission Mechanism: Proceedings of a conference* (Ottawa: Bank of Canada, 1995).

## Irreversibility and the Timing of Investment Decisions

Beneath the stock-demand-for-capital-leads-to-investment-flow model lies the idea that capital is "putty-putty." Goods are in a malleable form that can be transformed into capital by investment and then easily transformed back into general goods. Much capital is better described as "putty-clay." Once capital is built, it can't be used for much except its original purpose. A warehouse (putty-putty) may have high-valued alternative uses as a factory or an office building. A jetliner (putty-clay) isn't of much use except for flying. The essence of putty-clay investment is that it is irreversible. An irreversible investment will be executed not when it becomes merely profitable but, rather, when it does not pay to wait for any further improvement in profitability.[4]

## Residential Investment

Figure 15-7 shows residential investment spending as a percentage of GDP, together with the nominal mortgage interest rate. Residential investment is low when mortgage interest rates are high, and it declines in all recessions.

Residential investment consists of the building of single-family and multi-family dwellings, which we call *housing* for short. Housing is distinguished as an asset by its long life. Consequently, investment in housing in any one year tends to be a very small proportion—about 3 percent—of the existing *stock* of housing. The theory of residential investment starts by considering the demand for the existing stock of housing.

The demand for the housing stock depends on the net real return obtained by owning housing. The gross return—before taking costs into account—consists either of rent, if the housing is rented out, or of the implicit return that the homeowner receives by living in the home plus capital gains arising from increases in the value of the housing. In turn, the costs of owning the housing consist of interest costs, typically

---

### FIGURE 15-7

When the conventional mortgage interest rate rose sharply in the early 1980s and again in the early 1990s, residential investment fell in response.

**RESIDENTIAL INVESTMENT AND MORTGAGE INTEREST RATES, 1961-2002**

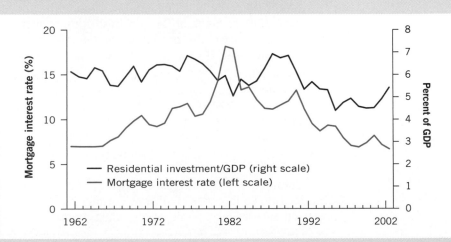

Source: Residential investment: CANSIM II V1992239; as a percentage of GDP: CANSIM II V1992259; five-year conventional mortgage rate: CANSIM II V122497.

---

[4] This statement is based on a sophisticated argument in terms of financial option theory. See Robert Pindyck, "Irreversible Investment, Capacity and Choice and the Value of the Firm," *American Economic Review*, December 1988, and Avinash K. Dixit and Robert S. Pindyck, *Investment Under Uncertainty* (Princeton, NJ: Princeton University Press, 1993).

the mortgage interest rate, plus any real estate taxes and depreciation. These costs are deducted from the gross return and, after tax adjustments, constitute the net return. An increase in the net return on housing, caused, for example, by a reduction in the mortgage interest rate, makes housing a more attractive form in which to hold wealth.

## OPTIONAL

### THE BUSINESS INVESTMENT DECISION: THE VIEW FROM THE TRENCHES

Businesspeople making investment decisions typically use discounted cash flow analysis.[5] Consider a businessperson deciding whether to build and equip a new factory. The first step is to figure out how much it will cost to get the factory into working order and how much revenue the factory will bring in each year after it starts operation.

For simplicity, consider a very short lived project, one that costs $100 to set up in the first year and then generates $50 in revenue (after paying for labour and raw materials) in the second year and a further $80 in the third year. By the end of the third year, the factory has disintegrated.

Should the project be undertaken? Discounted cash flow analysis says that the revenues received in later years should be discounted to the present in order to calculate their present value. If the interest rate is 10 percent, $110 a year from now is worth the same as $100 now. Why? Because if $100 is lent out today at 10 percent, a year from now the lender will end up with $110. To calculate the value of the project, the firm calculates the project's present discounted value at the interest rate at which it can borrow. If the present value is positive, the project is undertaken.

Suppose that the relevant interest rate is 12 percent. The calculation of the present discounted value of the investment project is shown in Table 15-1. The $50 received in year 2 is worth only $44.65 today: $1 a year from now is worth $1/1.12 = 0.893 today, and so $50 a year from now is worth $44.65. The present value of the $80 received in year 3 is calculated similarly. The table shows that the present value of the net revenue received from the project is positive ($8.41); thus, the firm should undertake the project. Note: If the interest rate had been much higher (say, 18 percent) the decision would have been not to undertake the investment. We thus see that the higher the interest rate, the less likely the firm will be to undertake any given investment project.

At any time, each firm has an array of possible investment projects and estimates of the costs and revenues from those projects. Depending on the level of the interest rate, the firm will want to undertake some of the projects and not undertake others. Adding the investment demands of all of the firms in the economy, we obtain the total demand for investment in the economy at each interest rate.

**TABLE 15-1** — **DISCOUNTED CASH FLOW ANALYSIS AND PRESENT VALUE** (dollars)

| | Year 1 | Year 2 | Year 3 | Present Discounted Value |
|---|---|---|---|---|
| Cash or revenue | −100 | +50 | +80 | |
| Present value of $1 | 1 | $1/1.12 = 0.893$ | $1/1.12^2 = 0.797$ | |
| Present value of costs or revenue | −100 | $50 \times 0.893$ = 44.65 | $80 \times 0.797$ = 63.76 | $-100 + 44.65 + 63.76$ = 8.41 |

[5] Discounted cash flow analysis and the rental-cost-equals-marginal-product-of-capital models are simply different ways of thinking about the same decision process. You will sometimes hear businesspeople discussing what we call the *marginal product of capital* as the *internal rate of return*.

## Monetary Policy and Residential Construction

Monetary policy has powerful effects on the housing market. Most of the loans obtained to finance new construction are mortgages provided by financial institutions, particularly chartered banks. When interest rates rise, the supply of mortgage funds is affected in two ways. First, the interest cost to financial institutions of attracting deposits rises as the return on alternative investments increases. Second, the proportion of assets channelled into mortgages falls as the yields on other securities rise.

The demand for housing is sensitive to interest rates, and the reason for this can be seen in Table 15-2. This table shows the monthly payment on a $100,000 mortgage with a 25-year amortization at various interest rates. Notice that the monthly payment nearly doubles when the interest rate doubles. Thus, an essential component of the cost of owning a house rises almost proportionately with the interest rate. It is, therefore, not surprising that the demand for housing is very sensitive to the interest rate.

**TABLE 15-2**

### MONTHLY PAYMENTS ON MORTGAGES

| Interest rate | 5% | 10% | 15% | 20% |
|---|---|---|---|---|
| Monthly payment | $584 | $908 | $1280 | $1816 |

Note: The assumed mortgage is $100,000, paid back over 25 years with equal monthly payments.

The above statement has to be qualified somewhat, since we should be concerned with the real and not the nominal interest cost of buying a house—and certainly much of the rise in the mortgage interest rate is a result of increases in the expected rate of inflation. However, the nominal interest rate also affects the homeowner. This results from the fact that a mortgage contract typically requires the borrower to pay a fixed amount each month over the lifetime of the mortgage. Even if the nominal interest rate has risen only because the expected rate of inflation has risen—and thus the real rate is constant—the payments that have to be made today by a borrower increase, but the inflation has not yet happened. Thus, the real payments made today by a borrower rise when the nominal interest rate rises, even if the real rate does not rise. Given the higher real monthly payments when the nominal interest rate rises, we should expect the nominal interest rate also to affect housing demand.

## Inventory Investment

Inventories consist of raw materials, goods in the process of production, and completed goods held by firms in anticipation of the products' sale.

Firms hold inventories for several reasons:

▶ Sellers hold inventories to meet future demand for goods, because goods cannot be instantly manufactured or obtained to meet demand.

▶ Inventories are held because it is less costly for a firm to order goods less frequently in large quantities than to order small quantities frequently—just as the average householder finds it is useful to keep several days' worth of groceries in the house to avoid having to visit the supermarket daily.

BOX

15-6

## Monetary Policy and Residential Construction

As we noted in the text, monetary policy has powerful effects on the housing market, as the demand for housing is very sensitive to short run interest rate changes brought about by monetary policy. After the events of September 11, 2001, monetary policy pushed interest rates to a level that had not been seen in almost 40 years. Almost immediately, residential construction began to increase. The increase was dramatic enough that many people were saying that the Canadian economy was going through a residential construction boom, as consumers took advantage of the low financing costs to move into the housing market or to trade up to more expensive housing.

The extent of the effect of this interest rate decline on residential construction can be seen in the figure below, which plots the five-year conventional mortgage interest rate with the ratio of residential construction to GDP. This is the same data that was used in Figure 15-7, only now it is measured quarterly and over a much shorter period of time. By mid-2003, mortgage interest rates were still low, and the construction boom showed no signs of slowing down.

### THE EFFECTS OF MONETARY POLICY ON RESIDENTIAL CONSTRUCTION, 1995 Q1–2003 Q2 (QUARTERLY

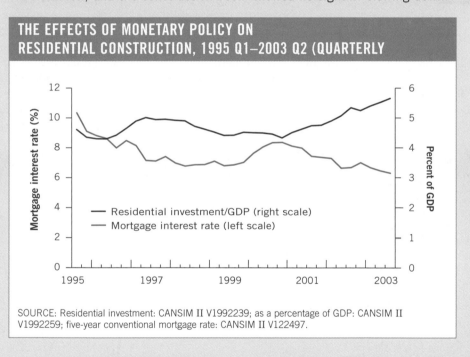

SOURCE: Residential investment: CANSIM II V1992239; as a percentage of GDP: CANSIM II V1992259; five-year conventional mortgage rate: CANSIM II V122497.

▶ Producers may hold inventories as a way of smoothing their production. Since it is costly to keep changing the level of output on a production line, producers may produce at a relatively steady rate even when demand fluctuates, building up inventories when demand is low and drawing them down when demand is high.

▶ Some inventories are held as an unavoidable part of the production process.

Firms have a desired ratio of inventories to final sales that depends on economic variables. The smaller the cost of ordering new goods and the greater the speed with which such goods arrive, the smaller the inventory-sales ratio. The inventory-sales ratio may also depend on the level of sales, with the ratio falling with sales because there is relatively less uncertainty about sales as sales increase.

Finally, there is the interest rate. Since firms carry inventories over time, the firms must tie up resources in order to buy and hold the inventories. There is an interest cost involved in such inventory holding, and the desired inventory-sales ratio should be expected to fall with increases in the interest rate.

### The Accelerator Model

**accelerator model**

Asserts that investment spending is proportional to the change in output and is not affected by the cost of capital.

All of these considerations notwithstanding, inventory investment can be explained surprisingly well with the simple **accelerator model**. The accelerator model asserts that investment spending is proportional to the change in output and is not affected by the cost of capital, $I = \alpha(Y - Y_{-1})$.[6] Figure 15-8 compares inventory investment to the change in GDP. Much, but not all, inventory investment can be explained this way. The connection of the *level* of inventory investment to the *change* in output is an important channel adding to the overall volatility of the economy.

### Anticipated versus Unanticipated Inventory Investment

*Inventory investment* takes place when firms increase their inventories. The central aspect of inventory investment lies in the distinction between anticipated (desired) and unanticipated (undesired) investment. Inventory investment could be high in two circumstances. First, if sales are unexpectedly low, firms would find unsold inventories accumulating on their shelves; that constitutes unanticipated inventory investment. Second, inventory investment could be high because firms plan to build up inventories; that is anticipated or desired investment.

The two circumstances obviously have very different implications for the behaviour of aggregate demand. Unanticipated inventory investment is a result of unex-

---

## FIGURE 15-8

The simple accelerator model of inventory investment asserts that there is a relationship between the change in GDP and the level of inventory investment.

**THE CHANGE IN GDP AND THE LEVEL OF INVENTORY INVESTMENT, 1962–2002**

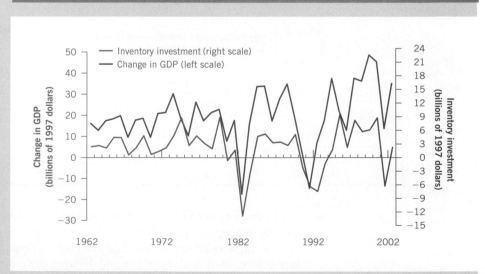

SOURCE: Inventory investment: CANSIM II V1992247; GDP: CANSIM II V1992259.

---

[6] The accelerator model is actually a special case of the flexible accelerator.

pectedly low aggregate demand. By contrast, planned inventory investment adds to aggregate demand. Thus, rapid accumulation of inventories could be associated with either rapidly declining aggregate demand or rapidly increasing aggregate demand.

### Inventories in the Business Cycle

Inventory investment fluctuates proportionately more in the business cycle than any other component of aggregate demand. In every post–World War II recession in Canada, there has been a decline in inventory investment between peak and trough. As a recession develops, demand slows down and firms add involuntarily to the stock of inventories. Thus, the inventory-sales ratio rises. Then production is cut, and firms meet demand by selling goods from inventories. At the end of every recession, firms were reducing their inventories, meaning that inventory investment was negative in the final quarter of every recession.

**inventory cycle**

Response of inventory investment to changes in sales that causes further changes in aggregate demand.

To understand the **inventory cycle,** consider the case of a hypothetical automobile dealer who sells, say, 30 cars per month and holds an average of one month's sales—namely, 30 cars—in inventory. As long as sales stay steady at 30 cars per month, the dealer will be ordering 30 cars each month from the factory. Now suppose sales drop to 25 cars per month, and it takes the dealer two months to respond to the change. During those two months, inventory will have climbed to 40 cars. In the future the dealer will want an inventory of only 25 cars on hand. Thus, when responding to the fall in demand, the dealer cuts the order from the factory from 30 cars to 10 in the third month to get the inventory back to one month's sales. After the desired inventory-sales ratio has been restored, the order will be 25 cars per month. We see in this extreme case how the drop in demand of 5 cars, instead of leading to a simple drop in car output of 5 cars per month, causes a drop in output of 20 cars in one month, followed by the longer run drop in output of 5 cars per month.

### Just-in-Time Inventory Management

**"just-in-time" inventory management**

Inventory management strategy; firms hold inventories for as short a time as possible by sending goods out as soon as they are produced, and ordering parts only as they are needed.

If inventories could be kept more closely in line with sales, or aggregate demand, fluctuations in inventory investment and in GDP would be reduced. As business methods are improving all the time, the hope is often expressed that new methods of management will enable firms to keep tighter control over their inventories and thus that the prospects for steadier growth can be improved. **"Just-in-time" inventory management** techniques, imported from Japan, emphasize the synchronization of suppliers and users of materials, thereby allowing firms to operate with small inventories, so production is "lean" in inventories. These improved methods help account for the downward trend in inventories. Indeed, in the 1990–91 recession, the inventory-final sales ratio increased very little, much less than in previous recessions.

## 15-3 | INVESTMENT AND AGGREGATE SUPPLY

Investment is an important component of aggregate demand. Investment also increases capital, increasing the productive capacity of the economy. Does investment matter for aggregate supply? In the short run, no, it doesn't. In the long run, yes, it does. A little back-of-the-envelope arithmetic can help us make sense of this apparent contradiction.

We saw in Box 15-1 that a year's worth of investment is typically about 1/15 of the capital stock. Suppose someone found a policy to increase investment by 25 percent more than it would have otherwise grown. (The historical record suggests no one has come up with an idea nearly this effective—but hope springs eternal!) Over the course of a year, the effect of the policy would be to increase capital by about 1/60 extra, or about 1.6 percent. Looking back at what we learned about growth accounting in Chapter 4 [see equation (2)], this would translate into an increase in GDP of about 4/10 of 1 percent. The notion that short run policy might increase investment by 25 percent is probably outlandish. The short run supply-side effect of any realistic policy will probably be too small to measure.

So claims of stimulating investment in hope of a short run supply-side effect are probably silly. But increasing investment may be among the most important tools for creating long-term prosperity. The effect of modest annual increases in the capital stock can cumulate to be quite large over long periods. We can see evidence by looking at the very high rates of investment as countries move into modern development with very high rates of growth sustained for considerable periods.

## Investment Around the World

One reason that high-growth countries are high-growth countries is because they devote a substantial fraction of their output to investment. Table 15-3 shows the ratio of gross fixed capital formation to GDP for several countries. The investment ratios are determined by both the demand for capital, as studied in this chapter, and the supply of savings.

http://strategis.ic.gc.ca/ SSG/ra01837e.html

Table 15-3 suggests that high rates of investment occur in rapidly growing countries but not necessarily in countries that have already become very wealthy. In both 1975 and 1997, Canada and the United States were wealthy countries with moderate growth rates. In 1975, Japan was a moderately well-off country with a high growth rate. Over this period, both Singapore and Korea grew very rapidly, due in part to their high rates of investment, but had not yet reached the income levels of the United States. In 1975, the two poor countries shown in the table, Bangladesh and Ethiopia, had investment rates too low to support rapid growth. By 1997, although both countries remained relatively poor, their investment rates had picked up considerably.

The relatively low rates of investment in Canada and the United States, compared to their international competitors, are a source of long run concern to policy makers.

| TABLE 15-3 | RATIO OF INVESTMENT TO OUTPUT (percent) | | |
|---|---|---|---|
| | Country | 1975 | 1997 |
| | Canada | 25.2 | 19.3 |
| | United States | 16.8 | 17.9 |
| | Japan | 32.8 | 28.5 |
| | Korea | 27.1 | 35.0 |
| | Singapore | 37.6 | 35.1 |
| | Bangladesh | 5.5 | 15.3 |
| | Ethiopia | 5.5 | 15.3 |

SOURCE: *International Financial Statistics Yearbook* 1998, ratio of gross fixed capital formation to GDP.

# Working with Data

In this chapter, we have stressed the important link between the real rate of interest and investment spending. For this exercise, you will need annual observations from 1961 to 2000 on business fixed investment (CANSIM II V1992240), the long-term government bond rate (CANSIM II V122487), and the Consumer Price Index (CANSIM II V735319). By now, you should know how to construct the inflation rate from the CPI and how to construct the real interest rate from the nominal interest rate and the inflation rate.

Use the real rate of interest and investment spending to construct a scatter plot. Can you see a negative relationship between these two variables? Now, construct two other plots. First, use data over the period 1961–81, and second, use data over the period 1982–2000. Can you see the negative relationship now?[7]

## CHAPTER SUMMARY

▶ Investment is spending that adds to the capital stock. Investment usually constitutes about 14 percent of aggregate demand in Canada, but fluctuations in investment account for a large share of business cycle movements in GDP. We analyze investment in three categories: business fixed investment, residential investment, and inventory investment.

▶ The neoclassical theory of business fixed investment sees the rate of investment being determined by the speed with which firms adjust their capital stocks toward the desired level. The desired capital stock is bigger the larger the expected output the firm plans to produce and the smaller the rental or user cost of capital.

▶ The real interest rate is the nominal (stated) interest rate minus the inflation rate.

▶ The rental cost of capital is higher the higher the real interest rate, the lower the price of the firm's stock, and the higher the depreciation rate of capital. Taxes also affect the rental cost of capital, in particular through the investment tax credit. The investment tax credit is, in effect, a government subsidy for investment.

▶ In practice, firms decide how much to invest using discounted cash flow analysis. This analysis gives answers that are consistent with those of the neoclassical approach.

▶ The accelerator model of investment is a special case of the gradual adjustment model of investment. It predicts that investment demand is proportional to the change in GDP.

▶ Because credit is rationed, firms' investment decisions are affected also by the state of their balance sheets, and thus by the amount of earnings they have retained.

---

[7] For those of you who are very curious, the reason this happens is that there is a structural break in the interest rate series in approximately 1981. This means that interest rates fell very quickly in 1981, and this masks the underlying relationship between the real rate of interest and investment spending.

▶ Empirical results show that business fixed investment responds with long lags to changes in output. The accelerator model, which does not take into account changes in the rental cost of capital, does almost as good a job of explaining investment as the more sophisticated neoclassical model.

▶ The theory of housing investment starts from the demand for the stock of housing. Demand is affected by wealth, the interest rates available on alternative investments, and the mortgage rate. The price of housing is determined by the interaction of the stock demand and the fixed stock supply of housing available at any given time. The rate of housing investment is determined by the rate at which builders supply housing at the going price.

▶ Housing investment is affected by monetary policy because housing demand is sensitive to the mortgage interest rate (real and nominal). Credit availability also plays a role.

▶ Monetary policy and fiscal policy both affect investment, particularly business fixed investment and housing investment. The effects take place through changes in real (and nominal, in the case of housing) interest rates and through tax incentives for investment.

▶ There are substantial lags in the adjustment of the investment spending to changes in output and other determinants of investment. Such lags are likely to increase fluctuations in GDP.

▶ Inventory investment fluctuates proportionately more than any other class of investment. Firms have a desired inventory-to-sales ratio. The ratio may get out of line if sales are unexpectedly high or low, and then firms change their production levels to adjust inventories. For instance, when aggregate demand falls at the beginning of a recession, inventories build up. Then when firms cut back production, output falls even more than did aggregate demand. This is the inventory cycle.

## KEY TERMS

business fixed investment, *299*
residential investment, *299*
inventory investment, *299*
flow of investment, *299*
stock of capital, *299*

rental (user) cost of capital, *301*
capital gains, *305*
*q* theory of investment, *306*
flexible accelerator model, *308*
dynamic behaviour, *308*

accelerator model, *316*
inventory cycle, *317*
"just-in-time" inventory
  management, *317*

## DISCUSSION QUESTIONS

1. If an economy has achieved its desired capital stock and wishes merely to maintain it, should any investment occur? If not, why not? If so, how much?

2. What effect has the recent shift toward investment in high-tech capital goods had on the rate of depreciation? Do you think there is a rate of depreciation associated with the stock of human capital?

3. If a firm invests out of retained profits rather than borrowed funds, will its investment decisions still be affected by the changes in the interest rate? Explain.

www.mcgrawhill.ca/college/dornbusch

4. The model of business fixed investment studied in Section 15-1 examines the benefits and costs to firms of owning capital goods. Its basic conclusion is that firms will increase their capital stock as long as the marginal product of their capital exceeds the marginal cost. What is Tobin's $q$, and how does it relate to the model in Section 15-1?

5. According to the description of business fixed investment in this chapter, how would you expect a firm's investment decisions to be affected by a sudden increase in the demand for its product? What factors would determine the speed of its reaction?

6. The number of small firms in the Canadian economy has grown substantially over the last decade. If small firms do, indeed, encounter more credit rationing than large firms, what effect might this have on output fluctuations (business cycles) in Canada?

7. **a.** Give at least two reasons why higher profits may increase the rate of investment.

   **b.** Explain why lenders may ration the quantity of credit rather than merely charge higher interest rates to more risky borrowers.

8. What is the relationship between the accelerator model of inventory investment and the flexible accelerator model of capital accumulation?

9. Can changes in inventories predict movements in the business cycle? Why does it matter whether these changes are planned or unplanned?

10. In the 1990–91 recession, the inventory-sales ratio did not rise appreciably. How do you explain this fact?

11. Why should (or shouldn't) policy makers be concerned about the relatively low levels of Canadian investment that have prevailed in the last decade?

12. In Chapter 6, you learned that when the aggregate supply curve is vertical, monetary policy has no effect on the real interest rate. Give two reasons why monetary policy might still affect investment even if it does not affect the interest rate.

## A P P L I C A T I O N    Q U E S T I O N S

1. Describe how a car rental agency would calculate the price at which it rents cars, and relate your description to the equation for rental cost given in the text.

2. The cash flows for an investment project are listed below. The firm will invest if the present value of the cash flows is positive.

   | Year 1 | Year 2 | Year 3 |
   |--------|--------|--------|
   | −200   | 100    | 120    |

   Should the firm undertake this project:

   **a.** If the interest rate is 5 percent?

   **b.** If the interest rate is 10 percent?

3. Suppose that an explicitly temporary tax credit is enacted. The tax credit is at the rate of 10 percent and lasts only one year.

   **a.** What is the effect of this tax measure on investment in the long run (say, after four or five years)?

   **b.** What is the effect in the current year and in the following year?

   **c.** How would your answers in (a) and (b) differ if the tax credit was permanent?

4. Given the following information, calculate Tobin's $q$ statistic: Let's suppose that a company has 1 million outstanding shares of stock, each valued at $25. Let us suppose also that the replacement cost of its physical capital stock is $18 million.

www.mcgrawhill.ca/college/dornbusch

    **a.** Should this firm invest (net) in more physical capital?

    **b.** Would your answer change if the replacement cost of its physical capital stock at this time was $25 million? $28 million?

**5.** (Optional) For this question use the Cobb-Douglas production function and the corresponding desired capital stock given by $K^* = g(rc, Y) = \theta Y/rc$. Assume that $\theta = 0.3$, $Y = \$5$ trillion, and $rc = 0.12$.

    **a.** Calculate the desired capital stock, $K^*$.

    **b.** Now suppose that $Y$ is expected to rise to $6 trillion. What is the corresponding desired capital stock?

    **c.** Suppose that the capital stock was at the desired level before the change in income was expected. Suppose further that $\lambda = 0.4$ in the gradual adjustment model of investment. What will be the rate of investment in the first year after expected income changes? In the second year?

    **d.** Does your answer in (**c**) refer to gross or net investment?

**6.** Go to CANSIM and retrieve the TSE 300 Index and business fixed investment. Calculate the average percentage change in each of these variables over the period 1961–91 and over the period 1992–2000. Discuss these averages in relation to the $q$ theory.

www.mcgrawhill.ca/college/dornbusch

# THE DEMAND FOR MONEY

## LEARNING OBJECTIVES

After reading and studying this chapter, you should be able to:

▶ *Understand that money is whatever asset is used in transactions, and that this varies over time and place.*

▶ *Understand that money demand is a demand for real balances, the number of nominal dollars divided by the price level.*

▶ *Understand that the demand for money rises with higher income and falls with higher nominal interest rates.*

**money**
The medium of exchange, whatever you use to pay for goods and services.

**W**hat is "money" and why does anyone want it?

This question is less frivolous than it appears, because economists use the term **money** in a special technical sense. By *money,* we mean the medium of exchange, whatever you use to pay for goods and services—the best example is cash. Be careful to distinguish the economists' use of the term *money* from the more everyday uses such as "I made a lot of money last year" (which really means income) or "That guy has a lot of money" (which really means wealth). When economists speak of the *demand for money*, we are asking about the stock of assets held as cash, chequing accounts, and closely related assets, specifically *not* generic wealth or income. Our interest is why consumers and firms hold money as opposed to an asset with a higher rate of return. The interaction between the demand for money and the supply of money provides the link through which the monetary authority, the Bank of Canada, affects output and prices.

Money is a means of payment or a medium of exchange. More informally, money is whatever is generally accepted in exchange. In the past, various commodities such as seashells, cocoa, or gold have been used as money.[1] Which assets constitute money? Discussions of the meaning of money are fluid for a simple reason: In the past, money was the means of payment generally accepted in exchange, but it also had the characteristic that it did not pay interest. Thus, the sum of currency and demand deposits (which did not earn interest in Canada) was the accepted definition of money for a long time. The aggregate is now known as *M*1.

In the course of the 1990s, however, a widening range of interest-bearing assets also became chequable. That has forced an ongoing review of where to draw the line between assets that form part of our definition of money and those that are just financial assets and not money proper. The issue is important not only conceptually but also for the evaluation of which monetary aggregate the Bank of Canada should try to control.

## 16-1 | COMPONENTS OF THE MONEY STOCK

**M1**
Those claims that can be used directly, instantly, and without restrictions to make payments.

**liquid asset**
An asset that can be used immediately, conveniently, and cheaply to make payments.

**M2**
*M*1 plus personal savings accounts and non-personal notice deposits.

There is a vast array of financial assets in any economy, from currency to complicated claims on other financial assets. The Bank of Canada publishes data on several monetary aggregates that are used as measures of the money supply. The major aggregates are shown in Table 16-1.[2]

*M*1 comprises those claims that can be used *directly, instantly,* and *without restrictions* to make payments. These claims are liquid. An **asset is liquid** if it can immediately, conveniently, and cheaply be used for making payments. *M*1 corresponds most closely to the traditional definition of money as a means of payment. *M*2 is a broader definition of the money supply that includes personal savings accounts and non-personal notice deposits.[3]

---

[1] One of the most unusual items ever used for money is the Yap Stone. This is a stone so big that it has a hole in the middle so that it can be carried with a large pole on the shoulders of two men. It is on display at the Bank of Canada Museum in Ottawa.

[2] All of the data in Table 16-1, as well as a wealth of other data, is available at the Bank of Canada's Internet site at www.bankofcanada.ca/en/wfsgen.htm.

[3] A notice deposit is an account on which the bank reserves the right to require notice before withdrawal can be made. Personal savings accounts have such a provision, but it is not normally enforced.

**TABLE 16-1**

| COMPONENTS OF THE MONEY STOCK, DECEMBER 2002 (billions of dollars, month-end) | | |
|---|---|---|
| Currency | $38.97 | |
| Personal chequing accounts | 28.72 | |
| Current accounts | 70.32 | |
| **M1** | | **138.01** |
| | | |
| M1 | 138.01 | |
| Non-personal notice deposits | 54.92 | |
| Personal savings deposits | 372.11 | |
| **M2** | | **570.04** |
| | | |
| M2 | 570.04 | |
| Deposits at trust and mortgage loan companies | 8.35 | |
| Deposits at credit unions and caisses populaires | 122.97 | |
| Annuities and deposits at government-owned savings institutions | 51.73 | |
| Money market mutual funds | 60.86 | |
| **M2+** | | **813.95** |
| | | |
| M2 | 570.04 | |
| Chartered bank non-personal term deposits plus foreign currency deposits | 206.41 | |
| **M3** | | **776.45** |

SOURCE: Bank of Canada Internet site: www.bankofcanada.ca/en/wfsgen.htm.

**M3**
Includes all Canadian dollar deposits in chartered banks and foreign currency deposits held by residents.

**M2+**
M2 plus deposits in other financial institutions such as trust companies, credit unions, and caisses populaires.

www.bankofcanada.ca/en/wfsgen.htm

Table 16-1 also shows the broader definition of the money supply, **M3**. M3 includes all Canadian dollar deposits in chartered banks and foreign currency deposits held by residents. The components of M3 that are not part of M1 or M2 are in general less liquid in that they cannot immediately and conveniently be used for making payments.

Although M2 includes the major assets that serve as means of payment, or can easily be converted into a means of payment, it includes only deposits in the chartered banks. **M2+** includes deposits in other financial institutions such as trust companies and credit unions.

In addition to the major monetary aggregates shown in Table 16-1, the Bank of Canada has published statistics on some new aggregates: $M2^{++}$ is equal to $M2^+$ plus Canada Savings Bonds plus non-money market mutual funds. $M1+$ is equal to $M1$ plus chequeable notice deposits held at chartered banks plus all chequable deposits at trust and mortgage loan companies, credit unions, and caisses populaires (excluding deposits of these institutions). Finally, $M1^{++}$ consists of $M1^+$ plus non-chequable notice deposits held at chartered banks, trust and mortgage loan companies, credit unions, and caisses populaires, with some adjustments. You are urged to go to the Bank of Canada Internet site at www.bankofcanada.ca/en/wfsgen.htm to see first-hand how all of these aggregates relate to each other.

Historically, there have often been changes in the types of assets that can be used as a means of payment, and simultaneous disagreements about what constitutes money in those circumstances. When cheques first began to be widely used in England early in the nineteenth century, there was disagreement over whether demand deposits should be regarded as part of the money stock. Now that point is not disputed. We can expect there to be continuing changes in the financial structure over the years, and consequent changes in the definitions of the various money supply concepts.

### Financial Innovation

www.bankofcanada.ca/en/
topic/top-fis.htm

Over the past 20 years, there have been a number of innovations in Canadian financial markets that have affected monetary aggregates.[4] Some of these have affected individual depositors; others have affected banking arrangements for businesses.

For individual depositors, a major change was the introduction of daily interest accounts. Prior to 1979, the standard savings account in a chartered bank paid interest on the minimum balance held over each calendar month. Most individuals were unable to earn interest on funds available for periods of less than a month and thus were likely to keep funds received from salary payments in chequing accounts. The introduction of savings accounts that pay interest on daily balances provided a new option that reduced the demand for $M1$.

In 1981, banks and other financial institutions began offering daily interest chequing accounts. A few years later, they began paying higher interest rates on balances above some minimum, such as $2000, and a much lower rate on balances below the minimum. Daily interest savings accounts with graduated interest rates were also introduced, with rates on large balances closely tied to rates on non-monetary assets such as Treasury bills. Similarly, businesses were induced to shift from non-interest-bearing chequing accounts to non-personal term deposits.

Another innovation affecting business depositors has been the provision of more cash management services that enable banks' customers to reduce their holdings of transactions balances and earn more interest. For example, there are arrangements under which surplus funds are automatically shifted at the end of each day to higher interest accounts. Such practices have served to reduce the demand for $M1$. The policy relevance of these issues is discussed in the Policy in Action feature later in this chapter.

## 16-2 | THE FUNCTIONS OF MONEY

Money is so widely used that we rarely step back to think how remarkable a device it is. It is impossible to imagine a modern economy operating without the use of money or something very much like it. In a mythical barter economy in which there is no money, every transaction has to involve an exchange of goods (and/or services) on both sides of the transaction. The examples of the difficulties of barter are endless. The economist wanting a haircut would have to find a barber wanting to listen to a lecture on economics; the actor wanting a suit would have to find a tailor

---

[4] Financial innovation in Canada is discussed in the following sources: C. Freeman, "Financial Innovation in Canada: Causes and Consequences," *American Economic Review,* May 1983; *Bank of Canada Review,* February 1991, pp. 3–14; C. Freedman, "The Canadian Banking System," *Bank of Canada Technical Report* No. 81, March 1998; C. Freedman and C. Goodlet, "The Financial Services Sector: Past Changes and Future Prospects," *Bank of Canada Technical Report* No. 82, March 1998; C. Freedman, "Monetary Policy Implementation: Past Present and Future—Will Electronic Money Lead to the Eventual Demise of Central Banking?", *International Finance,* vol. 3, no. 2, 2000, pp. 211–227.

**medium of exchange**
One of the roles of money; asset used to make payments.

wanting to watch a performance; and so on. Without a medium of exchange, modern economies could not operate. Money, as a **medium of exchange**, makes it unnecessary for there to be a "double-coincidence of wants," such as the barber and economist bumping into each other at just the right time.

There are four traditional functions of money, of which medium of exchange is the first.[5] The other three are store of value, unit of account, and standard of deferred payment. These stand on a different footing from the medium-of-exchange function.

**store of value**
Asset that maintains its value over time.

A **store of value** is an asset that maintains value over time. Thus, an individual holding a store of value can use that asset to make purchases at a future date. If an asset was not a store of value, it would not be used as a medium of exchange. Imagine trying to use ice cream as money in the absence of refrigerators. There would hardly ever be a good reason for anyone to give up goods for money (ice cream) if the money was sure to melt within the next few minutes. To be useful as money, an asset must be a store of value, but there are many stores of value other than money—such as bonds, stocks, and houses.

**unit of account**
Asset in which prices are denoted.

The **unit of account** is the unit in which prices are quoted and books kept. Prices are quoted in dollars and cents, and dollars and cents are the units in which the money stock is measured. Usually, the money unit is also the unit of account, but that is not essential. In many high-inflation countries, dollars become the unit of account even though the local money continues to serve as the medium of exchange.

**standard of deferred payment**
Asset normally used for making payments due at a later date.

Finally, as a **standard of deferred payment**, money units are used in long-term transactions, such as loans. The amount that has to be paid back in five or ten years is specified in dollars and cents. Dollars and cents are acting as the standard of deferred payment. Once again, though, it is not essential that the standard of deferred payment be the money unit. For example, the final payment of a loan may be related to the behaviour of the price level, rather than being fixed in dollars and cents. This is known as an *indexed loan*. The last two of the four functions of money are, accordingly, functions that money *usually* performs but not functions that it *necessarily* performs. And the store-of-value function is one that many assets perform.

There is one final point we want to re-emphasize. *Money is whatever is generally accepted in exchange.* In the past, an astounding variety of monies have been used: simple commodities such as seashells, then metals, pieces of paper representing claims on gold or silver, pieces of paper that are claims only on other pieces of paper, and then paper and electronic entries in banks' accounts.[6] However magnificently a piece of paper may be engraved, it is not money if it is not accepted in payment. And however unusual the material of which it is made, anything that is generally accepted in payment is money. There is thus an inherent circularity in the acceptance of money. Money is accepted in payment only because of the belief that it will later also be accepted in payment by others.

## 16-3 | THE DEMAND FOR MONEY: THEORY

In this section we review the three major motives underlying the demand for money, and we concentrate on the effects of changes in income and the interest rate on

---

[5] For the classic statement of the functions of money, see W.S. Jevons, *Money and the Mechanism of Exchange* (London: Kegan Paul, 1875).

[6] See Glyn Davies, *A History of Money from Ancient Times to the Present* (Aberystwyth: University of Wales Press, 1994).

**real balances**

Real value of the money stock (number of dollars divided by the price level).

money demand. Before we take up the discussion, we reiterate an essential point about money demand first raised in Chapter 3: The demand for money is a demand for **real balances**. In other words, people hold money for its purchasing power, for the amount of goods they can buy with it. They are not concerned with their *nominal* money holdings, that is, the number of dollar bills they hold. Two implications follow:

1. *Real* money demand is unchanged when the price level increases, and all real variables, such as the interest rate, real income, and real wealth, remain unchanged.

2. Equivalently, *nominal* money demand increases in proportion to the increase in the price level, given the real variables just specified.

In other words, we are interested in a money demand function that tells us the demand for real balances, $M/P$, not nominal balances, $M$. There is a special name for the behaviour described here. An individual is free from **money illusion** if a change in the level of prices, holding all real variables constant, leaves the person's real behaviour, including real money demand, unchanged.

**money illusion**

Belief that the numbers used to express prices have significance—that changes in the nominal price of a good are meaningful in and of themselves.

The theories we are about to review correspond to Keynes's famous three motives for holding money:[7]

▶ The **transactions motive**, which is the demand for money arising from the use of money in making regular payments.

▶ The **precautionary motive**, which is the demand for money to meet unforeseen contingencies.

▶ The **speculative motive**, which arises from uncertainties about the money value of other assets that an individual can hold.

**transactions motive**

The demand for money arising from the use of money in making regular payments.

**precautionary motive**

The demand for money to meet unforeseen contingencies.

**speculative motive**

Arises from uncertainties about the money value of other assets that an individual can hold.

In discussing the transactions and precautionary motives, we are mainly discussing $M1$, whereas the speculative motive refers more to $M2$ or $M3$, as we shall see.[8]

These theories of money demand *are built around a trade-off between the benefits of holding more money versus the interest costs of doing so.* Money ($M1$, that is, currency and some chequeable deposits) generally earns no interest or less interest than other assets. The higher the interest loss from holding a dollar of money, the less money we expect the individual to hold. In practice, we can measure the cost of holding money as the difference between the interest rate paid on money (perhaps zero) and the interest rate paid on the most nearly comparable other asset, such as a savings deposit or, for corporations, a certificate of deposit or commercial paper. The interest rate on money is referred to as the *own* rate of interest, and the *opportunity cost* of holding money is equal to the difference between the yield on other assets and the own rate.

---

[7] J.M. Keynes, *The General Theory of Employment, Interest and Money* (New York: Macmillan, 1936), Chapter 13.

[8] Although we examine the demand for money by looking at the three motives for holding it, we cannot separate a particular person's money holdings, say, $500, into three neat piles of, say, $200, $200, and $100, each being held from a different motive. Money being held to satisfy one motive is always available for another use. The person holding unusually large balances for speculative reasons also has those balances available to meet an unexpected emergency, so they serve, too, as precautionary balances. All three motives influence an individual's holdings of money.

## Transactions Demand

www.bankofcanada.ca/
publications/working.
papers/1999/aubry-
final.pdf

The transactions demand for money arises from the use of money in making regular payments for goods and services. In the course of each month, an individual makes a variety of payments for rent or a mortgage, groceries, the newspaper, and other purchases. In this section, we examine how much money an individual would hold to finance these purchases.

The trade-off here is between the amount of interest an individual forgoes by holding money and the costs and inconveniences of holding a small amount of money. To make the problem concrete, consider someone who is paid, say, $1800 each month. Assume the person spends the $1800 evenly over the course of the month, at the rate of $60 per day. Now at one extreme, the individual could simply leave the $1800 in cash and spend it at the rate of $60 per day. Alternatively, on the first day of the month, the individual could take $60 to spend that day and put the remaining $1740 in a daily interest savings account. Then, every morning, the person could go to the bank and withdraw that day's $60 from the savings account. By the end of the month, the depositor would have earned interest on the money retained each day in the savings account. That would be the *benefit* of keeping the money holdings down as low as $60 at the beginning of each day. The *cost* of keeping money holdings down is simply the cost and inconvenience of the trips to the bank to withdraw the daily $60.

The greater the number of trips to the bank, the larger the amount earning interest in the savings account. With one trip—everything taken as cash on the first day—no interest is earned. The cash balance falls smoothly from $1800 on the first day to $0 at the end of the month for an average balance of ($1800 − $0)/2 = $900, forgoing interest of $i \times$ $900. For two trips, the cash balance falls from $1800/2 to zero at midmonth and then repeats, for an average cash balance of ($1800/2 − $0)/2 = $450. We show in the appendix to this chapter that this generalizes so that starting with income $Y$, if $n$ trips are made, the average cash balance is $Y/2n$. If each trip costs $tc$, the combined cost of trips plus forgone interest is $(n \times tc) + i \times (Y/2n)$. Choosing $n$ to minimize costs and computing the implied average money holdings leads to the famous square-root Baumol-Tobin formula for the demand for money.[9]

$$\frac{M}{P} = \sqrt{\frac{tc \times Y}{2i}} \tag{1}$$

Equation (1) shows that the demand for money decreases with the interest rate and increases with the cost of transacting. Money demand increases with income, but less than proportionately, and with the level of income, but also less than proportionately. This point is sometimes put in different words by saying that there are *economies of scale* in cash management.

---

[9] The theory has quite general applicability for determining optimal inventories of goods as well as money. This inventory-theoretical approach to the demand for money is associated with the names of William Baumol and James Tobin: William Baumol, "The Transactions Demand for Cash: An Inventory Theoretic Approach," *Quarterly Journal of Economics,* November 1952; James Tobin, "The Interest Elasticity of Transactions Demand for Cash," *Review of Economics and Statistics,* August 1956.

BOX

16-1

## A Back of the Envelope Calculation Using Income Elasticity

You are now the monetary authority of the small country of Baumol-Tobinia. Real growth reliably averages 3 percent per year. How fast should you increase the money supply to stabilize the price level?

According to equation (1), 3 percent growth in GDP raises money demand 1.5 percent per year. If you increase the nominal money supply by the same 1.5 percent, real money supply and demand will stay in balance with a constant price level. If you had thought the income elasticity was 1 instead of $1/2$, you would have created money at 3 percent per year, in the erroneous belief that money demand was rising 3 percent per year, leading to a small but steady inflation.

Equation (1) makes two very strong predictions: The income elasticity of money demand is $1/2$, and the interest elasticity is $-1/2$.[10] Empirical evidence supports the signs of these predictions but suggests that the income elasticity is somewhat closer to 1 and that the interest elasticity is somewhat closer to zero.

## The Precautionary Motive

In discussing the transactions demand for money, we focused on transactions costs and ignored uncertainty. In this section, we concentrate on the demand for money that arises because people are uncertain about the payments they might want, or have, to make.[11] Realistically, an individual does not know precisely what payments she will be receiving in the next few weeks and what payments will have to be made. The person might decide to have a hot-fudge sundae, or need to take a cab in the rain, or have to pay for a prescription. If the person does not have money with which to pay, she will incur a loss.

The more money an individual holds, the less likely he or she is to incur the costs of illiquidity (that is, not having money immediately available). However, the more money the person holds, the more interest he or she is giving up. We are back to a trade-off similar to that examined in relation to the transactions demand. The added consideration is that greater uncertainty about receipts and expenditures increases the demand for money.

## The Speculative Demand for Money

The transactions demand and the precautionary demand for money emphasize the medium-of-exchange function of money, for each refers to the need to have money on hand to make payments. Each theory is most relevant to the $M1$ definition of money, although the precautionary demand could certainly explain some of the holding of savings accounts and other relatively liquid assets that are part of $M2$.

[10] Meaning that if income rises by 1 percentage point, or 100 basis points, money demand should rise by $1/2$ of 1 percentage point, or 50 basis points. You may want to review Box 8-1 in Chapter 8.

[11] See Edward H. Whalen, "A Rationalization of the Precautionary Demand for Cash," *Quarterly Journal of Economics*, May 1966.

# POLICY IN *ACTION*

## Is the Demand for *M*1 Stable?

Between 1975 and the early 1980s, monetary policy in Canada depended to a large extent on the demand for *M*1. One of the problems encountered in this policy was that the demand for *M*1 turned out to be less than stable. One explanation for this situation is that as monetary policy attempted to control *M*1, agents attempted to economize on their *M*1 balances. At the same time that this was happening, there was also an electronic revolution in the banking industry. As a result of these two occurrences, the income velocity of *M*1 climbed steadily throughout the late 1970s and into the 1980s. This increase in income velocity is shown in the figure below.

### THE INCOME VELOCITY OF *M*1, 1975–1985

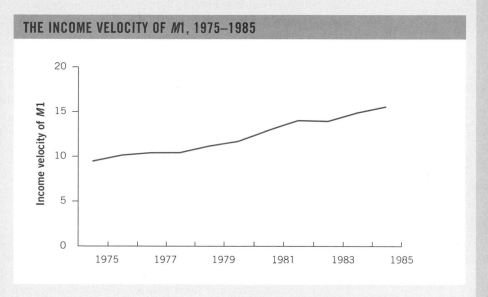

SOURCE: CANSIM II: *M*1: V737141; nominal GDP: V488918.

The Bank of Canada attempted to account for the instability in the *M*1 demand equation through sophisticated econometric techniques.* However, as a result of these changes, the Bank of Canada was eventually forced to conclude that *M*1 was no longer a good indicator of economic activity.

---

*This involved the use of complicated "dummy variables." See, for instance, S. Hendry, "The Long Run Demand for *M*1," *Bank of Canada Working Paper* 95-11, November 1995.

**portfolio**

The mix of assets someone owns.

**risky asset**

An asset whose future pay-off is uncertain.

Now we move over to the store-of-value function of money and concentrate on the role of money in the investment portfolio of an individual.

An individual who has wealth has to hold that wealth in specific assets. Those assets make up a **portfolio**. One would think an investor would want to hold the asset that provides the highest returns. However, given that the return on most assets is uncertain, it is unwise to hold the entire portfolio in a single **risky asset**. You may have the hottest tip that a certain stock will surely double within the next two years, but you would be wise to recognize that hot tips are far from infallible. The typical investor will want to hold some amount of a safe asset as insurance against capital losses on assets whose prices change in an uncertain manner. Money is a safe asset in that its nominal value is known with certainty.[12] In a famous article, James Tobin argued that money would be held as the safe asset in the portfolios of investors.[13] The title of the article, "Liquidity Preference as Behaviour Towards Risk," explains the essential notion. In this framework, the demand for money—the safest asset—depends on the expected yields as well as on the riskiness of the yields on other assets. Tobin shows that an increase in the expected return on other assets—an increase in the opportunity cost of holding money (that is, the return lost by holding money)—lowers money demand. By contrast, an increase in the riskiness of the returns on other assets increases money demand.

An investor's aversion to risk certainly generates a demand for a safe asset. However, that asset is not likely to be $M1$. From the viewpoint of the yield and risks of holding money, it is clear that time and savings deposits have the same risks as currency and chequeable deposits. However, the former generally pay a higher yield. Given that the risks are the same, and with the yields on time and savings deposits higher than those on currency and demand deposits, portfolio diversification explains the demand for assets such as time and savings deposits, which are part of $M2$, better than the demand for $M1$.

## 16-4 | EMPIRICAL EVIDENCE

**interest elasticity**

Percentage change in the demand for real money balances resulting from a 1 percent increase in the interest rate.

www.bankofcanada.ca/en/
topic/top-moa.htm

**income elasticity**

Amount that demand for real money balances changes, in percentage terms, when income increases by 1 percent.

This section examines the empirical evidence—the studies made using actual data—on the demand for money. We know from Chapters 11 and 12 that the **interest elasticity** of the demand for money plays an important role in determining the effectiveness of monetary and fiscal policies. We showed in Section 16-3 that there are good theoretical reasons for believing that the demand for real balances should depend on the interest rate. The empirical evidence supports that view. Empirical studies have established that the demand for money is negatively related to the interest rate.

The theory of money demand also predicts that the demand for money should depend on the level of income. The response of the demand for money to the level of income, as measured by the **income elasticity** of money demand, is also important from a policy viewpoint. As we shall see below, the income elasticity of money demand provides a guide for the Bank of Canada as to how fast to increase the money supply in order to support a given rate of GDP growth without changing the interest rate.

---

[12] Of course, when the rate of inflation is uncertain, the real value of money is also uncertain, and money is no longer a safe asset. Even so, the uncertainties about the values of equity are so much larger than the uncertainties about the rate of inflation that money can be treated as a relatively safe asset (countries at risk of hyperinflation excepted).

[13] James Tobin, "Liquidity Preference as Behavior Towards Risk," *Review of Economic Studies*, February 1958.

## Lagged Adjustment

The empirical work on the demand for money has introduced one complication that we did not study in the theoretical section—that the demand for money adjusts to changes in income and interest rates *with a lag*. When the level of income or the interest rate changes, there is first only a small change in the demand for money. Then, over the course of time, the change in the demand for money increases, slowly building up to its full long run change.

There are two basic reasons for these lags. First, there are costs of adjusting money holdings; second, money holders' expectations are slow to adjust. The costs of adjustment include the costs of figuring out the new best way to manage money and the cost of opening up a new type of account if that is needed. On the expectations side, if people believe that a given change in the interest rate is temporary, they may be unwilling to make a major change in their money holdings. As time passes and it becomes clearer that the change is not transitory, they are willing to make a larger adjustment.

## Empirical Results Using *M*1 Demand

There are several published studies of the demand for money in Canada using post-World War II data.[14] Table 16-2 shows the results for the demand for *M*1 in one of these. The table shows the elasticities of the demand for real balances with respect to real income and the interest rate. The interest rate used is that on commercial paper, an asset that is very liquid for investors who hold it instead of money for short periods of time.

In the short run (one quarter), the elasticity of demand with respect to real income is 0.22. This means that a 1 percent increase in real income raises money demand by 0.22 percent, which is considerably less than proportionately. The table shows that an increase in the interest rate reduces money demand. An increase in the interest rate on corporate paper from 4 to 5 percent—that is, a 25 percent increase ($5/4 = 1.25$)—reduces money demand by only 1.35 percent ($= 0.054 \times 0.25$).

The long run elasticities exceed the short run elasticities by more than 3, as Table 16-2 shows. The long run real income elasticity is 0.73, meaning that in the long run the increase in real money demand occurring as a result of an increase in real income is only 68 percent as large as a proportional increase in real income. The long run interest elasticity is $-0.18$, which means that an increase in the interest rate from 4 to 5 percent would reduce money demand by 4.5 percent.

| TABLE 16-2 | ELASTICITIES OF DEMAND FOR *M*1 | | |
| --- | --- | --- | --- |
| | | Income | Interest Rate |
| | Short run | 0.22 | $-0.054$ |
| | Long run | 0.73 | $-0.18$ |

SOURCE: S. Poloz, "Simultaneity and the Demand for Money in Canada," *Canadian Journal of Economics*, August 1980, page 413.

[14] See, for example, K. Clinton, "The Demand for Money in Canada, 1955–70," *Canadian Journal of Economics*, February 1973; N. Cameron, "The Stability of Canadian Demand for Money Functions," *Canadian Journal of Economics*, May 1979; S. Poloz, "Simultaneity and the Demand for Money in Canada," *Canadian Journal of Economics*, August 1980; and S. Hendry, "Long Run Demand for *M*1," *Bank of Canada Working Paper* 95-11, November 1995.

How long is the long run? That is, how long does it take the demand for money to adjust from the short run to the long run elasticities shown in Table 16-2? The answer is given in Table 16-3, which shows the elasticities of the demand for real balances in response to changes in the level of income and the interest rate after several quarters. Three-fourths of the adjustment is complete within the first year, and more than 90 percent of the adjustment is complete within the first two years.

**TABLE 16-3**

### DYNAMIC PATTERNS OF ELASTICITIES OF MONEY DEMAND WITH RESPECT TO REAL INCOME AND THE INTEREST RATE

| Quarters Elapsed | Income | Interest Rate |
|---|---|---|
| 1 | 0.22 | −0.054 |
| 2 | 0.37 | −0.092 |
| 3 | 0.48 | −0.119 |
| 4 | 0.55 | −0.138 |
| 8 | 0.69 | −0.172 |
| Long run | 0.73 | −0.182 |

SOURCE: Calculated using the elasticities shown in Table 16-2 and reported by Poloz, *op. cit.*

## Empirical Results for *M*2 Money Demand

Table 16-4 shows the long run elasticities obtained from a study of the demand for *M*2.[15] Compared with the value shown in Table 16-2, the income elasticity is lower (0.5 compared to 0.73), as would be expected because *M*2 includes assets that cannot be used directly as means of payment. In addition to the corporate paper rate, which represents the return on alternative assets, the rate on 90-day fixed term deposits is included. Since it represents an own rate of return, its elasticity has a positive sign. Further, the differential between this own rate and the rate offered by trust and mortgage loan companies is included to take account of the competition from non-bank institutions whose deposits are not included in *M*2. Taking all of the interest elasticities into account, a one-percentage-point increase in all rates would result in a reduction in demand for *M*2 of −0.16 (1.18 − 1.34).

**TABLE 16-4**

### LONG RUN ELASTICITIES OF DEMAND FOR *M*2

| Income | Interest Rates | | |
|---|---|---|---|
| | 90-day paper | Chartered bank term deposits | Term deposit differential |
| 0.50 | −1.34 | 1.18 | 3.56 |

SOURCE: F. Caramazza, "Technical Note: The Demand for *M*2 and *M*2+ in Canada," *Bank of Canada Review*, December 1989, Table 1.

---

[15] F. Caramazza, "Technical Note: The Demand for *M*2 and *M*2+ in Canada," *Bank of Canada Review*, December 1989, pp. 3–19.

In summary, we have so far described three essential properties of money demand:

1. The demand for real balances responds negatively to the rate of interest. An increase in interest rates reduces the demand for money.

2. The demand for money increases with the level of real income. However, because the income elasticity of money demand is less than 1, money demand increases less than proportionately with income.

3. The short run responsiveness of money demand to changes in interest rates and income is considerably less than the long run response.

---

**BOX 16-2**

## Money Demand and High Inflation

The demand for real balances depends on the alternative cost of holding money. That cost is normally measured by the yield on alternative assets, say, Treasury bills, commercial paper, or money market funds. But there is another margin of substitution. Rather than holding their wealth in financial assets, households or firms can also hold real assets: stocks of food or houses or machinery. This margin of substitution is particularly important in countries in which inflation is very high and capital markets do not function well. In that case, it is quite possible that the return on holding goods can even be higher than that on financial assets.

Consider a household deciding whether to hold $100 in currency or a demand deposit or to hold its wealth in the form of groceries on the shelf. The advantage of holding groceries is that, unlike money, groceries maintain their real value. Rather than having the purchasing power of money balances eroded by inflation, the household gets rid of money, buying goods and thus avoiding a loss.

This *flight out of money* occurs systematically when inflation rates become high. In a famous study of hyperinflations (defined in the study as inflation rates of more than 50 percent *per month*), Phillip Cagan of Columbia University found large changes in real balances taking place as inflation increased.* In the most famous hyperinflation, in Germany in 1922–23, the quantity of real balances at the height of the hyperinflation had fallen to one-twentieth of its preinflation level. The increased cost of holding money leads to a reduction in real money demand and, with it, to changes in the public's payment habits as everybody tries to pass money on like a hot potato.

In well-developed capital markets, interest rates will reflect expectations of inflation, and hence it will not make much difference whether we measure the alternative cost of holding money by interest rates or inflation rates. However, when capital markets are not free because interest rates are regulated or have ceilings, it is often appropriate to use inflation, not interest rates, as the measure of the alternative cost. Franco Modigliani has offered the following rule of thumb: The right measure of the opportunity cost of holding money is the higher of the two, interest rates or inflation.

---

*Phillip Cagan, "The Monetary Dynamics of Hyperinflation," in Milton Friedman (ed.), *Studies in the Quantity Theory of Money* (Chicago: University of Chicago Press, 1956).

There is one other important question to be considered: How does money demand respond to an increase in the level of prices? Here a number of researchers have found strong evidence that an increase in prices raises nominal money demand in the same proportion. We can add, therefore, a fourth conclusion:

4. The demand for nominal money balances is proportional to the price level. There is no money illusion; in other words, the demand for money is a demand for real balances.

## 16-5 | THE INCOME VELOCITY OF MONEY

**income velocity of money**

The number of times the stock of money is turned over per year in financing the annual flow of income.

Recall from Chapter 3 that the **income velocity of money** is the number of times the stock of money is turned over per year in financing the annual flow of income. It is equal to the ratio of nominal GDP to the nominal money stock. Thus, in 2000, GDP was about $1000 billion, the $M2$ money stock was $492 billion, and $M2$ velocity was therefore just about 2. The average dollar of $M2$ money balances financed $2.03 of spending on final goods and services, or the public held an average of 49 cents of $M2$ per dollar of income.

Income velocity is defined as[16]

$$V \equiv \frac{P \times Y}{M} = \frac{Y}{M/P} \tag{2}$$

that is, the ratio of nominal income to the nominal money stock or, equivalently, the ratio of real income to real balances.

The concept of velocity is important largely because it is a convenient way of talking about money demand. Let the demand for real balances be written $M/P = L(i,Y)$. Substituting into equation (2), velocity can be rewritten as $V = Y/L(i,Y)$. This is especially convenient if money demand is proportional to income, as is roughly true for long run $M2$ demand, so money demand can be written as $L(i,Y) = Y \times l(i)$. In this case, equation (2) is simply $V = 1/l(i)$, so velocity is a quick way to summarize the effect of interest rates on money demand—remembering that high velocity means low money demand.[17]

Figure 16-1 shows $M1$ velocity and the Treasury bill interest rate. $M2$ velocity has a strong tendency to rise and fall with market interest rates.

---

[16] Why do we say *income velocity* and not plain *velocity*? There is another concept, transactions velocity, which is the ratio of *total transactions* to money balances. Total transactions far exceed GDP for two reasons. First, many transactions involving the sale and purchase of assets do not contribute to GDP. Second, a particular item in final output typically generates total spending on it that exceeds the contribution of that item to GDP. For instance, a dollar's worth of wheat generates transactions as it leaves the farm, as it is sold by the miller, and so forth. Transactions velocity is thus higher than income velocity.

[17] In fact, while academic economists use *velocity* and *money demand* more or less interchangeably, "Bay Street" tends to focus directly on velocity as a measure.

**FIGURE 16-1**

This graph shows the change in *M2+* velocity and the change in the 90-day Treasury bill rate. Velocity tends to rise and fall with the nominal interest rate.

## *M2+* INCOME VELOCITY AND THE TREASURY BILL RATE

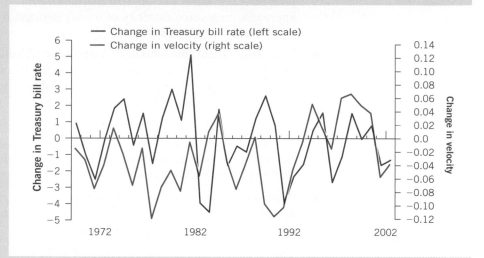

SOURCE: CANSIM II: *M2+*: V37131; nominal income: V498918; Treasury bill interest rate: V122484.

## *Working with Data*

In Figure 16-1, we graphed the change in velocity with the change in the 90-day Treasury bill rate. We are also interested in the trend in velocity over time. In order to see this, we ask you to calculate the income velocity for the different measures of the money stock from Table 16-1. Plot these different velocity measures and think about what they imply about the monetary aggregates.

## CHAPTER SUMMARY

▶ The demand for money is a demand for real balances. It is the purchasing power, not the number of dollar bills, that matters to holders of money.

▶ The money supply, *M1*, is made up of currency and chequeable deposits. A broader measure, *M2*, also includes savings and time deposits at depository institutions as well as some other interest-bearing assets.

▶ The chief characteristic of money is that it serves as a means of payment. The three classic reasons to hold money are for transactions purposes (*M1*) and for precautionary (*M1* and *M2*) and speculative reasons (*M2* and *M3*).

▶ Decisions to hold money are based on a trade-off between the liquidity of money and the opportunity cost of holding it when other assets have a higher yield.

www.mcgrawhill.ca/college/dornbusch

▶ The inventory-theoretic approach shows that an individual will hold a stock of real balances that varies inversely with the interest rate but increases with the level of real income and the cost of transactions. According to the inventory approach, the income elasticity of money demand is less than unity, implying that there are economies of scale.

▶ Uncertainty about payments and receipts in combination with transactions costs give rise to a precautionary demand for money. Precautionary money holdings are higher the greater the variability of net disbursements, the higher the cost of illiquidity, and the lower the interest rate.

▶ Some assets that are in *M2* form part of an optimal portfolio because they are less risky than other assets—their nominal value is constant. Because they earn interest, assets such as savings or time deposits dominate currency and demand deposits for portfolio diversification purposes.

▶ The empirical evidence provides support for a negative interest elasticity of money demand and a positive income elasticity. Because of lags, short run elasticities are much smaller than long run elasticities.

▶ The income velocity of money is defined as the ratio of income to money or the rate of turnover of money. The behaviour of velocity is closely tied to the demand for money, so an increase in the opportunity cost of holding money leads to an increase in velocity.

## KEY TERMS

money, *324*
*M1, 324*
liquid asset, *324*
*M2, 324*
*M3, 325*
*M2+, 325*
medium of exchange, *327*

store of value, *327*
unit of account, *327*
standard of deferred payment, *327*
real balances, *328*
money illusion, *328*
transactions motive, *328*
precautionary motive, *328*

speculative motive, *328*
portfolio, *332*
risky asset, *332*
interest elasticity, *332*
income elasticity, *332*
income velocity of money, *336*

## DISCUSSION QUESTIONS

1. What is money, and why does anyone want it?

2. To what extent would it be possible to design a society in which there was no money? What would the problems be? Could currency at least be eliminated? How? (Lest all this seem too unworldly, you should know that some people are beginning to talk of a "cashless economy" in the twenty-first century.)

3. Do you think credit card credit limits should be counted in the money stock? Why or why not?

4. Discuss the various factors that go into an individual's decision regarding how many traveller's cheques to take on a vacation.

5. Explain the concept of the opportunity cost of holding money.

6. The demand for nominal balances rises with the price level. At the same time, inflation causes the real demand to fall. Explain how these two assertions can both be correct.

7. "Muggers favour deflation." Comment.

## A P P L I C A T I O N   Q U E S T I O N S

1. Evaluate the effects of the following changes on the demand for $M1$ and $M2$. To which of the functions of money do they relate?

   **a.** "Instant cash" machines that allow 24-hour withdrawals from savings accounts at banks.

   **b.** The employment of more tellers at your bank.

   **c.** An increase in inflationary expectations.

   **d.** Widespread acceptance of credit cards.

   **e.** Fear of an imminent collapse of the government.

   **f.** A rise in the interest rate on time deposits.

2. **a.** Is velocity high or low relative to trend during recessions? Why?

   **b.** How can the Bank of Canada influence velocity?

 3. Go to CANSIM and retrieve the variables you will need to calculate the velocity of $M1B$. Plot this variable with the recession dates given in Chapter 6, Application Question 3. Relate this to your answer to Application Question 2, above.

The next two questions are related to the material in the appendix to this chapter.

*4. The transactions demand-for-money model can also be applied to firms. Suppose a firm sells steadily during the month and has to pay its workers at the end of the month. Explain how the firm would determine its money holdings.

5. **a.** Determine the optimal strategy for cash management for a person who earns $1600 per month, can earn 0.5 percent interest per month in a savings account, and has a transaction cost of $1. (*Hint:* Integer constraints matter here.)

   **b.** What is the individual's average cash balance?

   **c.** Suppose income rises to $1800. By what percentage does the individual's demand for money change?

---

* An asterisk denotes a more difficult problem.

---

### O P T I O N A L

#### APPENDIX: THE BAUMOL–TOBIN TRANSACTIONS DEMAND MODEL

The assumptions of the Baumol–Tobin transactions demand model are set out in the text and summarized here. An individual receives a payment, $Y$, at the beginning of each month and spends it at an even pace during the month. He or she can earn interest at the rate $i$ per month by holding money in a savings account (equivalently, bonds). There is a cost of $tc$ per transaction for moving between bonds and money. We denote by $n$ the number of transactions per month between bonds and money, and we assume, for convenience, that monthly income is paid into the savings account or paid in the form of bonds.

The individual minimizes the cost of money management during the month. Those costs consist of the transactions cost, $(n \times tc)$, plus the interest forgone by holding money instead of bonds during the month. The interest cost is $(i \times M)$, where $M$ is the average holdings of money during the month.

$M$, the average holdings of money, depends on $n$, the number of transactions. Suppose that each time the individual makes a transaction, she transfers amount $Z$ from bonds into money.[18] If the individual makes $n$ equal-sized withdrawals during the month, the size of each transfer is $Y/n$, since a total of $Y$ has to be transferred. Thus

$$nZ = Y \tag{A1}$$

Now, how is the *average* cash balance related to $n$? Figure 16A-1 helps answer this question. In Figure 16A-1(a), the average cash balance held during the month is $Y/2 = Z/2$, since the cash balance starts at $Y$ and runs down in a straight line to zero.[19] In the case of Figure 16A-1(b), the average cash balance for the first half of the month is $Y/4 = Z/2$, and the average cash balance for the second half of the month is also $Z/2$. Thus, the average cash balance for the entire month is $Y/4 = Z/2$. In general, the average cash balance is $Z/2$, as you might want to confirm by drawing diagrams similar to Figure 16A-1 for $n = 3$ or other values of $n$. Using equation (A1), it follows that the average cash balance is $Y/2n$.

The total cost of cash management is accordingly

$$\text{Total cost} = (n \times tc) + \frac{iY}{2n} \tag{A2}$$

The optimum number of transactions is found by minimizing total cost with respect to $n$.[20] That implies

$$n^* = \sqrt{\frac{zY}{2tc}} \tag{A3}$$

where $n^*$ is the optimal number of transactions. As we should expect, the individual makes more transactions the higher the interest rate, the higher the income, and the lower the transactions cost. The Baumol–Tobin result, equation (1) in the text, is obtained using equation (A3) and the fact that $M = iY/2n$.

*FIGURE 16A-1*

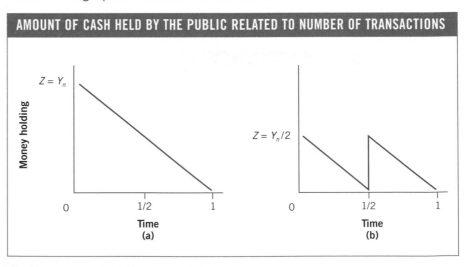

**AMOUNT OF CASH HELD BY THE PUBLIC RELATED TO NUMBER OF TRANSACTIONS**

---

[18] With simple interest being paid on the savings account, the individual's transactions between bonds and cash should be evenly spaced over the month.

[19] The average cash balance is the average of the amount of cash the individual holds at each moment during the month. For instance, if the balance held is $400 for 3 days and zero for the rest of the month, the average cash balance would be $40, or one-tenth (3 days ÷ 30 days) of the month times $400.

[20] If you can handle calculus, derive equation (A3) by minimizing the total cost with respect to $n$ in equation (A2).

In addition to deriving the square-root formula, we want also to show why for many people, it is optimal to make only one transaction between bonds and money. Consider the example in the text of an individual who receives $1800 per month. Suppose that the interest rate on deposits is as high as 0.5 percent per month. The individual cannot avoid making one initial transaction, since income is paid into the savings account to start with. Does it pay to make a second transaction? For $n = 2$, the average cash balance is $1800/2n = $450, so interest earned would be $(0.005 \times $450) = $2.25$.

If the transaction cost exceeds $2.25, the individual will not bother to make more than one transaction. And $2.25 is not an outrageous cost in terms of the time and nuisance of making a transfer between bonds (or a savings account) and money.

For anyone making only one transaction, the average cash balance is half his or her income. That means the interest elasticity of money demand for that person is zero—up to the point that the interest rate becomes high enough to make a second transaction worthwhile. And the income elasticity is 1, up to the point that income rises high enough to make a second transaction worthwhile. Since for some people the income elasticity is 1 and for others the Baumol–Tobin formula is closer to applying, we expect the income elasticity to be between 0 and 1; similarly, since for some the interest elasticity is zero while for others it is closer to $-\frac{1}{2}$, we expect the interest elasticity to be between $-\frac{1}{2}$ and zero.

# PART 6

# MONETARY AND FISCAL POLICY AND ADVANCED TOPICS

# POLICY

## *LEARNING OBJECTIVES*

After reading and studying this chapter, you should be able to:

▶ *Understand that uncertainty about the economy places limits on the reach of successful policy.*

▶ *Understand that imperfect knowledge of the economy sometimes argues for a "go-slow" approach in the application of economic policy.*

▶

*Understand that the choice of policy targets should be influenced by the limits of our knowledge as well as by the extent of our knowledge.*

S tabilization policy seems easy to design and implement according to the macroeconomic models set out so far in this book: In recession, use expansionary monetary and fiscal policy; in booms and when inflation is too high, use contractionary policy. If stabilization policy were that simple, recessions would be rare and brief, and inflation would always be low. Evidently, stabilization policy is not so simple. In part that is because the goals of keeping both inflation and unemployment low sometimes conflict, as we discussed in Chapters 6 through 8. In this chapter we discuss problems that arise in using stabilization policies even with a single agreed-on goal.

In this chapter, we discuss technical problems in policy making, which imply that policy cannot be expected to always keep the economy close to full employment with low inflation. In a nutshell, we will argue that a policy maker who (1) observes a disturbance, (2) does not know whether it is permanent or not, and (3) takes time to develop a policy that (4) takes still more time to affect behaviour, and (5) has uncertain effects on aggregate demand is very unlikely to do a perfect job of stabilizing the economy. When the economy is far from full employment, stabilization policy has a clear target and is bound to work. Near full employment, however, policies intended to stabilize the economy can easily go wrong.

## 17-1 | LAGS IN THE EFFECTS OF POLICY

Suppose that the economy is at full employment and has been affected by an aggregate demand disturbance that will reduce the equilibrium level of income below full employment. Suppose further that there was no advance warning of this disturbance and that, consequently, no policy actions were taken in anticipation of its occurrence. Policy makers now have to decide whether to respond at all and how to respond to the disturbance.

**permanent disturbance**

An exogenous change that shifts, say, the aggregate demand curve to a new position permanently.

**transitory disturbance**

An exogenous change that shifts, say, the aggregate demand curve, but the disturbance is short-lived and the curve shifts back to its original position.

The first concern is to distinguish whether a disturbance is **permanent**, or at least very persistent, or **transitory** and short-lived. Suppose the disturbance is only transitory, such as a one-period reduction in consumption spending. When the disturbance is transitory, so that consumption rapidly reverts to its initial level, the best policy may be to do nothing at all. You will recognize this as a similar policy prescription to the one that we applied to modern theories of the consumption function in Chapter 14.

Provided suppliers or producers do not mistakenly interpret the decrease in demand as permanent but, rather, perceive it as transitory, they will absorb it by production and inventory changes rather than by capacity adjustments. The disturbance will affect income in this period but will have very little permanent effect. Since today's policy actions take time to have an effect, today's actions would be hitting an economy that would otherwise have been close to full employment, and they would tend to move the economy away from the full employment level. Thus, if a disturbance is temporary and has no long-lived effects and policy operates with a lag, the best policy is to do nothing.

Figure 17-1 illustrates the main issue. Assume that an aggregate demand disturbance reduces output below potential, starting at time $t_0$. Without active policy intervention, output declines for a while but then recovers and reaches the full employment level again at time $t_2$. Consider next the path of GDP under an active stabilization policy, but one that works with the disadvantage of lags. Thus, expansionary policy might be initiated at time $t_1$ and start taking effect some time after. Output now tends

## FIGURE 17-1

If there are lags in stabilization policy, the economy may be driven away from full employment by the implementation of policy.

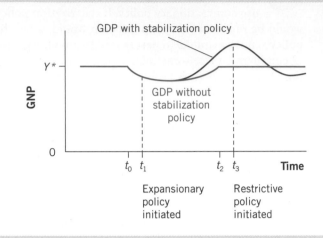

**LAGS AND DESTABILIZING POLICY**

www.bankofcanada.ca/en/
backgrounders/bg-p7.htm

to recover faster as a consequence of the expansion but, because of poor dosage and/or timing, actually overshoots the full employment level. By time $t_3$, restrictive policy is initiated and, some time after, output starts turning down toward full employment and may well continue cycling for a while. In this example, "stabilization" policy may actually *destabilize* the economy.

One of the main difficulties of policy making is establishing whether a disturbance is temporary. It was clear enough in the case of World War II that a high level of defence expenditures would be required for some years. However, in the case of the OPEC oil embargo of 1973–74, it was not at all clear how long the embargo would last or whether the high prices for oil that were established in late 1973 would persist. At the time, there were many who argued that the oil cartel would not survive and that oil prices would soon fall—that is, that the disturbance was temporary. "Soon" turned out to be 12 years.

Let us suppose, however, that it is known that the disturbance will have effects that will last for several quarters and that the level of income will, without intervention, be below the full employment level for some time. What lags do policy makers encounter?

We now consider the steps required before action can be taken after a disturbance has occurred. After that, we examine the process by which that policy action affects the economy. There are delays, or lags, at every stage, and these can be divided into two stages: an **inside lag**, which is the time period it takes to undertake a policy action—such as a tax cut or an increase in the money supply—and an **outside lag**, which describes the timing of the effects of the policy action on the economy. The inside lag, in turn, is divided into recognition, decision, and action lags.

**inside lag**
The time period it takes to undertake a policy action.

**outside lag**
The timing of the effects of the policy action on the economy.

**recognition lag**
The period that elapses between the time a disturbance occurs and the time the policy makers recognize that action is required.

## The Recognition Lag

The **recognition lag** is the period that elapses between the time a disturbance occurs and the time the policy makers recognize that action is required. This lag could, in principle, be *negative* if the disturbance can be predicted and appropriate policy actions considered *before* it even occurs. For example, we know that seasonal factors affect behaviour. Thus, it is known that during the December holiday period, the demand for currency is high. Rather than allow this to exert a restrictive effect on the money market, the Bank of Canada will accommodate this seasonal demand by an expansion of the money supply.

In general, however, the recognition lag is positive, so time elapses between the disturbance and the recognition that active policy is required. In the United States, there is some evidence that, on average, the recognition lag has been about five months. The lag appears to be somewhat shorter when the required policy is expansionary and somewhat longer when restrictive policy is required.

## The Decision and Action Lags

**decision lag**

The delay between the recognition of the need for action and the policy decision.

**action lag**

The lag between the policy decision and its implementation.

The **decision lag**—the delay between the recognition of the need for action and the policy decision—differs between monetary and fiscal policy. The Bank of Canada executives meet frequently to discuss and decide on policy. Thus, once the need for a policy action has been recognized, the decision lag for monetary policy is short. Further, the **action lag**—the lag between the policy decision and its implementation—for monetary policy is also short. The major monetary policy actions take the form of open market operations. These policy actions can be undertaken almost as soon as a decision has been made. Thus, the decision lag for monetary policy is short and the action lag practically zero.

However, fiscal policy actions are less rapid. Once the need for a fiscal policy action has been recognized, the administration has to prepare legislation for that action. Next, the legislation has to be considered and approved by both Houses of Parliament before the policy change can be made. That may be a lengthy process. Even after the legislation has been approved, the policy change still has to be put into effect. If the fiscal policy takes the form of a change in tax rates, it may be some time before the change in tax rates begins to be reflected in paycheques—that is, there may be an action lag.

## Automatic Stabilizers

The existence of the inside lag in policy making focuses attention on the use of automatic stabilizers. In Chapter 10, we defined an automatic stabilizer as any mechanism in the economy that automatically—that is, with case-by-case government intervention—reduces the amount that output changes in response to a change in some exogenous component of demand.

One of the major benefits of automatic stabilizers is that their inside lag is zero. The most important automatic stabilizer is the income tax, which stabilizes the economy by reducing the multiplier effects of any disturbance to aggregate demand. The multiplier for the effects of changes in autonomous spending on GDP is inversely related to the income tax rate, as we saw in Chapter 10.

Unemployment compensation is another automatic stabilizer. When workers become unemployed and reduce their consumption, that reduction in consumption demand tends to have multiplier effects on output. Those multiplier effects are reduced when a worker receives unemployment compensation because disposable income is reduced by less than the loss in earnings.

Although built-in stabilizers have desirable effects, they cannot be carried too far without also affecting the overall performance of the economy. The multiplier could be reduced to 1 by increasing the tax rate to 100 percent, and that would appear to be a stabilizing influence on the economy. But with 100 percent marginal tax rates, the desire to work, and consequently the level of GDP, would be reduced. Thus, there are limits on the extent to which automatic stabilizers are desirable.

## The Outside Lag

**discrete lag**

A lag that takes a fixed amount of time. Contrast *distributed lag*.

**distributed lag**

A lag that spreads the effects of policy over a variable amount of time.

The inside lag of policy is a **discrete lag**—so many months—from recognition to decision and implementation. The outside lag is generally a **distributed lag**: Once the policy action has been taken, its effects on the economy are spread over time. There may be a small immediate effect of a policy action, but other effects occur later.

The idea that policy operates on aggregate demand and income with a distributed lag is illustrated by the dynamic multiplier in Figure 17-2, where we show the effects over time of a once-and-for-all increase in the monetary base in period zero. The impact is initially very small, and it continues to increase over a long period of time. The lags of monetary policy are represented by the fact that any significant impact of money on spending and output takes several quarters and builds up only gradually.

What are the policy implications of the distributed lag encountered in the outside lag? If it was necessary to increase the level of employment rapidly to offset a demand disturbance, a monetary expansion would be necessary. But in later quarters, the large initial expansion would build up large effects on GDP, and those effects would probably overcorrect the unemployment, leading to inflationary pressures. It would then be necessary to reverse the expansion and conduct contractionary policies to avoid the inflationary consequences of the initial expansion.

Why are there such long outside lags? Consider the example of monetary policy. Because aggregate demand depends heavily on lagged values of income, interest rates, and other economic variables, expansionary monetary policy initially has

*FIGURE 17-2*

An increase in the monetary base causes GDP to increase by successively larger amounts as we move through time. The height of the bars shows the amount by which GDP exceeds the level that it would have reached in the absence of the policy change.

**DYNAMIC MULTIPLIERS FOR THE EFFECTS OF A CHANGE IN THE MONETARY BASE ON GDP**

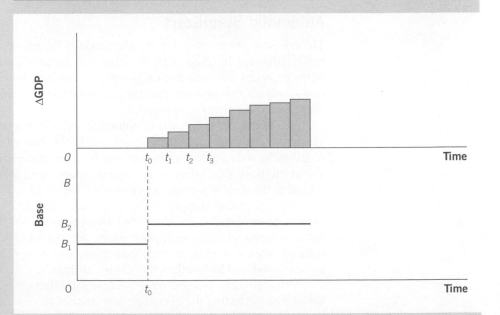

effects mainly on interest rates and not on income. The interest rates, in turn, affect investment with a lag, and also affect consumption by affecting the value of wealth. When aggregate demand is ultimately affected, the increase in spending itself produces a series of induced adjustments in output and spending. When policy acts slowly, with the impacts of policy building up over time as in Figure 17-2, considerable skill is required of policy makers if their own attempts to correct an initially undesirable situation are not to lead to problems that themselves need correcting.

## Monetary versus Fiscal Policy Lags

Fiscal policy—and certainly changes in government spending, which act directly on aggregate demand—affects income more rapidly than monetary policy. However, while fiscal policy has a shorter outside lag, it has a considerably longer inside lag. The long inside lag makes fiscal policy less useful for stabilization and means that fiscal policy tends to be used relatively infrequently to try to stabilize the economy.

Our analysis of lags indicates clearly one difficulty in undertaking stabilizing short-term policy actions: It takes time to set the policies in action, and then the policies themselves take time to affect the economy. But that is not the only difficulty. Further difficulties arise because policy makers cannot be certain about the size and the timing of the effects of policy actions.

---

**BOX 17-1**

### Two Nobel Laureates on Rules and Discretion

Nobel Laureate Milton Friedman is often associated with the term "long and variable lags." Friedman's point was that not only will the effects of monetary policy be felt through long lags in the economy (that is, the effects will be spread out over long periods of time), but also these lags will likely change each time a new monetary policy is implemented. Because of these long and variable lags, Friedman was a long-time advocate of conducting monetary policy according to rules, rather than discretion.

It is very interesting—and somewhat confusing—that later advocates of policy rules, most notably another Nobel Prize winner, Robert E. Lucas, Jr., often invoked the name of Milton Friedman whenever they advocated the use of rules rather than discretion. However, Lucas believes that an economy can be described by a set of market clearing equations, where agents possess rational expectations.

In the Lucas view of the world, the economy is always in equilibrium and, therefore, monetary policy cannot help the economy in any stabilization sense, so he advocates that policy should not be conducted according to discretion. In the Friedman view of the world, there are long adjustment lags that are not constant or predictable and, therefore, monetary policy should be conducted according to rules rather than discretion.

The same conclusion, but arising from two different views of the world!

---

## 17-2 | EXPECTATIONS AND REACTIONS

Uncertainty about the effects of policies on the economy arise because policy makers do not know the precise values of multipliers. The government is always uncertain about how the economy will react to policy changes. In practice, governments work

**econometric model**

A statistical description of the economy or some part of it.

with econometric models of the economy in estimating the effects of policy changes. An **econometric model** is a statistical description of the economy or some part of it.

Government uncertainty about the effects of policy arises partly because the government does not know the true model of the economy and partly because it does not know what expectations firms and consumers have. In this section, we concentrate on the role of expectations.

## Reaction Uncertainties

Suppose that in early 2010, because of weakness in the economy, the government decides to cut taxes. The tax cut is meant to be strictly temporary—a brief shot in the arm to get the economy moving and nothing more.

In figuring out how big a tax cut is needed, the government has to guess how the public will react to a temporary tax cut. One possible answer is that the tax cut raises permanent income by very little and hence leads to only a very small increase in spending. That suggests that to be useful, a temporary tax cut would have to be large. Alternatively, perhaps consumers will believe that the tax cut will last much longer than the government says—after all, the public knows that raising taxes is difficult. In this case, the marginal propensity to spend out of a tax cut announced as temporary would be larger. A smaller tax cut would be enough to raise spending a lot. If the government is wrong in its guess about consumers' reactions, it could destabilize rather than stabilize the economy.

## Changes in Policy Regime

A special problem emerges when the government changes the way it has traditionally responded to disturbances. For example, a government that has typically cut taxes in recessions and now no longer does so (e.g., because the deficit is large) may find that the cut had been expected and that there is an extra drop in demand when consumers realize taxes will not be cut this time.

It is particularly important to consider the effects of a given policy action itself on expectations, since it is possible that a new type of policy will affect how expectations are formed.[1] Suppose that the Bank of Canada announced that from now on its policy would be aimed *solely* at maintaining price stability and that in response to any price-level increase it would reduce the money supply (and vice versa). If people believed the announcement, they would not base expectations of money growth and inflation on the past behaviour of the inflation rate.

**credibility**

Announcements by policy makers are believed by economic agents.

However, people are not likely to fully believe such an announcement immediately. The policy makers are likely to lack full **credibility**. Policy makers have credibility when their announcements are believed by economic agents. Typically, policy makers have to earn credibility by behaving consistently over long periods, so that people learn to believe what they say.

Earning credibility is likely to be costly. Consider what happens if the Bank of Canada announces it will keep inflation low and is not believed. Then the expected inflation rate is above the actual inflation rate, and—as the Phillips curve shows—a recession follows. Only over time, as the new policies are understood, is credibility earned.

---

[1] The interactions of policy and expectations have been the focus of the rational expectations approach to macroeconomics (see Chapter 20). For a very early statement, see Thomas J. Sargent and Neil Wallace, "Rational Expectations and the Theory of Economic Policy," *Journal of Monetary Economics*, April 1976.

As an example, credibility issues are always a problem when governments promise to keep exchange rates fixed. In the 1980s, governments in the European Monetary System of quasi-fixed exchange rates announced that they would no longer respond to increases in wages and prices with devaluations. Initially, the policy makers lacked credibility, and inflation stayed high. But eventually, by holding fast, and with the aid of recessions, policy makers gained credibility and inflation came down. Then in 1992, under the macroeconomic impact of German unification, major devaluations were forced on reluctant governments, and their credibility was seriously dented.

## Econometric Policy Evaluation Critique

The public's reactions to changes in income, interest rates, and exchange rates depend on what people expect will be happening in the economy and what the policy responses of the government will be. This poses an acute dilemma for policy research. We would like to know what the public will do in response to this or that new policy. However, we cannot find the answer from historical relationships between variables and policies unless we know what expectations people held about policy.

This difficulty has been identified by Robert E. Lucas, of the University of Chicago, in a challenge to stabilization policy. Lucas argues in his **econometric policy evaluation critique** that existing macroeconometric models cannot be used to study the effects of policy changes because the way private agents (firms and consumers) respond to changes in income and prices depends on the types of policy being followed.[2]

Lucas claims that problems of this sort are pervasive in macroeconometric models. He does not argue that it will never be possible to use econometric models to study policy—only that existing models cannot be used for that purpose.

Accordingly, the Lucas critique is not one that rules out the use of econometric models.[3] It suggests, rather, that very careful modelling of the responses of consumers and firms to changes in income and prices, and particularly to changes in policy, is necessary for serious policy analysis.

**econometric policy evaluation critique**

Existing macroeconomic models cannot be used to study the effects of policy changes because the way private agents respond to changes in income and prices depends on the types of policy being followed.

## 17-3 | UNCERTAINTY AND ECONOMIC POLICY

Uncertainty about the expectations of firms and consumers is one reason that policy makers can go wrong in using active stabilization policy. Another reason is that it is difficult to forecast disturbances, such as changes in the price of oil, that might disturb the economy before policy takes effect.

A third reason is that economists and therefore policy makers do not know enough about the true structure of the economy. We distinguish between uncertainty about the correct model of the economy and uncertainty about the precise values of the parameters or coefficients within a given model of the economy, even though the distinction is not watertight.

First, there is considerable disagreement and therefore uncertainty about the correct model of the economy, as evidenced by the large number of macroeconometric

[2] See "Econometric Policy Evaluation: A Critique," in R.E. Lucas, Jr., *Studies in Business Cycle Theory* (Cambridge: MIT Press, 1981).

[3] The attempt of real business cycle theorists to uncover "deep parameters" (see Chapter 20) arose in part as a response to the Lucas critique.

## POLICY IN *ACTION*

### Did Policy Meet the Lucas Critique?

In the Policy in Action feature in Chapter 3, we discussed the Canadian monetarist experiment of the late 1970s. Recall that the Bank of Canada announced that it would begin running monetary policy by announcing annual target rates for the rate of growth of the money supply. The implementation of this policy required the Bank of Canada to estimate an econometric model of the demand for $M1$, one of the monetary aggregates. It was widely believed at the time that $M1$ was the best indicator of economic activity. The idea was that if $M1$ was growing too quickly, the short-term interest rate would be increased to lower the rate of growth of $M1$, which would eventually lower the rate of inflation.

After controlling the growth of $M1$ successfully for several years, it became apparent that $M1$ was becoming a less reliable indicator of the economy, and the use of $M1$ for policy purposes was discontinued. One view of what happened was that policy ran into the Lucas critique in the following manner: When $M1$ was not a target of policy, individuals behaved in a certain manner in terms of demand for $M1$, and this was reflected in the econometric model of $M1$ that was used. Once $M1$ was used for policy, individuals changed their behaviour, and the previous econometric model for $M1$ became invalid.

www.bankofcanada.ca/en/
res/wp00-10.htm

models. Reasonable economists can and do differ about what theory and empirical evidence suggest are the correct behavioural functions of the economy. Generally, each economist will have reasons for favouring one particular form and will use that form. But, being reasonable, the economist will recognize that the particular formulation being used may not be the correct one and will thus regard its predictions as subject to a margin of error. In turn, policy makers will know that there are different predictions about the effects of a given policy, and they will want to consider the range of predictions that are being made in deciding on policy.

Second, even within a given model, there is uncertainty about the values of parameters and multipliers. The statistical evidence does allow us to say something about the likely range of parameters or multipliers, so we can at least get some idea of the type of errors that could result from a particular policy action.[4]

Uncertainty about the size of the effects that will result from any particular policy action—because of uncertainty about expectations or about the structure of the economy—is known as **multiplier uncertainty**. For instance, our best estimate

**multiplier uncertainty**
Uncertainty about the size of the effects that will result from any particular policy action.

---

[4] We are discussing here confidence intervals about estimates of parameters; see Robert Pindyck and Daniel Rubinfeld, *Econometric Models and Economic Forecasts* (New York: McGraw-Hill, 1991), for further discussion.

of the multiplier of an increase in government spending might be 1.2. If GDP has to be increased by $60 billion, we would increase government spending by $50 billion. However, the statistical evidence might be better interpreted as saying only that we can be quite confident that the multiplier is between 0.9 and 1.5. In that case, when we increase government spending by $50 billion, we expect GDP to rise by some amount between $45 and $75 billion.

How should a policy maker react in the face of these uncertainties? The more precisely that policy makers are informed about the relevant parameters, the more activist the policy can afford to be. Conversely, if there is a considerable range of error in the estimate of the relevant parameters—in our example, the multiplier—then policy should be more modest. With poor information, very active policy runs a great danger of introducing unnecessary fluctuations in the economy.

## The Policy Portfolio Under Uncertainty

Consider the choice between monetary policy and fiscal policy when both monetary and fiscal policy multipliers are uncertain. When policy multipliers are known, either monetary policy or fiscal policy may be used to hit an output target, although one policy may be preferred over the other because of side effects on interest rates, exchange rates, or the budget deficit. We have, however, just argued that no policy should be used "full strength" when there is multiplier uncertainty.

**portfolio of policy instruments (diversification)**

A weaker dose of both monetary and fiscal policies.

The best procedure is to employ a **portfolio of policy instruments**—use a weaker dose of both monetary and fiscal policies. The reason for practising **diversification** in this way is that there is at least a chance that the errors in estimating one multiplier will be offset by the errors in estimating the other.[5] With good luck, errors in setting policy will partially cancel one another. Even if we are unlucky, we are no worse off than if we had relied fully on one instrument.[6]

---

### O P T I O N A L

**MULTIPLIER UNCERTAINTY AND POLICY: A FORMAL ANALYSIS**

Multipliers measure the quantitative effect of policy. The argument that the less certain we are about the size of a multiplier, the more cautious we should be in application of the associated policy instrument is intuitively plausible. This intuition was first given formal expression by William Brainard.[7] We present a simplified version here.

Suppose that our entire knowledge of the effect of monetary policy on the economy can be boiled down to one equation:

$$Y = \beta M \tag{1}$$

*continued...*

---

[5] If you have studied finance, you will be familiar with the notion of picking a *portfolio* of investments in order to reduce risk through *diversification*. The choice of words here is no coincidence—the principles of choosing a policy portfolio are the same as those involved in choosing an investment portfolio.

[6] The practice of coordinating monetary and fiscal policies has an interesting downside for macroeconomists. We are, of course, very interested in separating the effects of one type of policy from those of another. But if two policies are generally used in concert, it is very difficult to use historical data to learn which policy was responsible for the observed results.

[7] William Brainard, "Uncertainty and the Effectiveness of Policy," *American Economic Review*, May 1967.

OPTIONAL    cont'd

where $Y$ is output, $M$ is the money stock, and $\beta$ is the monetary policy multiplier. $Y^*$ is the target for output. Because we may not be able to hit the target precisely, we need a rule for evaluating the success of policy that measures the damage done when we miss the target. While we hope that $Y$ will hit $Y^*$ exactly, we recognize there will generally be some gap between actual and target outcomes, $Y - Y^*$. We "keep score"; that is, we measure the damage attributable to a "miss" with the **loss function**.

**loss function**

A mathematical formula to calculate how much damage is done when a policy misses its function.

**marginal loss function**

The loss function calculated with respect to changes is the policy instrument.

$$L = {}^1\!/_2\,(Y - Y^*)^2 \qquad (2)$$

Note that this loss function puts a much larger penalty on large losses than on small losses. We evaluate the success of a policy choice, $M$, by substituting $\beta M$ for the realized value of output, $Y$, in equation (2). The **marginal loss function**, with respect to changes in the policy instrument $M$, is

$$ML(M) = (\beta M - Y^*) \times \beta \qquad (3)$$

and, as usual in economics, one way to think about minimizing losses is to set the marginal loss to zero.

We now work out an example, first when the multiplier is known and then when it is uncertain. Suppose that our target is $Y^* = 3$ and that we somehow know the multiplier is exactly $\beta = \bar{\beta} = 1$. The appropriate policy is obviously to set $M = 3$, but to carry out the formal analysis, we set the marginal loss equal to zero in equation (4) and solve for the optimal policy in equation (5).

$$ML(M) = 0 = (\bar{\beta} M - Y^*) \times \bar{\beta} = (Y - Y^*) \times \bar{\beta} \qquad (4)$$

$$M = \frac{Y^*}{\bar{\beta}} \qquad (5)$$

So we choose $M = 3/1 = 3$, observe $Y = 1 \times 3 = 3 = Y^*$, hit the target exactly, and according to the rating from equation (2), achieve a perfect, zero-loss, score.

Now, suppose instead that $\beta$ is either 0.5 or 1.5, with a 50 percent chance for either value. The average value of $\beta$ remains $\bar{\beta} = (0.5 + 1.5)/2 = 1.0$, just as in the previous example; the difference is that we have introduced uncertainty. Suppose basing policy on this average value, we again set policy at $M = 3$. (This is called the **certainty equivalence policy**.) If $\beta$ is actually 0.5, we will undershoot the target; if $\beta$ equals 1.5, we will overshoot. However, we can do a little better by shading in the direction of undershooting rather than overshooting, because a low value of $\beta$ means that the marginal impact of the policy is lower.

**certainty equivalence policy**

A policy made under the assumption that there is no uncertainty regarding future events.

We can work out the optimal choice for $M$ in this case by weighting the marginal loss function with equal chances for each value of $\beta$. The weighted marginal loss function is

$$ML(M) = 0 = 50\% \times [(0.5M - Y^*) \times 0.5] + 50\% \times [(1.5M - Y^*) \times 1.5] \qquad (6)$$

$$M = \frac{Y^*}{1.25} \qquad (7)$$

Equation (7) tells us to set $M$ to 2.4 instead of 3—we are more conservative in our use of policy than we would be under certainty equivalence. Thus, Brainard's analysis affirms our intuition that uncertainty should lead to caution.

## 17-4 | DYNAMIC POLICY AND INFORMATION FEEDBACK

While textbook graphs generally portray a point-in-time snapshot, real policy plays out over time. We have already seen that lags in the implementation and effect of policy introduce a dynamic element. In this section, we look at how a go-slow approach can give the policy maker a chance to incorporate new information into a gradually evolving policy.

Faced with a given policy objective—for example, to reduce inflation—a policy maker must choose between "gradualist" and cold-turkey policies. Gradualist policies move the economy slowly toward the target, while cold-turkey policies are those that try to hit the target as quickly as possible. Cold-turkey policies generate a "shock effect," which can be bad if the shock is disruptive but good if dramatic action adds to the policy maker's credibility. Gradualist policies, in contrast, have the advantage of allowing for the incorporation of new information as the policy plays out.

### Targets, Instruments, and Indicators: A Taxonomy

Economic variables play a variety of roles in policy discussions. It is useful to divide variables into "targets," "instruments," and "indicators."[8]

**targets**
Identified goals of policy.

▶ **Targets**—Targets are identified goals of policy. While the ultimate target is "the good of society," we focus more specifically on output and prices, unemployment, and inflation. Targets are usefully subdivided into "ultimate targets" and "intermediate targets." An example of an ultimate target is "to achieve zero inflation." As part of overall economic policy, a particular policy-making unit may be assigned the task of hitting a particular intermediate target. For example, the central bank may be instructed to aim for 2 percent annual growth of the money stock. Even though money growth per se is not an ultimate economic goal, targeting money growth may be the appropriate task (intermediate target) to assign to the central bank.

**instruments**
The tools the policy maker directly manipulates.

▶ **Instruments**—Instruments are the tools the policy maker manipulates directly. For example, a central bank might have an exchange rate target. Its instrument would be the purchase or sale of gold or other reserves.

**indicators**
Economic variables that signal whether we are getting closer to our desired targets.

▶ **Indicators**—Indicators are economic variables that signal whether we are getting closer to our desired targets. As an example, increases in interest rates (an indicator) sometimes signal that the market anticipates increased future inflation (a target). So indicators provide information feedback that allows a policy maker to adjust the instruments in order to do a better job of hitting the target.

Most economists agree that the best way to reach ultimate targets is for policy makers to use indicators to provide additional information in computing the best adjustments to the available instruments.

The categorization of variables into target, instrument, or indicator is sometimes situational. For example, in some years, central banks have treated interest rates as intermediate targets. In other years, central banks have used interest rates as indicators of the success of money supply policy. Indeed policy makers often face a choice of whether to use a particular policy tool as an instrument, destroying its value as an indicator, or to keep the tool as an indicator and forgo its use as a direct instrument.

www.bankofcanada.ca/en/
conference/cn2000e1.
htm

---

[8] Credit for the terminology goes to Benjamin M. Friedman, "Targets, Instruments, and Indicators of Monetary Policy," *Journal of Monetary Economics*, October 1975.

## 17-5 | ACTIVIST POLICY

We started this chapter by asking why there are any fluctuations in the Canadian economy when the policy measures needed to iron out those fluctuations seem to be so simple. The list of difficulties in the way of successful policy making that we have outlined may have raised the opposite question: Why should one believe that policy can do *anything* to reduce fluctuations in the economy?[9]

Indeed, considerations of the sort spelled out in the previous four sections have led Milton Friedman and others to argue that there should be no use of active countercyclical monetary policy and that monetary policy should be confined to making the money supply grow at a constant rate. The precise value of the constant rate of money growth, Friedman suggests, is less important than the fact that monetary growth should be constant and that policy should *not* respond to disturbances. At various times, he has suggested growth rates for money of 2 or 4 or 5 percent. As Friedman has expressed it, "By setting itself a steady course and keeping to it, the monetary authority could make a major contribution to promoting economic stability. By making that course one of steady but moderate growth in the quantity of money, it would make a major contribution to avoidance of either inflation or deflation of prices."[10] Friedman thus advocates a simple monetary rule in which the central bank does not respond to the condition of the economy. Policies that respond to the current or predicted state of the economy are called **activist policies**. Interestingly, Friedman does make an exception to this rule in the face of extreme disturbances.

In discussing the desirability of activist monetary and fiscal policy, we want to distinguish between policy actions taken in response to major disturbances to the economy and **fine-tuning**, in which policy variables are continually adjusted in response to small disturbances in the economy. We see no case for arguing that monetary and fiscal policy should not be used actively in the face of major disturbances to the economy. Most of the considerations of the previous sections of this chapter indicate some uncertainty about the effects of policy, but sometimes there can be no doubt about the direction in which to move policy.

For instance, an administration coming to power in 1933 should not have worried about the uncertainties associated with expansionary policy that we have outlined. The economy does not move from 25 percent unemployment to full employment in a short time. Thus, expansionary measures, such as a rapid growth of the money supply, increased government expenditures, or tax reductions, or all three, would have been appropriate policy since there was no chance that the economy would have "overshot" into a boom. The measures would have an impact only after the economy was at full employment. Similarly, contractionary policies for private demand are called for in wartime. In the event of large disturbances in the future, activist monetary and/or fiscal policy should once again be used.

Fine-tuning presents more complicated issues. In the case of fiscal policy, the long inside lags make discretionary fine-tuning virtually impossible, although automatic stabilizers are in fact fine-tuning all the time. But with monetary policy decisions being made frequently, fine-tuning of monetary policy is indeed possible. The question, then, is whether a small increase in the unemployment rate should lead to

**activist policies**
Policies that respond to the current or predicted state of the economy.

**fine-tuning**
Policy variables are continually adjusted in response to small disturbances in the economy.

---

[9] An excellent discussion of the issues is by Steven Sheffrin, *The Making of Economic Policy* (Oxford: Basil Blackwell, 1989).

[10] Milton Friedman, "The Role of Monetary Policy," *American Economic Review*, March 1968. See also his book *A Program for Monetary Stability* (New York: Fordham University Press, 1959).

BOX

17-2

## Rules and Discretion and Governors of the Bank of Canada

In 1975, the Bank of Canada under Governor Gerald Bouey began a policy of monetary gradualism that, from the perspective of rules versus discretion, was designed to be non-discretionary policy. Throughout the 1980s and 1990s, economists were refining their arguments *against* fine-tuning and discretionary policy, and the policy of monetary gradualism seemed to be in concordance with this thinking.

By the early 1980s, however, it was very clear that monetary gradualism was not achieving its goal, and the Bank of Canada changed policy to a much more discretionary stance. This could be seen by the aggressive increasing of nominal and real interest rates over the period 1979–1981, which led to the recession of the early 1980s. This discretionary policy move certainly brought the inflation rate down, but at the expense of a very large increase in the unemployment rate.

In 1987, when John Crow took over as governor, inflation was still close to 5 percent when the Bank of Canada was faced with a potentially large crisis—the stock market crashed on October 19, 1987. The Bank of Canada and other central banks in the G7 injected liquidity into their economies to avoid financial panic.

Perhaps as a result of the injection of liquidity, inflationary pressures continued to rise through the end of the decade, and the Bank of Canada tightened monetary policy by raising interest rates. This drove the economy into a recession in the early 1990s. This last recession appears to have driven inflation out of the economy, as inflation is now low and stable.

The election of the Liberal government in 1993 roughly coincided with the end of John Crow's term as governor of the Bank of Canada. Rather than reappointing Crow, the job was given to Gordon Thiessen. The Thiessen years appear to represent somewhat of a change in monetary policy stance. By July 1998, the Canadian dollar was depreciating badly against the U.S. dollar, but Thiessen showed no interest in raising interest rates to protect the dollar. This is in direct contrast to the behaviour of his predecessors, and may have represented a movement away from direct stabilization policy on the part of the Bank of Canada.

In February 2001, Thiessen's term expired and David Dodge was appointed governor of the Bank of Canada. This was an interesting appointment, as Dodge was the first governor to be appointed who did not come from inside the Bank of Canada. Unfortunately for Dodge, he was very quickly confronted with the events of September 11, 2001. Dodge chose an aggressively activist intervention in response to these events, which most observers agree was the correct response.

Although it is still somewhat early to judge properly, through 2002 and early 2003, Dodge appears to be quite willing to continue a somewhat activist policy, as he has altered the direction of interest rate changes more than once.

a small increase in the growth rate of money or whether policy should not respond until the increase in unemployment becomes large, say more than 1 percent.

The problem is that the disturbance that caused the increase in unemployment may be either transitory or permanent. If it is transitory, nothing should be done. If it is permanent, policy should react to a small disturbance in a small way. Given uncertainty over the nature of the disturbance, the technically correct response is a small one, between the zero that is appropriate for a transitory shock and the full response that is appropriate for a permanent disturbance. Accordingly, fine-tuning is appropriate provided that policy responses are always kept small in response to small disturbances.

What does this say about the problems of discretionary policy? First, the inflationary bias of policy noted in the text can be reduced by having an independent central bank, charged with the task of maintaining the value of the currency or low inflation. Second, good policy makers make a difference. So does a good staff—and the Bank of Canada has an excellent professional staff.

However, the case for fine-tuning is a controversial one. The major argument against it is that in practice, policy makers do not in fact behave as suggested—making only small adjustments in response to small disturbances. If allowed to do anything, they may do too much. Instead of merely trying to offset disturbances, policy makers shift toward fine-tuning to keep the economy always exactly at full employment, with the risk of overdoing a good thing. The "full employment bias" in policies risks creating inflation.

The major lesson is not that policy is impossible but that overly ambitious policy is risky. The lesson is to proceed with extreme caution, always bearing in mind the possibility that policy itself may be destabilizing.

## Rules versus Discretion

**rules versus discretion**
A policy is set according to a rule if policy does not change in response to observed changes in the economy. A policy is set according to discretion if policy changes in response to observed changes in the economy.

If there is a risk that policy makers react to disturbances in unpredictable ways and use dosages that are excessively influenced by the perception of the day, and if all this is possibly one of the reasons for macroeconomic instability, why not put policy on automatic pilot? This is the issue of **rules versus discretion**. Should the monetary authority and also the fiscal authority conduct policy in accordance with pre-announced rules that describe precisely how their policy variables will be determined in all future situations, or should they be allowed to use their discretion in determining the values of the policy variables at different times?

One example of a rule is the constant-growth-rate rule, say at 4 percent, for monetary policy. The rule is that no matter what happens, the money supply will be kept growing at 4 percent. Another example would be a rule stating that the money supply growth rate will be increased by an additional 2 percent per year for every 1 percent unemployment in excess of, say, 5.5 percent. Algebraically, such a rule would be expressed as

$$\frac{\Delta M}{M} = 4.0 + 2(u - 5.5) \tag{8}$$

where the growth rate of money $\Delta M/M$ is an annual percentage rate, and $u$ is the percentage unemployment rate.

The activist monetary rule of equation (8) implies that at 5.5 percent unemployment, monetary growth is 4 percent. If unemployment rises above 5.5 percent, monetary growth is *automatically* increased. Thus, with 7.5 percent unemployment, monetary growth would be 8 percent, using equation (8). Conversely, if unemployment dropped below 5.5 percent, monetary growth would be lowered below 4 percent. The rule therefore gears the amount of monetary stimulus to an indicator of the business cycle. By linking monetary growth to the unemployment rate, an activist, anticyclical monetary policy is achieved, but this is done without any discretion.

The issue of rules versus discretion has been clouded by the fact that most proponents of rules have been non-activists, whose preferred monetary rule is a constant-growth-rate rule. Consequently, the argument has tended to centre on whether activist policy is desirable or not. The fundamental point to recognize is that we can design **activist rules**. We can design rules that have countercyclical features without, at the same time, leaving any discretion about their actions to policy makers. The point is made by equation (8), which is an activist rule because it expands money supply when unemployment is high and reduces it when unemployment is low. The equation leaves no room for policy discretion and in this respect is a rule.

Given that both the economy and our knowledge of it are changing over time, there is no economic case for stating permanent policy rules that would tie the hands of the monetary and fiscal authorities permanently.[11] Two practical issues, then, arise in the rules-versus-discretion debate. The first is where the authority to change the rule is located. At one extreme, the growth rate of money could be prescribed by the constitution. At the other, it is left to the Bank of Canada. In each case, policy can be changed, but changing the constitution takes longer than it takes the Bank of Canada to change its policy. In the trade-off between certainty about future policy and flexibility of policy, activists place a premium on flexibility, and those in favour of rules that are difficult to change place a premium on the fact that the Bank of Canada has often made mistakes in the past. Because the financial system responds very quickly to shocks and is so interconnected, many believe it essential that the Bank of Canada have considerable discretion and thus flexibility to respond to disturbances. But that is far from a universal judgement.

The second issue is whether the policy makers should announce in advance the policies they will be following for the foreseeable future. Such announcements are in principle desirable because they help private individuals forecast future policy.

**activist rules**

Rules that have countercyclical features without leaving any discretion about their actions to policy makers.

---

## BOX 17-3

### Fiscal Policy and Fine-Tuning—The Side Effects

Fiscal policy can be an inappropriate tool with which to tune the economy because of its side effects. Presumably the best tax rate is one that pays for the government while introducing minimal distortions in private decisions. Presumably the level of unemployment compensation is set so as to balance fairness to the unemployed against lost incentives to work. There is little reason that such choices will coincidentally be just the right ones to move the economy out of a recession.

So even if purely macroeconomic considerations argue for the use of fiscal rather than monetary policy, the existence of side effects limits the availability of fiscal policy for short run stabilization.

---

[11] For evidence on this point, see John B. Taylor, "Discretion and Policy Rules in Practice," *Carnegie-Rochester Conference Series on Public Policy*, December 1993.

## 17-6 | DYNAMIC INCONSISTENCY AND RULES VERSUS DISCRETION

**dynamic inconsistency**
Policy makers who have discretion will be tempted to take short run actions that are inconsistent with the economy's best long run interests.

The case for modest, activist, discretionary policy seems clear. Why then do countries, such as Canada, that follow such procedures sometimes seem to have a bias toward too much inflation? Is there any way to restructure stabilization policy to avoid this bias? The answer to these questions is found in an examination of the idea of **dynamic inconsistency**. Essentially, the argument is that policy makers who have discretion will be tempted to take short run actions that are inconsistent with the economy's best long run interests.[12] What's more, this is the natural outcome with rational, well-intentioned policy makers. In fact, the analysis of dynamic inconsistency begins with the assumption that the policy maker shares the public's dislike of both inflation and unemployment.

The key to understanding dynamic inconsistency lies in remembering that there is a short run trade-off between inflation and unemployment given by the short run Phillips curve, but that there is no long run trade-off because of the adjustment of inflationary expectations. The best long run position for the economy is full employment with zero (or at least low) inflation. However, if the policy maker announces a full employment–zero inflation policy, she will immediately be led to "cheat" by seeking lower unemployment and slightly higher inflation. It is this split between announced and executed plans that gives rise to the name "dynamic inconsistency."

One can model the interaction between policy maker and the economy as occurring in three sequential steps:

1. The policy maker announces a policy, say, zero percent inflation.

2. Economic decision makers choose a level of anticipated inflation consistent with the announced policy, implying the economy will be positioned on the short run Phillips curve at full employment.

3. The policy maker implements the best possible policy. Since the short run Phillips curve is now fixed, the policy maker can reduce unemployment at the expense of a little inflation. This policy is *optimal*, although it is *inconsistent* with the policy announced in step 1.

We use Figure 17-3 to illustrate the interactions between the policy maker and economic decision makers. The figure shows the Phillips curve trade-off between unemployment and inflation. Everyone, policy maker and the public, prefers to be at point A, with full employment and zero inflation. At point A, the policy maker promises and the public expects zero inflation, so the economy operates on the bottom short run Phillips curve. Suppose, through good fortune, that the economy reached the preferred point, A. What will the policy maker do? At zero inflation, everyone, policy maker and the public, is willing to accept a small amount of increased inflation in order to reduce unemployment. So the right thing for the policy-maker to do is increase inflation a little in order to reduce unemployment, sliding up and to the left along the bottom short run Phillips curve. The policy maker will push the

---

[12] The basic reference is Finn Kydland and Edward Prescott, "Rules Rather Than Discretion: The Inconsistency of Optimal Plans," *Journal of Political Economy*, June 1977. This is very difficult reading. See also V.V. Chari, "Time Consistency and Optimal Policy Design," Federal Reserve Bank of Minneapolis *Quarterly Review*, Fall 1988. See also Robert J. Barro and David B. Gordon, "A Positive Theory of Monetary Policy in a Natural Rate Model," *Journal of Political Economy*, August 1983, and "Rules, Discretion and Reputation in a Model of Monetary Policy," *Journal of Monetary Economics*, July 1983.

*FIGURE 17-3*

**THE PHILLIPS CURVE AND ECONOMIC POLICY**

The economy starts at point A with zero inflation. If policy moves the economy to point B to reduce unemployment, expectations will bring the economy to point C. If the policy maker attempts to push the economy back to point A, there is a credibility problem.

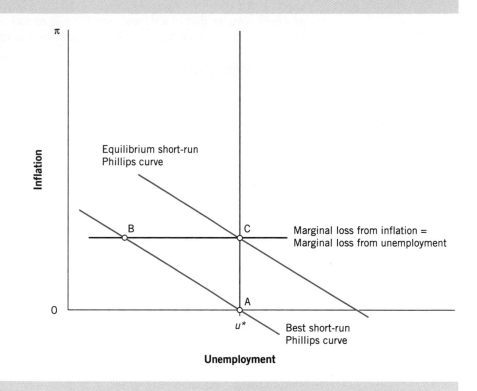

economy to point B, where inflation is just high enough that the marginal loss from more inflation equals the marginal benefit from lower unemployment.

At point B, inflation is greater than anticipated. Decision makers will come to anticipate higher inflation, and the short run Phillips curve will move to the upper Phillips curve. Eventually, the economy reaches equilibrium at point C, at full employment but with positive inflation. (At point C, the marginal loss from inflation is high enough that the policy maker is unwilling to increase inflation further to reduce unemployment; that is, there is no temptation to move further to the left along the upper Phillips curve.)

In equilibrium, the economy ends up with high inflation at point C, even though everyone prefers point A. The policy maker will gladly promise to return to zero inflation and stay at point A, but the promise isn't *credible*, because if the economy returned to point A, *everyone* would again agree to inflate back to B. It would be better if the policy maker kept her promises, but as soon as low inflation promises are believed, it is then in everyone's best interest to "cheat."

How can the temptation to engage in dynamic inconsistency be avoided, or at least minimized? First, a forward-looking policy maker will realize the value of maintaining a *reputation* for consistency. The difficulty is that there will always be outside pressures pushing for a short run inflationary bias. Second, the government can choose a policy maker whose personal tastes are more anti-inflationary than those of the public at large, so that the policy maker will lean against inflationary pressures. In terms of Figure 17-3, this means finding a policy maker with a black line lower than society's black line. Third, the policy maker can be given a contract with payments that reward low inflation. Fourth, low inflation "rules" can be adopted to prevent the policy maker from making the "discretionary" choices that lead to dynamic inconsistency. All these ideas have merit and all have been used to some extent. The problem remains that in a democracy, there is always a temptation to lower unemployment at the cost of higher inflation "just this one time."

OPTIONAL

### DYNAMIC INCONSISTENCY—A FORMAL APPROACH

In this section, we present an algebraic version of the model of dynamic inconsistency illustrated in Figure 17-3. We assume that the policy maker chooses the level of inflation, although in practice, the policy maker actually chooses monetary or fiscal policy and inflation is a result rather than a direct choice. The choice of inflation leads to the unemployment rate given by the short run Phillips curve in equation (9):

$$\pi = \pi^e + \epsilon(u^* - u) \tag{9}$$

The policy maker, and the public, prefers low unemployment and zero inflation. We "keep score" by specifying a loss function for the policy maker in equation (10):

$$L = a(u - u^*) + \pi^2 \tag{10}$$

The loss function in equation (10) says that high unemployment is bad and that any deviation from zero inflation is bad. The higher the coefficient $a$, the greater the relative weight given to lowering unemployment.

The three steps in the "game" played by the policy maker are (1) the policy maker chooses and announces an inflation policy (point A in Figure 17-3); (2) "the economy" picks anticipated policy, $\pi^e$ (point B); (3) the policy maker implements an actual policy, $\pi$, that minimizes the loss function in equation (10) (point C). In step 2, the decision makers look forward, guessing what the policy maker will do in step 3. In step 1, the policy maker is also looking forward, guessing what the economy will do in step 2 as it looks toward step 3. So early choices by the policy maker must anticipate later stages, which themselves depend on the choices made earlier. Decision makers work out their choices by starting at the end and working backward. This choice method is a simple example of **dynamic programming**.

**dynamic programming**

A process in which decision makers work out their choices by starting at the end and working backward.

The final "score" is calculated by inserting the actual policy, $\pi$, and anticipated inflation, $\pi^e$, into the loss function using the Phillips curve relationship to compute the deviation of unemployment from the natural rate. The final score is

$$L(\pi) = a\left[ -\frac{1}{\epsilon}(\pi - \pi^e) \right] + \pi^2 \tag{11}$$

The policy maker minimizes the loss in equation (11) by setting the marginal loss function in equation (12) equal to zero, giving the black line in Figure 17-3.

$$ML(\pi) = \frac{a}{\epsilon} + 2\,\pi = 0 \tag{12}$$

So the optimal policy is

$$\pi = \frac{a}{2\epsilon} \tag{13}$$

> ### O P T I O N A L   cont'd
>
> Note that the result in equation (13) holds for *any* level value of $\pi^e$.
>
> Everyone desires zero inflation, but in the last stage of the game, it always "pays" for the policy maker to choose a positive inflation rate. In fact, since anticipated inflation equals $a/2\epsilon$, if the policy maker chooses in the last step to set inflation below $a/2\epsilon$, a recession will result. The problem is that society has no way to *commit* to zero inflation.
>
> Note, in equation (13), that a loss function weighted heavily against unemployment—one with a high *a*—results in more inflation. This perverse result occurs because a high *a* increases the incentive in the last step to raise inflation to lower unemployment. However, if society can cede power to a policy maker who cares less about unemployment, one with a lower *a,* lower inflation will result.

## *Working with Data*

In Box 17-2, we discussed some of the monetary policy events over the last number of years. Recently, setting Bank of Canada interest rate policy has become very interesting, as there have been several events that have changed the course of the economy, starting with the events of September 11, 2001, and then the outbreak of SARS and BSE (mad cow disease).

Go to CANSIM and retrieve data on the bank rate and the Consumer Price Index. Use the latter to calculate the annual inflation rate. Plot these two variables over the period from January 2001 to the latest date that is available. Can you identify any reasons for bank rate changes in this graph?

## C H A P T E R   S U M M A R Y

▶ The potential need for stabilizing policy actions arises from economic disturbances. Some of these disturbances, such as changes in money demand, consumption spending, or investment demand, arise from within the private sector. Others, such as wars, may arise for non-economic reasons.

▶ Wise policy makers work with what we know about the economy while also recognizing the limits of our knowledge. Good policy design includes an assesssment of the risks associated with unforeseen errors.

▶ The three key difficulties of stabilization policy are that (*a*) policy works with lags; (*b*) the outcome of policy depends very much on private sector expectations, which are difficult to predict and may react to policy; and (*c*) there is uncertainty about both the structure of the economy and the shocks that hit the economy.

▶ When forming economic policy, policy makers must choose between sudden policy changes and gradual changes. Sudden policy changes may enhance the policy makers' credibility but are based on limited information. Gradual changes allow policy makers to incorporate new information as the economy moves toward its target.

www.mcgrawhill.ca/college/dornbusch

▶ For the purposes of policy, economic variables can be classified as targets (identified goals of policy), instruments (the tools of policy), and indicators (economic variables that signal whether we are getting close to our policy targets).

▶ There are clearly occasions on which active monetary and fiscal policy actions should be taken to stabilize the economy. These are situations in which the economy has been affected by major disturbances.

▶ Fine-tuning—continuous attempts to stabilize the economy in the face of small disturbances—is more controversial. If fine-tuning is undertaken, it calls for small policy responses in an attempt to moderate the economy's fluctuations, rather than to remove them entirely. A very active policy in response to small disturbances is likely to destabilize the economy.

▶ In the rules-versus-discretion debate, it is important to recognize that activist rules are possible. The two important issues in the debate are how difficult it should be to change policy and whether policy should be announced as far ahead as possible. There is a trade-off between the certainty about future policy that comes from rules and the flexibility of the policy makers in responding to shocks.

## KEY TERMS

permanent disturbance, *345*
transitory disturbance, *345*
inside lag, *346*
outside lag, *346*
recognition lag, *346*
decision lag, *347*
action lag, *347*
discrete lag, *348*
distributed lag, *348*
econometric model, *350*

credibility, *350*
econometric policy evaluation
     critique, *351*
multiplier uncertainty, *352*
portfolio of policy instruments
     (diversification), *353*
loss function, *354*
marginal loss function, *354*
certainty equivalence policy, *354*
targets, *355*

instruments, *355*
indicators, *355*
activist policies, *356*
fine-tuning, *356*
rules versus discretion, *358*
activist rules, *359*
dynamic inconsistency, *360*
dynamic programming, *362*

## DISCUSSION QUESTIONS

*1. Suppose there was a small, negative shock to demand. You—a policy maker—have a stack of papers in front of you detailing the magnitude of the shock and its devastating effects on the people of your country. You are tempted to use an active policy to offset these effects. Your advisers have estimated its impact on the economy, in both the long and short runs. What questions should you ask yourself before committing to this course of action? Why?

2. **a.** What is an inside lag?

   **b.** We can divide inside lags into three smaller, sequential lags. What are these, and in what order do they occur?

   **c.** Which has the smaller inside lag—fiscal or monetary policy? Why?

   **d.** What is the inside lag for automatic stabilizers?

---

*An asterisk denotes a more difficult problem.

3. **a.** What is an outside lag?

   **b.** Why does it generally take the form of a distributed lag?

   **c.** Which has the smaller outside lag—fiscal or monetary policy?

4. Which would you recommend be used to offset the effect of a temporary shock to output—fiscal or monetary policy? Why?

5. **a.** What is an econometric model?

   **b.** How might one be used?

   **c.** There is always some uncertainty with respect to predictions based on such models. Why? What is the source of this uncertainty?

6. Evaluate the argument that monetary policy should be determined by a rule rather than discretion. How about fiscal policy?

7. Evaluate the arguments for a constant-growth-rate rule for money.

8. What is dynamic inconsistency? Explain intuitively how it might arise in the case of the short run trade-off between inflation and unemployment.

9. How does nominal GDP targeting differ from real GDP targeting? Why is real GDP targeting the riskier of the two strategies?

## A P P L I C A T I O N    Q U E S T I O N S

1. Suppose that GDP is $40 billion below its potential level. It is expected that next-period GDP will be $20 billion below potential and that two periods from now it will be back at its potential level. You are told that the multiplier for government spending is 2 and that the effects of the increased government spending are immediate. What policy actions can be taken to put GDP back on target each period?

2. The basic facts about the path of GDP are as in Application Question 1, but there is now a one-period outside lag for government spending. Decisions to spend today are translated into actual spending only tomorrow. The multiplier for government spending is still 2 in the period that the spending takes place.

   **a.** What is the best that can be done to keep GDP as close to target as possible each period?

   **b.** Compare the path of GDP in this question with the path in Application Question 1 after policy actions have been taken.

3. Life has become yet more complicated. Government spending works with a distributed lag. Now when $1 billion is spent today, GDP increases by $1 billion this period and $1.5 billion next period.

   **a.** What happens to the path of GDP if government spending rises enough this period to put GDP back to its potential level this period?

   **b.** Suppose fiscal policy actions are taken to put GDP at its potential level this period. What fiscal policy will be needed to put GDP on target next period?

   **c.** Explain why the government has to be so active in keeping GDP on target in this case.

4. Suppose that you knew that the multiplier for government spending was between 1 and 2.5 but that its effects ended in the period in which spending was increased. How would you run fiscal policy if GDP would, without policy, behave as in Application Question 1?

5. Go to CANSIM and retrieve the TSE 300 Index and the 90-day Treasury bill interest rate. Graph the percentage change in the TSE 300 Index with the Treasury bill rate and relate this to the discussion in Box 17-2.

www.mcgrawhill.ca/college/dornbusch

*6. Suppose that, as the governor of the Bank of Canada, you decided to "put policy on automatic pilot" and require that monetary policy follow an established rule. When might each of the following two rules be appropriate? (*a*) Maintain a constant interest rate. (*b*) Maintain a constant money supply.

---

*An asterisk denotes a more difficult problem.

## CHAPTER 18

# THE MONEY SUPPLY AND MONETARY POLICY

## LEARNING OBJECTIVES

After reading and studying this chapter, you should be able to:

▶ Understand that money supply determination involves the interaction of the balance sheets of the Bank of Canada, the banking system, and the non-bank public.

▶ Understand that the money supply is determined by the monetary base (currency and reserves) and lending by chartered banks.

▶ Understand that the Bank of Canada controls the money supply in the short run by controlling the overnight interest rate.

▶ Understand that the implementation of monetary policy in an uncertain world involves the choice of ultimate and intermediate targets.

▶ Understand that the term structure of interest rates explains how long-term interest rates are related to short-term interest rates.

W
e have so far taken the money supply to be given and determined by the Bank of Canada. The Bank is indeed able to influence the money supply quite closely, but it does not set it directly. In this chapter we study how the actions of the Bank of Canada and the financial sector interact in determining the money stock. In addition, we shall examine in some detail how the Bank of Canada operates monetary policy.

## 18-1 | HOW IS THE MONEY SUPPLY DETERMINED?

In order to answer the question in the title of this section, it is helpful to think about how money has evolved in modern economies. In Section 16-2, we discussed the inefficiencies that arise in a barter economy. These inefficiencies surround the concept of the "double coincidence of wants." In a barter economy, if I grow corn and want to trade this for cows, I must find someone who wants my corn and at the same time is willing to trade cows. The existence of money as a medium of exchange and a unit of account overcomes these inefficiencies.

www2.bmo.com/content/
0,1151,divId-4_langId-1_
navCode-3227,00.html

www.bankofcanada.ca/en/
currency.htm

However, although the introduction of money into an economy is efficient from the point of view of trading goods, the practical question is: Who is going to issue the money? In the nineteenth century in Canada, private banks issued their own currency, the first being Montreal Bank (now the Bank of Montreal) in 1817.[1] However, as with any currency, if confidence in the currency erodes, people will no longer hold it or use it. In response to a rash of private bank collapses and lack of confidence in the private bank monies in the mid-1800s, the governing authority began to issue its own currency in 1866, but this currency still circulated with private bank money. In 1935, the Bank of Canada was created and private bank notes were gradually phased out, so that by approximately 1951, Canada had one common currency, issued and controlled by the central bank.

You can see that any discussion of the supply of money involves thinking about the actions of three groups of economic agents: the non-bank public, the private banks, and the Bank of Canada (the central bank). In order to organize our thoughts about money and the money supply, we can think of these groups as each having a consolidated balance sheet. This is summarized in Table 18-1.

Table 18-1 shows simplified balance sheets of the three sectors that play a role in determining the money supply. Money in the form of currency or deposits is an asset of the non-bank public. In addition, we show holdings of government securities (Treasury bills or government bonds) as an asset, and loans from chartered banks as a liability of this sector. These loans appear as an asset of the chartered banks, and deposits appear as a liability of the bank sector.

**cash reserves**
Currency held by chartered banks and chartered bank deposits at the Bank of Canada.

**settlement balances**
Deposits held by direct clearers at the Bank of Canada.

The other assets in the balance sheet of the chartered banks are government securities and **cash reserves**. Cash reserves are held by the chartered banks to meet (1) the demands of their customers for currency either directly or through automated teller machines, and (2) payments their customers make by cheques that are deposited in other banks. Cash reserves consist of currency held by the chartered banks (till money) and also of deposits held by the chartered banks at the Bank of Canada. The latter are referred to as **settlement balances**. A detailed balance sheet for the chartered banks is shown in Table 18-2.

---

[1] An interesting history of the evolution of money in Canada is contained in "A History of the Canadian Dollar" by James Powell, which can be found on the Bank of Canada Internet site at www.bankofcanada.ca/en/currency.htm.

## TABLE 18-1

### BALANCE SHEETS

| | Assets | Liabilities |
|---|---|---|
| Non-Bank Public | Money:<br>  Currency outside banks<br>  Deposits<br>Government securities | Bank loans |
| Chartered Banks | Cash reserves:<br>  Currency<br>  Settlement balances<br>Bank loans<br>Government securities | Deposits |
| Bank of Canada | Government securities | Monetary base:<br>  Currency in circulation*<br>  Deposits of chartered banks<br>  (settlement balances) |

*This item includes both the currency held by the non-bank public (currency outside banks) and the till money included in the cash reserves of the chartered banks.

Settlement balances appear as a liability in the balance sheet of the Bank of Canada. The chartered banks use their accounts at the Bank of Canada to settle the amounts owing as a result of the cheques written by their customers. If a customer of the Bank of Montreal makes a payment of $100 by a cheque that is then deposited in the Royal Bank, the cheque is settled by transferring $100 from the Bank of Montreal's account at the Bank of Canada to that of the Royal Bank. The process by which the net amounts owing among the banks are settled at the end of each day is referred to as the *clearing system*. Chartered banks and other financial institutions that are members of the Canadian Payments Association and that participate in the clearing system are referred to as *direct clearers* and are required to hold deposits at the Bank of Canada.

The other items shown in the simplified balance sheet of the Bank of Canada are government securities on the asset side and currency in circulation on the liability side (see Table 18-3 for a detailed balance sheet). The sum of currency in circulation

## TABLE 18-2

### BALANCE SHEET OF THE CHARTERED BANKS, DECEMBER 2002 (billions)

| Assets | | Liabilities | |
|---|---|---|---|
| Bank of Canada notes and deposits | 4.2 | Demand deposits | 101.2 |
| Loans and investments | | Personal savings deposits | 373.5 |
| Government of Canada securities | 97.1 | Non-personal term and notice deposits | 180.1 |
| Loans | 686.9 | Government of Canada deposits | 2.3 |
| Other securities | 125.8 | Other liabilities, net* | 256.9 |
| Total Canadian dollar assets | 914.0 | Total liabilities | 914.0 |

*Balancing item that includes net foreign currency liabilities and shareholders' equity.

SOURCE: Bank of Canada, *Weekly Financial Statistics:* www.bankofcanada.ca/en/wfsgen.htm.

### TABLE 18-3

**BALANCE SHEET OF THE BANK OF CANADA, DECEMBER 2002** (billions)

| Assets | | Liabilities | |
|---|---|---|---|
| Government of Canada securities | 40,074 | Notes in circulation | 39,059 |
| | | Deposits | |
| Advances | 402 | Chartered banks | 517 |
| Net foreign currency assets | 391 | Other Canadian Payments Association members | 387 |
| Other assets | 1,217 | Government of Canada | 1,705 |
| | | Other liabilities* | 416 |
| Total assets | 42,084 | Total liabilities | 42,084 |

*Excludes foreign currency liabilities that are netted against assets.

SOURCE: Bank of Canada, *Weekly Financial Statistics:* www.bankofcanada.ca/en/wfsgen.htm.

---

**monetary base**

The sum of currency in circulation and the deposits of the chartered banks at the Bank of Canada.

and the deposits of the chartered banks at the Bank of Canada is called the **monetary base**. Part of the currency is held by the non-bank public (*currency outside banks*), and the remainder is held by the chartered banks as till money.

## Open Market Operations

The Bank of Canada does not have direct control over the volume of bank deposits, but it can control the money supply indirectly through the monetary base that appears on the liability side of its balance sheet. An important means by which the Bank of Canada can accommodate a growing economy's need for a rising money supply is the use of **open market operations** to change the monetary base. Open market operations are purchases or sales of government securities by the central bank.

**open market operations**

Purchases or sales of government securities by the central bank.

www.bankof
canada.ca/en/bserv.htm

We examine the mechanics of an open market purchase, in which the Bank of Canada buys, say, $1 million of government bonds from individuals or businesses that make up the non-bank public. The accounting for the open market purchase is shown in Table 18-4. The Bank of Canada's holdings of government securities rise by $1 million and the non-bank public's holdings fall by the same amount. To pay for the bonds, the Bank of Canada writes a cheque on itself, and the seller deposits the proceeds in a chartered bank. The bank in turn sends the cheque to the Bank of Canada so that cash reserves increase by $1 million. Thus, the monetary base increases by the amount of the open market purchase.

If the seller of the bond chooses to hold some part of the proceeds in the form of currency rather than bank deposits, then the increases in cash reserves and deposits will be correspondingly reduced by the *currency drain*. Table 18-5 shows the case in which 5 cents out of each dollar is held in the form of currency. Cash reserves and

---

### TABLE 18-4

**AN OPEN MARKET PURCHASE FROM THE NON-BANK PUBLIC**

| | Assets | | Liabilities | |
|---|---|---|---|---|
| **Non-Bank Public** | Deposits | +1 | | |
| | Government securities | −1 | | |
| **Chartered Banks** | Cash reserves | +1 | Deposits | +1 |
| **Bank of Canada** | Government securities | +1 | Chartered bank deposits | +1 |

## TABLE 18-5

### AN OPEN MARKET PURCHASE WITH CURRENCY DRAIN

| | Assets | | Liabilities | |
|---|---|---|---|---|
| **Non-Bank Public** | Deposits | +.95 | | |
| | Currency | +.05 | | |
| | Government securities | −1 | | |
| **Chartered Banks** | Cash reserves | +.95 | Deposits | +.95 |
| **Bank of Canada** | Government securities | +1 | Chartered bank deposits | +.95 |
| | | | Currency | +.05 |

deposits will increase by $0.95 million, and if we assume that the chartered bank obtains the required currency from the Bank of Canada, then the liability side of the Bank of Canada's balance sheet will show an increase of $0.95 million of chartered bank deposits and $0.05 million of currency. However, the increase in the monetary base, the sum of currency and deposits at the Bank of Canada, will still be $1 million, the amount of the open market purchase. In general, an open market operation affects the monetary base by the amount of the purchase or sale *regardless of how changes in the money supply are split between currency and deposits*. The composition of the base is affected by this split, and it is for this reason that we view the central bank as controlling the monetary base as a whole rather than either of its components.

We have assumed so far that the open market purchase is made from the non-bank public. What will happen if the seller is a chartered bank? This case is illustrated in Table 18-6. The chartered bank receives a cheque from the Bank of Canada and exchanges it for a deposit. Thus, the monetary base is increased as in the previous case, but the transaction has no direct effect on the non-bank public.

## TABLE 18-6

### AN OPEN MARKET PURCHASE FROM A CHARTERED BANK

| | Assets | | Liabilities | |
|---|---|---|---|---|
| **Chartered Banks** | Cash reserves | +1 | | |
| | Government securities | −1 | | |
| **Bank of Canada** | Government securities | +1 | Chartered bank deposits | +1 |

## The Money Supply and the Monetary Base

A relationship between the monetary base and the money supply can be derived as follows. The money supply is defined in equation (1) as the sum of currency ($CU$) and deposits ($D$).

$$M = CU + D \qquad (1)$$

The monetary base ($B$) is:

$$B = CU + R \qquad (2)$$

where $R$ denotes cash reserves. Ignoring other items in the balance sheet of the chartered banks and denoting bank loans by $L$, we have

$$R + L = D \tag{3}$$

Thus, the money supply can be decomposed as follows

$$M = CU + D = CU + R + L = B + L \tag{4}$$

Here we see that the money supply is composed of the base, which is a liability of the Bank of Canada, and a component equal to the volume of loans made by the chartered banks. Thus, the money supply can be increased either by changes in the base initiated by the Bank of Canada or by the extending of credit by the chartered banks. The making of loans by the banks involves the creation of money, since the banks simply create deposits that show up on the liability side of their balance sheets to match the increase in loans on the asset side.

## Bank Lending and the Money Supply

To illustrate the creation of money by bank lending, we consider the granting of a loan of $1000 by Bank A to an individual or business in the non-bank sector. Table 18-7 shows the resulting changes in bank balance sheets. The loan appears as an asset of Bank A and the proceeds appear as an increase in deposits, which are a liability of the bank. (The balance sheet of the borrower will of course show the deposits as an asset and the loan as a liability.) Suppose, as is likely, that the proceeds are used to make a payment and that a cheque is written to someone who deposits it in Bank B. When the cheque is cleared, the deposits and the settlement balances are transferred from Bank A to Bank B. Thus, although the lending bank cannot count on being able to make loans without suffering a clearing loss (a loss of settlement balances), for the banking system as a whole, the net effect is an increase in loans and deposits with no change in the total amount of settlement balances.[2]

| *TABLE 18-7* | BANK LENDING AND MONEY CREATION |
| --- | --- |

(a)

**Bank A**

| Assets | Liabilities |
| --- | --- |
| Loans | Deposits |
| +1000 | +1000 |

(b)

**Bank A**

| Assets | Liabilities |
| --- | --- |
| Cash reserves | Deposits |
| −1000 | −1000 |

**Bank B**

| Assets | Liabilities |
| --- | --- |
| Cash reserves | Deposits |
| +1000 | +1000 |

---

[2] If, as in Table 18-5, some part of the proceeds are held in the form of currency, then there will be a reduction in total settlement balances equal to the amount of currency withdrawn, but there will be no change in the monetary base.

## The Money Multiplier

**money multiplier**

The ratio of the money supply to the monetary base.

Since the chartered banks can increase the money supply by making loans, what limits the size of the money supply given the size of the monetary base as determined by the Bank of Canada? The **money multiplier** provides an answer to this question. The money multiplier is defined as the ratio of the money supply to the monetary base.

The potential expansion of bank credit and the money supply is essentially limited by two factors. First, it depends on the proportion of the money supply that the non-bank public chooses to hold in the form of currency rather than deposits. Second, it depends on the ratio of cash reserves to deposits that the chartered banks choose to maintain.

Using equations (1) and (2), the ratio of the money supply to the monetary base can be written

$$\frac{M}{B} = \frac{CU+D}{CU+R} = \frac{CU/D+1}{CU/D+R/D}$$

Denoting the public's desired ratio of currency to deposits by $cu = CU/D$, and the banks' desired ratio of cash reserves to deposits by $re = R/D$, we can write the money multiplier as

$$\frac{M}{B} = \frac{cu+1}{cu+re} \tag{5}$$

It is clear from equation (5) that the money multiplier is greater than 1. For this reason, the monetary base is sometimes referred to as *high-powered money*. It is also clear that the smaller the reserve ratio, *re*, and the smaller the currency-deposit ratio, *cu*, the larger is the money multiplier.

## The Value of the Multiplier

Table 18-8 shows the calculation of the money multiplier for *M*2 as given by equation (5) using the actual values of the components that existed in December 2002. The same result can be obtained by taking the ratio of the *M*2 money stock to the sum of currency and reserves.

What determines the values of the two ratios that enter into the money multiplier? The currency-deposit ratio is determined primarily by payment habits. It has a strong seasonal pattern and is highest around the December holiday season. The cash reserve ratio reflects two distinct components of the banks' demand for reserves. The first is the level of the *minimum required cash reserve ratio* prescribed under the Bank

**TABLE 18-8** — CALCULATION OF THE *M*2 MULTIPLIER, DECEMBER 2002

| Currency (CU) | Deposits (D) | Cash Reserves (R) | cu = CU/D | re = R/D | Multiplier $=\frac{cu+1}{cu+re}$ |
|---|---|---|---|---|---|
| 38.9 | 531.1 | 5.7 | .073 | .011 | 12.77 |

SOURCE: Bank of Canada, *Weekly Financial Statistics:* www.bankofcanada.ca/en/wfsgen.htm.

Act. From 1985 to 1992, there was a 10 percent requirement for demand deposits and a lower ratio for other deposits. Under the 1991 Bank Act, these requirements were phased out over the two years ending July 1994. Since then, a system of zero reserve requirements has been in effect.

The second factor affecting the reserve-deposit ratio is the amount of cash reserves held by the chartered banks to meet their customers' demands for currency and to meet any indebtedness to other banks arising from the clearing of cheques. In a system with minimum reserve requirements, only excess cash reserves held beyond the required level are available for this purpose. With the abolition of reserve requirements, total holdings of cash reserves can be used.

As a result of a downward trend in the ratio of currency to demand deposits, changes in the required minimum reserve ratios, and changes in the proportions of demand and savings deposits, there has been an upward trend in the money multiplier. For example, the *M*2 multiplier was about 6 in 1980 as compared with the value of 12.77 calculated above for 2002.

## 18-2 | SHORT RUN CONTROL OF THE MONEY SUPPLY

The money multiplier is useful for determining the upper limit of the money supply given the monetary base and the two ratios that represent the behaviour of the public and the chartered banks. However, it is of little relevance to how the Bank of Canada influences the money supply in the short run. To see why this is so, we have to examine in detail the rules governing the holding of cash reserves under the Bank Act.

### Policy Implementation with Minimum Required Reserve Ratios

As indicated in the previous section, prior to 1994, the chartered banks were required to maintain minimum cash reserve ratios. These requirements were not applied to each day's holdings of cash reserves, but to the average level over a specified period (beginning in 1969, the reserve averaging period was set at two weeks). This was to allow for the fact that an individual bank is subject to erratic day-to-day fluctuations in its cash position as cheques are cleared and deposits are transferred from one bank to another.

Furthermore, the level of required cash reserves in effect at any time was not based on the current volume of deposits, but rather on the average volume of deposits during the preceding month. Thus, an expansion of loans and deposits did not affect total excess reserves during the current month, but increased the level of required reserves that would have to be held in the following month. Of course, to the extent that the banks did not all expand their loans at the same rate, deposits and cash were redistributed, so that the faster-growing banks tended to lose cash reserves to the slower-growing ones.

Chartered bank holdings of Bank of Canada notes that were counted toward reserve requirements were also calculated as an average over the preceding month. This means that changes in the public's demand for currency had no effect on a bank's cash reserve position in the current month unless they induced the bank to reduce or replenish its till money by respectively increasing or running down its deposits at the Bank of Canada.

These institutional arrangements had the following important implication for the implementation of monetary policy. The Bank of Canada could control not only the total base, but also the cash reserve component of the base. Further, since required cash reserves were determined by deposits in the preceding month, effective control could be exercised over the excess cash reserves of the chartered banks. This principle carries over into the new system with zero reserve requirements.

## The Zero Reserve Requirement System

**zero reserve requirements**
The system under which direct clearers are not required to keep a minimum cash reserve ratio.

As indicated in Section 18-1, a system of **zero reserve requirements** came into effect in July 1994.[3] In view of the argument given above, required cash reserves were seen to be unnecessary for purposes of central bank control of the money supply. In addition, they put the chartered banks at a disadvantage compared with other financial institutions such as trust companies, which offered banking services and had access to the clearing system but were not subject to minimum required cash reserve requirements.

The new rules apply to all direct clearers, that is, to chartered banks and other members of the Canadian Payments Association that participate in the clearing system and settle through the Bank of Canada. These institutions are required to maintain a zero or positive balance each day in their accounts at the Bank of Canada. In addition, they must maintain an average balance over each month that equals or exceeds zero.[4]

www.bankofcanada.ca/en/
res/wp97-8.htm

**drawdowns and redeposits**
The transfer of government deposits between the direct clearers and the Bank of Canada.

The process by which the Bank of Canada implements monetary policy under this system involves control of the supply of settlement balances (Bank of Canada deposits) available to chartered banks and other direct clearers for settlement of payments. One of the means by which changes in the supply of balances are brought about is the **drawdown/redeposit** procedure, that is, the transfer of government deposits between the direct clearers and the Bank of Canada.

## Government Deposits and Settlement Balances

The detailed balance sheets of the chartered banks and the Bank of Canada, in Tables 18-2 and 18-3 earlier in this chapter, show Government of Canada deposits on the liability side. The account maintained at the Bank of Canada is used by the federal government for receipts and payments. In the absence of offsetting transactions, fluctuations in government revenues and expenditures would thus be reflected in fluctuations in the supply of settlement balances. For example, in a period in which the government receives more than it spends, there would be a transfer of deposits from the accounts of the public at the chartered banks and other direct clearers to the government's account at the Bank of Canada and a consequent reduction in settlement balances.

To avoid these effects, the Government of Canada maintains deposits with the direct clearers as well as with the Bank of Canada. Transfers of these deposits between the direct clearers and the Bank of Canada can then be used to offset the effects of government transactions. In addition, these transfers provide a convenient means of bringing about changes in the supply of settlement balances desired by the Bank of Canada.

---

[3] The details of the new system are described in a series of papers prepared by the Bank of Canada. See "The Transmission of Monetary Policy in Canada," available online at www.bankofcanada.ca/en/pdf/hermes.pdf.

[4] The monthly average requirement is an additional constraint since it applies to the sum of all positive daily settlement balances less the sum of all daily overdraft loans taken to avoid a negative daily position. See the reference in footnote 3.

An increase in the supply of settlement balances can be brought about by a *redeposit*, that is, a transfer of government deposits from the Bank of Canada to the direct clearers. Conversely, a decrease in settlement balances results from a *drawdown* of government deposits, as illustrated in Table 18-9. In this case, the reduction of deposit liabilities in chartered banks and other direct clearers is matched by a reduction in assets in the form of settlement balances. These changes are mirrored on the liability side of the balance sheet of the Bank of Canada.

*TABLE 18-9*

### A DRAWDOWN OF GOVERNMENT DEPOSITS

|  | Assets |  | Liabilities |  |
|---|---|---|---|---|
| **Direct Clearers** | Settlement balances | −1 | Government deposits | −1 |
| **Bank of Canada** |  |  | Government deposits | +1 |
|  |  |  | Settlement balances | −1 |

## The Overnight Rate and the Transmission of Monetary Policy

**overnight rate**

The interest rate at which banks borrow or lend so that they do not have a shortage or excess of settlement balances.

The aim of the short run goal of monetary policy is to affect the overnight rate. The **overnight rate** is the interest rate at which banks borrow or lend so that they do not have a shortage or excess of settlement balances. The Bank of Canada believes that changes in the overnight rate will affect other interest rates, and then this will affect spending (aggregate demand) and eventually inflation. The process by which this happens is described by the aggregate demand-aggregate supply model we have studied in this book.

Since 1994, the Bank of Canada has announced target bands for the overnight rate of 0.5 percentage points, and is aided in implementing this target band by lending and taking deposits from direct clearers. In addition, chartered banks are now aided in clearing their settlement balances by the large-value transfer system, which was introduced by the Canadian Payments Association in 1999.[5]

The Bank of Canada can take measures to ensure that the overnight rate stays in the target band. Suppose that the overnight rate was edging toward the top of the Bank of Canada target band. Since the Bank of Canada does not want this rate to go above its target range, it will lend to direct clearers at a rate equal to the top of the target band. (This is the item labelled Advances in Table 18-3.) This effectively puts a ceiling on the overnight rate. Of course, if the overnight rate was edging toward the bottom of the target band, the Bank of Canada would take deposits and pay an interest rate equal to the bottom of the target band.

Now suppose that the Bank of Canada wishes to tighten monetary policy. You can think of this as decreasing the money supply and shifting the *LM* curve to the left. In our *IS-LM* model, this would cause the interest rate to rise. How would the Bank of Canada implement this? First, it would announce an increase in the target band for the overnight rate. The Bank of Canada will now take deposits at a higher rate, which encourages the chartered banks to lend to the Bank of Canada. On the asset side of the Bank of Canada balance sheets, advances decrease and therefore, on the liability side, the monetary base decreases. This leads to a decrease in the money supply. Thus, there is a negative relationship between the money supply and interest rates.

[5] Details on this can be found in Donna Howard, "A Primer on the Implementation of Monetary Policy in the LVTS Environment," *Bank of Canada Review*, Autumn 1998.

**bank rate**

The upper end of the Bank of Canada's target band on the overnight rate.

The **bank rate** is equal to the upper end of the Bank of Canada's target band on the overnight rate. The mechanism by which the bank rate is set has changed a number of times. For example, between 1962 and 1980, it was administered directly and changed from time to time. In 1980, a floating bank rate was adopted under which the rate was set each week at 1/4 of 1 percent above the Treasury bill rate. Beginning in February 1996, this procedure was abandoned in favour of daily setting of the bank rate.[6] In general, it is set in relation to short-term money market rates so as to encourage direct clearers to adjust their settlement balances by means other than overdraft loans or advances from the Bank of Canada.

## 18-3 | TARGETS AND THE IMPLEMENTATION OF MONETARY POLICY

In the previous section, we examined the process by which the Bank of Canada controls the overnight rate on a day-to-day basis. However, the ultimate goal of monetary policy is to have a low and stable inflation rate. In terms of the theory of economic policy discussed in Chapter 17, this means that the overnight rate is the instrument of monetary policy and the inflation rate is the target of monetary policy.

Although the inflation rate has always been the ultimate target of monetary policy, this policy has in the past been implemented in different ways. Prior to the early 1970s, Bank of Canada policy was formulated primarily in terms of target levels of interest rates, as well as other measures of the cost and availability of credit. By 1973, the central bank had become dissatisfied with this approach and was beginning to move toward greater emphasis on controlling the money supply.

In 1975, the Bank of Canada announced a new policy of monetary gradualism. This involved setting target ranges for the rate of growth on narrowly defined money ($M1$) and gradually lowering these target ranges over time. The initial target rate of growth was established in late 1975 at 10 to 15 percent per year. This target was gradually lowered over time, as summarized on Table 18-10. In this policy, $M1$ growth can be thought of as an intermediate target and inflation as the ultimate target.

**TABLE 18-10**

### BANK OF CANADA TARGET GROWTH RATES OF $M1$, 1975–81

| Base Period | Target Band | Base Period | Target Band |
|---|---|---|---|
| 2nd Qtr. 1975 | 10–15% | June 1978 | 6–10% |
| Feb.–Apr. 1976 | 8–12 | 2nd Qtr. 1979 | 5–9 |
| June 1977 | 7–11 | Aug.–Oct. 1980 | 4–8 |

SOURCE: Bank of Canada Annual Report, 1976, 1977; *Bank of Canada Review*, November 1991, notes to Table 14.

### The Current Implementation of Monetary Policy

In recent years, the Bank of Canada has made a concerted effort to be more open about the conduct of monetary policy. In an attempt to be more transparent, the

[6] For a detailed description of the current procedure, see *Bank of Canada Review*, "Notes to the Tables," Table F1.

## BOX 18-1

### What Happened to Monetary Gradualism?

In 1975, the Bank of Canada announced a policy of monetary gradualism. The aim of the policy was to slowly lower the rate of growth of narrow money, $M1$, thereby eventually lowering the long run inflation rate. Even though the central bank was very successful in meeting its target growth rates for $M1$, the inflation rate did not respond in the manner predicted. We can examine this policy using the models developed in this book. Lowering the rate of growth of money will shift the aggregate demand curve inward. In the short run, this will shift the economy along a very flat short run Phillips curve, and inflation will drop only moderately. In the long run, the rate of inflation will go down substantially only if inflationary expectations decrease in response to the implementation of this policy.

What happened was a combination of bad timing and questionable implementation. The bad timing was that this policy was instituted at a time when actual inflation as well as inflationary expectations were both rising. Part of this was due to a series of oil price shocks between 1973 and 1979, which shifted the aggregate supply curve leftward. In addition to this, or possibly because of this, it appeared that the public just did not believe that the policy would work, so it did not have the desired effect on expectations. The questionable implementation was the decision to implement this policy gradually over time, rather than just lowering the rate of the growth of money all at once to the long run target. Most economists now believe that the policy was too gradual.

Unfortunately, even though the Bank of Canada met its target bands quite well, this policy had only limited success in terms of bringing down the long run rate of inflation. In the early 1980s, the practice of announcing target bands for $M1$ growth was discontinued. The Bank of Canada then moved to a policy of targeting inflation directly. In early 1991, the governor of the Bank of Canada and the minister of Finance jointly announced that monetary policy would be directed toward achieving target rates of inflation. The targets were specified as 3 percent by the end of 1992, declining to 2 percent by the end of 1995. During the recession of 1990–91, the inflation rate fell below 3 percent, and by early 1992 the target of 2 percent by the end of 1995 had already been reached. A target band of 1 to 3 percent was then established, which remains in effect today.

Bank of Canada has a very good description of monetary policy implementation and goals on its Internet site.[7]

As noted earlier, the current Bank of Canada policy is to set the overnight rate. Therefore, we can think of this as conducting policy according to an interest rate rule. The central bank sets the rate so as to control aggregate demand. However, the interest rate is not the only policy variable that affects aggregate demand. In a flexible exchange rate regime, the exchange rate can also affect aggregate demand through the net export channel. Given this, the Bank of Canada publishes a Monetary Conditions Index.

---

[7] See www.bankofcanada.ca/en/monetary.htm.

## What Is the Correct Inflation Rate for Monetary Policy?

When formulating monetary policy with an ultimate goal of low and stable inflation, the Bank of Canada has in mind the *long run* rate of inflation. Unfortunately, there is no precise definition of this concept. When individuals speak of inflation, they most often refer to the rate of change in the Consumer Price Index (CPI). However, the inflation rate as measured by the CPI can be quite volatile over some periods of time. When thinking about the long run inflation rate, the central bank would like to exclude these temporary volatile periods. Given this, the Bank of Canada watches several measures of inflation in formulating policy. Three other measures that the central bank uses to calculate inflation are: core inflation, inflation as measured by the CPIXFET, and inflation measured by the CPIW.

Core inflation is calculated using the CPI minus the eight most volatile components: fruit, vegetables, gasoline, fuel oil, natural gas, mortgage interest, intercity transportation, and tobacco products, as well as the effect of changes in indirect taxes on the remaining components. Inflation measured using the CPIXFET is calculated from the CPI less food, energy, and indirect taxes. Finally, if inflation is calculated using the CPIW, each component of the total CPI is multiplied by an additional weight that is inversely proportional to the component's volatility, so that the more volatile the component, the less it influences the overall index. Each of these measures of the inflation rate can be viewed on the Bank of Canada Internet site at www.bankofcanada.ca/en/cpi.htm.

www.bankofcanada.ca/en/
res/r954c-ea.htm

The Monetary Conditions Index (MCI) is a measure of the effects of changes in the interest rate and the exchange rate on aggregate demand. The Bank of Canada is interested in this because it must gauge whether a shock to aggregate demand has a positive or negative stimulative effect. Technically, the MCI is a weighted average of the 90-day commercial paper interest rate and the C-6 exchange rate. Research at the central bank has determined that it takes a 3 percent change in the exchange rate to have the same effect on aggregate demand as a 1 percent change in the interest rate. This observation gives the weights in the average.

Consider the following hypothetical example. Suppose that there is a depreciation shock to the exchange rate of 6 percent, caused by political developments. If the desired monetary conditions have not changed, then the Bank of Canada may feel obligated to offset the aggregate demand effects of this shock. The effects of the demand shock could be neutralized by raising interest rates by 2 percent. The calculated change in the MCI would be $2 \times 1 + (1/3) \times (-6) = 0$.

The Monetary Conditions Index is published in the Bank of Canada's semi-annual *Monetary Policy Report*, and is also available online.[8]

Monetary policy is currently undertaken in a forward-looking framework. The Bank of Canada has a sophisticated model of the Canadian economy that it uses to forecast the future path of economic activity in Canada. Given this forecast, the central bank sets a desired path for monetary conditions that will produce an inflation

---

[8] See www.bankofcanada.ca/en/graphs/a1-table.htm.

## BOX 18-3

### Rules versus Discretion: The Taylor Rule

As we saw in the previous chapter, there are advocates of tying the hands of a central bank by requiring that monetary policy be conducted according to some fixed rule. These rules could be some version of the Monetary Conditions Index or some other method of policy action when monetary conditions change. In the United States, John Taylor (U.S. Under Secretary of Treasury for International Affairs) has advocated a rule that has come to be called the *Taylor rule*. The Taylor rule would involve central bank intervention based on two conditions: the percent deviation of current output from full employment output, and the current four-quarter average rate of inflation relative to some inflation target.

We could write an equation for the Taylor rule for Canada as:

$$i - \bar{\pi} = 0.02 + 0.5y + 0.5(\bar{\pi} - 0.02)$$

where $i$ is the overnight rate (the policy rate); $\bar{\pi}$ is the average rate of inflation over the last four quarters; $y = (Y_t - Y^*)/Y^*$ is the percentage deviation of current output from full employment; and 0.02 is the midpoint of the current Bank of Canada inflation target. Notice that this rule is based on the *real* overnight rate.

The "rule" would be that the Bank of Canada would intervene by raising the nominal overnight rate if the economy was operating beyond full employment ($y > 0$) or if inflation was above 2 percent.

## BOX 18-4

### The Relationship Between Long-Term and Short-Term Interest Rates

In macroeconomics, we often proceed as if there was only one interest rate in the money market. However, in reality, there are many interest rates for many different maturities. The word *maturity* in this context refers to when the bond comes due. For instance, a 90-day Treasury bill has a maturity of 90 days.

The relationship between interest rates of different maturities is called the *term structure of interest rates*. The figure below shows the relationship between interest rates on bonds with four different maturities: the 90-day Treasury bill, 1- to 3-year government bonds, 5- to 10-year government bonds, and government bonds with maturities greater than 10 years.

BOX

18-4

## The Relationship Between Long-Term and Short-Term Interest Rates cont'd

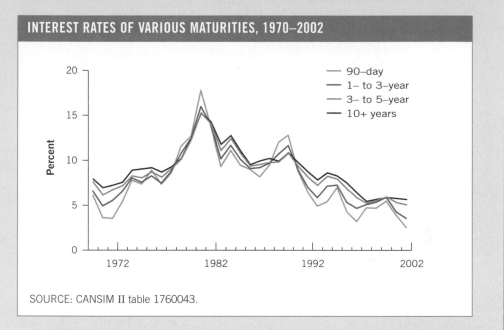

**INTEREST RATES OF VARIOUS MATURITIES, 1970–2002**

SOURCE: CANSIM II table 1760043.

The figure above shows three interesting features of the term structure of interest rates. First, interest rates of different maturities mostly go up and down together. Second, the gap between long-term and short-term interest rates varies. In 1988, the interest rates on 10+-year bonds and 90-day Treasury bills were about equal, but in 1994, the 10+-year rate was about 4 percent higher than the 90-day rate. Third, long-term rates are usually higher than short-term rates.

rate in the future in the target band of 1 to 3 percent. As shocks to the economy will change monetary conditions, the Bank of Canada adjusts its policy stance accordingly.

In this framework, the intermediate target is the output gap, which we discussed in Chapter 6. Remember that the Phillips curve tells us that if aggregate demand is greater than full employment output, then the output gap is positive and this will lead to inflation. Thus, the ultimate target of monetary policy is the inflation rate. However, the Bank of Canada must also deal with the additional problem of "managing expectations"; that is, if the central bank has policy credibility, individuals will believe that it is capable of keeping inflation low and stable, and the Phillips curve will not shift upward. The end result will be that the economy will have low and stable inflation.

## POLICY IN *ACTION*

### Interest Rates, the Exchange Rate, and Aggregate Demand: The MCI in Action

If the monetary conditions index is increasing, this is indicative of a tightening of monetary conditions, and if it is decreasing, monetary conditions are loosening. We have graphed a five-week moving average of the change in the monetary conditions index in the following figure.

#### THE MONETARY CONDITIONS INDEX, JANUARY 2001–MAY 2002

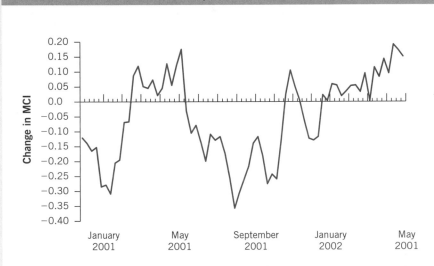

SOURCE: Bank of Canada Internet site: www.bankofcanada.ca/pdf/wfs.pdf.

After the events of September 11, 2001, monetary policy in Canada clearly became somewhat less restrictive. In response to this, the Canadian economy began to grow very strongly throughout 2002, and inflation edged up toward the upper band of the Bank of Canada's target range. The governor of the central bank raised interest rates somewhat, but in early 2002, there was widespread belief that interest rates in Canada would have to increase further. However, in early 2003, the Canadian exchange rate began to appreciate strongly. This appreciation pressure caused the monetary conditions index to show enough tightening that the Bank of Canada no longer felt the need to raise interest rates to cool off aggregate demand.

## Working with Data

In this exercise, we ask you to calculate the Monetary Conditions Index (MCI) yourself. Remember that the MCI is a weighted average of the 90-day commercial paper interest rate and the C-6 exchange rate. The weight is 1 for the interest rate and 1/3 for the exchange rate. The CANSIM II source for the interest rate is V121812, and for the exchange rate, it is V37451.

## CHAPTER SUMMARY

▶ The supply of money can be controlled by the Bank of Canada through its control of the monetary base, which appears on the liability side of its balance sheet. The monetary base is the sum of currency in circulation and deposits of the chartered banks at the Bank of Canada. The base can be controlled by the Bank of Canada using open market operations, that is, the purchases and sales of government securities.

▶ Chartered banks and other members of the Canadian Payments Association maintain deposits at the Bank of Canada (called *settlement balances*) in order to participate in the clearing system. This involves the settlement of the net amounts owing among these institutions as a result of the clearing of cheques and other payments.

▶ The money supply can be expressed as the sum of the base and the amount of bank credit. The money multiplier is the ratio of the money supply to the monetary base. It shows how, given the base, the size of the money supply is limited by the currency deposit ratio and the cash reserve ratio.

▶ The Bank of Canada determines interest rates and the money supply in the short run through the overnight rate. This is accomplished using a drawdown or redeposit of government deposits in the banks and other financial institutions—that is, a transfer of these deposits to or from the Bank of Canada.

▶ During the period 1975–1981, the Bank of Canada operated policy according to monetary gradualism, setting annual target rates for the growth rate of $M1$. This was abandoned in approximately 1981.

▶ The current Bank of Canada policy is to set the overnight rate. Therefore, we can think of this as conducting policy according to an interest rate rule. The central bank sets the rate so as to control aggregate demand so that the output gap will lead to an inflation rate in the target band of 1 to 3 percent.

▶ The "Monetary Conditions Index" is a weighted average of the short-term interest rate and the exchange rate, with the exchange rate receiving one-third of the weight of the interest rate.

www.mcgrawhill.ca/college/dornbusch

## K E Y   T E R M S

cash reserves, *368*

settlement balances, *368*

monetary base, *370*

open market operations, *370*

money multiplier, *373*

zero reserve requirements, *375*

drawdowns and redeposits, *375*

overnight rate, *376*

bank rate, *377*

## D I S C U S S I O N   Q U E S T I O N S

1. How do open market operations affect the monetary base and the money supply?

2. What is meant by the clearing system and what role is played by the deposits of banks and other institutions in the Bank of Canada?

3. Can the Bank of Canada affect the currency deposit ratio?

4. Discuss the impact of credit cards and automated teller machines on the money multiplier.

5. A *bank run* is a large-scale withdrawal of funds on deposit with banks precipitated by a fear that the banks may fail and be unable to meet the demands of their depositors. What effect would this have on the money supply and the money multiplier?

6. The Canada Deposit Insurance Corporation insures deposits in chartered banks and other financial institutions against bank default. What are the implications for the money multiplier?

7. Under what circumstances should the central bank conduct monetary policy by targeting mainly (a) interest rates, or (b) the money supply?

8. Why might the central bank choose intermediate targets for its monetary policy rather than directly pursuing its ultimate targets?

## A P P L I C A T I O N   Q U E S T I O N S

1. Show the effects on the balance sheets of the non-financial public, the individual banks, and the Bank of Canada of the following transactions:

   a. Bank A makes a loan of $1000 to a customer who initially holds the proceeds in Bank A.

   b. The borrower writes a cheque for $1000 to someone who deposits it in Bank B.

   c. Bank A sells a $1000 Treasury bill in exchange for a cheque drawn on Bank B.

   d. What is the net effect on the balance sheets of all of the above transactions?

2. Table 18-5 shows the effect of an open market purchase with currency drain. If the reserve ratio is 0.10, what would be the amount of bank lending in the next round of expansion? What would be the total expansion of the money supply arising from the money multiplier process? (*Note:* The currency deposit ratio is $0.05/0.95 = 0.0526$.)

3. A scheme for "100 percent banking," involving a reserve deposit ratio of unity, has been proposed to enhance control over the money supply.

   a. Why would such a scheme improve money supply control?

   b. What would bank balance sheets look like?

   c. How would banking remain profitable?

 www.mcgrawhill.ca/college/dornbusch

4. Illustrate using balance sheets how the Bank of Canada can increase the supply of settlement balances by using the redeposit procedure.

5. What requirements must the banks meet under the zero reserve requirement system and what is the penalty for failure to meet them?

6. **a.** What is the relationship between the rates of interest on a ten-year bond and on the series of one-year bonds covering the same period? Assume that all interest rates are known in advance, so there is no uncertainty.

   **b.** Suppose that the interest rate on the ten-year bond is 12 percent and the interest rates on one-year bonds, for the next ten years, are expected to remain at 10 percent. What must the term premium be on the ten-year bond?

7. Go to CANSIM and retrieve $M1B$ and the monetary base. Calculate the money supply multiplier [see equation (5)] and plot this variable. Comment on the movements of the money multiplier.

## CHAPTER 19

# DEFICITS, DEBT, AND FISCAL POLICY

## *LEARNING OBJECTIVES*

After reading and studying this chapter, you should be able to:

▶ *Understand that, between 1975 and 1996, the federal government ran fiscal deficits. By the end of the 1990s, the federal government was in a budgetary surplus position.*

▶ *Understand that the budgetary deficit is composed of the operating deficit plus interest on the public debt.*

▶ *Understand that the debt to GDP ratio has exhibited three peaks: during the Great Depression, during World War II, and in the mid-1990s, when the federal government began reducing budget deficits.*

▶ *Understand that when the government finances its deficit by issuing money, the government is imposing an inflation tax.*

n this chapter, we are going to examine government and how it is financed. Discussions about the levels of taxation and government spending are discussions about fiscal policy. However, you should bear in mind that fiscal policy discussions are quite a bit different from monetary policy discussions. Recall from Chapter 18 that monetary policy has very powerful, very rapid effects on our economy. Fiscal policy does not operate with such speed. For instance, for 22 straight years, from 1975 to 1996, the federal government ran consistent budgetary deficits. These fiscal deficits certainly exerted some stimulative effect on aggregate demand, but this was spread out over long periods of time.

With the change in federal government in 1993, a concerted effort was made to reduce these deficits. It took until the end of the 1990s before the federal government was in a consistent surplus position. This slow change in the stance of fiscal policy has prompted a great deal of debate concerning government revenue in the form of taxes, government spending, and the size of the deficit. In this chapter, we look at the numbers involved in this debate, as well as some of the issues surrounding deficits and debt.

## 19-1 | REVENUES, EXPENDITURES, AND DEFICITS

In this section, we examine the size of government involvement in the economy. Be sure that you understand what we mean when we say *government*. There are at least three levels of government: the federal government, the provincial governments, and municipal and local governments. We begin our examination of the data by looking at revenue and expenditure items for total government; that is, all levels of government aggregated. We then look at the taxing, spending, debt, and deficit patterns of the federal government.

### Revenue and Expenditure for All Levels of Government Combined

Figure 19-1 shows total revenue and subcategories of revenue for all levels of government. In this figure, we have divided sources of revenue into direct and indirect taxes and other revenue. **Direct taxes** are taxes directly applied to persons and corporations, and include items such as personal and corporate income taxes, while **indirect taxes** are levied on goods. An example of the latter would be the federal Goods and Services Tax. The final category, other revenue, is mostly composed of investment income, although in latter years, there has been a growth in the sale of government assets.

Figure 19-1 shows that total revenue for all levels of government combined has been more or less steadily increasing from just under 30 percent of GDP in 1961 to just over 40 percent of GDP in 2002. Since the early 1970s, governments have become more reliant on direct taxes, rather than indirect taxes.

Figure 19-2 shows the major sources of expenditures for all levels of government. In this figure, we have divided total government spending into three categories: government purchases, transfers, and interest payments.

**Government purchases** are composed of government spending on currently produced goods and services. You will recognize this as *G* from the national accounts identity that is used throughout this book. **Transfer payments** include a wide variety of spending for which the government does not receive goods or services in return. This

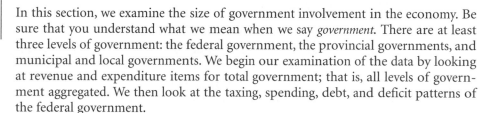

www.fin.gc.ca/purl/
frt-e.html

**direct taxes**

Taxes directly applied to persons and corporations, including personal and corporate income taxes.

**indirect taxes**

Taxes levied on goods, such as the federal Goods and Services Tax.

**government purchases**

Government spending on currently produced goods and services.

**transfer payments**

Spending for which the government does not receive goods or services in return (e.g., welfare payments, which are transfers to individuals).

## FIGURE 19-1

Government revenue from all sources has been steadily increasing as a percent of GDP. Direct taxes are now the largest component of revenue.

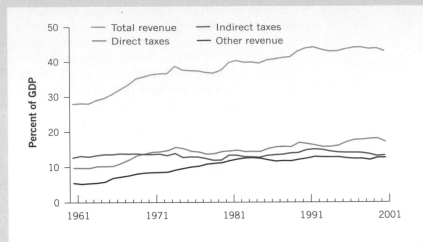

**TOTAL REVENUE AND COMPONENTS, ALL LEVELS OF GOVERNMENT, 1961–2001 (PERCENT OF GDP)**

SOURCE: Department of Finance Canada, Fiscal Reference Tables, Table 32: www.fin.gc.ca/frt/2002/frt02_5e.html#Table 32

**interest payments**

The amounts that individuals receive for holding government debt such as Treasury bills and long-term bonds.indirect taxes

category includes various components of social spending such as welfare payments, which are transfers to individuals, and also includes subsidies to businesses.[1] The final category is **interest payments**, which is the amount that individuals receive for holding government debt such as Treasury bills and long-term bonds. Figure 19-2 shows that

## FIGURE 19-2

Expenditure for all levels of government trended upward until the early 1990s.

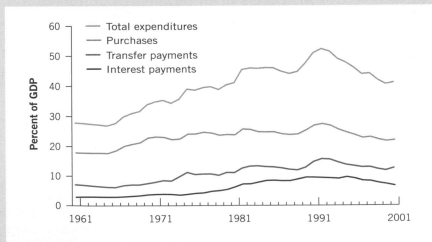

**TOTAL EXPENDITURE AND COMPONENTS, ALL LEVELS OF GOVERNMENT, 1961–2001 (PERCENT OF GDP)**

SOURCE: Department of Finance Canada, Fiscal Reference Tables, Table 33: www.fin.gc.ca/frt/2002/frt02_6e.html.

---

[1] You should be aware that approximately 30 percent of *federal* transfers go to provincial governments. These are netted out in Figure 19-2.

## Fiscal Policy, the Great Depression, and Keynesian Economics

The table below describes the performance of the Canadian economy during the Great Depression years. Between 1929 and 1933, real income in Canada fell by 30 percent and the price level fell by 20 percent. Of course, most of the world economies suffered during this period. Even today, this event is considered to be one of the greatest economic crises that the world has seen.

Classical economics at the time had no well-developed theory to explain persistent high unemployment, nor were there any policy prescriptions to solve the problem. Keynesian economics arose from this economic crisis. It was widely believed that the experience of this depression showed that the private economy was inherently unstable. The very first Keynesian models, simple aggregate demand models similar to those in Chapter 10, arose from the Great Depression experience. Most analysts believe that this marked the birth of Keynesian economics and modern fiscal policy.

### THE DEPRESSION YEARS, 1929–1939

|      | GNP   | Gov't Exp. (billions of 1961 dollars) | Exports | GNE Deflator (1961 = 100) | Gross Investment | Budget Surplus (% of GNP) | Unemployment Rate (%) | Stock Market Index (1961 = 100) |
|------|-------|-------|---------|-------|-------|-------|-------|-------|
| 1929 | 12.24 | 1.70  | 3.10    | 50.2  | 22.2  | −0.2  |       | 49.0  |
| 1930 | 11.71 | 1.93  | 2.70    | 48.8  | 18.9  | −3.9  |       | 35.0  |
| 1931 | 10.23 | 1.94  | 2.41    | 45.9  | 15.5  | −6.6  | 11.6  | 21.9  |
| 1932 | 9.17  | 1.79  | 2.24    | 41.6  | 8.8   | −7.3  | 17.6  | 14.2  |
| 1933 | 8.56  | 1.47  | 2.26    | 40.8  | 6.8   | −5.0  | 19.3  | 17.6  |
| 1934 | 9.59  | 1.58  | 2.55    | 41.4  | 7.7   | −4.7  | 14.5  | 22.1  |
| 1935 | 10.34 | 1.68  | 2.81    | 41.6  | 8.6   | −4.0  | 14.2  | 23.6  |
| 1936 | 10.80 | 1.67  | 3.38    | 42.9  | 10.0  | −0.7  | 12.8  | 30.7  |
| 1937 | 11.89 | 1.79  | 3.46    | 44.1  | 11.8  | −0.6  | 9.1   | 32.6  |
| 1938 | 11.98 | 1.93  | 3.12    | 44.0  | 11.3  | −2.8  | 11.4  | 26.8  |
| 1939 | 12.87 | 2.02  | 3.44    | 43.7  | 10.3  | −0.8  | 11.4  | 25.8  |

SOURCE: Statistics Canada, 11–505.

government expenditure peaked in the early 1990s and then began declining as various levels of government began to balance their budgets.

## Federal Government Revenues and Expenditures

Figure 19-3 shows revenues for the federal government over the period 1961–2001. Notice that revenue grew faster than GDP from 1970 to 1975, but grew more slowly in the second half of the 1970s as a result of the slowing down of income growth and the

**FIGURE 19-3**

Federal government revenue grew faster than GDP from 1970 to 1975, but grew more slowly in the second half of the 1970s as a result of the slowing down of income growth and the introduction of various tax reductions.

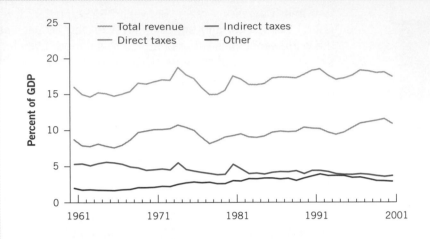

**TOTAL REVENUE AND COMPONENTS, FEDERAL GOVERNMENT, 1961–2001 (PERCENT OF GDP)**

SOURCE: Department of Finance Canada, Fiscal Reference Tables, Table 35: www.fin.gc.ca/frt/2002/frt02_6e.html.

introduction of various tax reductions. The Department of Finance has estimated that the cumulative effect of tax changes made in budgets over the period 1972–1981 was a reduction in revenue in the 1982–1983 fiscal year of nearly $25 billion.[2] During the 1980s and 1990s, there were large increases in personal taxes, causing revenue to grow faster than GDP.

Figure 19-4 shows federal government expenditures over the period 1961–2001. Until the 1990s, the fastest-growing item on the expenditure side was interest on the public debt. This increase was due to the large accumulation of debt caused by the ongoing budgetary deficits that started in the 1970s and also to the increase in interest rates over this period. Notice that total expenditures as a percent of GDP began to decline rapidly after the early 1990s, as the federal government embarked on an ambitious deficit-reduction program.

## 19-2 | MEASURING THE FEDERAL DEFICIT

In Chapter 10, we defined the budget surplus as the excess of revenue over expenditure. When the budget surplus is negative, the government is running a deficit. Figure 19-5 shows total revenue expenditure and the federal government surplus or deficit position between 1961 and 2001.

Figure 19-5 shows that, until the early 1970s, the federal government had a budget that was roughly balanced. For every year between 1975 and 1996, the federal government spent more than it collected in revenue, and ran a budget deficit. It was not until the late 1990s that this deficit problem was addressed through fiscal changes on the part of the federal government. Figure 19-5 appears to show that the bulk of the deficit reduction was undertaken on the expenditure side. This was a major fiscal policy change on the part of the federal government. However, there is some evidence that this

---

[2] See Department of Finance Canada, *The Federal Deficit in Perspective, 1983*, Annex D.

**FIGURE 19-4**

Until the 1990s, the fastest-growing item on the expenditure side was interest on the public debt. This increase was due to the large accumulation of debt caused by the ongoing budgetary deficits that started in the 1970s and also to the increase in interest rates over this period.

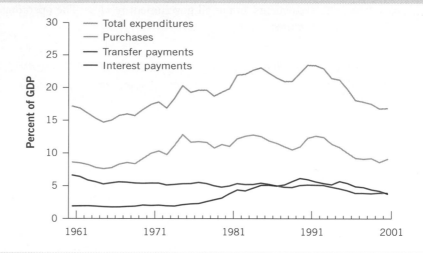

**TOTAL EXPENDITURE AND COMPONENTS, FEDERAL GOVERNMENT, 1961–2001 (PERCENT OF GDP)**

SOURCE: Department of Finance, Fiscal Reference Tables, Table 36: www.fin.gc.ca/frt/2002/frt02_6e.html.

reduction in expenditure simply shifted the responsibility for certain types of spending to the provinces. This issue is discussed in Box 19-2.

Measuring the federal deficit is complicated by the fact that most of the later deficit can be accounted for by interest payments on the national debt. So most of the deficit represents not the excess of current spending over revenues but the legacy of past deficits. We distinguish between two components of the budget deficit: the operating deficit and interest payments on the public debt.

**FIGURE 19-5**

For every year between 1975 and 1996, the federal government spent more than it collected in revenue, and ran a budget deficit. It was not until the late 1990s that this deficit problem was addressed through fiscal changes on the part of the federal government.

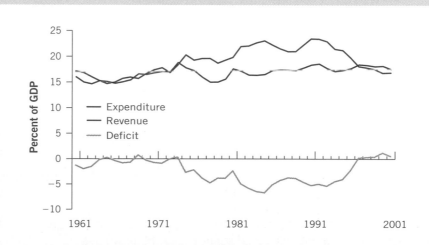

**REVENUE, EXPENDITURE, AND DEFICIT, FEDERAL GOVERNMENT, 1961–2001 (PERCENT OF GDP)**

SOURCE: Department of Finance Canada, Fiscal Reference Tables, Table 36: www.fin.gc.ca/frt/2002/frt02_6e.html

**operating (or non-interest) deficit**

The budget deficit excluding interest payments.

$$\text{Total deficit} \equiv \text{Operating deficit} + \text{Interest payments} \qquad (1)$$

The **operating deficit** (or surplus) represents all government outlays, except interest payments, minus all government revenue. The operating deficit is also called the *non-interest deficit*.

---

**BOX 19-2**

## Fiscal Federalism—or—How Did the Federal Government Reduce Its Deficit?

We noted in the text that the major portion of the federal deficit reduction appears to have fallen on the expenditure side. However, an argument can be made that the federal government simply shifted the burden of some expenditures to the provinces. As part of the deficit-reduction strategy of the early 1990s, the Canada Health and Social Transfer (CHST) to the provinces was reduced. The CHST involves items such as expenditures for health, post-secondary education, and social assistance. A reduction in transfers from the federal government to the provinces is often called *off-loading*. The effects of this can be seen in the figure below.

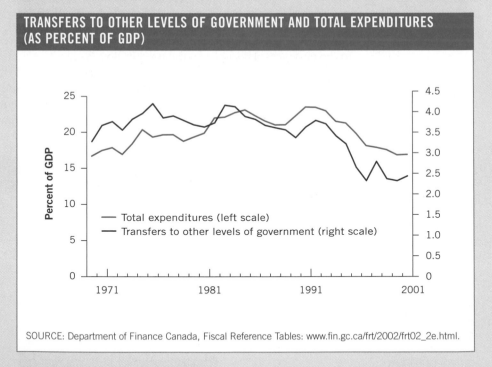

### TRANSFERS TO OTHER LEVELS OF GOVERNMENT AND TOTAL EXPENDITURES (AS PERCENT OF GDP)

Total expenditures (left scale)
Transfers to other levels of government (right scale)

SOURCE: Department of Finance Canada, Fiscal Reference Tables: www.fin.gc.ca/frt/2002/frt02_2e.html.

www.fin.gc.ca/wp/
2001-23e.html

You can see from this figure that the federal government appeared to manage a great deal of its expenditure reductions in the mid-1990s through decreases in transfers to the provinces. Thus, a great deal of the deficit reduction policy of the federal government may be attributed to off-loading responsibility for social spending to the provinces.

Figure 19-6 shows the budgetary and operating federal deficit as a percentage of GDP. Notice that even though Canada was running deficits between 1974 and 1997, the operating deficit has been in surplus since 1987.

When interest payments are large, as they are in Canada, proper measurement of the deficit is complicated by the distinction between real and nominal interest rates. Since the nominal interest rate equals the real interest rate plus inflation, interest payments on the debt can be divided into real payments and payments due to inflation. The latter do not cost the government anything in real terms, because they are exactly offset by the decrease in the real value of the nominal debt.[3] During periods of high inflation most of the interest payments are offset by inflation. Even during periods of low inflation, nearly half the interest payments may be offset in this way.

### FIGURE 19-6

The budgetary deficit is composed of the operating deficit plus interest paid on the public debt. The federal operating deficit has been in surplus since approximately 1987.

**BUDGETARY DEFICIT, PRIMARY DEFICIT, AND INTEREST ON THE PUBLIC DEBT, FEDERAL GOVERNMENT, 1961–2001**

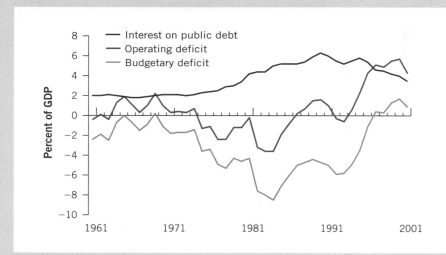

SOURCE: Department of Finance Canada, Fiscal Reference Tables, Table 45: www.fin.gc.ca/frt/2002/frt02_8e.html.

## The Burden of the Debt

As deficits continue, the national debt piles up. The Canadian (gross) national debt at the end of 2001 exceeded $600 billion. In per capita terms, the national debt amounts to about $21,000 per person. Do we actually have to pay off this debt? It is the notion that every person in the country owes a large debt that makes the existence of the debt seem so serious.

However, by and large, we owe the national debt to ourselves. Each individual shares in the obligation to repay the public debt, but many individuals own the national debt in the form of Treasury bonds held directly or indirectly through financial intermediaries. As a first step, one could think of the liability that the debt represents as cancelling out the asset that the debt represents to the individuals who hold

---

[3] See Mario Blejer and Adrienne Cheasty, "The Measurement of Fiscal Deficits: Analytical and Methodological Issues," *Journal of Economic Literature*, December 1991.

claims on the government. In this case, the debt would not be a net burden on society. However, this argument is limited by the fact that a large portion of the debt is owned by foreigners. The portion of the debt owned by foreigners does represent a future tax burden to be borne by Canadian taxpayers.

A more important sense in which the debt may be a burden is through the potential long run effects of the deficit and debt on the capital stock. We saw earlier that debt financing increases the interest rate and reduces investment. Hence, the capital stock will be lower with debt financing than otherwise, and output will be lower as a result of debt financing of a deficit. This *is* a real burden.

Thus, if the debt is a burden, it is a burden for reasons very different from those suggested by the statement that every person in Canada has a debt of $21,000 as a share of the national debt. The major source of burden arises from the possible effects of the national debt on the country's net national worth: An increase in the national debt can reduce the capital stock and/or increase the nation's external debt.

## Debt, Growth, and Instability

The national debt of Canada has been rising almost every year for the last 50 years. However, at the same time, the economy has been growing. Figure 19-7 shows the debt-to-income ratio for Canada since 1926. Notice the two spikes corresponding to the Great Depression and World War II. The debt-to-income ratio had been falling since World War II, but when Canada started running large budget deficits in 1974, it began rising again.

How could this happen? It is helpful to look at the definition of the **debt-income ratio**:

**debt-income ratio**

Ratio of national debt to GDP.

$$\text{Debt ratio} = \frac{\text{Debt}}{PY} \qquad (2)$$

where $PY$ represents nominal GDP. The ratio of debt to GDP falls when nominal GDP grows more rapidly than the debt. To see this point, it is useful to look separately at the numerator and denominator of the debt-GDP ratio. The numerator, the debt, grows because of deficits. The denominator, nominal GDP, grows as a result of both inflation and real GDP growth.

Why is it useful to look at the ratio of debt to income rather than at the absolute value of the debt? The reason is that GDP is a measure of the size of the economy, and the debt-GDP ratio is thus a measure of the magnitude of the debt relative to the size of the economy. A national debt of $620 billion would have been overwhelming in 1929 when Canadian GDP was about $6 billion: Even if the interest rate had been only 1 percent, the government would have had to raise 50 percent of GDP in taxes to pay interest on the debt. But when GDP is over $800 billion, a $620 billion debt is large—but certainly not overwhelming.

## 19-3 | DEFICITS AND THE INFLATION TAX

### The Government's Budget Constraint

The federal government as a whole, consisting of the Department of Finance plus the Bank of Canada, can finance its budget deficit in two ways. It can either sell bonds or "print money." The Bank of Canada "prints money" when it increases the stock of high-powered money, typically through open market purchases that buy up part of the debt that the Department of Finance is selling.

## FIGURE 19-7

The federal debt-to-income ratio has three distinct peaks: during the Great Depression, during World War II, and in the mid-1990s, when the federal government began reducing budget deficits.

### FEDERAL GOVERNMENT DEBT-TO-INCOME RATIO, 1926–2001

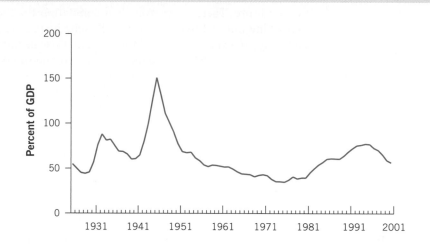

SOURCE: 1961-2001: Gross debt: Department of Finance Canada, Fiscal Reference Tables, Table 14, available online at www.fin.gc.ca/frt/2002/frt02_8e.html; nominal GDP: CANSIM II V498918; historical data on nominal GDP: Statistics Canada, *Historical Statistics*: www.statcan.ca/english/freepub/11-516-XIE/sectiona/toc.htm; historical data on gross debt: CANSIM II V151537.

**government budget constraint**

A limit that says the government can finance its deficits only by selling bonds (accumulating debt) or by increasing the monetary base.

The **government budget constraint** is

$$\text{Budget deficit} = \text{Sales of bonds} + \text{Increase in money base} \qquad (3)$$

There are two types of possible links between budget deficits and money growth. First, in the short run, an increase in the deficit caused by expansionary fiscal policy will tend to raise nominal and real interest rates. If the Bank of Canada is targeting interest rates in any way, it may increase the growth rate of money in an attempt to keep the interest rate from rising. Second, the government may deliberately be increasing the stock of money as a means of obtaining government revenue over the long term.

We examine first the short run links between money and deficits that come from central bank policy and then the use of money printing as a means of financing government budgets. Finally, we link the short and long run aspects.

## The Bank of Canada's Dilemma

The Bank of Canada is said to monetize deficits whenever it purchases a part of the debt sold by the Department of Finance to finance the deficit. In Canada, the monetary authorities enjoy independence from the Department of Finance and therefore can choose whether to monetize or not.[4]

---

[4] In other countries the central bank may enjoy much less independence; for instance, it might be under the control of the Treasury, and then it may simply be ordered to finance part or all of the deficit by creating high-powered money. It is noteworthy that the Maastricht Accord strictly prohibits the European Central Bank from financing government deficits.

The Bank of Canada faces a dilemma in deciding whether to monetize a deficit. If it does not finance the deficit, the fiscal expansion, not being accompanied by accommodating monetary policy, raises interest rates and thus crowds out private expenditure. There is accordingly a temptation for the Bank of Canada to prevent crowding out by buying securities, thereby increasing the money supply and hence allowing an expansion in income without a rise in interest rates.

But such a policy of accommodation, or **monetization**, runs a risk. If the economy is near full employment, the monetization feeds inflation. Often the Bank of Canada should *not* accommodate; that is, it should let the interest rate increase and keep the growth rate of money constant. An unwise fiscal expansion would be made even more potent by fuelling it with a monetary expansion.

There are other circumstances, though, in which the risks of igniting inflation are much more remote. Certainly in a deep recession, there is no reason to shy away from accommodating a fiscal expansion with higher money growth.

In any particular case, the Bank of Canada has to judge whether to pursue an accommodating monetary policy or whether to stay with an unchanged monetary target or even offset a fiscal expansion by a tightening of monetary policy. To make that decision, the Bank of Canada must decide what relative weight it attaches to inflation and to unemployment whenever expansionary policy threatens to cause inflation.

### The Canadian Evidence

It would be interesting to know if the Bank of Canada has been monetizing the fiscal deficits of the government to any significant degree. If it has been monetizing deficits, this would make the Bank of Canada's policy of tight money to fight inflation somewhat difficult to implement. Figure 19-8 shows a scatter diagram of the change in the growth rate of the monetary base and the change in the budget deficit (as a percentage of GDP).[5] There would appear to be no noticeable pattern to these data points, which is consistent with lack of monetization on the part of the Bank of Canada.

Of course, we would like to have a more sophisticated study of the data, but even then it would be difficult to know whether the Bank of Canada is reacting to the deficit or other macroeconomic variables such as unemployment or inflation.

### The Inflation Tax

In discussing monetization of deficits in Canada, we paid no attention to the fact that financing government spending through the creation of high-powered money is an alternative to explicit taxation. For Canada, and for most of the industrialized economies, the creation of high-powered money is a fairly minor source of revenue. Other governments can—and some do—obtain significant amounts of resources year after year by printing money, that is, by increasing high-powered money. This source of revenue is sometimes known as **seigniorage**, which is the government's ability to raise revenue through its right to create money.

When the government finances a deficit by creating money, it in effect keeps printing money, period after period, that it uses to pay for the goods and services it buys. This money is absorbed by the public. But why would the public choose to increase its holdings of nominal money balances period after period?

**monetization**
When the Bank of Canada purchases part of the debt sold by the Department of Finance to finance the federal government budget deficit.

**seigniorage**
Revenue derived from the government's ability to print money.

[5] The monetary base is the relevant aggregate, because the deficit can be financed either by the sale of bonds or by the creation of high-powered money (or monetary base).

## *FIGURE 19-8*

This scatter diagram plots the relationship between the monetary base and the federal budget deficit. The fitted trend line through these points has a slope very close to zero, showing that, in Canada, there is no relationship between these two variables. This is evidence that the Bank of Canada is not actively engaged in monetizing the federal debt.

### MONEY AND DEFICITS, 1963–2001

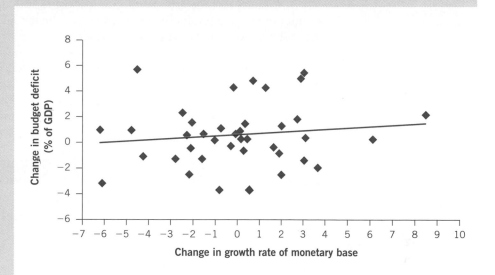

SOURCE: Federal deficit: Department of Finance Canada, Fiscal Reference Tables, Table 45: www.fin.gc.ca/frt/2002/frt02_8e.html; monetary base: CANSIM II V37145.

The only reason, real income growth aside, for the public's adding to its holdings of nominal money balances would be to offset the effects of inflation. Assuming there is no real income growth, in the long run, the public will hold a constant level of *real* balances. But if prices are rising, the purchasing power of a given stock of *nominal* balances is falling. To maintain the real value of its money balances constant, the public has to be adding to its stock of nominal balances at a rate that will exactly offset the effects of inflation.

When the public is adding to its stock of nominal balances in order to offset the effects of inflation on holdings of real balances, it is using part of its income to increase holdings of nominal money. Suppose a person has to add, say, $300 to a bank account just to maintain the real value of his or her money holdings. That $300 is not available for spending. The person seems to be saving $300 in the form of money holdings, but in fact all that person is doing is preventing her or his wealth from decreasing as a result of inflation.

*Inflation acts just like a tax because people are forced to spend less than their income and pay the difference to the government in exchange for extra money.*[6] The government thus can spend more resources, and the public less, just as if the government had raised taxes to finance extra spending. When the government finances its deficit by issuing money, which the public adds to its holdings of nominal balances to

---

[6] There is one complication in this analysis. As noted above, the amount that is received by the government is the increase in the stock of *high-powered money*, because the Bank of Canada is buying Department of Finance debt with high-powered money. However, the public is increasing its holdings of both bank deposits and currency, and thus part of the increase in the public's holdings of money does not go to the government to finance the deficit. This complication in no way changes the essence of the analysis.

**inflation tax**

Revenue gained by the government because of inflation's devaluation of money holdings.

maintain the real value of money balances constant, we say the government is financing itself through the **inflation tax**.[7]

How much revenue can the government collect through the inflation tax? The amount of revenue produced is the product of the tax rate (the inflation rate) and the object of taxation (the real monetary base).

$$\text{Inflation tax revenue} = \text{Inflation rate} \times \text{Real money base} \qquad (4)$$

Table 19-1 shows data on the inflation tax for Latin American countries in the 1983–1988 period.[8] Clearly the amounts are very significant, as are the inflation rates at which these amounts of revenue are obtained by the government.

### TABLE 19-1

**INFLATION AND INFLATION TAX, 1983–1988** (percent)

| Country | Inflation Tax, % of GDP | Average 1983–1988 Annual Inflation Rate | Peak Year Inflation Tax, % of GDP |
|---|---|---|---|
| Argentina | 3.7 | 359 | 5.2 |
| Bolivia | 3.5 | 1,797 | 7.2 |
| Brazil | 3.5 | 341 | 4.3 |
| Chile | 0.9 | 21 | 1.1 |
| Colombia | 1.9 | 22 | 2.0 |
| Mexico | 2.6 | 87 | 3.5 |
| Peru | 4.7 | 382 | 4.5 |

SOURCE: M. Selowsky, "Preconditions Necessary for the Recovery of Latin America's Growth," World Bank, June 1989 (mimeographed).

The amount of revenue the government can raise through the inflation tax is shown by curve *AA* in Figure 19-9. When the inflation rate is zero, the government gets no revenue from inflation.[9] As the inflation rate rises, the amount of inflation tax received by the government increases. But, of course, as the inflation rate rises, people reduce their real holdings of the money base—because the base is becoming increasingly costly to hold. Individuals hold less currency, and banks hold as few excess reserves as possible. Eventually, the real monetary base falls so much that the total amount of inflation tax revenue received by the government falls. That starts to happen at point C and signifies that there is a maximum amount of revenue the government can raise through the inflation tax; the maximum is shown as amount *IR** in the figure.

---

[7] Inflation is often referred to as the "cruelest tax." This refers not to the above analysis of the inflation tax but, rather, to the redistribution of wealth and income associated particularly with unanticipated inflation, which was discussed in Chapter 3.

[8] Hyperinflation has been a frequent plague for much of Latin America. For more information on both the monetary and real sides of Latin American economies, see Eliana Cardoso and Ann Helwege, *Latin America's Economy: Diversity, Trends, and Conflicts* (Cambridge, MA: MIT Press, 1995).

[9] When the economy is growing, the government obtains some revenue from seigniorage even if there is no inflation. That is because when the demand for the real monetary base is growing, the government can create some base without producing inflation.

**FIGURE 19-9**

As the inflation rate rises, revenue from the inflation tax also increases. However, as inflation increases, it becomes increasingly costly to hold money. Therefore, eventually the revenue from the inflation tax must decrease. This happens at point C, where the maximum revenue from the inflation tax is obtained from an inflation rate of $\pi^*$.

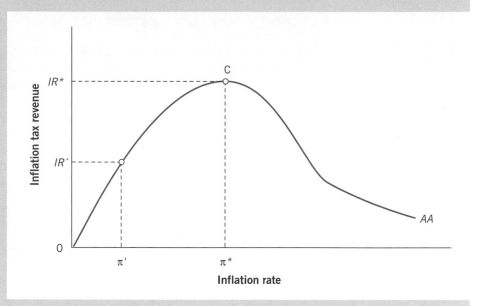

There is a corresponding inflation rate, denoted $\pi^*$: the inflation rate at which the inflation tax is at its maximum.[10]

Suppose that in Figure 19-9, the economy is initially in a situation where there is no deficit and no printing of money. Inflation is zero and the economy is at point 0 in the figure. Now the government cuts taxes and finances the deficit by printing money. We assume that the deficit is equal to amount $IR'$ in Figure 19-9, and thus it can be financed entirely through the inflation tax. Money growth is permanently increased, and inflation in the long run moves to the rate $\pi'$, corresponding to the inflation tax revenue $IR'$.

It is clear from Figure 19-9 that the more revenue the government wishes to raise through the inflation tax, the higher the inflation rate must be—as long as the economy is on the rising part of the curve. The figure raises the question of what happens if the government tries to finance a deficit larger than $IR^*$ by printing money. That cannot be done.

## Inflation Tax Revenue

The amounts of inflation tax revenue obtained in the high-inflation developing countries in Table 19-1 are very large. In the more industrialized economies, in which the real money base is small relative to the size of the economy, the government obtains only small amounts of inflation tax revenue. For instance, in Canada,

---

[10] Miguel A. Keguel and Pablo Andres Neumeyer, in "Seigniorage and Inflation: The Case of Argentina," *Journal of Money, Credit and Banking,* August 1995, consider whether Argentina went past the revenue-maximizing point in the 1980s. They estimate that the revenue-maximizing inflation rate was in the range of 20 to 30 percent per month. With the exception of spring 1989, inflation in Argentina was generally below these levels.

BOX

19-3

## Real Balances and Inflation

A sustained increase in money growth and in inflation ultimately leads to a reduction in the real money stock.

Here is a very important result that might seem a bit puzzling: Increased nominal money growth reduces the long run real money stock. Conversely, reduced nominal money growth raises the long run real money stock. The reason is that higher inflation raises the nominal interest rate and hence raises the opportunity cost of holding money. Hence, money holders will reduce the amount of real balances they choose to hold. This reduction in real balances is an important part of the adjustment process to an increase in money growth. It means that, on average, in the period of adjustment to an increase in money growth, prices must rise faster than money.

Higher money growth means higher inflation in the long run, and therefore higher interest rates and lower real money balances, $\overline{M}/P$. For $\overline{M}/P$ to drop, $P$ must at some point grow faster than $M$ grows. During this transition, inflation is higher than the long run inflation rate. Empirically, this extra "transitional" inflation can be quite high.

the base is about 4 percent of GDP. At a 5 percent inflation rate, the government would, from equation (4), be collecting about 0.2 percent of GDP in inflation tax revenue. That is not a trivial amount, but it is not a major source of government revenue either. It is hard to believe that the inflation rate in Canada is set with the revenue aspects of inflation as the main criterion. Rather, the Bank of Canada chooses policies to influence the inflation rate on the basis of an analysis of the costs and benefits of inflation.

In countries in which the banking system is less developed and in which people therefore hold large amounts of currency, the government obtains more revenue from inflation and is more likely to give much weight to the revenue aspects of inflation in setting policy. And, as we will see in the next section, under conditions of high inflation in which the conventional tax system breaks down, the inflation tax revenue may be the government's last resort to keep paying its bills. But whenever the inflation tax is used on a large scale, inflation invariably becomes extreme.

## 19-4 | INTERGENERATIONAL ACCOUNTING

There is no hard-and-fast economic principle that describes what is fair and not fair in allocating burdens among generations. Nonetheless, politicians and non-politicians have strong views on how burdens should be shared across generations. Such decisions, of course, have to be based on an accounting of just how much current policies impose burdens on different generations. **Intergenerational accounting** evaluates the costs and benefits of the entire fiscal (tax and spending) system for various age groups in society.

Laurence Kotlikoff of Boston University has made a systematic estimate of the intergenerational redistribution involved in U.S. fiscal policies. He comes up with a stark and controversial finding:

**intergenerational accounting**

Evaluate the costs and benefits of taxes and spending for various age groups in society.

The big winners from fiscal policy in the 1980s were Americans over forty at the time. Americans under forty were hurt by the policies. Young women were particularly hard hit by the decline in real welfare benefits and the rise in excise taxation.[11]

As the last sentence of the quotation suggests, Kotlikoff arrives at his unexpected conclusion by taking into account not only the future tax burdens imposed by the growing debt but also the burdens and benefits that different generations derive from government tax and spending programs.

## The Size-of-Government Debate

There has been a worldwide trend over the last 30 years toward an increased share of government in GDP. In Canada, government (all levels) purchases were 18 percent of GDP in 1960 and rose to nearly 26 percent in the 1990s. This increase reflects in large measure the broadening of government social programs, especially the growth of transfer programs.

How large should the government be? That is, of course, a difficult question to answer. Clearly, some government programs are widely regarded as desirable; for instance, relatively few dispute the need for adequate national defence. Other programs, such as social security, also command wide support, although just how large such programs should be is controversial. According to the fiscally conservative political parties in Canada, government is far too large, and hence the deficit—and the pressures it puts on interest rates and financial stability—is undesirable. Deficit-reduction pressure, in this view, is the best way to get spending cuts.

In practice, of course, the issue of how much government spending there should be is handled by the political process. In the 1930s and in the 1960s, the rules and traditions of fiscal policy were changed by activist government policy in pursuit of full employment and widening social objectives. Today, there is widespread sentiment that things have gone too far and need to be brought under control by a return to "sound fiscal policy." The fiscal revolt reflects a disagreement in society on how best to use resources. At the same time, there is a strand of thinking that calls for a resumption of government activity, from infrastructure to education. The debate is not over, and the acute fiscal problem is bound to keep the difficult trade-offs involved at the forefront of the discussion.

## The Barro-Ricardo Problem

Does the size of the deficit matter? That is, given the size of government spending, does it matter whether sufficient taxes are levied to pay for what we spend? The traditional aggregate supply-aggregate demand model gives a clear answer: Lower taxes mean higher aggregate demand, higher interest rates, more crowding out, and less investment for the future. New classical economists, led by Robert Barro,[12] give a surprisingly different answer: Deficits don't matter. The logic behind this answer follows directly from the LC-PIH studied in Chapter 14 and goes as follows: Suppose first that government spending increases $100 per family and that taxes also increase $100. Each family has $100 less in lifetime resources to allocate and makes choices to

---

[11] Laurence Kotlikoff, *Generational Accounting* (New York: Free Press, 1992), p. 184.

[12] See Robert Barro, "The Neoclassical Approach to Fiscal Policy," in R. Barro (ed.), *Modern Business Cycle Theory* (Cambridge, MA: Harvard University Press, 1989).

reduce lifetime spending accordingly. Suppose, instead, that the government had raised spending $100 per family but had left taxes unchanged and borrowed the $100. Just as in the first case, the "representative family" has $100 less in allocable resources *today,* but now it is because the family has loaned the money to the government. Since the family is in the same financial position in this $100-deficit case as it would be in the zero-deficit case, the family will make the same decisions. The deficit doesn't matter.

There is one *apparent* difference in the $100-deficit case: The family now owns a $100 government bond. However, the family also realizes that at the time its bond comes due, the government will find it has to raise taxes to pay off the principal and interest due on the bonds it issued to finance the deficit. So ownership of the bond does not affect the family's decisions because the value of the bond is exactly offset by the value of its implicit future tax liability.

The issue raised by this argument is sometimes posed as the question "Are government bonds net wealth?" The question goes back at least to the classical English economist David Ricardo. Renewed by Robert Barro,[13] it is known as the *Barro-Ricardo equivalence proposition,* or **Ricardian equivalence**. The proposition is that debt financing by bond issue merely postpones taxation and therefore, in many instances, is strictly equivalent to current taxation. (Incidentally, after raising this as a theoretical possibility, Ricardo rejected its practical significance.)

The strict Barro-Ricardo proposition that government bonds are not net wealth turns on the argument that people realize their bonds will have to be paid off with future increases in taxes. If so, an increase in the budget deficit unaccompanied by cuts in government spending should lead to an increase in saving that precisely matches the deficit.

There are two main theoretical objections to the Barro-Ricardo proposition. First, given that people have finite lifetimes, different people will pay off the debt than those who are receiving the tax cut today. This argument assumes that people now alive do not take into account the higher taxes their descendants will have to pay in the future. Second, it is argued that many people cannot borrow, and so do not consume according to their permanent income. They would like to consume more today, but because of liquidity constraints—their inability to borrow—they are constrained to consuming less than they would want according to their permanent income. A tax cut for these people eases their liquidity constraint and allows them to consume more.[14]

These theoretical disagreements mean that the Barro-Ricardo hypothesis has to be settled by examining the empirical evidence. The sharp decline of the Canadian private savings rate in the 1980s in the face of increased public deficits is one piece of evidence against the proposition. Less casual empirical research continues in an

**Ricardian equivalence**
Debt financing by bond issue merely postpones taxation and therefore, in many instances, is strictly equivalent to current taxation.

[13] The original article is Robert Barro, "Are Government Bonds Net Wealth?" *Journal of Political Economy,* December 1974. See also, by the same author, "The Ricardian Approach to Budget Deficits," *Journal of Economic Perspectives,* Spring 1989. Theoretical challenges to the Barro-Ricardo view include Olivier Blanchard, "Debts, Deficits and Finite Horizons," *Journal of Political Economy,* April 1985, and Douglas Bernheim, "A Neoclassical Perspective on Budget Deficits," *Journal of Economic Perspectives,* Spring 1989.

[14] Barro himself pointed out another qualification to the equivalence proposition. Changes in marginal tax rates change tax-induced distortions in private decision making. Deficits that allow low tax rates today at the expense of high tax rates in the future may create greater overall distortion than would a constant-over-time medium tax rate.

attempt to settle the issue of whether the debt is wealth.[15] We believe the evidence to date is, on balance, unfavourable to the Barro-Ricardo proposition, but we recognize that the issue has not yet been decisively settled.

## 19-5 | THE CANADA PENSION PLAN

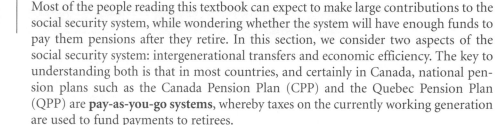

www.fin.gc.ca/wp/
2003-04e.html

**pay-as-you-go (social
security) system**
Social security system in
which payments to
retirees are made with
funds provided, not by
their social security taxes,
but by the social security
taxes of the working
populace.

Most of the people reading this textbook can expect to make large contributions to the social security system, while wondering whether the system will have enough funds to pay them pensions after they retire. In this section, we consider two aspects of the social security system: intergenerational transfers and economic efficiency. The key to understanding both is that in most countries, and certainly in Canada, national pension plans such as the Canada Pension Plan (CPP) and the Quebec Pension Plan (QPP) are **pay-as-you-go systems**, whereby taxes on the currently working generation are used to fund payments to retirees.

### CPP/QPP as Intergenerational Transfer

Pay-as-you-go social security systems such as the CPP and QPP may transfer resources from the young to the old for three reasons: (1) because of population growth, (2) because of real income growth, and (3) because of the political process. We deal with each in turn. As a benchmark, we ask first what benefits and payments would look like in a no-resource-transfer system.

Suppose the typical person works and makes contributions to the CPP system from age 26 through 65 and receives benefits from age 66 through 81. Since there are 40 years of work for 10 years of retirement, there will be four active contributors for each active beneficiary.[16] This means that the CPP budget will balance if each beneficiary receives the payments of four workers. And since each worker pays in for four times the number of years the worker receives benefits, over a lifetime the worker's contributions and benefits will balance.

### Intergenerational Transfers Because of Population Growth

Growing populations have a higher ratio of young to old than do stable populations. The higher ratio arises simply because each succeeding generation is larger than the one before it. For example, if population growth is 2 percent per year, the ratio of the working age to retirement age population in the example above will be 7 to 1 instead of 4 to 1. Thus, the benefit-contribution ratio can be much higher in a growing population than in a stable population.

Taking advantage of population growth to increase the benefit-contribution ratio is understandably politically attractive. The problem with such a set-up is that one day population growth may end. To maintain expected benefits, contributions by the working generations will have to increase drastically. (In the example we've

---

[15] See, for example, Joseph Altonji, Fumio Hayashi, and Laurence Kotlikoff, "Parental Altruism and Inter Vivos Transfers: Theory and Evidence," *Journal of Political Economy*, December 1997; Joseph J. Altonji, Fumio Hayashi, and Laurence Kotlikoff, "Is the Extended Family Altruistically Linked? Direct Tests Using Micro Data," *American Economic Review*, December 1992; and John J. Seater, "Ricardian Equivalence," *Journal of Economic Literature*, March 1993.

[16] We pick a round number, four, for purposes of illustration. Real social security systems have more complicated rules for computing taxes and benefits.

been using, contributions would have to nearly double, increasing by a ratio of 7 to 4.) This is exactly what has happened as most of the world's industrialized countries have moved toward zero population growth (ZPG).

Table 19-2 gives projections of the working-age to retirement-age population for seven industrialized countries. You can see that in the future in all these countries, pay-as-you-go social security will have to either increase contributions from each worker or cut benefits to each retiree.[17]

| TABLE 19-2 | THE RATIO OF WORKING-AGE POPULATION TO RETIREMENT-AGE POPULATION |

| Year | Canada | France | Germany | Italy | Japan | United Kingdom | United States |
|------|--------|--------|---------|-------|-------|----------------|---------------|
| 1960 | 7.7 | 5.3 | 6.3 | 7.5 | 10.5 | 5.6 | 6.5 |
| 1990 | 5.9 | 4.7 | 4.5 | 4.7 | 5.8 | 4.3 | 5.3 |
| 2010 | 4.7 | 4.1 | 2.8 | 3.9 | 3.4 | 4.5 | 5.3 |
| 2030 | 3.5 | 3.3 | 3.0 | 3.4 | 3.0 | 3.9 | 4.9 |
| 2040 | 2.6 | 2.6 | 2.1 | 2.4 | 2.6 | 3.0 | 3.1 |

SOURCE: Patricia S. Pollard, "How Will Demographics Affect Social Security," Federal Reserve Bank of St. Louis, *International Economic Trends*, August 1996, based on OECD data.

## Intergenerational Transfers Because of Income Growth

Younger generations have a higher standard of living than older generations that is simply due to economic growth.[18] Suppose that contributions are set at a certain percentage of income, rather than a fixed dollar level. In a pay-as-you-go system, retired workers receive benefits higher than their own contributions because the source of the contributions is the higher income of the younger generation. At reasonable levels of productivity growth, this effect allows benefits to be much higher than would otherwise be possible. If long run economic growth was to falter, the system would collapse. But as long as economic growth continues, each generation can count on receiving extra benefits based on the productivity of the young.

## Intergenerational Transfers Because of the Political Process

Social security systems are in trouble in many countries. Put simply, social security has been set up to pay out more in benefits than can be supported by the level of contributions, even considering population and income growth. This worked to the advantage of early recipients, but the day of reckoning having arrived, young people today can expect to receive a far lower benefit per dollar of contribution than did their parents. This situation has a political rather than purely economic explanation. Older people vote more than younger people, and current generations can vote for benefit programs without consulting the not-yet-born generations who will be required to pay for them. Older generations are, at least sometimes, in a position to enforce intergenerational transfers through the political system.

---

[17] For projections on the effect of possible social security reforms in the major industrial countries, see "Fiscal Challenges Facing Industrial Countries," *World Economic Outlook* (International Monetary Fund), May 1996.

[18] Not every member of every generation is better off than his or her parents, of course. For example, in Canada today, young workers with low levels of education generally have a standard of living no higher than that of their parents.

## Social Security and Economic Efficiency

There is a strong economic argument in favour of a social security system. As a society, there is a minimal standard of living that we find acceptable for the elderly. Social security is a roundabout way of forcing everyone to undertake at least some saving for old age. Without a social security system, we would have to choose between seeing some of the elderly go hungry and having younger generations support older generations who had insufficient savings.

Unfortunately, in a pay-as-you-go system, society as a whole does not save for the future. Since contributions are immediately disbursed, no productive capital is created. So while social security forces some people to save who otherwise would not, it also reduces the effectiveness of investment by those who would have saved anyway by a remarkable amount.

In a pay-as-you-go system, $100 in contributions produces $100 in benefits. In our pay-in-40-year/take-out-10-year example, a worker would pay in $25 per year to sustain a $100 per year benefit level. Contrast this return with the compound return on real investment. At 5 percent interest, $25 per year in contributions sustains a $391 per year benefit level.[19] The difference between the $391 per year and the $100 per year benefit level is the economic cost of society's forgoing productive investment.[20]

Social security contributions almost certainly do not crowd out private (productive) retirement savings one for one. But each dollar of private saving that is displaced significantly reduces the size of society's nest egg.

## POLICY IN *ACTION*

### Unfunded Liabilities

When discussing the federal deficit or surplus, we measure current revenue and current expenditures. However, there is a class of obligations of the government that is often called *unfunded liabilities*. These are liabilities in the future under such programs as the Canada and Quebec Pension Plans, Old Age Security, and the health care system.

According to the Fraser Institute, these unfunded liabilities have been growing, and this is not generally counted in deficit calculations. Although there was a drop of approximately $54 billion in debt for all levels of government in 2001, this was more than offset by the increase in unfunded liabilities. The Fraser Institute suggests that, due to increases in program obligations since 1996, the 2000–2001 liabilities for all levels of government add up to $172,416 per Canadian taxpayer or $83,927 per Canadian citizen.*

---

*Canadian Government Debt 2003: A Guide to the Indebtedness of Canada and the Provinces*, published by the Fraser Institute. Information on this article can be obtained from the Fraser Institute Internet page at www.fraserinstitute.ca.

---

[19] This calculation is sensitive to the real interest rate used in the calculation. We use 5 percent per year, a number commonly used by universities in computing a rate at which endowments may be drawn on. At 2 percent annual interest, the benefit would be $168; at 8 percent the benefit would be $965.

[20] You can also think of the efficiency argument in terms of the effect of lower saving reducing economic growth and lowering very long run output. We studied this point in Chapters 4 and 5.

## *Working with Data*

A wealth of statistical information is available on the Department of Finance Canada Internet site, which can be accessed at www.fin.gc.ca/toce/2002/frt_e.html. In Table 55, you can see how the fiscal performance in Canada compares to other major countries in the world. Retrieve this data, plot the fiscal balances of various countries, and comment on these relative to the Canadian performance.

## CHAPTER SUMMARY

▶ The federal government ran budget deficits for each year between 1973 and 1996, which led to increases in debt and a resultant increase in the debt-GDP ratio. By the end of the 1990s, the federal government was in a budgetary surplus position.

▶ The budgetary deficit is composed of the operating deficit plus interest on the public debt.

▶ The debt-GDP ratio has exhibited three peaks: during the Great Depression, during World War II, and in the mid-1990s, when the federal government began reducing budget deficits.

▶ When the government finances its deficit by issuing money, the government is imposing an inflation tax.

▶ Social security is financed as a pay-as-you-go system.

## KEY TERMS

direct taxes, *387*
indirect taxes, *387*
government purchases, *387*
transfer payments, *387*
interest payments, *388*

operating (or non-interest)
    deficit, *392*
debt-income ratio, *394*
government budget constraint, *395*
monetization, *396*
seigniorage, *396*

inflation tax, *398*
intergenerational accounting, *400*
Ricardian equivalence, *402*
pay-as-you-go (social security)
    system, *403*

## DISCUSSION QUESTIONS

1. **a.** To what extent do we need to worry about the component of our total deficit that consists of interest payments on the public debt? (Hint: Ask yourself how much of this component is a real cost to the government.)

    **b.** To what extent do we need to worry about the national debt? In what way or ways is it a burden on society?

2. Should we require that the budget be balanced? Discuss.

3. Why is it more useful to look at the ratio of debt to GDP than at the absolute value of the debt?

www.mcgrawhill.ca/college/dornbusch

4. **a.** Why might a pay-as-you-go social security system transfer resources from the young to the old?

   **b.** What are the consequences of such a system on economic efficiency?

   ***c.** Are there other ways to structure a social security system that might alleviate some of the problems associated with this one? Explain.

5. When should, and shouldn't, the Bank of Canada monetize deficits?

6. How can inflation create government revenue?

7. German unification involved massive expenditures for infrastructure in the east, as well as transfer payments to many former East Germans. Should such expenditures have been financed by (a) money creation because of their transitory, exceptional nature, (b) debt, or (c) taxes? Justify your answer.

8. Discuss what you think might happen in the Canadian economy if the federal government was to pursue expansionary fiscal policy, while one or more of the provinces pursued contractionary fiscal policy at the same time.

## A P P L I C A T I O N    Q U E S T I O N S

1. Go to the Department of Finance Canada Fiscal Reference Tables cited in this chapter and retrieve the federal government deficit. Plot this with the recession dates given in Chapter 6, Application Question 3. Can you see any relationship between these variables?

2. Go to the Department of Finance Canada's Fiscal Reference Tables and retrieve the tables pertaining to federal government revenue: www.fin.gc.ca/toce/2002/frt_e.html

   **a.** Calculate the percentage change in revenue for each year since 1970.

   **b.** The individual income tax was the largest component of federal revenue in the 1970s and remains the largest today. The second-largest component has changed dramatically, however. What was it in the 1970s, and what has it been since?

3. If the growth rate of output averaged roughly 4 percent per year and the growth rate of the national debt averaged 5 percent, what would happen to the ratio of debt to GDP over time? Why?

4. Suppose the money base is 10 percent of GDP. Suppose also that the government is considering raising the inflation rate from 0 to 10 percent per annum and believes that doing so will increase government revenue by 1 percent of GDP. Explain why the government must be overestimating the revenue it will receive from the resulting inflation tax.

5. In the Department of Finance's Fiscal Reference Tables at www.fin.gc.ca/toce/2002/frt_e.html, there is a category for local governments.

   **a.** Reproduce Figures 19-1 and 19-2 for this level of government.

   **b.** For all of the available years, calculate the percent contribution of local government to the total government revenue and expenditure.

---

* An asterisk denotes a more difficult problem.

# ADVANCED TOPICS

## *LEARNING OBJECTIVES*

After reading and studying this chapter, you should be able to:

▶ *Understand that in a rational expectations model, people form expectations that are consistent with the way the economy operates. Anticipated monetary policy has no real effects in the short run or the long run.*

▶ *Understand that the random walk theory of GDP argues that most shifts in output are permanent, as opposed to transitory booms and recessions, and that changes in aggregate demand are much less important than changes in aggregate supply.*

▶ *Understand that real business cycle theory argues that money is very unimportant and that economic fluctuations are due largely to changes in technology.*

▶ *Understand that New Keynesian models of price stickiness offer "microfoundations" explaining why the price level does not always adjust quickly to changes in the money supply.*

T This chapter offers advanced material presenting the revolution in macroeconomics that has developed over the last 25 years. These ideas are exciting and controversial. When introduced, each seemed as if it would forever change macroeconomics in both teaching and practice. Some of the dramatic impact has failed to materialize, in part because empirical support for these challenging ideas has not been as full and convincing as had been hoped by their proponents. What's more, the ideas in part contradict each other—as well as the traditional aggregate supply-aggregate demand model. Even so, the impact of these concepts on both research and policy has been revolutionary. And while the ideas continue to be contested, each remains an active component of the economics research agenda.

We look at four new theories in this chapter:

▶ Rational expectations.

▶ The random walk of GDP.

▶ Real business cycle theory.

▶ New Keynesian models of price stickiness.

These models yield contrasting conclusions about the conduct of monetary policy, but they are alike in their emphasis on the importance of consistency between macroeconomic and microeconomic theory.

These theories are at the forefront of research, and their exposition is necessarily more technical than is most of the text. For this reason, we begin with an informal overview.

## 20-1 | AN OVERVIEW OF THE NEW MACROECONOMICS

### Rational Expectations

**rational expectations equilibrium**

A model in which expectations are formed rationally, and markets are always in equilibrium.

In a **rational expectations equilibrium**, markets clear and there is nothing systematic that monetary policy can do to affect output or unemployment. The rational expectations approach is most closely associated with Nobel Laureate Robert Lucas of the University of Chicago.

The term *rational expectations equilibrium* identifies two key features of this approach. First, it places weight on the role of expectations and specifically *rational* expectations. Economic agents do not know the future with certainty and therefore have to base their plans and decisions, including price setting, on their forecasts or expectations of the future. If these expectations are made in a rational fashion, agents use all available information as well as possible to come out with the best possible forecasts. Second, the rational expectations model insists on *equilibrium:* Markets clear immediately. Phenomena such as insider-outsider effects, as seen in the preceding chapter, simply do not come into play.

The full neoclassical theory of aggregate supply asserts that unemployment is always at the natural rate, that output is always at the full employment level, and that any unemployment is purely frictional. Changes in the price level—for example, as a result of an increase in the money stock—leave output and employment unchanged. Money wages will rise, but since the real wage is unchanged, neither the quantity of labour supplied nor that demanded will change. The analysis of the Classical case in Chapter 6 applies in full: Neither monetary nor fiscal policy changes will have any effect on output. The rational expectations equilibrium approach, first presented in "the Lucas model," offers a qualified departure from that conclusion.

Lucas presents a neoclassical model with one changed assumption: Some people do not know the aggregate price level but do know the nominal (dollar) wage or price at which they can buy and sell. For instance, at a given moment in time, a worker knows that the going nominal wage rate is $12 per hour but does not know the aggregate price level, and thus does not know the real wage (the nominal wage divided by the price level, equal to the amount of goods the wage will buy). Suppose all nominal prices and wages rise in proportion. The real wage is unchanged, but if workers do not realize that prices have also risen, they will think that the real wage has risen and will supply more labour, so output will rise.

We turn now to the **rational expectations** aspect of this approach. How are firms and workers to form expectations of the price level? The rational expectations approach assumes that people use all relevant information in forming expectations of economic variables. In particular, it assumes that workers and firms will think through the economic mechanisms underlying the determination of the actual price level and then use the implied value of the actual price level as the expected price level.

Households' and firms' best guess is that full employment will prevail, although they recognize that this guess may be wrong in either direction. The expected price level, $p^e$, will be the price level consistent with full employment, or the price level that equates aggregate demand and supply, that is, $AS = AD$. The central implication of the rational expectations approach is that people may not always get forecasts right but they do not make *systematic* errors.

We are now ready to see the central implication of the Lucas approach, namely, *the differential reaction of the economy to anticipated versus unanticipated changes in the money supply*. In response to an anticipated change in the money supply, agents will expect an equiproportionate change in the price level. Both $p$ and $p^e$ will change in proportion to the change in the money supply, the real money supply will remain unchanged, and the economy will remain at full employment. In contrast, an unanticipated change in money will have its full $AS = AD$ effect—precisely because an unanticipated change will not affect $p^e$. Of course, agents will discover any change in the money supply relatively quickly, so even "unanticipated" changes will have real effects only in the very short run.

**rational expectations**

Theory of expectations formation in which expectations are based on all available information about the underlying economic variables; frequently associated with New Classical macroeconomics.

www.bankofcanada.ca/en/res/wp02-30.htm

## Policy Irrelevance

At first sight, the Lucas model seems to be almost the same as the Classical model: Both models predict **policy irrelevance**—that neither monetary nor fiscal policy can affect the equilibrium level of income in the long run. The Lucas model is more interesting than the Classical model, though, because it allows at least *transitory* deviations from full employment. However, these transitory deviations are the result of expectational errors, and they last only as long as the errors last—and that cannot be very long.

Moreover, there is no room for monetary policy in this world of rational expectations and market clearing. Suppose agents believe that the price level is lower than it actually is. The government need simply announce the correct statistics, and the market will, by itself, immediately go back to full employment. There is no need for accommodating monetary or fiscal policy to hasten the return to full employment. Thus, policy does not matter. In fact, in some versions of this approach, policy responses are problematic because they make it more complicated for economic agents to determine exactly what is happening in the economy and how best to adjust to it. This is a radically different perspective from a Keynesian world, where policy offers relief from unemployment.

**policy irrelevance**

Refers to the inability of monetary or fiscal policy to affect output in rational expectations equilibrium models.

## The Random Walk of GDP

Are fluctuations in output mainly transitory or mainly permanent? If fluctuations are primarily permanent, changes in aggregate demand—the heart of Keynesian macroeconomics—must be of relatively little importance. The logic is as follows: (1) According to the $AS = AD$ model, the effect of aggregate demand shocks wears off with time because the long run aggregate supply curve is vertical. (2) Therefore, if the effect of shocks is permanent, their source must be something other than aggregate demand.

This argument was first advanced by Charles Nelson and Charles Plosser, who presented careful statistical evidence in favour of the dominant role of permanent shocks.[1] Nelson and Plosser's work does not suggest that the $AS = AD$ model is theoretically flawed, but it does argue that the aggregate demand side is simply not very important. Their work serves as the inspiration for much of the real business cycle literature, discussed below.

**random walk**
A variable in which changes over time are unpredictable.

The idea that changes in output are permanent is sometimes described by saying that GDP follows a **random walk**, meaning that, having wandered up or down, GDP has no tendency to return to trend. This contrasts with the implicit model in the text. We think of the path of output over time as following a growth trend, explained largely by technological improvement and capital accumulation, plus a business cycle of transitory fluctuations, explained by our aggregate supply aggregate demand model. Since the fluctuations are transitory, output in our model tends to revert to the growth trend.

Inevitably, there has been a counterreaction to the random walk argument. The evidence is clear that large permanent changes to output are important, but a number of economists have argued that these permanent changes are infrequent and that in between such changes, aggregate demand is the primary source of fluctuations.

## Real Business Cycle Theory

**real business cycle (RBC) theory**
Theory that recessions and booms are due primarily to shocks in real activity, such as supply shocks, rather than to changes in monetary factors.

Equilibrium **real business cycle (RBC) theory** asserts that fluctuations in output and employment are the result of a variety of real shocks that hit the economy, with markets adjusting rapidly and remaining always in equilibrium.[2] Real business cycle theory is the natural outgrowth of the theoretical implication of the rational expectations approach—that anticipated monetary policy has no real effect—and of the empirical implication of random walk theory—that aggregate demand shocks are not an important source of fluctuations.[3]

http://papers.nber.org/
papers/w7534

---

[1] Charles R. Nelson and Charles I. Plosser, "Trends and Random Walks in Macroeconomic Time Series: Some Evidence and Implications," *Journal of Monetary Economics*, September 1982.

[2] To read more about the real business cycle approach, see S. Rao Aiyagari, "On the Contribution of Technology Shocks to Business Cycles," Federal Reserve Bank of Minneapolis *Quarterly Review*, Winter 1994; John H. Cochrane, "Shocks," *Carnegie-Rochester Conference Series on Public Policy*, Spring 1994; and Mark W. Watson, "Measures of Fit for Calibrated Models," *Journal of Political Economy*, December 1993. For a forceful negative view of real business cycle theory, see Lawrence Summers, "Some Skeptical Observations on Real Business Cycle Theory," Federal Reserve Bank of Minneapolis *Quarterly Review*, Fall 1986. See also Charles Plosser, "Understanding Real Business Cycles," and N. Gregory Mankiw, "Real Business Cycles: A New Keynesian Perspective," both in *Journal of Economic Perspectives*, Summer 1989.

[3] Real business cycle theory also has some methodological differences from other areas of macroeconomics with regard to the best way to identify underlying economic parameters. For a methodological and historical perspective on some of these differences, see Robert G. King, "Quantitative Theory and Econometrics," Federal Reserve Bank of Richmond *Economic Quarterly*, Summer 1995. For a somewhat more catholic view on methodology in empirical macroeconomics, see Christopher A. Sims, "Macroeconomics and Methodology," *Journal of Economic Perspectives*, Winter 1996.

With monetary causes of the business cycle assumed out of the way, real business cycle theory is left with two tasks. The first is to explain the shocks, or disturbances, that hit the economy, causing fluctuations in the first place. The second is to explain the **propagation mechanisms**. A propagation mechanism is a mechanism through which a disturbance is spread through the economy. In particular, the aim is to explain why shocks to the economy seem to have long-lived effects. We start with propagation mechanisms.

## Propagation Mechanisms

The propagation mechanism that is most associated with equilibrium business cycles is the **intertemporal substitution of leisure**. Any theory of the business cycle has to explain why people work more at some times than at others: During booms, employment is high and jobs are easy to find; during recessions, employment is lower and jobs are hard to find. A simple, but unsatisfactory, equilibrium explanation would be that people voluntarily supply more labour in response to a higher wage. (Remember that the equilibrium approach requires that people be on their supply and demand curves at all times.) However, the empirical evidence does not support this explanation. The elasticity of the labour supply with respect to the real wage is very small, and the real wage changes very little over the business cycle.

RBC models explain large movements in output with small movements in wages as follows: There is a high elasticity of labour supply in response to *temporary* changes in the wage. Or, as the argument is put, people are very willing to substitute leisure intertemporally. The argument is that people care about their total work effort but care very little about *when* they work. Suppose that within a two-year period they plan to work 4000 hours at the going wage (50 weeks each year at 40 hours a week). If wages are equal in the two years, they would work 2000 hours each year. But if wages were just 2 percent higher in one year than the other, they might prefer to work, say, 2200 hours in one year, forgoing vacations and working overtime, and 1800 hours in the other. By substituting between years, they work the same total amount but earn more total income. Note that the intertemporal substitution of leisure does not mean that the labour supply is sensitive to *permanent* changes in wages. If the wage rises, and will stay higher, there is nothing to be gained by working more this period than next. So it is quite possible for the response of labour supply to a permanent change in wages to be very small, even though the response to a temporary wage change is large.

This intertemporal substitution of leisure is clearly capable of generating large movements in the amount of work done in response to small shifts in wages—and thus could account for large output effects in the cycle accompanied by small changes in wages. However, there has not been strong empirical support for this view.

## Disturbances

The mechanisms that propagate business cycles are set in motion by events or *disturbances* that change the equilibrium levels of output and employment in individual markets and the economy as a whole. The most important disturbances isolated by equilibrium business cycle theorists are shocks to *productivity*, or supply shocks, and shocks to *government spending*. A **productivity shock** changes the level of output produced by given amounts of inputs. Changes in the weather and new methods of production are examples. Suppose there is a temporary favourable productivity shock this period. Individuals will want to work harder to take advantage of the

---

**propagation mechanisms**
Mechanisms by which current economic shocks cause fluctuations in the future, for example, intertemporal substitution of leisure.

**intertemporal substitution of leisure**
The extent to which temporarily high real wages cause workers to work harder today and enjoy more leisure tomorrow.

**productivity shock**
Change in technology that affects workers' productivity. See also *supply shock*.

higher productivity. In working more this period, they raise output. They also invest more, thus spreading the productivity shock into future periods by raising the stock of capital. If the effect of the intertemporal substitution of leisure is strong, even a small productivity shock could have a relatively large effect on output.

Real business cycle theory has been, and continues to be, a major area of research for many macroeconomists. However, proponents of this view have been less successful at converting the rest of the profession to their view than they had once hoped. In part, this is because the evidence for the importance of money seems persuasive. Most policy makers continue to rely on the aggregate supply-aggregate demand model we have studied throughout the book.

## New Keynesian Models of Price Stickiness

**New Keynesians**
Those who develop models whose basis is rational behaviour and conclude that the economy is not inherently efficient and that, at times, the government ought to stabilize output and unemployment.

**price stickiness**
When prices do not move with the infinite speed assumed in the Classical model.

**menu cost**
Small cost incurred when the nominal price of a good is changed; for example, the cost for a restaurant of reprinting its menus when it raises/lowers its prices.

**imperfect competition**
Form of competition in which firms have market power—firms can choose, to some extent, the price at which they will sell the goods they produce.

The models described above are all in the equilibrium-market clearing tradition. These models have become important in part because of their merits but also in part because economists have found rational decision making and market clearing to be a sound guiding principle. However, these models are inconsistent with the aggregate supply-aggregate demand behaviour that many economists believe characterizes the real world. **New Keynesians** accept the premise of individual rational behaviour, but develop models in which markets do not quickly reach the full Classical equilibrium and prices do not always adjust to changes in the money supply.[4]

We focus on a particular model of **price stickiness** developed by Gregory Mankiw. Suppose that the money supply increases. According to equilibrium theories, firms should all increase prices proportionately. But suppose there is a small cost, a **menu cost**, of actually making the price change. Might firms choose to leave their price at its old—now "wrong"—value? The traditional answer is no, because the benefit of getting the price right surely outweighs any very small cost of changing it.

Mankiw invoked **imperfect competition** to show that the losses to a firm from having the "wrong" price may be a very small fraction of the value to society of having the correct price. This suggests that menu costs can be quite small compared to fluctuations in output but still be large enough that no single firm is willing to incur the costs and change prices. So an increase in the nominal money supply may leave prices unchanged, and the resulting increase in real money increases output.

We turn now to more detailed—and more technically challenging—considerations of these ideas.

## 20-2 | THE RATIONAL EXPECTATIONS REVOLUTION

In this section, we work through a basic rational expectations model in several steps. First, we give a simplified version of our *AS-AD* model and solve it with exogenously given price expectations. We show that, except by coincidence, the

---

[4] For overviews of this literature, see Jean-Pascal Bénassy, "Classical and Keynesian Features in Macroeconomic Models with Imperfect Competition," Huw D. Dixon and Neil Rankin, "Imperfect Competition and Macroeconomics: A Survey," and Richard Startz, "Notes on Imperfect Competition and New Keynesian Economics," all in Huw D. Dixon and Neil Rankin (eds.), *The New Macroeconomics: Imperfect Markets and Policy Effectiveness* (Cambridge, UK: Cambridge University Press, 1995). See also Robert J. Gordon, "What Is New Keynesian Economics?" *Journal of Economic Literature* 28 (1990), and Jacquim Silvestre, "The Market-Power Foundations of Macroeconomic Policy," *Journal of Economic Literature* 31 (1993). See footnote 31 for more readings.

price predicted by the model will be inconsistent with the price that people expected. We turn then to a perfect-foresight model—a model in which we assume that people use the model's own predictions to form their price expectations. Finally, we change the perfect-foresight assumption to the weaker assumption of rational expectations, where agents do use the model to form price expectations but do so with only partial information. In both the perfect-foresight and rational expectations models, anticipated monetary policy will have no real effects. This is a direct consequence of the fact that actual and expected prices are consistent with one another and that the expectations-augmented Phillips curve asserts that deviations of unemployment from the natural rate are tied to the difference between realized inflation and expected inflation.

In each step of the model's development, you should focus on the link between the specification of expectations and the monetary policy multiplier. In the simplified $AS = AD$ model with exogenous expectations, the monetary policy multiplier is relatively large. In the perfect-foresight model, where expectations adjust perfectly, the monetary policy multiplier is *zero*. Finally, the rational expectations model combines the assumptions of the $AS = AD$ and perfect-foresight models. Expectations adjust perfectly with respect to anticipated changes in the money supply, but not at all to unanticipated changes; the monetary policy multiplier is zero with respect to anticipated changes in the money supply and relatively large with respect to unanticipated changes.

## A Simple Aggregate Supply-Aggregate Demand Model

We begin with a simplified version of the aggregate supply-aggregate demand model, stripping out much of the detail developed in earlier chapters. We begin by specifying a simple aggregate demand schedule.

$$AD: \quad m + v = p + y \tag{1}$$

Equation (1) is called the *quantity theory equation: m* is (the log of) the money supply; $v$ is velocity and is assumed to be constant; $p$ is the price level; and $y$ is GDP.[5]

We next specify a simple short run aggregate supply curve, one that emphasizes the role of price expectations.

$$p = p^e + \lambda(y - y^*) \tag{2}$$

where $p$ is again the price level, $p^e$ is the *expected* price level, $y$ is again GDP, and $y^*$ is potential GDP. The parameter $\lambda$ gives the slope of the aggregate supply curve. If $\lambda$ is large, an increase in output above potential output causes a steep rise in prices above what had been expected. If $\lambda$ is small, the short run response of prices to output is small.

---

[5] We employ here a quite technical, but quite useful, "trick." Equation (1), and the equations that follow, are written using the natural logarithms of the indicated variables. The quantity equation is usually written $MV = PY$, where $M$ is the money supply, $P$ is the price level, and so on. We use lower-case letters to represent logarithms, so $m = \ln(M)$, and so on. Thus, we get to equation (1) by writing $\ln(MV) = \ln(PY) = \ln M + \ln V = \ln P + \ln Y = m + v = p + y$. Using logarithms has the advantage that a change in $m$ can be interpreted as the *percentage* change in $M$. Having said all this, if you aren't comfortable with logarithms, no noticeable harm will be done if you just think of $m$ as the money supply. Note that we call $m$ "the money supply" in the text without continually qualifying the definition by saying "the logarithm of."

The aggregate demand and aggregate supply equations can be combined to solve for output [equation (3)] and prices [equation (4)] in terms of the money supply and other variables:[6]

$$y = \frac{1}{1+\lambda}m + \frac{1}{1+\lambda}(v - p^e) + \frac{\lambda}{1+\lambda}y^* \qquad (3)$$

$$p = \frac{\lambda}{1+\lambda}(m + v - y^*) + \frac{1}{1+\lambda}p^e \qquad (4)$$

Together, equations (3) and (4) tell us the equilibrium output and prices in our model economy. If the money supply rises 1 percent, output rises $1/(1 + \lambda)$ percent and prices rise $\lambda/(1 + \lambda)$ percent. To be concrete, suppose $\lambda$ is ½: then a 1 percent increase in the money supply causes a ⅔ percent increase in output and a ⅓ percent increase in the price level.

Now we use equations (3) and (4) to illustrate the standard approach to making an economic "forecast." (Be warned that this forecast will be subject to the Lucas critique, below.) For our fabricated example, suppose that $\lambda$ equals ½ and the values for the money supply, velocity, and potential GDP are $m = 2$, $v = 3$, $y^* = 4$, respectively. Most particularly, we assume that *agents in the economy expect* the price level to be $p^e = 5$. *What do you expect the price level to be?* What do you expect output to be? Try working out the answers for yourself. Our answers appear in the next paragraph.

Plugging the values given into equation (3), we find output is $y = 1\frac{1}{3} = \frac{2}{3}(2) + \frac{2}{3}(3 - 5) + \frac{1}{3}(4)$. From equation (4), we expect the price to be $p = 3\frac{2}{3} = \frac{1}{3}(2 + 3 - 4) + \frac{2}{3}(5)$.

So the output from our model is that we expect the price to be $3\frac{2}{3}$, taking as an input to the model that the expected price is 5! Shouldn't rational agents, who have a great deal at stake, make forecasts that are consistent with the way the economy (represented here by our simple model) actually operates? This is the essence of the **Lucas critique:** The standard aggregate supply-aggregate demand model assumes that economic agents make predictions for the economy that are inconsistent with the predictions the model itself makes.

Suppose that economic decision makers accept our forecast and change their expectation of the price level to $p^e = 3\frac{2}{3}$. Reworking equations (3) and (4) would then lead to predicting $y = 2\frac{2}{9} = \frac{2}{3}(2) + \frac{2}{3}(3 - 3\frac{2}{3}) + \frac{1}{3}(4)$ and $p = 2\frac{7}{9} = \frac{1}{3}(2 + 3 - 4) + \frac{2}{3}(3\frac{2}{3})$. Now the expected price input to and the price predicted as output from the model are closer, but they're still not the same. Modifying the model so that the predicted value of $p$ and the input value $p^e$ are equal leads to the idea of a perfect-foresight model.

## A Perfect-Foresight Model

We now assume that agents *do* use the $AS = AD$ model to forecast prices and that they have all the information necessary to make the forecast. Agents are said to have **perfect foresight**. Rather than assuming $p^e$ is given from outside the model, we

**Lucas critique**
Points out that many macroeconomics models assume that expectations are given by a particular function, when that function can change.

**perfect foresight**
Assumption that people know the future value of all relevant variables, or that their expectations are always correct.

---

[6] If you want to work through the algebra yourself, a useful first step is to rewrite equation (1) with price on the left, as in $p = m + v - y$. Use this expression to substitute out for the price level in equation (2), giving an equation with $y$ on both sides, $m + v - y = p^e + \lambda(y - y^*)$. Collecting terms and solving for output gives equation (3). Putting equation (3) back into $p = m + v - y$ and solving for the price level gives equation (4).

assume agents use the model itself to compute $p^e$. In other words, agents compute $p$ based on $m$, $\nu$, $p^e$, and so forth. Agents then set their predicted price at $p^e = p$. Since $p$ itself depends on $p^e$, the two must be solved for simultaneously.

Assume that our model correctly describes the economy, so that economic decision makers use equation (4) to *predict prices and compute $p^e$*, so $p^e = p$.

$$p^e = p = \frac{\lambda}{1 + \lambda}(m + \nu - y^*) + \frac{1}{1 + \lambda}p^e \tag{5}$$

Collecting terms containing $p^e$,[7] we can rearrange equation (5) to give the perfect-foresight forecast and solution for the price level and the corresponding solution for output.

$$p^e = p = m + \nu - y^* \tag{6}$$

$$y = y^* \tag{7}$$

The perfect-foresight predictions in equations (6) and (7) are quite different from the original $AS = AD$ predictions embodied in equations (4) and (3). The latter assume *exogenously* given price expectations; the former assume that price expectations are formed *endogenously* and, specifically, that expectation formation is consistent with the predictions of the model.

The switch to such consistently formed expectations has dramatic implications for the effectiveness of monetary policy. According to equation (4), a 1 percent increase in the money supply increases prices by $\lambda/(1 + \lambda)$ percent, but under perfect foresight, a 1 percent increase in the money supply leads to exactly a 1 percent increase in the price level. According to equation (3), a 1 percent increase in the money supply increases output by $1/(1 + \lambda)$ percent, but under perfect foresight, a 1 percent increase in the money supply leads to no increase at all in output. Notice that these perfect-foresight short run results are the same as the long run $AS = AD$ results. Under perfect foresight, prices rise not only as a direct result of the increase in the money supply but also because of the increase in price expectations. This extra boost raises prices just enough to completely offset the increase in the money supply.

Under perfect foresight, monetary policy is neutral in the short run as well as in the long run.

A perfect-foresight model has two important shortcomings. First, it requires that economic decision makers know everything about the economy. Second, it implies that the economy is always at full employment.[8] Neither of these shortcomings is really critical, as we will see when we consider a rational expectations model in the next section.

## A Rational Expectations Model

A *rational expectations model* assumes that agents make the best use of whatever information is available to them and that expectations are formed in a manner consistent with the way the economy actually operates. A rational expectations model is much like a perfect-foresight model in which some of the key variables are uncertain.

---

[7] Write $p^e\left(1 - \dfrac{1}{1+\lambda}\right) = \dfrac{\lambda}{1+\lambda}(m + \nu - y^*)$, and then multiply through by $1 + \lambda$.

[8] You can see in equation (2) that $p^e = p$ implies $y = y^*$.

To illustrate, suppose that before the money supply is known, economic decision makers expect the money supply to equal $m^e$. If the money supply actually turns out to be $m$, we can define the difference between the agents' expectation and the actual money supply

$$\epsilon_m = m - m^e$$

as the agents' money forecast error. (Analogously, suppose agents expect potential output to be $y^{*e}$. Since potential output is actually $y^*$, the agents' potential output forecast error is $\epsilon_{y^*} = y^* - y^{*e}$.) We show below that the monetary policy multiplier with respect to *anticipated money*, $m^e$, is zero, just as in the perfect-foresight model. The monetary policy multiplier with respect to *unanticipated* money, $\epsilon_m$, is zero, just as in the $AS = AD$ model.

The forecast errors in a particular quarter may be either positive (the money supply, for instance, turned out to be larger than anticipated) or negative (the money supply turned out to be smaller than anticipated), but on average, rational forecast errors equal zero. The argument here is straightforward. Suppose $\epsilon_m$ averaged 7. In this case we could improve our forecasts by just raising every forecast $m^e$ by 7. So while rational forecast errors may be either large or small, depending on the quality of information available, they average zero. Another way to express this is $(\epsilon_m)^e = 0$.

We next ask what the price level will be in equilibrium. We begin by repeating equation (4) but substituting $m^e + \epsilon_m$ for $m$ and $y^{*e} + \epsilon_y$ for $y^*$.

$$p = \frac{\lambda}{1 + \lambda}\left[\left(m^e + \epsilon_m\right) + v - \left(y^{*e} + \epsilon_{y^*}\right)\right] + \frac{1}{1 + \lambda}p^e \tag{8}$$

We assume that agents form their expectations, $p^e$, on the basis of the price forecast in equation (8). However, we recognize that forecasts are based only on the information the agents have.[9]

$$p^e = \frac{\lambda}{1 + \lambda}(m^e + v - y^{*e}) + \frac{1}{1 + \lambda}p^e \tag{9}$$

Simplifying equation (9) gives

$$p^e = m^e + v - y^{*e} \tag{10}$$

Notice that the expected price under rational expectations, in equation (10), is the same as that under perfect foresight, in equation (6), except that it is based only on the limited information available to those making the forecast: $m^e$ rather than $m$, for example. The equilibrium solutions for price and output are[10]

$$y = y^{*e} + \frac{1}{1 + \lambda}\epsilon_m + \frac{\lambda}{1 + \lambda}\epsilon_{y^*} \tag{11}$$

$$p = m^e + v - y^{*e} + \frac{\lambda}{1 + \lambda}(\epsilon_m - \epsilon_{y^*}) \tag{12}$$

---

[9] The expectation of $\epsilon_m$, for instance, is zero, and the expectation of $m^e$ is $m^e$. We assume, for simplicity of illustration, that $v$ and $\lambda$ are known exactly.

[10] If you're working out the algebra for yourself, replace $p^e$ in the price level equation, (8), with the value from equation (10) to find

$$p = \frac{\lambda}{1 + \lambda}\left[\left(m^e + \epsilon_m\right) + v - \left(y^{*e} + \epsilon_{y^*}\right)\right] + \frac{1}{1 + \lambda}\left(m^e + v - y^{*e}\right)$$

Simplify and make the analogous substitutions for output in equation (3) to derive equations (11) and (12).

## Rational Expectations Forecast Errors Are Unpredictable

Rational expectations differ from perfect foresight in that rational expectations forecasts are imperfect. They may be too high or too low, although the forecast is right on average. Rational expectations forecasts make the best use of the information available to the agents making the forecasts. As a consequence, the best guess of the forecast error, based on the information available when the forecast is made, is zero.

Suppose agents forecast $p$ to be $p^e$. The forecast error, $\epsilon$, is the difference between the realized value of $p$ and the forecast.

$$\epsilon = p - p^e$$

It's straightforward to show that the expected value of the forecast error, call it $\epsilon^e$, is zero. The expected forecast error is the difference between the average value of $p$ and the average value of $p^e$. But these two are equal on average, precisely because agents adjust $p^e$ to make them equal on average. If $p^e$ was higher on average than $p$, agents could improve their guesses just by lowering $p^e$.

What is the effect of an increase in the money supply under rational expectations? The question must now be broken down into two parts: What is the effect of an anticipated increase in the money supply? And what is the effect of an unanticipated increase in the money supply?

From examination of equation (11), we see that under rational expectations, an anticipated increase in money supply has no effect at all on output but an unanticipated increase in the money supply increases output, by $1/(1 + \lambda)$. Notice that anticipated changes operate just as predicted by the perfect-foresight model above and that unanticipated changes operate just as predicted by our initial, exogenous price expectation, $AS = AD$ model. In effect, anticipated monetary policy is neutral; unanticipated policy has its full $AS = AD$ effects.

You should use equations (11) and (12) to check the effects of supply shocks ($y^{*e}$ and $\epsilon_{y^*}$) and of shocks on the price level to see that these also behave as in the perfect-foresight model when anticipated and as in the $AS = AD$ model when unanticipated.

### The Rational Expectations Equilibrium Approach: Empirical Evidence

The rational expectations model has the very strong prediction that anticipated monetary policy should have no effect on output. Early studies seemed consistent with this view, finding evidence that only unanticipated changes in the money stock increase output.[11] However, these results did not stand up to further testing.[12]

---

[11] See, for instance, Robert Barro, "Unanticipated Money, Output, and the Price Level in the United States," *Journal of Political Economy*, August 1978.

[12] Two influential, if difficult, articles are John Boschen and Herschel Grossman, "Tests of Equilibrium Macroeconomics with Contemporaneous Monetary Data," *Journal of Monetary Economics*, November 1982, and Frederic Mishkin, "Does Anticipated Monetary Policy Matter? An Econometric Investigation," *Journal of Political Economy*, February 1982.

We give here the flavour of these empirical tests. We wish to ask whether anticipated money growth increases output, as the $AS = AD$ model predicts, or whether there is no effect, as suggested by rational expectations models. The test involves two steps. First, we have to estimate anticipated money growth. Second, we compare anticipated money growth to changes in output.

Figure 20-1 shows $M2$ growth from 1973 through 2003. The actual growth rate is split into anticipated growth and unanticipated growth. In other words, we show three lines: $m = m^e + \epsilon_m$. Anticipated money growth is a statistical forecast based on the preceding four quarters of money growth.[13] Unanticipated growth is the difference between the forecast and the growth that actually occurred.

### FIGURE 20-1

We decompose the growth of $M2$ into an anticipated component and an unanticipated component. This is based on the assumption that the growth rate from the last four periods can be used to anticipate the current growth rate. Anticipated follows actual reasonably closely. Notice that the unanticipated component is centred on zero, so there is no consistent forecast error.

### ACTUAL, ANTICIPATED, AND UNANTICIPATED M2 GROWTH, 1973–2003

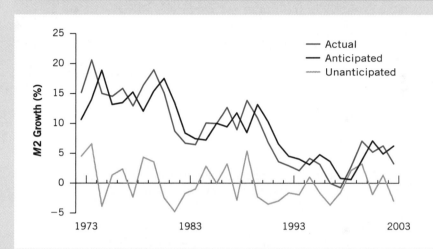

SOURCE: CANSIM II V37128 and calculations by the authors.

We plot output growth against our estimate of anticipated money growth in Figure 20-2, showing also the line that best fits the data. Two aspects of Figure 20-2 are salient: (1) anticipated money growth does a very poor job of explaining output growth (many of the data points are far from the line); and (2) there is actually a small negative slope to the line. Thus the statistical evidence is not very supportive of a strict interpretation of the rational expectations model.

## Recap

▶ Rational expectations models predict that anticipated changes to the money supply change the overall price level proportionately, leaving output unchanged.

▶ With respect to anticipated money growth, rational expectations models operate as if the long run aggregate supply curve applied instantaneously, not just in the long run.

▶ While the intellectual appeal of rational expectations models is very strong, the empirical evidence is less supportive.

---

[13] For the statistically curious, the forecast is based on a least-squares regression of $M2$ growth on four lags of $M2$ growth.

*FIGURE 20-2*

**EXPECTED MONEY GROWTH AND GROWTH OF OUTPUT, 1973–2002**

This figure shows that there is very little relationship between anticipated *M*2 growth and the growth rate of real output. Many of the points are very far from the estimated line, and the line actually has a small negative slope.

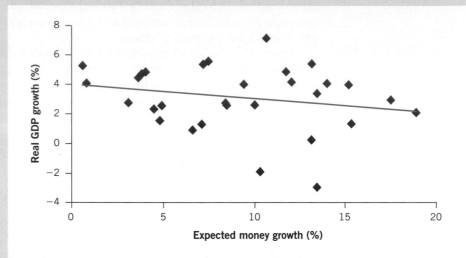

SOURCE: GDP: CANSIM II V1992259; expected money growth estimated by the authors; see Figure 20-1.

# POLICY IN *ACTION*

## Rational Expectations, Equilibrium, and Monetary Policy

The rational expectations model studied in this chapter has a very strong prediction: Anticipated changes in the money supply should have no effect on real output. This is the prediction of policy irrelevance. From a monetary policy perspective, this means that if the Bank of Canada announces policy and then implements the announced policy, this policy cannot affect real output. As we saw in Chapter 18, the Bank of Canada is very transparent in its implementation of monetary policy, yet it still affects real output in the short run.

The reason for this is that the policy ineffectiveness proposition, *as a theoretical proposition*, depends crucially on two important assumptions: First, agents must make expectations in a rational manner and, second, the equilibrium model that is used to derive this proposition must be the correct model of the economy. From the perspective of short run implementation of monetary policy, neither of these assumptions appears to be relevant.

We saw the first point in Chapter 7. If agents have static expectations, changes in the money supply will affect output in the short run. Put another way, there is a *short run* trade-off between inflation and real output. Regarding the second point, as we have seen in various places in this book, an equilibrium model really describes the economy only over the long run. We have

## POLICY IN *ACTION*

### Rational Expectations, Equilibrium, and Monetary Policy cont'd

learned that, in the very short run, monetary policy can change the real interest rate and real output. In these models, it does not matter whether agents have rational expectations—monetary policy can still affect real output.

We have learned in this book that, in the long run, equilibrium models are a more relevant description of the economy. It is also quite possibly true that, over longer time horizons, agents have rational expectations. From a monetary policy perspective, this simply means that policy irrelevance is something we knew all along: *In the long run*, monetary policy controls only the inflation rate, not real output, as we learned in Chapter 3.

---

## 20-3 | THE MICROECONOMICS OF THE IMPERFECT INFORMATION AGGREGATE SUPPLY CURVE[14]

An important feature of the inflation-expectations-augmented aggregate supply curve is that output is high ($y > y^*$) when the nominal price level is higher than expected ($p > p^e$). This feature plays a central role in both the aggregate supply-aggregate demand model of Chapter 6 and the rational expectations model just presented. In this section, we examine Lucas's **imperfect-information model** of the aggregate supply curve.[15,16]

**imperfect-information model**

Forecasts based on imperfect information will be less than fully accurate, although not necessarily biased.

Why does output sometimes rise when the overall price level rises? Lucas's answer is that firms usually observe prices only in their own market. A high price might be due to high demand, or it might just reflect an increase in the overall price level. In the former case, the firm would like to increase production; in the latter case, the price change should be neutral and production should be unchanged. But information is imperfect: When the firm sees a high price for its product, it doesn't know whether the cause is high demand or high overall prices. The firm, rationally, acts as if each cause was partially responsible and raises production a small amount. At the aggregate level, an unanticipated overall price increase is "misinterpreted" by every firm as a possible signal of higher demand, so the overall price increase leads to increased output. This connection gives us the Phillips curve relationship we see in real-world data. We turn now to a simplified version of Lucas's original model.

---

[14] This section and Section 20-5 are by far the most technically difficult in the book. You may wish to skip them on first reading.

[15] See Robert E. Lucas, Jr., "Expectations and the Neutrality of Money," *Journal of Economic Theory*, April 1972. Also see Edmund S. Phelps, "Introduction," in Edmund S. Phelps et al., *Microeconomic Foundations of Employment and Inflation Theory* (New York: Norton, 1970).

[16] We strip many of the details from Lucas's original presentation. For a more thorough presentation, see David Romer, *Advanced Macroeconomics* (New York: McGraw-Hill, 1995), Chapter 6.

Suppose the economy is composed of distinct markets—Lucas originally suggested a parable in which each market was on an isolated island. Inhabitants of each island produce goods and then meet at a central location to trade. People on island $i$ are willing to work longer hours when the output from their island is expected to fetch a price, $p_i$, which is high relative to the overall price level in the economy, $p$. The supply of output produced on the $i^{th}$ island $i$ would be

$$y_i = \alpha(p_i - p) \tag{13}$$

if island $i$'s inhabitants knew the overall price level.[17] We assume, instead, that they have to make a guess as to the overall price level. Call this guess the expectation of the price level given the information available on island $i$, $E(p|\text{island } i)$, so the supply is

$$y_i = \alpha[p_i - E(p|\text{island } i)] \tag{14}$$

The price that will be paid for goods produced on island $i$ depends on the overall price level, $p$, and on a demand shock specific to the particular kind of goods made on island $i$, $z_i$. We suppose the inhabitants of the island know their local price, $p_i$, but observe neither the demand shock nor the overall price level. They must therefore infer the overall price level from $p_i$. High $p_i$ might mean that $z_i$ is high *or* that $p$ is high. So when the inhabitants observe a high $p_i$, they increase their estimate of $p$, but not by too much, because sometimes high $p_i$ is due to high $z_i$ and normal levels of $p$. The best guess of $p$ is

$$E(p|p_i) = k_0 + \frac{1}{\alpha}\beta p_i, \quad 0 < \beta < 1 \tag{15}$$

where $E(p|p_i)$ indicates that the only information used in making a guess is the local price,[18] and $a$ is a constant reflecting the slopes of the supply and demand curves.[19] If most changes in local prices, $p_i$, are due to changes in the overall price level, $p$, then $\beta$ will be close to 1; if most changes are due to local demand shocks, $z_i$, then $\beta$ will be close to zero.[20] *The value of $\beta$ is the key to the slope of the aggregate supply curve— we see below that if $\beta = 1$, the aggregate supply curve will be vertical.*

We can use equation (15) to express supply as

$$y_i = \alpha\left[p_i - \left(k_0 + \frac{1}{\alpha}\beta p_i\right)\right] = \alpha\left[\left(1 - \frac{\beta}{\alpha}\right)p_i - k_0\right] \tag{16}$$

Demand for the product of island $i$ depends on aggregate GDP, $y$, on the demand shock for the product of the island, $z_i$, and on the relative price of the island's product, $p_i - p$. That is

$$y_i = y + z_i - \gamma(p_i - p) \tag{17}$$

---

[17] As before, lower-case $y$ and $p$ really represent logarithms of output and price. Nothing of any importance rests on this point.

[18] Since we don't permit the islanders any aggregate information, we must be implicitly assuming that the anticipated inflation rate is zero.

[19] The intercept $k_0$ is not of any particular interest. It appears for technical reasons.

[20] Engineers will recognize this as a signal extraction problem, where $p$ is the signal and $z_i$ is the noise; $\beta$ will be close to 1 if there is a high signal-to-noise ratio.

The equilibrium price on an island is found by equating supply [equation (16)] and demand [equation (17)].

$$\alpha\left[\left(1 - \frac{\beta}{\alpha}\right)p_i - k_0\right] = y + z_i - \gamma(p_i - p) \tag{18}$$

Equation (18) gives the equilibrium relationship between shocks, prices, and output for a particular island. But any one island is *representative* of the economy as a whole. Islands differ from one another because of idiosyncratic shocks, but the aggregate economy is just the average of the economies on the individual islands. Specifically, this means that aggregate output $y$ is the average of the $y_i$ values, that the overall price level $p$ is the average of the $p_i$ values, and that the $z_i$ values average out to zero. If we average both sides of equation (18), we get

$$y = \alpha\left[\left(1 - \frac{\beta}{\alpha}\right)p - k_0\right] \tag{19}$$

## BOX 20-2

### A Visual Example of Forming an Expectation

Expectations formation plays a key role in the derivation of the imperfect-information aggregate supply curve. Equation (15) can be derived algebraically by using statistical theory, but we present here a more visual approach. The figure below shows three possible relationships between observed $p_i$ and the rational guess $E(p)$. Suppose the value of $p_i$ contains no information about $p$. As shown on the horizontal line, a rational person would guess $p$ independently of the value of $p_i$. (This is the $\beta = 0$ case.) If all movements in $p_i$ were movements in $p$, the best guess would be along the 45° line. (This is the $\beta = 1$ case.) With imperfect information, the optimal guess lies partway between the no-information and the perfect-information cases.

#### VISUAL EXAMPLE OF FORMING AN EXPECTATION

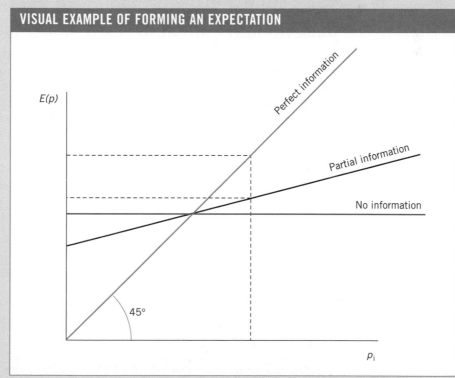

Equation (19) is the aggregate supply curve for the economy. With some further algebra, we can show that $a = 1$,[21] so the final expression for the aggregate supply curve is

$$p = \frac{1}{\alpha(1 - \beta)} \times (y + \alpha k_0) \tag{20}$$

The slope of the aggregate supply curve depends on both the slope of individual supply curves, $\alpha$, and the relative importance of aggregate versus idiosyncratic shocks, $\beta$. If shocks to the overall price level play a dominant role, $\beta$ will be close to 1 and the aggregate supply curve will be relatively steep. Thus, when most price shocks are attributed to changes in the overall price level, price shocks will be largely neutral, with little effect on output.

## Recap

▶ Agents forecast the overall price level on the basis of imperfect information. Agents are uncertain whether a price increase in an individual market is due to increased aggregate demand or to increased market-specific demand. As a result, increases in market-specific prices are attributed partially to increases in the overall price level and partially to increases in real demand.

▶ Unanticipated increases in the overall price level, $p$, generate partial increases in the anticipated price level, $p^e$, and partial increases in output, $y$. The positive associations between increases in $p$ and $y$ become the Phillips curve that we see in the data.

## 20-4 | THE RANDOM WALK OF GDP: DOES AGGREGATE DEMAND MATTER, OR IS IT ALL AGGREGATE SUPPLY?

In the orthodox model of the economy, the business cycle is presented as fluctuations of GDP around a smooth trend line. These fluctuations last from a few quarters to several years. Shocks to aggregate demand are presumed to be the primary cause of these transitory fluctuations. In 1982, Charles Nelson and Charles Plosser offered a heterodox challenge by suggesting that the trend is not so smooth but, rather, is subject to large and frequent shocks that have a permanent effect on the level of GDP.[22] If the Nelson and Plosser view is correct, aggregate demand shocks, which are transitory in nature, are less important than aggregate supply shocks, which may be permanent.

---

[21] If you want to do the algebra, use equation (19) to substitute for $y$ in equation (18). Collect terms and simplify to show that

$$p_i = \frac{1}{\gamma + (1-\beta)\alpha} z_i + p$$

The generic expression for $p_i$ is $p_i = a_0 + a_i z_i + ap$, and the implicit coefficient of $p$ in the expression just given shows that $a = 1$.

[22] Charles R. Nelson and Charles I. Plosser, "Trends and Random Walks in Macroeconomic Time Series: Some Evidence and Implications," *Journal of Monetary Economics*, September 1982. See also Stephen Beveridge and Charles R. Nelson, "A New Approach to Decomposition of Economic Time Series into Permanent and Transitory Components with Particular Attention to Measurement of the Business Cycle," *Journal of Monetary Economics*, March 1981; John Y. Campbell and N. Gregory Mankiw, "Are Output Fluctuations Transitory," *Quarterly Journal of Economics*, November 1987; and John H. Cochrane, "How Big Is the Random Walk in GNP?" *Journal of Political Economy*, October 1988.

trend (secular)
component of GDP
Potential output.

cyclical component of
GDP
Fluctuations of output
around its trend; the
output gap.

Think of output as composed of a **trend, or secular, component**, perhaps the result of the growth processes discussed in Chapter 4, and a **cyclical component**, representing perhaps the business cycle. Figure 20-3 presents a stylized view of trend growth and fluctuations around the trend. In studying business cycles, we are interested in the fluctuations. Therefore, the first step in most studies of the economy is to create a *stationary* picture of the economy, that is, to *detrend* the data. Nelson and Plosser showed that the method used to model the trend plays a critical role in identifying shocks.

### FIGURE 20-3

A standard view of the business cycle is that it is represented as fluctuations of actual GDP around trend, or potential output. (You may recognize this as Figure 6-1.)

### A STYLIZED BUSINESS CYCLE

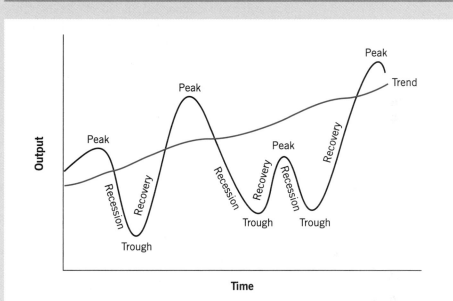

## Two Equivalent Representations of Trend and Shock

Suppose the trend in $y$ can be represented by a literal time trend, as in

$$y_t = \alpha + \beta t \tag{21}$$

Equation (21) states that $y$ rises by $\beta$ in each time period. By subtracting $y_{t-1} = \alpha + \beta(t-1)$ from each side of equation (21), we get

$$y_t - y_{t-1} = (\alpha + \beta t) - [\alpha + \beta(t-1)] \tag{22}$$

or

$$y_t = y_{t-1} + \beta \quad or \quad \Delta y_t = \beta \tag{23}$$

where $\Delta y$ is defined as $y_t - y_{t-1}$. Equation (23) also states that $y$ rises by $\beta$ in each time period.

## Is the Effect of Shocks Permanent or Transitory?

Equations (21) and (23) are precisely equivalent to one another. But suppose we add an output shock, $u_t$, to equation (21) or to equation (23). If we add the shock to equation (21), we have

$$y_t = \alpha + \beta t + u_t \qquad or \qquad \Delta y_t = \beta + u_t - u_{t-1} \qquad (24)$$

If we, instead, add the shock to equation (23), we have

$$y_t = y_{t-1} + \beta + u_t \qquad or \qquad y_t = \alpha + \beta t + u_t + u_{t-1} + u_{t-2} \cdots u_0 \qquad (25)$$

According to equation (24), the effect of a shock lasts one period, or, said differently, shocks to the change in $y$ reverse themselves after one period. In sharp contrast, according to equation (25), the effect of a shock on the level of $y$ is permanent, or, said differently, shocks to $y$ accumulate over time. A variable that behaves as described by equation (24)—that can be made stationary by taking out a time trend—is called **trend stationary**. A variable that behaves as described by equation (25)—that can be made stationary by differencing—is called **difference stationary**. A difference-stationary process is dominated by permanent shocks; a trend-stationary process is dominated by transitory shocks.

Whether GDP is better described by equation (24) or by equation (25) sounds at first like a question of arcane statistical interest only. But the distinction strikes to the heart of the relevance of aggregate demand theory. According to the $AS = AD$ model, business cycles caused by aggregate demand fluctuations are relatively short lived, a matter of a few quarters or, at most, a few years. In contrast, shocks to aggregate supply may be permanent if they derive from permanent productivity improvements.

Nelson and Plosser showed that GDP includes both permanent and transitory shocks but that the GDP process is dominated by permanent shocks. Their evidence struck a blow against arguments that aggregate demand is important in explaining the economy.

Figure 20-4 illustrates the importance of permanent shocks. Potential GDP shows the trend of GDP estimated from 1961 through 1973 and then projected forward. The left side of the figure, covering years prior to 1974, appears quite consistent with the idea of fluctuations around a trend. But if we project the same trend to the present, it is clear that something has shifted output permanently downward. It is hard to believe that the gap between output and the projected trend on the right-hand side of Figure 20-4 represents the actions of aggregate demand.

The idea that shocks with long-lasting impact are important to the economy is now generally accepted. The inference that aggregate demand is relatively unimportant remains controversial. An alternative view is that large and relatively permanent aggregate supply shocks occur, but only on rare occasions; in between, aggregate demand shocks dominate. Pierre Perron is the original exponent of this point of view.[23] Perron argues that while there are occasional permanent breaks in trend, within decades-long subperiods, the economy does have important short run fluctuations around trend. In Figure 20-5, we estimate separate trends for output before 1974 and after 1974. Within each subperiod, output appears to be well modelled as transitory fluctuations around trend. This view of the world argues that there are

**trend stationary**

A variable is trend stationary when temporary shocks do *not* permanently affect its level. Changes in $AD$, for example, can only temporarily affect output. If changes in output were driven primarily by demand shocks, output would be trend stationary.

**difference stationary**

Temporary shocks to a variable permanently affect its level. A random walk is an example of a difference-stationary process.

---

[23] Evidence for this view is given in an influential, but difficult, article by Pierre Perron, "The Great Crash, the Oil Shock and the Unit Root Hypothesis," *Econometrica*, November 1989.

## FIGURE 20-4

Actual and potential GDP were approximately equal until the early 1970s. There appears to have been a permanent shock in the 1970s that drove output away from its pre-1970s growth path. The fact that this may have been the result of a productivity shock was discussed in Box 4-2 in Chapter 4.

### ACTUAL AND POTENTIAL GDP, 1961–2002

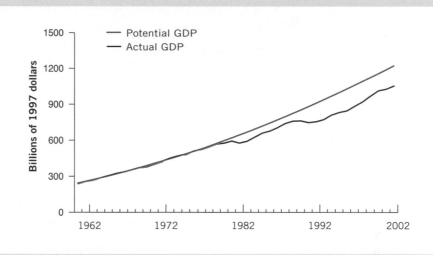

SOURCE: CANSIM II V1992259; potential output estimated by authors as a linear regression of output on trend and trend squared.

**trend stationary with breaks**

Trend stationary, but with a trend that sometimes changes.

large and permanent but infrequent aggregate supply shocks and that, in between these shocks, aggregate demand shocks dominate year-to-year fluctuations.

Because the dispute between believers in *difference stationary* and believers in **trend stationary with breaks** rests on measurements of long-lasting phenomena, the dispute can't be easily settled by statistical analysis of the relatively short data periods

## FIGURE 20-5

If potential GDP is modelled as a separate trend function after 1973, then it appears that business cycles can still be thought of as temporary fluctuations around (a new) trend.

### ACTUAL AND TWO ESTIMATES OF POTENTIAL GDP, 1961–2002

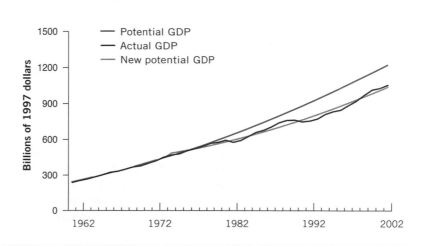

Source: CANSIM II V1992259; potential output estimated by authors as a linear regression of output on trend and trend squared.

currently available. The importance of aggregate demand shocks is likely to remain a controversial area.

## Recap

▶  There is significant empirical evidence that macroeconomic fluctuations are dominated by shocks with permanent effects. Since aggregate demand shocks do not have permanent effects, this evidence argues that aggregate demand fluctuations are less important than aggregate supply fluctuations. Changes due to aggregate supply shocks, in particular shocks to technology, could well be permanent.

▶  An alternative view of the evidence is that there are occasional episodes of large, permanent aggregate supply shocks, but that between these episodes, aggregate demand shocks predominate.

## 20-5 | REAL BUSINESS CYCLE THEORY

Rational expectations provided a theoretical basis for the notion that monetary policy should not have terribly important effects. The work of Nelson and Plosser casts doubt on the empirical importance of aggregate demand shocks. These ideas supported the development of *equilibrium real business cycle theory*.[24] Real business cycle (RBC) theory asserts that fluctuations in output and employment are the result of a variety of real shocks that hit the economy, with markets adjusting rapidly and remaining always in equilibrium.

RBC theorists also differ from more traditional macroeconomists on how to measure the economic parameters that govern a model's behaviour. RBC theorists generally prefer using *calibration* or *quantitative theory* techniques. In practice, this means choosing a small number of parameters that are crucial to the behaviour of a model and estimating the value of each parameter from microeconomic studies, rather than from the macroeconomic data itself. We explore here a very simple RBC model that focuses attention on a single parameter: the *intertemporal elasticity of substitution of labour.*

### A Simple Real Business Cycle Model

Real business cycle theorists create models in which firms choose optimal investment and hiring plans and individuals make optimal consumption and labour supply choices—all choices being made in a dynamic, uncertain environment. The resulting models are technically complex. In fact, they can be solved only by use of relatively sophisticated mathematics combined with computer simulation. We present here a simple model that gives the flavour of real business cycle models and focuses on the question of the intertemporal substitution of labour. In this simple model, the firm buys labour and produces output in each of the many periods. The representative worker sells her labour and buys consumption goods each period. If she wishes, she can save her consumption goods for another period.[25]

---

[24] See footnote 2 for further readings.

[25] The pattern of capital investment and shifts in interest rates play important roles in real business models. We are omitting both in the interest of simplicity.

Each period, the representative firm buys labour, $L_t$, and uses it to produce output, $Y_t$, according to the production function

$$Y_t = \alpha_t L_t \tag{26}$$

where $a_t$ is the marginal product of labour in period $t$. (Looking ahead, we know the real wage rate will end up equalling $a_t$ because in a competitive market the real wage rate equals the marginal product of labour.) Changes in the marginal product of labour are the source of real shocks in this simple model.

The representative worker has up to $\overline{L}$ hours available to sell in each period. Her leisure is $\overline{L}$ hours less the time she sells, so leisure equals $\overline{L} - L_t$. Each period, the representative worker receives utility from leisure and from consumption, $C_t$. We assume that the worker's utility function in a given period can be expressed as[26]

$$U(C_t, \overline{L} - L_t) = C_t^\gamma (\overline{L} - L_t)\beta \tag{27}$$

The worker's lifetime budget constraint states that the sum of lifetime consumption must equal the sum of lifetime earnings.[27]

$$C_t + C_{t+1} + C_{t+2} + \ldots = w_t L_t + w_{t+1} L_{t+1} + w_{t+2} L_{t+2} + \ldots \tag{28}$$

where $w_t$ is the real wage rate in period $t$. The worker chooses consumption and leisure each period in amounts that will maximize the sum of lifetime utility subject to the budget constraint in equation (28).

It will prove helpful to note that the marginal utility of leisure is

$$MU_{\text{leisure}} = \beta C_t^\gamma (\overline{L} - L_t)^{\beta - 1} = \frac{\beta U_t}{\overline{L} - L_t} \tag{29}$$

How do we find the worker's optimal trade-off defining her intertemporal substitution of leisure? If the worker reduces leisure one hour this period, she earns $w_t$ more, which permits her to add $w_t/w_{t+1}$ hours of leisure the following period. It follows that the marginal utility of leisure this period must equal $w_t/w_{t+1}$ times the marginal utility of leisure next period.

$$MU_{\text{leisure}_t} = (w_t/w_{t+1}) \times MU_{\text{leisure}_{t+1}} \tag{30}$$

Equating the values of the marginal utilities of present and future leisure—using equation (29) twice in equation (30)—gives us the worker's intertemporal substitution of leisure.

$$\frac{\overline{L} - L_t}{\overline{L} - L_{t+1}} = \left(\frac{w_{t+1}}{w_t}\right)^{\frac{1-\gamma}{1-\gamma-\beta}} \tag{31}$$

Equation (31) tells us that if the wage in period $t+1$ increases 1 percent while the wage in other periods remains constant, leisure in period $t+1$ will fall by $(1 - \gamma)/(1 - \gamma - \beta)$. Depending on the values of $\beta$ and $\gamma$, leisure may be very responsive or quite unresponsive to temporary changes in the wage rate.

---

[26] We assume that $\gamma$ and $\beta$ are both positive.

[27] Note again that we are implicitly assuming a zero interest rate.

Our model needs to be consistent with the empirical observation that *permanent* wage changes have little effect on labour supply. We can check this by computing the long run response of leisure to a permanent wage change. Suppose the wage was constant over time, say, $w^*$. In this case, consumption and labour supply would also be constant over time, say, $C^*$ and $L^*$. From the budget constraint [equation (28)], it must be true that $C^* = w^*L^*$. Combine this with the worker's *consumption-leisure trade-off,* $\bar{L} - L_t = (\beta/\gamma)(C_t/w_t)$, to derive the long run labour supply, and we find

$$\bar{L} - L^* = \frac{(\beta/\gamma)(w^*L^*)}{w^*} \qquad \text{or} \qquad L^* = \frac{\gamma}{\beta + \gamma}\bar{L} \tag{32}$$

Equation (32) shows that the long run response of labour to the wage rate is zero, since $w^*$ drops out of equation (32) entirely. So in this aspect, our model is in accord with the facts.[28]

Consider now the effect of intertemporal substitution of labour as a *propagation mechanism.* Suppose there is a transitory technology shock in period $t$ and thus the marginal product of labour rises by $\%\Delta a$. We know that the wage rate equals the marginal product of labour, so the wage rate will increase along with the increase in $a$. The total change in output will be

$$\%\Delta Y = \%\Delta a + \%\Delta L \tag{33}$$

The propagation mechanism is the "extra kick" to output $\%\Delta L$. We know from equation (31) that leisure will decrease by $[(1-\gamma)/(1-\gamma-\beta)] \times \%\Delta a$. Since leisure hours are roughly three times labour hours,[29] the percentage increase in labour should be approximately $\%\Delta L = 3 \times [(1-\gamma)/(1-\gamma-\beta)] \times \%\Delta a$. The total change in output will be

$$\%\Delta Y = \left(1 + 3 \times \frac{1-\gamma}{1-\gamma-\beta}\right) \times \%\Delta a \tag{34}$$

**deep parameters**

Parameters that describe the preferences of individuals and the production of firms, and that can be identified from macroeconomics studies.

The parameters $\beta$ and $\gamma$ are examples of what are called **deep parameters** in the real business cycle literature. RBC theorists argue that our models should depend on the parameters that describe the preferences of consumer-workers and the parameters that describe the production function of firms. These parameters can be identified from microeconomic studies. In our very simple model, if $\beta + \gamma$ is close to 1, the intertemporal substitution of leisure will be very strong and the propagation mechanism in equation (34) will translate relatively small technology shocks into much larger output shocks. In contrast, if the intertemporal substitution of leisure is weak, this propagation mechanism will be relatively unimportant. The empirical evidence, based on microeconomic data, favours the view that intertemporal substitution is relatively weak.[30]

---

[28] Empirically, the long run supply of labour is slightly backward bending. In the long run, higher wages reduce labour supply somewhat as people prefer to spend some of their higher income on increased leisure.

[29] Suppose one works 2000 out of $8760 = 24 \times 365$ hours.

[30] See Joseph Altonji, "Intertemporal Substitution in Labor Supply: Evidence from Micro Data," *Journal of Political Economy*, June 1986, and David Card, "Intertemporal Labor Supply: An Assessment," NBER Working Paper 3602, January 1991.

## Recap

▶ Real business cycle theory models the macroeconomy through the optimizing decisions about work and consumption made by individuals and the optimizing decisions about production made by firms. The model presented above is a simple version of the non-linear, dynamic models deployed by RBC theorists.

▶ Real business cycle theory minimizes the role of nominal fluctuations and money.

▶ RBC theorists try to identify deep parameters that can be measured in microeconomic studies. The elasticity of the intertemporal substitution of leisure is a key example. The conclusions from the measurement of such parameters are not always favourable to the RBC models.

## 20-6 | A NEW KEYNESIAN MODEL OF STICKY NOMINAL PRICES

http://papers.nber.org/
papers/w9069

The introduction of rational expectations theory and real business cycle theory instituted a *New Classical* revolution against the Keynesian orthodoxy of the aggregate supply-aggregate demand model. New Classical theories are grounded in rational, maximizing behaviour, characteristics that economists, by training, greatly prefer. On the other hand, these theories leave little or no role for the kind of sluggish nominal price adjustment that Keynesian economists believe they see in the real economy. Beginning in the mid-1980s and continuing today, a *New Keynesian* counter revolution has arisen. New Keynesian models try to play by the intellectual rules of the New Classicists—that is, reflect rational, maximizing behaviour—while still giving $AS = AD$-like results.

New Keynesian models generally rely on an assumption of imperfect competition. Under perfect competition, the individual actions of firms and consumers lead society to an "efficient" equilibrium. But under imperfect competition, individual decisions need not lead to efficient social outcomes. New Keynesian models explain how individually rational decisions under imperfect competition lead to socially undesirable booms and busts. In this section, we examine one New Keynesian model, Mankiw's model of nominal price stickiness. Mankiw's model explains why individual, imperfectly competitive firms might leave nominal prices unchanged ("sticky") in the face of a change in the nominal money supply.

The intellectual problem that Mankiw faced is that according to economic theory, *nominal* prices are just measures based on an arbitrary unit of account. Microeconomic theory makes clear that only *relative* prices matter. In fact, microeconomic theory makes a very clear prediction related to the neutrality of money. Suppose that the economy initially has money supply $\overline{M}$ and that, through the supply and demand process, it reaches equilibrium with prices $p_1$, $p_2$, $p_3$, and so forth, for an average price level $p$. Now suppose that the money supply is $2\overline{M}$ instead. Microeconomic theory predicts that markets will reach the identical equilibria as previously, this time with prices $2p_1$, $2p_2$, $2p_3$, and an average price level $2p$. Nothing *real* has changed. The real money supply remains $2\overline{M}/2p = \overline{M}/p$, and the ratio of prices in any pair of markets, say, markets 1 and 3, remains unchanged, $2p_1/2p_3 = p_1/p_3$. So the Keynesians faced the question of how to reconcile rational, microeconomically justified economic theory with the idea that the nominal price level might not immediately reflect changes in the nominal money supply.

The beginning of the answer lay in recognizing that setting and changing prices is itself an economic activity. Since changing prices uses economic resources, firms will change prices only when the benefits from the price change outweigh the costs. On the surface, this seems a reasonable explanation for leaving prices unchanged in the face of a change in the money supply. The problem with this argument is that the cost of changing prices is surely very small and swings in the economy are in the order of several percent of GDP. It would seem that the benefits of a price change would nearly always outweigh the cost.

In 1985, Greg Mankiw solved this conundrum by using very basic microeconomic theory to show that the *private* benefits of changing a price can be much smaller than the *social* benefits if there is substantial monopoly power in the economy.[31] Firms base their decisions on the private benefit only, so it is possible that in the face of changed demand each firm will decide to hold constant the price it charges, even though the social benefit of changing the price outweighs the social cost. We present a simplified version of Mankiw's analysis.

Suppose the production side of the economy consists of many small firms, each with some element of monopoly power in its own market. Indexing the markets by $i$, we can write the demand facing firm $i$ as

$$Y_i = \left(\frac{P_i}{P}\right)^{-\epsilon} \frac{M}{P} \tag{35}$$

where $P_t$ is the price charged by firm $t$, $P$ is the overall price level, and $\epsilon$ ($\epsilon > 1$) is the elasticity of demand. Suppose labour is the only input, the marginal product of labour is $a$, and the nominal wage is $W$. A monopolist sets its price as a markup over costs. Since marginal cost is $W/a$, the firm will charge[32]

$$P_i = \left(\frac{\epsilon}{\epsilon - 1}\right) \frac{W}{a} \tag{36}$$

and the firm's nominal profit will be

$$\left(P_t - \frac{W}{a}\right) Y_i \tag{37}$$

To provide a base of comparison for looking at sticky prices, we first ask what happens in the neoclassical model when the money supply increases by, say, 2 percent. Since money is neutral in a neoclassical model, we know that all nominal prices and wages will rise by 2 percent. We see that both the left and the right sides of equation (36) rise by 2 percent. Since $M$, $P$, and all of the $P$s rise by 2 percent, real demand in equation (35) is unchanged. From equation (37), nominal profits rise 2 percent, but since overall prices have risen, real profits are unchanged. So everything in our model is consistent with the neutrality of money.

Suppose now that each firm has to undertake a small expenditure, $z$, called a *menu cost*, if it raises its price. Each firm will compare the cost of maintaining its now "too low" price with the potential increase in profit if it raises prices 2 percent.

[31] N. Gregory Mankiw, "Small Menu Costs and Large Business Cycles: A Macroeconomic Model of Monopoly," *Quarterly Journal of Economics*, May 1985. See also George A. Akerlof and Janet L. Yellen, "A Near Rational Model of the Business Cycle, with Wage and Price Inertia," *Quarterly Journal of Economics*, Supplement, 1985. These and a number of related articles are reprinted in N. Gregory Mankiw and David Romer (eds.), *New Keynesian Economics* (Cambridge, MA: MIT Press, 1991). For an overview, see Laurence Ball and N. Gregory Mankiw, "A Sticky-Price Manifesto," *Carnegie-Rochester Conference Series on Public Policy*, December 1994.

[32] Equation (35) can be derived from solving the monopolist's profit maximization problem. If you have had an intermediate microeconomics course, you may have seen the formula there.

Mankiw showed that the potential profit can be very small—literally "second order"—when two conditions hold:

▶ If the deviation between optimal price and existing price is small, the profit opportunity is *very* small.

▶ If the elasticity of firm demand is low, profit is relatively less sensitive to getting the price exactly right.

As an example, Figure 20-6 shows profit losses, measured as a percentage of optimal output, on the vertical axis and the percentage deviation of price from optimal price on the horizontal axis. The blue line shows profit losses for a modestly monopolistic firm (as it happens, one with a demand elasticity of 20). Suppose the firm's current price is 2 percent below optimal. Then, reading across on the blue line, we see that the firm is forgoing potential profit equal to 0.5 percent of output. If the menu cost is more than this, the firm will leave its price unchanged. Since other firms face similar choices, they too leave prices unchanged. The net effect is that all nominal prices remain fixed, the overall price level remains fixed, the real money supply increases, and aggregate demand rises along with the real money supply. From equation (35), we see that the real money supply (*M/P*) and output will rise 2 percent. Note that the 2 percent gain in societal output is four times the privately forgone firm profits.

The key to Mankiw's breakthrough is the assumption that firms face a downward sloping demand curve. In a perfectly competitive market, every firm faces a horizontal (infinitely elastic) demand curve, even though the demand curve for the market as a whole can have an arbitrary slope. If the demand curve facing an individual firm is horizontal, or nearly so, a small deviation of price from the optimal price causes a

**FIGURE 20-6**

**PROFIT LOSS AND DEVIATION FROM OPTIMAL PRICE**

In this diagram, if a firm is operating at, say, 2 percent below optimal price, then the profit loss will be approximately 0.5 percent. If menu costs are greater than this amount, the firm has no incentive to alter price. This reasoning has been used to justify sticky prices.

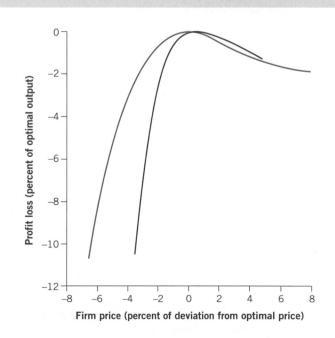

huge swing in demand and a correspondingly huge swing in profits. So in a competitive market, the private profit from getting prices right always outweighs a small menu cost.[33] In contrast, with a downward sloping demand curve facing each firm, a small menu cost may well be bigger than potential profit changes.

Mankiw's work provides a rigorous microeconomic justification for nominal price stickiness. Since New Classical economists attack the rigour of the underpinnings of Keynesian models, such justification is a key piece of the Keynesian response to rational expectations and real business cycle models. Not everyone agrees on the empirical significance of Mankiw's formulation, but the work is certainly a milestone in the New Keynesian counterrevolution.

## Recap

▶ The New Keynesians try to build models based on maximizing behaviour that result in aggregate supply-aggregate demand-like behaviour.

▶ Most New Keynesian models rely on imperfect competition.

▶ Prices can be sticky, even though the menu costs of adjustment are quite small, because the increased profit from resetting prices is even smaller.

## *Working with Data*

In this section we will show you how to produce an estimate of potential GDP, as we did in Figure 20-4. Technically, we ran a linear regression of actual GDP on a constant, trend and trend squared, over the period 1961–1973, using annual data. Trend is just a variable that takes on a value of 1 in 1961, 2 in 1962, etc. The estimated equation that we used was

$$GDP = 225.98 + 13.61^*T + 0.238^*\,T^2 \qquad (38)$$

You can use this equation to calculate potential GDP in each period. You should now be able to reproduce Figure 20-4.

## C H A P T E R  S U M M A R Y

▶ Modern theories emphasize the consistency of macroeconomic and microeconomic theories.

▶ The rational expectations approach emphasizes the consistency of public expectations about the behaviour of the economy.

▶ Rational forecasts make errors, but not predictable ones.

---

[33] The black line in Figure 20-6 shows potential profits for a relatively more competitive firm. The same 2 percent mispricing here costs more than 2 percent of output, about four times the cost in the less competitive, (blue line) case. By manipulating the elasticity, $\epsilon$, one can make the contrast between the lines as large or small as desired.

▶ The rational expectations approach suggests that anticipated monetary policy is neutral even in the short run.

▶ An imperfect-information approach will explain a short run upward-sloping aggregate supply curve, but one in which the trade-off between output and inflation cannot be exploited through anticipated monetary policy.

▶ The random walk model of output suggests that economic fluctuations are highly persistent—and therefore not due to changes in aggregate demand.

▶ The real business cycle approach builds models of a dynamic economy in which real shocks are propagated. These models minimize the role of the monetary sector.

▶ New Keynesian models attempt to reintegrate aggregate demand, especially sticky prices, with solid microeconomic foundations.

## KEY TERMS

rational expectations equilibrium, *409*
rational expectations, *410*
policy irrelevance, *410*
random walk, *411*
real business cycle (RBC) theory, *411*
propagation mechanisms, *412*
intertemporal substitution of leisure, *412*

productivity shock, *412*
New Keynesians, *413*
price stickiness, *413*
menu cost, *413*
imperfect competition, *413*
Lucas critique, *415*
perfect foresight, *415*
imperfect-information model, *421*

trend (secular) component of GDP, *425*
cyclical component of GDP, *425*
trend stationary, *426*
difference stationary, *426*
trend stationary with breaks, *427*
deep parameters, *430*

## APPLICATION QUESTIONS

1. This chapter covers four broad classes of research—rational expectations theory, random walk in output, real business cycle theory, and models that endeavour to explain why output can diverge, in the short run, from its full employment level. To what extent do these models complement or contradict one another? Discuss.

*2. What are rational expectations? How do rational expectations differ from perfect foresight? Is monetary policy neutral under both assumptions?

3. Describe a propagation mechanism used in real business cycle theory. Explain, briefly, how it works.

*4. What are the similarities and differences between Mankiw's menu-cost model of aggregate supply and Lucas's imperfect-information one? Classify each as New Keynesian or New Classical.

*5. What is the key assumption in Mankiw's menu-cost model of aggregate supply?

*6. What are deep parameters, in the sense used by proponents of real business cycle theory?

*7. In Lucas's imperfect-information model of aggregate supply, when will aggregate shocks (shocks to the economy at large, rather than to particular regions or markets) have the strongest effect on output? Explain.

---

* An asterisk indicates a more difficult problem.

**\*8. a.** What is the difference between trend-stationary and difference-stationary output?

   **b.** Why is this an important distinction, and how does our belief regarding which of these best characterizes output affect our forecasting strategy?

   **c.** Perron suggested that output might best be characterized as trend stationary with breaks. How does this help resolve the question of the importance of shocks to aggregate demand?

---

## D I S C U S S I O N   Q U E S T I O N S

**1.** Go to CANSIM and retrieve $M2$ and real GDP. Reproduce Figure 20-2 using actual $M2$ growth rather than expected $M2$ growth. Do you see any difference between these two graphs? Comment.

**\*2. a.** Use equations (3) and (4) to forecast both the price level and the level of output that result from the simple $AS = AD$ model of Section 20-2. You may assume that the slope of the aggregate supply curve is 2/3; that the values of the money supply, velocity, and potential GDP are 9, 8, and 7, respectively; and that the expected price level is 5.

   **b.** Evaluate your forecast in light of the Lucas critique.

   **c.** How does this forecast differ from that which would result from a perfect-foresight model?

   **d.** Is this forecast better or worse? Explain.

**\*3.** Use equations (11) and (12) to check the effects of anticipated and unanticipated supply shocks on the level of output. Show that they behave as they would in a perfect-foresight model when anticipated and as they would in the standard $AS = AD$ model when unanticipated.

**4.** Does empirical evidence support the rational expectations result that anticipated monetary policy should have no effect on output? Explain.

**\*\*5. a.** Suppose, in the simple RBC model developed in Section 20-5, that $\gamma = 0.35$ and $\beta = 0.05$. How much of an output increase will result from a 10 percent increase in the marginal product of labour, given these parameter values? [*Hint:* Use equation (34).]

   **b.** Would there be strong intertemporal substitution of leisure in using the parameters given in part (a)? Why or why not?

**\*6. a.** What does empirical evidence suggest regarding the extent to which people substitute leisure over time?

   **b.** What does this suggest regarding the role of intertemporal substitution in propagating shocks throughout the economy and regarding the ability of small technology shocks to generate large output shocks?

**\*7.** This question relates to expectations formation in the Lucas imperfect-information model of aggregate supply.

   **a.** If $\alpha = 1$ and $\beta = 0.75$, what is the expected change in the overall price level when local prices, $p_i$, rise to four times their original level? [*Hint:* Use equation (18).]

   **b.** If $\alpha$ (the slope of the "local" supply function) is ½ for a particular region, by how much will output increase in the region as a result of this increase in its local prices?

   **c.** How would this result change if $\beta$ was 0.25 instead of 0.75, and what would it mean for $\beta$ to have such a small value?

   **d.** What if $\beta$ was 1?

---

\* An asterisk indicates a more difficult problem.

\*\* Two asterisks indicates a highly technical question.

# EPILOGUE: WHAT HAVE WE LEARNED?

I f you ever get a chance to look at a macroeconomics textbook from some 30 years ago, you will notice that it is quite a bit different from this book. This reflects the fact that there have been major developments in macroeconomics over the last 30 years. These developments have come from careful analysis of a great deal of macroeconomic data, as well as from recent intellectual developments in macroeconomic theory and policy. Of course, these developments are not independent of each other, because much of macroeconomics is data-driven. In this book, we have paid careful attention to this interaction of economic theory and observed movements in major macroeconomic variables. Indeed, modern macroeconomics grew largely out of analysis of movements in macroeconomic aggregates.

We often call John Maynard Keynes the "father of modern macroeconomics." A form of macroeconomics existed before Keynes, but it was not called *macroeconomics*; rather, it was just standard economic theory applied to aggregates, and it was sometimes called *aggregate economics*. To a large extent, the reigning intellectual paradigm before Keynes was very similar to what we have called the *Classical market clearing paradigm* in this book. The research agenda of these pre-Keynesian economists was to explain observed movements in macro aggregates, assuming that the appropriate model was one where all markets cleared and all prices were flexible.

It was the writings of Keynes, especially in his book *The General Theory of Employment, Interest and Money*, that essentially pointed out that there are circumstances in which we cannot depend on flexible prices and, therefore, not all markets clear at all times. Early Keynesian economists would often use the example of the Great Depression and state that it was very difficult to explain how 25 percent of the workforce actually chose to be unemployed, which, to some extent, was the Classical explanation. Thus, Keynesian economics arose from attempts to explain the observed behaviour of the macro economy.

Thirty years ago, macroeconomics textbooks generally reflected a somewhat narrow (by today's standards) Keynesian view of the discipline. Textbooks in the 1960s were almost exclusively full of Keynesian models, and they all shared a common theme: extremely detailed modelling of the demand side of the economy, with very little (if any) thought given to aggregate supply. These demand-side Keynesian models seemed to naturally evolve into what was called the *Keynesian prescription*. In the 1960s and 1970s, the Keynesian prescription involved the belief that if Keynesian models said that markets do not clear, then the government must have a role in stabilization policy. The pervasiveness of this view was summarized by Franco Modigliani, a Nobel Prize winner in Economics, who stated:

> [Keynesian economists] accept what I regard to be the fundamental practical message of *The General Theory* that a private enterprise economy using an intangible money needs to be stabilized, can be stabilized, and therefore should be stabilized by appropriate monetary and fiscal policies.[1]

Even Milton Friedman, another Nobel winner and staunch anti-Keynesian, has been quoted as saying "We are all Keynesians now."[2]

---

[1] Franco Modigliani, "The Monetarist Controversy or, Should We Forsake Stabilization Policies?" *American Economic Review*, March 1977, p. 1 (presidential address to the American Economic Association).

[2] It is not clear whether Friedman actually said this, although it has been attributed to him many times. Unfortunately, it has also been attributed to former U.S. president Richard Nixon.

Keynesian economics encountered very troubled times in the 1970s and 1980s, both intellectually and through macroeconomic events. As an example, we have seen that inflation gradually increased through the 1960s and 1970s, and the prevailing Keynesian models did not seem to be able to explain this. This is not surprising, given the lack of emphasis on the supply side of the economy. In response to this perceived failure of the Keynesian model, a group of economists led by Nobel Prize winner Robert Lucas, Jr., at the University of Chicago, essentially revived pre-Keynesian Classical thinking. This resulted in the New Classical models that we studied in Chapters 7 and 20, which rely on the assumptions of full market clearing and rational expectations. Interestingly, this class of models largely emphasized the supply side of the economy, and the only role for the demand side was to ensure that the quantity theory of money held. These models were widely viewed as an intellectual improvement over early Keynesian models. However, the empirical validity of these models was subject to severe criticism.

For a while in macroeconomics, it appeared as though we had two separate research agendas: one broadly Keynesian and non-market clearing, and another largely Classical and market clearing. This should be viewed as healthy intellectual discourse, and has left macroeconomics with the consensus that we have emphasized in this book: Market clearing analysis is most relevant for long run questions, and non-market clearing analysis is most relevant for short run questions. So, here we are, 30 years later, with a macroeconomics textbook that reflects the importance of both the demand and supply sides of the economy.

In Chapter 1, we asked the question: How is it that you can hear two macro-economists on the news appearing to give opposite answers to the same question? The answer to this question is not that there is a fundamental difference of opinion concerning how the macro economy works, but rather there is some difference of opinion concerning whether the short run or the long run is more important. All economists use models to address questions of importance, and in macroeconomics, our major model is the aggregate demand-aggregate supply model. However, the assumptions about adjustment that are built into this model depend on the time frame over which you analyze macroeconomic phenomena. In the short run, there are some real adjustments that must take place, and these may result in markets not clearing. In this case, if you want to analyze the economy over the short run, you would use some Keynesian sticky or fixed price assumptions. In the long run, any stickiness in the economy should have had time to be worked out and, therefore, adjustment takes place and markets generally clear. In this case, if you wanted to analyze the economy over the long run, you would use Classical market clearing assumptions. Essentially, one important lesson that can be learned from comparing textbooks today to those of 30 years ago is that both aggregate demand and aggregate supply matter.

Given this framework, what can we say about the current state of macroeconomics and the Canadian economy? The following are some lessons that we have learned:

▶ **In the very long run, growth is important.**

If you look back at Figure 1-5, you will see that output per capita is much higher now (in real terms) than it was a hundred years ago. In the very long run, aggregate supply is really all that matters, and output per capita is still our best measure of the economic well-being of Canadians. We saw in Chapters 3 and 4 that our ability to produce goods and services depends on our factors of production (mainly labour and capital) and our use of technology to aid in the process of turning factors of production into output.

From a policy perspective, most economists agree that there is a role for public policy in fostering long run growth. We saw in Chapter 4 that policies aimed at increasing the savings rate may help with capital accumulation and increase our ability to produce goods in the future. Also, there is a strong correlation between education and growth, so that government policies that promote education may lead to stronger future growth. There is a lot of discussion in the news concerning what is often called the "productivity gap" between Canada and the United States. Unfortunately, there is much disagreement about how to properly measure productivity, and even if we could show that productivity in Canada is low by some standards, there is no generally accepted method to raise productivity.

▶ **In the long run, the Bank of Canada controls the rate of inflation.**

This is a lesson that we first encountered in Chapter 3: Over the long run, the quantity theory of money will hold. Put another way, we cannot have a long run sustained rate of inflation without the Bank of Canada accommodating this through continual increases in the money stock. Certainly the evidence presented in Figure 3-12 appears to be consistent with this proposition, and most economists and policy makers accept that this is true over the long run. This is an important lesson to understand. We know that, in the short run, monetary policy can change the course of real variables. This is the theory of the Phillips curve that we discussed in Chapter 7 (see the discussion below). However, this stabilization policy can be thought of as only a short run phenomenon. If, for instance, the Bank of Canada was to continually stimulate the economy, in the long run, this would result in inflation. If you think about it, you will see that this lesson is summarized in the old adage "There is no free lunch."

▶ **In the short run, policy makers face a trade-off between inflation and unemployment.**

We saw in Chapter 7 that there is a good deal of empirical support for the existence of a short run Phillips curve. This represents the trade-off that policy makers face in the short run. However, it is important to bear in mind the discussion in the second point above: *There is no long run trade-off.*

The fact that a short run trade-off exists does not necessarily imply that policy makers should exploit this trade-off. The New Classical models developed by Robert Lucas (and most of the later variants discussed in Chapter 20) can be used to argue that short run stabilization policy, in the form of exploiting the short run Phillips curve, can actually have a negative effect on the economy.

Should policy makers engage in short run stabilization? This question represents an active debate in macroeconomics. There are those who argue that, although continual pursuit of short run stabilization policy could potentially lead to problems, there are situations where a shock may be large enough that policy makers should react. The example most often cited (prior to the events of September 11, 2001) to support this view is the monetary policy reaction to the stock market meltdown that occurred in October 1987. In order to stem the flow of financial capital out of equity markets, most central banks injected liquidity into their countries' economies, which immediately lowered interest rates. In the framework of the *IS-LM* model, the *LM* curve shifted outward. This appeared to slow the drop in equity prices. The problem with this type of example is that, once policy makers intervene in the economy, there is no manner in which we can know what the reaction of the economy would have been in the absence of this intervention. In essence, we can never know whether we are better off as a result of policy intervention.

Since the events of September 11, 2001, there has been a great deal of discussion in Canada over this very question. David Dodge became governor of the Bank of Canada in early 2001, and between that point and the time of the writing of this Epilogue in late 2003, there have been several episodes of *both* tightening *and* loosening of monetary policy. Critics of Dodge say that he is too quick to attempt to exploit the short run Phillips curve trade-off. Proponents say that he is simply protecting the economy in turbulent times. As with the events of October 1987, this type of discussion really centres on the question of how big a shock has to be in order to justify policy intervention. Almost no one disagrees that the shock of September 11, 2001, required strong monetary policy intervention. However, the apparent seesaw movements in subsequent monetary policy in 2002 and 2003 are still debated, and there is no clear answer to the question of the efficacy of short run stabilization policy in Canada. The lesson here is that stabilization policy must be applied with caution, as there is probably still much that we do not understand.

▶ **In Canada, the exchange rate matters.**

Canada is a very open economy. For instance, in 2002, exports accounted for more than 40 percent of our GDP and imports were 37 percent of GDP. Compared to our largest trading partner—the United States—we are also a small economy. In this situation, not only do movements in foreign variables impact our economy, but movements in the foreign exchange rate—both nominal and real—are also extremely important.

We saw in Chapter 12 that interest differentials and capital flows play a large role in short run movements in the nominal exchange rate. In the short run, movements in the nominal exchange rate lead to changes in terms of trade and, therefore, lead to changes in net exports and output. In 2003, the Canadian nominal exchange rate underwent a rather sharp, sudden appreciation. As we write this Epilogue, we know that this will have a dampening affect on aggregate demand. This has led some observers to call for the Bank of Canada to lower interest rates in order to offset the effects on aggregate demand caused by the appreciation. This is a typical Canadian short run economic policy situation and is one of the reasons why the concept of the Monetary Conditions Index (introduced in Chapter 18) plays an important role in the Canadian economy. This index gives us an indication of the state of aggregate demand, given movements in the short-term interest rate and the nominal exchange rate.

In terms of the nominal exchange rate in the long run, we understand the fundamental determinants of the long run level of the exchange rate that are given by the purchasing power parity (PPP) theorem that was discussed in Chapter 5. We know that if our inflation performance in Canada is significantly better than that of our major trading partners (mainly the United States), this will lead to a nominal exchange rate appreciation. Unfortunately, very little is understood about the timing of PPP movements. We know that short run speculation can drive the exchange rate from equilibrium for a non-trivial amount of time. This is likely the reason why some many observers (including the Bank of Canada) were surprised by the appreciation of 2003, which many economists were warning about as early as 1999.

# GLOSSARY

## A

**absolute convergence** Tendency of both the levels and growth rates of output in different countries to approach each other over time, and for their steady-state values to be the same.

**accelerator model** Asserts that investment spending is proportional to the change in output and is not affected by the cost of capital.

**action lag** The lag between the policy decision and its implementation.

**activist policies** Policies that respond to the current or predicted state of the economy.

**activist rules** Rules that have countercyclical features without leaving any discretion about their actions to policy makers.

**adaptive expectations** Individuals are assumed to take an average of past actual price levels to form their expectation of the current price level.

**aggregate demand** The total amount of goods demanded in the economy.

**aggregate demand (*AD*) curve** Shows combinations of the price level and the level of output for which the demanders of goods and services are in equilibrium.

**aggregate demand–aggregate supply model** The major macroeconomic model that will be used throughout this book. The *AD* curve shows, for each price level, the amount of demand from the goods and money market simultaneously. The aggregate supply curve shows, for each price level, the amount that firms are willing to supply.

**aggregate demand curve** Maps out the *IS-LM* equilibrium holding autonomous spending and the nominal money supply constant and allowing prices to vary.

**aggregate supply (*AS*) curve** Relationship between the amount of final goods and services produced in an economy and the price level.

**arbitrage** Buying/selling assets to take advantage of differences in returns.

**automatic adjustment mechanisms** Mechanisms that automatically act to eliminate balance-of-payments problems.

**automatic stabilizer** Any mechanism in the economy that automatically reduces the amount by which output changes in response to a change in autonomous demand.

## B

**balance of payments** A record of the transaction of a country with the rest of the world.

**balance of trade** The difference between exports and imports.

**balanced budget multiplier** Increase in output that results from equal increases in taxes and government purchases.

**bank rate** The upper end of the Bank of Canada's target band on the overnight rate.

**beggar-thy-neighbour policy** A depreciation-induced change in the trade balance that exports unemployment or creates domestic employment at the expense of the rest of the world.

**budget constraint** A line that shows the combinations of consumption today and consumption next period that the consumer can choose, given real income and the real interest rate.

**budget deficit** An excess of expenditures over revenues.

**budget surplus** The excess of the government's revenues, taxes, over its total expenditures, consisting of purchases of goods and services and transfer payments.

**buffer stock** Excess consumer savings used to maintain consumption when income is lower than usual (saving for a rainy day).

**business cycle** The more or less regular pattern of expansion (recovery) and contraction (recession) in economic activity around full employment output.

**business fixed investment** Annual increase in machinery, equipment, and structures used in production.

# C

**capital and financial account** Financial account records direct investment and portfolio investment, while capital account includes items such as inheritances and trade in intellectual property.

**capital gains** The amount an asset appreciates in value over time.

**capital-labour ratio** The number of machines per worker.

**cash reserves** Currency held by chartered banks and chartered bank deposits at the Bank of Canada.

**central bank** Bank that has control over the money supply. In Canada, the Bank of Canada. In the United States, the Federal Reserve. In Europe, the European Central Bank.

**chain weighted GDP** Is calculated by averaging the base over two years, the current and the preceding year, and so the averaging moves over time as the current year moves over time.

**Classical aggregate supply curve** Long run vertical $AS$ curve; output equals potential output.

**Classical, or market clearing, paradigm** A paradigm that uses the assumption that all prices are flexible, and, therefore, that all markets clear at all times.

**clearing system** The process by which the net amounts owing among the banks are settled at the end of each day.

**closed economy** An economy that does not engage in any international trade.

**Cobb-Douglas production function** $Y = AK^\theta N^{1-\theta}$

**competitive depreciation** Occurs when every country tries to depreciate to attract world demand.

**conditional convergence** Tendency of growth rates of output in different countries to approach each other over time, and for their steady-state values to be the same.

**constant dollar, or real, GDP** Measuring GDP between two periods, holding the price level constant.

**Consumer Price Index (CPI)** A measure of the average cost consumers face when purchasing goods and services.

**consumption function** Describes the relationship between consumption spending and disposable income.

**consumption spending** Total current spending by consumers in the economy.

**contraction (recession)** That period of time in a business cycle when output is falling below full employment.

**cost-of-living adjustment (COLA)** Links increases in wages to increases in the price level.

**credibility** Announcements by policy makers are believed by economic agents.

**crowding out** Occurs when expansionary fiscal policy causes interest rates to rise, thereby reducing private spending, particularly investment.

**currency appreciation or depreciation** A change in the price of foreign exchange under flexible exchange rates.

**current account** Net exports, net income from assets, and net transfers.

**current dollar, or nominal, GDP** Measuring GDP between two periods, while allowing the price level to change between the two periods.

**cyclical component of GDP** Fluctuations of output around its trend; the output gap.

**cyclical unemployment** Unemployment in excess of frictional unemployment; occurs when output is below its full employment level.

# D

**debt–income ratio** Ratio of national debt to GDP.

**decision lag** The delay between the recognition of the need for action and the policy decision.

**deep parameters** Parameters that describe the preferences of individuals and the production of firms, and that can be identified from macroeconomics studies.

**demand for real balances** Quantity of real money balances people wish to hold.

**depreciation** The wearing out of capital as it is being used to produce output.

**difference stationary** Temporary shocks to a variable permanently affect its level. A random walk is an example of a difference-stationary process.

**diminishing marginal product** A characteristic of a production function whereby the marginal product of a factor falls as the amount of the factor increases while all other factors are held constant.

**diminishing marginal product of labour** As labour use increases, the amount of extra output that is gained from an increase in labour input becomes smaller.

**direct clearers** Members of the Canadian Payments Association (large banks and trust companies) that hold balances at the Bank of Canada for settlement purposes.

**direct taxes** Taxes directly applied to persons and corporations, including personal and corporate income taxes.

**discouraged workers** Individuals who have been in the labour force, could not find employment, and have now given up looking for work. Because these individuals are not in the labour force, they are not counted among the unemployed.

**discrete lag** A lag that takes a fixed amount of time. Contrast *distributed lag.*

**discretionary fiscal policy** When a government changes a variable under its control (e.g., government spending) in response to a change in the economy.

**distributed lag** A lag that spreads the effects of policy over a variable amount of time.

**disposable income** Income available for consumption or saving.

**drawdowns and redeposits** The transfer of government deposits between the direct clearers and the Bank of Canada.

**dynamic behaviour** Behaviour that depends on values of economic variables in periods other than the current period.

**dynamic inconsistency** Policy makers who have discretion will be tempted to take short run actions that are inconsistent with the economy's best long run interests.

**dynamic programming** A process in which decision makers work out their choices by starting at the end and working backward.

# E

**econometric model** A statistical description of the economy or some part of it.

**econometric policy evaluation critique** Existing macroeconomic models cannot be used to study the effects of policy changes because the way private agents respond to changes in income and prices depends on the types of policy being followed.

**endogenous growth** Self-sustaining growth.

**endogenous variables** Variables determined within the model.

**equilibrium level of output** The quantity of output produced is equal to the quantity demanded.

**excess sensitivity** Consumption responds too strongly to predictable changes in income.

**excess smoothness** Consumption responds too little to surprise changes in income.

**exchange rate expectations** When individuals feel that the current exchange is about to appreciate or depreciate.

**exogenous variables** Variables determined outside of the model.

**expansion (recovery)** A sustained period of rising real income.

**expectations-augmented Phillips curve** Phillips curve that includes inflationary expectations as a determinant of the inflation rates.

**expectations theory of term structure** States that long-term interest rates are equal to the average of current and expected future short-term interest rates, plus a term premium.

**expected or anticipated inflation** Inflation that people expect.

**expected real interest rate** The nominal interest rate minus the rate of inflation that is expected in the future.

# F

**factor payments** Payments made to factors, such as wages and interest payments.

**factors of production** Inputs such as labour and capital.

**final goods and services** Goods and services that are sold to firms, the public, or the government for any purpose other than use as an input to production; all goods excluding intermediate ones.

**fine-tuning** Policy variables are continually adjusted in response to small disturbances in the economy.

**fiscal policy** The policy of the government with regard to the level of government purchases, the level of transfers, and the tax structure.

**fiscal policy multiplier** Shows how much an increase in government spending changes the equilibrium level of income, holding the real money supply constant.

**Fisher effect** A long run increase in the inflation rate will increase the nominal interest rate, so that the real interest rate will not change due to inflation.

**fixed rate system** Central banks buy and sell currency at a fixed rate in terms of foreign exchange.

**flexible accelerator model** Asserts that firms plan their invetsment to close a fraction of the gap between their actual capital stock and their desired capital stock; a result is that more firms with a larger gap inbetween their actual and desired capital stocks accumulate capital more quickly than other firms.

**flexible (or floating) exchange rate** The central bank allows the exchange rate to be determined by the foreign exchange market.

**flexible prices** Prices that are assumed to move very quickly after an exogenous change.

**flow of investment** The addition to the capital stock over some period of time.

**foreign exchange rate** The price that foreign citizens must pay for one Canadian dollar, or, equivalently, the price that Canadians must pay for one unit of foreign currency.

**foreign (or world) real rate of interest** The real interest rate that prevails in international capital markets; individuals, businesses, and governments are assumed to be able to borrow and lend at this rate.

**frictional unemployment** The unemployment that exists when the economy is at full employment.

**full employment** Occurs when all members of the labour force are employed; individuals not working are not in the labour force and therefore are not counted as being unemployed.

**full employment budget surplus** The budget surplus at the full employment level of income or at potential output.

## G

**GDP deflator** The ratio of nominal GDP in a given year to real GDP of that year.

**GDP per capita** The ratio of GDP to population.

**government budget constraint** A limit that says the government can finance its deficits only by selling bonds (accumulating debt) or by increasing the monetary base.

**government expenditure** Transfers plus purchases.

**government purchases** Government spending on goods and services. Contrast *government expenditure.*

**government savings** The budgetary surplus or deficit; the difference between total revenue and total expenditure.

**Great Depression** A historical period of very low output and very high unemployment that occurred during the years 1929–37 in Canada and the United States. A number of other countries also experienced severe depressions during this period.

**gross domestic product (GDP)** The dollar value of all final goods and services produced in an economy over some specified period of time, usually one year.

**gross investment** Investment including depreciation.

**gross national product (GNP)** Measure of the value of all final goods and services produced by domestically owned factors of production.

**growth accounting equation** A summary of the contributions of input growth and changes in productivity to the growth of output.

## H

**heterodox approach to stabilization** Coordinated use of monetary, fiscal, and exchange rate policies accompanied by wage and price control.

**human capital** The knowledge and ability to produce that is embodied in the labour force.

**hyperinflation** Very rapid price increase, usually defined as over 100 percent per month.

## I

**imperfect competition** Form of competition in which firms have market power—can choose to some extent, the price at which they will sell the goods they produce.

**imperfect-information model** Forecasts based on imperfect information will be less than fully accurate, although not necessarily biased.

**income effect** The change in consumption due to the fact that the consumer can now reach a higher indifference curve.

**income elasticity** Amount that demand for real money balances changes, in percentage terms, when income increases by 1 percent.

**income velocity of money** The number of times the stock of money is turned over per year in financing the annual flow of income.

**indexation** Ties the terms of contracts to the behaviour of the price level.

**indicators** Economic variables that signal us as to whether we are getting closer to our desired targets.

**indifference curve** A graphical representation of consumer preferences, showing combinations of current and future consumption for which total utility is constant.

**indirect taxes** Taxes levied on goods, such as the federal Goods and Services Tax.

**industrial product price index (IPPI)** A measure of the price index at the level of the first commercial transaction. This measure is a signal of price changes that are likely to show up later in the CPI.

**inflation rate** The rate of change in the CPI.

**inflation tax** Revenue gained by the government because of inflation's devaluation of money holdings.

**inside lag** The time period it takes to undertake a policy action.

**instruments** The tools the policy maker manipulates directly.

**interest differential** The level of domestic interest rate minus the level of the foreign interest rate.

**interest elasticity** Percentage change in the demand for real money balances resulting from a 1 percent increase in the interest rate.

**interest elasticity of the money supply** A parameter that measures how much the central bank changes the money supply in response to an interest rate change.

**interest payments** The amounts that individuals receive for holding government debt such as Treasury bills and long-term bonds.

**interest rate rule** Monetary policy is conducted according to an interest rate rule whenever the money supply is changed in response to a change in the demand for money in order to keep interest rates constant.

**intergenerational accounting** Evaluate the costs and benefits of taxes and spending for various age groups in society.

**intermediate goods** Goods used to produce other goods or services; flour purchased by bakers is an example.

**internal balance** Occurs when output equals potential output.

**International Monetary Fund (IMF)** International organization created to promote international monetary cooperation; makes its resources temporarily available, under stringent conditions, to member countries experiencing balance-of-payments problems.

**intertemporal choice** Choice that involves decisions over more than one period of time.

**intertemporal substitution of leisure** The extent to which temporarily high real wages cause workers to work harder today and enjoy more leisure tomorrow.

**intervention** Occurs when the central bank has to buy or sell foreign currency to make up for any excess supply or demand arising from private transactions.

**inventory cycle** Response of inventory investment to changes in sales that causes further changes in aggregate demand.

**inventory investment** Increase in the stock of goods on hand.

**investment spending** Additions to the physical stock of capital.

**IS curve (goods market equilibrium curve)** Shows combinations of the interest rate and income for which the goods market is in equilibrium.

**IS-LM model** Interaction of *IS* and *LM* curves determines the real interest rate and the level of income for a given price level, for which both goods and money markets are in equilibrium.

## J

**J-curve effect** Observation that when a currency depreciates, the value of net exports rises temporarily and then falls.

**"just-in-time" inventory management** Inventory management strategy; firms hold inventories for as short a time as possible by sending goods out as soon as they are produced, and ordering parts as soon as they are needed.

## K

**Keynesian aggregate supply curve** Very short run horizontal aggregate supply curve.

**Keynesian, or non-market clearing, paradigm** A paradigm that uses the assumption that (at least some) prices move slowly, or, in some cases, are even fixed.

## L

**labour force** The total number of individuals who are employed, plus the number of individuals who are actively seeking employment but do not have jobs.

**labour force participation rate** Number of individuals in the labour force as a percentage of the adult population.

**leisure** Non-work activities.

**life-cycle hypothesis** Emphasizes choices about how to maintain a stable standard of living in the face of changes in income over the course of life.

**lifetime utility** The sum of period-by-period utilities.

**liquid asset** An asset that can be used immediately, conveniently, and cheaply to make payments.

**liquidity constraints** Exist when a consumer cannot borrow to sustain current consumption in the expectation of higher future income.

**liquidity trap** A situation that arises when the *LM* curve is horizontal because the interest elasticity of money demand is infinite.

*LM* **curve (money market equilibrium curve)** Shows combinations of interest rates and levels of output such that money demand equals money supply.

**long run** The time frame in which all prices are considered to be flexible, and all markets are assumed to be in equilibrium at all times, but the productive capacity of the economy is assumed to be fixed.

**Lucas critique** Points out that many macroeconomics models assume that expectations are given by a particular function, when that function can change.

# M

*M1* Those claims that can be used directly, instantly, and without restrictions to make payments.

*M2* *M1* plus personal savings accounts and non-personal notice deposits.

*M2+* *M1* plus deposits in other financial institutions such as trust companies, credit unions and caisse populaires.

*M3* Includes all Canadian dollar deposits in chartered banks and foreign currency deposits held by residents.

**managed, or dirty, floating** Central banks intervene by buying or selling foreign currency and attempt to influence exchange rates.

**marginal lifetime utility of consumption** The increase in utility from a small increase in consumption.

**marginal product of capital (MPK)** Increment to output obtained by adding one unit of capital, with other factor inputs held constant.

**marginal product of labour (MPN)** The amount that output increases for each additional unit increase in labour input.

**marginal propensity to consume** The increase in consumption per unit increase in income.

**marginal propensity to import** The increase in the demand for imports that results from a one-unit increase in domestic income.

**marginal propensity to save** The increase in saving per unit increase in income.

**marginal rate of substitution** The rate at which a consumer is willing to give up an amount of consumption today in order to receive increased consumption in the next period, holding total utility constant.

**maturity (or term) of a bond** Length of time until a bond expires.

**medium of exchange** One of the roles of money; asset used to make payments.

**menu cost** Small cost incurred when the nominal price of a good is exchanged; for example, the cost for a restaurant of reprinting its menus when it raises/lowers its prices.

**merchandise trade balance** The difference between exports of goods and import of goods.

**models** Simplified representations of the world.

**monetary accommodation** The central bank prints money to buy the bonds with which the government pays for its deficit.

**monetary approach** The emphasis on monetary considerations in the interpretation of external balance problems.

**monetary base** The sum of currency in circulation and the deposits of the chartered banks at the Bank of Canada.

**monetary policy** Any choice made by the Bank of Canada concerning the level of the nominal money stock.

**monetary policy multiplier** Shows how much an increase in the real money supply increases the equilibrium level of income, keeping fiscal policy unchanged.

**monetization** When the Bank of Canada purchases part of the debt sold by the Department of Finance to finance the federal government budget deficit.

**money** The medium of exchange, whatever you use to pay for goods and services.

**money multiplier** The ratio of the money supply to the monetary base.

**money stock (or money supply)** The total amount of money available in an economy; consists of any asset that can be used for immediate payment.

**money supply rule** A policy stance where the central bank holds the level (or growth rate) of the money supply constant.

**multilateral exchange rate** Measures the value of one currency against a basket of other currencies.

**multiplier** The amount by which equilibrium output changes when autonomous aggregate demand increases by one unit.

**Mundell-Fleming model** The analysis extending the standard *IS-LM* model to the open economy under perfect capital mobility.

**myopia** The idea that consumers are not as forward-thinking as the LC-PIH suggests.

# N

**national income accounting identity**

$$Y \equiv C + I + G + NX$$

*National Income and Expenditure Accounts* A measure of current activity in the Canadian economy, published quarterly by Statistics Canada.

**natural rate of unemployment** Rate of unemployment at which the flows into and out of the unemployment pool balance; also, the point on the augmented Phillips curve at which expected inflation equals actual inflation.

**neoclassical growth theory** Focuses on capital accumulation and its link to savings decisions and the like.

**net domestic product at factor cost** The total payments to factors of production.

**net domestic product at market prices** Indirect taxes (net of subsidies) are added to net domestic product at factor cost.

**net exports** The difference between exports and imports.

**net foreign investment** The amount that domestic residents are lending to foreigners.

**net investment** Gross investment minus depreciaton.

**New Keynesians** Those who develop models whose basis is rational behaviour and conclude that the economy is not inherently efficient and that, at times, the government ought to stabilize output and unemployment.

**nominal exchange rate** The number of Canadian dollars that must be given up in order to purchase a unit of foreign currency.

**nominal interest rate** Measures how much money you received (or paid) above the amount that you invested (or borrowed), expressed as a percentage.

**normal good** Any good is said to be a normal good if an increase in income causes the demand for this good to increase.

# O

**official reserves** Assets held by central banks that can be used to make international payments.

**Okun's law** The hypothesized relationship between changes in unemployment and change in real GDP.

**open economy** An economy that engages in a substantial amount of international trade.

**open economy aggregate demand curve** The aggregate demand curve that takes into account changes in the real exchange rate.

**open market operations** Purchases or sales of government securities by the central bank.

**operating (or noninterest) deficit** The budget deficit except for interest payments.

**opportunity cost** What is forgone to take an action. For example, one opportunity cost of attending university or college is the lost wages the student could be earning in a full-time job.

**output gap** Measures the difference between actual output and the output that could be produced at full employment, or potential output.

**outside lag** The timing of the effects of the policy action on the economy.

**overnight rate** The interest rate at which banks borrow or lend so that they do not have a shortage or excess of settlement balances.

# P

**pay-as-you-go (social security) system** Social security system in which payments to retirees are made with funds provided, not by their social security taxes, but by the social security taxes of the working populace.

**perfect capital mobility** Occurs when investors can purchase assets in any country they choose, quickly, with low transaction costs, and in unlimited amounts.

**perfect foresight** Assumption that people know the future value of all relevant variables, or that their expectations are always correct.

**perfectly/imperfectly anticipated inflation** Inflation is perfectly anticipated when all agents correctly anticipate the future inflation rate. Inflation is imperfectly anticipated when inflation is unexpected.

**permanent disturbance** An exogenous change that shifts, say, the aggregate demand curve, to a new position permanently.

**permanent income** The steady rate of consumption a person could maintain for the rest of his or her life, given the present level of wealth and the income earned now and in the future.

**permanent-income theory** Says that people form expectations of their future income and choose how much to consume based on those as well as their current income.

**Phillips curve** An inverse relationship between the rate of unemployment and the rate of change in the nominal wage.

**policy irrelevance** Refers to the inability of monetary or fiscal policy to affect output in rational expectations equilibrium models.

**policy mix** A combination of monetary and fiscal policies.

**policy trade-off** The choice made by policy makers of different combinations of unemployment and inflation rates.

**portfolio** The mix of assets someone owns.

**potential GDP** Output that is produced when all factors of production are fully employed.

**price stickiness** When prices do not move with the infinite speed assumed in the Classical model.

**private savings** Saving by individuals, by families, and by firms; saving by everyone other than government.

**production function** Technological relationship showing how much output can be produced for a given combination of inputs.

**productivity shock** Change in technology that affects workers' productivity.

**propagation mechanisms** Mechanisms by which current economic shocks cause fluctuations in the future, for example, intertemporal substitution of leisure.

**purchasing power parity (PPP)** In the long run, the nominal exchange rate moves primarily as a result of difference in price level behaviour between two countries.

# Q

**q theory of investment** Investment theory emphasizing that investment will be high when assets are valuable relative to their reproduction cost. The ratio of asset value to cost is called $q$.

**quantity equation** $MV = PT$

**quantity theory of money** Predicts that if the nominal money stock increases, the nominal price level will increase and real income will remain constant.

# R

**random walk** A variable in which changes over time are unpredictable.

**random-walk model of consumption** Consumption tomorrow should equal consumption today plus a truly random error.

**rate of time preference** The rate at which you are willing to give up consumption today if you are compensated by increased consumption in the future.

**rational expectations** (1) Individuals do not make systematic errors in forming their expectations; expectational errors are corrected immediately, so that on average, expectations of the price level are correct. (2) Theory of expectations formation in which expectations are based on all available information about the underlying economic variables; frequently associated with New Classical macroeconomics.

**rational expectations equilibrium** A model in which expectations are formed rationally, and markets are always in equilibrium.

**real balances** Real value of the money stock (number of dollars divided by the price level).

**real business cycle (RBC) theory** Theory that recessions and booms are due primarily to shocks in real activity, such as supply shocks, rather than to changes in monetary factors.

**real exchange rate (or terms of trade)** The ratio of foreign prices to Canadian prices, measured in a common currency.

**real interest rate** The nominal interest rate minus the rate of inflation.

**real rate of interest** Return on an investment measured in dollars of constant value; roughly equal to the difference between the nominal interest rate and the rate of inflation.

**real wage** Payment to labour measured in terms of output; calculated as the nominal wage divided by the price level.

**recognition lag** The period that elapses between the time a disturbance occurs and the time the policy makers recognize that action is required.

**rental (user) cost of capital** The cost of using one more unit of capital in production.

**residential investment** Investment in housing.

**Ricardian equivalence** Debt financing by bond issue merely postpones taxation and therefore, in many instances, is strictly equivalent to current taxation.

**risky asset** An asset whose future pay-off is uncertain.

**rules versus discretion** A policy is set according to a rule if policy does not change in response to observed changes in the economy. A policy is set according to discretion if policy changes in response to observed changes in the economy.

## S

**sacrifice ratio** The percentage of output lost for each 1 percentage-point reduction in the inflation rate.

**seigniorage** Revenue derived from the government's ability to print money.

**settlement balances** Deposits held by direct clearers at the Bank of Canada.

**short run** The time frame in which prices are assumed to be sticky.

**short run aggregate supply (SRAS) curve** A relationship derived from the Phillips curve that shows how output can deviate from its full employment level in the short run.

**speed of adjustment** The amount of time it takes a price to adjust so that a market returns to equilibrium.

**spillover (interdependence) effects** Occur when policy changes or supply/demand shocks in one country affect output in another.

**standard of deferred payment** Asset normally used for making payments due at a later date.

**static expectations** Individuals form their expectations by assuming that the expected price level equals last period's actual price level.

**steady-state equilibrium** The combination of per capita GDP and the capital-labour ratio where the economy will remain at rest.

**sticky prices** Prices that are unable to adjust quickly enough to keep markets in equilibrium.

**short run** The time frame in which prices are assumed to be sticky or even fixed.

**short run aggregate supply (SRAS) curve** A relationship derived from the Phillips curve that shows how output can deviate from its full employment level in the short run.

**stock of capital** The value of all building machinery and inventories at a point in time.

**store of value** Asset that maintains its value over time.

**structural unemployment** Long-term unemployment that arises because of a lack of matching between the skills of workers and the needs of employers.

**structural unemployment** The idea that cutting tax rates will increase aggregate supply enormously—so much, that the tax collections will rise rather than fall.

**substitution effect** All else being equal, an increase in the real rate of interest will cause current consumption to go down and savings to go up.

**supply-side economics** The idea that cutting tax rates will increase aggregate supply enormously—so much, that the tax collections will rise rather than fall.

## T

**targets** Identified goals of policy.

**tariff** A tax on an import.

**term structure of interest rates** The relationship between interest rates on bonds of different maturities.

**terms of trade (or real exchange rate)** The ratio of foreign prices to Canadian prices, measured in a common currency.

**total factor productivity** Rate at which productivity of inputs increases; measure of technological progress.

**transactions motive** The demand for money arising from the use of money in making regular payments.

**transfer payments** Payments that are made to people without their providing a current service in exchange.

**transitory disturbance** An exogenous change that shifts, say, the aggregate demand curve, but the disturbance is short-lived and the curve shifts back to its original position.

**transmission mechanism** The process by which changes in monetary policy affect aggregate demand.

**trend (secular) component of GDP** Potential output.

**trend stationary** A variable is trend stationary when temporary shocks do not permanently affect its level. Changes in *AD*, for example, can only temporarily affect output. If changes in output were driven primarily by demand shocks, output would be trend stationary.

**trend stationary with breaks** Trend stationary, but with a trend that sometimes changes.

**twin deficit** In a small open economy, a government budget deficit leads to a balance of trade deficit.

## U

**ultimate targets** Variables such as the inflation rate, the unemployment rate, or real GDP growth.

**unemployed person** Someone who is out of work and (1) has actively looked for work in the previous four weeks, or (2) is waiting to be recalled to a job after having been laid off, or (3) is waiting to report to a new job within four weeks.

**unemployment hysteresis** The phenomenon that when unemployment is high, it tends to remain high and come down only slowly.

**unemployment pool** The number of unemployed people at any point in time.

**unemployment rate** A measure of the number of people who are actively in the labour force seeking jobs, but who cannot find work.

**unit of account** Asset in which prices are denoted.

## V

**value added** Increase in value of output at a given stage of production. Equivalently, value of output minus cost of inputs.

**velocity of money** A measure of the speed with which money circulates in an economy.

**very long run** The time frame in which growth theory is studied; all prices are flexible and all markets are in equilibrium at all times.

**very short run** The time frame in which prices are assumed to be fixed.

## W

**wealth redistribution** When inflation is not anticipated, those who hold financial assets have some of their purchasing power transferred to those who issue financial assets.

**World Trade Organization (WTO)** International organization that works out rules of trade between its member nations; created January 1, 1995, as a result of the Uruguay Round of the General Agreement on Tariffs and Trade (GATT).

## Y

**yield curve** Shows how interest rates change as bond maturities increase.

## Z

**zero reserve requirements** The system under which direct clearers are not required to keep a minimum cash reserve ratio.

# INDEX

458    INDEX

## FIGURE 1-7

Over the very short run, output varies substantially. This figure shows the rate of change in real GDP per person quarterly. In this diagram, you can see clearly the quarterly ups and downs in GDP, as well as the economic downturn in 2001, with the beginning of the recovery in 2002. In this very short run time framework, we assume that the AS curve is horizontal and shifts in AD determine changes in GDP.

### REAL GDP PER CAPITA, PERCENTAGE CHANGE, 1998 QUARTER 1 TO 2002 QUARTER 4

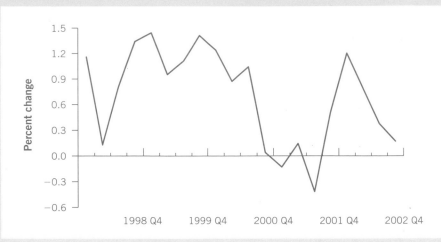

SOURCE: Real GDP: CANSIM II V1992259; population: CANSIM II V1.

## FIGURE 6-3

The unemployment rate increases during recessions, and decreases during expansions.

### THE CYCLICAL BEHAVIOUR OF THE UNEMPLOYMENT RATE, 1968–2002

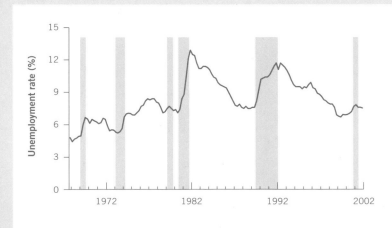

SOURCE: 1968–1975: *Bank of Canada Review*, various issues; 1976–2002: CANSIM II V2062815.